Effective Management of Long-Term Care Facilities

Douglas A. Singh, PhD, MBA
Associate Professor
School of Public and Environmental Affairs
Indiana University-South Bend
South Bend, Indiana

D0075155

WITHDRAWN

JONES AND BARTLETT PUBLISHERS
Sudbury, Massachusetts
BOSTON   TORONTO   LONDON   SINGAPORE

World Headquarters

Jones and Bartlett Publishers
40 Tall Pine Drive
Sudbury, MA 01776
978-443-5000
info@jbpub.com
www.jbpub.com

Jones and Bartlett Publishers
Canada
2406 Nikanna Road
Mississauga, ON L5C 2W6
CANADA

Jones and Bartlett Publishers
International
Barb House, Barb Mews
London W6 7PA
UK

Library of Congress Cataloging-in-Publication Data

Singh, Douglas A., 1946–
    Effective management of long-term care facilities / Douglas A. Singh.
        p. cm.
    Includes bibliographical references and index.
    ISBN 0-7637-4801-3 (pbk.)
    1. Long-term care facilities—Administration.   2. Nursing homes—Administration.
I. Title.
    RA999.A35S56 2004
    362.16′068—dc22

                                                                                    2004004949

Production Credits
Publisher: Michael Brown
Production Manager: Amy Rose
Associate Production Editor: Tracey Chapman
Editorial Assistant: Kylah McNeill
Marketing Manager: Matthew Payne
Manufacturing Buyer: Amy Bacus
Composition: Auburn Associates, Inc.
Cover Design: Diana Coe
Printing and Binding: Malloy, Inc.
Cover Printing: Malloy, Inc.

Printed in the United States of America
08 07 06 05 04   10 9 8 7 6 5 4 3 2 1

Table of Contents

Foreword

You may read this book as a student of health care administration while you prepare for the professional licensure examination, when you need a ready reference, or when you consider a career in long-term care administration. You will not be disappointed. Dr. Singh provides a compendium of information needed for successful administration in long-term care.

This book clearly defines an administrator's scope of responsibility in these four dimensions of care: physical, social, mental, and spiritual. Although regulations require that you create a "home-like" environment in the nursing home, elders and their families yearn for it to be a "home." By using the physical design judiciously, empowering the staff, and engaging the community as partners in care, the leader-administrator creates an environment that both elders and caregivers want.

Dr. Singh frames many of these issues in a manner that familiarizes the reader with important theories and models, such as theories of aging and quality improvement models. He demonstrates to the reader the importance of functioning in an "open system" that is integrally linked to the external environment. The text clearly points out that using models, systems, and processes is essential for excellent outcomes in all areas of quality of life and quality of care.

Leaders must understand the realities of today while visioning the possibilities of tomorrow. While detailing what you must know to deal with today's standards, the author also points to models that contain the seeds of future realities.

The challenges of managing long-term care are numerous. Our society demands near perfection in care, but does not support an adequate reimbursement system. Although regulation is highly prescriptive, it mandates maximum autonomy and choice. Students and candidates in health care

professions are frequently discouraged from working in long-term care by those oblivious to its many rewards. Being a leader in long-term care is one of the most rewarding and challenging positions in health care. As a health care administrator, you must ensure quality of care. As a leader in long-term care, you will create the quality of life experienced by those entrusted to you.

The American College of Health Care Administrators, the professional association for administrators in long-term care, conducted a survey of administrators in the fall of 2002. Their written comments were voluminous. This quote from one of those surveyed speaks to the reason that people working in the field find such rewards: *This is more than a job. I am in a position to affect change, to improve lives, to touch hearts. As administrators we should revel in the chance to make major differences in lives, patients, families, and staff. It is our privilege and our responsibility. Done correctly, the rewards are immeasurable.*

I hope that you will experience both the professional and personal rewards from working in long-term care.

Mary Tellis-Nayak, RN, MSN, MPH
President/CEO
American College of Health Care Administrators

Introduction

ABOUT THIS BOOK

The primary focus of this book is to provide an in-depth source on how an effectively managed skilled-nursing facility should operate, and how prospective, as well as currently employed, nursing home administrators can hone their skills to deliver quality services cost-effectively.

The chapters are arranged in three major sections. The book begins with an overview of long-term care (LTC) and an explanation of the key external factors that can significantly affect long-term care organizations. The next section focuses on the organization of a nursing home, detailing how the physical structures, human resources, and delivery of services are arranged and integrated to provide total patient care. The final section concentrates on management and leadership skills that are necessary for managing the internal organization, as well as the external environment.

Using the open-system theoretical framework, the first two chapters emphasize why it is essential to understand changes in the facility's external environment and how value-based community and client exchanges can be managed to accomplish strategic objectives. The legal and regulatory environment (Chapter 3) and financing and reimbursement (Chapter 4) are often regarded as the most critical external factors. The eight chapters in Part II (Chapters 5–12) cover building layout and architectural designs; contemporary systems of client-centered care; and traditional processes, personnel roles, and departmental functions that must be organized to deliver patient care and adjunct services. Achieving an appropriate blend of clinical and socio-residential aspects of care is the goal that guides the way in which the facility's structures and processes are

managed to deliver holistic care. The internal structures and processes must also respond to the external demands, because major environmental forces change over time and compel the facility to either respond to external challenges or face adverse consequences. Hence, management practices must face current challenges and foresee the likely impact of new developments. The five chapters in Part III (Chapters 13–17) cover the management of the internal systems, the human resources, and the external environment. The critical roles of leadership, strategy, and management tools are discussed in Chapter 13. The remaining chapters cover human resource management and staff development; marketing, public relations, and customer relations; budgeting and financial controls; and improvement of productivity and quality.

As a college textbook, a major objective of this work is to enable the student to gain both a conceptual and "nuts-and-bolts" knowledge of health care faciliy management. After mastering the concepts in this book, the student can step into a management position as an administrator, assistant administrator, or trainee administrator, and find a level of comfort in dealing with various operational issues and problems encountered in day-to-day management situations. To accomplish this goal, the book incorporates numerous theories, models, illustrations, and examples to help the reader grasp the complexities of managing a long-term care facility. Practicing administrators can use this book as a handy reference for improving their skills, becoming more effective leaders in their organizations and their communities, and serving their noble profession by meeting the needs of the residents under their care. This book is also a valuable resource for administrator-in-training programs run by various nursing home corporations. Administrators can also use this book as a manual for training their department heads and other key personnel.

Each chapter begins with a list of learning modules. The chapters follow the learning modules, which describe the critical areas that students should master in order to develop their long-term care management skills. Discussion questions at the end of each chapter have been designed to provoke thought, and to make the student reason beyond what is obvious in the text itself. Some questions are designed to apply what is discussed in the text. A list of websites is included at the end of each chapter to promote further inquiry.

At the end, the book contains a comprehensive glossary, which is to be used as a dictionary of key terms encountered in the text. When first used in the text, each technical term has been highlighted. When the reader encounters the same term in subsequent readings, the Glossary can be used as a ready reference. Throughout the text, certain terms have been used interchangeably. Examples include: nursing home, nursing facility, facility, and long-term care facility; and patient, resident, and elder.

LONG-TERM CARE ADMINISTRATION

Skilled nursing care facilities are traditional nursing homes, which have evolved and developed into clinical centers for institution-based LTC. These are complex organizations to manage and have been the target of much regulatory oversight and public criticism. Yet demographic trends, especially the aging of more than 75 million baby boomers, suggest that these organizations will be needed more than ever before. Despite healthy lifestyles, advances in medical technology, and growth of community-based LTC services, the sheer number of people reaching old age and living longer implies that chronic conditions, comorbidity, and accompanying impairments will create high demand for nursing home care. It also means that a greater number of well-trained administrators will be needed to organize and manage skilled nursing, subacute care, and other types of long-term care services.

Nursing home administration entails much more than overseeing the various functions in an organization or following set routines. Of course, organizational stability and certain standard routines are signs of an effectively managed nursing facility. Such organizations also have predictable outcomes, according to recognized measures of patient care and financial expectations. In the long run, however, successes are achieved by (1) serving the community and creating meaningful partnerships with other health agencies and care delivery organizations, (2) understanding and working within the confines of what reimbursements will allow, (3) adapting to changing demands while complying with legal and regulatory requirements, (4) organizing internal operations within a nursing home to develop an integrated system in which services are delivered in a seamless fashion, and (5) managing the operations through effective leadership, human resource development, strategic marketing, financial control, and

quality improvement. The evidence of the dynamic nature of LTC delivery is ample, because in the past few years market competition has intensified, Medicare and Medicaid rules have placed new demands on managers, public scrutiny has increased, and litigation has intensified. Risk taking and innovation will mark successful administrators of the future.

To be the person in charge of a long-term care facility that takes care of frail and vulnerable individuals is a solemn responsibility. The nursing home administrator (NHA) must understand the clinical, social, and residential aspects of care delivery and also be directly responsible for managing the facility as a business. The NHA position is, in many respects, similar to that of a general manager in a complex human-service delivery organization. The NHA must have a 24-hour-a-day, 7-days-a-week commitment to an organization that must meet the patients' clinical needs, ensure their social and emotional well-being, preserve their individual rights, promote human dignity, and improve their quality of life. In addition, the NHA must manage staff relations, budgets and finances, marketing, and quality. Hence, NHAs typically have a broad range of management responsibilities and are closely involved with day-to-day operational details. Being an NHA is a rewarding career, both financially and professionally. The psychological rewards that can come from delivering quality care to patients, helping family members, supporting community health initiatives, coaching the staff, and building excellence into the organization often exceed the financial rewards.

Becoming a Nursing Home Administrator

Since all NHAs must be licensed to practice, the first step is to contact the state's licensing agency and obtain a copy of the state's licensure requirements. The prospective administrator must meet the minimum educational qualifications. Most states require a college degree; some states also require completion of a short course in long-term care. All states require passing a national examination prepared by the National Association of Boards of Examiners of Long-Term Care Administrators (NAB). In most states, certain private firms hold a one- or two-day seminar, which many have found to be quite adequate to prepare for the NAB examination. In addition to the NAB, there is also a shorter examination on state nursing home regulations. Some states may also require an internship with a state-certified preceptor who is also a practicing NHA. Many states have reciprocity agreements, meaning that an administrator licensed in one state

can obtain a license in another state if that state has a reciprocity agreement with the other state.

Administrator Licensure Issues

At least one major reason that U.S. nursing homes have been targets of national scandals for delivering poor quality of care can be traced to a lack of proper NHA training. Since the licensing of NHAs is a state function, qualifications required for managing nursing facilities vary widely from one state to another. Only a handful of states stipulate a bachelor's degree in health services administration as an educational requirement. Over the years, state and national licensing policies have been crafted under the false assumption that a degree in English or History, a self-study course on long-term care, a score of 75% on a 150-question multiple-choice NAB test, and some internship hours with an experienced NHA adequately qualify someone to become responsible for the care of 100 or more residents in a nursing home. When most of the nation's NHAs have educational backgrounds in areas that are totally unrelated to delivering long-term care to the elderly, it should come as no surprise that substandard quality is rampant. At least two landmark reports by the Institute of Medicine have reached this conclusion. In fact, administrative skills and behavioral factors associated with NHAs may be more important for delivering quality than facility constraint or resource factors. While there is growing evidence that high turnover among NHAs may be associated with low-quality patient care, many administrators find the challenges of managing a nursing home to be overwhelming. The starting point to remedy these circular problems is a licensure requirement of a bachelor's degree in health care management.

LONG-TERM CARE POLICY OVERVIEW

The LTC delivery system in the United States comprises various types of community-based and institutional options, and there are wide variations in payment for services and regulation of different kinds of facilities. For instance, residential care facilities, such as board-and-care homes, sheltered-care facilities, and assisted living are not even licensed in some states. Also, the type and level of services can vary substantially because of a lack of standard terminology and criteria for differentiating between

various levels of care. However, nursing homes, which health care professionals generally know by their regulatory title as skilled nursing facilities (SNFs), have been the prime targets of policy oversight.

Public policy in long-term care has evolved in three main directions: financing, utilization, and quality. The evolutionary process, however, did not progress according to some planned design. This follows the general pattern of American health policymaking. Since the U.S. does not have a national health insurance system, which would be more amenable to uniform and comprehensive policymaking, issues pertaining to health care financing and delivery in the U.S. are addressed incrementally, in a piecemeal fashion. Long-term care policy has been no exception to this disjointed, ad hoc approach.

The three policy areas discussed here have a tremendous impact on the management of long-term care facilities, because nursing homes must render services that meet at least the minimum standards defined by regulations, implement operating systems to comply with laws and regulations, and manage within the financial parameters set by reimbursement levels. Health policy can also have a major effect on access to services, shifts in utilization, market competition, and an adequate and well prepared workforce.

Financing

The major initiatives in LTC policy can be traced back to 1965, when the Medicare and Medicaid programs were created under Social Security Amendments. Of these two programs, Medicare was never designed to pay for long-term care. Although Medicare was designed primarily to finance hospital-based acute care services for the elderly, short-term post-acute convalescence was included as a benefit for two main reasons: (1) to ensure continuity of care after discharge from a hospital, and (2) to save money on otherwise lengthy and more expensive hospital stays once the acute phase of an illness was over. Medicaid rules, on the other hand, provide for comprehensive medical care services for the indigent who meet the state-established income criteria. Medicaid benefits include financing for nursing home care, and the length of nursing home stay is generally not limited, as long as need is demonstrated.

The problem with such fragmented public policies is that access becomes restricted for many who need the services for a long period of time, because Medicare pays only for post-acute short-term stays, and

Medicaid requires people to exhaust their financial resources to become eligible. Thus, Medicaid has become the payer of last resort for many middle-class elderly who have run out of their own private funds to pay for nursing home care. But many elders who do not qualify for either program have to pay on a private basis. In 2000, 44.4% of the funding for nursing home care was derived from Medicaid, and only 9.5% came from Medicare. Private out-of-pocket payments financed 24.9%, and 7.4% was financed through privately purchased long-term care insurance (Friedland 2003).

Despite the gaps in access, policymakers have shown little concern for LTC coverage. Some believe that this neglect can be attributed to fears that improving the system will result in increased health care expenditures, especially because family members currently provide most LTC to their elderly parents or relatives in their private homes without getting paid for the services they render (Friedland 2003). However, gains in life expectancy which, for a newborn, has risen from 68.2 years in 1950 to 77.2 years in 2001[1]; over 75 million baby boomers who are about to enter retirement age in 2011 and beyond; and dwindling birth rates[2] have already set in motion the demographic imperative, with potentially serious consequences at two main fronts: (1) With fewer working people and a burgeoning elderly population, the financial burden for LTC on future generations is expected to be enormous (Shi and Singh 2004, 412). This is an impending dilemma that policymakers are reluctant to bring up for public policy debates. (2) A labor force crisis for LTC delivery is already beginning to emerge, as a smaller proportion of people from a shrinking pool of new workers are choosing employment in health care delivery settings (Stone and Wiener 2001). Stone (2003) believes that a shortage of stable and qualified workforce may be the most important and most neglected policy concern. Training in geriatrics is particularly lacking among physicians, nurses, therapists, and social workers, and there are not enough trained administrators to provide leadership in the long-term care field. There is also a need to prepare and sustain a qualified workforce of direct-care personnel, such as certified nursing assistants, who provide

---

[1]According to data from the U.S. Department of Health and Human Services.

[2]The crude birth rates (live births per 1,000 population) were 24.1 for 1950 and 14.5 for 2001 according to data from the U.S. Department of Health and Human Services.

most of the daily hands-on care to patients in nursing homes. According to Stone (2003), policies are needed to promote collaboration between education, labor, welfare, and immigration agencies to evaluate the labor issues and to create positive incentives for workforce development.

Other policy issues related to financing surround the levels of reimbursement from Medicare and Medicaid. Nursing home operators have long contended that payments from public payers have been inadequate to support quality services. On the other hand, Medicaid and Medicare administrators have been concerned about rising expenditures, while the public is not inclined to pay more in taxes. Even though independent experts continue to voice their opinions that reimbursement levels should be raised, the demographic imperative suggests that the government will have to find new ways to keep payments in check. The irony is that, unlike many other industries, nursing home care is highly labor intensive, and few options are available to increase productivity or slash operating costs.

Coverage for nursing-home services from private long-term care insurance has increased slightly in recent years, but fewer than 10% of people 50 years of age and older purchase private insurance for LTC (Seff 2003). The elderly population most likely to benefit from private LTC coverage also has a lower average income than the general population. Hence, LTC insurance is difficult to market, because premiums must be high enough to cover costs but low enough to attract clients. Insurance is based on the principle of adequately spreading risk among a large segment of the population. However, younger healthy groups have shown little interest in buying LTC insurance because they see the need for LTC only as a remote possibility (Shi and Singh 2004, 412). A few states offer tax deductions or credits for purchasing private LTC insurance, but the incentives appear to be too small to induce many people to purchase LTC plans (Wiener et al. 2000). Thus, financing for nursing home care is likely to remain a major dilemma as time progresses. In such an environment, NHAs will have to be skillful leaders who can motivate their staff to become more efficient providers of care. NHAs are also challenged to find cost-effective ways to deliver services without compromising the quality of care.

Utilization

Table 1 provides capacity and utilization data for nursing home beds. Even though capacity has increased, occupancy rates have been falling during the decade of the 1990s. However, both capacity and utilization have declined since the early 1980s (although accurate data are not available because of

Table 1 Utilization of Nursing Home Beds (selected years)

	1992	1995	2000
Number of nursing homes	15,846	16,389	16,886
Number of beds	1,692,123	1,751,302	1,795,388
Occupancy rate	86.0%	84.5%	82.4%
Beds utilized	1,455,226	1,479,850	1,479,400

Sources: Data from Health, United States 1996–97, p. 248; Health, United States 2002, pp. 284–85.

inconsistencies in data reporting methods). The downward trend in nursing home utilization during the last decade is very likely a function of shifting configurations of the services offered by various long-term care providers (Bishop 2003). During the 1980s, nursing homes entered the post-acute (or subacute) and rehabilitation market, mainly as a result of the DRG-based prospective payment system implemented in hospitals, which created incentives for early discharge of acute-care patients. The trend accelerated during the 1990s, as the proliferation of managed care put further pressures on reducing the length of stay in hospitals. While these trends should have increased nursing home utilization, other factors in play since the 1980s promoted the use of alternative settings such as home health care, other community-based long-term care services, and assisted-living care, an industry that has experienced tremendous growth. For example, the implementation of the Pre-admission Screening and Annual Resident Review (PASARR) program restricted placement in nursing homes of persons with psychiatric diagnoses (Institute of Medicine 2001). The Omnibus Budget Reconciliation Act of 1987 (OBRA-87) gave states the authority to implement Home and Community-Based Services programs as an alternative to institutional care through Medicaid waivers created under section 1915(c) of the Social Security Act. Almost all states opted for the 1915(c) waivers as a means of reducing their financial burden by curtailing nursing home utilization and providing less costly community-based long-term care services. Using a combination of federal grant money and their own matching funds, a number of states have programs, although limited in scope, to cover adult day care, home health care, homemaker services, and assisted living for some of the neediest people.

The 1988 court ruling on a class-action lawsuit, *Duggan v. Bowen*, opened up broad access to Medicare-covered home health services, and for some time, home health had become the fastest growing health care ser-

vice in the U.S. On the other hand, private paying patients have found the residential and social lifestyles in assisted living facilities to be much more appealing than those in skilled nursing facilities. Many people have figured that they might as well spend their personal savings in an upscale assisted living home, and later apply for Medicaid if they need care in a skilled nursing facility. However, the impending demographic shifts will increase the number of people with functional impairments who will need nursing home services. On the other hand, policymakers will continue to explore new ways for providing cost-effective LTC services without turning LTC into an expanded social program. As part of these efforts, funding for community alternatives will continue, but many recipients of care in the home and community-based settings will eventually need to be institutionalized. Nursing home administrators with the savvy to establish community exchange partnerships (discussed in Chapters 1 and 2) will be ahead of the curve in an increasingly competitive environment.

Quality

Quality has been a well-recognized issue in long-term care for some time. Since Medicare and Medicaid have financed more than half of the nation's nursing home care, government regulations have played a major role in establishing standards to ensure at least the minimum level of quality. Research has demonstrated that the effects of this regulation have been positive. For example, the sharp decline in the use of physical and chemical restraints has been attributed to the requirements of OBRA-87. Other positive care practices since the implementation of OBRA-87 standards include more accurate medical records, comprehensive care planning, greater use of advance directives, increased use of incontinence training programs, and increased participation of residents in activity programs (Hawes et al. 1997; Marek et al. 1996; Teno et al. 1997). OBRA-87 also mandated a comprehensive patient assessment program, which led to the development of a standardized Resident Assessment Instrument. The assessment protocols are designed to help a nursing facility identify and treat or manage chronic conditions, the onset of acute illnesses, adverse effects of medications, or other factors that caused or contributed to a clinical problem (Hawes 2003). In future, successful nursing facilities will go beyond the minimum quality standards enforced by regulations, will make total quality management a part of the daily operations, and will build organizations in which a culture of quality will prevail.

INTERNET RESOURCES FOR FURTHER LEARNING

National Association of Boards of Examiners of Long-Term Care Administrators (NAB). This organization administers the national licensure examination for nursing home administrators. It has publications available to prepare for the examination. The website also provides links to the licensing agencies in all states.
http://www.nabweb.org

Improving the Quality of Care in Nursing Homes (1986)
Institute of Medicine (IOM). The full text of this publication is available online.
http://books.nap.edu/books/0309036461/html/243.html#pagetop

Improving the Quality of Long-Term Care (2001)
Institute of Medicine (IOM). The full text of this publication is available online.
http://www.nap.edu/books/0309064988/html/

REFERENCES

Bishop, C. 2003. Long-term care needs of elders and persons with disability. In *Long-term Care and Medicare Policy: Can We Improve the Continuity of Care?*, eds. D. Blumenthal et al., 21–39. Washington, DC: National Academy of Social Insurance.

Friedland, R.B. 2003. Planning for and financing long-term care. In *Long-term Care and Medicare Policy: Can We Improve the Continuity of Care?*, eds. D. Blumenthal et al., 48–67. Washington, DC: National Academy of Social Insurance.

Hawes, C. 2003. Ensuring quality in long-term care settings. In *Long-term Care and Medicare Policy: Can We Improve the Continuity of Care?*, eds. D. Blumenthal et al., 131–143. Washington, DC: National Academy of Social Insurance.

Hawes, C., et al. 1997. The impact of OBRA-87 and the RAI on indicators of process quality in nursing homes. *Journal of the American Geriatrics Society* 45, no. 8: 977–985.

Institute of Medicine. 2001. *Improving the Quality of Long-term Care.* Eds. G.S. Wunderlich and P.O. Kohler. Washington, DC: National Academy Press.

Marek, K.D., et al. 1996. OBRA '87: Has it resulted in positive change in nursing homes? *Journal of Gerontological Nursing* 22, no. 12: 32–40.

Seff, M.K. 2003. Clearing up health care myths. *Golden Lifestyles* (Jan. Feb. Mar.): 7.

Shi, L., and D.A. Singh. 2004. *Delivering Health Care in America: A Systems Approach*. 3rd ed. Sudbury, MA: Jones and Bartlett Publishers.

Stone, R. 2003. Reality of caring for the long-term care population. In *Long-term Care and Medicare Policy: Can We Improve the Continuity of Care?*, eds. D. Blumenthal et al., 40–47. Washington, DC: National Academy of Social Insurance.

Stone, R., and J. Wiener. 2001. *Who Will Care for Us? Addressing the Long-term Care Workforce Crisis*. Washington, DC: Urban Institute and the American Association of Homes and Services for the Aging.

Teno, J., et al. 1997. The early impact of the Patient Self-determination Act in long-term care facilities: Results from a ten-state sample. *Journal of the American Geriatrics Society* 45, no. 8: 939–944.

Wiener, J.M., et al. 2000. Federal and state initiatives to jump start the market for private long-term care insurance. *Elder Law Journal* 8, no. 1: 57–102.

PART I

System Perspectives and Environmental Exchanges

This book takes the *open system* approach. In modern management, the open system theory has found a strategic role in operating a successful enterprise in a changing environment. To be successful, an organization must adapt to external change.

According to the open system theory, organizations are viewed as living entities that exist within, and are part of, a larger environment. The external environment consists of numerous forces, which can be classified into six broad environmental domains: social, political, economic, technological, informational, and ecological. Forces in these domains have varying degrees of influence on an entire industry and its member organizations. The nursing home industry is no exception. Over time, the long-term care industry in America has been shaped by such factors as innovations in medical care and technology, government regulations, national health policy, consumer advocacy groups, and people's attitudes and commitments at work and home. Such external influences will continue to pressure the industry to change. While broad forces influence the whole industry, individual long-term care facilities are affected by their local

environment. Examples include market competition, shifts in local demographics, and makeup of the labor force in the area.

In the open system approach to long-term care management, facility administrators view their organizations as integrally linked to the external environment. Because the various environmental forces remain dynamic, administrators must be keen observers of emerging trends. They must assess the nature and degree of change in the environment, and evaluate the potential impact of external changes on the organization. Certain environmental changes can have a lasting effect on an individual facility's or a nursing home corporation's long-range survival. For example, when new competition enters the market, new regulations take effect, or payment methods are changed, they generally have lasting effects on long-term care facilities. Hence, the difference between success and failure often depends on the ability of top-level managers to identify changes in the external environment, evaluate their potential effect on the organization, make decisions, and take action. The dynamic environment not only presents challenges, it also opens up new opportunities. Long-term care administrators who understand and are attuned to external factors and their potential effect on the organizations they manage are likely to outperform those who do not pay attention to the changes or do not grasp their implications for the facility. Achieving this kind of success requires that nursing home administrators develop a high level of conceptual skills. They must be active in their local communities, exchange ideas with managers in other health care organizations, and actively participate in professional associations representing the long-term care industry.

A clear understanding of the external environment is essential for four main reasons:

- To meet the variety of care needs of all the patients served by a facility, the administrator must establish effective exchanges between the facility and key external agencies that are best suited to provide the services that the facility does not produce.
- Administrators must pursue opportunities to forge partnerships with external agencies that would result in serving the organization's best interests.
- Administrators must persistently improve operational efficiencies as new health policies emerge, new regulations are passed, and new reimbursement methods are implemented.

- The long-range direction of a facility must be driven by the current and anticipated changes in the external environment.

Strategic decision-making is vital for an organization's long-term success. Examples of strategy include deciding whether to add new services to meet changing health care demands or to curtail services for which the demand is declining; whether to expand an existing facility or to build a new one; and whether to acquire a facility or to merge with another organization. Periodically, all health facility administrators must confront external threats, take action to meet new environmental challenges, or take advantage of some opportunity to gain market share.

The major environmental components are discussed in this Part of the book. Chapter 1 explains the six environmental domains and discusses their implications. It also gives an overview of the long-term care system, describing the various services that can be arranged along a continuum of care. From a facility's perspective, some of the services are competitive whereas others are complementary. The chapter also addresses how long-term care services ought to be rationally linked to the rest of the health care delivery system. Chapter 2 provides more specific illustrations of the types of exchange relationships a nursing facility can establish with external agencies. Using a systems model of value exchanges, it emphasizes value-driven partnerships as the basis on which meaningful exchanges are built. Chapter 3 centers on the legal and regulatory environment. Chapter 4 covers details of financing and reimbursement, which constitute the life blood necessary for sustaining an organization.

The significance of the environmental domains for strategic management, and how the concepts of open and closed systems should be integrated into management practice, are more fully addressed later in Part III.

CHAPTER 1

System Concepts and Long-Term Care Delivery

LEARNING MODULES

1. Differences between closed and open systems. Open system cycle of exchanges. Organizational outputs that benefit the external agencies in open system partnerships. Outputs and benefits as necessary conditions to attract desirable resource inputs.

2. Application of open system theory to strategic management. An overview of the six environmental domains that influence the operation of a long-term care facility. Implications of environmental factors for long-term care delivery.

3. Operation of environmental influences in primary and secondary proximities, and at four proximal levels that require different types of responses from administrators. Competitive and complementary services, and their implications for nursing home administration.

4. Six main characteristics of long-term care. Differences between care based on the medical model and the holistic model. Reasons that a variety of services must be appropriately balanced. Four distinct categories for clas-

continues

sifying the variety of long-term care services. Two major aspects of medical care.

5. Reasons that mental health needs may go unattended. The facility's responsibility for total care. Importance of integrating social and residential services.

6. Physical and mental dysfunction and the goal of long-term care. Integration of holistic aspects and quality-of-life features into the delivery of care.

7. Three main components of the long-term care continuum. Common types of community-based long-term care services. General objectives of community-based services. Intramural and extramural services.

8. Types of institution-based long-term care services. Main differences between a skilled nursing facility and other types of institutional settings. Challenges posed by skilled nursing care.

9. Subacute care and specialized care services.

10. Common types of non-long-term health care services. Their relationship to long-term care. Rational integration of long-term care and other services. How integration can be improved.

If we can find a logical point of departure to discuss effective management of long-term care organizations, it will be recognizing that no organization is self-contained. Organizations are not self-sufficient and cannot function effectively if isolated from their external environments. Organizational success requires establishing linkages with external agencies. It requires adapting to a changing environment. It requires managers to be proactive in assessing the potential effects of emerging trends. It requires perception, understanding, analysis, decision-making, and action on the part of managers. The open system theory embodies these concepts. An organization that is capable of pulling resources from its environment remains dynamic. Over time, it builds internal strengths that enable it to attract clients, serve them well, improve profitability, develop its staff, and benefit the community. Such an organization gains a certain momentum,

enabling it to meet new challenges and profit from new opportunities when other organizations may remain inert and suffer from atrophy.

In general, long-term care includes a complex array of services that have remained fragmented because no attempts have been made to integrate them into a seamless system of long-term care delivery. Nursing care facilities are a part of this uncoordinated "system," and facility administrators should understand the other pieces of the long-term care puzzle. For example, a nursing home administrator should become familiar with complementary long-term care services available in the community. These services include home health care, outpatient rehabilitation, subacute care, specialized services for Alzheimer's patients, and a variety of supportive living options for the elderly or disabled. A knowledge of other health care agencies and social services outside the long-term care sector is also critical.

THE CLOSED AND OPEN SYSTEMS

A system can be defined as "a set of elements standing in interrelation among themselves and with the environment" (Von Bertalanffy 1972). Whether or not an organization's internal systems are linked to the external environment is what differentiates between closed and open systems.

Closed System

Organizations that function as a **closed system** emphasize only the interrelationships between the various internal components, while the interaction with the external environment is largely ignored. A closed system typically focuses on procedures for monitoring outputs, comparison of outputs with preset standards, evaluation of discrepancies between actual outputs and preset standards, and mechanisms for taking action to rectify negative variances between actual outputs and preset standards (Brown 1977). Effective closed systems management is essentially focused on organizational structures, productivity, effectiveness, cost control, profitability, and quality. In an effectively functioning closed system, the various departments of a nursing facility work together cohesively, support each other, and develop systems to improve quality and efficiency. Clearly, management must focus on improving the internal operations. However, even though these aspects of management are extremely important, a closed system functions as a self-contained entity, isolated from its environment. No matter how efficient the internal systems of an organization may become,

without the open system approach a nursing facility will stagnate and eventually lose any competitive advantage it may have once enjoyed.

Open System

An **open system** recognizes the effects of external factors and views internal operations in relation to changes in the external environment. The open system approach is based on the premise that "no organization can survive for long if it ignores government regulations, supplier relations, or the myriad external constituencies upon which the organization depends" (Robbins 2000, 606). The open system approach is necessary because organizations do not function in a stable and predictable environment. In this approach, internal operations are evaluated in terms of the demands of a changing environment. External forces impose new pressures and challenges, compelling the organization to respond, conform, adapt, and innovate. Appropriate responses to external demands also result in interactions that benefit the organization as well as the constituencies the organization serves. The organization depends on the environment to receive essential inputs, it transforms those inputs and supplies outputs that benefit the environment (Brown 1977).

Open systems theory suggests that an organization's interface with its external environment should be viewed as an exchange relationship—a give-and-take relationship—between the organization and its environment. At the receiving end, the organization obtains from its environment various inputs in the form of resources such as staff, supplies, loans, fire and police protection, clients, and payments for services. At the giving end, the organization returns to the environment what it has produced in the form of jobs, taxes, market competition, education, and improved community health. Dill (1958) identified four factors in the environment that are particularly relevant for organizational goal setting and goal attainment. The four factors are:

- Customers
- Suppliers of labor, materials, capital, etc.
- Competitors for both markets and resources
- Regulatory groups

When properly exploited by astute management, each of these factors makes a contribution toward making a nursing facility more effective in delivering services.

Cycle of Exchanges

The relationship between an organization and its environment goes through a complete cycle of exchange, which has four identifiable phases, as illustrated in Figure 1-1.

Resource Inputs

Organizations rely on the environment to obtain the critical resources needed to accomplish their goals and objectives. Some of the major resources are human resources, capital financing, supplies and equipment, technology, complementary services needed by the organization's clients, licensure by the state, and federal certification. These basic inputs are critical to a long-term care facility's ability to deliver appropriate levels of patient care.

Clients and Payments

The nursing facility must attract clients who will benefit from the services provided by the organization. Clients establish the primary exchange whereby the organization produces services: clients receive services tailored to meet their individual needs, and the facility gets paid for the services it has rendered. This exchange relationship among the facility, its clients, and payers generates revenues that make an indispensable contribution to a nursing facility's profitability.

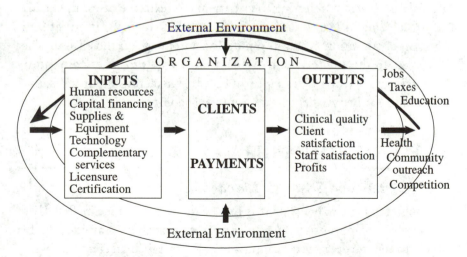

FIGURE 1-1 Organizational Interface with the External Environment

Production of Outputs

As they deliver services to clients, nursing care organizations transform the resources obtained from the environment into critical outputs such as clinical quality, client satisfaction, staff satisfaction, and profits. Effectiveness and consistency in producing these outputs determine the long-range success of a nursing facility.

Returns to the Environment

Organizations provide jobs, pay taxes, contribute to cost-efficiency within the health care system by actively competing in the marketplace, engage in community outreach by providing education and information, and positively influence a community's health and well-being. Thus, the organization creates external benefits by what it produces and returns to the environment. Finally, the cycle is completed as external agencies take into account a facility's outputs and benefits returned to the community when the facility needs resources to sustain its operations. A facility's ability to attract desirable resource inputs is often conditional upon its outputs and returns to the environment. For example, a long-term care facility that produces poor quality outputs will find it difficult to attract the most qualified staff members, a key resource the facility must obtain from the external environment. Such a facility is also likely to face difficulties attracting clients. Other health care providers, such as hospitals and physicians, may stop referring their patients. In extreme cases, the facility may risk losing its license and certification, which may put it out of business. An organization builds its reputation and image on the basis of what it delivers to the environment. When a facility fails to meet community expectations, it jeopardizes its prospects for attracting quality resource inputs and further weakens its ability to stay competitive.

THE ENVIRONMENT

Open System and Strategic Management

Although strategic management is one of the main themes in Part III of this book, it is appropriate here to emphasize that there is an inextricable link between the open system approach and strategic management. Figure 1-2 gives an overview of the strategic management process and includes examples of strategic planning and actions. Strategy formulation is a top-

FIGURE 1-2 Relationship Between the Open System Approach and Strategic Management

management function that is driven primarily by environmental change. The purpose of strategy is to keep the nursing facility afloat during adverse circumstances and to make it more profitable by gaining a competitive edge. When a nursing facility administrator adopts the open system approach to management, he or she will monitor changes in the environment; decide on the type of strategic response that would be in the organization's best interest according to organizational mission and values; plan a course of action; and carry out the plan. Using various formal and informal processes to identify significant trends and events on an ongoing basis is called **environmental scanning**. A formal analysis and evaluation of environmental trends to understand their potential implications for a facility's long-term success is called **environmental assessment**. In strategic planning, administrators assess major trends and directions and make decisions to avert threats and pursue new opportunities

that may emerge. A careful environmental assessment is also often necessary when planning major changes in the internal operations.

Environmental Domains

Environmental scanning and assessment activities are greatly facilitated by a conceptual model that classifies the macro-environment of a long-term care facility into six main domains: social, political, economic, technological, informational, and ecological (Figure 1-3).

Social Factors

Social factors include demographic trends, social change, cultural factors, and lifestyle preferences. The demand for long-term care and the type of services are influenced by changes in the population's demographic composition, such as age, gender, and prevalence of disability. Greater longevity has given rise to the "sandwich generation" of middle-aged families who must take responsibility for their teenage and college-age children on the one hand, and for elderly parents on the other. An increasing number of women in the workforce means that married couples may need formal help

_ _ _   Primary Proximity (local community and county)

————   Secondary Proximity (state and national)

FIGURE 1-3 Environmental Influences in the Primary and Secondary Proximities of an Organization

to care for their elderly parents. Strong family and social support enable people with disabilities to continue to live independently. Other trends, such as job mobility, often require making appropriate arrangements for the elderly parents who are left behind as close family members move away. Migration of retired people to areas of the country that offer a more temperate climate has important implications for the development of long-term care services in those areas. Lifestyle preferences of baby-boomers are giving rise to a new demand for nursing care settings that emphasize personal independence and lifestyle choices.

Political Factors

The **policy agenda** that sets priorities for political action, tax policy, the appropriation of tax dollars to various programs, and laws and regulations have a tremendous impact on the management of long-term care facilities. For instance, high taxes chip away profit margins in for-profit businesses. Federal and state funding appropriations for the Medicare and Medicaid programs determine how much nursing facilities will get paid. Federal and state legislatures pass new laws, and government agencies craft regulations. The political clout of the long-term care industry can influence how state and federal funds are appropriated or how the industry is regulated. Administrators can participate in the political process by establishing contacts with their state and federal representatives, by voicing their opinions, and by becoming members of professional associations representing their interests.

Economic Factors

Economic growth or recession, industrial development, and unemployment create demographic shifts that can bring people into an area or make them leave. Economic factors may also dictate whether people can afford to pay for long-term care, especially when public financing does not cover certain services. Changes in the labor market affect the availability of skilled workers and hence a facility's ability to recruit qualified staff members. Tight labor markets, for example, ease up recruitment of nursing assistants, cooks, and housekeepers, because those workers have difficulty finding jobs in restaurants, hotels, motels, and other low-skilled service industries. The job market also governs wages and benefits necessary to attract and retain employees. Competition from other facilities, and from substitute services such as home health care, present challenges

that nursing home administrators must not ignore. Other major economic events, such as the growth of managed care since the late 1980s, have an enormous impact on every aspect of health care delivery, including long-term care.

Technological Factors

Technological innovation in medical sciences will continue to revolutionize health care. It also has social implications as people live longer and healthier lives, and as the elderly seek more independent lifestyles. Technology has enabled many individuals to receive long-term care services in less restrictive or non-institutional settings instead of getting that care in traditional nursing homes. Home health care, for instance, is not only a cheaper alternative to nursing homes, but is also preferred by clients when services such as intravenous antibiotics, **oncology** therapy, **hemodialysis**, and **parenteral** and **enteral** nutrition can be provided by home-care agencies. On the other hand, technology has enabled nursing care facilities to provide specialized services and has allowed these facilities to care for acutely ill patients who previously could receive such services only in a hospital. Examples include AIDS care, **ventilator** care, head trauma services, and post-orthopedic **rehabilitation**.

Informational Factors

Computer-based information systems and the Internet have numerous applications. Adoption of information systems is changing many of the processes of health care delivery. It is also providing more effective tools for managing health care organizations. Areas of application where information systems have made a positive difference include clinical records, patient assessment and care planning, patient-care protocols, inventory management, data collection and analysis, advertising, and computer support systems for both clinical and management decision-making. The Internet has also opened access to a barrage of information for practitioners and consumers alike.

Ecological Factors

New infections and diseases, as well as a carry-over of certain medical conditions into older populations will affect long-term care delivery. The incidences of infection with Human Immunodeficiency Virus (HIV) and Hepatitis C virus have shown the need for training in precautionary

measures and practice of stringent infection-control procedures. Also, new treatments seem to delay the onset of Acquired Immune Deficiency Syndrome (AIDS). As people infected with HIV live longer, AIDS is likely to become more prevalent among older people. People with developmental disabilities are also living longer and need specialized care. Other ecological factors such as natural disasters (earthquakes, floods, hurricanes, snowstorms, tornadoes, etc.) require that facilities undertake adequate planning and prepare for unforeseen eventualities, particularly if they are located in areas that may be prone to such events. The possibility of **bioterrorism** has raised new concerns for patient safety. It also requires that health care facilities work in close collaboration with local civil defense and public health agencies to address potential threats.

Environmental Proximity

Environmental proximity determines how closely certain influences surround the organization. An organization's relationship to its environment and the degree of control it may have over environmental issues is often governed by the proximity. For instance, a facility administrator generally has much more control over managing relationships with the local hospital than he or she does over state or national policy that affects nursing home regulations and reimbursement.

First, in rather broad terms, we can think of primary and secondary proximities (Figure 1-3). The primary proximity is closer to the organization, and the six environmental domains operate in a local environment such as the community, which can be a neighborhood, a local district, or an entire metropolitan area. In other instances, such as facilities serving rural areas, an entire county would constitute the primary proximity. The secondary proximity consists of environmental domains operating at the state and national levels. Primary proximity offers the administrator opportunities for direct involvement in the community, it helps identify local agencies with which exchange relationships should be established, it creates heightened expectations for the organization's social responsibility toward the community, and it influences the market's competitiveness.

Another way to illustrate the interplay of external factors is through four proximal levels shown in Figure 1-4. In this four-level model, the first three levels comprise the primary proximity; the fourth level forms the secondary proximity.

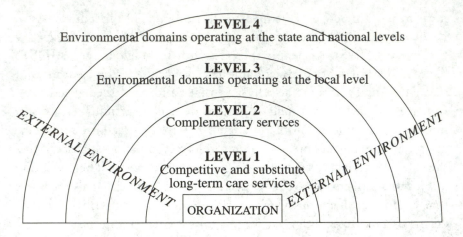

FIGURE 1-4 Four Levels of Environmental Proximity

Level One Proximity

The most proximal influence surrounding a nursing home is other similar facilities and substitute services that directly or indirectly compete against the organization. **Substitute services** are other long-term care options that clients may choose from. For example, home health can be a substitute for institutional care. Three-fourths of all elderly patients receiving home health care require nursing services, and almost 30% need physical therapy (U.S. Bureau of the Census 2003), which are services that are also provided by nursing care facilities. Competition is generally viewed as a threat, but it may also drive the organization to innovate and expand its range of services. For example, a nursing home may open an outpatient rehabilitation center, or expand into delivering home health care. Well thought-out strategic actions can maintain or enhance a facility's competitive advantage.

Level Two Proximity

Level 2 proximity includes a wide variety of **complementary services**. These are services that are not directly rendered by the facility in which the patient resides, but are necessary to address the total health care needs of a patient. A nursing home must assume responsibility for the total care of all patients. **Total care** means recognizing any health care need that may arise, and ensuring that the need is evaluated and addressed by appropriate clinical professionals. When evaluation and treatment are beyond the

nursing home's scope of services, a timely referral to an outside provider is necessary. For example, a skilled care facility is not a mental health institution. It must, however, recognize mental health needs when they arise, and coordinate the delivery of appropriate mental health care. In some cases, it may be necessary to move a patient temporarily to an acute care hospital. In other instances, a patient may need to be referred to a dentist, optometrist, or podiatrist. Community outreach efforts, marketing decisions, and liaisons with complementary service providers that would facilitate ready access to services needed by a facility's patients can only be undertaken with a keen understanding of the level 2 proximity. Administrators must forge meaningful relationships with external providers with the goal of establishing a two-way patient referral system. For example, it is common for nursing homes to have contracts with selected dentists, **podiatrists**, **optometrists**, acute care hospitals, and other providers. Skilled nursing facilities can also make informal agreements with retirement centers, assisted living facilities, and home health agencies to transfer patients among them to accommodate the changing needs of their clients.

Level Three Proximity

At level 3, we can think of the environmental factors operating in a facility's primary proximity. These are local environmental factors and various community and civil services that are not directly associated with health care delivery. Examples include the local economy, demographic shifts in the county, local job conditions, the level of local police- and fire-protection services, and local ordinances.

Level Four Proximity

Level 4 environmental factors affect the nursing home industry at the state and national levels. But in many instances these changes also affect local nursing homes. Examples are changes in the government's payment methods for patients on public assistance, changes in rules and regulations, reports on nursing homes by state or national media, and major industry trends that may eventually become more localized, such as the spread of managed care or growth of substitute services. These influences often shape decisions that administrators must make. Administrative decisions in response to state or national influences often have long-range consequences for the nursing facility, and the type of response is generally quite different from what would be appropriate for the previous three lev-

els of proximity. The first three levels of proximity primarily call for establishing community exchanges and involvement, and for adapting facility services to meet local needs. Level 4 proximity generally requires changes in internal operations to respond to broader issues. Level 4 proximity also requires active participation in the professional and trade associations that represent the industry. Some of the major long-term care associations include the American Health Care Association (AHCA), the American Association of Homes and Services for the Aging (AAHSA), the Assisted Living Federation of America (ALFA), and the American College of Health Care Administrators (ACHCA). These organizations closely follow major economic and political developments, and they keep their members informed about these developments. These organizations maintain active lobbying efforts at the state and national levels in order to influence long-term care policy. From time to time, they also engage in mobilizing grass-root campaigns by directing their members to contact their elected representatives and to educate those representatives about specific nursing home issues.

THE NATURE OF LONG-TERM CARE

This section gives an overview of the main characteristics of long-term care. These characteristics are common to all long-term care services, regardless of whether they are delivered in an institution or in a community-based setting.

Long-term care can be defined as a variety of individualized services that are designed to promote the maximum possible independence for people with functional limitations, and these services are provided over an extended period of time to meet the patients' physical, mental, social, and spiritual needs while maximizing their quality of life. This comprehensive definition covers six main aspects which apply to both institutional and non-institutional long-term care:

- variety of services
- individualized services
- promotion of maximum possible functional independence
- extended period of care
- meeting the patient's physical, mental, social, and spiritual needs
- maximizing quality of life

Variety of Services

The delivery of most types of medical services is based on what is called the **medical model**, according to which health is viewed as the absence of disease. When a patient suffers from some disorder, clinical interventions that are widely accepted by the medical profession are used to relieve the patient's symptoms. Prevention of disease and promotion of optimum health are relegated to a secondary status. By contrast, in long-term care, medical interventions are only a part of an individual's total care. Emphasis is also placed on non-medical factors such as social support and residential services.

By its very nature, effective long-term care is holistic; medical and nursing care make up only one aspect of meeting the needs of the whole individual. On the other hand, the need for long-term care is not deter-mined solely by social and residential factors. The need is triggered by physical factors, mental factors, or both; but once the need for long-term care has been established, a holistic approach must be used in the delivery of care.

Long-term care encompasses a variety of services so that needs that vary from one individual to another can be adequately addressed. The range of services an individual needs is determined by the nature and degree of his or her functional disability, and the presence of any other medical conditions and emotional requirements that the individual may have.

The full range of long-term care can be categorized into four distinct types of services: medical care, mental health, social support, and residen-tial amenities. Although understanding the distinctive features of these services is important, in actual practice they should be appropriately inte-grated into the total package of care in accordance with individual needs.

Medical Care

Medical interventions in long-term care are primarily governed by the presence of two main health conditions: chronic illness and comorbidity. First, as opposed to the care for acute conditions, long-term care focuses on chronic ailments, particularly when they have already caused some physical or mental dysfunction. **Acute conditions** are episodic, require short-term but intensive medical interventions, generally respond to med-ical treatment, and are treated in hospitals, emergency departments, or outpatient clinical settings. **Chronic conditions**, on the other hand, per-

sist over time, are generally irreversible, but must be kept under control. If not controlled, serious complications can develop. Examples of chronic conditions include **hypertension**, diabetes, arthritis, asthma, heart disease, cancer, and **multiple sclerosis**. The mere presence of chronic conditions, however, does not indicate a need for long-term care. When chronic conditions are compounded by the presence of **comorbidity**—coexisting multiple health problems—they often become the leading cause of an individual's disability and erode that individual's ability to live without assistance. This is when long-term care is needed. The prevalence of comorbidity and disability rise dramatically in aging populations.

Services, devices, and living arrangements that enable a functionally impaired person to live independently are a part of long-term care. Examples include assistive devices for mobility, self-care, or eating. Intermittent assistance with household chores can promote independent living. And living with a family member or friend who can routinely give needed assistance, with or without external services, is also considered long-term care. Institutional care generally becomes necessary when part-time help or assistive devices can no longer compensate for a person's loss of function caused by some health-related complications.

The medical aspect of long-term care has two main areas of focus:

- Preventing complications from chronic conditions by routine monitoring, promotion of healthful practices, medical treatment, and coordination of care with other providers, such as dentists, podiatrists, or optometrists
- Delivering treatment after acute episodes.

Preventing Complications

Onset of complications arising from chronic conditions can be prevented or postponed through preventive medicine that includes nutrition, vaccination against pneumonia and influenza, and well-coordinated primary-care services. Each nursing home patient must be under the medical care of a qualified primary-care physician, and the overall care regimen must emphasize prevention through adequate nutrition, **hydration**, **ambulation**, and various other preventive services. Ongoing monitoring and appropriate therapeutic regimens are important to keep chronic conditions under control and to minimize the development of medical complications. Coordination of care with various medical providers such as the

attending physicians, dentists, optometrists, podiatrists, **dermatologists**, or **audiologists** is often required to prevent complications or to deal with the onset of impairments at an early stage.

Delivering Treatment After Acute Episodes

Onset of an acute episode requires medical evaluation and treatment in a hospital where the treatment plan must also take into account the presence of chronic conditions and disabilities. Long-term care will generally continue after the acute condition is stabilized. Post-acute long-term care often consists of **skilled nursing care,** which is physician-directed care provided by licensed nurses and may include such treatments as intravenous feeding, wound care, dressing changes, or clearing of air passages. The patient may also require rehabilitation therapies such as physical therapy, occupational therapy, speech therapy, or respiratory therapy. Rehabilitation therapies are supplemented by ongoing restorative care from the nursing staff. Medical services associated with long-term care are typically provided by nurses and other professional staff members under the supervision of a physician, rather than directly by a physician who may only make periodic rounds for general follow-up.

Mental Health

Long-term care patients frequently suffer from mental conditions, most notably anxiety disorders, depression, and dementia. Mental disorders range in severity from problematic, to disabling, to fatal. Mental illness represents a grave threat, especially for older adults, who also have the highest rates of suicide in the United States (Hoyert et al. 1999). Approximately two-thirds of nursing home residents suffer from mental disorders, including Alzheimer's and related dementias (Burns et al. 1993). It is erroneous, however, to believe that mental disorders are normal in older people or that older people cannot change or improve their mental health. But major barriers must be overcome in the delivery of mental health care. Efforts to prevent mental disorders among older adults have been inadequate because present knowledge about effective prevention techniques is not as extensive as our understanding of the diagnosis and treatment of physical disorders. On the other hand, treatment of many elderly people may be inadequate because assessment and diagnosis of mental disorders in older people can be particularly difficult: the elderly often focus on physical ailments rather than psychological

problems (Department of Health and Human Services [DHHS] 1999). Another drawback is that many elder-care providers, including primary care physicians, are often not adequately trained in the diagnosis and treatment of mental health problems.

Mental health services are generally delivered by specialized providers in both ambulatory (outpatient) and inpatient facilities. Because long-term care facilities are responsible for a patient's total care, nursing home employees must be trained to recognize the need for mental health care, and the facility must arrange to obtain needed services from qualified providers in the community.

Social Support

Social and emotional support are necessary for elderly residents to cope with changing life events. Various stressors commonly accompany the aging process itself and create such adverse effects as frailty, pain, increased medical needs, and the inability to do common things for one-self, such as obtaining needed information or running errands. Other stressors are event-driven. Events that force an unexpected change in a person's lifestyle or emotional balance—such as moving to an institution, adjusting to a new environment, or the loss of a loved one—require coping with stress or grief. Even the thought of change brings on anxiety. Many people go through a period of "grieving" when coming to terms with change, which is a normal part of the transition process. Grieving may manifest in reactions such as anger, denial, confusion, fear, despondency, and depression (McLeod 2002). Social support is needed to help buffer these adverse effects (Feld & George 1994; Krause & Borawski-Clark 1994).

Social support includes both concrete and emotional assistance provided by families, friends, neighbors, volunteers, staff members within an institution, organizations such as religious establishments and senior centers, or by other private or public professional agencies. Such assistance may also include coordination of simple logistical problems that may otherwise become "hassles" of daily life, providing information, giving reminders, counseling, and spiritual guidance.

Residential Amenities

Housing is a key component of long-term care because housing features must be carefully planned to compensate for people's disabilities to the

maximum extent possible. Residences for the disabled must have physical features and amenities that are designed to promote independence. Some simple examples include access ramps that enable people to go outdoors; wide doorways and corridors that allow adequate room to navigate wheelchairs; railings in hallways to promote independent mobility; extra-large bathrooms that facilitate wheelchair negotiation; grab bars in bathrooms to prevent falls and promote unassisted toileting; raised toilets to make it easier to sit down and get up; and pull-cords in the living quarters to summon help in case of an emergency. Adequate space, privacy, safety, comfort, and cleanliness are basic necessities. In addition, the residential environment must feel home-like, it must encourage social activities, it must promote recreational pursuits, and the décor must be both pleasing and therapeutic.

Individualized Services

Long-term care services are specifically tailored to the needs of the individual patient. Those needs are determined by an assessment of the individual's current physical, mental, and emotional condition, as well as that individual's past history of these conditions. A social history is also incorporated into the assessment. The social history encompasses the individual's family relationships, former occupation, community involvement, leisure activities, and cultural factors such as racial or ethnic background, language, and religion. An individualized plan of care is developed so that each type of need can be appropriately addressed through customized interventions. Assessment and plan of care are addressed in Part II of this book.

Functional Limitations and Promotion of Independence

A key determinant of the need for long-term care is the degree to which an individual is unable to independently perform certain common tasks of daily living. The goal of long-term care is to enable the individual maintain functional independence to the maximum level that is practicable. Restoration of function may be possible to some extent through appropriate rehabilitation therapy, but in most cases a full restoration of normal functioning is an unrealistic expectation. The individual must be taught to use adaptive equipment such as wheelchairs, walkers, special eating utensils, or portable oxygen devices. Staff members must render care and assistance whenever the patient is either unable to do things for himself or herself, or absolutely refuses to do so.

In keeping with the goal of maximizing functional independence for the patient, nursing home staff members should concentrate on maintaining whatever ability to function the patient still has and on preventing further decline of that ability. For example, a patient may be unable to walk independently but may be able to take a few steps with the help of trained staff members. Assistance with mobility helps maintain residual functioning. Progressive functional decline may be slowed by appropriate assistance and ongoing restorative care, such as assisted walking, range of motion exercises, bowel and bladder training, and cognitive reality-orientation. However, in spite of these efforts, it is reasonable to expect a gradual decline in an individual's functional ability over time. As this happens, services must be modified in accordance with the changing condition. In other words, long-term care must "fill-in" for all functions that can no longer be carried out independently. For instance, a comatose patient who is totally confined to bed presents an extreme case in which full assistance from employees is required. In most other instances, staff members motivate and help the patient do as much as possible for himself or herself.

Extended Period of Care

For most long-term care patients, the delivery of various services extends over a relatively long period because most recipients of care will at least require ongoing monitoring to note any deteriorations in their health and to address any emerging needs. Certain types of services, such as professional rehabilitation therapies, post-acute convalescence, or stabilization, may be needed for a relatively short duration, generally less than 90 days. In other instances, long-term care may be needed for years. In either situation, the period during which care is given is much longer than it is for acute-care services, which generally last only for a few days. Because patients stay in nursing care facilities over an extended time, holistic care and quality of life (discussed in the next two sections) must be integrated into every aspect of long-term care delivery.

Physical, Mental, Social, and Spiritual Needs

In sharp contrast to the medical model, the **holistic model** of health proposes that health care delivery should focus not merely on a person's physical and mental needs, but should also go beyond those concerns to emphasize well-being in every aspect of what makes a person whole and complete. In this integrated model, a patient's mental, social, and spiritual

needs and preferences should be incorporated into medical care delivery and all aspects of institutional living.

The social aspects of health care include housing, transportation services, information, counseling, recreation, and social contact with other residents, staff members, family, and other members of the outside community. For example, community members can participate in the lives of nursing home residents through a variety of volunteer programs. The success of such programs depends on a facility's ability to form links with the outside community. Also, family and friends must be encouraged to visit the facility as often as possible. The social aspects of institutional living are explored in greater detail in some of the later chapters.

Spirituality and spiritual pursuits are very personal matters, but, for most people, they also require continuing interaction with other members of the faith community. The facility's main responsibility is to make every reasonable accommodation that would allow each individual total freedom to practice or not to practice his or her faith. Most long-term care facilities invite local congregations to hold religious services for their residents' convenience. Participation in these services is important to many residents, but others should have the freedom to refrain from any participation. The facility should also encourage a resident's faith community to maintain contact with the patient through regular personal visits. Clearly, an important factor in building exchange relationships with the community (discussed in Chapter 2) should be to enhance the social and spiritual well-being of the facility's residents.

Quality of Life

For institutionalized patients, **quality of life** refers to the total living experience that results in overall satisfaction with one's life. It is particularly relevant to long-term care facilities because people typically reside there for an extended period. Quality of life is a multifaceted concept that recognizes at least five factors: lifestyle pursuits, living environment, clinical palliation, human factors, and personal choices. Quality of life can be enhanced by integrating these five factors into the delivery of care.

- Lifestyle factors are associated with personal enrichment and making one's life meaningful through activities one enjoys. For example, almost everyone enjoys warm friendships and social relationships. Elderly people's faces often light up when they see children. Many residents may still enjoy pursuing their former leisure activities, such

as woodworking, crocheting, knitting, gardening, and fishing. Many residents would like to engage in spiritual pursuits, or spend some time alone. Even those patients whose functioning has decreased to a vegetative or comatose state can be creatively engaged in something that promotes sensory awakening through visual, auditory, and tactile stimulation.

- The living environment must be comfortable, safe, and appealing to the senses. Cleanliness, décor, furnishings, and other aesthetic features are critical.

- Clinical palliation should be available for relief from unpleasant symptoms such as pain or nausea.

- Human factors refer to employee attitudes and practices that emphasize caring, compassion, and preservation of human dignity in the delivery of care. Institutionalized patients generally find it disconcerting to have lost their autonomy and independence. Quality of life is enhanced when residents have some latitude to govern their own lives. Residents also desire an environment that promotes privacy. For example, one field study of nursing home residents found that dignity and privacy issues were foremost in residents' minds, overshadowing concerns for clinical quality (Health Care Financing Administration 1996).

- The nursing facility should make every effort to accommodate patients' personal choices. For example, food is often the primary area of discontentment, which can be addressed by offering a selection of dishes. Many elderly resent being awakened early in the morning when nursing home staff begin their responsibilities to care for patients' hygiene, bathing, and grooming. Patient privacy is compromised when a facility can offer only semi-private accommodations. But, in that case, the facility can at least give the patients some choice in deciding who their roommates would be.

THE LONG-TERM CARE DELIVERY SYSTEM

Nursing home administrators should have an understanding of the competitive environment. They must also understand the array of complementary services within the long-term care delivery system. The broad

discussion presented in this section provides an overview of the system. The full range of long-term care services is referred to as the **continuum of long-term care**.

The long-term care-delivery system has three major components:

- The informal system
- The community-based system
- The institutional system

The first component, informal care, is the largest, but it generally goes unrecognized. It is largely unfinanced by insurance and public programs, but it includes private-duty nursing arrangements between private individuals. The other two components have formalized payment mechanisms to pay for services, but payment is not available for every type of community-based and institutional service. In many situations, people receiving these services must pay for them out of their personal resources.

Although institutional management is the key focus of this book, the other two components, informal care and community-based service, also have important implications for administrators who manage long-term care institutions. The community-based services and informal systems compete with the institutional system in some ways, but are also complementary. As such, the community-based and informal components of long-term care are very much a part of the external environment of the institutional component.

The three subsystems that form the continuum of long-term care are illustrated in Figure 1-5. The patients' levels of **acuity** and the complexity of services they need increase from one end of the continuum to the other. Informal care provided mainly by family members or friends involves basic assistance, and is at one extreme of the continuum. Next on the continuum are the various community-based in-home services and ambulatory services. Finally, there are different levels of institutional settings.

An evaluation of the extent of disability and personal needs determines which services on the continuum may be best suited, but client preferences often play a significant role. Most people in need of long-term care, for instance, prefer to stay at home or in an institution where the environment is less clinical than in a traditional nursing home. Medical needs, however, may override one's personal preferences. Generally, a patient is admitted to a nursing facility when medical needs become the overriding

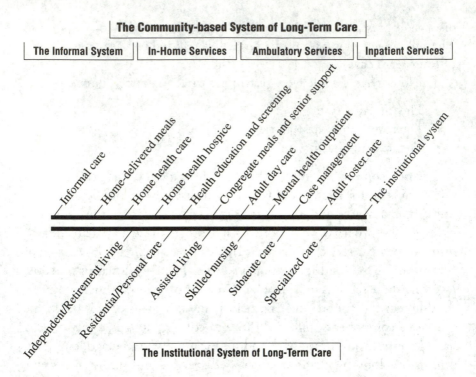

FIGURE 1-5 The Continuum of Long-Term Care

factor, and a patient's long-term care needs cannot be adequately addressed in a less restrictive setting.

In recent years, numerous public and private health care organizations have proliferated, organizations that offer information to consumers on how to care for someone at home, how to find and pay for community-based services, and how to find an appropriate institutional setting. A list of Web sites at the end of this chapter names several such agencies.

The Informal System

The informal long-term care system is very large. An accurate estimate of its size is difficult, mainly because the system is not formally organized and it cannot even be called a system in the true sense. Hence, there is no reporting on how many people are cared for informally at home, and exactly what type of services family, friends, or privately paid help may be providing. For the most part, services rendered are believed to be basic, such as general supervision and monitoring, running errands, dispensing

medications, cooking meals, assistance with eating, grooming and dressing, and, to a lesser extent, assistance with mobility and **transfer**.

The extent of informal care that an individual receives is highly dependent on the extent of the social support network the individual has. People with close family, friends, neighbors, or surrogates, such as members of a religious community, can often continue to live independently much longer than those who have little or no social support. For those who do not have an adequate informal support network, community-based services provided by formal agencies can become an important resource for allowing an individual to continue to live independently.

The Community-Based System

Community-based long-term care consists of formal services provided by various health care agencies. Community-based long-term care services have a threefold objective:

(1) To supplement informal caregiving when more advanced skills are needed than what family members or surrogates can provide to address the patients' needs,
(2) To delay or prevent institutionalization, and
(3) To provide temporary respite to family members from caregiving stress.

Community-based long-term care services can be categorized as intramural and extramural.

Intramural Services

Intramural services are taken to patients who live in their own homes, either alone or with family. The most commonly used intramural services include home health care and **meals-on-wheels** (home-delivered meals). Limited social-support programs that provide services such as homemaker, chores and errands, and handyman assistance also exist, but the funding to pay for such services is not well-established and varies from community to community. In **home health care**, services such as nursing, therapy, and health-related homemaker or social services are brought to patients in their own homes because such patients do not need to be in an institution and yet are generally unable to leave their homes safely to get the care they need.

Extramural Services

Extramural services require that patients come and receive the services at a community-based location. This category mainly includes ambulatory services, such as adult day care, mental health outpatient clinics, and congregate meals provided at senior centers. Respite care is another type of service that can be classified as extramural.

Adult day care enables a person to live with family but receive professional services in a daytime program in which nursing care, rehabilitation therapies, supervision, and social activities are available. Adult day-care centers generally operate programs during normal business hours five days a week. Some programs also offer services in the evenings and on weekends. **Senior centers** are local community centers where seniors can congregate and socialize. Many centers offer a daily meal. Others sponsor wellness programs, health education, counseling services, information and referral, and some limited health care services. **Respite care** can include any kind of long-term care service (adult day care, home health, or temporary institutionalization) when it allows family caregivers to take time off while the patient's care is taken over by the respite care provider. It allows family members to get away for a vacation or deal with other personal situations without neglecting the patient.

The Institutional System

A variety of long-term care institutions form the institutional continuum, with facilities ranging from independent-living or retirement centers at one extreme to subacute care and specialized care facilities at the other extreme (See the lower section of Figure 1-5). Based on the level of services they provide, institutional long-term care facilities may be classified under six distinct categories, keeping in mind, however, that the distinctions among these facilities are not always clear-cut because services provided in some of the settings frequently overlap:

- Independent or Retirement Living
- Residential or Personal Care
- Assisted Living
- Skilled Nursing
- Subacute Care
- Specialized Care

A **continuing-care retirement community** (CCRC) integrates and coordinates the independent living and institutional components of the long-term care continuum. CCRCs offer the advantage and convenience of having a range of living and care options located on one campus. Based on the concept of aging-in-place, people's changing needs are met within the same organizational setting. In addition to retirement and residential living apartments or cottages, CCRCs have personal care and assisted living services available in an adjoining facility. A separate skilled nursing facility provides intermittent as well as permanent accommodations based on changing needs.

Independent or Retirement Housing

Independent housing units and retirement living centers are not long-term care institutions in the true sense. They do not deliver clinical care but emphasize privacy, security, and independence. Their special features and amenities are designed to create a physically supportive environment to promote an independent lifestyle. The living quarters are equipped with emergency call systems. Many of these facilities provide monthly blood pressure and vision screenings, and most organize programs for social activities, recreation, and local outings for shopping and entertainment. **Hotel services** such as meals, housekeeping, and laundry may or may not be included. Apartment units or detached cottages, equipped with kitchenettes and private baths, are the most common types of retirement institutions. Common laundry rooms are often shared with other residents. Nursing or rehabilitation services, when needed, can be arranged with a local home health agency. Many upscale retirement centers abound, in which one can expect to pay a fairly substantial entrance fee plus a monthly rental or maintenance fee. But some communities have government-subsidized housing units available for low-income elderly and disabled people.

Residential or Personal Care Homes

Domiciliary care facilities, board-and-care homes, and foster-care homes fall into this category. Residential or personal care can be defined as nonmedical **custodial care** which is characterized by the least intensive level of inpatient care. In addition to providing a physically supportive environment, these facilities generally provide light assistive care such as medication use management, and assistance with bathing and grooming.

Other basic services such as meals, housekeeping, laundry, and social and recreational activities are also included. Beyond the very basic nursing care, more advanced services can be arranged with a local home health agency on an as-needed basis.

For many people, adult foster-care homes, which are also called **group homes**, have become a preferred alternative to large institutions. **Adult foster care** (AFC) is defined as a service characterized by small, family-run homes that provide room, board, and varying levels of supervision, oversight, and personal care to non-related adults who are unable to care for themselves (AARP Studies Adult Foster Care 1996). The environment in these homes promotes the feeling of being part of a family unit because caregiving families reside in part of the home, and the number of residents is relatively small, generally between 6 and 10. Employed staff generally consists of nursing **paraprofessionals**, such as personal-care aides who do not require a license or professional certification to deliver care. Similar workers employed in nursing homes must be certified by the state.

Because personal care homes are located within residential communities, they are sometimes regarded as a community-based rather than an institutional service.

Assisted Living Facilities

In the past few years, **assisted living** has been the fastest-growing type of long-term care facility in the United States. An assisted-living facility can be described as a residential setting that provides personal care services, 24-hour supervision, scheduled and unscheduled assistance, social activities, and some nursing care services (Citro and Hermanson 1999). Common nursing services include assistance with eating, bathing, dressing, toileting and ambulation, which are rendered by paraprofessionals. Most residents also require help with medications. Some facilities have a skeleton staff of licensed nurses, generally licensed practical (or vocational) nurses, who perform admission assessments and deliver basic nursing care. Advanced nursing care and rehabilitation therapies can be arranged through a home-health agency. The services are specially designed for people who cannot function without assistance and therefore cannot be accommodated in a retirement-living or residential-care facility. Due to increased acuity level, approximately one-third of the residents in assisted-living facilities are discharged because they need the higher level of service that is provided in skilled care nursing homes.

Assisted living is paid for on a private basis for the most part. Monthly fees are between $2,000 and $2,800, but costs vary according to amenities, room size and type (e.g., shared versus private), and the services required by the resident. Most facilities charge a basic monthly rate that covers rent, board, and utilities. Additional fees are charged for nursing services. Many facilities also charge a one-time entrance fee, which may be equal to one month's basic rent. In some states, assisted-living care may be covered under the Medicaid program for SSI recipients, or may be funded through Title XX Social Services Block Grants or 1915(c) HCBS (home and community-based services) waivers. The main purpose of these grants and waivers is to extend Medicaid services to people who otherwise would have to reside in nursing homes at a much higher cost to the Medicaid program. Although most states license assisted-living facilities, the trend is toward increasing the regulatory oversight of these facilities.

Because of the phenomenon of aging-in-place, the distinction between residential/personal care and assisted living is being blurred, from the standpoint of the level of services. However, compared to personal-care homes, assisted-living facilities are generally larger in size and offer some nursing services that were previously available only in traditional nursing homes.

Skilled Nursing Facilities

These are the typical nursing homes at the higher end of the institutional continuum that will be the focus of attention in the remainder of this book. Skilled nursing care is medically oriented care provided by a licensed nurse. It includes monitoring of unstable chronic conditions, evaluation of the patient's care needs, and nursing and therapy treatments. The patient's treatment plan is individualized and involves multidisciplinary input from various health care professionals, such as the attending physician, nurses, the social worker, the dietician, therapists, and others. Compared to the institutions discussed earlier, the environment in skilled nursing facilities is more institutionalized and clinical. Yet, many facilities have implemented creative ideas in layout and design to make their living environments as pleasant and homelike as practicable. Some of these ideas are discussed in Chapters 5 and 6.

These facilities employ full-time administrators who must understand the varied concepts of clinical and social care and have been trained in management and leadership skills. The facility must be adequately equipped to care for patients who require a high level of nursing services

and medical oversight, yet the quality of life must be maximized. A variety of disabilities—including problems with ambulation, incontinence, and behavioral episodes—often coexist among a relatively large number of patients. Compared to other types of facilities, nursing homes have a significant number of patients who are cognitively impaired, besides having physical disabilities and conditions requiring medical intervention. The social functioning of many of these patients has also severely declined. Hence, the nursing home setting presents quite a challenge to administrators in the integration of the four service domains discussed earlier—medical care, mental health care, social support, and residential services.

Subacute Care Units

Subacute care is a blend of intensive medical, nursing, and other services. It has become a substitute for services that were previously provided in acute care hospitals, and it has grown because it is a cheaper alternative to hospital stay. Now, patients who no longer need hospital-based acute care, but require more nursing intervention than what is typically included in skilled nursing care, can receive subacute services in specialized settings. The patients may still have an unstable condition requiring active monitoring and treatment, or they may require technically complex nursing treatments such as wound care, intravenous therapy, blood transfusion, or AIDS care. According to the National Subacute Care Association (NSCA), the severity of a patient's condition often requires active physician contact, professional nursing care, involvement of an interdisciplinary team in total care management, and complex medical or rehabilitative care (NSCA 1996). Subacute services are generally found in two types of locations:

(1) Long-term care units, known as **transitional care units** (TCUs) or **extended care units** (ECUs), located in acute care hospitals. Hospitals entered into this service after they started facing severe occupancy declines because of payment restrictions from the government, starting in the mid-1980s.

(2) Many nursing homes have opened subacute units by raising the staff skill mix by hiring additional registered nurses and having therapists on staff. Some subacute type services are also rendered by community-based home health agencies.

Specialized Care Units or Facilities

By their very nature, both subacute care and specialized care place high emphasis on medical and nursing services. Some nursing homes have opened specialized-care units for patients requiring ventilator care, treatment of Alzheimer's disease, special rehabilitation, or closed head trauma care. There are also freestanding facilities that specialize only in treating Alzheimer's or in rehabilitation. Other specialized facilities include intermediate care facilities for the mentally retarded (ICF/MR). The key distinguishing feature of the latter institutions is specialized programming and care modules for patients suffering from mental retardation and associated disabilities. Physical incapacity and mental retardation often accompany **developmental disabilities** arising in early childhood. Specialized pediatric long-term care facilities fulfill the care needs for such children.

THE NON-LONG-TERM HEALTH CARE SYSTEM

Health care services described in this section are complementary to long-term care. Even though these services fall outside the long-term care domain, they are often needed by long-term care patients. Hence, ideally, the two systems—long-term care and non-long-term care—should be rationally linked. Following are the main non-long-term care services that are complementary to long-term care:

- Primary care delivered by community-based physicians located in solo or group practices and walk-in clinics. By definition, **primary care** is medical care that is basic, routine, continuous over time and coordinated. It is rendered and coordinated by a primary-care physician or a mid-level provider such as a physician's assistant or nurse practitioner. Primary care is brought to the patients who reside in nursing homes, whereas those residing in less institutionalized settings such as retirement living communities or personal care homes commonly visit the primary care physician's office.
- Mental health care delivered by community-based mental-health outpatient clinics and psychiatric inpatient hospitals.
- Specialty care delivered by community-based physicians in specialty practices, such as cardiology, ophthalmology, dermatology, or oncology. Certain services are also delivered by free-standing **chemother-**

apy, radiation, and dialysis centers. Other services are provided by dentists, optometrists, opticians, podiatrists, chiropractors, and audiologists in community-based clinics or mobile units that can be brought to a nursing home. In case of frequently needed services, such as dental, optometric, and podiatric care, nursing homes establish contracts with providers, and in many instances these providers make periodic rounds of the facility for screening and preventive care.

- Acute care delivered by hospitals and outpatient surgery centers. Acute care is short-term, intense medical care for an episode of illness or injury, which generally requires hospitalization. Hence, acute conditions require transfer to a hospital by ambulance. Depending on the patient's condition, surgical procedures may be performed in an outpatient center or a hospital.

- Diagnostic and health screening services offered by hospitals, community-based clinics, or mobile medical services. Some common types of services brought to nursing homes include preventive dentistry, x-ray, and optometric care.

- Hospice care that can be directed from a hospital, home health agency, nursing home, or free-standing hospice. Also referred to as end-of-life care, the term **hospice** is used for a cluster of special services for the terminally ill. It blends medical, spiritual, legal, financial, and family-support services. However, the emphasis is on comfort and pain management, and on social support over medical intervention. The option to use hospice means that temporary measures to prolong life will be suspended. The services are generally brought to the patient, although a patient may choose to go to a free-standing hospice center if one is available.

Rational Integration of Long-Term Care and Complementary Services

The system of long-term care is part of a larger continuum of health care services. Types of services comprising the broader health care continuum are summarized in Table 1-1. Long-term care patients, regardless of where they may be residing, frequently require a variety of services along the health care continuum, dictated by the changes in the patient's condition and episodes that occur over time. As an example, a person living at home may undergo partial mastectomy for breast cancer, return home under the

Table 1-1 The Continuum of Health Care Services

Types of Health Services	Delivery Settings
Preventive care	Public health programs Community programs Personal lifestyles
Primary care	Physician's office or clinic Self-care Alternative medicine
Specialized care	Specialist provider clinics
Chronic care	Primary care settings Specialist provider clinics Home health Long-term care facilities Self-care Alternative medicine
Long-term care	Long-term care facilities Home health
Subacute care	Special subacute units (hospitals, long-term care facilities) Home health Outpatient surgical centers
Acute care	Hospitals
Rehabilitative care	Rehabilitation departments (hospitals, long-term care facilities) Home health Outpatient rehabilitation centers
End-of-life care	Hospice services provided in a variety of settings

care of a home health agency, require hip surgery after a fall in the home, and subsequently be admitted to a skilled nursing facility for rehabilitation. This individual will need recuperation, physical therapy, chemotherapy, and follow-up visits to the oncologist. Once she is able to walk with assistance and her overall condition is stabilized, she may wish to be moved to an assisted living facility. To adequately meet the changing needs of such a patient, the system requires rational integration, but the flow of care is not always as smooth as it should be. Integrated care also requires an evaluation of the patient's needs in accordance with the type and degree of impairment, and a reevaluation as conditions change. Depending on the change in condition and functioning, the patient may move between the various levels and types of long-term care services and may also need transferring between long-term care and non-long-term care services. Figure 1-6 illustrates these concepts.

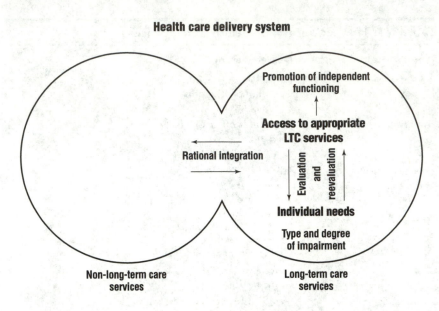

KEY CHARACTERISTICS

1. The LTC system is rationally integrated with the rest of the health care delivery system. This rational integration facilitates easy access to services between the two components of the health care delivery system.
2. Appropriate placement of the patient within the LTC system is based on an assessment of individual needs. For example, individual needs determine whether and when institutionalization may be necessary.
3. The LTC system accommodates changes in individual needs by providing access to appropriate LTC services as determined by a reevaluation of needs.
4. LTC services are designed to compensate for existing impairment and have the objective of promoting independence to the extent possible.

FIGURE 1-6 Key Characteristics of a Well-Designed LTC System

Having primary responsibility for ensuring that each patient's total health care needs are met, administrators must institute working relationships with external agencies. As basic needs change, or episodes occur, the facility must coordinate delivery of appropriate services. In some instances, the patient may be actually moved to a more appropriate facility. This responsibility includes determining which residential setting will be the most appropriate, given the level of support offered by community-based services. Linkages with agencies in both the long-term care and the broad health care delivery sectors are established through contracts in some cases, and through mutual working relationships in others. Some types of transfer arrangements, such as those with acute care hospitals, are

mandated by state and federal regulations. Alliances with other service providers often create mutual advantages for the two parties in each exchange when a patient referral base is established. Administrators can also develop community outreach programs, such as screening and educational programs, case management, or meals-on-wheels, to enhance their facility's image and to create goodwill in the community. A clear understanding of the continuum of services can also enable the administrator to see strategic opportunities to establish new services. For instance, a nursing home can open a home health agency, a hospice program, an outpatient rehabilitation clinic, a respite-care program, specialized care units, or other types of operations.

CONCLUSION

Effective management is founded on open system theory. To obtain critical resources, a nursing facility has no choice but to depend on the external environment. What the facility receives is a function of what it gives back. Also, external trends and events shape management decisions and strategic action. To guide major decision-making, nursing facility administrators should understand the six external environmental domains to identify the nature of external demands and their likely impact on the facility's internal operations.

The need for long-term care services is triggered by the degree of functional impairment, but a variety of services must be provided in a holistic context to meet the varied needs of a long-term care patient with the goal of promoting the maximum level of self-functioning. Long-term care comprises a number of different services along a continuum of care to address the changing needs of patients over time. The rational integration model suggests that facility administrators must institute working relationships with external agencies—both long-term care and non-long term care—because the administrators are primarily responsible for ensuring that each patient's total health care needs are met.

DISCUSSION AND APPLICATION QUESTIONS

1. As a nursing home administrator, would you adopt the closed-system or the open-system approach to management? Explain.

2. Is the open-system approach needed only when the organization faces challenges or tries to take advantage of emerging opportunities? Explain?

3. W.R. Dill identified four environmental factors that are necessary for organizational goal achievement: (1) customers; (2) suppliers of labor, materials, capital, etc.; (3) competitors for both markets and resources; and (4) regulatory groups. What contribution, if any, does each of these factors make in enhancing the organizational effectiveness of a nursing facility? What is the interrelationship between these four factors?

4. Both formal and informal processes can be employed to carry out environmental scanning. Discuss some of the formal and informal means that a nursing home administrator can employ to identify significant environmental trends.

5. Identify the various entities in a nursing facility's primary proximity. What influences might each have on the organization? Again, using the four-level model of proximities, discuss the influences various entities may have on a nursing facility.

6. How does long-term care differ from other types of medical services?

7. Why is it important that employees in nursing facilities not perform every task of daily living for a patient? How much should employees do for patients who have functional impairments?

8. What type of exchanges can be created to enhance the social and spiritual well-being of a facility's patients?

9. Identify some staff practices that will promote each individual resident's privacy and dignity.

10. As an administrator of a skilled nursing facility, how can an understanding of the long-term care continuum help you operate the facility effectively?

INTERNET RESOURCES FOR FURTHER LEARNING

AARP (formerly, American Association of Retired Persons): The nation's foremost consumer-oriented agency that concerns itself with numerous issues related to aging and long-term care.

www.aarp.org

Alliance for Aging Research: The nation's leading citizen advocacy organization for improving the health and independence of Americans as they age. The Alliance was founded in 1986 to promote medical and behavioral research into the aging process.
http://www.agingresearch.org

ARCH National Respite Network and Resource Center: This organization assists and collaborates with those who run programs that provide respite for caregivers of adults and the elderly.
http://www.archrespite.org

Assisted Living Federation of America: A group that offers basic consumer-oriented information on assisted living and gives a directory of assisted living facilities. This trade organization represents assisted living and other senior housing facilities.
www.alfa.org

Family Caregiver Alliance: A nonprofit organization set up to provide information and resources to address the needs of families and friends providing long-term care at home.
http://www.caregiver.org

The George Washington Institute for Spirituality and Health: Affiliated with the George Washington University, the Institute is a leading organization on educational and clinical issues related to spirituality and health.
http://www.gwish.org/

Hospice Foundation of America: A nonprofit organization that provides leadership in the development and application of hospice and its philosophy of care.
http://www.hospicefoundation.org

The Meals On Wheels Association of America: This organization represents those who provide congregate and home-delivered meal services to people in need.
www.mowaa.org

Medicaid: A jointly funded federal-state health insurance program for the indigent.
http://cms.hhs.gov/medicaid

Medicare: A federal program of health insurance for the elderly and some disabled persons.
http://cms.hhs.gov/medicare

National Adult Day Services Association: This organization represents the adult day-care industry and also furnishes consumer information.
http://www.nadsa.org/

National Association for Home Care and Hospice: The nation's largest trade association representing the interests and concerns of home care agencies, hospices, home care aide organizations, and medical equipment suppliers.
http://www.nahc.org

National Citizens' Coalition for Nursing Home Reform: This consumer watchdog organization lobbies to influence long-term care policy, promotes quality standards, and works to empower nursing home residents.
www.nccnhr.org

National Council on Aging: A private, nonprofit organization providing information, training, technical assistance, advocacy, and leadership in all aspects of care for the elderly. It provides information on training programs and in-home services for older people. Publications are available on topics such as lifelong learning, senior center services, adult day care, long-term care, financial issues, senior housing, rural issues, intergenerational programs, and volunteers serving the aged.
www.ncoa.org

National Family Caregiver Support program: A government program established under the Administration on Aging to provide information and support services to family caregivers.
http://www.cfda.gov/public/viewprog.asp?progid=1547

National Hospice Foundation: A nonprofit, charitable organization affiliated with the National Hospice and Palliative Care Organization that provides support and information about hospice care options.
www.hospiceinfo.org

National Mental Health Association: The country's oldest and largest nonprofit organization that addressess all aspects of mental health and mental illness.
www.nmha.org

REFERENCES

AARP studies adult foster care for the elderly. 1996. *Public Health Reports* 111, no. 4: 295.

Brown, W.B. 1977. Systems theory, organizations, and management. In *Long-Term Care Administration: A Managerial Perspective-Volume I*, eds. S. Levey and N.P. Loomba. New York: Spectrum Publications, Inc.

Burns, B. et al. 1993. Mental health service use by the elderly in nursing homes. *American Journal of Public Health*, 83, 331–337.

Citro, J., & S. Hermanson. 1999. *Fact sheet: Assisted living in the United States.* Washington, DC: American Association of Retired Persons.

DHHS. 1999. *Mental health: A Report of the Surgeon General.* Rockville, MD: U.S. Department of Health and Human Services.

Dill, W.R. 1958. Environment as an influence on managerial autonomy. *Administrative Science Quarterly*, 2, 409–443.

Feld, S. & George, L.K. 1994. Moderating effects of prior social resources on the hospitalizations of elders who become widowed. *Journal of Aging and Health*, 6, 275–295.

Health Care Financing Administration. 1996. Nursing home quality of life study spotlights residents' concerns. *Health Care Financing Review* 17, no. 3: 324.

Hoyert, D.L., Kochanke, K.D., & Murphy, S.L. 1999. Deaths: Final data for 1997. *National Vital Statistics Reports, 47* (9). Hyattsville, MD: National Center for Health Statistics.

Krause, N., & Borawski-Clark, E. 1994. Clarifying the functions of social support in later life. *Research on Aging, 16,* 251–279.

McLeod, B.W. 2002. *And Thou Shalt Honor: A Caregiver's Companion.* Wiland-Bell Productions, distributed by Rodale at www.rodalestore.com.

NSCA. 1996. Definition of subacute care as developed and approved by the NSCA board of directors, June 27, 1996. Available: http://www.nsca.net/info/definition.htm

Robbins, S.P. 2000. *Managing Today,* 2nd ed. Upper Saddle River, NJ: Prentice Hall.

U.S. Bureau of the Census. 2003. *Statistical Abstract of the United States: 2003.* Washington, DC.

Von Bertalanffy, L. 1972. The history and status of general systems theory. *Academy of Management Journal* 15, no. 4: 407–427.

Community and Client Exchanges

LEARNING MODULES

1. The importance of returning outputs to the community. Need for the administrator's leadership, team building, budget allocation, and liaison with the governing body.

2. Systems model of value exchanges. Primary service value flow to clients and its implications for the facility. Stakeholders as secondary exchange partners in a value network.

3. Exchange partnerships with the community as part of a facility's mission. Premises on which value-added partnerships are built.

4. Becoming a community resource on long-term care by using a six-point plan. Recognizing opportunities for building a community resource program.

5. Establishing linkages along the health care continuum. Exchange linkages as inconspicuous sources of patient referral. Ways to participate in the long-term care continuum. Partnerships with advocacy agencies. Partnerships with the non-long-term sector.

6. Building value-based partnerships. Sustaining relationships through commitment, continuity, and consistency. Role of a community advisory board.

continues

7. Facility outputs as ingredients necessary for building client exchanges. Exchange relationships lay the foundation for marketing. What the administrator expects from the exchanges.
8. Long-term care clients: older adults, disabled children and young adults, people with AIDS, and people requiring sub-acute or specialized care.
9. Risk factors associated with nursing home demand. How the hospital serves as a gateway to nursing home admissions.
10. Decision-makers for nursing home placement. Influence of physicians and social workers on the decision process.
11. State of the long-term care industry. Demographics that favor future growth. Health policy favors community-based services over institutional care. Quality to receive increasing attention from policymakers and consumers.

As discussed in Chapter 1, a long-term care facility is an integral part of the local community. Based on the open system model, a nursing facility's primary responsibility is to serve the community upon which it depends for resource inputs and for patients who need the facility's services. The quality of these inputs often depends on how well the nursing facility benefits its local community by returning some of its outputs, and on the meaningful partnerships it is able to establish with other agencies. Primarily, the returned benefits help shape the collective opinions of key stakeholders, and these opinions determine the facility's image and repu-tation in the community. The term **stakeholder** can apply to any con-stituent group that has an interest in what a nursing facility stands for and what outcomes it produces. In this sense, stakeholders can be a facility's own employees, and externally, they include family members, other health care providers, advocacy groups, and regulators. Key stakeholders are often important opinion leaders and decision-makers.

Building partnerships with external agencies to meet the total needs of all patients is the basis for rational integration (see Chapter 1). However, these partnerships must extend beyond the health care delivery system. Exchanges with the community in areas outside health care can be critical

for the ongoing well-being of a facility's patients, such as in meeting their social and spiritual needs.

ROLE OF THE ADMINISTRATOR

The administrator plays a major leadership role in deciding which community exchanges will be of most benefit to the facility and its patients. Establishing appropriate linkages is often a key factor in positioning the facility at the forefront in the public's perceptions. The administrator should take the lead in initiating external relationships, and if the facility employs liaison staff or marketing personnel, they should be introduced to these external agencies for continuous contact. Large nursing facilities may employ a marketing director, who will shoulder the major follow-up responsibilities of furnishing updates and information to the external agencies, but the administrator should periodically monitor and nurture those relationships. The facility's key departmental managers, such as the social worker, the director of nursing, and activity director also have some external involvement within their respective areas of responsibility. For example, the social worker has to work closely with the discharge planner at the local hospital, the director of nursing maintains contact with community physicians, and the activity director establishes liaisons with community volunteers and social organizations such as churches and schools. By building a professional team through coaching and providing support, eventually the administrator can rely on subordinate members of the team to carry out most routine engagements and community contacts.

Besides initiating and coaching key staff members through positive leadership, and intermittent monitoring and nurturing of the exchange relationships, the administrator's role also interfaces with the **governing body** or board, especially in formulating or redefining the facility's **mission** and in allocating funds in the **budget**. The facility's responsibilities toward the community should be clearly articulated in the mission statement. By incorporating its social obligations in the mission statement, a facility makes a long-range commitment to becoming an active partner with the community and other stakeholder agencies (Formulation of mission is discussed in Chapter 13). The size of the community-relations budget will depend on the extent of a facility's planned involvement in the activities that are described later in this chapter. Most nursing facilities operate under tight budgets, and governing boards may be reluctant to

approve funds for community relations. Generally, administrators who have a close working relationship with the board members, and who prepare clearly articulated yearly plans that enumerate the goals to be achieved have better success in obtaining funds. The yearly plan and goals should relate to the facility's mission.

EXCHANGE RELATIONSHIPS

A Systems Model of Value Exchanges

Exchange relationships are founded on value received by each partner in the exchange. Conceptually, a nursing home organization creates **value** when the facility produces benefits that exceed, or at least equal, the inputs brought by outsiders into the input-output exchange relationships illustrated in Figure 1-1. More generally, value is perceived when a party expects to receive more than it gives up in an exchange. Miller (1986) argued that seeking any value-based objectives by an organization requires some sacrifice or paying a price. If the organization desires value but is not committed to paying the price, then the value is no more than a wish. As stated in the previous section, a facility's long-range commitment requires paying a price that is set aside in the annual budget. Conversely, a facility may also eventually pay a price through the erosion of its standing in the community if it does not make sacrifices to build community partnerships.

A systems model built on value exchanges (Figure 2-1) is a basic operating model that governs a total pattern of values received, generated, and distributed through the facility's ongoing relationships with its clients and stakeholders. Allee (2000) has called such a pattern of value exchanges as the **value network**, which in today's information- and knowledge-driven era can be applied to almost any type of organization. The values flowing mainly to patients and family members can be regarded as primary service values, which are generated by building and managing the structures and processes of long-term care delivery (covered in Part II of the book) and by managing these resources effectively (covered in Part III of the book). Clients assess the value received through clinical outcomes and their satisfaction with the services. Values return from clients to the nursing facility in the form of revenue and increased profitability. However, there are also intangible benefits that go beyond those accounted for in traditional financial measures (Allee 2000). For example, satisfaction with services

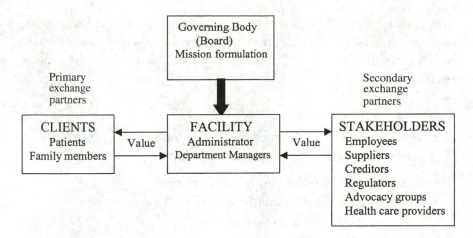

FIGURE 2-1 Systems Model of Value Exchanges

builds customer loyalty. The facility benefits from word-of-mouth marketing when satisfied clients say positive things about the facility to people they know. Caregivers obtain personal gratification (psychic wage) and find their jobs more satisfying when they receive positive feedback from clients. Some loyal family members choose to become volunteers for the facility and serve in areas that enrich the lives of residents. Over time, the facility's enhanced image can produce immeasurable benefits for all major stakeholders in the value network.

On the other side of the exchange, illustrated in Figure 2-1, are the stakeholders who can be regarded as secondary exchange partners. The relationship between the facility and its stakeholders is interdependent because value can be exchanged with mutual advantage to each individual partner. The entire system must be maintained in equilibrium (homeostasis) through management decisions and actions.

Mission-driven Partnerships

Although a facility's primary mission is to provide appropriate long-term care services to members of the community who need those services, its role in the community extends beyond that. In accordance with the facility's formal mission, the administrator must also set up other types of exchanges and partnerships with the community. This broader mission is driven by the facility's social accountability to the community that is met by engaging in various activities to benefit the community. That estab-

lishing such partnerships is in the facility's own best interest should be evident from the open system model discussed in the previous chapter. But, the question arises, "What kind of partnerships should the facility establish?"

Premises for Partnership

Four main partnering principles can help guide the administrator in establishing appropriate community relationships:

- Become a community resource for long-term care.
- Form linkages along the continuum of health care services.
- Establish value-based partnerships.
- Build trust and commitment.

Becoming a Community Resource for Long-term Care

Allee (2000) considers knowledge to be an important medium of exchange in a value network. Every long-term care facility administrator can find some avenue by which the facility can become a valuable resource, because most facilities have expertise in caring for the elderly. A facility can garner expertise by hiring and retaining the most qualified professionals in key positions, and by forming alliances with well-positioned professionals in the community. Staff training is another avenue for acquiring expertise that can be used in exchange partnerships. A six-point plan for community outreach is presented in Exhibit 2-1.

The effective administrator constantly evaluates what expert resources the facility possesses, how the existing resources can be supplemented and enhanced, and how they can be deployed to benefit the community. Depending on the extent of its planned outreach, the facility can establish partnerships with numerous agencies such as hospitals, physicians, local Area Agencies on Aging, local chapters of organizations such as the American Cancer Society, insurance and managed care organizations, etc. The following list of examples will help administrators recognize various opportunities for the facility to become an active community resource:

- Participation in community health fairs or a fair held at the facility
- Free blood-pressure and blood-sugar screening for community residents
- Seminars on caring for chronically disabled family members at home

EXHIBIT 2–1

Six-point Outreach Plan

1 Inventory current resources and level of expertise

2 Begin small programs using existing resources

3 Evaluate success

4 Plan programs for further outreach

5 Establish partnerships with appropriate external agencies. Evaluate the need for staff training.

6 Implement. Evaluate. Modify as necessary.

- Seminars on using adaptive equipment at home
- Seminars on creating safe home environments
- Support groups for dementia-related problems
- Support groups on handling personal guilt and anxiety associated with institutional placement
- Educational seminars on nutritional needs of the elderly
- Educational seminars on Medicare, Medicaid, and private long-term care insurance
- Information on managed care and its role in long-term care delivery
- Information on the role of long-term care ombudsmen
- Education on respite care
- Fund-raising events for health-related non-profit groups or foundations
- Fund-raising events for local charity
- Other events to benefit the community

Lending such expertise to the community is a goodwill gesture. In almost all instances, the programs should be offered free to the public, except to cover the cost of any materials the facility may provide to the participants. Light refreshments are often served to promote social bonding. By sponsoring such programs, the facility creates name recognition for itself and builds a positive image. Many of these events also allow the public to visit the facility and see the premises first hand.

Forming Linkages Along the Continuum of Health Care Services

Partnerships can be established with the various long-term care and non-long-term service sectors. Such linkages also rationally integrate the system to best address patient needs.

Linking the Informal System

Some of the community exchanges discussed above form linkages with the informal sector of long-term care. Informal caregivers often need support and assistance with their personal stress and burnout. Many are seeking answers on how to cope with parents or relatives who suffer from memory loss, depression, behavioral episodes, or incontinence. Although the facility establishes such exchanges with no expectation of returns, over time the partnerships become inconspicuous sources of patient referral. The facilities that have forged effective community relationships over time stand a better chance of attracting new clients than competitors who have not forged such relationships. As Figure 2–2 shows, almost one-third of all new geriatric admissions to nursing homes come from private residences.

Linking Across the Long-Term Care Continuum

Different types of linkages can be formed with the formal long-term care sector for participating in the continuum of services. Examples include: becoming a food preparation center for the local meals-on-wheels program, developing an adult day care center or participating in one at another site, establishing partnerships with retirement homes or personal-care homes to lend expert assistance to their residents when needed, and formalizing transfer arrangements with these institutions to best accommodate the changing needs of their residents.

Linking with Advocacy Agencies

An often overlooked area for meaningful exchanges is the local **Area Agency on Aging** and the Ombudsman. Area Agencies on Aging were established in local communities under the 1973 amendments to the federal Older Americans Act of 1965 to address the needs of Americans aged 60 and over. Among other services, these agencies assess clients' needs and determine eligibility for services best suited to meet their needs. Amendments to the Older Americans Act in 1978 mandated that each state have an ombudsman program, which is administered by the Agencies on Aging. An **ombudsman** is a trained professional who works

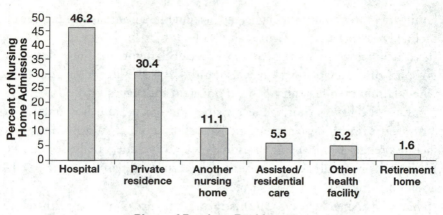

Source: Data from Statistical Abstract of the United States: 2003, p. 129. U.S. Census Bureau (Based on the 1999 National Nursing Home Survey).

FIGURE 2-2 Living Quarters Before Nursing Home Admission for People 65 Years Old and Over.

independently with nursing home residents and their families in resolving concerns they may have about their lives in a facility. As an advocate for residents of nursing homes, board-and-care homes, and assisted living facilities, the ombudsman investigates and resolves complaints on behalf of facility residents and informs consumers on how to obtain quality care. For instance, an ombudsman helps educate the public and facility staff on complaint filing, new laws governing facilities, and the best practices used in improving quality of care and evaluating long-term care options (Institute of Medicine 2001). The ombudsman also informs public agencies about the problems of older adults residing in nursing facilities. A facility can form positive working relationships with its local ombudsman by inviting the ombudsman to the facility, and by involving him or her in the facility's resident council and family-council programs.

Linking with the Non-Long-Term Sector

As discussed in Chapter 1, the non-long-term care sector is complementary to long-term care. Complementary services enable a long-term care facility to address the total care needs of a patient. Therefore, it is incumbent upon the facility administrator to establish linkages with community physicians and hospitals. Physicians often struggle with questions from

family members about nursing home placement. They may or may not be inclined to make a direct recommendation but are likely to suggest two or three facilities for a family member to check out before making a decision. Hospital discharge planners may also find themselves in similar situations where family members may depend on them for suggestions. Also, many communities have a shortage of nursing home beds, and hospitals often struggle to find long-term care beds at short notice. At a minimum, a facility's relationship with the hospitals would include a daily or periodic phone call or e-mail message updating the discharge planners on the availability of beds.

Savvy nursing facility administrators are also working with acute care providers, positioning themselves to meet the needs of managed care organizations looking for high-quality, low-cost health care. Beck (1996) recommends three different ways (discussed in Chapter 4) in which hospitals and nursing facilities can establish partnerships: through sponsorship agreements, bed reserve arrangements, or shared service agreements.

Establishing Value-Based Partnerships

Value-based exchanges between any two or more entities require win-win opportunities for the parties to the exchange. All too often, facility administrators focus only on how to get more patients to fill empty beds. Such thinking is short-sighted because the administrator seeks to benefit only the facility and often exhibits little regard for what is in the patient's best interest. The first type of exchange discussed above, in which the facility becomes a community resource for long-term care and provides helpful services to the community, may appear to be a one-sided exchange that benefits only the community. But in the long run, such exchanges often benefit the facility as well. Administrators who have established ongoing exchanges with the community generally have little reason to worry about future patient referrals to the facility.

Partnerships with the formal long-term care sector and with the non-long-term care sector are also based on the mutual-value concept. A win-win situation adds value for all partners, so value is potentially lost when the same exchange relationship is not formed. Added value also benefits the patients. For example, collaboration between a nursing home and hospice adds value because research documents superior outcomes for residents who enroll in hospice for end-of-life care (Miller and Mor 2002). Since one in four Americans who reach the age of 65 will likely spend their

last days in a nursing home (Hanson et al. 2002), linking nursing home and hospice services can deliver added value to patients. Value creation in long-term care is often founded on such patient service initiatives.

The implication of value-added partnerships for administrators is that they need to think about how a potential exchange relationship can add value for the other partner and for the patients. What each party will put into the exchange and the potential benefits to be derived should be openly discussed in order for such exchanges to materialize. A simple question the other party will ask itself is, "What is in it for my agency?" Before they agree to formalize any relationships, the other parties have to be convinced that "there is something in it for them." This type of a value-based proposition can be called win-win. On the other hand, potential future rewards are often accompanied by certain risks. Partnerships are built on an open discussion of possible risks and rewards, and a willingness to share both.

One caveat must be kept in mind while building partnerships. The facility must refrain from any activities that may amount to payment for referral of patients or clinical services. The anti-kickback legislation (discussed in Chapter 4) makes it illegal to knowingly and willfully offer, pay, solicit, or receive remuneration to induce referrals for which payment may be made by Medicare or Medicaid, the two major public financing programs that pay for nursing home services.

Building Trust and Commitment

Trust is built over time in an environment of mutual understanding and respect. It requires open and frequent communication, congruent goals and objectives, and joint problem solving (Kaluzny and Zuckerman 1999). A win-win proposition is the first step toward building trust, but it requires a long-range strategy driven by commitment, continuity, and consistency, the "3 Cs" that are indispensable for sustaining partnerships over time.

Commitment requires two things: (1) Determining where the greatest needs are. Evaluate the expertise the facility is able to provide and decide on programs that will optimize mutual benefits for the community, other exchange partners, and the facility. (2) Funding appropriate expenditures in the annual budget to carry out the community-oriented programs. The budget may also require salary appropriations for a full-time or part-time staff position responsible for coordinating the programs and getting the word out into the community. Once a facility has made the commitment

to provide goodwill exchanges, they must be carried out with consistency. Occasional exchanges do not form sustainable relationships.

Continuity is based on long-range commitment. It also requires designating a liaison staff member to manage the relationship on an ongoing basis, and to handle details as they arise. It also requires that the administrator monitor and nurture the relationship by occasional contact.

Consistency is based on written policies that are used as a basis for understanding. Written policies also provide continuity despite turnover of administrators or key staff members. These policies must be incorporated in the training and orientation of new staff members.

Once trust is established, community stakeholders can be the facility's "eyes and ears." They can be included in discussions for improving existing services, and in strategic decisions such as adding a new service, or if necessary, discontinuing an existing program.

A community advisory board consisting of key stakeholders can be instrumental in helping the facility fulfill its ongoing mission. A **community advisory board** is distinct from the main governing body. Unlike the governing body, the advisory board does not oversee facility operations or evaluate the administrator's performance. Composed of key community leaders, the advisory board functions as the "eyes and ears" for the facility. Through their influence, the advisory board members can also assist the administrator form meaningful partnerships discussed in this section.

INGREDIENTS FOR BUILDING CLIENT EXCHANGES

Client exchanges are built not on what a facility expects to receive but on what it is willing and able to give. But willingness and ability are not enough. The administrator must also actively engage in building exchange partnerships, as discussed in the previous section. This section focuses on the outputs needed for creating exchanges, and the facility's expectations from the exchanges.

Facility Outputs As Key Ingredients

Long-term care facilities produce four major outputs that are necessary to build exchange links with the community (see Figure 1-1):

- Care quality
- Client satisfaction

- Staff loyalty
- Profits.

The first three—care quality, client satisfaction, and staff loyalty—are marketing ingredients. They are essential for creating the goodwill necessary to make the facility attractive to potential exchange partners. Once the exchange relationships have been established, they often function as powerful avenues through which the facility can market its services to the community. But for such marketing strategies to succeed the facility must pay utmost attention to the three quality outputs as they become the determining factor in shaping the facility's reputation and image in the community. The fourth output, profits, provides the financial resources necessary for achieving the other three outputs. Profits also provide the means for funding the community-oriented programs carried out as a goodwill gesture by the facility when it functions as an expert resource on various long-term care issues.

Expectations from the Exchanges

At this point, the facility administrator may ask the question, "What is in it for my facility if I have to initiate all the exchanges?" The answer is, the facility generally realizes no direct and immediate reward. The establishment of exchange relationships should be viewed as an investment in the facility's future. Like any other investment, this is a long-range proposition. But, over a period of time, the facility can expect to gain some healthy indirect returns on the investment. The facility is dependent on the community to get patients who need its services. The exchanges established by the facility help build its reputation, not only among the general public but also among professional agencies that are part of the exchange. Whenever these agencies come across clients who need nursing home services, these entities will be more inclined to refer those clients to a facility that is in an exchange relationship with them than to one that is not. Creation of referral sources is one marketing strategy the facility can employ (details are given in Chapter 15).

CLIENTS OF LONG-TERM CARE

According to the 1999 National Nursing Home Survey, there were 18,000 nursing homes operating in the United States, caring for 1.6 million residents. The average number of beds per nursing home was 105.

The average occupancy rate[1] was 87% and the discharge rate[2] was 134 residents per 100 beds. Nursing homes are actually used by a much greater number of people than the 1.6 million residents counted at the time of the survey, because many residents are admitted for a short duration and then discharged to a community setting. Of the 2.5 million discharges in 1999, 68% stayed in the facility for less than three months. About 24% had deceased. The 1999 data also show that the average length of time a patient stays in a nursing home is 272 days (National Center for Health Statistics 2002). Approximately 90% of all nursing home residents are elderly; the remaining 10% are younger than 65 (DHHS 2003, 322). Besides older adults (geriatric patients), nursing homes also serve the young disabled, people with acquired immune deficiency syndrome (AIDS), and people that require subacute or specialized care. At present, reliable data are not available on facilities other than nursing homes, such as assisted living facilities and board-and-care homes. Services most commonly used by young and old nursing home patients are included in Table 2-1.

Older Adults

The elderly, people 65 years of age or older, are the primary clients of long-term care. Most of the elderly, however, are in good health. According to household interviews of the elderly civilian non-institutionalized population, only 27% described their health as fair or poor (DHHS 2003, 208). It is reasonable to assume that the segment of the elderly population in fair-to-poor overall health is likely to require long-term care at some point. Even for those in good or excellent health, short-term long-term care (needed for 90 days or less) may become necessary after an accident, surgery, or acute illness. The household interviews just mentioned also indicated some important differences in health according to population characteristics. Those in fair or poor health are more likely to be black, Hispanic, or American Indian rather than white or Asian; financially poor or near poor; and rural rather than urban residents. A person's health status is also likely to decline with age.

A person's age, or the presence of chronic conditions, by itself does not predict the need for long-term care. However, as a person ages, chronic

---

[1]The occupancy rate is calculated by dividing residents by the number of beds.
[2]The discharge rate is calculated by dividing discharges by the number of beds.

Table 2-1 Services Most Commonly Used by Nursing Home Residents

	Age	
	Under 65 years	65 years and over
Service used	Percent of Residents	Percent of Residents
Dental care	30.8	31.8
Equipment or devices	51.2	53.4
Hospice services	*	1.9
Medical services	92.3	90.3
Mental health services	36.0	21.5
Nursing services	97.1	96.2
Nutritional services	77.7	72.9
Occupational therapy	22.6	18.1
Personal Care	83.2	90.7
Physical therapy	29.3	26.3
Prescribed and non-prescribed medicines	93.8	94.2
Social services	78.2	70.8
Speech or hearing therapy	7.3	7.7
Transportation	30.3	22.5
Other	7.1	7.5

Source: National Nursing Home Survey 1999. *Vital Health Statistics*, Series 13, No. 152 (2002), p. 26. National Center for Health Statistics.

ailments, comorbidity, disability, and dependency tend to follow each other. This progression is associated with increased probability that a person would need long-term care (Figure 2-3). Even though only a small percentage of the elderly are actually in need of nursing home care (see Table 2-2), many more require assistance at home or in less clinical institutional settings. In 2001, only about 4.2% of the total U.S. elderly population was residing in nursing homes (DHHS 2003). Their demographic characteristics appear in Figure 2-4.

Disability is commonly assessed in terms of a person's physical ability to perform certain key everyday activities, even though disability can also be mental. Chronic mental impairments are often assumed to eventually manifest in physical dysfunction, but that is not always the case. Yet disability assessment concentrates primarily on physical limitations. Individuals with certain chronic mental illnesses may be able to perform most everyday activities but may require supervision and monitoring. Severe dementias, on the other hand, which are mostly confined to older people, are commonly accompanied by physical functional limitations.

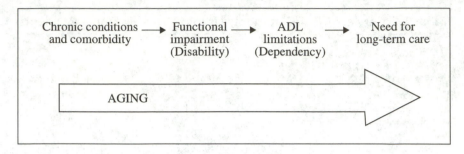

FIGURE 2-3 Progressive Steps Toward the Need for Long-Term Care Among the Elderly

Two measures of disability assessment are commonly used. The first **activities of daily living (ADL)** scale is used to determine whether an individual needs assistance in performing six basic activities: eating, bathing, dressing, using the toilet, maintaining continence, and getting into or out of a bed or chair (transferring). Grooming and walking a distance of eight feet are sometimes added to evaluate self-care and mobility. The ADL scale is the most relevant measure for determining the need for assistance in a long-term care facility. Therefore, ADLs are a key input in determining a facility's aggregate patient acuity level. **Acuity** is a term used to denote the level of severity of a patient's condition, and consequently the amount of care the patient would require. ADLs are also a key component of Medicare and Medicaid payment methodologies, as discussed in Chapter 4. According to the 1999 National Nursing Home Survey, three quarters of the residents in U.S. nursing homes required assistance with 3 or more ADLs (Figure 2-5). Most residents received help with bathing/showering, dressing, using the toilet, eating, and transferring in or out of bed or chair (Figure 2-6).

The second commonly used measure is called **instrumental activities of daily living (IADL)**. This measure focuses on a variety of activities that are necessary for independent living. Among the IADLs are doing housework, cooking, doing laundry, grocery shopping, taking medication, using the telephone, managing money, and moving around outside the home (Lawton and Brody 1969). The measure is most helpful when a nursing home patient is being discharged for community-based long-term care or independent living. It helps in assessing how well the individual is likely to adapt to living independently and what type of supportive services may be most appropriate to ensure that the person can live independently.

Table 2-2 Elderly population, nursing home residence, functional status, and common chronic conditions

AGE GROUPS	65 and over (All elderly)	65–74	75–84	85 and over
1999 data				
Elderly population (% of total U.S. population)	12.7	6.7	4.5	1.5
Age segments (% of total elderly population)	100	52.7	35.2	12.1
Nursing home residence[1] (per 1000 elderly pop.)	42.9	10.8	43.0	182.5
Nursing home resident age distribution (% of all residents)	90.3	12.0	31.8	46.5
Functional status of elderly nursing home residents (% with specified functional disabilities):				
Dependent mobility	80.4	73.9	77.8	83.8
Incontinent (bowels and/or bladder)[2]	65.7	58.5	64.2	68.6
Dependent eating	47.4	43.1	46.6	49.0
All three of the above	37.0	31.7	35.4	39.4
2000 data				
				75 and over
Functional status of non-institutionalized population (% with any activity limitation[3])	34.7	26.1		45.1
1998 data				
Functional limitations among the elderly[4]:				
(% of elderly in each age group who have functional limitations)				
No limitations		72.4	53.7	25.2
IADL only		15.6	20.7	20.7
1 or 2 ADL		8.2	14.7	22.6
3 to 5 ADL		3.8	11.0	31.6

Common chronic conditions among non-institutionalized persons age 70 and over:
Arthritis
Hypertension
Heart disease
Diabetes
Respiratory illnesses (asthma, chronic bronchitis, and emphysema)
Stroke
Cancer

[1]Excludes residents in personal care or domiciliary care homes
[2]Includes those with ostomy or indwelling catheter
[3]Limitation caused by chronic conditions
[4]Medicare beneficiaries age 65 and over
Sources: Health United States 1999, pp. 41, 42; Health United States 2002, pp. 79, 189, 266, 267, 302, 326.

Gender

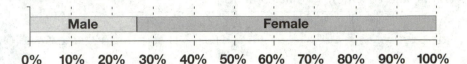

Age

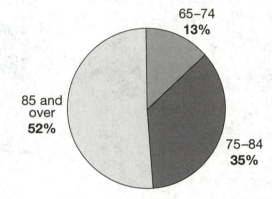

Source: Data from *Statistical Abstract of the United State: 2003*, p. 129. U.S. Census Bureau (Based on the 1999 National Nursing Home Survey).

FIGURE 2-4 Demographic Characteristics of Nursing Home Elderly Residents.

The Non-Elderly

Disability is not necessarily age dependent. People who develop functional impairments can be children or adults of any age. Generally, different types of health problems create the need for long-term care among children and adolescents, and among young adults. Common conditions leading to a need for long-term care among the non-elderly are summarized in Figure 2-7.

Children and Adolescents

In children, functional impairments are often birth related, such as brain damage which can occur before or during childbirth. Examples of birth-related disorders include **cerebral palsy**, **autism**, **spina bifida**, and **epilepsy**. These children grow up with physical disability, and need help with ADLs. The term **developmental disability** describes the general physical incapacity such children may face at a very early age. Those who

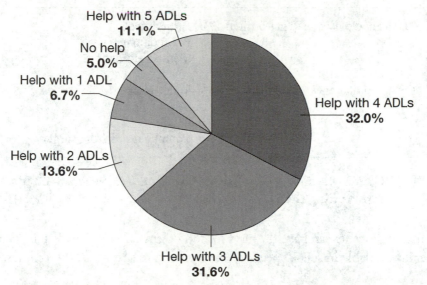

NOTE: ADL is activities of daily living

Source: Data from *Statistical Abstract of the United States: 2003*, p. 129. U.S. Census Bureau (Based on the 1999 National Nursing Home Survey).

FIGURE 2-5 Percent Distribution of Residents With Dependencies in Activities of Daily Living and Numbers of Dependencies.

acquire such dysfunctions are referred to as developmentally disabled, or DD for short. **Mental retardation**, that is, below-average intellectual functioning, also leads to developmental disability in most cases. The close association between the two is reflected in the term **MR/DD**, which is short for mentally retarded/developmentally disabled. Thus, some children

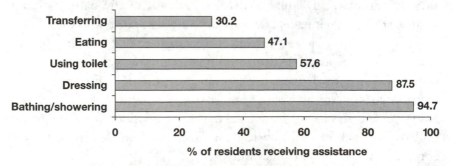

Source: Data from *Statistical Abstract of the United States: 2003*, p. 129. U.S. Census Bureau (Based on the 1999 National Nursing Home Survey).

FIGURE 2-6 Type of ADL Assistance Received by Nursing Home Elderly Residents.

Children/adolescents (ages birth to 17):	Birth defects
	Brain damage
	Mental retardation
Young adults (ages 18-64):	Major injury
	Serious illness
	AIDS
	Complications from surgery

FIGURE 2-7 Common Conditions Creating the Need for Long-Term Care Among the Non-elderly

and adolescents can have the need for long-term care services that are generally available in special pediatric long-term care and MR/DD facilities.

Young Adults

Permanent disability among young adults commonly stems from **neurological** malfunctions, degenerative conditions, traumatic injury, or surgical complications. For example, **multiple sclerosis** is potentially the most common cause of neurological disability in young adults (Compston and Coles 2002). Severe injury to the head, spinal cord, or limbs can occur in victims of vehicle crashes, sports mishaps, or industrial accidents. Other serious diseases, injuries, and respiratory or heart problems following surgery can make it difficult, or even impossible, for a patient to breathe naturally. Such individuals, who cannot breathe (or ventilate) on their own, require a ventilator. A **ventilator** is a small machine that takes over the breathing function by automatically moving air into and out of the patient's lungs. Ventilator-dependent patients also require total assistance with their ADLs.

Many MR/DD victims are entering adulthood. The aging process begins earlier in people with mental retardation, and the age of 50 has been suggested to demarcate the elderly segment in this population (Altman 1995). An increasing number of people with MR/DD are now living beyond the age of fifty. Hence, this population will manifest not only severe mental and physical impairments but also the effects of chronic conditions and comorbidity.

Evidence suggests that MR/DD patients may function better in community-based residential settings than in traditional nursing homes. Studies of patients who had moved out of nursing homes to community

settings demonstrated that these patients had higher levels of adaptive behavior, lifestyle satisfaction, and community integration than residents who remained in nursing homes (Heller et al. 1998; Spreat et al. 1998). A more attractive physical environment and greater opportunity for choice-making were associated with higher levels of adaptive behavior. Greater opportunity to make choices, small facility size, and family involvement were associated with higher levels of community integration (Heller et al. 1999; Heller et al. 2002).

People with AIDS

Care of AIDS patients in long-term care facilities dates back to the late-1980s. Before this time, care for patients with HIV/AIDS was focused on ambulatory and acute-care services. However, most nursing facilities at the time were not prepared to admit AIDS patients because their primary focus was on geriatric care. Some of the concerns expressed by nursing homes for their reluctance to admit AIDS patients included inadequate preparation to provide care; age differences and interest disparities between the younger AIDS patients and the predominantly elderly nursing home population; negative reactions from the families of existing patients; inadequate financing to support care; and the potential for increased regulation (Marder and Linsk 1995). Mainly in response to the looming threat of discrimination complaints against nursing homes that refused to admit patients with AIDS, the industry responded by training staff members, and some facilities designated sections of the facility to care for AIDS patients. Some states, such as New York, on the other hand, took a more practical approach. The state of New York established incentives to attract health care providers, including a financing mechanism that recognized the increased cost of providing services to the AIDS population (Hoos et al. 2000). A number of states since then have developed a continuum of services that includes AIDS adult day-care programs, AIDS home health care, AIDS residential care facilities, nursing home beds dedicated to AIDS patients, and AIDS hospices.

In the United States, a little over 3,000 nursing home beds are designated specifically for AIDS (AARP 1998). However, a number of states still have not taken this type of initiative. On the other hand, it has been difficult to estimate the demand for AIDS care beds.

When it was first discovered, AIDS was a fatal disease that resulted in a relatively painful death shortly after HIV infection developed into AIDS.

In recent years, the introduction of protease inhibitors, antiretroviral therapy, and antibiotics for the treatment of AIDS-related infections has vastly improved the health condition of HIV/AIDS patients. These treatments have slowed the progression of the disease from the appearance of first symptoms to death. Consequently, AIDS has evolved from an end-stage terminal illness to a chronic condition. Over a period of time, people with AIDS are subject to a number of debilitating conditions, which create the need for assistance. For instance, nervous system disorders are common in AIDS patients even though the patients may survive for several years. Infections of the nervous system, such as cytomegalovirus, can cause blindness and dementia. It remains unpredictable whether the improvements in the clinical status of HIV/AIDS population will continue, or if morbidity and intense-care needs will increase in the future (Hoos et al. 2000). However, the accompanying disabilities of AIDS patients, in spite of the advanced treatments just mentioned, have actually increased the demand for long-term care as the patient's health condition changes over time (Montoya et al. 1996).

People Requiring Subacute or Specialized Care

A growing number of nursing facilities have developed sub-acute and specialized care services. Subacute care includes services for people who require convalescence from acute illness or surgical episodes. These patients are recovering but are still subject to illness or complications while in recovery. The patients are transferred from the hospital to a nursing home after the acute condition has been treated, or after surgery. Some common orthopedic episodes include hip and knee replacement. Other subacute and specialized services are needed for patients who require ventilator care, head trauma victims, comatose patients, and those with progressive Alzheimer's disease.

NURSING HOME DEMAND AND DECISION-MAKING

Risk Factors Creating Demand

Nursing home demand is driven by certain risk factors that increase the probability of institutional care. The risk factors include both clinical and social-support attributes. Based on research findings, clinical factors asso-

ciated with institutionalization in a nursing home include physical disability, impaired mental functioning, and age. Prior hospitalization and prior nursing-home admission also increase the probability of nursing-home placement (Giacalone 2001, 36, 37). Other clinical factors are diabetes, fracture, dementia, and bowel incontinence (Rivo 1995).

Various attributes associated with the patient's social support network are also significant predictors of nursing-home placement. For example, it has been demonstrated that older persons who have a family network and have regular contact with kin have a lower risk of institutionalization, whereas living alone is a significant risk factor for institutionalization. For men, having a spouse is the most important factor in reducing the probability of entry into a nursing home. For women, having regular contact with at least one family member reduces the risk (Freedman et al. 1994). Overall, married older persons have about half the risk of nursing home admission of unmarried older adults (Freedman 1996). Caregiver problems in a community setting are also a significant predictor, among which the most significant are (1) caregiver living separately from the patient, (2) time conflicts because of a job, and (3) caregiving stress (Rivo 1995).

A substantial number of nursing home admissions are direct transfers from hospitals (Figure 2-2). Also, elderly persons residing in nursing homes have a much higher incidence of hospital admission than those living in the community. In the former case, those who are hospitalized from a nursing home frequently return to a nursing home after hospitalization (Freiman and Murtaugh 1995). Because the hospital serves as a gateway to nursing home admissions, acute-care hospitals should be among the prime candidates with which administrators should establish exchange partnerships. The close interactions between hospitals and nursing homes also have implications for improving the level of care in nursing homes. To reduce the need for hospitalization, nursing home administrators ought to find ways to reduce infections, prevent falls and accidents, and ensure appropriate dietary intake.

Decision-Makers for Nursing Home Placement

Not surprisingly, the decision to go to a nursing home is typically involuntary, from the perspective of both the patient and the family. Despite having severe impairments, older adults would rather stay in their own homes. Except in circumstances such as pre-planned surgery, which may require subsequent rehabilitation in a nursing home, the

need for institutionalization often develops abruptly and is frequently a crisis situation.

Wiseman and Roseman (1979) describe nursing home admission as a two-stage process. Stage One is characterized by unplanned events, or "push factors," that trigger the decision to move a patient to a nursing home. Unplanned admissions to nursing homes often occur due to sudden deteriorations in health or unexpected hospitalizations. Once such crisis-oriented triggers arise, the decision process has to move rapidly. At this stage, people who influence the patient socially, such as family, friends, physicians, and other health care professionals, are frequently involved in the decision process. Stage Two is characterized by the search for a suitable nursing facility. This search is most commonly undertaken by close family members. The patient's adult children, and sometimes the spouse, are most likely to be the primary decision-makers. The patients themselves are generally not active participants in the decision, especially if their functioning is diminished.

Past research demonstrates that physicians have a strong influence on decisions leading to nursing home admissions. The physician may not actually choose the facility, but is likely to be consulted by family, and can be very influential in the decision process. African-American families are actually unlikely to consider nursing home placement unless this alternative is first mentioned by a physician (Belgrave et al. 1993). Hospital social workers also play an influential role, followed by nurses, although nurses are not as frequently consulted as physicians and social workers. African Americans are particularly likely to consider social workers and nurses as key players in nursing-home placement decisions (McAuley and Travis 1997).

STATE OF THE LONG-TERM CARE INDUSTRY

As long-term care administrators contemplate the exchange relationships they can form, it will be helpful to understand the current direction of the long-term care industry. These trends are also likely to set the industry's future direction. As explained in Chapter 1, such dynamics are part of the external environment that must be studied for strategic decision-making and effective management of nursing facilities.

Older people use a disproportionately large share of total health care services in the United States. Although people over age 65 represent only about 13% of the U.S. population, this group consumes one-third of all national health care spending, and occupies one-half of all physician time. The elderly population is growing. With the aging of the baby boomers, the number of Americans over 65, which today is 35.3 million, will double in size and approach 20% of the population by 2030. The number of Americans over 85 is expected to nearly quadruple by mid-century from its current census of 4.4 million. While healthcare services needed by the elderly are expected to multiply, there is currently a critical shortage of physicians, nurses, and pharmacists who are certified in geriatric medicine.

Health policy trends have clearly shown a preference for allowing the elderly to remain in their own homes or communities. Nursing homes are not the only long-term care option available to the elderly. Consequently, the growth of community- and home-based services has outstripped the growth of institutional services. This development does not mean, however, that the need for institutional long-term care will decline. But it does underscore the importance of establishing community exchanges by nursing facility administrators to get future referrals.

Policy initiatives are also increasingly focusing on quality of care in nursing facilities. Quality data and nursing facility ratings based on such data have been made public, which means that consumers will also begin paying increasing attention to published quality information on individual nursing homes. Government oversight is clearly going to focus on facilities that consistently have problems with quality. Any negative publicity ensuing from government action can seriously hamper a facility's ability to sustain existing partnerships or to forge new ones. Therefore, administrators must pay close attention to quality as a key facility output that helps to build exchange relationships.

CONCLUSION

Establishing value-based community exchanges is a vital responsibility of the nursing home administrator. The governing body and the administrator must work together to formulate a mission and make budget allocations for carrying out various programs of service for the community. The systems model of value exchanges underscores the importance of value-based objectives for client and stakeholder exchanges. Value-based exchanges also

have strategic significance for marketing the facility. A facility that excels in producing value-added outcomes positions itself to benefit from an inflow of referrals, provided that the exchanges can be sustained over time through commitment, continuity, and consistency, the "Three Cs." In formulating exchange relationships, particular attention should be paid to entities that make or influence decisions regarding nursing-home placement.

DISCUSSION AND APPLICATION QUESTIONS

1. Discuss some leadership traits that may be helpful in building a professional team for enhancing a nursing facility's commitment to establish exchange relationships.
2. Nursing home administrators generally view regulators and consumer advocates as adversaries. How can these entities be included in value-based partnerships?
3. Develop a mission statement that incorporates an organization's commitment to value-based exchanges. Incorporate into the mission some of the elements illustrated in Figure 1-1.
4. As an administrator, how would you convince the governing board to allocate funds in the annual budget to carry out the facility's outreach mission?
5. A new discharge planner has just replaced the previous one at your local hospital. At your very first meeting with her, you get bombarded by a number of negative comments about your facility. How would you respond?

INTERNET RESOURCES FOR FURTHER LEARNING

National Association of Area Agencies on Aging (N4A): The umbrella organization for the 655 area agencies on aging (AAAs) and more than 230 Title VI Native American aging programs in the U.S. Through its presence in Washington, D.C., N4A advocates on behalf of the local aging agencies to ensure that needed resources and support services are available to older Americans.
http://www.n4a.org/

National Citizens' Coalition for Nursing Home Reform: A grassroots advocacy group that provides information and leadership on federal and state regulatory and legislative policy development and models and strategies to improve care and life for residents of nursing homes and other long term care facilities. http://www.nccnhr.org/

National Long Term Care Ombudsman Resource Center: An organization that provides support, technical assistance and training to the 53 State Long Term Care Ombudsman Programs and their statewide networks of almost 600 regional (local) programs. http://www.ltcombudsman.org/

REFERENCES

AARP. 1998. *Across the States 1998: Profiles of Long-Term Care Systems.* 3rd ed. Washington, DC: Public Policy Institute, American Association of Retired Persons.

Allee, V. 2000. Reconfiguring the value network. *Journal of Business Strategy* 21, no. 4: 36–39.

Altman, B.M. 1995. *Elderly Persons With Developmental Disabilities in Long-Term Care Facilities.* AHCPR Pub. No. 95-0084. Rockville, MD: Agency for Health Care Policy and Research (now Agency for Healthcare Research and Quality), July.

Beck, D.C. 1996. Partnerships may tame subacute rivalry. *Contemporary Long-term Care* 19, no. 7: 72.

Belgrave, L.L. et al. 1993. Health, double jeopardy, and culture: The use of institutionalization by African Americans. *The Gerontologist* 33: 379–385.

Compston, A., and A. Coles. 2002. Multiple sclerosis. *Lancet* 359, no. 9313: 1221–1231.

DHHS. 2003. *Health, United States, 2003.* Hyattsville, MD: U.S. Department of Health and Human Services.

Freedman, V.A. et al. 1994. Family networks: predictors of nursing home entry. *American Journal of Public Health* 84, no. 5: 843–845.

Freedman, V.A. 1996. Family structure and the risk of nursing home admission. *Journal of Gerontology: Social Sciences* 51B: S61–S69.

Freiman, M.P., and C.M. Murtaugh. 1995. Interactions between hospital and nursing home use. *Public Health Reports* 110, no. 5: 546–554.

Giacalone, J.A. 2001. *The U.S. Nursing Home Industry.* Armonk, NY: M.E. Sharp, Inc.

Hanson, L.C., et al. 2002. As individual as death itself: a focus group study of terminal care in nursing homes. *Journal of Palliative Medicine* 5, no. 1: 117–125.

Heller, T., et al. 1998. Impact of age and transitions out of nursing homes for adults with developmental disabilities. *American Journal of Mental Retardation* 103, no. 3: 236–248.

Heller, T., et al. 1999. Autonomy in residential facilities and community functioning of adults with mental retardation. *Mental Retardation* 37, no. 6: 449–457.

Heller, T., et al. 2002. Eight-year follow-up of the impact of environmental characteristics on well-being of adults with developmental disabilities. *Mental Retardation* 40, no. 5: 366–378.

Hoos, D. et al. 2000. HIV/AIDS and long-term care: A state perspective. *Journal of Urban Health: Bulletin of the New York Academy of Medicine* 77, no. 2: 232–243.

Institute of Medicine. 2001. *Improving the Quality of Long-Term Care*, eds. G.S. Wunderlich and P.O. Kohler. Washington, DC: National Academy Press.

Kaluzny, A.D., and H.S. Zuckerman. 1999. Alliances in a changing industry. In *The 21st Century Health Care Leader*, ed. R.W. Gilkey, 149–157. San Francisco: Jossey-Bass Publishers.

Lawton, M.P., and E.M. Brody. 1969. Assessment of older people: Self-maintaining and instrumental activities of daily living. *Gerontology* 9: 179–186.

Marder, R., and N.L. Linsk. 1995. Addressing AIDS long-term care issues through education and advocacy. *Health and Social Work* 20, no. 1: 75–80.

McAuley, W.J., and S.S. Travis. 1997. Positions of influence in the nursing home admission decision. *Research on Aging* 19, no. 1: 26–45.

Miller, R.L. 1986. Toward a more complete theory of objectives: A systems model of corporate value exchanges. *American Business Review* 4, no. 1: 1–13.

Miller, S.C., and V.N. Mor. 2002. The role of hospice care in the nursing home setting. *Journal of Palliative Medicine* 5, no. 2: 271–277.

Montoya, et al. 1996. Drug abuse, AIDS, and the coming crisis in long-term care. *Journal of Nursing Management* 4, no. 3: 151–162.

National Center for Health Statistics. 2002. *The National Nursing Home Survey: 1999 Summary. Vital and Health Statistics*, series 13, no. 152. Hyattsville, MD: Department of Health and Human Services.

Rivo, M. 1995. Predictors of nursing home placement in elderly patients. *American Family Physician* 52, no. 5: 1547–1548.

Spreat, S., et al. 1998. Improve quality in nursing homes or institute community placement? Implementation of OBRA for individuals with mental retardation. *Research in Developmental Disabilities* 19, no. 6: 507–518.

Wiseman, R.F., and C.C. Roseman. 1979. A typology of elderly migration based on the decision-making process. *Economic Geography* 55: 324–337.

Legal and Regulatory Environment

LEARNING MODULES

1. The general purposes of laws and regulations. Reasons why health care is more heavily regulated than other industries.
2. Sources of law: common law, statutory law, and administrative law. Differences between civil and criminal law.
3. Civil law: distinction between tort and breach of contract. Nature and purpose of a contract. Application of contract law to patient care. Regulations carry the force of law.
4. Types of ownership structures and their legal implications. Facility governance and main responsibilities of the governing body. Licensing of nursing home administrators and other professionals.
5. Personal liability, negligence, and intentional torts. Four necessary conditions for negligence. Main types of intentional torts.
6. Corporate liability, *respondeat superior*, and agency.
7. Purpose of licensure, certification, and accreditation and differences between them.
8. Overview of the requirements of participation in Medicare and Medicaid. The survey and enforcement process. Types of surveys. Survey process and protocols.

continues

9. Overview of patient rights. Informed consent and advance
   directives. Three types of advance directives. Protection of
   patient privacy.

Laws serve a protective purpose in civilized societies. An organized society formulates laws to prescribe rules of conduct that are enforced by public authority under threat of punishment for violating the laws. In business transactions, laws and regulations are designed to protect all parties involved. For instance, laws have been written to protect businesses, agencies, and individuals who may have business dealings with an organization. Laws protect the employees working for an organization, the clients receiving services from the organization, suppliers furnishing goods and services to the organization, and the community in which the organization conducts business. Further, the organization itself is protected against illegal activities of others. Finally, in a free society, private organizations are also protected against unlawful government action.

The health care sector has been the object of numerous regulations, for two main reasons: (1) The government is a major payer for individuals receiving health care services under Medicare, Medicaid, and other public programs (discussed in Chapter 4). By committing a significant amount of tax dollars to the delivery of health care, the government retains a vested interest in how the money is spent by private organizations that deliver health care. (2) Health care in general, and long-term care in particular, provides services to the frailest and most vulnerable individuals in society. Many of them are physically or mentally incapacitated and have no one else to act on their behalf. The legal system is deemed obligated, in the best interests of society, to protect vulnerable populations against negligence and abuse, to ensure that they receive needed services for which they are eligible, and to ensure that the services provided meet at least certain minimum standards of quality.

Nursing home malpractice has become an area ripe for litigation. Actually, during the 1990s, the nursing home industry became the fastest growing area of health-care litigation. Nationwide, nursing home litigation claims in 2001 were estimated to be between $1.4 and $2.3 billion (Stevenson and Studdert 2003). The following news reports also highlight why administrators, to be effective, must remain on top of legal and regulatory issues:

- In cases tried before juries, nursing homes lost in three out of five cases. Although most verdicts were between $200,000 and $290,000, approximately 4% of the awards were in excess of $10 million (Haymarket Media Inc. 2001).
- A large nursing home chain settled civil and criminal charges after two patients died and six others suffered severe dehydration. As part of this settlement, the company agreed to meet state and federal regulations, significantly boost staff training, and commit major capital funds to improve the air conditioning system (Haymarket Media Inc. 2001).
- Under a special rule, the Occupational Safety and Health Administration will start issuing citations for workplace injuries. Compared to other industries, skilled nursing facilities encounter as much as three times more employee injuries (Haymarket Media Inc. 2002).
- A large nursing home chain refunded $5.78 million to the government to settle allegations that the company inflated Medicare and Medicaid bills for certain medical supplies (U.S. Attorney, District of New Mexico, 1996).

Like other organizations, health care providers can use laws to protect their own interests. For example, in some states, nursing homes have sued to stop proposed cuts in payment from government sources.

The legal and regulatory environment is vast and complex. The purpose of this chapter is to provide basic knowledge necessary for day-to-day management of nursing care facilities. This information is intended to help administrators take steps to avoid certain legal problems. However, if issues with potentially substantial legal ramifications do arise, the administrator should have access to expert legal counsel. Large multifacility corporations generally have their own corporate attorneys. Small corporations and independent facilities should engage a reputable law firm to help the administrator deal with legal and regulatory issues when they crop up. Many law firms specialize in nursing-home law, including regulatory and reimbursement issues. Getting to know the legal experts and seeking consultations before minor issues turn into major problems are vital elements of effective management.

This chapter summarizes some key aspects of business law as it applies to nursing facilities. It also includes an overview of licensure and certification, the survey and enforcement process, patient rights, and privacy requirements. Other legal issues are addressed in later chapters, within the

context of the topics covered in those chapters. For instance, Medicare and Medicaid fraud and abuse are discussed in Chapter 4. Employment laws are covered in Chapter 14.

LAWS AND REGULATIONS

In the context of health-care delivery, most people have come across expressions such as negligence, malpractice, injury, or wrongful action. In law, these expressions carry specific meanings, which may be quite different from the meanings they commonly carry. Malpractice, for instance, finds its meaning within the context of tort law, which focuses on negligent and intentional wrongs. **Negligence** may involve commission or omission. **Injury** can be in the form of physical, financial, or emotional harm. The legal system differentiates between two main categories of laws—civil law (private law) and criminal law (public law). To determine whether certain behaviors fall under civil or criminal jurisdiction, the U.S. judicial system relies on three sources of law: common law, statutory law, and administrative law. **Common law** is the body of legal principles and precedents that have been handed down in the form of court decisions. In rendering a decision, a court must review the merits of the case before it. However, it is also obligated to apply settled principles of law from previous cases embracing similar facts and involving similar principles (Landry 1997). **Statutory law** comprises statutes passed by legislative bodies, such as the U.S. Congress, state legislatures, or legislative bodies of local governments. States and local jurisdictions can enact and enforce only those laws that do not conflict with federal law (Pozgar 2002, 5). **Administrative law** is formulated by the departments or agencies of the executive branch of government. It consists of rules and regulations, which are generally used to implement statutory laws crafted by the legislative branch. Rules and regulations established by an agency must be consistent with the statute under which they are promulgated (Pozgar 2002, 6). Civil and criminal laws operate within the bounds of common, statutory, and administrative laws.

Civil and Criminal Laws

Civil law is the body of laws governing private legal affairs, such as private rights and duties, contracts, and commercial relations. In civil law, a private party (individual or corporation) files the lawsuit and becomes the

plaintiff (Standler 1998). Civil penalties in the form of monetary damages—as opposed to jail terms—ensue from a breach of what the law prescribes. Within the body of civil law, two main types of laws are commonly encountered: tort law and contract law (discussed later).

The second category of law, **criminal law**, defines crimes and provides punishments for them. A **crime** is an offense committed against the general public, regardless of the number of individuals wronged. Jail terms, fines, or both may be imposed for criminal offenses. Examples of crime include theft, murder, disorderly conduct, and sexual abuse. In addition to such common criminal acts, other types of actions particular to health care may also constitute crimes. Billing the Medicare program for services that may not be medically necessary or for services that were not performed, or gross violation of commonly recognized standards of care, may constitute Medicare fraud, which is a criminal offense. A reckless disregard for the safety and well-being of patients may constitute criminal negligence. Crimes are ranked as felonies and misdemeanors. A crime classified as a **felony** is of a serious nature and is subject to a jail term of more than one year. A **misdemeanor** is a less serious crime that is punishable by a jail term of less than one year.

The wrongdoer who commits a crime is subject to prosecution by the state. Often a public prosecutor, not a private party, brings the case before a court. Prosecution of an action that has been deemed a crime may still allow the wronged party to pursue civil action. Sometimes the same conduct may violate both criminal and civil laws.

Tort Law

Civil law distinguishes between tort and breach of contract. A **tort** is described as a civil wrong—other than a breach of contract—committed against a person or a corporation. Tort may also be defined as interference with another's rights, either intentionally or otherwise (discussed later under Personal Liability).

In broad terms, a tort almost always constitutes the violation of some duty. It can be in the form of wrongdoing, that is, something was done incorrectly or something that should have been done was omitted (Miller and Hutton 2000, 361). On admitting a patient, the facility becomes duty-bound to meet the patient's total care needs. If the facility is not equipped to meet all of the patient's needs, because of staff shortages, lack of training, or any other reason, the patient should not be admitted. If an

admitted patient's condition deteriorates so that a higher level of care—perhaps available only in a hospital—would be more appropriate, the facility must make the needed transfer arrangements, including safe transportation to another facility.

In a civil case under tort law, monetary damages are generally awarded to "make the person whole again." However, the court may also award **punitive damages** in excess of the actual losses suffered. Punitive damages are also called exemplary damages because their intent is to make a public example of the **defendant**, supposedly to deter future wrongful conduct by others. Punitive damages are generally awarded when the defendant's conduct was egregious. Such conduct generally falls into four categories: (1) malicious intent (i.e., desire to cause harm), (2) gross negligence (i.e., conscious indifference), (3) blatant disregard for the rights of others, and (4) fraud. Punitive damages are particularly important in torts involving harm to the plaintiff's dignity (e.g., invasion of privacy) or other breaches of civil rights, where the actual monetary injury to the plaintiff may be small (Standler 1998). A landmark 2001 verdict from Texas, *Fuqua v Horizon/CMS Healthcare Corporation*, illustrates the kind of circumstance in which punitive damages may be warranted. In one of the largest ever jury verdicts in a nursing home malpractice lawsuit, brought by Cecil Fuqua on behalf of the Estate of his mother, Wyvonne Fuqua, the plaintiff was awarded $2.7 million in compensatory damages and an additional $310 million in punitive damages. The suit was filed after the death of 76-year-old Wyvonne Fuqua in 1997. Fuqua had been admitted to a nursing home in Fort Worth, Texas in 1994, following a stroke. In late 1996, Fuqua began developing severe **pressure ulcers**. As her condition deteriorated, the nursing home staff allegedly did not apprise the family of Fuqua's condition and did not discharge her to a facility that could adequately treat her pressure ulcers. In April 1997, Ms. Fuqua's adult children moved her to a local hospital. She arrived in a state of malnutrition, with 16 pressure ulcers, of which 9 were Stage III and 5 were Stage IV (the most severe type, in which bone or muscle may be exposed). Two months after she left the nursing home, Fuqua died (Schabes 2002).

Contract Law

A civil wrong involving the violation of a specific agreement between two parties constitutes a **breach of contract**, not a tort. In a civil case, the remedy is often in the form of recovery of damages. However, the injured

party has the duty to mitigate, i.e., reduce potential damages. For example, an employee who is separated from an organization in breach of a contract that existed between the employee and the organization has the duty to try to find other employment. Punitive damages are not available in breach of contract cases.

Many business relationships are governed by contracts. Contracts may concern patients or parties responsible for them, certain employees, independent providers of services to the facility's patients, construction contracts, lease contracts, loan agreements, purchasing contracts, etc. A **contract** is a legally binding agreement between two or more parties to carry out a legal purpose. For instance, two parties cannot enter into a contract to commit fraud. Although most contracts are executed in writing, certain verbal agreements can also be legally viewed as contracts. A contract essentially represents a mutual assent or "meeting of the minds."

For most contracts to be legally enforceable, two main conditions must be met: (1) An offer and acceptance should have occurred, indicating that an agreement has actually been reached. Generally, all parties to a contract sign a written document to affirm the agreement. (2) Promise of a price or benefit—called consideration—should be stated. A **consideration** is something of value promised to another in exchange for something else of value. The party that is being required to perform under the contract will receive the consideration upon performance.

Only contracts executed between competent parties are considered legal. To be considered **competent**, the parties must be of sound mind and of legal age. Thus, agreements with minors or those who do not have the mental capacity to enter into a contract because of mental illness, mental retardation, dementia, or substance abuse are not enforceable. In most cases, competence can be determined by a physician. In more difficult situations, the matter is referred to a court. Agreements reached under duress may also be unenforceable. Unless a court determines it to be invalid, and therefore nonenforceable, a contract is held "sacred," which means that the parties must perform according to its provisions. Otherwise, the aggrieved party can bring a complaint before a court for breach of contract and recover damages.

When admitting a patient, a nursing home enters into a contract with the patient or a party, such as a family member, who acts on behalf of the patient. The contract, or admission agreement, generally spells out the services the nursing home will provide and the cost of

those services. The nursing home can be sued for breach of contract if a patient is harmed, and the harm is determined to have resulted because services promised in the contract were not delivered.

Regulations

Regulations distinguish between statutory law and administrative law. Regulations are issued pursuant to the enacted statutes. They provide administrative interpretations of the statutes and contain details for carrying them out. Hence, they have the force of law. For example, it is illegal to operate a nursing home without a facility license, or for the administrator to practice without an administrator's license. Regulations also govern facility certification under Medicare and Medicaid rules (discussed later in the chapter). Administrative agencies have the power to enforce the rules and regulations that they formulated. The most important federal agency regulating nursing facilities is the Centers for Medicare and Medicaid Services (CMS), an administrative agency under the U.S. Department of Health and Human Services (DHHS).

In June 2003, based on nursing home regulations with which facilities are required to comply, a facility in New York State pleaded guilty to criminal charges stemming from its failure to provide an adequate level of care to patients because of severe staff shortages. According to charges filed in the county court, this amounted to a willful violation of the public health laws, a misdemeanor. The nursing home also admitted that its employees falsified its business records to conceal the fact that licensed practical nurses were unlawfully performing medical assessments, a felony. As part of its plea agreement, the facility was required to pay $1 million in restitution to the state's Medicaid program before sentencing, and a total of $17,000 in fines. Moreover, the two owners must divest themselves of their nursing home operations. The administrator is required to forfeit his nursing home administrator's license, and the owners and the administrator are permanently enjoined from having any further involvement in the management, operation, or ownership of any nursing home in New York State. The Attorney General's Medicaid Fraud Control Unit followed this nursing home's problems from 1999 to 2001. The investigation was sparked, in part, by repeated citations from the state Department of Health (DOH) for violations of regulatory standards that the facility failed to correct. Specifically, DOH inspectors found that the nursing home failed repeatedly to prevent and treat dan-

gerous pressure sore wounds, to give patients medications on schedule, and to provide treatments and evaluations, as well as other quality of life care requirements. DOH concluded that numerous residents had suffered harm because of these deficiencies. According to the complaint filed in court, the administrator knew as early as April 2000 that staffing was at a critically low level and that resident care was at risk. Throughout this same period, however, patient admissions were aggressively pursued, and the owners withdrew more than $1 million in profits (Office of New York State Attorney General 2003).

LEGAL STRUCTURE AND RESPONSIBILITY

A nursing facility is a legal entity, meaning that it has been established as an organization under law. An organization's ownership structure defines, in a broad sense, its rights and responsibilities. This structure has implications for how the organization and the owners are taxed, whether the organization or the owners have liability for civil offenses, and what rights and responsibilities the organization and its owners have. For nursing homes, key responsibilities of ownership include governance, appointment of a qualified nursing home administrator, and appointment of other qualified personnel to manage and deliver patient care. Statutes concerning the rights and responsibilities of private corporations may be loosely referred to as **corporate law**.

Ownership

There are three main classes of ownership (national data for nursing homes and beds for the three types of ownership are shown in Figure 3-1):

- public
- private non-profit
- private for-profit (proprietary). There are three types of proprietorships:
  - corporations
  - partnerships
  - sole proprietorships

Public Facilities

A **public**, or government-owned, facility may be established under a specific statute enacted by a city or county. That statute would include the

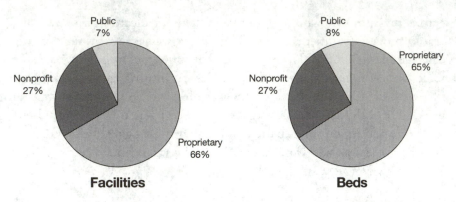

Source: Data from the National Nursing Home Survey 1999. *Vital Health Statistics*, Series 13, No. 152 (2002), p. 6. National Center for Health Statistics.

FIGURE 3-1 Percentage Distribution of Nursing Homes and Beds by Ownership

specific duties and limitations for the organization. Often, such statutes specifically outline the charity mission for which the institute may have been created. In some instances, the statute may prohibit leasing of the facility to a private corporation. Other aspects of facility management may be governed by statute. In a broad sense, then, the rights and responsibilities of a government-owned facility are subject to the statute that created the organization.

Private Non-profit Facilities

A privately-owned facility incorporated as a **non-profit** (also called not-for-profit) entity is prohibited from distributing its profits to individuals. A non-profit nursing facility is not prohibited from earning a profit, but the facility must serve a charitable purpose. Non-profit corporations are exempt from federal taxation under Section 501(c)(3) of the Internal Revenue Code, 1986. The law provides for federal exemption from taxation to any organization operated exclusively for "religious, charitable, scientific or educational purposes." These organizations are also exempt from state income and sales taxes and may be exempt from local taxes, such as property taxes. Tax law also enables non-profit entities to obtain private donations, for which the donors can claim a charitable deduction on their income tax returns. The owners and administrators of non-profit facilities must be particularly careful that the privileges afforded under the law are not abused. "Charity" does not mean that the facility is required

to provide free care to anyone. It does mean that the facility must make its services available to the public at the lowest feasible cost, and that it should not force anyone who cannot pay for services to move out. To provide care to residents who are unable to pay, the facility may participate in government funding programs such as Medicaid, obtain private donations, or cover such costs out of its own profits.

Private For-profit Facilities

A privately-owned for-profit (also called proprietary) corporation is created to generate a profit that can be distributed to its owners or shareholders. Proprietary enterprises are also required to pay all federal, state, and local taxes. For-profit corporations may be owned by a group of private investors or by a parent corporation, such as a long-term care chain or a proprietary hospital. The parent corporation may also be publicly owned, in which case the company's stock is available to any investor through the stock market.

A **partnership** is another type of private ownership which is described as an association of two or more individuals or organizations for the purpose of conducting business for profit. A partnership is specifically created for the purpose of sharing profits among the partners. They also share the expenses and liabilities of the partnership. In a **general partnership**, there is no limit on the potential liability of the partners. However, a **limited partnership** can be established to limit the individual liability of partners. Limited partners are liable only to the extent of their investment, as long as they do not participate in the management and control of the operations (Miller and Hutton 2000, 25). So, limited partners can be viewed as mere investors in a business enterprise.

A **sole proprietorship** consists of a single owner who has not incorporated the business. All income of the business is taxed as personal income of the owner, and the owner's potential liability is unlimited. Because of the many complex tax and legal issues they entail, nursing facilities are rarely operated as sole proprietorships.

Governance

Nursing facilities are required by law to have a **governing body**, which is also called the board of directors, the governing board, or the board of trustees. The only real difference between these entities is in the name a corporation chooses to use.

The ultimate legal responsibility for the facility's operations and for their outcomes is vested in the governing body (or board). Responsibility for daily management is delegated to the administrator. Thus, a close relationship—based on trust, mutual commitment, communication, and professionalism—should exist between the board and the administrator. The administrator reports to the board and looks to it for general direction. A good match in business values and operational philosophies and ongoing positive relationships between the two are essential for effective management.

The main responsibilities of the governing body are summarized below:

- Appoint a qualified administrator to manage the facility, periodically review the administrator's performance, determine compensation, and make decisions about the administrator's continuing employment.
- Establish the **mission** and **vision** for the facility and assist the administrator in establishing a strategic plan that is periodically updated to accommodate changes in the environment (see Chapters 1 and 2).
- Establish broad policies that provide adequate guidelines to the administrator in making decisions pertaining to finance, budgets, quality of patient care, building and equipment, staffing, legal and ethical conduct, and the facility's relationship to its external environment.
- Written policies must also assure protection of patient rights.
- Provide needed support to the administrator by procuring technical expertise when necessary and by committing adequate resources so that the facility can be effectively managed and an acceptable level of patient care can be delivered.
- Be involved in overseeing the facility's operations and outputs. Because of its legal accountability, the board must ensure the facility's compliance with quality standards, financial goals, and legal and ethical expectations.

Although the board has the primary responsibility for these functions, the administrator should be actively involved in developing policies, mission and vision, and strategic direction for the facility. The board must exercise due vigilance, but without undue interference. It should not step

over the administrator's authority to make operational decisions, yet it must maintain adequate control.

Health care organizations generally have **self-perpetuating boards**, in which the board itself selects new members to succeed the ones who will no longer serve. Selection of board members should be guided by the ownership structure and by the organization's mission. For example, the board of a public or private non-profit facility will include people who can best represent the organization's charity mission. The board may include one or two city or county administrative and health officials, a representative of the local social services department, one or two community physicians, a public health nurse, and an official from the local hospital. A private for-profit facility's board may include similar representatives from the community, plus some local business leaders. Boards of private for-profit and non-profit corporations should also include some corporate officers.

In the public (government) sector, the governing body will focus particularly on the facility's charity mission, while also ensuring that the facility remains financially viable. In the non-profit sector, the special focus should be on meeting the health care needs of the community, which should include a charity function to justify the corporation's tax-exempt status. In the for-profit sector, maximizing profits and creating value for the shareholders are the main goals. But the facility must also establish meaningful exchange relationships with the community and provide services of a quality that is acceptable to the community, and comply with all regulatory standards. In addition, long-term care facilities operated by various religious organizations, which are private non-profit entities, may adhere to certain religious tenets, spiritual values, and moral commitments upheld by the sponsoring organizations.

Certain key officers of the corporation may serve as *ex officio* members of the board; the administrator may be one of them. Others should be carefully selected from among respected leaders in the community on the basis of their qualifications and character. The skills and social standing of potential board members should be carefully reviewed to help select people who can assist the administrator in establishing positive exchange relationships; provide technical expertise in health care, finance, law, or public relations; represent the community and clients; and bring their own individual perspectives to the operation of the facility.

Nursing Home Administrator

The nursing home administrator (NHA) functions as chief executive officer (CEO) for a nursing facility and reports to the governing body. The NHA acts as the agent of the governing body and is responsible for the day-to-day management of the nursing facility.

Federal and state regulations require that the NHA be licensed. Licensure standards establish minimum qualifications for NHAs. Because licensure of NHAs is a state function, the prescribed qualifications vary from state to state. In recent years, the trend has been toward requiring a bachelor's degree. However, a bachelor's degree with an academic major in health care administration is required only by a few states. In this respect, current health policy presents a paradox. A great deal of concern has been expressed about the quality of patient care in nursing facilities. Little or no concern has been expressed, however, about raising the qualifications required for an NHA license. In many instances, NHAs hold key leadership positions in long-term care with no more than a high school diploma or a bachelor's degree in an academic discipline that may be totally unrelated to providing services to infirm elderly people residing in nursing homes. The governing body is required to select as NHA an individual who is competent to maintain acceptable levels of patient care. Yet, health policy-makers, by paying so little attention to NHA qualifications, have been largely responsible for creating a shortage of qualified NHAs.

To be licensed, a prospective NHA must pass an examination that has two components: a short component focusing on state regulations and standards, and a longer component focusing on five broad areas called the **domains of practice**. These domains, established by the National Association of Boards of Nursing Home Administrators (NAB), focus on resident care management, personnel management, financial management, environmental management, and governance and organizational management. To qualify for a license in some states, the prospective administrator must also complete an internship or administrator-in-training (AIT) program under the supervision of a certified preceptor. Many of the large multifacility chains have established their own AIT programs.

Other Professionals

Nursing facilities employ various health professionals, such as nurses, social workers, and sometimes therapists and dieticians. Most facilities

contract with professionals such as therapists and dieticians, however, to provide services. A nursing facility must also appoint a licensed physician to serve as the medical director. In almost all instances, the medical director is a physician practicing in the community with whom the facility has established a contract. All states license nurses, therapists, and physicians. Many also license dieticians, social workers, and other health care professionals. Licensing laws in each state specify the minimum qualifications various professionals must possess in order to provide services to patients. Licensing laws also define the scope of practice for each classification of professionals and prohibit health care professionals from using patients' confidential medical information inappropriately. The administrator should ensure that all professionals working in the facility comply with state licensure statutes, whether they are employees of the facility or are working as contractors. Documentation should be maintained on the qualifications, current licensure status, and other credentials of all such personnel.

LIABILITY

Liability refers to the potential damages ensuing from legal action. Liability may be ascribed to an individual or a corporation. Generally speaking, individual members of the governing body are not held personally liable for negligence amounting to errors of judgment. They may, however, be held liable for gross or willful negligence. Hence, board members, acting in good faith, can have wide latitude in fulfilling their roles and responsibilities. Acting in good faith generally means how a reasonable person would have acted under similar circumstances. On the other hand, board members may be held criminally liable, for instance, in cases involving fraud or taking of bribes for personal benefit.

Personal Liability

As a general rule, both tort law and criminal law ascribe personal liability to an individual who commits wrongful acts. For example, falsification of medical or business records may be grounds for criminal prosecution. Administrators and other employees of a long-term care facility can be held liable when their actions result in injury to someone else. To incur personal liability, an individual must do something wrong or fail to do something he should have done. Individuals may also be held liable for

unlawful acts, whether or not those acts result in injury to others. An example of this kind of unlawful act would be possession or use of illegal drugs. Personal tort liability may result from either negligent or intentional acts.

Negligence

Negligence is the failure to exercise the degree of care that a reasonable person would have exercised in similar circumstances. It is generally associated with a breach of duty. A nursing facility has a duty to exercise due care. For instance, it must have adequate equipment and staff to provide services as required by the needs of its patients.

An act of negligence is not sufficient for establishing liability unless it has resulted in injury. An administrator who fails to install an alarm system to monitor patients who may wander out of the facility is not liable unless a patient has actually wandered away and sustained injury. For a plaintiff to establish injury from negligence, four conditions must be present:

- A duty must be owed. For instance, nursing facilities have the duty to maintain a safe environment and provide services that meet acceptable standards.
- There must be a breach of duty.
- An injury must be sustained.
- A direct cause-and-effect relationship must be present between the breach of duty and the injury sustained.

In health care, duty is commonly defined in terms of standards of care. Judgments about standards of care are often determined on the basis of common sense or best professional judgment, established regulations, written procedures or policies of the facility, or expert opinion. The duty that is breached can be in the form of an act of commission, such as a nurse giving the wrong medication, or it can be an act of omission, such as a nurse failing to give the prescribed medication.

Intentional Acts

An **intentional tort** is a willful act that violates the rights or interests of others. Willful means that a person knows and desires the consequences of his or her acts. Actions commonly regarded as intentional torts are assault, battery, false imprisonment, invasion of privacy, defamation of character, fraud, and intentional infliction of mental distress.

An **assault** creates a threatening environment in which a person fears being touched in an offensive, insulting, provoking, or potentially injurious manner. No physical contact has to occur, but the assaulted individual must reasonably believe that the aggressor has the ability to carry it out presently. If the aggressor actually touches the other individual without consent, that action results in **battery**. In this context, restraining a patient without a physician's order or the patient's consent may amount to battery.

False imprisonment is the unlawful restriction of freedom. Unlawful use of restraints may constitute false imprisonment in addition to battery. Restraints are regarded as an intervention, and harm caused by medical intervention can make the nursing home liable (Yorker 1988). Also, generally accepted medical procedures and the state health code must be followed when isolating patients who have a contagious disease.

Invasion of privacy concerns both privacy and confidentiality. A patient's name, pictures, or private affairs should not be made public without proper authorization. Unreasonable search or intrusion, such as opening personal mail without consent, is a violation of a patient's privacy rights. Patients' medical records belong to the long-term care facility, but these records are confidential. Release of information to persons not involved in patient care requires the patient's authorization, or its release may be governed by law.

Defamation of character involves making false reports that result in damage to someone's reputation. The false reports may be in written form (constituting a **libel**) or they may be communicated verbally (constituting a **slander**).

Fraud occurs when harm or loss is incurred because of willful misrepresentation. As mentioned earlier, certain types of fraudulent activities may constitute a crime, not just a civil tort.

Intentional infliction of mental distress is considered intentional tort when some outrageous conduct results in mental or emotional trauma. Patients and their families must be treated in a civilized manner. Health care professionals can be held liable when outbursts of anger, abusive language, or other irrational behavior results in mental distress.

Corporate Liability

The law regards corporations as individuals, and as entities separate from their owners. The corporation is often held liable for actions of its directors, officers, and employees, notwithstanding the personal liability of

individuals. The main areas with which health facility administrators should become familiar are summarized below:

Respondeat Superior

All people are responsible for their own tortious conduct (behavior that constitutes a tort). At times, however, the law will hold liable for a tort not only the tortfeasor (person who commits the tort), but also the organization that hired the tortfeasor. A corporation's liability for the acts of its officers or employees is known as **vicarious liability**, which is founded on the legal doctrine of *respondeat superior* (let the master respond). In most instances, the nursing facility is held liable for the wrongful acts of its employees when such acts are committed during the course of their employment. It does not matter if the organization takes all reasonable steps in selecting, training, and supervising its employees. Under the doctrine, a supervisor is not regarded as an employer and is not held liable except for his or her own personal acts, as described in the previous section. *Respondeat superior* does not absolve the employee of personal liability, nor does it obligate the employer to provide liability protection to its employees.

The doctrine of *respondeat superior*, however, does not apply to the wrongful acts of an independent contractor, who is responsible for his own acts. Hence, it is important to differentiate between an employee and a contractor, but this distinction is not always clear in law. For instance, from an administrative standpoint, a therapist may be working on contract with a facility. But, if the facility exercises some measure of control over the therapist, such as patient scheduling, billing, and compliance with the facility's policies, and if he or she is represented to clients as an employee of the facility, the therapist may not qualify as an independent contractor under law. On the other hand, a facility is not liable for the actions of a non-employed attending physician who generally is not under the control of the facility's staff. However, the facility can be held liable if it fails to review the qualifications and credentials of providers who may be rendering services to the facility's residents as independent contractors. The administrator should also ensure that all personnel providing services to patients are duly licensed if they are required to be licensed under state laws. The administrator should also ensure that licensed professionals do not provide services outside their scope of practice. The administrator also has the responsibility to report any professional misconduct to the appropriate licensing authority.

Agency

An **agent** is someone a corporation authorizes to represent it or to act on its behalf. In this case, the corporation (called the principal) would be liable for the acts of commission or omission of its agent. The nursing home administrator may be regarded as an agent of the corporation. Individual partners in a partnership, or institutions in a joint venture, are considered each others' agents. For example, partners are liable for tortious actions of other partners.

LICENSURE, CERTIFICATION, AND ACCREDITATION

These three terms carry different meanings, but all three procedures serve at least one main purpose—to establish minimum standards of quality and to enforce compliance with those standards. Exhibit 3-1 provides a summary of the main distinctions between licensure and certification.

Licensure

The regulatory oversight of long-term care facilities begins with **licensure**. The licensure process starts at the planning stage, before a new facility can even be built. Acquiring an existing facility requires the facility to be relicensed. Once a facility has been built or acquired, its licensure status must be maintained, generally through an annual renewal process. Many states have a certificate of need (CON) program for building a new facility or for expanding an existing one. In some states, transfer of ownership must also go through the CON process. State CON requirements define several aspects of building or acquiring a facility:

- the type of expenditures that are subject to review. A state may allow a certain number of beds to be built without the CON review
- the criteria for evaluating need for additional beds or services
- the procedures for review, which include public hearings

Licensure is a state function, and a nursing facility must have a license to operate. The licensure function generally falls within the purview of each state's health department. A license is granted on the condition that the facility meets standards that specify minimum thresholds for staffing, adequacy of services, building construction specifications, and compli-

EXHIBIT 3–1

Differences between Nursing Home Licensure and Certification

Licensure	Certification
• State function	• Federal function
• Mandatory	• Optional
• Basic requirement for operating a nursing home	• A facility must first be licensed before it can apply for certification
• Does not make a facility eligible for public funds	• Required for receiving public funds
• There is one licensing category for nursing care facilities	• There are three categories depending mainly on the source of government funding and types of patients served: 1. SNF—Medicare, post-acute, short stay 2. NF—Medicaid, long stay (if the patient qualifies) 3. ICF/MR—Medicaid, long stay, MR/DD patients only
• With the exception of the Life Safety Code, licensing standards differ between states	• Uniform federal standards for all states

ance with fire and safety regulations mandated by the Life Safety Code. The Life Safety Code standards are national (see Chapter 5 for more details). Standards in the remaining areas are developed by each state, and they vary from one state to another.

Licensing also requires that the facility supply information about the professional credentials of the principal owners and key employees, such as the administrator and the director of nursing. If a principal owner or key officer has had a criminal conviction, facility license may be denied or revoked.

Certification

All facilities must be licensed, but a licensed facility may or may not be certified. In contrast to licensure, which is a state function, **certification** is a federal function. The Centers for Medicare and Medicaid Services (CMS)—a federal agency, called Health Care Financing Administration (HCFA) before 2001—promulgates certification standards with which nursing facilities must comply to retain their certification status. CMS also oversees enforcement of certification standards, although the actual monitoring is undertaken by each state. Monitoring is carried out through an annual inspection (called a survey) of each facility, which assesses compliance with both licensure and certification standards.

Unlike licensure, participation in the certification program is voluntary—to the extent that a facility will not be admitting patients enrolled in the Medicaid or Medicare programs. If a nursing facility plans to admit Medicaid or Medicare patients, it must seek federal certification and comply with the federal standards.

Until 1989, federal statutes classified nursing homes into two types: skilled nursing facilities (SNFs) for residents enrolled in either Medicare or Medicaid, and intermediate care facilities (ICFs) for those covered by Medicaid only. Patients requiring a higher level of care were eligible for admission to a SNF that was required to have a licensed nurse on duty 24 hours a day and a registered nurse (RN) on the day shift. By contrast, ICFs were required to have a licensed nurse on duty only on the day shift.

The Nursing Home Reform Act, passed in 1987, as part of the Omnibus Budget Reconciliation Act of 1987 (OBRA-87, PL 100-203) removed the distinctions between ICFs and SNFs for both Medicare and Medicaid. The new law created two categories of nursing homes, but for certification purposes only.

A nursing home certified to admit Medicare patients is now called a **SNF (skilled nursing facility)**. Such a facility can be free-standing or a **distinct part**, that is, a section of a nursing home that is certified apart from the rest of the facility. When SNF certification applies to a distinct part, Medicare patients can be admitted only to that particular section of the facility. SNF certification conforms to the original intent of the Medicare legislation (Social Security Amendment of 1965) according to which Medicare would cover only post-hospital services in a nursing facility.

A long-term care facility serving only Medicaid patients (but not Medicare patients) is certified as a **NF (nursing facility)**. SNF and NF are both legal terms associated with certification, not necessarily with the level of services. A facility may be dually certified as both an SNF and an NF. Facilities that have **dual certification** can admit Medicare and Medicaid patients to any part of the facility. The federal standards for the delivery of care in SNFs and NFs are the same. For federal certification purposes, the former ICF category has been abolished. However, because Medicaid is a state-administered program, some states distinguish among levels of care within the NF category. The state of Tennessee, for example, created level I NF (NF-1) and level II NF (NF-2) categories. In the NF-1 category, services are less intensive than they are at the NF-2 level. Other states maintain the ICF category to provide services to Medicaid patients who do not require the degree of care and treatment that a skilled nursing facility is designed to provide. These states pay nursing homes a lesser amount for the ICF level of care. National data on the distribution of facilities and beds according to certification appear in Figure 3-2.

Federal regulations prohibit an SNF or an NF from serving patients who have severe mental diseases. A separate certification category, Intermediate Care Facility for the Mentally Retarded (ICF/MR), has been created for specialized facilities that provide health and rehabilitative ser-

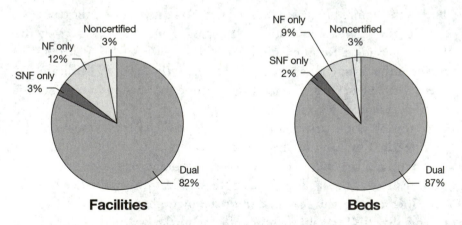

Source: Data from the National Nursing Home Survey 1999. *Vital Health Statistics*, Series 13, No. 152 (2002), p. 6. National Center for Health Statistics.

FIGURE 3-2 Percentage Distribution of Nursing Homes and Beds by Type of Certification

vices to patients with mental retardation and related conditions. T\
tification enables these facilities to participate in the Medicaid pro
To qualify for Medicaid reimbursement, ICF/MRs must be licensed by
the state and must comply with federal standards. The Conditions of
Participation, found in Federal regulations at 42 CFR Part 483, Subpart I,
Sections 483.400- 483.480, specify eight areas in which standards must be
met: management, client protections, facility staffing, active treatment
services, client behavior and facility practices, health care services, physical
environment, and dietetic services. ICF/MR services may be furnished in
a distinct part of a facility, provided the distinct part is ICF/MR certified.

According to certification regulations, the term "facility" does not necessarily imply a separate physical structure. The term can be used for the
facility as a whole or, within the context of licensure and certification, it
may apply more specifically to distinct parts: different sections or units of
a building that have different types of certifications or no certification.

A few facilities have elected not to participate in the Medicaid and
Medicare programs. As such, they can admit only those patients who have
a private source of funding for nursing home care. Such facilities are **non-
certified**. However, they must be licensed under the state licensure regulations. Medicare and Medicaid patients cannot be admitted to noncertified facilities. But **private-pay patients**, those who have a personal or
private source of funding, are not restricted to noncertified facilities. Such
patients may be admitted to SNF or NF certified beds as well. Figure 3-3
illustrates how a facility can have distinctly-certified sections.

The certification standards in the Medicare and Medicaid programs are
called **Requirements of Participation**. The standards currently in place,
authorized under OBRA-87, are widely regarded as minimum standards of
quality for nursing facilities. The Requirements of Participation include
roughly 185 different standards, which are classified under 15 major categories. A summary of the broad requirements appears in Exhibit 3-2, which
is meant for illustrative purposes only. The actual regulations can be found
in the Code of Federal Regulations, Title 42, Part 483. The regulations and
their application are periodically clarified by CMS. These interpretive
guidelines (now called Guidance to Surveyors) are contained in the current
edition of the State Operations Manual produced by CMS (See the internet
resources listed at the end of this chapter for accessing the State Operations
Manual online). It is imperative for health facility administrators to become
thoroughly familiar with the **interpretive guidelines**. The law defines **sub-**

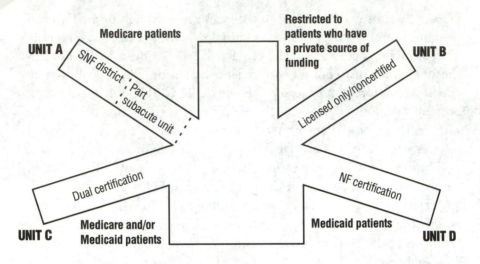

The entire facility must be licensed by the state

Source: Shi, Leiyu and Singh, Douglas. Delivering Health Care in America, p. 401, 2004

FIGURE 3-3 Distinctly Certified Units in a Nursing Home.

stantial compliance as "a level of compliance with requirements of participation such that any identified deficiencies pose no greater risk to patient health and safety than the potential for causing minimal harm." In simple language, it means that violation of a certification standard should not endanger the health and safety of a patient. If a facility meets this criterion, it is deemed to be in substantial compliance. Enforcement of the certification standards is based on substantial compliance rather than "zero tolerance," because perfect compliance sets expectations that are unrealistic in most instances. Enforcement of zero tolerance could disqualify most nursing facilities from providing services to Medicare and Medicaid patients.

Accreditation

In contrast to licensure and certification, which are government functions, **accreditation** is a private function. Hence, accreditation is totally voluntary. The Joint Commission on Accreditation of Healthcare Organizations (JCAHO)—a private non-profit organization—accredits hospitals, nursing homes, and other types of health care sites and has issued its own standards for the purpose of accreditation. Compared to hospitals, relatively few nursing facilities have opted to seek accreditation. From its inception, Medicare regulations have conferred **deemed status**

EXHIBIT 3–2

Requirements of Participation for SNF, NF, and Dual Certification (condensed)

(1) Resident rights. These rights provide for a physician of one's choice, to be fully informed of one's medical condition and treatments, to refuse treatment, to formulate advance directives, to authorize the facility to manage personal funds and require accounting for the funds, right to personal privacy and confidentiality, and the right to voice grievances without fear of retaliation. In addition, residents cannot be prevented, coerced, or discriminated against in the course of exercising their rights as citizens of the facility or citizens of the United States.

(2) Admission, transfer, and discharge rights. These rights provide residents certain safeguards against transfer or discharge from a facility and allow one to return to the same facility after brief periods of hospitalization or therapeutic leave. It also requires equal access and delivery of services regardless of the source of payment.

(3) Resident behavior and facility practices. It limits the facility's use of physical and chemical restraints and prohibits mistreatment, neglect, or abuse of residents.

(4) Quality of life. The facility must promote each resident's individuality, dignity, and respect. Exercise of choice and self-determination must be allowed. Residents have the right to interact with the community. Residents can organize resident and family groups for mutual support and planned activities, or to air grievances. The facility must make reasonable accommodation for individual preferences, such as meals and roommates. The facility must provide an ongoing program of activities and medically related social services. The standard also requires a clean, safe, comfortable, and homelike environment that will promote maintenance or enhancement of the quality of life of each resident.

(5) Resident assessment. Within fourteen days of admission and at least annually thereafter the facility must undertake a comprehensive assessment of each patient's func-

continues

EXHIBIT 3–2 *continued*

tional capacity and medical needs. The assessment must be reviewed at least quarterly. Based on the need assessment, the facility must develop a comprehensive plan of care for each resident and provide the services necessary to provide that care.

(6) Quality of care. Each resident must receive and the facility must provide the necessary care and services to attain or maintain the highest practicable physical, mental, and psychosocial well-being in accordance with the comprehensive assessment and plan of care. The facility must provide appropriate treatments to maintain or improve a resident's functioning and range of motion, unless it is unavoidable. The facility must ensure that residents receive proper treatment and assistive devices to maintain vision and hearing abilities. Other patient care requirements include adopting measures to prevent pressure sores, providing appropriate treatment for pressure sores, ensuring adequate nutrition and hydration, providing special treatments as necessary, limiting use of antipsychotic drugs, and confining medication errors rates to less than five percent. The standards also address appropriate use of urinary catheters and nasogastric tubes.

(7) Nursing services. The facility must have sufficient nursing staff, including licensed nurses, to provide necessary care on a 24-hour basis.

(8) Dietary services. The facility must provide a nourishing, palatable, and well-balanced diet that meets the daily nutritional and special dietary needs of each resident.

(9) Physician services. A physician must approve each admission, and each resident must remain under the care of a physician. Unless otherwise prohibited, the physician may delegate tasks to a physician assistant, nurse practitioner, or clinical nurse specialist.

(10) Specialized rehabilitative services. The facility must provide specialized rehabilitative therapies by qualified personnel under written orders of a physician.

(11) Dental services. The facility must assist residents in obtaining routine and 24-hour emergency dental services.

(12) Pharmacy services. The facility must provide pharmaceutical services with consultation from a licensed pharmacist. If state law permits it, unlicensed personnel may administer drugs, but only under the general supervision of a licensed nurse. The standard also requires monthly review of drug regimen for each resident and appropriate labeling and storage of drugs.

(13) Infection control. The facility must have an infection control program and maintain records of incidents and corrective actions.

(14) Physical environment. The facility must comply with the Life Safety Code of the National Fire Protection Association. The facility should provide for emergency electrical power in case of power failure. The building must have adequate space and equipment for dining, health services, and recreation. Resident rooms must meet certain requirements as to size and furnishings.

(15) Administration. The facility must operate in compliance with all applicable federal, state, and local regulations and must be licensed by the state. The governing body has legal responsibility for the management and operation of the facility. The governing body must appoint a licensed nursing home administrator to manage the facility. Nurses aides working at the facility must receive required training, a competency evaluation, periodic performance review, and needed in-service education. The facility must also designate a physician to serve as medical director. The facility must provide or obtain needed laboratory, radiology, and other diagnostic services. The facility must maintain clinical records on each resident, have detailed written plans and procedures to meet all potential emergencies and disasters, have a written transfer agreement with a hospital that participates in the Medicare and Medicaid programs, and maintain a quality assessment and assurance committee.

on hospitals accredited by JCAHO. Deemed status means an accredited hospital is deemed to meet the Medicare conditions of participation. Nursing facilities, however, are not given deemed status on the basis of accreditation. But accreditation has its advantages: accreditation status is highly correlated with performance on certification surveys. Compared to non-accredited facilities, accredited ones also perform better on various quality measures and have lower exposure to risk, such as malpractice lawsuits (Grachek 2002). On the other hand, many facilities find that accreditation fees are high in relation to the benefits reaped.

Deemed status currently does not apply to swing beds in rural hospitals, but the acute care sector has been lobbying to have all Medicare rules removed from long-term care services delivered in an acute care setting. Small rural hospitals frequently have an excess of hospital acute care beds, and the communities in which they are located often have a scarcity of SNF beds for Medicare beneficiaries. The **swing-bed** program allows rural hospitals with fewer than 100 beds to use their beds interchangeably as either acute-care or SNF beds, giving these facilities greater flexibility in meeting fluctuating demands for acute and long-term care. These hospitals are currently required to comply with SNF standards.

SURVEY AND ENFORCEMENT

CMS has delegated to each state the responsibility for surveying (that is, inspecting) nursing facilities and making recommendations to CMS to determine the provider's eligibility to participate in the Medicare and Medicaid programs. Regulations governing survey and enforcement procedures are published in the Code of Federal Regulations, Title 42, Part 488. The State Operations Manual, published by CMS, contains a detailed description of the survey protocols and procedures. All facility surveys are unannounced. The enforcement process is not confined to weekdays and normal business hours; surveys may also be conducted in the evening (after 6 PM), early in the morning (before 8 AM), or on weekends.

Types of Survey

The State Operations Manual provides for five different types of surveys:

- Standard
- Abbreviated

- Extended
- Special
- Validation

The **standard survey** is the most common type of survey. This periodic survey is conducted for the purpose of certification renewal and is generally conducted within nine to fifteen months of the previous survey.

An **abbreviated survey** is a standard survey of shorter duration and more limited scope than usual. States may determine that an abbreviated survey may suffice in a facility that has been consistently in compliance with the certification standards. An abbreviated survey may also be used to conduct a focused review, for example in case of a specific complaint against a facility.

An **extended survey**, in which the scope and duration of a standard survey is expanded, may be necessary when indications are present that quality of care may be substandard. An extended survey requires a more detailed investigation of problems and a closer review of the facility's policies and procedures.

A **special survey** may be conducted in case of a change in ownership or key personnel, such as the administrator or director of nursing, to ensure continuity of patient care.

A **validation survey** is carried out by federal surveyors to confirm the findings of a survey conducted by the state. CMS has adopted a policy of validating at least five percent of the surveys conducted by the states. When a validation survey is conducted, federal findings take precedence over a state's findings.

Survey Process and Protocols

The State Operations Manual contains details of the actual survey process. A standard survey consists of seven successive tasks, summarized below:

- Off-site preparation
- Entrance conference
- Initial tour
- Resident sample selection
- Information gathering
- Information analysis and deficiency determination
- Exit conference

Task 1: Off-site preparation

This task is primarily governed by information generated by the minimum data set (MDS), discussed in Chapters 4 and 8. This is the instrument used by nursing facilities for patient assessment on initial admission and periodically thereafter. Facilities are required to electronically transmit the MDS data to the state. The MDS information is used by the state to compile certain quality indicators (QI) and develop a Facility Quality Indicator Profile. Off-site preparation before the actual visit to the facility includes preselection of residents and potential areas of concern based on the QI and facility profile information. During the actual visit, surveyors will initially focus on determining whether the pre-identified concerns indeed exist. Other elements that may require specific focus may include previous complaints about patient care and any issues brought before the ombudsman's office.

Task 2: Entrance conference

The survey team coordinator has an on-site meeting with the administrator (or other person in charge of the facility at the time) to provide introductions, explain the purpose of the visit, and obtain some basic information that would facilitate the survey. Signs are posted to notify the residents, employees, and the general public that a survey is in progress and that the surveyors are available to meet with any concerned individual.

Task 3: Initial tour

The tour may take approximately two hours. Members of the survey team may go around independently, with or without members of the facility's staff accompanying them. The surveyors talk to residents, employees, and visitors in the facility; visit some patient rooms and key departments, such as the kitchen; and make general observations. The purpose is to make a general assessment in conjunction with the information compiled during offsite preparation. The main focus is on quality of care and quality of life concerns (see Exhibit 3-2).

Task 4: Resident sample selection

Information gathered during off-site preparation and the tour is used to develop a resident sample for detailed investigation of patient care. The sampling method is called "case mix stratified," meaning that the sample should include patients who require heavy care as well as those who

require light care; it should also include residents who have sufficient memory and comprehension to be interviewed. To the extent possible, the sample should include residents who may be particularly vulnerable, such as those who have indwelling catheters, are tube fed, are mentally impaired, or have speech or hearing disorders. Patients who have sustained a weight loss, those at hydration risk, those with pressure ulcers, or those with other associated risk factors are also sampled.

Task 5: Information gathering

This phase of the process is designed to investigate areas such as patient care, medication errors, food preparation and dining services, residents' quality of life, facility environment and safety, and procedures for protecting residents against abuse and neglect. Most of the surveyors' time in the facility is spent on this investigative phase. Even though this task is investigative in nature, the State Operations Manual recommends that dialogue between the surveyors and facility staff members be ongoing, to prevent any surprises for the staff on the surveyors' conclusions at the end of the survey.

Task 6: Information analysis and deficiency determination

The surveyors determine the facility's compliance with each of the standards associated with the Requirements for Participation. A **deficiency** is cited for each of the standards not met. Deficiencies are characterized as resident-centered or facility-centered. Resident-centered requirements must be met for each resident, and a violation affecting any single resident is cited as a deficiency. Facility-centered violations refer to the operational systems such as staffing, food preparation, and infection control. Deficiencies are also evaluated in terms of their severity and scope. Severity is determined by the extent of actual or potential harm and negative health outcomes. Scope describes how widespread a problem is in the facility. At this stage, the surveyors may also discuss whether indications of substandard quality of care have been noted that may warrant an extended survey.

Task 7: Exit conference

In the exit conference, the surveyors meet face to face with facility officials to present their findings and any citations for deficiencies. The administrator may request a copy of the patient sample, provide additional infor-

mation that may have been overlooked, or ask for further clarifications. The facility also has the right to record any disagreements with the survey findings.

Enforcement and Remedies

The Statement of Deficiencies is a federal document that records the deficiencies cited as a result of a survey. Facilities must respond to the deficiencies with a **plan of correction** (POC) and take corrective action to reach compliance within a specified period of time. The POC is a public document, so the information can be accessed by the press and the general public.

Depending on the severity and scope of the deficiencies, the state may impose a **directed plan of correction** if state regulators do not believe that the facility can formulate and implement an effective POC on its own. For example, the state may require the facility to retain a nurse consultant. Other remedies that the state can impose include denial of payment for services, civil monetary penalties (fines), temporary management appointed by the state, or termination from the Medicare and Medicaid programs.

The CMS now posts on its Medicare Web site information on all facilities, with data for national and state comparisons. Called Nursing Home Compare, the information includes the number and types of deficiencies each facility had on its most recent survey.

PATIENT RIGHTS

Patients in nursing facilities and those seeking admission to a facility have all the rights of citizenship that are guaranteed to every American by the Constitution of the United States. Additional protections against discrimination are included in federal and state laws. Title VI of the Civil Rights Act of 1964 applies to programs receiving federal funds. The law prohibits denial of benefits on the basis of race, color, or national origin. Denial of benefits may be construed to mean discrimination in admission, segregation by race or ethnicity, and unequal treatment in other respects. Section 504 of the Rehabilitation Act of 1973 prohibits any facility receiving federal funds from discriminating on the basis of physical or mental handicap. Admission to a facility may be denied only if that facility does not provide the level of services that a patient in a protected

category requires. Individuals with HIV/AIDS are also protected under the Rehabilitation Act. The Americans with Disabilities Act (ADA) of 1990 goes beyond the requirements of the Rehabilitation Act. It specifically states that "no individual shall be discriminated against on the basis of disability in the full and equal enjoyment of the goods, services, facilities, privileges, advantages, or accommodations of any place of public accommodation." A **handicap** or disability, according to these laws, is physical or mental impairment that substantially limits one or more of a person's major life activities.

In health care facilities, patients must be informed of their rights. The Patient Self-Determination Act of 1990 also requires health care providers to protect and promote patient rights. Many states require that health care facilities develop a patient's bill of rights. Other states have taken the initiative in proposing these rights (see Exhibit 3-3 for an illustration of the rights proposed by North Carolina). Whether or not required by state law, facilities should have a bill of rights in printed form to inform residents and family members of these rights. Facilities are required to preserve patients' privacy in the delivery of care and treatments. It is important for nursing home staff members to realize that the facility is considered the patients' home. Facility administration should institute practices such as knocking before entering a patient's room, drawing privacy curtains for personal care, and ensuring appropriate dressing and grooming of residents. Facilities are also required to keep patient information confidential. The responsibilities of nursing homes, however, go far beyond ensuring the basic rights to privacy, dignity, and confidentiality. OBRA-87 added further rights regarding freedom from resident abuse, neglect, and misappropriation of resident property in nursing homes. **Abuse** is defined as "willful infliction of injury, unreasonable confinement, intimidation or punishment with resulting physical harm, pain or mental anguish." **Neglect** means "failure to provide goods and services necessary to avoid physical harm, mental anguish, or mental illness." **Misappropriation of resident property** means "deliberate misplacement, exploitation, or wrongful, temporary, or permanent use of a resident's belongings or money without the resident's consent." More recently, the Balanced Budget Act of 1997 required denial of payment under Medicare and Medicaid to facilities charged with abuse and mistreatment of patients. The law also directed the states to establish nurse-aide registries. Part of the information contained in the registry pertains

EXHIBIT 3-3

North Carolina's Bill Of Rights for Nursing Home Residents (Condensed Version)

EVERY RESIDENT SHALL HAVE THE FOLLOWING RIGHTS:

(1) To be treated with consideration, respect, and full recognition of personal dignity and individuality.

(2) To receive care, treatment, and services that are adequate and appropriate, and in compliance with relevant federal and State statutes and rules.

(3) To receive at the time of admission and during stay, a written statement of services provided by the facility, including those required to be offered on an as needed basis, and of related charges. Charges for services not covered under Medicare and Medicaid shall be specified. The patient will sign a written receipt upon receiving the above information.

(4) To have on file physician's orders with proposed schedule of medical treatment. Written, signed evidence of prior informed consent to participation in experimental research shall be in patient's file.

(5) To receive respect and privacy in his medical care program. All personal and medical records are confidential.

(6) To be free of mental and physical abuse. Except in emergencies, to be free of chemical and physical restraint unless authorized for a specified period of time by a physician according to clear and indicated medical need.

(7) To receive from the administration or staff of the facility a reasonable response to all requests.

(8) To associate and communicate privately and without restriction with persons and groups of the patient's choice at any reasonable hour. To send and receive mail

continues

EXHIBIT 3–3 *continued*

promptly and unopened. To have access to a telephone where the patient may speak privately. To have access to writing instruments, stationery and postage.

(9) To manage his/her own financial affairs unless other legal arrangements have been implemented. The facility may also assist the patient, but is required to follow stringent guidelines.

(10) To have privacy in visits by the patient's spouse, and if both are patients in the same facility, they shall be given the opportunity, where feasible, to share a room.

(11) To enjoy privacy in his/her room.

(12) To present grievances and recommend changes in policies and services personally, through other persons or in combination with others, without fear of reprisal, restraint, interference, coercion, or discrimination.

(13) To not be required to perform services for the facility without personal consent and the written approval of the attending physician.

(14) To retain, to secure storage for, and to use his personal clothing and possessions, where reasonable.

(15) To not be transferred or discharged from a facility except for medical, financial, or their own or other patient's welfare, nonpayment for the stay or when mandated by Medicare or Medicaid. Any such transfer shall require at least five days' notice, unless the attending physician orders immediate transfer, which shall be documented in the patient's medical record.

(16) To be notified within ten days after the facility's license is revoked or made provisional. The responsible party or guardian must be notified as well.

Source: North Carolina Division of Aging
http://www.dhhs.state.nc.us/aging/rights.htm

to findings of abuse, neglect, and misappropriation of resident property. This information is designed to ban aides who have been abusive in the past from employment in nursing facilities. The Patient Self-Determination Act of 1990 also governs a patient's right to make decisions about treatment and covers issues regarding advance directives, which are briefly discussed below. The Health Insurance Portability and Accountability Act of 1996 makes it incumbent upon facilities to develop policies and procedures to protect patient privacy. All documents pertaining to patients' rights should be appropriately maintained in their medical records.

Informed Consent

Informed consent is the right of a patient to make an informed choice about medical care. To make an informed choice, the resident must be given sufficient information to make a decision. A resident has the right to refuse treatment, even when the treatment is medically advisable. Legal consent, however, requires that the patient has actually understood whatever he or she is consenting to. So, if a resident is not legally competent to give consent, another individual who has legal authority to act on the patient's behalf must give consent. Obtaining consent from family members is a widely accepted practice, but it may give rise to legal issues, especially if the family consents to withhold treatment against medical advice. A patient who is legally incompetent may have a **guardian** who is legally empowered and responsible for making decisions in the patient's best interest. The legal guardian's decisions overrule those of family members. Express consent may, however, be waived or implied under certain circumstances, such as emergency situations in which a physician may determine that delay incurred in the process of obtaining consent may result in harm to the patient.

Substitute decision-making (decision by someone other than the patient) is not generally a simple matter. Clear communication between the decision makers and clinicians about the benefits and risks of expected clinical interventions, participation of decision makers in the deliberations of ethics committees, and joint decisions regarding what the patient would have desired, given the circumstances, are some of the means employed for making decisions on behalf of a patient. Other alternatives available when the patient loses the capacity to make decisions and indicate consent are discussed in the next section.

Advance Directives

When a patient lacks decision-making capacity, an **advance directive** provides an avenue for the patient to convey his or her wishes about medical treatment in the event of cognitive impairment. Advance directives must be prepared before a person loses his or her competency for making decisions. Three types of commonly used advance directives include a living will, a do-not-resuscitate order, and a durable power of attorney. A **living will** specifies a person's wishes regarding medical treatment in the event this person becomes incompetent. The main drawback with this approach is that it cannot possibly conceive all possible situations in which the advance directive may become necessary. A **do-not-resuscitate order** specifies that the person does not wish to have heartbeat or breathing restored in the event of a cardiac or respiratory arrest. By executing a **durable power of attorney**, a person appoints another individual to make decisions on his or her behalf. Unlike a power of attorney that expires when a patient becomes incompetent, a durable power of attorney continues even after the patient is declared legally incompetent. Compared to a living will, this approach provides more flexibility. But the drawback is that the appointed person may not act in the same manner in which the patient would have acted had he or she remained competent.

Patient Privacy

The Health Insurance Portability and Accountability Act (HIPAA) of 1996 contains some of the strongest provisions ever to protect patient privacy in all types of health care settings, including nursing facilities. This law made it illegal to gain access to personal medical information for reasons other than health care delivery, operations, and reimbursement. HIPAA legislation mandated strict controls on the transfer of personally identifiable health data between two entities, provisions for disclosure of protected information, and civil and criminal penalties for violation (Clayton 2001). Under the law, nursing facilities are required to provide a notice to patients detailing the ways in which the facility will use or disclose the patient's **protected healthcare information**, which is defined as individually identifiable health information that relates to the past, present, or future physical or mental health of, or the provision of healthcare to, a patient (Battaglia 2003).

To comply with the law, a nursing facility must have a detailed privacy policy in place (see Exhibit 3-4 for guidelines on developing a policy statement). At the time of admission, a copy of the policy should be given

EXHIBIT 3–4

Elements to be Included in a Facility's Privacy Policy under HIPAA

- A statement as a header and prominently displayed must declare: THIS NOTICE DESCRIBES HOW MEDICAL INFORMATION ABOUT YOU MAY BE USED AND DISCLOSED AND HOW YOU CAN GET ACCESS TO THIS INFORMATION. PLEASE REVIEW IT CAREFULLY.

This requirement is easily followed, but note that the statement must be in all caps and worded exactly as set forth above.

- Information relating to the uses and disclosures of the individual's PHI (protected healthcare information), including a description and one example for each of the types of uses and disclosures that the facility is permitted to make for the purposes of treatment, payment, and healthcare operations; a description of each of the other purposes that the facility is permitted or required to perform without consent, such as public health, governmental health oversight, judicial and administrative proceedings, law enforcement, and work-related illness or injury; and enough detail to clarify the uses and disclosures that are permitted or required by the Privacy Rule or other applicable laws.

This section may be lengthy because it will list the multiple ways that PHI is used and disseminated. You may want to consider for inclusion in the privacy policy: treatment purposes including creation of the healthcare records at the facility and for referrals to other healthcare providers, payment purposes, or healthcare operations such as quality improvement, business associates, facility directory, notifications to family members, marketing, fundraising, public health requirements, law enforcement requirements, and reports required by

continues

EXHIBIT 3–4 *continued*

health oversight agencies, including your survey and certification office.

- **Information that other disclosures and uses will be made only with the resident's written authorization and that he or she may revoke this authorization.**

This information can be placed anywhere in the document and can state that revocation is possible, and the request for revocation must be in writing.

- **Statement that describes the resident's rights concerning his or her PHI and how those rights may be exercised, such as (i) to request restrictions concerning certain uses and disclosures of PHI, (ii) to receive confidential communications of PHI, (iii) to inspect and copy PHI, (iv) to amend PHI, (v) to receive an accounting of disclosures of PHI, and (vi) to obtain a paper copy of the privacy notice on request even if the individual has agreed to receive the notice electronically.**

Again, this provision will result in a lengthy disclosure. Under section i, the facility wants to make clear that while the resident can request that PHI not be disclosed, the facility is under no obligation to grant the request. Medicare and Medicaid facilities can state that there are times when the request cannot be honored—including emergencies, if the resident is being transferred to another healthcare facility, or the disclosure is required by law. Under section iii, remember to indicate that if the resident wants copies of his/her medical record, HIPAA allows the facility to charge a reasonable copying fee. Section iv indicates that amending PHI is allowed, and requests for amendment should be made in writing with information to support the requested change. The accounting provisions listed under section v should be conditioned, and the policy should state that

continues

EXHIBIT 3–4 *continued*

an accounting can only go back six years, and that no accounting will be given for disclosures for reason of treatment, payment, or healthcare operations; for disclosures made to the resident, the resident's legal representative, or any other individual
involved in the resident's care; for disclosures to law enforcement officials; or for disclosures for national security purposes.

- **The facility is required by law to maintain the privacy of
  the resident's PHI with a list of the duties and practices
  of the facility with respect to PHI; and further, the facility is required to abide by the terms of the notice currently in effect. The notice should state that the facility
  reserves the right to change the terms of its notice and
  to make new notice provisions effective for all PHI that
  it maintains. The facility must also describe how it will
  provide residents with a revised notice.**

Facilities can choose to use a "layered notice," where this
information is included on a summary page (or first layer)
along with a summary of the resident's rights, then have a
"second layer" that contains all of the elements required by
the Privacy Rule.

Source: Excerpted from Battaglia SK. HIPAA compliance requires facilities to have
privacy policy. *Nursing Homes Long Term Care Management* 2003; 52(3):30–31. Used
with permission of Medquest Communications LLC.

to the patient or guardian, and receipt of the privacy notice must be
acknowledged in writing. The policy must also be posted at a prominent
location within the facility, and on the facility's Web site, if any.

The enforcement process is complaint-driven, which provides for progressive steps to penalize violators. For example, the first violation might
yield a warning, and subsequent violations might bring increasing fines.
The DHHS Office of Civil Rights will enforce civil violations of the
Privacy Rule, and the Department of Justice will enforce criminal violations (Edwards 2003).

CONCLUSION

Laws and regulations protect individuals as well as organizations. They also impose certain obligations that govern managers' decision-making and behaviors. Not only must nursing homes comply with general business law, they must also operate under a variety of regulations, such as the Life Safety Code and licensure and certification standards. In particular, certification standards establish minimum standards of quality, and adherence to them gives at least some assurance to patients and their families that the facility provides adequate care. Protection of patient rights is also paramount.

DISCUSSION AND APPLICATION QUESTIONS

1. What specific lessons can a nursing home administrator learn from *Fuqua v Horizon/CMS Healthcare Corporation*? What do you think may have been the basis for awarding huge punitive damages in this case?
2. In a case in which charges were filed against a New York nursing home and in which the owners and the administrators pleaded guilty to the charges, why do you think this was a criminal rather than a civil case?
3. What attitudes do you think nursing home administrators ought to have toward regulations that are often regarded as onerous?

INTERNET RESOURCES FOR FURTHER LEARNING

Centers for Medicare and Medicaid Services (CMS): The entire State Operations Manual and interpretive guidelines are available online in PDF format. The survey protocol and procedures, plus detailed regulatory standards and their interpretations (guidance to surveyors) for long-term care facilities can be accessed by clicking on Appendices Part P-PP [per link on the CMS site].
    http://www.cms.hhs.gov/manuals/pub07pdf/pub07pdf.asp

Free Advice: The site offers free legal information on civil law and proceedings.
http://law.freeadvice.com

MEDLINEplus health information: A comprehensive Web resource, with search options, for consumers and professionals; provided by the U.S. National Library of Medicine and the National Institutes of Health.
http://www.nlm.nih.gov/medlineplus/nursinghomes.html

Nursing Home Compare: Comparative reports on all nursing homes are accessible through the Medicare website.
http://www.medicare.gov/

Nursing Home Deficiency Trends and Survey and Certification Process Consistency (March 2003): A report compiled by the Office of Inspector General, Department of Health and Human Services.
http://oig.hhs.gov/oei/reports/oei-02-01-00600.pdf

REFERENCES

Battaglia, S.K. 2003. HIPAA compliance requires facilities to have privacy policy. *Nursing Homes Long Term Care Management* 52, no. 3: 30–31.

Becker, S. 2001. *Health Care Law: A Practical Guide*. 2nd ed. Newark, NJ: Matthew Bender & Company, Inc.

Clayton, P.D. 2001. Confidentiality and medical information. *Annals of Emergency Medicine* 38, no. 3: 312–316.

Edwards, D.J. 2003. DHHS lays out plan for HIPAA enforcement. *Nursing Homes Long Term Care Management* 52, no. 6: 12–13.

Grachek, M.K. 2002. Reducing risk and enhancing value through accreditation. *Nursing Homes Long Term Care Management* 51, no. 11: 34–36.

Haymarket Media Inc. 2001. *McKnight's Long-term Care News*. New York, NY. October 29.

Haymarket Media Inc. 2002. *McKnight's Long-term Care News*. New York, NY. April 12.

Landry, P. 1997. The common law: tradition and *stare decisis*. A Blupete Essay. http://www.blupete.com/Literature/Essays/BluePete/LawCom.htm

Miller, R.D., and R.C. Hutton. 2000. *Problems in Health Care Law*. 8th ed. Gaithersburg, MD: Aspen Publishers Inc.

Office of New York State Attorney General. 2003. Upstate nursing home chain admits to criminal charges relating to understaffing and falsification of records. Press release dated June 30, 2003.

Pozgar, G.D. 1992. *Long-Term Care and the Law: A Legal Guide for Health Care Professionals*. Gaithersburg, MD: Aspen Publishers Inc.

Pozgar, G.D. 2002. *Legal Aspects of Health Care Administration*. 8th ed. Gaithersburg, MD: Aspen Publishers Inc.

Schabes, A.E. 2002. Liability: Hints of 'sweet reason' from the Midwest. *Nursing Homes Long Term Care Management* 51, no. 9: 52–53.

Standler, R.B. 1998. Differences between civil and criminal law in the USA. http://www.rbs2.com/cc.htm

Stevenson, D.G., and D.M. Studdert. 2003. The rise of nursing home litigation: Findings from a national survey of attorneys. *Health Affairs* 22, no. 2: 219–229.

U.S. Attorney, District of New Mexico. Press release dated December 31, 1996.

Yorker, B.C. 1988. The nurse's use of restraint with a neurologically impaired patient. *Journal of Neuroscience Nursing* 20: 390–392.

CHAPTER 4

Financing and Reimbursement

LEARNING MODULES

1. Basic concepts of financing and reimbursement. Overview of the main sources of financing nursing home care.
2. Private payment and private insurance. Use of reverse mortgages. Establishing private pay rates. State of private long-term care insurance plans. Plan provisions to check when admitting a patient who has private insurance.
3. Eligibility for Medicare. Long-term care coverage under Medicare. Part A and Part B of Medicare. Coverage limitations, deductibles and copayments.
4. Covered and non-covered services under Medicare Part A. Services covered under Medicare Part B.
5. Medicare's prospective payment system. Case mix and its determination using the resident assessment instrument. Role of assessment in prospective reimbursement. Seven major RUG-III Groups. Using the major groups and ADL scores to determine RUG-III classification.
6. The Medicaid program, eligibility, services, and reimbursement.

continues

7. Managed care and its role in long-term care financing. Partnerships with hospitals and health systems. Veterans Health
   Administration contracts.
8. Civil and criminal penalties under fraud and abuse laws. *Qui
   tam* provision of the False Claims Act.

Financing and reimbursement are viewed as the backbone of long-term care services because they provide the financial resources necessary for sustaining internal facility operations. For the most part, health care financing is governed by external factors, notably politics, social changes, the economy, competition, and changes in the broader health care delivery system.

Much of the information covered in this chapter is of value to more than just nursing home corporations and administrators. Social workers and patient-accounts managers should also have a clear understanding of financing so they can furnish advice and assistance to current and prospective patients, families and guardians, and the community.

Financing is the means by which patients receiving services in nursing facilities pay for those services. Institutional long-term care is expensive. In 2003, the estimated average cost of skilled nursing care for someone paying out of his or her personal funds ranged between $4,000 and $5,000 a month. Few patients or their families can afford such costs if they pay with their own funds. Although individual long-term care insurance has grown, it is not widely popular, and only a small fraction of national nursing home expenditures are paid for by private insurance. Public financing, mainly Medicaid and Medicare, remains the predominant source of financing nursing home care. Figure 4-1 shows the primary expected source of payment at the time of admission. Total national expenditures for nursing home care, and the distribution of different types of financing, are illustrated in Figure 4-2.

Often the critical issue for nursing facility operators is how much the various publicly-financed programs would pay, that is, how much **reimbursement** (or payment) they can expect for services delivered to patients receiving public benefits. Reimbursement covers two aspects of financing: The method used by a payer to determine the amount of payment, and the amount that is actually paid to a facility on behalf of a patient.

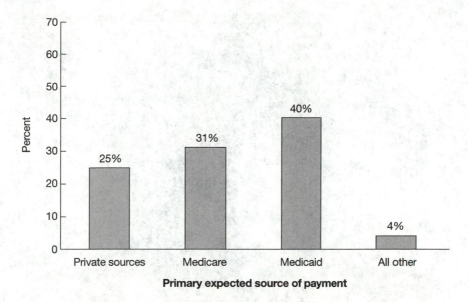

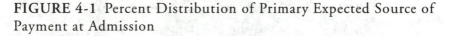

Primary expected source of payment

Source: National Nursing Home Survey 1999. *Vital Health Statistics*, Series 13, No. 152 (2002), p. 4. National Center for Health Statistics.

FIGURE 4-1 Percent Distribution of Primary Expected Source of Payment at Admission

Trends in nursing-home financing show that people's ability to pay for long-term care out of their own funds continues to decline. For example, in 1990, out-of-pocket payments financed 37.5% of nursing home care nationwide. By 2001, only 27.2% was paid out of pocket (Department of Health and Human Services 2003). Consequently, the public programs have to shoulder the growing burden. As discussed in Chapter 3, as a major financier for health care services, the government has been actively involved in regulating the delivery of health care. Financing and reimbursement have also been the subject of recent laws and regulations.

A growing elderly population in the United States requires more and more health care services. Moreover, total health care expenditures have been escalating, even after factoring out the effects of an aging population. Since 1965, when the Medicaid and Medicare programs were created, reimbursement for health care services has undergone some revolutionary changes. The main objective of any new government initiative has been to restrain the escalating expenditures, mainly by reducing the amount of reimbursement. Some cuts have been imposed directly through reduced reimbursement from Medicaid and Medicare; others

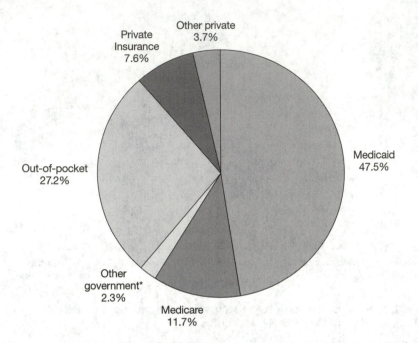

*Other government expenditures include, for example, care funded by the Department of Veterans Affairs.

Source: Data from *Health, United States, 2003*, p. 311, National Center for Health Statistics, Department of Health and Human Services.

FIGURE 4-2 Sources of Funding for Nursing Home Care (non-hospital affiliated facilities), 2001

have come indirectly by enrolling patients with managed care organizations that receive fixed payments from the government for an enrolled population and then seek cost-efficient health care for the enrollees. More recently, fraud and abuse by providers participating in the public programs have come under increased government scrutiny and have resulted in numerous criminal as well as civil prosecutions.

The Centers for Medicare and Medicaid Services (CMS) establishes Medicare reimbursement rates, whereas each state sets its own rates for Medicaid payment. The actual rate-setting mechanisms are quite complex. Nursing home administrators can obtain details of the Medicaid rate-setting methodology from their own state agencies. Rate-setting methods used by Medicare and a number of Medicaid programs are illustrated later in this chapter.

PRIVATE FINANCING

Of the two types of private financing, direct out-of-pocket payment is the most common. The other type, presently much smaller in size, is private long-term care insurance.

Private Pay

Private pay refers to out-of-pocket financing for long-term care. It may come from cash savings, stocks, bonds, or annuities. For some people, such resources may provide adequate income to pay for nursing home care. In most instances, however, assets may have to be sold to generate cash.

A home is often the largest asset that most people have. Reverse mortgaging is a new creative way to tap into the built-up equity in a home without having to sell the property. But the owner has to continue to live in the home, which makes this option unavailable for nursing home care, although it can be used for in-home medical and housekeeping services. It can also be used to purchase private long-term care insurance. A **reverse mortgage** is a type of loan against the equity in a home. It is available to people 62 and older who own their home and have few or no mortgage payments left. By using this method, an individual can choose to receive either a one-time loan against the equity or monthly cash payments. Even though it is a loan, the borrower does not make any loan payments, and does not have to repay the loan as long as he or she lives in the home. The lending institution retains a financial interest in the home. The borrowed amount is paid back to the lender when the borrower dies or sells the home.

Long-term care facilities are free to establish their own private pay rates or prices. For non-certified beds (see Chapter 3), a facility may label its services as "intermediate care," "personal care," or "residential care." No clear-cut definitions exist for these terms, and a facility can establish its own criteria for determining its different levels of services and how much it will charge for those services. The terms all signify a level of care that is clinically much less complex than what is provided in SNF and NF certified facilities (see Chapter 3). For such custodial levels of care, nursing facilities may establish private pay per-diem rates that are lower than Medicare or Medicaid rates. Private pay rates can be lower as long as the services are provided in non-certified beds. On the other hand, when private pay patients are placed in a section of the facility that is certified as SNF or NF, administrators must be careful when setting private pay rates.

They risk having the Medicare and Medicaid rates reduced if the all-inclusive private-pay rate happens to be lower than what the public programs are paying. Generally, private pay rates are the highest, and admission of private-pay patients often helps subsidize services provided to Medicaid patients because of low reimbursement.

Even though private pay rates may be established at any level, they are governed by market forces and competition. Additional factors such as amenities, comforts, and the ambiance that a facility offers should also be considered and compared with those of its competitors while setting private pay rates. Patients and their families who have sufficient private funds available are often willing to pay extra for a better living environment. A facility with a reputation for providing high-quality care also can charge its private-pay clients a premium.

As discussed in chapter 3, federal certification enables a facility to serve Medicare or Medicaid clients. Although certified beds can also be used for private-pay patients, these patients cannot be provided better quantity or quality of services for clinical needs that are similar to those of patients on public assistance. For example, certified beds occupied by private-pay patients cannot have extra staffing or extra amenities such as a more exclusive menu, because these extra services would be construed as discrimination against patients on public assistance if they do not get these extra services. For these reasons, many facilities have a separate non-certified section to care for private-pay patients because then the facility can deliver extras and charge for them.

Private-pay rates may be set as all-inclusive (or bundled) rates although this option is not the general practice. A **bundled rate** (also called package price) is one set price that includes all services that a patient may require. Generally, the rates are unbundled, meaning that each particular level of care has a basic room-and-board rate, which includes nursing care, meals, social services, activities, housekeeping, and maintenance services. Charges are added for ancillaries such as pharmaceuticals; supplies such as catheters, dressings, and incontinence pads; and services such as oxygen therapy or rehabilitation therapy. The basic rates and the charges for ancillary products and services are spelled out in a contract between the facility and the patient.

Private Insurance

General health insurance plans sponsored by employers may have limited coverage for long-term care services. Some retirees may also have similar

limited coverage available under their company's health insurance plan for retirees. In most instances, however, people have to buy their own long-term care policies, which are sold to them by various private insurance companies. Some insurers may allow the use of life insurance death benefits in an existing policy to cover the cost of long-term care. However, this option will reduce the dollar amount of the death benefit that the beneficiary will receive.

Long-term care insurance is available in a wide range of choices in services covered and prices. In addition to nursing home care, insurance also generally covers community-based services such as home health care or adult day-care. Insurance policies (or plans) also vary in terms of the dollar amount of benefits to be paid on a daily basis. Depending on the policy, there may or may not be a maximum limit on the benefits. To be eligible for benefits, the insured person must meet the criteria for disability specified in the policy. Such criteria may include cognitive dysfunction or inability to perform certain activities of daily living (ADLs). Other criteria may be more loosely stated, such as medical necessity. In almost all instances, physician certification for the need of long-term care services is required.

When admitting patients with private insurance coverage, the facility's business office manager should carefully review the coverage, such as the type of care covered by the policy. Some policies pay for only the skilled level of nursing home care that is authorized by a physician, whereas other policies are more comprehensive and may cover various community-based services as well. Other elements to check include the length of coverage, amount the policy will pay each day, and coverage for ancillaries such as supplies and therapies.

The cost of premiums for long-term care insurance is generally quite high, especially if a plan is purchased in later years of one's life. Although a plan purchased early in life is comparatively less expensive and, at least theoretically, it may be affordable for most working-age adults, people in younger age groups generally face other financial priorities in their lives, such as saving for retirement, their children's college education, life insurance, and buying a home. The need for long-term care in the distant future is often seen as a much lower priority (Merlis 2003). For these reasons, only a relatively small number of people, most of them affluent, have chosen to purchase long-term care insurance. Nevertheless, purchase of long-term care insurance has increased steadily in recent years. Between

1992 and 1998, the number of long-term care insurance plans sold in the United States doubled from approximately 3 million to 6 million (Coronel 2000). By the end of 2001, almost 8.3 million long-term care policies had been sold nationwide. For several years now, the market for private long-term care insurance has been growing at an average rate of 18 percent per year. The average age at which individuals purchase a long-term care policy has also gone down from 72 in 1990 to 62 in 2001 (Health Insurance Association of America 2003). The main financial incentive offered by many insurance companies is guaranteed premiums that do not increase over time. A premium is the cost of purchasing an insurance policy, which is usually paid every month to keep the policy active. Many policies have a waiver of premium feature which means that the insured individual does not pay the premiums during the period benefits are used. The AARP publishes consumer information on long-term care insurance, which can be accessed at its Web site.

MEDICARE

Medicare, which is also called Title 18 of the Social Security Act, is a federal program. It finances medical care for three categories of people: (1) persons who are age 65 and over, (2) disabled individuals who are entitled to Social Security benefits, and (3) people who have end-stage renal disease. The program is operated under the administrative oversight of the Centers for Medicare and Medicaid Services (CMS). Medicare is not a comprehensive program. Actually, the benefits for long-term care are very limited. Medicare consists of two separate insurance programs, called Part A and Part B.

Part A of Medicare and Eligibility

Part A, also called Hospital Insurance (HI), provides for care in a facility certified as SNF (see Chapter 3) for a period not to exceed 100 days. This limit means that a patient may be covered for less than 100 days. In fact, during 1999, the average days of care in a SNF amounted to 23 days per admission (Centers for Medicare and Medicaid Services 2002). Apart from being short-term, the Medicare benefit for SNF is a post-acute program. Before it will pay for services in a SNF, Medicare requires hospitalization for at least three consecutive days, not counting the day of dis-

charge. The patient must be in need of skilled nursing care as certified by a physician and be admitted to a SNF within 30 days after discharge from the hospital.

The maximum of 100 days of care is allowed within each benefit period. A **benefit period** is a period that begins when a patient is hospitalized for a particular spell of illness and ends when the beneficiary has not been hospitalized nor has received care in a SNF for 60 consecutive days for that particular spell of illness. Three key criteria determine a benefit period:

- A spell of illness or principal condition for which a patient is hospitalized. Different spells of illness can trigger new benefit periods.
- Hospitalization, treatment in a SNF, or both. If a spell of illness for which a patient is hospitalized subsequently requires skilled nursing care in a SNF, the benefit period continues.
- A given benefit period associated with a given spell of illness ends when the patient remains out of the hospital or SNF for 60 consecutive days.

After discharge, a patient may be readmitted to the hospital for the same spell of illness. On discharge from the hospital the patient may or may not go to a SNF. The initial benefit period remains in force after discharge and ends only when the patient remains out of the hospital or SNF for 60 consecutive days. If the patient goes into the hospital after one benefit period has ended, a new benefit period begins. The number of benefit periods a patient can have is unlimited. Part A also covers hospital inpatient services, home health services for intermittent or part-time skilled nursing care, and hospice care in a Medicare-certified hospice.

At the time of admission, the facility's business office manager should determine eligibility for Part A coverage by finding out whether the patient had a hospital stay of at least three days, whether the patient is being admitted within 30 days of discharge from the hospital, and the number of SNF days that may already have been used up in the benefit period. Details on admission and billing procedures are published in the Medicare Skilled Nursing Facility Manual (See Web site listed at the end of this chapter). A summary of eligibility for SNF care appears in Exhibit 4-1; covered services are discussed later in this chapter. Medicare does not pay for services provided in facilities that are not certified as SNF (see Chapter 3).

EXHIBIT 4-1

SNF Eligibility under Medicare Part A

Medicare Part A will pay for skilled nursing care if a Medicare beneficiary meets all of the following conditions:

- The patient's condition requires daily skilled nursing or skilled rehabilitation services which can only be provided in a skilled nursing facility (SNF).

- Before being admitted to a SNF, the patient has been an inpatient in a hospital for 3 consecutive days or more, not counting the day of discharge from the hospital.

- The patient is admitted to the SNF within 30 days after leaving the hospital.

- Care in the SNF is for a condition that was treated in the hospital.

Part B of Medicare and Eligibility

Part B of Medicare, also called Supplementary Medical Insurance (SMI), covers outpatient services. In general, these services include physician services, X-rays, laboratory tests, other diagnostic tests, ambulance services, and outpatient rehabilitation therapies (services provided by physical, occupational, and speech therapists). These services are generally delivered by providers other than SNFs, and the providers bill Medicare directly for the services.

From an eligibility standpoint, there is a major difference between Part A and Part B. Medicare Part A is a true entitlement program. People who qualify for one of the three categories mentioned earlier are eligible for benefits without having to pay any premiums, because all working Americans pay a Medicare payroll tax that funds Part A. Medicare Part B, on the other hand, requires voluntary enrollment and payment of a monthly premium, which was $66.60 in 2004. Because Part B premiums are heavily subsidized by general taxes, 95% of the Medicare beneficiaries have chosen to purchase Part B coverage. At the price the elderly pay to purchase Part B coverage, they will not be able to buy a similar plan in the private insurance market. For those who also qualify for Medicaid, the state pays the Part B premiums.

Coverage Limitations, Deductibles and Copayments

Medicare is more accurately described as a program for short-term post-hospital care, rather than a long-term care program. It covers a wide array of skilled-nursing and skilled-rehabilitation services for post-acute conditions. But it falls short of meeting the long-term needs of a person who requires ongoing assistance. For example, it does not pay for care in an assisted living facility or in the various community-based programs, such as adult day-care. Hence, Medicare is not a comprehensive long-term care program. Even in a SNF, the average length of stay per admission is only 23 days because based on their clinical needs as outlined in Medicare rules very few patients qualify for the full 100 days of care.

A **copayment** is the amount an insured patient must pay out of pocket each time a particular type of service is used. Medicare fully pays for just the first 20 days of SNF care in a benefit period. From days 21 through 100, the patient must pay a copayment, which was $109.50 per day in 2004. Medicare pays nothing after 100 days, even if the patient's condition may justify the need for ongoing services in a nursing facility.

Medicare Part A also requires the payment of a deductible, which was $876 per benefit period in 2004. A **deductible** is the amount the patient must first pay when a benefit period begins. Medicare starts paying only after the patient has paid the deductible. In almost all instances, however, the deductible requirement is met during the three-day hospitalization before a patient comes to the SNF. During the SNF stay, the patient becomes responsible only for the applicable copayment after completing the first 20 days of stay. The copayments, and payment for services beyond the 100 days, must be paid either privately or by Medicaid, provided the patient meets the eligibility criteria for Medicaid coverage (discussed later).

It is illegal for nursing facilities to attempt to recover any payments that exceed the applicable deductible and copayments for services covered under the public programs.

Medicare Covered Services: Skilled Nursing Care

Part A SNF benefits are summarized in Exhibit 4-2. The definition of skilled nursing care, as it applies to SNFs under the Medicare program, includes subacute care services. Hence, the same rules govern skilled nursing care and subacute care. According to Medicare law, skilled nursing care may include skilled nursing or skilled rehabilitation services. It has specific characteristics, summarized below:

EXHIBIT 4-2

SNF Benefits Under Medicare Part A

- Semi-private room

- Meals

- Skilled nursing care

- Physical, occupational, and speech therapy

- Medical social services

- Medications, medical supplies, medical equipment used in the facility

- Ambulance transportation to nearest provider of needed services when the SNF does not provide those services, and when other types of transportation may endanger the patient's health

- Dietary services

- The services must be ordered by a physician.
- The care furnished must be for treating conditions for which the patient was hospitalized, or for conditions that arose while the patient was receiving care in a SNF.
- Skilled services must be needed and must be provided seven days a week, except for skilled rehabilitation, which must be needed and provided five days a week.
- The services must require the skills of, and must be furnished directly by or under the supervision of, registered nurses (RNs), licensed practical (or vocational) nurses (LPNs or LVNs), physical therapists, occupational theapists, or speech pathologists.

"Under the supervision of" means that some of the actual hands-on care can be provided by paraprofessionals, such as certified nursing assistants, physical therapy assistants, and occupational therapy assistants. Skilled services are inherently complex and are required for medical conditions that can be treated safely and effectively only by the personnel just mentioned. Examples of complex nursing services include intravenous or intramuscular injections; enteral feeding (delivery of liquid feedings through a

tube); nasopharyngeal aspiration (suctioning through the nose and pharynx); tracheostomy (direct opening into the windpipe for breathing); insertion and irrigation of urinary catheters; dressings for the treatment of infections; treatment of pressure ulcers or widespread skin disorders; heat treatments; start of oxygen therapy; and rehabilitation nursing. Examples of skilled rehabilitation include assessment of rehabilitation needs and restorative potential (probability of functional improvement), therapeutic exercises or activities, gait training, range-of-motion exercises, maintenance therapy that requires the skills of a professional therapist, ultrasound treatment, short wave treatment, application of hot packs, infrared treatments, paraffin baths, whirlpool treatments, services needed for the restoration of speech or hearing, and therapy for swallowing disorders. The skilled-care criteria do not require that a potential for restoration be present. Even if recovery or improvement is not possible, preventing further deterioration is a sufficient justification for providing skilled care. If a patient requires only **custodial care**, such as assistance with ADLs, he or she does not qualify for SNF. Additional examples of custodial care include administration of routine oral medications, eye drops, or ointments; general maintenance of colostomy (attachment of colon to a **stoma**) and ileostomy (attachment of the small intestine to a stoma); routine maintenance of bladder catheters; dressings for noninfected conditions; care of minor skin problems; care for routine incontinence; periodic turning and positioning; and other routine and basic nursing-care services.

Medicare Covered Services: Other Services

According to Title 42 of the Code of Federal Regulations (Part 409, Subpart C), post-hospital services provided in a SNF include the following, many of which are incidental to the nursing home stay:

- Nursing care provided by or under the supervision of a registered nurse (RN).
- Bed and board (i.e., lodging and meals) in connection with the furnishing of nursing care. Medicare pays for semi-private accommodations. However, Medicare will pay for a private room if the patient's condition requires clinical isolation, or if the SNF does not have semi-private accommodations available.
- Physical, occupational, or speech therapy furnished by the facility or under arrangements made by the facility. If a SNF makes arrange-

ments with a company to provide therapeutic services to its patients, that service company cannot bill Medicare directly for Part A services. The facility is responsible for paying that company.

- Medical social services, which include services such as assessment and treatment of social and emotional issues, adjustment to the facility, and discharge planning.
- Drugs, biologicals (medical preparations—serums, vaccines, etc.— made from living organisms), supplies, appliances, and equipment. Medicare pays for these items during the inpatient stay. To facilitate a patient's discharge from the facility, Medicare pays for only a limited supply of the drugs and equipment that the patient must continue to use after leaving the facility.
- Other services that are generally provided by (or under arrangements made by) SNFs.

SNF benefits do not cover services that only a hospital can provide. Also, Medicare does not pay for services of a private-duty nurse or attendant.

Medicare Covered Services—Part B

Although Part B does not include SNF services, it is essential for nursing home administrators and business office personnel to understand Part B benefits. Certain services are paid under Part B while the patient is receiving SNF services under Part A. An example is physician services that are billed under Part B by the patient's attending physician. Similarly, diagnostic services and outpatient mental health care are covered under Part B. Other services, such as therapies, can be covered under Part B even after a patient's Part A benefits expire, and the patient may continue to stay in the nursing home as a private payer or as a Medicaid beneficiary. Certain preventive health screenings and immunizations, authorized under the Balanced Budget Act of 1997, are also included in Part B. Exhibit 4-3 summarizes Part B benefits.

Medicare Prospective Payment System

Section 4432(a) of the Balanced Budget Act of 1997 required Medicare to develop a prospective payment system (PPS) to reimburse SNFs. When it was implemented in 1998, PPS replaced the retrospective cost-based reimbursement system. The new method provides for a per-diem (daily) rate based on a facility's case mix.

EXHIBIT 4–3

Benefits Under Medicare Part B

Medically Necessary Services

- Physicians' services
- Outpatient medical and surgical services and supplies
- Diagnostic tests
- Outpatient therapy*
- Outpatient mental health services
- Some preventive health care services
- Other medical services

Preventive Services

- Bone mass measurement
- Colorectal cancer screening
- Diabetes services and some supplies
- Glaucoma screening
- Mammogram screening
- Pap test/pelvic exam/clinical breast exam
- Prostate cancer screening
- Vaccinations such as flu and pneumonia shots

Other Part B Services

- Clinical laboratory services, such as blood test and urinalysis
- Home health care: Part-time skilled care, and home health aide services
- Durable Medical Equipment (DME) when supplied by a home health agency (HHA) while delivering Medicare-covered home health care
- Outpatient hospital services
- Blood when needed as an outpatient
- Ambulance service

*As of September 1, 2003, Medicare limits how much it covers for outpatient physical (PT), occupational (OT), and speech (SLP) therapy. The limits are $1,590 per calendar year for PT and SLP combined, and $1,590 per calendar year for OT. After the patient has paid the $100 yearly Medicare Part B deductible, Medicare pays 80% of the cost up to the maximum limits.

Case-Mix Based Reimbursement

The aggregate level of clinical severity (acuity level) of patients in a facility is referred to as its *case-mix*. The case mix varies from facility to facility. The level of case mix rises as the number of seriously ill patients increases. Patients who are more seriously ill require more intensive use of resources and incur greater cost to the facility. Therefore, a higher case mix calls for greater reimbursement.

A case-mix adjusted rate of reimbursement is based on the level of care needed by patients in a SNF. It is based on the premise that a nursing home should be paid in accordance with the use of resources necessary for delivering care to its patients. For example, some residents require total assistance with their ADLs and have complex nursing-care needs. Other residents may require less assistance with ADLs, but may require rehabilitation or restorative nursing services. Residents with heavy care needs require more staff resources, so payment levels for their care are higher than they are for those residents with less intense care needs. The recognition of these differences is the premise on which a case-mix system is based.

The per-diem rate is facility-specific. Also, the rate is all-inclusive, which means that it is a bundled rate that includes payment for all SNF services that a Medicare recipient is eligible to receive under the program.

The former retrospective cost-based system reimbursed, with some limitations, the actual costs for routine services, ancillary service costs, and cost of capital. These same costs are now consolidated in the PPS rate. The basic rate is determined by the mean costs of various SNF facilities in a base year and adjusted for inflation according to a market-basket index. The market-basket index is used to reflect inflationary cost increases between cost determination periods. This market-adjusted basic rate requires further adjustments, which are discussed later.

Role of Assessment in Prospective Reimbursement

Patient assessment plays a critical role in prospective reimbursement because it is used to determine the case mix. A trained registered nurse (RN) in the facility oversees the assessment process for which a standardized resident assessment instrument (RAI) called the **minimum data set** (MDS 2.0 is the current version in use, MDS 3.0 is being developed) must be used to conduct a comprehensive assessment of each patient's needs. The MDS contains extensive information on the resident's nursing

care needs, ADL impairments, cognitive status, behavioral problems, and medical diagnoses (See Appendix 4-I).

A SNF must complete an initial assessment on a patient by the fifth day of admission. Subsequent assessments must be completed by the fourteenth day and again by the thirtieth day. For patients staying longer than 30 days for Part A services, assessments must also be done by the sixtieth and ninetieth days, as the case may be. MDS information is electronically transmitted to the state, and the state transmits it to the CMS.

The facility's case mix is derived from a patient-classification system called **resource utilization groups**, version 3 (RUG-III). The MDS data provide the input for classifying each patient in one of the 44 RUG-III classes, which are mutually exclusive; a resident can be classified in only one class, and the patient is assigned a code for that class. When classified, the patient goes into the highest group for which he or she is eligible, based on the MDS assessment (Baker 2000). RUG-III classification can be viewed as a three-step process:

Step 1—Seven Major RUG-III Groups

The system first groups the residents into one of seven categories, known as the seven major RUG-III groups. Each of the major groups has a certain number of RUG categories, and all categories together total forty-four. The major groups are described below with illustrative examples, and the number of RUG categories in each group is given in parentheses:

1. **Rehabilitation** (14). This category is subdivided into five levels based on the number of minutes of rehabilitation therapy per week needed by the patient. For example, the highest level, labeled 'ultra-high intensity,' requires therapy for more than 720 minutes per week in at least two rehabilitation disciplines. At the lowest level, labeled 'low intensity,' therapies are delivered for at least 45 minutes per week.

2. **Extensive services** (3). These services require a high level of technical skills. Examples include intravenous feeding, tracheostomy care, suctioning, or ventilator/respirator.

3. **Special care** (3). This category includes patients with serious medical conditions such as **quadriplegia**, multiple sclerosis, **cerebral palsy**, surgical wounds, or open lesions. Also included are patients with problems such as fever with vomiting or dehydration. In

addition, patients who show a weight loss, are tube fed, or receive radiation treatment are included.

4. **Clinically complex** (6). Patients in this category require skilled nursing management and treatments. Examples include burns, coma, **septicemia**, pneumonia, internal bleeding, and **hemiplegia**. This category also includes patients requiring oxygen, transfusions, chemotherapy, or dialysis.

5. **Impaired cognition** (4). Patients with impaired cognition include those with cognitive impairment in decision-making, recall, and in short-term memory. They must first qualify for skilled nursing care under the Medicare guidelines.

6. **Behavioral problems** (4). Residents displaying behavior such as wandering, verbally or physically abusive or socially inappropriate behavior, or who experience hallucinations or delusions. These patients must first qualify for skilled nursing care under the Medicare guidelines.

7. **Reduced physical function** (10). Residents whose care needs primarily require assistance with ADLs and general supervision. Again, these patients must first qualify for skilled nursing care under the Medicare guidelines.

The seven groupings are hierarchical. For example, residents in the Rehabilitation groups have the highest level of combined nursing and rehabilitation need, while residents in the Extensive Services groups have the next highest level of need.

Step 2—ADL Score

Each of the seven categories is further divided by the intensity of the resident's ADL needs. Appendix 4-II shows a worksheet to illustrate the calculation of the total ADL score. The scores are derived from section G of the MDS. For example, the ADL score for bed mobility from section G1a of the MDS is 4 (See Appendix 4–II), based on ADL code 3 in column A (self-performance requiring extensive assistance) and ADL code 2 in column B (support provided as one person physical assist) of the MDS. According to the ADL worksheet, the combined value of column A code 3 and column B code 2 results in a score of 4 for the patient identified as 007163. See Discussion item 3 at the end of the chapter for the remainder of this worksheet. The total ADL scores can range between 4 and 18.

Step 3—RUG-III Classification

After determining a resident's total ADL score, the RUG classi[fication]
process begins starting with Rehabilitation, the first major group. Again,
the information is obtained from the MDS. A hierarchical process, beginning with Ultra High Intensity (see Appendix 4-III), is again used to
determine whether a patient could be classified in one of the 14 RUG
classes of the Rehabilitation group. For example, a patient who received
ultra-high intensity therapy (720 minutes or more of therapy per week,
and at least two disciplines, one of which is at least 5 days per week, and
the second for at least 3 days) based on the MDS and has a total ADL
score of between 16 and 18 will be coded RUC according to the RUG-III
classification system (see Appendix 4-III). If a patient cannot be classified
into any of the Rehabilitation RUG-III codes, the formula for inclusion
in the next major group, Extensive Services, is used to determine whether
the patient could be classified into one of the three RUG-III codes in that
group, and so on. Notice that for illustrative purposes only the section on
Rehabilitation has been included in the Appendices. See Internet Resources
listed at the end of this chapter for obtaining the other six sections.

Index Maximizing and Rate Adjustments

Although the worksheets in Appendices 4-II and 4-III can be used to
manually determine the RUG-III classification for a patient, commercial
software programs are used to convert the MDS data into RUG classes.
CMS has also designed its own software program, called the Resident
Assessment Validation and Entry (RAVEN) system, which is available free
of charge from the CMS Web site.

The manual hierarchical method described above helps one understand the relationship between the clinical needs of patients and their
classification for reimbursement purposes. However, Medicare PPS and
Medicaid payments in most states are based on an Index Maximizing
Classification rather than the hierarchical method discussed above. The
difference between the two methods is relatively small.

Medicare uses a Case Mix Index (CMI), which is a weight developed
by CMS (see Appendix 4-IV for an example of weights used by CMS in
2002). The weights represent the amount of time required for nursing
care and rehabilitation therapies. As in the hierarchical method, index
maximizing begins by going through all seven major groups. But in the
hierarchical method, the process stops once a patient is classified into the

first group in which he or she qualifies, beginning at the top with Rehabilitation. In index maximizing, the process continues and all 44 RUG III groups are evaluated because a resident can sometimes qualify for more than one RUG-III group. The CMI for each of the qualifying groups is then recorded, and the patient is classified in the group with the highest CMI. The higher the CMI, the higher the per diem payment to the facility.

The case-mix adjusted reimbursement rates for the RUG-III classes are published in the Federal Register. The basic per-diem rate for a facility is adjusted for the qualifying RUG categories to account for the relative use of resources by different patients in the facility. The per-diem rate is also adjusted for geographic variation in wages by separating the costs of care into their labor and non-labor components. A wage index is used to adjust the labor component depending on where the facility is located. The rate then undergoes one final adjustment according to whether the facility is located in a rural or urban area. Facilities located in a **Metropolitan Statistical Area** (MSA) receive an urban per-diem rate; those outside an MSA receive a rural per diem rate.

SNFs are required to submit Medicare claims (i.e., billings) to their designated **fiscal intermediary**. These are private insurance companies contracted by Medicare to process claims from providers.

With additional research, the RUG categories currently in use are likely to evolve. CMS is further refining the methodology to more accurately reflect the resource utilization for the numerous types of patient conditions that require skilled nursing care. The revised MDS version 3.0 is targeted for implementation in 2005.

MEDICAID

Medicaid is a jointly-funded federal-state health insurance program that is also called Title 19 of the Social Security Act. Medicaid is a welfare program for the indigent. People with very low incomes and those with little or no assets generally qualify. The eligibility criteria are set by the different states, so they vary from state to state. However, states are also required to follow federal guidelines. Under the guidelines, people receiving supplemental security income (SSI) are required to be covered under Medicaid. It includes many of the elderly, the blind, and the disabled.

States have the option to include people regarded as "medically needy" and many states have opted to do so. This option allows states to extend

Medicaid eligibility to individuals who may have too much income to qualify otherwise. People who have excess income or assets to qualify outright for Medicaid have the option to "**spend down**" to Medicaid eligibility thresholds by incurring medical or remedial care expenses to offset their excess income, thereby reducing it to a level below the maximum allowed by that state's Medicaid plan. The resource limits for spend down, meaning the amount of funds a person may keep in order to apply for Medicaid, generally vary between $2,000 and $3,000. This provision is particularly significant for nursing facilities because it allows middle-class elderly patients to qualify for Medicaid once they have exhausted their personal assets. An estimated one-fourth of the patients who are initially admitted to a nursing facility on a private-pay basis eventually switch over to the Medicaid program after their personal assets have been exhausted. If individuals who qualify for Medicaid receive income from any sources, they are required to apply most of that income toward nursing home expenses; Medicaid will then pay the rest. Under federal law, it is a felony to shelter or distribute personal assets with the intention of making oneself eligible for Medicaid coverage.

The spend-down provision of Medicaid was modified under the Medicare Catastrophic Coverage Act (MCCA) of 1988. Although much of the MCCA was repealed, the portions affecting Medicaid remain in effect. The law protects the assets of an institutionalized person's spouse if the spouse must remain at home. The law was designed to prevent the impoverishment of the spouse remaining in the community. When one spouse enters a nursing home, there is a maximum amount of resources that the spouse at home is allowed to keep. This maximum amount, which varies from one state to another, is called Community Spouse Resource Allowance (CSRA). The community spouse is also allowed to keep a portion of the monthly income, an amount referred to as Community Spouse Monthly Income Allowance (MIA), which guarantees the spouse at home a basic monthly allowance for living expenses. Medicaid eligibility rules are complex, and they vary from state to state. Specific details can be obtained from a local social services office.

Unlike Medicare, Medicaid is a comprehensive health care program. Medicaid has no limit on the number of days a person may stay in a nursing facility. Hence, Medicaid pays the largest share of national expenditures for nursing home services (Figure 4-2). Many states also pay for eyeglasses, hearing aids, dental care, and other needed services. Also, a number of states cover community-based long-term care services such as adult day care, adult foster care, residential care, and assisted living,

because services comprising personal care in community settings is more cost-effective than the more skilled services provided in nursing homes.

Determination of reimbursement rates for nursing facilities is left up to each state. States employ diverse methods and policies to determine the per diem rates, and the amount of the per-diem reimbursement varies greatly from one state to another. Many states have adopted a case-mix method similar to the Medicare prospective payment system discussed earlier. Of all payers, Medicaid generally has the lowest reimbursement rates.

Some states, notably, Indiana, Iowa, Ohio, and Pennsylvania, are using "modified pricing" systems of reimbursement. It uses a prospective payment method, but the component for direct care, such as nurse staffing, is tied to the amount a facility actually spends on direct care. The American Association of Homes and Services for the Aging (AAHSA) has argued that such methods should be more broadly adopted, because they provide an incentive to facilities to have adequate staffing to deliver better care. Reimbursement methods could include other factors related to quality of care, such as the use of standardized protocols for pressure ulcer risk assessment to identify high-risk patients (Edwards 2003).

MANAGED CARE AND HEALTH-SYSTEM PARTNERSHIPS

The growing health care burden for an aging population will, by necessity, make public financing more stringent. It means that nursing home administrators will have to find innovative ways to increase revenues from private sources, something that will increasingly involve other organizations for financing and delivery of care.

Managed Care

Since the 1990s, managed care has become the primary mechanism for delivering the vast array of health care services in the United States. Most of employer-based health insurance (about 95% in 2002) provided to American workers is through various types of managed care plans. Some states have also opted to enroll their Medicaid beneficiaries in managed care plans. Nationwide, 57% of all Medicaid recipients are enrolled in managed care (Aventis Pharmaceuticals 2003). The Balanced Budget Act of 1997 authorized the Medicare+Choice program (now named Medicare

Advantage) with the objective of channeling Medicare beneficiaries into managed care plans, although Medicare allows beneficiaries to remain in the traditional fee-for-service program. Approximately 18% of Medicare beneficiaries nationwide are enrolled in managed care (Department of Health and Human Services 2003).

Managed care includes organizations such as health maintenance organizations (HMOs) and preferred provider organizations (PPOs). In Medicare terminology, the terms Health Maintenance Organizations and Competitive Medical Plans (HMO/CMPs) sometimes refer to entities that contract for and deliver services through various managed care organizations (MCOs). All MCOs are private organizations, but they can contract with Medicare or Medicaid to deliver health care to beneficiaries covered by these public programs. To invite participation from a broader array of risk-bearing organizations under the Medicare+Choice program, the term now being used is "M+C" organization. An M+C organization must be authorized under state law to operate as a risk-bearing entity that may offer health benefits. A risk-bearing organization assumes financial risk just like an insurance company does. In their simplest form, these organizations take the responsibility to deliver health care services to a large number of enrollees at a fixed contracted price per enrollee. The organization takes financial risk because the fixed payment may not be adequate to cover the cost of all the services the enrollees may need. Because, under the terms of the contract, the organization must pay for those services, it can lose money.

The key to understanding the general concept of managed care is the delivery of services on a prepayment basis, which means that an MCO must provide all needed services to enrolled beneficiaries in exchange for a fixed monthly payment agreed to in advance. This method of financing is called **capitation**. In determining the capitation rates, a method called risk adjustment is used to account for variations in beneficiary health status. **Risk adjustment** accounts for the expected consumption of health care resources in accordance with the patients' health status. For example, the MDS-based RUG system (discussed earlier) is a risk-adjustment method used for setting payment levels. In a nutshell, the idea of capitation incorporates the prepayment of a predetermined rate per person, and secondly, the capitation payment includes all covered services. Thus, an MCO is required to provide all covered services needed by the enrollees, and the cost of providing the services must be managed within the capi-

tation amount received. Therefore, MCOs seek services that are cost-effective. Capitation is designed to control inappropriate use of services and to control the escalating costs of health care delivery.

For the Medicaid program, the federal government has created Section 1915(b) and Section 1915(c) waivers that allow states to provide a variety of long-term care services by contracting with MCOs. These services may include both community-based and institution-based long-term care.

MCOs generally negotiate per-diem rates with nursing facilities. A nursing facility could have contracts with several different MCOs to provide services to clients covered under private or public financial arrangements. Refinements in basic per-diem reimbursement are likely to be made as administrators become savvy in associating costs with case-mix variations. The MDS-driven RUG classification method, discussed earlier, can effectively be used for managed care contracting. However, MCOs are interested in three to four levels of services instead of the forty-four in the RUG-III system, but the system can be modified to accommodate MCOs' needs.

The growth of managed care has serious implications for health facility administrators. They must now include MCOs as key stakeholders in the exchange environment. To manage costs, M+C organizations and MCOs have a financial incentive to minimize the length of stay in acute care hospitals and to put greater emphasis on subacute care. Although cost is the primary concern in the managed care environment, the M+C organizations are also held accountable by the payers for quality of care. Hence, incentives are in place for these organizations to contract with only those facilities that can offer an acceptable level of quality at the lowest price.

Nursing facility administrators are faced with both an opportunity and a challenge to meet higher demands for subacute care. They must also develop contracting and negotiating skills to deal with MCOs, skills at costing and pricing skilled care and subacute services, and skills to manage clinical services that have become increasingly complex. On the other hand, many hospitals have developed transitional care (or extended care) units that deliver postacute services after a patient is discharged from acute care. This puts hospitals in the driver's seat to steer patients away from nursing homes when these patients require postacute care in a skilled nursing facility. That means stiffer competition for freestanding community nursing facilities. On the other hand, not all hospitals have postacute care units. In either case, a nursing facility can estab-

lish partnerships with area hospitals to at least serve the overflow of patients that may require postacute care. An MCO may also partner with a hospital-based health system and one or two nursing facilities. Getting a piece of the action unquestionably presents difficult challenges for nursing home administrators. The task can be daunting without administrative leadership that is firmly based on the open system model discussed in Chapter 1.

Hospital and Health-System Partnerships

Partnership between a hospital and nursing home can be attractive to MCOs because MCOs look for organizations that can offer a full range of services, along with high quality and low cost. Beck (1996) proposed four different partnership options that nursing home administrators can explore: (1) One relatively low-risk form of partnership with a hospital is in the form of a sponsorship agreement. Under this arrangement, a hospital "sponsors" skilled nursing care for a specific patient or patients, essentially acting as a third-party payer for the patient at a predetermined rate. The hospital benefits by discharging a patient who no longer needs to be hospitalized and for whom the hospital will have to absorb the costs under PPS and capitation payment methods. The nursing facility can benefit from a relatively high payment from the hospital. (2) A second form of partnership is a bed-reserve agreement. Under this plan, a hospital pays a fixed amount for each bed that it reserves in a SNF for use by its patients. Unlike sponsorship, bed-reserve agreements may not be patient-specific. In fact, payment must be made even if the reserved beds are not used. In this case, it is important to check with the state's Medicaid program that such an arrangement would be acceptable. (3) Nursing facilities and hospitals can initiate a shared service arrangement. Such an arrangement is desirable when either a hospital needs long-term care expertise to establish a subacute program or a SNF needs specific expertise to upgrade its level of care. Monetary arrangements between the providers are determined by the services provided. (4) A hospital that seeks to establish a skilled nursing unit for subacute care can contract with a nursing home to manage that unit. Frequently the nursing facility is paid a management fee, which is usually a percentage of the profits generated from the operation. The hospital holds the license, and the nursing facility handles day-to-day operations. The nursing home can admit the overflow of patients to its own facility.

Summa Health System, an integrated health system in northeastern Ohio, is an example of the type of partnerships that can be formed between various organizations. In this case, Summa and skilled nursing providers in northeastern Ohio have come together to be part of a system-wide Care Coordination Network (CCN) that is designed to meet the complex, post-discharge needs of older adult patients. Summa has partnered with twenty-five SNFs that have been designated as preferred providers. In order to provide a seamless transfer of patients, the network developed a communication program and defined methods of transfer. Each facility works closely with Summa to set clinical guidelines and works to improve the outcomes of patients who are transferred from Summa (Kohn et al. 2003).

Veterans Health Administration Contracts

The VHA is responsible for providing nursing home care to any veteran in need of such care. The care may be provided directly in VHA's own facilities, or the veterans needing care may be placed in community nursing homes. To participate in the program, a nursing facility must enter into a contractual arrangement with the VHA. Roughly one in five nursing homes has a contract with the VHA. The contract is generally for a one-year term and is renewable. Reimbursement is contractually established between the facility and the VHA.

FRAUD AND ABUSE

Fraud and abuse by providers who participate in the Medicare and Medicaid programs have been a growing concern in recent years. Because fraud and abuse siphon off resources that otherwise could be used for providing legitimate services to needy people, the government has been cracking down on providers who abuse the system. Both criminal and civil laws can be enforced.

Federal Fraud and Abuse Law

The federal Fraud and Abuse law is a criminal statute. The legislation has evolved over time in the form of amendments to the Social Security Act. Most recently, the statute was expanded in the form of the Health Insurance Portability and Accountability Act (HIPAA) of 1996. The law

gives the government expanded powers to investigate and prosecute fraud in the delivery of health care services. Here are the main provisions of the Fraud and Abuse statute:

(A) It is a felony to make false statements or claims regarding services provided to Medicare or Medicaid patients. Violations are punishable with fines up to $25,000 or imprisonment of up to five years. Examples of violations include false billings, or attempts to obtain payments for services not provided. **Upcoding**, that is, billing for services that procure a higher reimbursement than the services actually provided, and which should have been billed at a lower rate of reimbursement, is also a felony. For example, manipulating the MDS to increase the case mix would be considered upcoding.

(B) It is a felony to induce referrals of Medicare or Medicaid patients by offering or receiving any kind of remuneration, kickback, or bribe, regardless of whether they are in cash or kind. Same penalties as in (A) apply. This category would include gifts to physicians or other referral agents. Anti-kickback provisions may also apply to situations in which the nursing home refers services to external providers, such as pharmacies, laboratories, and medical equipment suppliers, in exchange for services received. For example, a nursing facility may ask a clinical laboratory for free services such as chart review or infection control. These are services that nursing homes are required to provide, and they are included in the reimbursements nursing homes receive from Medicare and Medicaid. The clinical laboratory is in a position to financially benefit from referral of clinical tests and other laboratory work from the facility. Under these circumstances, free services to the nursing home may be construed as inducement for referrals to the laboratory. Either offering or receiving any kind of remuneration to induce referrals violates the anti-kickback statute.

(C) Under HIPAA, any felony conviction for fraud, theft, embezzlement, or other financial misconduct by a health care provider must also result in the provider's exclusion from Medicare and Medicaid programs.

False Claims Act

The Civil False Claims Act (FCA) was originally enacted in 1863 during the Civil War as a measure against fraud by companies furnishing supplies

to the Union Army. The law was amended in 1986, under the Reagan presidency, to curtail widespread reports of fraud in the defense industry. In the health care industry, the law relates primarily to the making of false or fraudulent claims for payment from public payers such as Medicare and Medicaid. For example, it makes it illegal to provide and bill for services that are medically unnecessary, to provide and bill for services that are not covered under a federal program, or to try to claim payment for unbundled services by submitting separate bills when in fact the services should be bundled. Damages under the False Claims Act are severe. For all claims made after September 29, 1999, an entity that violates the act must repay three times the amount of damages suffered by the government plus a mandatory civil penalty of at least $5,500 and no more than $11,000 per claim.

Apart from penalizing facilities for filing fraudulent claims, the FCA has also been used to punish facilities who fail to provide adequate care. For example, in 1996, the U.S. Attorney's Office for the Eastern District of Pennsylvania filed a civil complaint against the owner and former administrator of a nursing facility in Philadelphia. The government contended that the defendants had violated the FCA when they submitted claims for payment, despite the fact that the residents did not receive adequate care, because three residents in the facility had suffered from malnutrition and inadequate wound care. The case was settled for a $600,000 fine and consent by the facility to implement quality-of-care standards. Failure to hire adequate staff to provide sufficient care may be regarded as deliberate intent to render substandard services and can fall under the provisions of the FCA.

An important feature of the FCA that has been widely credited for its success is the *qui tam* (informer or whistleblower) provision. Any individual who has knowledge that a person or an entity is submitting false claims or otherwise defrauding the federal government can bring a lawsuit on behalf of the government and can share in the damages recovered as a result of the lawsuit. The person who brings the case is referred to as a ***qui tam relator*** or whistleblower, who is often an employee or a former employee of a company. But a competitor, a subcontractor, a patient or a family member can also be a relator. The whistleblower does not need to have personal knowledge of the fraud to file a False Claims Act case. The lawsuit can be based on information the relator learned from a friend, a relative, a competitor, etc. As long as the information is not publicly disclosed and the government has not already sued the individual or company for the fraud, the relator may bring a *qui tam* lawsuit. Depending on

various factors, the relators are entitled to between 15 and 30% of whatever amount the government recovers as a result of their *qui tam* lawsuits (Phillips and Cohen 2003).

CONCLUSION

Financing will always be a key issue in nursing home management. Growth of private long-term care insurance plans will be necessary to sustain adequate financing levels for the growing elderly population. When the baby boomers start retiring around 2011, increased dependency on public funds for long-term care services could become unsustainable in the long run particularly as a shrinking American workforce is overburdened with higher taxes. Hence, the future of reimbursement from public sources does not appear too bright. However, savvy administrators are finding ways to collaborate with managed care organizations and health systems in mutually rewarding relationships. To serve future needs of the elderly, nursing home administrators also need to understand risk adjustment; MDS is a valuable tool for this purpose.

A number of high-profile prosecutions in recent years show the need for deterrence against fraud and abuse. Nursing home corporations and administrators must understand the criminal and civil aspects of fraud and abuse laws.

DISCUSSION AND APPLICATION QUESTIONS

1. Suppose you have just been appointed the administrator of a chain-affiliated 110-bed facility in which all the beds are dually certified. Your superior who is a corporate official comments on the low percentage of private-pay patients in the facility even though the overall occupancy rate has been 98%. In your discussions, the supervisor suggests that whenever a bed is vacant you should wait for a private-pay patient to occupy it, and that you can advise Medicaid and Medicare clients that no beds are available. How will you address this issue with your superior?

2. Mabel Brown resides in an assisted-living facility and is admitted to a hospital following a stroke. After a hospital stay of 8 days, Ms.

Brown returned to her apartment at the assisted living center, but she needs assistance with personal care and some speech therapy. Will Medicare pay for the personal care services and speech therapy? Explain.

3. Using the ADL score worksheet (Appendix 4-II), calculate the ADL scores for transfer and toilet use in Step #1 for the patient identified as 007163 in Appendix 4-I. Continue with Steps 2 and 3 and calculate this patient's total RUG-III ADL score.

4. Can the patient identified as 007163 be classified into any one of the 14 RUG-III codes for Rehabilitation?

5. As an administrator of a nursing facility, what actions can you take to protect your organization against fraud and abuse?

INTERNET RESOURCES FOR FURTHER LEARNING

AARP (American Association of Retired Persons): The nation's foremost consumer-oriented agency that concerns itself with numerous issues related to aging and long-term care.
www.aarp.org

MDS 2.0 Manuals and Forms
http://www.cms.hhs.gov/quality/mds20/
Note: Other sections of Appendix 4-III can be obtained by clicking on "Chapter 6" under "RAI User's Manual by Chapter."

MDS version 3.0 (draft version formulated April 2, 2003).
http://www.cms.hhs.gov/quality/mds30/DraftMDS30.pdf

Medicaid: A jointly-funded federal-state health insurance program for the indigent.
http://cms.hhs.gov/medicaid

Medicare: A federal program of health insurance for the elderly and some disabled persons.
http://cms.hhs.gov/medicare

Medicare Skilled Nursing Facility Manual.
http://www.cms.hhs.gov/manuals/12_snf/sn400.asp

REFERENCES

Aventis Pharmaceuticals. 2003. *Managed Care Digest Series: HMO-PPO/ Medicare-Medicaid Digest.* Bridgewater, NJ: Aventis Pharmaceuticals, Inc.

Baker, J.J. 2000. *Prospective Payment for Long-Term Care: 2000–2001.* Gaithersburg, MD: Aspen Publishers, Inc.

Beck, D.C. 1996. Partnerships may tame subacute rivalry. *Contemporary Longterm Care* 19, no. 7: 72.

Centers for Medicare and Medicaid Services. 2002. Program information. www.cms.hhs.gov/charts/series/sec3-D.ppt

Coronel, S.A. *Long-Term Care Insurance in 1997–1998.* Washington, DC: Health Insurance Association of America.

Department of Health and Human Services. 2003. *Health, United States, 2003.* Hyattsville, MD: National Center for Health Statistics.

Edwards, D.J. 2003. AAHSA seeks to link quality and payment. *Nursing Homes Long Term Care Management* 52, no. 9: 8.

Health Insurance Association of America. 2003. *Long-Term Care Insurance in 2000–2001: Executive Summary Research Findings.* Washington, DC: Health Insurance Association of America.

Kohn, C., et al. 2003. Network brings skilled nursing facilities together. *Managed Care Weekly Digest* (June 9): 22–23.

Merlis, M. 2003. *Private Long-Term Care Insurance: Who Should Buy it and What Should They Buy?* Unpublished manuscript.

Phillips and Cohen: Attorneys at Law. 2003. The False Claims Act: How It Works. http://www.whistleblowers.com/HTML/FRM/howks_f.htm

APPENDIX
4–I

MINIMUM DATA SET (MDS)—VERSION 2.0
FOR NURSING HOME RESIDENT ASSESSMENT AND CARE SCREENING
FULL ASSESSMENT FORM
(Status in last 7 days, unless other time frame indicated)

SECTION A. IDENTIFICATION AND BACKGROUND INFORMATION

1. RESIDENT NAME

a. (First)	b. (Middle Initial)	c. (Last)	d. (Jr./Sr.)

2. ROOM NUMBER

2	2	3	-	1

3. ASSESSMENT REFERENCE DATE

a. Last day of MDS observation

0	9	–	1	3	–	2	0	0	3
Month			Day			Year			

b. Original (0) or corrected copy of form (enter number of correction) [ ]

4a. DATE OF REENTRY — Date of reentry from most recent temporary discharge to a hospital in last 90 days (or since last assessment if less than 90 days)

		–			–				
Month			Day			Year			

5. MARITAL STATUS
1. Never married 2. Married 3. Widowed 4. Separated 5. Divorced → **2**

6. MEDICAL RECORD NO.

0	0	7	1	6	3				

7. CURRENT PAYMENT SOURCES FOR N.H. STAY
(Billing Office to indicate; check all that apply in last 30 days)

a. Medicaid per diem		f. VA per diem	
b. Medicare per diem **X**		g. Self or family pays for full per diem	
c. Medicare ancillary part A **X**		h. Medicaid resident liability or Medicare co-payment	
d. Medicare ancillary part B		i. Private insurance per diem (including co-payment)	
e. CHAMPUS per diem		j. Other per diem	

---

3. MEMORY/RECALL ABILITY
(Check all that resident was normally able to recall during last 7 days)

a. Current season	
b. Location of own room	
c. Staff names/faces	
d. That he/she is in a nursing home	
e. NONE OF THE ABOVE are recalled	**X**

4. COGNITIVE SKILLS FOR DAILY DECISION-MAKING — (Made decisions regarding tasks of daily life)
0. INDEPENDENT—decisions consistent/reasonable
1. MODIFIED INDEPENDENCE—some difficulty in new situations only
2. MODERATELY IMPAIRED—decisions poor; cues/supervision required
3. SEVERELY IMPAIRED—never/rarely made decisions → **2**

5. INDICATORS OF DELIRIUM—PERIODIC DISORDERED THINKING/AWARENESS — (Code for behavior in the last 7 days.) [Note: Accurate assessment requires conversation with staff and family who have direct knowledge of resident's behavior over this time.]
0. Behavior not present
1. Behavior present, not of recent onset
2. Behavior present, over last 7 days appears different from resident's usual functioning (e.g., new onset or worsening)

a. EASILY DISTRACTED—(e.g., difficulty paying attention; gets side-tracked)	**1**
b. PERIODS OF ALTERED PERCEPTION OR AWARENESS OF SURROUNDINGS—(e.g., moves lips or talks to someone not present; believes he/she is somewhere else; confuses night and day)	**1**
c. EPISODES OF DISORGANIZED SPEECH—(e.g., speech is incoherent, nonsensical, irrelevant, or rambling from subject to subject; loses train of thought)	**1**
d. PERIODS OF RESTLESSNESS—(e.g., fidgeting or picking at skin, clothing, napkins, etc.; frequent position changes; repetitive physical movements or calling out)	**0**
e. PERIODS OF LETHARGY—(e.g., sluggishness; staring into space; difficult to arouse; little body movement)	**2**
f. MENTAL FUNCTION VARIES OVER THE COURSE OF THE DAY—(e.g., sometimes better, sometimes worse; behaviors sometimes present, sometimes not)	**1**

6. CHANGE IN COGNITIVE STATUS — Resident's cognitive status, skills, or abilities have changed and compared to status of 90 days ago (or since last assessment if less than 90 days)
0. No change 1. Improved 2. Deteriorated → **0**

1. HEARING — (With hearing appliance, if used)

8.	REASONS FOR ASSESSMENT [Note—If this is a discharge or reentry assessment, only a limited subset of MDS items need be completed]	a. Primary reason for assessment		0	1
		1. Admission assessment (required by day 14)			
		2. Annual assessment			
		3. Significant change in status assessment			
		4. Significant correction of prior full assessment			
		5. Quarterly review assessment			
		6. Discharged—return not anticipated			
		7. Discharged—return anticipated			
		8. Discharged prior to completing initial assessment			
		9. Reentry			
		10. Significant correction of prior quarterly assessment			
		0. NONE OF ABOVE			
		b. Codes for assessments required for **Medicare PPS or the State**			1
		1. Medicare 5 day assessment			
		2. Medicare 30 day assessment			
		3. Medicare 60 day assessment			
		4. Medicare 90 day assessment			
		5. Medicare readmission/return assessment			
		6. Other state required assessment			
		7. Medicare 14 day assessment			
		8. Other Medicare required assessment			

9.	RESPONSI-BILITY/ LEGAL GUARDIAN	(Check all that apply)	
		a. Legal guardian	Durable power of attorney/ financial d.
		b. Other legal oversight	Family member responsible e. X
		c. X Durable power of attorney/health care	Patient responsible for self f.
			NONE OF THE ABOVE g.

10.	ADVANCED DIRECTIVES	(For those items with supporting documentation in the medical record, check all that apply)	
		a. Living will	Feeding restrictions f.
		b. X Do not resuscitate	Medication restrictions g.
		c. Do not hospitalize	Other treatment restrictions h.
		d. Organ donation	NONE OF THE ABOVE i.
		e. Autopsy request	

SECTION B. COGNITIVE PATTERNS

1.	COMATOSE	(Persistent vegetative state/no discernible consciousness)	0
		0. No 1. Yes (If yes, skip to Section G)	

2.	MEMORY	(Recall of what was learned or known)	
		a. Short-term memory OK—seems/appears to recall after 5 minutes	1
		0. Memory OK 1. Memory problem	
		b. Long-term memory OK—seems/appears to recall long past	1
		0. Memory OK 1. Memory problem	

SECTION C. COMMUNICATION/HEARING PATTERNS

1.	HEARING		0
		0. HEARS ADEQUATELY—normal talk, TV, phone	
		1. MINIMAL DIFFICULTY when not in quiet setting	
		2. HEARS IN SPECIAL SITUATIONS ONLY—speaker has to adjust tonal quality and speak distinctly	
		3. HIGHLY IMPAIRED/absence of useful hearing	

2.	COMMUNI-CATION DEVICES/ TECH-NIQUES	(Check all that apply during last 7 days)	
		a. Hearing aid, present and used	
		b. Hearing aid, present and not used regularly	
		c. Other receptive comm. techniques used (e.g., lip reading)	
		d. X NONE OF THE ABOVE	

3.	MODES OF EXPRESSION	(Check all used by resident to make needs known)	
		a. X Speech	American sign language or Braille c.
		b. Writing messages to express or clarify needs	Signs/gestures/sounds d.
			Communication board e.
			Other f.
			NONE OF THE ABOVE g.

4.	MAKING SELF UNDER-STOOD	(Expressing information content—however able)	2
		0. UNDERSTOOD	
		1. USUALLY UNDERSTOOD—difficulty finding words or finishing thoughts	
		2. SOMETIMES UNDERSTOOD—ability is limited to making concrete requests	
		3. RARELY/NEVER UNDERSTOOD	

5.	SPEECH CLARITY	(Code for speech in the last 7 days)	1
		0. CLEAR SPEECH—distinct, intelligible words	
		1. UNCLEAR SPEECH—slurred, mumbled words	
		2. NO SPEECH—absence of spoken words	

6.	ABILITY TO UNDER-STAND OTHERS	(Understanding verbal information content—however able)	2
		0. UNDERSTANDS	
		1. USUALLY UNDERSTANDS—may miss some part/intent of message	
		2. SOMETIMES UNDERSTANDS—responds adequately to simple, direct communication	
		3. RARELY/NEVER UNDERSTANDS	

7.	CHANGE IN COMMUNI-CATION/ HEARING	Resident's ability to express, understand, or hear information has changed as compared to status of **90 days ago** (or since last assessment if less than 90 days)	0
		0. No change 1. Improved 2. Deteriorated	

= When box blank, must enter number or letter   a. = When letter in box, check if condition applies

█ = When box blank, check if condition applies

SECTION D. VISION PATTERNS

2.	**VISION**	*(Ability to see in adequate light and with glasses if used)* **0. ADEQUATE**—sees fine detail, including regular print in newspapers/books **1. IMPAIRED**—sees large print, but not regular print in newspapers/books **2. MODERATELY IMPAIRED**—limited vision; not able to see newspaper headlines, but can identify objects **3. HIGHLY IMPAIRED**—object identification in question, but eyes appear to follow objects **4. SEVERELY IMPAIRED**—no vision or sees only light, colors, or shapes; eyes do not appear to follow objects	**0**
2.	**VISUAL LIMITATIONS/ DIFFICULTIES**	Side vision problems—decreased peripheral vision (e.g., leaves food on one side of tray, difficulty traveling, bumps into people and objects, misjudges placement of chair when seating self) Experiences any of following: sees halos or rings around lights; sees flashes of light; sees "curtains" over eyes NONE OF THE ABOVE	a. ☐ b. ☐ c. **X**
3.	**VISUAL APPLIANCES**	Glasses; contact lenses; magnifying glasses **0.** No. **1.** Yes	**1**

SECTION E. MOOD AND BEHAVIOR PATTERNS

1.	**INDICATORS OF DEPRESSION, ANXIETY, SAD MOOD**	*(Code for indicators observed in last 30 days, irrespective of the assumed cause)* **0.** Indicator not exhibited in last 30 days **1.** Indicator of this type exhibited up to five days a week **2.** Indicator of this type exhibited daily or almost daily (6, 7 days a week)	

VERBAL EXPRESSIONS OF DISTRESS

a.	Resident made negative statements—e.g., *"Nothing matters; Would rather be dead; What's the use; Regrets having lived so long; Let me die"*	**0**
b.	Repetitive questions— e.g., *"Where do I go; What do I do?"*	**0**
c.	Repetitive verbalizations— e.g., calling out for help (*"God help me"*)	**0**
h.	Repetitive health complaints—e.g., persistently seeks medical attention, obsessive concern with body functions	**0**
i.	Repetitive anxious complaints/concerns (non-health related) e.g., persistently seeks attention/ reassurance regarding schedules, meals, laundry/clothing, relationship issues	**0**

SLEEP-CYCLE ISSUES

j.	Unpleasant mood in morning	**0**

SECTION F. PSYCHOSOCIAL WELL-BEING

1.	**SENSE OF INITIATIVE/ INVOLVE-MENT**	At ease interacting with others At ease doing planned or structured activities At ease doing self-initiated activities Establishes own goals Pursues involvement in life of facility (e.g., makes/keeps friends; involved in group activities; responds positively to new activities; assists at religious services) Accepts invitations into most group activities NONE OF THE ABOVE	a. **X** b. **X** c. ☐ d. ☐ e. ☐ f. ☐ g. ☐
2.	**UNSETTLED RELATION-SHIPS**	Covert/open conflict with or repeated criticism of staff Unhappy with roommate Unhappy with residents other than roommate Openly expresses conflict/anger with family/friends Absence of personal contact with family/friends Recent loss of close family member/friend Does not adjust easily to change in routines NONE OF THE ABOVE	a. ☐ b. ☐ c. ☐ d. ☐ e. ☐ f. ☐ g. **X** h. **X**
3.	**PAST ROLES**	Strong identification with past roles and life status Expresses sadness/anger/empty feeling over lost roles/status Resident perceives that daily routine (customary routine, activities) is very different from prior pattern in the community NONE OF THE ABOVE	a. ☐ b. ☐ c. **X** d. ☐

SECTION G. PHYSICAL FUNCTIONING AND STRUCTURAL PROBLEMS

1.	**(A) ADL SELF-PERFORMANCE**—*(Code for resident's PERFORMANCE OVER ALL SHIFTS during last 7 days—Not including setup)* **0. INDEPENDENT**—No help or oversight—OR—Help/oversight provided only 1 or 2 times during last 7 days **1. SUPERVISION**—Oversight, encouragement or cueing provided 3 or more times during last 7 days—OR—Supervision (3 or more times) plus physical assistance provided only 1 or 2 times during last 7 days **2. LIMITED ASSISTANCE**—Resident highly involved in activity; received physical help in guided maneuvering of limbs or other nonweight bearing assistance 3 or more times—OR—More help provided only 1 or 2 times during last 7 days **3. EXTENSIVE ASSISTANCE**—While resident performed part of activity, over last 7-day period, help of following type(s) provided 3 or more times: —Weight-bearing support —Full staff performance during part (but not all) of last 7 days **4. TOTAL DEPENDENCE**—Full staff performance of activity during entire 7 days **8. ACTIVITY DID NOT OCCUR during entire 7 days**	

(B) ADL SUPPORT PROVIDED—(Code for MOST SUPPORT PROVIDED OVER ALL SHIFTS during last 7 days; code regardless of resident's self-performance classification)		(A) SELF	(B) SUPT
0. No setup or physical help from staff 1. Setup help only 2. One person physical assist	3. Two+ persons physical assist 8. ADL activity itself did not occur during entire 7 days		
a. BED MOBILITY	How resident moves to and from lying position, turns side to side, and positions body while in bed	3	2
b. TRANSFER	How resident moves between surfaces—to/from: bed, chair, wheelchair, standing position (EXCLUDE to/from bath/toilet)	3	3
c. WALK IN ROOM	How resident walks between locations in his/her room	8	8
d. WALK IN CORRIDOR	How resident walks in corridor on unit	8	8
e. LOCOMOTION ON UNIT	How resident moves between locations in his/her room and adjacent corridor on same floor. If in wheelchair, self-sufficiency once in chair	4	2
f. LOCOMOTION OFF UNIT	How resident moves to and returns from off unit locations (e.g., areas set aside for dining, activities, or treatments). If facility has only one floor, how resident moves to and from distant areas on the floor. If in wheelchair, self-sufficiency once in chair	4	2
g. DRESSING	How resident puts on, fastens, and takes off all items of street clothing, including donning/removing prosthesis	3	2
h. EATING	How resident eats and drinks (regardless of skill). Includes intake of nourishment by other means (e.g., tube feeding, total parenteral nutrition)	3	2
i. TOILET USE	How resident uses the toilet room (or commode, bedpan, urinal); transfers on/off toilet, cleanses, changes pad, manages ostomy or catheter, adjusts clothes	4	2
j. PERSONAL HYGIENE	How resident maintains personal hygiene, including combing hair, brushing teeth, shaving, applying makeup, washing/drying face, hands, and perineum (EXCLUDE baths and showers)	3	2

---

	d. Persistent anger with self or others—e.g., easily annoyed, angered at placement in nursing home; anger at care received	0	k. Insomnia/change in usual sleep pattern	0
	SAD, APATHETIC, ANXIOUS APPEARANCE l. Sad, pained, worried facial expressions—e.g., furrowed brows m. Crying, tearfulness	0		
	e. Self deprecation—e.g., "I am nothing; I am of no use to anyone"	0	n. Repetitive physical movements—e.g., pacing, hand wringing, restlessness, fidgeting, picking	0
	f. Expressions of what appears to be unrealistic fears—e.g., fear of being abandoned, left alone, being with others	0	LOSS OF INTEREST o. Withdrawal from activities of interest—e.g., no interest in long standing activities or being with family/friends	0
	g. Recurrent statements that something terrible is about to happen—e.g., believes he or she is about to die, have a heart attack	0	p. Reduced social interaction	0
2. MOOD PERSISTENCE	One or more indicators of depressed, sad or anxious mood were not easily altered by attempts to "cheer up", console, or reassure the resident over last 7 days 0. No mood 1. Indicators present, indicators easily altered		2. Indicators present, not easily altered	0
3. CHANGE IN MOOD	Resident's mood status has changed as compared to status of 90 days ago (or since last assessment if less than 90 days) 0. No change 1. Improved 2. Deteriorated			0
4. BEHAVIORAL SYMPTOMS	(A) Behavioral symptom frequency in last 7 days 0. Behavior not exhibited in last 7 days 1. Behavior of this type occurred 1 to 3 days in last 7 days 2. Behavior of this type occurred 4 to 6 days, but less than daily 3. Behavior of this type occurred daily (B) Behavioral symptom alterability in last 7 days 0. Behavior not present OR behavior was easily altered 1. Behavior was not easily altered			

		(A)	(B)
a. WANDERING (moved with no rational purpose, seemingly oblivious to needs or safety)		0	0
b. VERBALLY ABUSIVE BEHAVIORAL SYMPTOMS (others were threatened, screamed at, or cursed at)		0	0
c. PHYSICALLY ABUSIVE BEHAVIORAL SYMPTOMS (others were hit, shoved, scratched, sexually abused)		0	0
d. SOCIALLY INAPPROPRIATE/DISRUPTIVE BEHAVIORAL SYMPTOMS (made disruptive sounds, noisiness, screaming, self-abusive acts, sexual behavior or disrobing in public, smeared/threw food/feces, hoarding, rummaged through others' belongings)		0	0
e. RESISTS CARE (resisted taking medications/injections, ADL assistance, or eating)		0	0

5. CHANGE IN BEHAVIORAL SYMPTOMS	Resident's behavior status has changed as compared to status of 90 days ago (or since last assessment if less than 90 days) 0. No change 1. Improved 2. Deteriorated	0

Resident ______________________ Numeric Identifier **007163**

2.	**BATHING**	How resident takes full-body bath/shower, sponge bath, and transfers in/out of tub/shower (EXCLUDE washing of back and hair). ***Code for most dependent in self-performance and support.*** **(A)** BATHING SELF-PERFORMANCE codes appear below. **0.** Independent—No help provided **1.** Supervision—Oversight help only **2.** Physical help limited to transfer only **3.** Physical help in part of bathing activity **4.** Total dependence **8.** Activity itself did not occur during entire 7 days ***(Bathing support codes are as defined in Item 1, code B above)***	**(A)** 3 **(B)** 2
3.	**TEST FOR BALANCE (See training manual)**	(*Code for ability during test in the **last 7 days***) **0.** Maintained position as required in test **1.** Unsteady, but able to rebalance self without physical support **2.** Partial physical support during test; or stands (sits) but does not follow directions for test **3.** Not able to attempt test without physical help	
		a. Balance while standing	3
		b. Balance while sitting—position, trunk control	1
4.	**FUNCTIONAL LIMITATION IN RANGE OF MOTION (See training manual)**	(*Code for limitations during **last 7 days** that interfered with daily functions or placed resident at risk of injury*) **(A)** *RANGE OF MOTION*: **0.** No limitation; **1.** Limitation on one side; **2.** Limitation on both sides **(B)** *VOLUNTARY MOVEMENT*: **0.** No loss; **1.** Partial loss; **2.** Full loss	**(A)** / **(B)**
		a. Neck	0 / 0
		b. Arm—including shoulder or elbow	0 / 0
		c. Hand—including wrist or fingers	2 / 1
		d. Leg—including hip or knee	2 / 1
		e. Foot—including ankle or toes	0 / 0
		f. Other limitation or loss	0 / 0
5.	**MODES OF LOCOMOTION**	***(Check all that apply during last 7 days)*** Cane/walker/crutch — a. Wheeled self — b. Other person wheeled — c. X Wheelchair primary mode of locomotion — d. X *NONE OF ABOVE* — e.	
6.	**MODES OF TRANSFER**	***(Check all that apply during last 7 days)*** Bedfast all or most of time — a. Bed rails used for bed mobility or transfer — b. X Lifted manually — c. Lifted mechanically — d. Transfer aid (e.g., slide board, trapeze, cane, walker, brace) — e. *NONE OF ABOVE* — f.	
7.	**TASK SEGMENTATION**	Some or all of ADL activities were broken into subtasks during last 7 days so that resident could perform them **0.** No **1.** Yes	0

4.	**CHANGE IN URINARY CONTINENCE**	Resident's urinary continence has changed as compared to status of **90 days ago** (or since last assessment if less than 90 days) **0.** No change **1.** Improved **2.** Deteriorated	0

SECTION I. DISEASE DIAGNOSES

Check only those diseases that have a relationship to current ADL status, cognitive status, mood and behavior status, medical treatments, nursing monitoring, or risk of death. (Do not list inactive diagnoses)

1. DISEASES (*If none apply, **CHECK the NONE OF ABOVE** box*)

ENDOCRINE/METABOLIC/NUTRITIONAL		Hemiplegia/Hemiparesis	v.
Diabetes mellitus	a.	Multiple sclerosis	w.
Hyperthyroidism	b.	Paraplegia	x.
Hypothyroidism	c.	Parkinson's disease	y. X
HEART/CIRCULATION		Quadriplegia	z.
Arteriosclerotic heart disease (ASHD)	d.	Seizure disorder	aa.
Cardiac dysrhythmias	e.	Transient ischemic attack (TIA)	bb.
Congestive heart failure	f.	Traumatic brain injury	cc.
Deep vein thrombosis	g.	**PSYCHIATRIC/MOOD**	
Hypertension	h. X	Anxiety disorder	dd.
Hypotension	i.	Depression	ee.
Peripheral vascular disease	j.	Manic depression (bipolar disease)	ff.
Other cardiovascular disease	k.	Schizophrenia	gg.
MUSCULOSKELETAL		**PULMONARY**	
Arthritis	l. X	Asthma	hh.
Hip fracture	m.	Emphysema/COPD	ii.
Missing limb (e.g., amputation)	n.	**SENSORY**	
Osteoporosis	o.	Cataracts	jj.
Pathological bone fracture	p.	Diabetic retinopathy	kk.
NEUROLOGICAL		Glaucoma	ll.
Alzheimer's disease	q.	Macular degeneration	mm.
Aphasia	r. X	**OTHER**	
Cerebral palsy	s.	Allergies	nn.
Cerebrovascular accident (stroke)	t.	Anemia	oo.
Dementia other than Alzheimer's disease	u. X	Cancer	pp. X
		Renal failure	qq.
		NONE OF ABOVE	rr.

2.	INFECTIONS	(If none apply, CHECK the NONE OF ABOVE box)		
		Antibiotic resistant infection (e.g. Methicillin resistant staph)	a.	
		Clostridium difficile (c. diff.)	b.	
		Conjunctivitis	c.	
		HIV Infection	d.	
		Pneumonia	e.	
		Respiratory infection	f.	
		Septicemia	g.	
		Sexually transmitted diseases	h.	
		Tuberculosis	i.	
		Urinary tract infection in last 30 days	j.	
		Viral hepatitis	k.	
		Wound infection	l.	
		NONE OF ABOVE	m.	X

3.	OTHER CURRENT OR MORE DETAILED DIAGNOSES AND ICD-9 CODES		
	a.	PARALYSIS AGITANS	3 3 2 . 0
	b.	ARTERIOSCLER DEMEN	2 9 0 . 4 0
	c.	BONE & CARTILAGE DIS	7 3 3 . 9 0
	d.	HYPERLIPIDEMIA NEC/	2 7 2 . 4
	e.	SECOND MALIG NEO BR	1 9 8 . 8 1

SECTION J. HEALTH CONDITIONS

1.	PROBLEM CONDITIONS	(Check all problems present in last 7 days unless other time frame is indicated)		
	INDICATORS OF FLUID STATUS	Weight gain or loss of 3 or more pounds within a 7 day period	a.	
		Inability to lie flat due to shortness of breath	b.	
		Dehydrated; output exceeds input	c.	
		Insufficient fluid; did NOT consume all/almost all liquids provided during last 3 days	d.	
		OTHER		
		Delusions	e.	
		Dizziness/Vertigo	f.	
		Edema	g.	
		Fever	h.	
		Hallucinations	i.	
		Internal bleeding	j.	
		Recurrent lung aspirations in last 90 days	k.	
		Shortness of breath	l.	
		Syncope (fainting)	m.	
		Unsteady gait	n.	
		Vomiting	o.	
		NONE OF ABOVE	p.	X

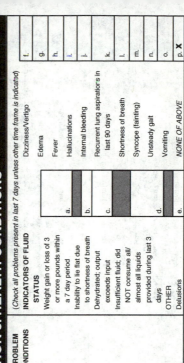

8.	ADL FUNCTIONAL REHABILITATION POTENTIAL	Resident believes he/she is capable of increased independence in at least some ADLs	a.	X
		Direct Care staff believe resident is capable of increased independence in at least some ADLs	b.	X
		Resident able to perform tasks/activity but is very slow	c.	
		Difference in ADL Self-Performance or ADL Support, comparing mornings to evenings	d.	
		NONE OF ABOVE	e.	

9.	CHANGE IN ADL FUNCTION	Resident's ADL self-performance status has changed as compared to status of 90 days ago (or since last assessment if less than 90 days)		
		0. No change 1. Improved 2. Deteriorated	2

SECTION H. CONTINENCE IN LAST 14 DAYS

1.	CONTINENCE SELF-CONTROL CATEGORIES

(Code for resident's PERFORMANCE OVER ALL SHIFTS)

0. CONTINENT—Complete control (includes use of indwelling urinary catheter or ostomy device that does not leak urine or stool)
1. USUALLY CONTINENT—BLADDER, incontinent episodes once a week or less; BOWEL, less than weekly
2. OCCASIONALLY INCONTINENT—BLADDER, 2 or more times a week but not daily; BOWEL, once a week
3. FREQUENTLY INCONTINENT—BLADDER, tended to be incontinent daily, but some control present (e.g., on day shift); BOWEL, 2-3 times a week
4. INCONTINENT—Had inadequate control. BLADDER, multiple daily episodes; BOWEL, all (or almost all) of the time

a.	BOWEL CONTINENCE	Control of bowel movement, with appliance or bowel continence programs, if employed	4
b.	BLADDER CONTINENCE	Control of urinary bladder function (if dribbles, volume insufficient to soak through underpants), with appliances (e.g., foley) or continence programs, if employed	4

2.	BOWEL ELIMINATION PATTERN	Bowel elimination pattern regular—at least one movement every three days	a.	
		Constipation	b.	
		Diarrhea	c.	
		Fecal impaction	d.	
		NONE OF ABOVE	e.	X

3.	APPLIANCES AND PROGRAMS	Any scheduled toileting plan	a.	
		Bladder retraining program	b.	
		External (condom) catheter	c.	
		Indwelling catheter	d.	
		Intermittent catheter	e.	
		Did not use toilet room/commode/urinal	f.	
		Pads/briefs used	g.	X
		Enemas/irrigation	h.	
		Ostomy present	i.	
		NONE OF ABOVE	j.	

SECTION M. SKIN CONDITION

			Number at Stage
1.	ULCERS (Due to any cause)	(Record the number of ulcers at each stage—regardless of cause. If none present at a stage, record "0" (zero). Code all that apply during last 7 days. Code 9 = 9 or more.) (Requires full body exam.)	
		a. **Stage 1.** A persistent area of skin redness (without a break in the skin) that does not disappear when pressure is relieved.	0
		b. **Stage 2.** A partial thickness of skin layers that presents clinically as an abrasion, blister, or shallow crater.	0
		c. **Stage 3.** A full thickness of skin is lost, exposing the subcutaneous tissues—presents as a deep crater with or without undermining adjacent tissue.	0
		d. **Stage 4.** A full thickness of skin and subcutaneous tissue is lost, exposing muscle or bone.	0
2.	TYPE OF ULCER	(For each type of ulcer, code for the highest stage in the last 7 days using scale in item M1—i.e., 0 = none; stages 1, 2, 3, 4)	
		a. Pressure ulcer—any lesion caused by pressure resulting in damage of underlying tissue	0
		b. Stasis ulcer—open lesion caused by poor circulation in the lower extremities	0
3.	HISTORY OF RESOLVED ULCERS	Resident had an ulcer that was resolved or cured in **LAST 90 DAYS** 0. No 1. Yes	0
4.	OTHER SKIN PROBLEMS OR LESIONS PRESENT	(Check all that apply last 7 days)	
		Abrasions, bruises	a.
		Burns (second or third degree)	b.
		Open lesions other than ulcers, rashes, cuts (e.g., cancer lesions)	c.
		Rashes—e.g., intertrigo, eczema, drug rash, heat rash, herpes zoster	d.
		Skin desensitized to pain or pressure	e.
		Skin tears or cuts (other than surgery)	f.
		Surgical wounds	g.
		NONE OF THE ABOVE	h. X
5.	SKIN TREAT-MENTS	(Check all that apply during last 7 days)	
		Pressure relieving device(s) for chair	a.
		Pressure relieving device(s) for bed	b. X
		Turning/repositioning program	c. X
		Nutrition or hydration intervention to manage skin problems	d.
		Ulcer care	e.
		Surgical wound care	f.

2.	PAIN SYMPTOMS	(Code the highest level of pain present in the last 7 days)	
		a. FREQUENCY with which resident complains or shows evidence of pain — **0**	b. INTENSITY of pain
		0. No pain (skip to J4)	1. Mild pain
		1. Pain less than daily	2. Moderate pain
		2. Pain daily	3. Times when pain is horrible or excruciating
3.	PAIN SITE	(If pain present, check all sites that apply in last 7 days)	
		Back pain — a.	Incisional pain — f.
		Bone pain — b.	Joint pain (other than hip) — g.
		Chest pain while doing usual activities — c.	Soft tissue pain (e.g., lesion, muscle) — h.
		Headache — d.	Stomach pain — i.
		Hip pain — e.	Other — j.
4.	ACCIDENTS	(Check all that apply)	
		Fell in past 30 days — a. X	Hip fracture in last 180 days — c.
		Fell in past 31–180 days — b.	Other fracture in last 180 days — d.
			NONE OF THE ABOVE — e.
5.	STABILITY OF CONDITIONS	Conditions/diseases make resident's cognitive, ADL, mood or behavior patterns unstable—(fluctuating, precarious, or deteriorating) — a. X	
		Resident experiencing an acute episode or flare-up of a recurrent or chronic problem — b.	
		End-stage disease, 6 or fewer months to live — c.	
		NONE OF THE ABOVE — d.	

SECTION K. ORAL/NUTRITIONAL STATUS

1.	ORAL PROBLEMS	Chewing problem	a.
		Swallowing problem	b. X
		Mouth pain	c.
		NONE OF THE ABOVE	d.
2.	HEIGHT AND WEIGHT	Record (a.) height in inches and (b.) weight in pounds. Base weight on most recent measure in last 30 days; measure weight consistently in accord with standard facility practice—e.g., in a.m. after voiding, before meal, with shoes off, and in nightclothes.	a. HT (in.) 6 6 b. WT (lb.) 1 3 7
3.	WEIGHT CHANGE	a. Weight loss—5% or more in last 30 days; or 10% or more in last 180 days 0. No 1. Yes	0
		b. Weight gain—5% or more in last 30 days; or 10% or more in last 180 days 0. No 1. Yes	0

Application of dressings (with or without topical medications) other than to feet			g.
Application of ointments/medications (other than to feet)			h.
Other preventative or protective skin care (other than to feet)			i. X
NONE OF THE ABOVE			j.

6.	FOOT PROBLEMS AND CARE	(Check all that apply during last 7 days)	
		Resident has one or more foot problems—e.g., corns, calluses, bunions, hammer toes, overlapping toes, pain, structural problems	a.
		Infection of the foot—e.g., cellulitis, purulent drainage	b.
		Open lesions on the foot	c.
		Nails/calluses trimmed during last 90 days	d.
		Received preventative or protective foot care (e.g., used special shoes, inserts, pads, toe separators)	e.
		Application of dressings (with or without topics medications)	f.
		NONE OF THE ABOVE	g. X

SECTION N. ACTIVITY PURSUIT PATTERNS

1.	TIME AWAKE	(Check appropriate time periods over last 7 days) Resident awake all or most of time (i.e., naps no more than one hour per time period) in the:	
		Morning	a.
		Afternoon	b. X
		Evening	c.
		NONE OF THE ABOVE	d.
		(IF RESIDENT IS COMATOSE, SKIP TO SECTION O)	

2.	AVERAGE TIME INVOLVED IN ACTIVITIES	(When awake and not receiving treatments or ADL care) 0. Most—more than 2/3 of time 1. Some—from 1/3 to 2/3 of time 2. Little—less than 1/3 of time 3. None	1

3.	PREFERRED ACTIVITY SETTINGS	(Check all settings in which activities are preferred)	
		Own room	a. X
		Day/activity room	b. X
		Inside NH/off unit	c. X
		Outside facility	d.
		NONE OF THE ABOVE	e.

4.	GENERAL ACTIVITY PREFER-ENCES (Adapted to resident's current abilities)	(Check all PREFERENCES whether or not activity is currently available to resident)	
		Cards/other games	a.
		Crafts/arts	b.
		Exercise/sports	c.
		Music	d. X
		Reading/writing	e.
		Spiritual/religious activities	f. X
		Trips/shopping	g.
		Walking/wheeling outdoors	h.
		Watching TV	i.
		Gardening or plants	j.
		Talking or conversing	k. X
		Helping others	l.
		NONE OF THE ABOVE	m.

4.	NUTRITIONAL PROBLEMS	Complains about the taste of many foods	a.	
		Leaves 25% or more of food uneaten at most meals	c. X	
		Regular or repetitive complaints of hunger	b.	
		NONE OF THE ABOVE	d.	

5.	NUTRITIONAL APPROACH-ES	(Check all that apply in last 7 days)		
		Parenteral/IV	a.	
		Feeding tube	b.	
		Mechanically altered diet	c. X	
		Syringe (oral feeding)	d.	
		Therapeutic diet	e. X	
		Dietary supplement between meals	f.	
		Plate guard, stabilized built-up utensil, etc.	g.	
		On a planned weight change program	h.	
		NONE OF THE ABOVE	i.	

6.	PARENTERAL OR ENTERAL INTAKE	(Skip to Section L if neither 5a nor 5b is checked)
		a. Code the proportion of total calories the resident received through parenteral or tube feedings in the last 7 days
		0. None 1. 1% to 25% 2. 26% to 50% 3. 51% to 75% 4. 76% to 100%
		b. Code the average fluid intake per day by IV or tube in last 7 days
		0. None 1. 1 to 500 cc/day 2. 501 to 1000 cc/day 3. 1001 to 1500 cc/day 4. 1501 to 2000 cc/day 5. 2001 or more cc/day

SECTION L. ORAL/DENTAL STATUS

1.	ORAL STATUS AND DISEASE PREVEN-TION	Debris (soft, easily movable substances) present in mouth prior to going to bed at night	a.
		Has dentures or removable bridge	b. X
		Some/all natural teeth lost—does not have or does not use dentures (or partial plates)	c.
		Broken, loose, or carious teeth	d.
		Inflamed gums (gingiva); swollen or bleeding gums; oral abscesses; ulcers or rashes	e.
		Daily cleaning of teeth/dentures or daily mouth care—by resident or staff	f. X
		NONE OF THE ABOVE	g.

Resident _____

Numeric Identifier _____ **007163**

5.	PREFERS CHANGE IN DAILY ROUTINE	Code for resident preferences in daily routines
		0. No change 1. Slight change 2. Major change
		a. Type of activities in which resident is currently involved — [0]
		b. Extent of resident involvement in activities — [0]

SECTION O. MEDICATIONS

1.	NUMBER OF MEDICA-TIONS	(Record the number of different medications used in the last 7 days; enter "0" if none used) — [1][1]
2.	NEW MEDICA-TIONS	(Resident currently receiving medications that were initiated during the last 90 days) 0. No 1. Yes — [1]
3.	INJECTIONS	(Record the number of DAYS injections of any type received during the last 7 days; enter "0" if none used) — [1]
4.	DAYS RECEIVED THE FOLLOWING MEDICATION	(Record the number of DAYS during last 7 days; enter "0" if not used. Note—enter "1" for long-acting meds used less than weekly)
		a. Antipsychotic [0] d. Hypnotic [0]
		b. Antianxiety [0] e. Diuretic [0]
		c. Antidepressant [5]

SECTION P. SPECIAL TREATMENTS AND PROCEDURES

1. SPECIAL TREAT-MENTS, PROCE-DURES, AND PROGRAMS

a. SPECIAL CARE—Check treatments or programs received during the last 14 days

TREATMENTS

a. Chemotherapy		l. Ventilator or respirator	
b. Dialysis		**PROGRAMS**	
c. IV medication		m. Alcohol/drug treatment program	
d. Intake/output		n. Alzheimer's/dementia special care unit	
e. Monitoring acute medical condition	**X**	o. Hospice care	
f. Ostomy care		p. Pediatric unit	
g. Oxygen therapy		q. Respite care	
h. Radiation		r. Training in skills required to return to the community (e.g., taking medications, house work, shopping, transportation, ADLs)	**X**
i. Suctioning		s. NONE OF THE ABOVE	
j. Tracheostomy care			
k. Transfusions			

4.	DEVICES AND RESTRAINTS	(Use the following codes for last 7 days:)
		0. Not used
		1. Used less than daily
		2. Used daily
		Bed rails
		a.—Full bed rails on all open sides of bed [0]
		b.—Other types of side rails used (e.g., half rail, one side) [2]
		c. Trunk restraint [0]
		d. Limb restraint [0]
		e. Chair prevents rising [0]
5.	HOSPITAL STAY(S)	Record the number of times resident was admitted to hospital with an overnight stay in last 90 days (or since last assessment if less than 90 days). (Enter 0 if no hospital admissions) — [0][1]
6.	EMERGENCY ROOM (ER) VISIT(S)	Record the number of times resident visited ER without an overnight stay in last 90 days). (Enter 0 if no ER visits) — [0][0]
7.	PHYSICIAN VISITS	In the LAST 14 DAYS (or since admission if less than 14 days in facility) how many days has the physician (or authorized assistant or practitioner) examined the resident? (Enter 0 if none) — [0][1]
8.	PHYSICIAN ORDERS	In the LAST 14 DAYS (or since admission if less than 14 days in facility) how many days has the physician (or authorized assistant or practitioner) changed the resident's orders? Do not include other renewals without change. (Enter 0 if none) — [0][1]
9.	ABNORMAL LAB VALUES	Has the resident had any abnormal lab values during the last 90 days (or since admission)? 0. No 1. Yes — [1]

SECTION Q. DISCHARGE POTENTIAL AND OVERALL STATUS

1.	DISCHARGE POTENTIAL	a. Resident expresses/indicates preference to return to the community
		0. No 1. Yes — [1]
		b. Resident has a support person who is positive toward discharge
		0. No 1. Yes — [1]
		c. Stay projected to be of a short duration—discharge projected within 90 days (do not include expected discharge due to death)
		0. No 2. Within 31–90 days
		1. Within 30 days 3. Discharge status uncertain — [2]
2.	OVERALL CHANGE IN CARE NEEDS	Resident's overall self-sufficiency has changed significantly as compared to status of 90 days ago (or since last assessment if less than 90 days)
		0. No change
		1. Improved—receives fewer supports needs, less restrictive level of care
		2. Deteriorated—receives more support — [2]

b. THERAPIES —*Record the number of days and total minutes each of the following therapies was administered (for at least 15 minutes a day) in the **last 7 calendar days** (Enter 0 if none or less than 15 min. daily)* [NOTE—count only post admission therapies]—

		DAYS (A)	MIN (B)
	(A) = # of days administered for **15 minutes or more** in **last 7 days**		
	(B) = total # of minutes provided in **last 7 days**		
a.	Speech-language pathology and audiology services	0 0	0 0 0
b.	Occupational therapy	2 0	0 7 6
c.	Physical therapy	3 0	1 1 9
d.	Respiratory therapy	0 0	0 0 0
e.	Psychological therapy (by any licensed mental health professional)	0 0	0 0 0

2.	INTERVEN-TION PROGRAMS FOR MOOD, BEHAVIOR, COGNITIVE LOSS	(Check all interventions or strategies used in **last 7 days**— no matter where received)	
		Special behavior symptom evaluation program	a.
		Evaluation by a licensed mental health specialist in **last 90 days**	b.
		Group therapy	c.
		Resident-specific deliberate changes in the environment to address mood/behavior patterns—e.g., providing bureau in which to rummage	d.
		Reorientation—e.g., cueing	e. X
		NONE OF THE ABOVE	f.

3.	NURSING REHABILI-TATION/ RESTORATIVE CARE	*Record the NUMBER OF DAYS each of the following rehabilitation or restorative techniques or practices was provided for **more than or equal to 15 minutes per day** in the last 7 days (Enter 0 if none or less than 15 min. daily.)*	
		a. Range of motion (passive)	0
		b. Range of motion (active)	0
		c. Splint or brace assistance	0
		TRAINING AND SKILL PRACTICE IN:	
		d. Bed mobility	0
		e. Transfer	0
		f. Walking	0
		g. Dressing or grooming	0
		h. Eating or swallowing	0
		i. Amputation/prosthesis care	0
		j. Communication	0
		k. Other	0

SECTION R. ASSESSMENT INFORMATION

1.	PARTICI-PATION IN ASSESSMENT	a. Resident:	0. No	1. Yes	1
		b. Family:	0. No	1. Yes	1
		c. Significant other	0. No	1. Yes	0

2. SIGNATURES OF PERSONS COMPLETING THE ASSESSMENT:

a. Signature of RN Assessment Coordinator (sign on above line)

b. Date RN Assessment Coordinator signed as complete

0 9	–	1 5	–	2 0 0 3
Month		Day		Year

SECTION T. THERAPY SUPPLEMENT FOR MEDICARE PPS

1.	SPECIAL TREAT- MENTS AND PROCE- DURES	a. **RECREATION THERAPY**—*Enter number of days and total minutes of recreation therapy administered (for at least 15 minutes a day) in the last 7 days (Enter 0 if none)*		

			DAYS	MIN
			(A)	(B)
		(A) = **# of days** administered for 15 minutes or more	0	0 0 0 0
		(B) = **total # of minutes** provided in last 7 days		

Skip unless this is a Medicare 5 day or Medicare readmission/return assessment.

b. **ORDERED THERAPIES**—*Has physician ordered any of following therapies to begin in FIRST 14 days of stay—physical therapy, occupational therapy, or speech pathology service?*

    0. No   1. Yes   **1**

If not ordered, skip to Item 2

c. Through day 15, provide an estimate of the number of days when at least 1 therapy service can be expected to have been delivered.   **0 8**

d. Through day 15, provide an estimate of the number of therapy minutes (across the therapies) than can be expected to be delivered.   **0 7 5 0**

2.	WALKING WHEN MOST SELF SUFFICIENT	**Complete item 2 if ADL self-performance score for TRANSFER (G.1.b.A) is 0, 1, 2, or 3 AND at least one of the following are present:**

- Resident received physical therapy involving gait training (P.1.b.c)
- Physical therapy was ordered for the resident involving gait training (T.1.b)
- Resident received nursing rehabilitation for walking (P.3.f)
- Physical therapy involving walking has been discontinued within the past 180 days

Skip to item 3 if resident did not walk in last 7 days

(FOR FOLLOWING FIVE ITEMS, BASE CODING ON THE EPISODE WHEN THE RESIDENT WALKED THE FARTHEST WITHOUT SITTING DOWN. INCLUDE WALKING DURING REHABILITATION SESSIONS.)

a. **Furthest distance walked without sitting down during this episode.**

    0. 150+ feet   3. 10–25 feet
    1. 51–149 feet   4. Less than 10 feet
    2. 26–50 feet

b. **Time walked without sitting down during this episode.**

    0. 1–2 minutes   3. 11–15 minutes
    1. 3–4 minutes   4. 16–30 minutes
    2. 5–10 minutes   5. 31+ minutes

c. **Self-performance in walking during this episode.**

0. *INDEPENDENT*—No help or oversight

1. *SUPERVISION*—Oversight, encouragement or cueing provided

2. *LIMITED ASSISTANCE*—Resident highly involved in walking; received physical help in guided maneuvering of limbs or other nonweight bearing assistance

3. *EXTENSIVE ASSISTANCE*—Resident received weight bearing assistance while walking

d. **Walking support provided associated with this episode (code regardless of resident's self-performance classification).**

0. No setup or physical help from staff

1. Setup help only

2. One person physical assist

3. Two+ persons physical assist

e. **Parallel bars used by resident in association with this episode.**

0. No   1. Yes

3.	CASE MIX GROUP	Medicare	R H C 0 7	State	R M C 0 1

APPENDIX
4–II

CALCULATION OF TOTAL "ADL" SCORE
RUG-III, 44 GROUP HIERARCHICAL CLASSIFICATION

The ADL score is used in all determinations of a resident's placement in a RUG-III category. It is a very important component of the classification process.

►STEP # 1

To calculate the ADL score use the following chart for Gla (bed mobility), Glb (transfer), and Gli (toilet use). **Enter the ADL scores to the right**.

Column A =		Column B =	ADL score =	SCORE
-, 0 or 1	**and**	(any number)	= 1	Gla=_____
2	**and**	(any number)	= 3	Glb=_____
3, 4, or 8	**and**	-, 0, 1 or 2	= 4	Gli= _____
3, 4, or 8	**and**	3 or 8	= 5	

►STEP # 2

If K5a (parenteral/IV) is checked, the eating ADL score is 3. If K5b (feeding tube) is checked and <u>EITHER</u> (1) K6a is 51% or more calories <u>OR</u> (2) K6a is 26% to 50% calories and K6b is 501cc or more per day fluid enteral intake, then the eating ADL score is 3. **Enter the ADL eating score (G1h) below and total the ADL score. If not,** *go to Step #3.*

►STEP # 3

If neither K5a or K5b (with appropriate intake) are checked, evaluate the chart below for G1hA (eating self-performance). *Enter the score to the right* and total the ADL score. This is the RUG-III **TOTAL ADL SCORE**. (The total ADL score range possibilities are 4 through 18.)

Column A (G1h) =	ADL score =	EATING SCORE
-, 0 or 1	= 1	G1h = ____
2	= 2	
3, 4, or 8	= 3	

TOTAL RUG-III ADL SCORE _____

Other ADLs are also very important, but the researchers have determined that the late loss ADLs were more predictive of resource use. They determined that allowing for the early loss ADLs did not significantly change the classification hierarchy or add to the variance explanation.

Revised—December 2002

APPENDIX
4–III

CATEGORY I: REHABILITATION
RUG-III, 44 GROUP HIERARCHICAL CLASSIFICATION

After determining a resident's total ADL score, you start the classification process beginning at the Rehabilitation level. Rehabilitation therapy is any combination of the disciplines of physical, occupational, or speech therapy. This information is found in Section P1b. Nursing rehabilitation is also considered for the low intensity classification level. It consists of providing active or passive range of motion, splint/brace assistance, training in transfer, training in dressing/grooming, training in eating/swallowing, training in bed mobility or walking, training in communication, amputation/prosthesis care, any scheduled toileting program, and bladder retraining program. This information is found in Section P3 and H3a,b of the MDS Version 2.0.

➤STEP # 1

Determine if the resident's rehabilitation therapy services satisfy the criteria for one of the RUG-III Rehabilitation groups. **If the resident does not meet all of the criteria for one Rehabilitation group (e.g., Ultra High Intensity), then move to the next group (e.g., Very High Intensity).**

A. **Ultra High Intensity Criteria**
In the last 7 days (section P1b [a,b,c]):
720 minutes or more (total) of therapy per week **AND**
At least two disciplines, 1 for at least 5 days, **AND**
2nd for at least 3 days

RUG-III ADL Score	RUG-III Class
16–18	RUC
9–15	RUB
4–8	RUA

B. **Very High Intensity Criteria**
In the last 7 days (section P1b [a, b, c]):
500 minutes or more (total) of therapy per week **AND**
At least 1 discipline for at least 5 days

RUG-III ADL Score	RUG-III Class
16–18	RVC
9–15	RVB
4–8	RVA

Revised—December 2002

C. **High Intensity Criteria** (either (1) or (2) below may qualify)
   (1) In the last 7 days (section P1b [a, b, c]):
        325 minutes or more (total) of therapy per week **AND**
        At least 1 discipline for at least 5 days

   (2) **If this is a Medicare 5-Day or a Medicate Readmission/Return Assessment, then the following apply** (section T1b, T1c, T1d and section P1b [a, b, c]):
        Ordered Therapies, T1b is checked **AND**
        In the last 7 days:
            Received 65 or more minutes, P1b [a,b,c] **AND**
        In the first 15 days from admission:
            520 or more minutes expected, T1d **AND**
            rehabilitation services expected on 8 or more days, T1c.

RUG-III ADL Score	RUG-III Class
13–18	RHC
8–12	RHB
4–7	RHA

D. **Medium Intensity Criteria** (either (1) or (2) below may qualify)
   (1) In the last 7 days: (section P1b [a,b,c])
        150 minutes or more (total) of therapy per week **AND**
        At least 5 days of any combination of the 3 disciplines

   (2) **If this is a Medicare 5-Day or a Medicare Readmission/ Return Assessment, then the following apply**: (section T1b, T1c, T1d):
        Ordered Therapies, T1b is checked **AND**
        In the first 15 days from admission:
            240 or more minutes are expected, T1d **AND**
            rehabilitation services expected on 8 or more days, T1c.

RUG-III ADL Score	RUG-III Class
15–18	RMC
8–14	RMB
4–7	RMA

E.   **Low Intensity Criteria** (either (1) or (2) below may qualify):
    (1) In the last 7 days (section P1b [a, b, c] and P3):
        45 minutes or more (total) of therapy per week **AND**
        At least 3 days of any combination of the 3 disciplines **AND**
        2 or more nursing rehabilitation services* received for
            at least 15 minutes each with each administered for 6 or more
            days.

    (2) **If this is a Medicare 5-Day or a Medicare Readmission/
        Return Assessment, then the following apply** (section P3 and
        section T1b, T1c, T1d):
        Ordered therapies T1B is checked **AND**
        In the first 15 days from admission:
            75 or more minutes are expected, T1d **AND**
            rehabilitation services expected on 5 or more days, T1c **AND**
            2 or more nursing rehabilitaiton services* received for at least
                15 minutes each with each administered for 2 or more days,
                P3.

Nursing Rehabilitation Services

*H3a,b***	*Any scheduled toileting program and/or bladder retraining program*
*P3a,b***	*Passive and/or active ROM*
P3c	*Splint or brace assistance*
*P3d,f***	*Bed mobility and/or walking training*
P3e	*Transfer training*
P3g	*Dressing or grooming training*
P3h	*Eating or swallowing training*
P3i	*Amputation/Prosthesis care*
P3j	*Communication training*

***Count as one service even if both provided*

RUG-III ADL Score	RUG-III Class
14–18	RLB
4–13	RLA

RUG-III Classification _____

If the resident does not classify in the Rehabilitation Category, *proceed to Category II.*

APPENDIX
4–IV

Major Category	Number of RUG Groups	Nursing Care Index	Therapy Index
Rehabilitation	14	0.80–1.30	0.43–2.25
Extensive Services	3	1.17–1.70	NA
Special Care	3	1.10–1.13	NA
Clinically Complex	6	0.75–1.12	NA
Impaired Condition	4	0.53–0.69	NA
Behavior Problems	4	0.48–0.68	NA
Reduced Physical Function	10	0.46–0.79	NA
Total	44		

PART II

Clinical Organization and Process Integration

This section makes a transition from studying external influences on a facility to understanding the facility's internal organization and processes that are essential for patient care delivery. However, many internal structures and processes are influenced by external forces. For instance, the evolution of nursing homes (discussed in Chapter 6) has been driven primarily by external factors.

In this section of the book, Chapter 5 discusses the physical structures, such as building layout and design. Nursing home design has undergone a gradual evolution in creating settings that promote independence in a socially supportive living environment. In response to changing expectations about long-term care, current trends suggest a gradual transformation from traditional hospital-inspired facilities to contemporary architectural features with a more residential look and feel. Contemporary models of client-centered care are based on a philosophy that integrates physical layout and design with empowerment of the residents, families, and staff. Chapter 6 describes these emerging concepts and innovations. The remaining six chapters in this section represent the six main organizational departments that oversee the processes essential to delivering total care in a typical nursing facility: Chapter 7 covers social services; Chapter 8 explains medical and nursing care; Chapter 9 looks at recreational activ-

ities; Chapter 10 discusses dietary services; Chapter 11 describes plant and environmental services; and Chapter 12 covers administrative offices. The organizational chart of a typical skilled nursing facility includes these functional departments as illustrated in Figure II-1. From a managerial standpoint, most facilities separate plant maintenance and housekeeping into two departments (as shown in Figure II-1), although they both have a common mission of environmental support.

In a mid-sized facility of 120 to 150 beds, each of these services is managed by a department head. Some of these managers are actually working supervisors. For example, depending on a facility's size, a housekeeping supervisor may clean some rooms or polish floors but also supervise a crew of housekeepers. In spite of this organizational arrangement, in which qualified individuals are put in charge of different departments, the nursing home administrator has a "hands-on" role in coordinating and overseeing the integration of the clinical and adjunct processes. The various support services are adjuncts to the central nursing care process and must interface with clinical care using a multidisciplinary approach. Building a multidisciplinary team requires the administrator's involvement, and the administrator must develop an organizational culture of interdepartmental communication and cooperation to address patient needs in a holistic system of care. Materials covered in this section are intended to help administrators understand the purpose and function of each department. This knowledge will improve the administrator's own effectiveness in managing the facility and should be useful in hiring qualified supervisors when vacancies occur.

In an integrated multidisciplinary approach to patient care, professionals who provide medical, nursing, social services, recreational activities, and dietary services share their observations, discuss clinical goals, and develop interventions in which a variety of services interface. Professionals in each discipline are aware of what others are doing to address the multifaceted needs of each patient. Developing an individual plan of care for each patient is a multidisciplinary effort. The overarching goal is to address all aspects of a patient's needs without duplicating or disregarding any needed services. Often, problems and issues are addressed in committees, with service providers from all pertinent disciplines interacting and providing their professional inputs.

The Omnibus Budget Reconciliation Act of 1987 mandated that nursing facilities provide necessary care and services with the objective of pro-

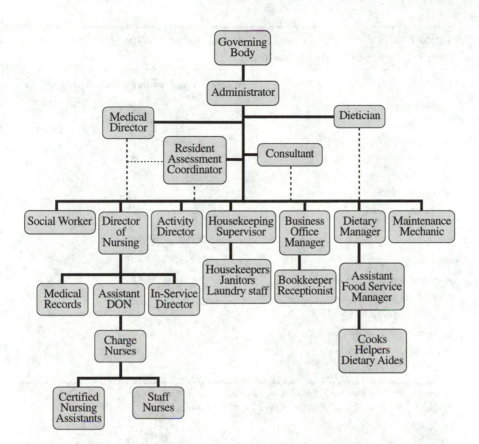

Note: The above chart is illustrative only, because variations exist according to facility size. For instance, some large facilities may have additional positions such as Assistant Administrator, Director of Marketing, or Admissions Coordinator. These positions report to the Administrator. The Medical Records position may report to the Administrator instead of Director of Nursing. The nursing department may have Shift Supervisors, either in addition to or instead of the Assistant Director of Nursing. The Social Worker, Activity Director, and Maintenance Mechanic may have assistants. For example, the maintenance mechanic may have a groundskeeper. The Resident Assessment Coordinator may report to the administrator or the Director of Nursing. Similarly, the In-service Director may report to either the Administrator or Director of Nursing.

------ indicates advisory relationships (referred to as 'staff relationships' in management)

—— indicates supervisor-subordinate relationships (called 'line relationships' in management)

FIGURE II-1 Organizational Chart of a Typical Skilled Nursing Facility

moting the highest practicable level of well-being for each patient. This section describes the process of fulfilling this mandate. Some of the most commonly provided services are listed in Table II-1.

Table II-1 Types of Services Commonly Provided by Nursing Homes, either Directly or through Contracts.

	% of all nursing facilities providing the service
Dental services	80.0
Help with oral hygiene	97.1
Hospice services	74.6
Medical services	96.1
Mental health services	79.7
Nursing services	99.5
Nutrition services	99.2
Occupational therapy	94.0
Personal care	96.7
Physical therapy	96.9
Podiatry services	89.2
Prescribed and nonprescribed medications	98.0
Social services	97.5
Speech therapy and audiology	93.5
Transportation	81.7
Equipment and devices	95.3

Source: Data from the National Nursing Home Survey 1999. *Vital Health Statistics*, Series 13, No. 152 (2002), p. 9. National Center for Health Statistics.

Unlike other health care institutions, nursing facilities must combine both medical and social services. Although patients are admitted to skilled nursing facilities primarily to receive therapeutic interventions, these services must be delivered within a human context that emphasizes a homelike setting, personal choice, independence, dignity, and self-esteem as overarching factors that govern the clinical and socio-residential elements of service delivery. Achieving the appropriate blend of clinical and socio-residential services is the goal that guides the way in which the facility's structures are developed and processes are implemented. Figure II-1 classifies nursing home services into their clinical and socio-residential components. When human factors are integrated into the two components, it creates a total living environment in which a person's physical, mental, social, and spiritual needs are met.

Overarching Human Factors		
Personal preferences		
Independence		
Dignity		
Self-esteem		
Socio-Residential Component		**Clinical Component**
Room and Board	**Amenities**	**Clinical Care**
Accommodation • Privacy • Safety • Cleanliness • Comfort Meals • Nutrition • Choice • Adequacy • Attractiveness • Palatability	Private rooms Personal space Social space Dining rooms Layout Décor and aesthetics Barber/beauty salon Gift shop Library Chapel	Medical oversight Nursing care Rehabilitation Social services Dietary services Recreational activities End-of-life care

FIGURE II-2 Clinical, Residential, and Human Components of Nursing Home Services

Clinical, Social, and Residential Structures

continues

6. Compatibility, dining, and companionship as key factors in the public domain to counter loneliness and isolation. The nursing facility's duty to facilitate opportunities for relationship-building and socializing.

7. Residential designs and small group settings, particularly for patients with dementia. Creating small neighborhoods with cluster arrangements and nested single-room architecture to integrate residential features with clinical and social aspects.

8. Creating a safe environment. Compliance with the Life Safety Code.

9. Accessibility and the Americans with Disabilities Act. Wayfinding to promote self-orientation.

10. Positive stimulation and distraction. Aesthetics: lighting, color, and furnishings. Creating a homelike environment and incorporating safety and comfort factors.

The physical characteristics of a nursing home influence the living environment which affects the patients' sense of well-being. At least some evidence suggests that the physical environment can also affect social behavior and certain clinical outcomes. For example, in a pilot study, Brush and colleagues (2002) found that improved lighting and table setting contrast had a positive effect on food consumption and functional abilities of patients with dementia. When the environment provides too many stressors (discussed later in this chapter under Positive Stimulation and Distraction) and few opportunities to relax, dysfunctional behaviors are observed among patients with dementia (Rader 1991). Therefore, building layout, design, décor, furnishings and other amenities should be used to support clinical, residential, and social structures.

Unlike acute-care hospitals, a nursing facility is both a clinical and a social establishment. In the hospital, the **sick-role model** proposed by Parsons (1972) governs patients' social relationships. The patient is expected to relinquish individual control to hospital personnel and comply with their directives. The sick-role promotes an institutional orientation to patient care, which is manifested in four ways: rigid daily routines; social distance between staff members and the patient; care

practices that lend to depersonalization, such as loss of privacy; and "blocking routines" that require patients to do certain things at pre-arranged times (Kruzich and Berg 1985). A social and residential orientation in patient care, on the other hand, is characterized by shared control between the patient and the facility personnel. Indeed, social and residential elements of long-term care extend beyond their immediate context of medical- and nursing-care delivery to a philosophy that embraces the idea that a long-term care facility is not merely a clinical setting; it is also a place that many people call home.

In a nursing facility, the clinical and social dimensions should complement each other, promoting effective clinical care and, at the same time, maximizing quality of life. The internal structures and processes must be designed to meet the needs of the residents and the needs of families and visitors. Striking the right balance between clinical and social aspects of care is not always easy, because traditional nursing home care has been based on an expert approach to meeting the physical and medical needs of patients (Collopy 1995). Well-meaning staff members are often ill-prepared to reconcile their own training and priorities with the fact that residents are entitled to make their own choices. As a result, caregivers may experience difficulty relating to residents because of this conflict (Chapman et al. 2003).

The **clinical structure** of long-term care is designed primarily to address the medical needs of patients. Although the clinical structure is associated with the sick role and the institutional dimension, it is irrational to think that this structure can be dispensed with entirely. For example, giving medications and other treatments in a patient population of any size requires certain routines based on medical directives. Medical examinations result in some loss of personal control by the patient. Necessary staff assistance with daily living activities does create some dependency. But, the clinical and socio-residential structures must complement each other.

The **social structure** is what lends a living and vibrant personality to a long-term care facility. The social structure includes numerous elements that promote individual satisfaction within a stable communal environment, in which people engage in individual pursuits and meaningful social relationships. The social structure encourages interaction, independence, engagement, activity, and leisure among the residents, while facility staff maintains its responsibility of oversight and support.

Individual rights are respected, but interventions are undertaken when necessary to promote the total well-being of all residents. Social structures also promote individual autonomy and decision-making, even when a resident's decision-making capacity is limited.

The **residential structure** emphasizes making living arrangements homelike. A homelike environment is safe, clean, comfortable, and aesthetically pleasing, and it gives a reasonable amount of privacy.

INTEGRATING THE THREE STRUCTURES

The clinical organization of care delivery has been grounded in medical science, borrowing many of its salient features from hospitals. Medical structures are designed to facilitate efficient care delivery to a relatively large number of patients. Social structures, on the other hand, are largely based on a philosophy of holistic care. Residential structures emphasize architectural designs and interior décor. The extent to which social and clinical aspects are integrated varies according to the services a facility provides. Within the institutional continuum of long-term care (see Figure 1-5), social aspects are given greater emphasis in personal care and assisted living facilities, whereas clinical aspects get more emphasis in skilled nursing and subacute care facilities.

In all long-term care settings, the ultimate challenge is to deliver patient care while maximizing quality of life, which requires properly integrating human factors, the clinical component, and the socio-residential component to create a total living environment (Figure 5-1). Such an environment is holistic. It allows each resident's physical, mental, social, and spiritual needs to be met, and it enables residents to live their lives as normally as possible. Modern architectural features also facilitate the delivery of clinical care in an environment of intimacy by allowing familiarity and bonding between caregivers and patients.

THE HOLISTIC AND REALISTIC CONTEXTS

As described in Chapter 1, the objective of long-term care is to address a patient's medical care needs within a delivery structure that integrates social, emotional, and spiritual support in a homelike physical setting. A

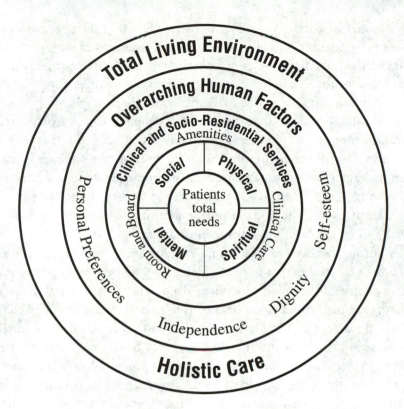

FIGURE 5-1 An Integrated Model of a Total Living Environment That Promotes Holistic Care

nursing facility should strive to achieve this objective for every patient, regardless of his or her physical or mental condition.

Holistic Model of Health Care

A holistic model of health care, as proposed by Shi and Singh (1998), emphasizes well-being: every aspect of what makes a person whole and complete. The authors propose that holistic health care incorporate four dimensions or contexts:

- physical (the human body in a medical context)
- mental (the mind in an emotional and behavioral context)
- social (emotional fulfillment in social relationships)
- spiritual (personal beliefs, values, and commitments in a religious and spiritual context)

The model of total living environment (Figure 5-1) suggests that a patient's total needs should be evaluated and understood within the confines of the four dimensions of holistic health. Holistic long-term care then governs the clinical and socio-residential structures and aspects of care by promoting each individual's quality of life through comfort, security, aesthetics, private space, personal independence, personal preferences, dignity, and self-esteem. Each patient is allowed to feel at ease and in harmony with the environment that has become the patient's home. It means that the environment itself must promote healing of the body, mind, and spirit. Because a patient's stay in a nursing facility generally involves an extended period of time, long-term care falls short of its objective if it does not have this holistic integration.

A nursing facility has a legal and moral duty to provide clinical care according to acceptable standards. Regulatory standards set a minimum quality threshold for clinical services. To a lesser degree, regulations also identify the main social components. But, in both areas, nursing facilities must go beyond the minimum requirements. The culture of nursing home administration suffers from paranoia of the regulatory system. Collopy (1995, 149) argued that the nursing home industry is often slow to respond and is largely reactive in the way that it invokes moral values, mainly to protect itself against possible regulatory sanction. Such a highly risk-averse stance mutes the providers' own moral agency, so regulators and advocates for the elderly have seized the ethics agenda and have taken the initiative to prescribe minute regulatory details. Such a state of affairs will change only when the industry's leadership asserts the values that are most desired by its clients.

The Realistic Context

Even though a total living environment of holistic care is an ideal that nursing homes must strive to achieve, numerous constraints keep the ideal from being fully attained. Inadequate financing is often a major constraint that limits a facility's ability to obtain or use resources. Some constraints are patient centered. Examples include behavioral problems, such as frequent combativeness or screaming episodes, that can disrupt the environment. Therefore, the delivery of clinical and socio-residential services in nursing homes must also be placed in a realistic context. Patients in nursing facilities are in a clinical environment 24 hours a day,

seven days a week. Nursing facilities exist because of economic necessity. If it were feasible, almost every nursing home patient would choose to be cared for in a private residence by a private-duty nurse. The reality, however, is that unless an individual is very wealthy neither the individual patient nor the society can afford to incur the expense that private-duty care would entail. Expensive as it is, delivery of care in a nursing facility is highly cost-effective compared to private-duty nursing. From this perspective, the residential nature of a nursing facility should not be construed to mean that it is a private residence. It must, by necessity, provide services to a relatively large number of patients. In spite of suggestions to downplay or to criticize the institutional nature of nursing facilities, the fact remains that nursing facilities must function as organizations. As organizations, they must provide services as efficiently as possible, although focusing on efficiency will dilute social and residential aspects to some degree.

By its very nature, any group living arrangement, whether large or small, creates an environment in which small-scale conflicts of everyday life are likely to occur. First, respecting autonomy can be "vexatious because the conditions that bring elders into long-term care—confusion, dementia, wandering, and a host of diseases associated with being old— are such that the very capacity for choice and rational decision making is seriously compromised, if not absent" (Agich 1995, 113). In a relation of dependence, it may be quite natural for a caregiver to simply take over the care-delivery process. Yet, an effort must be made to return to the elder patient some of the responsibilities for his or her own health care in a caring and respectful way. Thus, a delicate balance exists between the clinical and social aspects of caregiving. The caregivers' primary task is to help the patients reorient themselves in their effort to "make or remake their world," which is an important but often overlooked aspect of adaptation to loss, pain, and suffering (Scarry 1985). However, there is no standard rule that can be followed to help people adapt to change in their lives. People try to adapt in their own unique ways through various interpretive efforts. The nursing facility, however, can provide physical surroundings and a basic sense of personal space to help the process of adjustment. Familiarity and closeness in the caregiver-patient relationship that is built on the foundation of respect for the patient can also help patients maintain their sense of identity despite the ravages of impairment (Agich 1995).

In a nursing facility, each resident's desires, interests, and actions can directly affect the interests and legitimate expectations of other residents (Arras 1995). For example, patients who wander into others' rooms, rummage through others' belongings, dip their hands into other diners' plates, make yelling noises, or display combativeness disrupt the quality of life of other residents. To deal with such conflicts in an institutional setting, the facility must achieve an appropriate balance between the needs of these groups. Arras (1995) suggested that a model other than the one in which the patient's best interest becomes the overriding goal is necessary. This alternative model is based on the notions of fairness, accommodation, compromise, and negotiation. Again, each situation is going to be different, but as a general rule, no one patient's interests are legitimately outweighed by the competing interests of other patients.

CLINICAL ORGANIZATION

This section describes the clinical set-up in a traditional skilled nursing facility. Many newer facilities are being built using innovative design concepts to downplay the clinical structures, as discussed later in this chapter. The concept of a Green House, a sort of small, cottage-like structure, is presented in Chapter 6.

Nursing Units

A nursing unit or wing is a section of a facility that consists of a certain number of patient rooms served by a nursing station. Depending on its size, a facility may have clinically distinct nursing units, each providing a somewhat distinct level of care, such as rehabilitation, dementia care, or specialized care. Distinct nursing units can also be designated according to the type of certification (see Figure 3-3). To achieve staff efficiency, most clinical units are self-contained, having their own bathing rooms, dining or feeding rooms, and lounges for patients and visitors. An adequate number of clean linen closets should be located in the hallways of each nursing unit. An enclosed area or a hallway nook for depositing soiled linens should be located in the unit, with marked containers to ease sorting and to separate lightly soiled linens from those that are heavily soiled. When utility closets are easily accessible to staff, hallways are kept free of clutter and odors are kept to a minimum. An enclosed soiled-utility area

is ideal, because it can be equipped with a rinse tub to eliminate heavy wastes. Modern ventilation and waste-elimination systems are designed to keep odors to a minimum. Also, staff members ought to be trained in sanitation and odor control methods. Chemical deodorizers should not be used to mask odors.

A facility of 80 or more beds is likely to have more than one nursing unit. To the extent that it can do so, a facility should segregate patients based on clinical criteria. Distinctly separate specialized care units are often provided for subacute care or Alzheimer's care. Such a specialized unit allows the facility to match staff skills to special patient needs. Restorative aides (paraprofessionals who follow up on rehabilitation therapies), for instance, are most appropriately stationed in the SNF unit where most of the Medicare patients are located. A separate nursing unit, however, is not feasible to have for every type of specialization. Several clinically complex services such as ventilator care, head trauma care, care for spinal injuries, and treatment for pressure ulcers and wounds can be located on one unit that is served by the same nursing station. On the other hand, neatly categorizing patients in terms of their needs for care is not always practical. Comorbidities often present a challenge to long-term care clinicians about where a patient with given health conditions can be best accommodated. However, facilities must give due consideration to each patient's clinical needs as well as the patient's quality of life. For instance, every effort should be made to segregate patients with cognitive impairments or behavioral problems from those who do not have such disabilities.

Some facilities focus on private-pay clients by furnishing a separate non-certified unit where the living environment is enhanced and amenities are upgraded. This type of segregation in a non-certified section allows a facility to provide upscale services to private-pay clients without discriminating against those on public assistance. It also shelters the non-certified section from certification surveys (see Chapter 3).

Nursing Station

The hub of clinical care is an appropriately located, adequately staffed, and well-furnished nursing station. This station can be regarded as a service center from where all nursing care is delivered to a certain number of patients, generally on an entire nursing unit.

Location of Nursing Stations

A nursing station should be centrally located, to enable the nursing staff to observe and supervise a certain number of patient rooms and to respond effectively to patient needs. A facility may have more than one station, depending on its size, acuity level of patients, and complexity of care. On the other hand, having too many stations would be inefficient, because each station must be individually staffed. As a general rule, a nursing station serves each clinical unit in a facility. The maximum distance allowed from a nursing station to the farthest patient room is generally specified in state licensure regulations.

Other areas of a clinical unit that may be adjacent to the nursing station include rooms for bathing and showering, special dining areas, and patient lounges, including the lounges designated for smokers. Of course, not all patient dining rooms and lounges must be in the vicinity of a nursing station—only those where supervision from staff is necessary. Also, not every type of specialized service requires a separate nursing station. Services for patients who need ventilators, head trauma care, spinal injury care, and treatment for pressure ulcers and wounds can all be provided from the same nursing station.

Staffing of Nursing Stations

Staffing is one of the most important issues in nursing homes. State licensure regulations often specify minimum staff-to-patient ratios, and facility administrators may tend to believe that those minimum standards represent adequate staffing levels. State standards set a minimum requirement, which is at best arbitrary, because it does not take into account the level of patients' clinical acuity and other aspects of patient mix discussed above. Clinical load rather than state regulations should govern staff-to-patient ratios, and higher ratios are needed in specialized and heavy-care units (discussed in Chapter 14). Staff-hours per patient specify total staff hours for a given number of patients. Two additional staffing considerations are necessary:

- The skill-mix—the mix between registered nurses (RNs), licensed practical/vocation nurses (LPNs/LVNs), and certified nurse aides (CNAs)—must be carefully evaluated. Skill-mix considerations also include any specialized training, experience, and actual staff performance and productivity. For example, the staff may require spe-

cial training to adequately address cognitive and behavioral issues. Matching the skill-mix to patient needs is important, as indicated by a composite case mix based on patient assessment.

- Distribution of staff hours between the three main shifts—day, evening, and night—requires a proper balance. Generally, the day shift needs the heaviest staffing, and the night shift requires the least. But, different nursing units are likely to require different day-to-evening and day-to-night staffing ratios. Even within the same shift, certain time periods have heavier patient loads than others. For instance, the morning wake-up and grooming time, the lunch hour, and evening meal time generally require more staff assistance than at other times. The feasibility of adding staff hours to meet peak patient load demands should be assessed.

Nursing Station Furnishings

The layout and furnishing of a nursing station should enhance staff effectiveness. The station itself is an enclosed area, with a counter behind which nurses and other staff members perform administrative tasks. No one but authorized staff members should have access to the area behind the counter. Among other things, a nursing station's furnishings must include three important components: a patient-call signal system, medical records, and a pharmaceuticals room.

Patient Call Signals

A call system is a critical component of a nursing unit. The system connects devices at all patient bedsides and next to all toilets to the nursing station. Ideally, it should also connect the station to the bathing-and-shower rooms, dining areas, and lounges located on a given nursing unit. The system enables the patients themselves and staff members working with patients to summon help when needed. Ideally, the system should have audio-visual as well as voice capabilities. A patient uses a sensory device—such as a call button—that sets off the audio-visual signal at the nursing station. This audio-visual signal consists of a light and a buzzer or bell to alert the staff that a patient is calling for assistance and also to identify the patient who needs help. A voice or "talk-back" feature is useful when the staff member attending to a patient needs to communicate with

staff members located at the station; this device saves time that otherwise will be spent walking back and forth from the nursing station.

Medical Records

Located at the nursing station, there must be a separate medical chart for every patient on the unit. The medical records must be readily accessible to all authorized staff members. Confidentiality, however, must be maintained at all times. Medical records are increasingly being automated by using computer-based information systems. Automation can greatly facilitate the tasks of keeping records up to date and retrieving them quickly. But keeping them secure and confidential is challenging (see Chapter 12).

Pharmaceuticals Room

The pharmaceuticals room, or "medication room," as it is commonly called, should be quickly accessible from the nursing station. This room is locked to adequately safeguard all medications. A system that allows separate storage of medications for each patient should be used. The pharmaceuticals room is also commonly used to store nursing treatment supplies and a first-aid box. The room is furnished with a refrigerator for storing certain medications that require refrigeration. The room also contains a locked storage area for controlled substances that must be kept double-locked. A system must be in place to adequately account for all used and unused medications for each patient.

The prescription, dispensing, and use of **controlled substances**—narcotics, stimulants, depressants, hallucinogens, anabolic steroids, and chemicals—are governed by the Controlled Substances Act (CSA), Title II of the Comprehensive Drug Abuse Prevention and Control Act of 1970. Except as provided under the law, possession or use of controlled substances is illegal. Controlled substances are listed in Schedules I through VI of the CSA. Many of these drugs have a useful and legitimate medical purpose when appropriately prescribed by a physician, but their abuse generally has a substantial and detrimental effect on health and general welfare; hence the need for strict control of these substances. A facility must store controlled substances in a double-locked cabinet and implement proper recordkeeping and verification systems. Federal regulations also require all controlled substances to be destroyed—and that this destruction be duly witnessed—if an order for controlled substances is discontinued for any reason.

SOCIAL ASPECTS

Although a nursing facility is considered a patient's home, it is also a community. The social aspects of long-term care entail the influences that the physical and social environments have on the patients' physical, mental, social, and spiritual well-being. A positive environment is therapeutic for the patient, and it should also relieve the clinical infrastructure of pressures that might otherwise be imposed on it from social conflict or individual ill-adjustment. As mentioned earlier, clinical segregation plays a role in shaping the social environment, and it enables a facility to reach a better balance between the clinical and social domains. Segregating patients with severe dementia and those with behavioral problems from other patients is particularly important. A disruptive environment creates commotion and confusion and is unhealthy for those who prefer quietude and wish to engage in productive social, mental, and spiritual pursuits. The facility's set-up should also make it easier for patients to explore their compatibilities with others and engage in social interactions in accordance with personal preferences. Thus the social environment has both personal and public domains.

Personal Domain

At a personal level, the main concerns people have are security, autonomy, and privacy. In coping with change, opportunities for introspection, a sense of personal space, and the respect of others may be more important for the patient than the ability to socialize with others.

Security

Security is a basic human need. It entails not only physical safety and psychological peace of mind but also the commonality rather than separateness of person (Parmelee and Lawton 1990). Security includes a variety of conditions that contribute to freedom from risk, danger, anxiety, or doubt (Schwarz 1996). A nursing facility is responsible for its patients' personal security and the safekeeping of their belongings and private funds if the latter are deposited in a patient's trust account that the facility manages. Security considerations often vary from one patient to another. A patient may have a tendency to wander out unnoticed, another may insist on wearing expensive jewelry that someone could remove or that could get lost, and another may hallucinate and imagine that someone is assaulting her. It can

be therapeutic for a patient to wander out into a protective environment, such as a fenced-in walkway. On the other hand, any major safety concerns should be incorporated into the patient's plan of care, and they ought to be addressed by a multidisciplinary team of professionals, because the patient may require therapeutic intervention from trained staff.

Autonomy

Autonomy can be defined as "a cluster of notions including self-determination, freedom, independence, and liberty of choice and action. In its most general terms, autonomy signifies control of decision-making and other activity by the individual. It refers to human agency free of outside intervention and interference" (Collopy 1988). In any type of health care delivery, the patient assumes a dependent role in relation to the provider of care, as observed by Talcott Parsons (1972) in the sick-role model; the patient must concede some degree of autonomy. This dependence, however, does not mean that the patient should be made to give up all choice and decision-making. To the contrary, because health care by its very nature creates dependency, providers have an obligation to ensure the maximum preservation of patient autonomy. Patient rights, discussed in Chapter 3, are founded on both legal and ethical principles. Patient autonomy is the ethical principle governing patient rights. Therefore, any attempt to minimize patient autonomy is unethical. In this respect, the ethical principle goes beyond whatever is prescribed by law. On the other hand, a patient's autonomy cannot be taken to an extent that it infringes on the rights of others.

Autonomy for patients also requires that they be allowed to personalize their living quarters with familiar things, and such personal items as radios, small television sets, family pictures, mementos, artifacts, plants, music, personal furniture, bed accessories, etc. For people with dementia, in particular, a link to the past becomes essential for exercising their remaining capabilities, because their long-term memory remains relatively intact until the later stages of the disease (Cohen and Day 1993). Emotions and memories from past experiences and events often stimulate conversation and social interaction. Although space is almost always limited, a display shelf in each room can help people personalize their space by displaying memorabilia and other items. Certain personal belongings may also pose safety concerns. For instance, too many electrical gadgets may overload the circuits and create a fire hazard. Long extension cords and floor rugs pose a tripping hazard.

Autonomy also means that a patient must be able to make informed choices. Although the nursing facility must encourage informed choice, it also has the responsibility to do what is in the patient's best interest. Occasionally, conflicts may arise between a patient's autonomy and the facility's duty toward the patient. Such conflicts should be resolved by taking into consideration legal requirements, regulatory constraints, and ethics. Such situations are often not clear-cut. For instance, should a nursing facility use funds out of a patient's trust account to purchase new glasses or new hearing aids after the patient has already broken or lost two or three of them? Such decisions can be best addressed in a multidisciplinary forum in which decision-makers take into account the patient's wishes and past practices if the patient is unable to participate in decision-making. But, if the patient can participate, his or her wishes must be carried out.

Privacy

Almost all individuals require at least some privacy in terms of space, time, and person. In a health-care facility privacy of space is first determined by the type of accommodation: private or shared. Many facilities maintain a small number of private rooms for single accommodation. As a general rule, however, occupying a private room is considered a luxury for which someone has to pay more. Unless a medically determined need exists for private accommodation, public as well as private insurers do not cover it. So, in most instances, a patient must spend out-of-pocket funds if a private room is desired. Hence, for most patients, shared accommodation is the norm, which in most modern facilities constitutes double occupancy (rather than triple or quadruple accommodation). In these circumstances, privacy rests on how much physical space each individual has, including closet and storage space. Privacy also entails the need for intimacy (Westin 1967). **Intimacy** is a person's privacy during visits with family, friends, and legal or spiritual counselors. Residents can also express their sexuality in a private environment if their intimacy is assured. Because privacy is generally compromised in a multiple-occupancy setting, the facility should provide secluded areas that may be used for intimate dining experiences with family and friends, for private visits, or for sexual intimacy. Even a recessed nook with a small table and two chairs can provide an area for private visitation.

Privacy of time is often compromised by clinical routines that are established for the sake of staff efficiency. However, such routines tend to

make patients' lives regimented. In most nursing homes, wake-up and morning-hygiene chores must be completed before breakfast. Because assigning staff members to every resident at the same time is not possible, certain residents must wake up before others, and there may be little provision for patients to sleep in late. Meal hours are also generally fixed. Bathing and shower routines are scheduled ahead of time. Yet, within the parameters of such scheduled routines, patients' individual preferences should be accommodated whenever possible. Privacy of time also includes the need for personal reclusion, that is, have time for oneself and be free from unwanted intrusion, to be alone for quiet reflection. For this purpose quiet and secluded spaces such as small libraries and chapels are highly desirable.

A disregard of privacy of person is dehumanizing. Privacy of person can be equated with dignity. Privacy of person should always be protected, because some aspects of privacy depend not on space or time but on the practices and processes of care delivery. A basic rule for facilities to follow is to treat every person with dignity, regardless of whether he or she can perceive indignities (Kane 2001). Knocking at the door before entering a patient's room, closing the door for a patient while that patient is using the toilet, drawing privacy curtains during treatment, providing appropriate personal covering for a trip to the common bathing-and-shower area, providing proper grooming during a trip to the therapy room or dining room, and giving lap robes to female patients in wheelchairs are examples of how personal privacy is respected to preserve individual dignity.

Public Domain

Loneliness and isolation are common concerns among the elderly. Unless a person chooses to remain alone, opportunities must be provided for wholesome social interaction. The range of such opportunities depends on how well a nursing facility functions as a social community. The three most important experiences from this perspective are compatibility, the dining experience, and socializing.

Compatibility

Social interactions in the public domain are primarily driven by compatibility, because compatible relationships are something people naturally seek. The issue of compatibility first arises when a new patient is admitted to the facility and has to share a room with another patient who is a com-

plete stranger. Gender compatibility has been a long-established practice. Room sharing by two individuals of the opposite sex is permitted only in case of legitimate couples. Apart from such obvious types of compatibility, the main consideration in assigning a room to two people is how well the two individuals are likely to get along and engage in a meaningful social rapport. Compatibility is also an important consideration in other situations requiring social groupings, such as dining at the same table or participating in social and recreational events.

Relationship-building and bonding can be facilitated in several ways. Some nursing home residents assist other residents with simple tasks, such as escorting a friend to the dining room or assisting someone in a wheelchair. People who have disabilities of their own can find meaning in being helpful to others; it builds their own self-esteem. Nursing home residents can also develop such appropriate relationships with volunteers and staff members.

Dining

In the social context, dining is more than just something done for physical sustenance and good nutrition. Dining can provide opportunities for people to interact with others in a social setting. Seating arrangements should be such that they create opportunities for those who can socially interact. Of course, a patient's clinical condition will determine to what extent interaction is possible. For patients who require feeding assistance or who may have other special needs, dining may become a clinical event, but staff interaction can still help make it a social event. To the extent possible, clinical dining areas for those who cannot eat on their own should be separated from social dining areas, so that those who are able to dine in a social setting can enjoy the dining experience without interruption or distraction.

The dining environment should be relaxed. Comfortable chairs, tablecloths or placemats, cloth napkins, table center-pieces, and soft music contribute to a relaxed and enjoyable experience. A facility should also have some special tables to accommodate wheelchairs, but ambulatory and wheelchair patients should be allowed to sit and dine together.

Socializing

Socializing often depends on an individual's capacity to interact with others. Well-planned facilities offer varied spaces where people can spend time in the company of others. Effectively managed facilities offer numer-

ous daily opportunities for patients to socialize according to their personal interests. Social events also enable patients with dementia and other limitations to receive sensory stimulation by just being present. Events should be held in both interior and exterior spaces. Interior spaces include lounges, dining areas, craft and game rooms, and chapels. Exterior spaces include courtyards, patios, balconies, terraces, vegetable and flower patches, gazebos, and the spaces around bird feeders and fountains. The building's design should permit all residents easy access to the exterior. The outdoor spaces should have appropriate seating arrangements so that the patients can spend time relaxing, socializing, and simply enjoying the surroundings. Interior spaces should be comfortable and pleasing, with appropriate furniture, lighting, fixtures, and décor that allow people to associate with one another in pleasant surroundings. Modern facilities also have spaces such as mini-malls, ice cream parlors, and barber and beauty shops where residents can enjoy in similar fashion some of the social activities they once pursued.

RESIDENTIAL FEATURES

'Homelike' is the buzzword often used in discussing the residential context of long-term health care facilities. Indeed, the design of the residential structure should be founded on the home concept. To be realistic, though, one should also take into account the clinical domain. The point is that patients are admitted to nursing facilities only because they have clinical needs. The clinical and residential elements of care, therefore, must complement each other. Otherwise, residential features that detract from a high level of clinical care, particularly in subacute care settings, can be counterproductive.

A pleasant and comfortable environment is necessary for maximizing the patients' quality of life. A homelike environment is achieved by a facility's structural design, furnishings, décor, and a proper emphasis on the social structures discussed earlier. This section will address some of the physical features necessary for creating a residential environment. Most of the design features that will be addressed are particularly applicable to planning a new facility or remodeling or expanding an existing one. Other elements of residential-structure design can be incorporated into existing facilities with little expense. In addition, the safety and accessibility features that the nursing facilities' buildings must have are governed by laws with which the nursing facilities must comply.

For people with dementia, in particular, small groupings of residents in a setting that resembles a home—and not a large institution—provide a more effective therapeutic setting. The smaller scale of the living quarters reduces the stress that such patients may experience from the overwhelming effect of being placed in complex, unfamiliar surroundings. The medical character of the facility can be further deemphasized by eliminating the traditional nursing station and creating more shared spaces for social contact (Cohen and Day 1993). Large institutions can often modify a section of the main building to create a smaller, self-contained unit with its own kitchenette and common room, which can serve as a multipurpose room for dining, activities, and socializing.

Residential Designs

The average size of a nursing facility has increased by 40% from 75 beds in 1973 to 105 beds in 1999 (National Center for Health Statistics 2002). Although the larger size creates operational efficiencies, it detracts from a residential environment. In response, some innovative architectural plans have emerged. Modern residential designs promote privacy and neighborhood social activities. Increasingly, in new constructions, private rather than shared rooms are in vogue, to give patients more personal space. In addition, current architectural designs no longer feature the traditional long corridors that are lined with rooms on both sides, which often get cluttered with all kinds of barrels and carts and create an institutional look and feel. High-pitched roofs, varied plan configurations, and the connection of indoor to outdoor spaces can make a building seem more like a condominium than a nursing home (Nursing home architecture 1997).

Cluster Arrangement

The cluster design is gradually replacing the traditional corridor design in modern nursing home architecture. The design places decentralized self-contained clusters within the larger clinical units, creating relatively small residential groupings. Even though a nursing station is present, the design helps de-emphasize it. The cluster concept is sometimes called "neighborhood living," and the clusters may be called "household clusters." Each cluster functions as a residential unit or neighborhood, with its own living room and a room for various activities and for dining, surrounded by resident rooms (Dunkelman 1992). Seating configurations are designed to

create intimate social spaces. The design allows for plenty of windows for natural lighting and a somewhat panoramic view of the exterior. Clusters also tend to offer better flexibility in segregating residents than traditional layouts do. For instance, patients requiring heavy care could be accommodated in the same cluster.

Clusters are typically designed for between eight and twelve residents, and three or more clusters are grouped together for staffing efficiency (Browning 2003). For example, Figure 5-2 illustrates three nine-bed clusters, totaling 27 beds. High construction costs for clusters present a major challenge to facilities although better functional efficiencies are often gained. By decentralizing staff and services and giving staff members quick access to utilities, a cluster layout can make employees more productive and the delivery of care can be improved. Small nurse-aide stations—generally no more than a desk and chair—enable the staff to be in close proximity to residents, allowing for prompt attention to their needs. In Figure 5-2, each of the three clusters has its own nurse-aide station. The self-contained clusters also have their own bathing rooms, linen closets, and soiled utility closets. Staff members can function more efficiently, because this arrangement shortens walking distances and saves time. Services are brought to each cluster, instead of transporting residents to the nursing station, dining room, or therapy room (Dunkelman 1992). A group of permanent caregivers assigned to each cluster can also provide opportunities for interaction and bonding between caregivers and residents.

Nested Single Rooms

To counter the high cost of constructing private rooms, the architectural firm of Engelbrecht & Griffin (now named EGA, PC) pioneered the design of nested single rooms. Cost is conserved by efficient use of space. Although nested rooms are much smaller than regular rooms, they are self-contained bedrooms with their own private half-bathrooms that have a toilet and a sink (Figure 5-3). Nested single rooms offer privacy, and when they are placed in a cluster setting, they can also provide opportunities for socializing through "neighborhood living" arrangements (Figure 5-4). Easy access to common lounge areas in the vicinity of the rooms encourages residents to get out of their rooms to meet and converse with familiar neighbors, and provides a comfortable setting for visiting with family and friends.

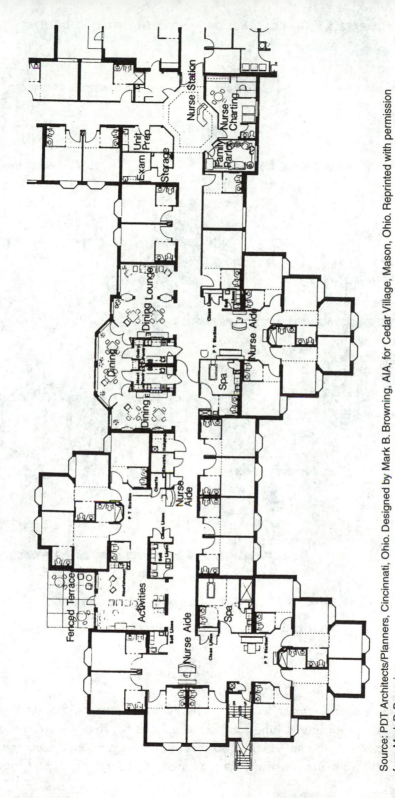

Source: PDT Architects/Planners, Cincinnati, Ohio. Designed by Mark B. Browning, AIA, for Cedar Village, Mason, Ohio. Reprinted with permission from Mark B. Browning.

FIGURE 5-2 27-Bed Wing Plan in a Cluster Arrangement of Private Rooms

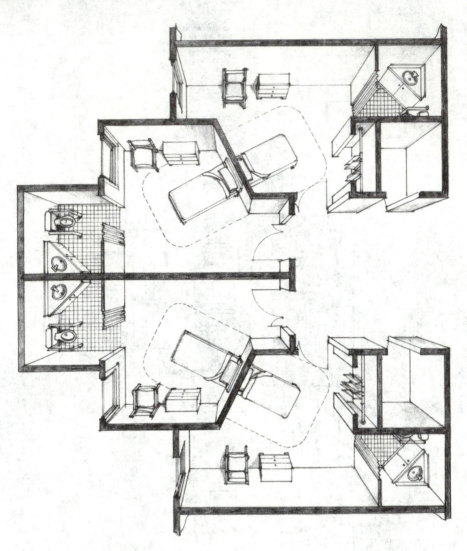

Source: EGA, P.C. "Designs for Living." Reprinted with permission from EGA, P.C.

FIGURE 5-3 Overhead One-Point Interior Perspective of Nested Rooms

Safety

Safety is a paramount concern in all living environments. But safety is especially important in long-term care facilities because these facilities house residents who have various degrees of disability. In building design, safety requirements are primarily governed by federal, state, and local

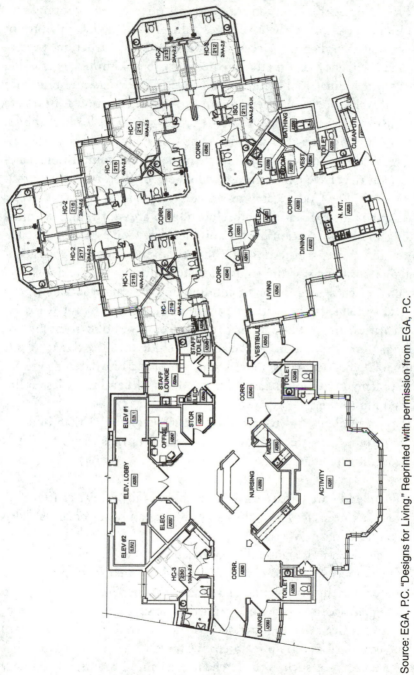

Source: EGA, P.C. "Designs for Living." Reprinted with permission from EGA, P.C.

FIGURE 5-4 Partial Floor Plan of Cluster Scheme

codes and regulations. Among these, the Life Safety Code of the National Fire Protection Association (an international private non-profit agency) provides the most comprehensive set of rules. The Code has the force of law; so total compliance is necessary. It addresses construction, protection, and occupancy features that are necessary to minimize danger to life from fire, including smoke, fumes, or panic. Fire barriers; fire resistance ratings of walls, doors, and ceilings; and other construction features are minutely detailed in the Code. Flame-retardant standards for furnishings, curtains, and upholstery are specified. The Code requires that waste baskets and trash cans used in the facility be made of non-combustible materials or that they have Underwriters Laboratory or Factory Mutual product markings. The Code establishes criteria for means of egress, as well as written plans for evacuation and relocation to areas of refuge within a building and for evacuation from a building. The Code specifies installation, maintenance, and testing of safety equipment such as emergency generators, sprinkler systems, smoke detectors, fire alarms, fire doors, and exit signs. It sets standards for air conditioning, heating, ventilation, and electrical systems. It also outlines minimum requirements for fire drills that facilities must conduct on a regular basis. Publications by the National Fire Protection Association include a Life Safety Code Handbook, which contains not only the text of the Life Safety Code but also supplementary interpretations in the form of commentaries, examples, and illustrations.

Safety of residents is determined by many factors other than building requirements. These are common safety considerations that staff members must remember at all times:

- The elderly are particularly vulnerable to falls. Great caution and vigilance needs to be exercised around wet floors, power cords, fallen objects, and throw rugs.
- Potential hazards should be eliminated or closely monitored. Access to products such as drugs, lotions, and ointments on medication and treatment carts should be adequately supervised. Patients could also gain access to other unattended toxic substances, such as cleaning chemicals left unattended on housekeeping carts, or sharp objects, such as certain maintenance tools.
- Access to areas such as the kitchen, mechanical rooms, and laundry are generally prohibited. However, kitchen and laundry areas can provide stimulating and meaningful engagement for some patients,

including those with dementia. With some supervision, cooking or laundry activities can add to patient's quality of life, particularly when smaller kitchenettes are included in the facility's design.

Not all nursing homes are located in safe neighborhoods. The administrator must evaluate external security concerns, which include protecting residents and their property from intruders. To the extent that patients can feel safe and secure, they can choose to spend time indoors and outdoors.

Accessibility and Wayfinding

Nursing home buildings and facilities must be accessible by individuals with disabilities. A **disability** can be a physical or mental impairment that substantially limits one or more major life activities. Accessibility for disabled people is required under the Americans with Disabilities Act (ADA) of 1990. The legislation is a general civil rights law designed to protect the rights of handicapped people in all aspects of their lives, including employment, recreation, and their use of buildings and facilities. The ADA also covers access to transportation and communication. ADA prohibits discrimination in public accommodations (i.e., businesses open to the public) on the basis of disability. Although the law does not specifically mention nursing facilities, health care establishments fall within the category of public accommodation. The law requires that certain adaptations, whenever necessary be made to provide access by the disabled to such public accommodations. For example, there should be no architectural barriers that might prevent access to the building from sidewalks and parking areas. Inside the building, barriers to accessibility should also be removed. Examples of things a facility can do to make its services accessible include positioning telephones, water coolers, and vending machines so that they are easy to reach and use; installing elevator control buttons with raised markings; using flashing fire alarm lights; installing raised toilet seats and grab bars in the bathrooms, and allowing enough room to maneuver a wheelchair; and avoiding high-pile carpeting that makes steering a wheelchair difficult.

The ADA also requires facilities to provide auxiliary aids for effective communication. Such aids include interpreters, telecommunication devices for the deaf, audio recordings, and large-print books and publications. However, the facility is not required to provide personal devices and services such as eyeglasses and hearing aids (American Association of

Retired Persons, undated). Any segregation of patients within the facility should be based on clinical factors, not on a person's disability, because segregation based solely on disability is discriminatory. Another law, the Fair Housing Amendments Act of 1988, prohibits disability-based discrimination in public and private living quarters. The American National Standards Institute (ANSI) has published detailed design specifications for accessibility (see ANSI 1986).

Due to a decline of various senses, residents in nursing homes are often susceptible to disorientation. Sameness and repetition—similar layouts, regular pattern of doors, and similar furniture throughout a facility—are the common sources of disorientation (Drew 1992). **Wayfinding** is the term used to describe features that can help people find their way through a large institution with relative ease. Orientation involves much more than use of signs. In addition to clear and readable signage, wayfinding can be facilitated by using a variety of means such as employing different color schemes and patterns in different sections of the facility; color-coding handrails; varying furniture styles; varying layout and arrangement; using pictures, photographs, tapestry, hanging quilts, and window displays; and placing public accessories such as telephones and water coolers in planned locations. Pathways for wandering, residential kitchens and laundries, and contained outdoor gardens are particularly helpful in caring for patients with dementia (Regnier 1998). On the other hand, doors leading to utility rooms and areas not meant for residents should be painted to blend with the adjacent walls.

Positive Stimulation and Distraction

In long-term care facilities, chronic understimulation and lack of positive distraction for patients can pose a substantial threat to wellness (Ulrich 1995). A nursing facility should be organized to function efficiently but design and décor should also promote health by creating physical surroundings that are psychologically and emotionally supportive for patients, visitors, and staff members. Supportive surroundings help reduce stress.

A psychologically supportive environment—also called an enhanced environment—is one that provides a moderate degree of positive stimulation and distraction. If the degree of stimulation caused by sounds, intense lighting, bold colors, etc., is too high, the effect can be quite stressful. On the other hand, prolonged exposure to low levels of environ-

mental stimulation can lead to boredom, negative feelings, and depression. In the absence of positive distractions, patients begin to focus on their own problems and end up increasing their level of stress. Positive distractions elicit good feelings, hold attention, and generate interest. Happy faces, laughter, people passing by, pets, fish in aquariums, birds, flowers, trees, plants, water, pleasant aromas, and soothing music can all be positive distractions. Negative distractions, on the other hand, are stressors. They simply assert their unwanted presence because it is difficult to ignore them. Visual stimulation from pictures, artwork, and television-watching can be positive for patients, but abstract art and uncontrolled loud noise from television are negative distractions. Other loud sounds, such as frequent paging over the intercom, are also distressing. Modern wireless communication devices, such as portable pagers, reduce institutional noises and enhance staff efficiency.

Aesthetics and Comfort[1]

Light and color play a role in more than just the illumination and aesthetics of a facility. They also influence patients' sleep, wakefulness, emotions, and health. The proper aesthetics are necessary to promote a sense of well-being, but aesthetically appealing surroundings are not necessarily comfortable. Aesthetics and comfort must be integrated.

Lighting

Natural sunlight is known to have positive effects on overall health. Facility design should incorporate as much natural lighting as possible, while also incorporating artificial light. Patios and porches provide residents with a place to be outdoors and enjoy direct sunlight. Windows, skylights, atriums, and greenhouse windows can be used to bring some of the natural daylight indoors. Low windows in patient rooms, lounges, and corridors allow residents to see the exterior grounds from their beds and wheelchairs. Window treatments should be used to regulate sunlight and minimize glare. Horizontal mini-blinds are generally preferable to vertical blinds, but light-filtering pleated shades are considered even better. Valances can be added to create a homelike look.

---

[1]For much of the information in this section, the author is indebted to the excellent work by Elizabeth C. Brawley 1997. See References.

Lighting needs of the elderly are quite different from those of younger people. As their sight and visual acuity decline, the elderly require higher levels of illumination; glare must be minimized, however, because many patients are not able to modify their environment to avoid glare. Poor lighting and glare can lead to depression, agitation, confusion, and falls. A facility can ensure proper lighting for patients and also enhance the homelike feel by using chandeliers, wall sconces, recessed lighting, table- and floor-lamps, and other light fixtures. In resident rooms, night-lights are essential. Along with clear pathways to the toilet, night-lights can facilitate safe trips to the bathroom and help patients avoid falls.

Color

Colors can help lift spirits and create cheerful and soothing environments. Colors used in health care settings have changed dramatically in recent years. Traditional colors such as white, bold yellow, beige, and green are no longer considered appropriate. More pleasing and stimulating colors have now become popular, colors such as soft apricot, peach, salmon, coral, soft yellow-orange, and a variety of earth-colored tones. Patterns and colors in wallcoverings and decorative borders can liven up some otherwise unexciting areas. Bedrooms, bathrooms, dining rooms, living rooms, and alcoves are all appropriate places where wallcovering can enhance residential quality. Coated wallcoverings can be used in areas such as hallways, where soiling is a serious problem. Handrails are necessary in hallways and other areas, but with a natural wood finish, they help maintain the residential look.

Colors are also used to promote safety. Aging reduces a person's ability to distinguish colors. To compensate for this reduced visual function, high-contrast colors should be used. For example, the color of grab bars in the toilet should contrast sharply with the color of the wall, to ensure maximum visibility. Countertop colors should stand out strongly from those of floors. For many nursing home residents, being able to use the toilet may depend on being able to locate it. In a totally white bathroom, some patients will find it difficult to distinguish the toilet from the floor or the adjacent wall. Colored toilet seats create visible contrasts against the surroundings and can facilitate locating the toilet. Conversely, a colored wall can provide visual contrast against a white toilet. For patients with Alzheimer's, however, sharp color contrasts and patterns can be disturbing. Pastel colors tend to work best for these patients (Kretschmann 1995).

Furnishings

Carpeting adds warmth and softens sounds. It also provides cushioning against falls and can prevent serious fractures of the hip or wrist. Today's high-performance carpets, which are resistant to stains and odors, are also cost-effective. New carpets are treated with a vinyl moisture barrier and an antimicrobial coating (Yarme and Yarme 2001). Proper installation and regular maintenance can make carpeting last for several years. Of course, carpeting is not appropriate for all areas in the building. Slip resistant tile is by far the most widely used flooring material. Resilient flooring with low sheen can be used in certain high-use areas without creating an institutional appearance. For example, these hard-surface floorings also come in beautiful wood-grain patterns that add a homelike touch. Also available are new soft-surface floorings that are made of easy-to-maintain sheet vinyl material with a dense, soft, carpet-like surface and a cushioned backing. These materials have been tested to ensure that they reduce injuries from falls (Yarme and Yarme 2001). Highly-polished and buffed surfaces are not recommended for the elderly, because they produce glare, appear wet or slick, and can be a source of anxiety and confusion.

A variety of furniture is now available that is specifically designed for long-term care facilities. Lounge chairs, sofas, and rocking chairs can add charm and variety as well as comfort. Use of upholstered furniture has actually become quite common. Some manufacturers are producing foam cushions that are soft enough to be comfortable and yet firm enough for residents to rise easily from chairs and sofas (Child 1999). Brawley (1997) comments on several enhancements in high-tech finishing of upholstery fabrics. These include soil- and stain-resistant finishes, lamination with vinyl, fluid barriers, and anti-microbial finishes. For nursing home use, these fabrics must also be flame-retardant. "Super fabrics," such as Crypton, have built-in stain and moisture resistance and have been tested for fire and microbial resistance. These new fabrics have replaced vinyl coverings for chairs and sofas, and a range of colors, textures, and patterns are now available to enhance the residential environment in nursing facilities.

CONCLUSION

The delivery of long-term care in the nation's nursing facilities continues to evolve as the holistic model of health care delivery transcends the sick-role

model as the basis for delivering care. As the sharp differences between acute care and long-term care are recognized and acknowledged, innovative approaches increasingly are being used to integrate the clinical organization of care with its social aspects and residential features. In fact, the residents' quality of life cannot be maximized without integrating a number of factors that include clinical care, an environment that respects and promotes the personal domain, opportunities for compatible social relationships, and various aesthetic features that enhance the residential environment, with due regard for safety and positive stimulation. The next chapter describes some emerging concepts that in some ways build upon the concepts discussed in this chapter and in other ways go a step beyond.

DISCUSSION QUESTIONS

1. What actions can a nursing home administrator take to integrate the clinical and social structures in a skilled nursing facility?

2. Discuss the integration of clinical, social, and residential elements necessary for creating a therapeutic environment for patients with Alzheimer's disease.

REFERENCES

Agich, G.J. 1995. Actual autonomy and long-term care decision making. In *Long-Term Care Decisions: Ethical and Conceptual Dimensions*, eds. L.B. McCullough and N.L. Wilson, 113–136. Baltimore: Johns Hopkins University Press.

American Association of Retired Persons. Undated. *ADA: Accessibility for Older Persons with Disabilities*. Washington, DC: AARP.

American National Standards Institute. 1986. *American National Standard for Buildings and Facilities: Providing Accessibility and Usability for Physically Handicapped People*. New York: ANSI.

Arras, J.D. 1995. Conflicting interests in long-term care decision making: Acknowledg-ing, Dissolving, and resolving conflicts. In L.B. McCullough and N.L. Wilson, eds. *Long-Term Care Decisions: Ethical and Conceptual Dimensions* (pp. 197–217). Baltimore: Johns Hopkins University Press.

Brawley, E.C. 1997. *Designing for Alzheimer's Disease: Strategies for Creating Better Care Environments*. New York: John Wiley & Sons, Inc.

Browning, M.B. 2003. Letter to the author dated August 18, 2003 on cluster design plan.

Brush, J.A., et al. 2002. Using the environment to improve intake for people with dementia. *Alzheimer's Care Quarterly* 3, no. 4: 330–338.

Chapman, S.A., et al. 2003. Client-centered, community-based care for frail seniors. *Health and Social Care in the Community* 11, no. 3: 253–261.

Child, M. 1999. Comfort is the key. *Nursing Homes Long Term Care Management* 48, no. 9: 61–62.

Cohen, U., and K. Day. 1993. *Contemporary Environments for People with Dementia*. Baltimore: The Johns Hopkins University Press.

Collopy, B.J. 1988. Autonomy in long-term care: some crucial distinctions. The *Gerontologist* 28 (supplement): 10–17.

Collopy, B.J. 1995. Safety and independence: Rethinking some basic concepts in long-term care. In L.B. McCullough and N.L. Wilson, eds. *Long-term care decisions: Ethical and conceptual dimensions* (pp. 137–152). Baltimore: Johns Hopkins University Press.

Drew, S.G. 1992. Designing for special needs of the elderly. In A. Bush-Brown, and D. Davis, eds. *Hospitable Design for Healthcare and Senior Communities*. New York: Van Nostrand Reinhold.

Dunkelman, D.M. 1992. Individualized cluster. In A. Bush-Brown, and D. Davis, eds. *Hospitable Design for Healthcare and Senior Communities*. New York: Van Nostrand Reinhold.

Kane, R.A. 2001. Long-term care and a good quality of life: Bringing them closer together. *The Gerontologist* 41, no. 3: 293–304.

Kretschmann, A. 1995. Design touches to make the SCU a "home." *Nursing Homes Long Term Care Management* 44, no. 6: 31–34.

Kruzich, J.M. and W. Berg. 1985. Predictors of self-sufficiency for the mentally ill in long term care. *Community Mental Health Journal* 21 (3): 198–207.

National Center for Health Statistics. 2002. The national nursing home survey: 1999 summary. *Vital and Health Statistics*, series 13, no. 152. Hyattsville, MD: Department of Health and Human Services.

National Fire Protection Association. 2000. *Life Safety Code*. Quincy, MA: NFPA.

Nursing home architecture. 1997. *Contemporary Longterm Care* 20, no. 8: 43–44.

Parmelee, P.A., and M.P. Lawton. 1990. The design of special environments for the aged. In J.F. Birren, and W. Schaie, eds. *Handbook of the Psychology of Aging* (3rd ed.). New York: Academic Press.

Parsons, T. 1972. Definitions of health and illness in the light of American values and social structure. In *Patients, Physicians and Illness: A Sourcebook in Behavioral Science and Health*. 2nd ed., ed. E.G. Jaco. New York: Free Press.

Rader, J. 1991. Modifying the environment to decrease use of restraints. *Journal of Gerontological Nursing* 17, no. 2: 9–13.

Regnier, V. 1998. Look homeward. *Contemporary Longterm Care* 21, no. 3: 92–94.

Scarry, E. 1985. *The Body in Pain: The Making and Unmaking of the World*. New York: Oxford University Press.

Schwarz, B. 1996. *Nursing Home Design: Consequences of Employing the Medical Model*. New York: Garland Publishing Inc.

Shi, L., and D.A. Singh. 1998. *Delivering Health Care in America: A Systems Approach*. Gaithersburg, MD: Aspen Publishers, Inc.

Ulrich, R.S. 1995. Effects of healthcare interior design on wellness: Theory and recent scientific research. In S.O. Marberry, ed. *Innovations in Healthcare Design*. New York: Van Nostrand Reinhold.

Westin, A. 1967. *Privacy and Freedom*. New York: Atheneum Press.

Yarme, J., and H. Yarme. 2001. Flooring and safety. *Nursing Homes Long Term Care Management* 50, no. 10: 82–83.

CHAPTER 6

Nursing Home Evolution and Cultural Change

LEARNING MODULES

1. Recognition of a slowly occurring cultural and social change that calls for lifestyle and quality-of-life changes in nursing homes.
2. History of nursing homes. The social-welfare function of the poorhouses and poor farms of the colonial period.
3. The Social Security Act and government assistance for living in private old-age homes. The closing of poorhouses and poor farms. Absence of regulatory standards for old-age homes.
4. The construction boom, direct reimbursement, and nursing home licensing during the 1950s. Hospital infrastructure adapted for nursing home construction and clinical care. Issues of poor quality of care emerge.
5. Industry growth fueled by Medicare and Medicaid, without regulations until 1974. Regulatory standards focus on the clinical infrastructure. The medical model is firmly entrenched in nursing home care.
6. Social and cultural change that began during the 1990s. Alternatives to the medical model based on the philosophy

continues

of person-centered care in personal communities. Theoretical foundations for the alternative models.

7. The Eden Alternative, its main concepts, and steps toward edenizing. The Eden environment and its likely benefits. Management and organizational implications of edenizing. Outcomes of edenizing. Deterrents to edenizing.

8. The Green House architecture and organization. Empowerment and delivery of care in the Green House setting. Cultural protocols for Green Houses.

9. The grassroots movement called the Pioneer Network. Its philosophy and methods for bringing about cultural change.

10. Sensory stimulation through Snoezelen. Basic approach of the Wellspring Model.

Nursing home design, its residential and social features, and methods of care delivery have followed the general evolutionary course of health care delivery and its financing and regulation. As hospitals in the United States developed along with the advancements in medical science and technology, the poorhouses of the 18th and 19th centuries, which were institutions of social welfare, were abandoned in favor of a health-care model. Evolving from the poorhouses, nursing homes also became health care institutions. The predominant hospital model influenced the traditional nursing home design, characterized by long corridors, shared occupancy, and large cafeteria-style dining rooms. When government financing for hospital and nursing home construction became available during the 1950s, a construction boom got underway, but for lack of an alternative design, nursing homes again relied on institutional architecture. Licensing and certification rules further reinforced the hospital design, because the nursing home was viewed as a place where convalescent treatment would continue following discharge from hospitals, as laid out in Medicare rules. Thus, by default, hospital design was adapted for nursing home construction. Clinical set-ups and processes in nursing homes have also followed the hospital-based **medical model**, with central nursing stations, buzzers and call signals, noisy shower and bathing rooms, lack of privacy, sched-

uled routines, and hallways cluttered with medication carts, soiled linen hampers, food carts, housekeeping carts and similar items.

During the 1980s, construction of new nursing facilities and renovation of existing ones began emphasizing the socio-residential and aesthetic features discussed in Chapter 5. These changes were triggered mainly by market competition, which created the need to attract new patients to keep the beds filled and prompted the efforts by nursing facilities to cater to the private-pay clientele. Most facilities operating today have taken at least some steps toward creating homelike and social environments that are better than those found in older facilities. Also, long-term care policy since the 1980s has favored the development of community-based options for care, mainly because these alternatives are cheaper than nursing homes. Medicare rules were relaxed to qualify a growing elderly population for home health services. Care in the patient's home was a cheaper alternative for Medicare, and the home setting was preferred by most patients needing care. On the other hand, private-paying patients have found the residential and social lifestyles in many assisted living facilities to be much more appealing than skilled nursing facilities.

The proliferation of these new choices and alternatives to traditional nursing home care have affected people's expectations, at least to some extent, and a cultural and social change is underway, with clients demanding that nursing home environments be made more appealing and less institutionalized. A move away from the medical model, and toward a more holistic socio-residential model that allows individuals to pursue their own lifestyles—rather than be governed by established routines and schedules—is what we find today in nursing home evolution. As part of this evolutionary process, long-term care vocabulary has also changed, as reference to patients has switched from "inmates" to "patients" to "residents" to "elders."

From the experiences of placing their own parents in nursing facilities, middle-aged adults who make up the baby-boom generation do not wish the same quality of life for themselves later in life. However, the nursing home industry has been slow in adopting the socio-residential model, and most nursing facilities continue to operate primarily as clinical institutions. Although it is too early to tell whether the emerging concepts, discussed later in this chapter, will become mainstream, nursing homes, as we know them today, are likely to undergo some major transformations. This chapter provides insights into how external factors can be instrumental in directing an entire industry to adopt new attitudes and vision.

EVOLUTION OF THE NURSING HOME INDUSTRY

The evolution of nursing homes can be traced through five distinct stages. The progression is marked by facilities that served a welfare function, federal old-age assistance, rapid growth of a new industry in which nursing homes adopted hospital architecture and methods of care delivery, regulations to monitor quality of care, and grassroots movements calling for a cultural change.

Stage I—County-operated Poorhouses

Historically, the origin of nursing homes can be traced back to the American poorhouses (also known as almshouses) of colonial times. The **poorhouse** was not a nursing home or a hospital in the true sense, but an institution where the destitute of society, including the elderly, the homeless, orphans, the ill, and the disabled, were given food and shelter. Conditions were often squalid. In many ways, a poorhouse was an infirmary, an old-age facility, a mental asylum, a homeless shelter, and an orphanage all rolled into one institution. Some basic nursing care was delivered to the sick, but the poorhouse was a far cry from today's health care facilities. Because most people received health care in their own homes, and physicians sometimes traveled long distances to make house calls in rural America, the main purpose of poorhouses was to "put away" the annoying and disruptive elements of society.

In some rural communities, poor farms (or "pauper farms") were established to house and support paupers at public expense. The following account provides a glimpse into the tightly-regimented routines practiced in a poor farm established in 1854 and run by Ramsey County in Minnesota (Ramsey County 2003):

> ". . . the matron was . . . largely concerned with the rules she found
> necessary for her institution. Inmates were required to take a weekly
> bath. Once a week clean clothes were issued upon the return of the
> soiled. At this time the weekly issue of tobacco or snuff was given out
> to the men. Women received lemon drops. A bell was rung 15 minutes
> before meals so that all may prepare themselves. No talking was
> allowed in the dining room and all were required to leave their place at
> the table in an orderly manner."

A little over a century later, in 1957, this poor farm was moved to a different location and was reestablished as the Ramsey County Nursing Home, licensed for 285 beds.

These poorhouses also functioned as "hospitals" in most parts of the country until the latter part of the 19th century when hospitals were built, and when separate institutions called old-age homes were established for the elderly (Brown 2003).

Stage II—Private Old-Age Homes

In the second evolutionary phase, elder-care transitioned from county poorhouses to private old-age homes or boarding homes for the elderly. These latter institutions emerged after the Social Security Act was passed in August 1935 under President Franklin D. Roosevelt. The Act provided matching grants to the states for Old Age Assistance (OAA). But people living in public institutions, such as poorhouses, were not eligible for the payments because the government purposely intended to discourage the use of poorhouses because of their ill repute. Consequently, private for-profit institutions for nursing care developed so people could move into them and still collect the OAA payments. At the same time, poorhouses and poor farms closed down in large numbers. Private operators acquired various types of buildings—old schools, hotels, and dormitories—and converted them into old-age homes. At this time, building standards and oversight for care delivery were practically non-existent. The boarding homes provided basic nursing care and supervision, much as today's personal care homes do, and the very sick stayed in hospitals. The typical length of stay in hospitals was much longer than it is today. But the nursing home industry was born. It would go through rapid expansion and take on its current form during the next two stages, described below.

Stage III—Nursing Home Construction Boom

In the third stage, direct reimbursement from public funds became available to providers. In August 1950, a National Conference on Aging was convened by the Federal Security Agency, and President Harry Truman signed the 1950 Social Security Amendments, which expanded coverage under the old-age assistance program. The law also required the states to license nursing care facilities. In 1954, during Dwight Eisenhower's presidency, Public Law 482 was passed; this law expanded federal aid for the construction of hospitals, but also provided funds to build other health care facilities such as facilities for the chronically ill, nursing homes, diagnostic and treatment facilities, and rehabilitation facilities. The Hospital

Survey and Construction Act, commonly known as Hill-Burton, had been passed earlier in 1946 to build new hospitals across the country. Now government financing was made available to build nursing homes under both for-profit and non-profit types of ownership. During the late 1950s, not only did the government become the primary payer for nursing home services, it also fueled a nursing home construction boom with legislation in 1958 and 1959 that authorized the Small Business Administration and the Federal Housing Administration to aid the construction of for-profit nursing homes.

By this time, hospitals functioned as the primary institutional core of medical care delivery. The hospital layout and clinical arrangements were adapted for nursing home architecture. Building codes for nursing home construction were also adapted from hospitals. As this relatively new industry underwent rapid growth, concerns about inadequate patient care, noncompliance with staffing and building-code requirements, and financial irregularities also began to emerge, soon reaching scandalous proportions.

Stage IV—Explosive Industry Growth, Financing, and Regulations

The fourth stage of the development of nursing homes was marked by an explosive growth of nursing homes, increased financing, and rigid regulations soon after the Medicare and Medicaid programs were created in 1965. Thanks to these two landmark programs, the number of nursing homes in the U.S. jumped from 9,582 in 1960 to 23,000 in 1970, and the number of nursing home patients increased from 290,000 (1.8% of the population aged 65 and over) in 1960 to 900,000 (4.5% of the population aged 65 and over) in 1970 (U.S. Senate Special Committee on Aging 1974). Total nursing home expenditures escalated from $0.8 billion in 1960 to $4.2 billion in 1970 (Department of Health and Human Services 1999, p. 289). Figure 6-1 illustrates this remarkable growth in nursing homes, patients, and expenditures. According to these data, over the entire decade of 1960-1970, the number of nursing homes, number of patients, and total dollars spent increased by 140%, 210%, and 425% respectively. The massive infusion of dollars into the nursing home industry, which already had acquired a tarnished image, prompted regulations to hold individual nursing homes accountable for meeting minimum

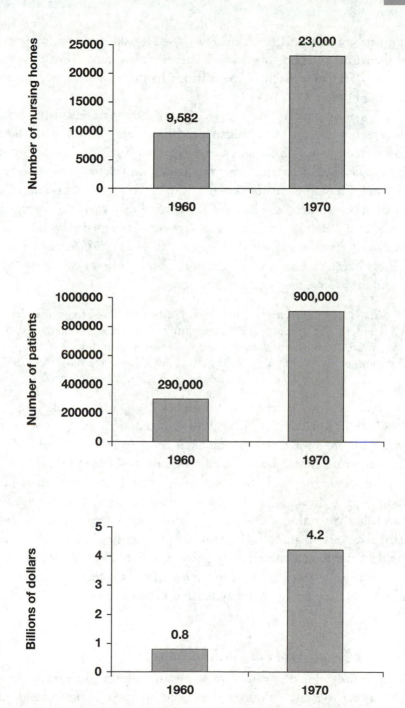

FIGURE 6-1 Growth in the Number of Nursing Homes, Patients, and Expenditures: 1960–1970

standards of care. In 1968, Congress passed legislation, commonly known as the Moss Amendments (named after Senator Frank Moss), that paved the way for comprehensive regulations to improve care in the nation's nursing homes.

It was not until 1974, during Richard Nixon's administration, that final regulations for skilled nursing facilities were promulgated, and their enforcement began in earnest. Compliance with standards such as staffing levels, staff qualifications, fire-safety codes, and delivery of services now became a requirement for certification. Again, these regulations had a medical orientation, emphasizing the clinical infrastructure for the delivery of care. Yet despite widespread adoption of the medical model, quality of care in general remained very poor. In late 1974, Senator Frank E. Moss, chair of the subcommittee on long-term care of the Senate Special Committee on Aging, exclaimed:

> "Laws have been passed; national commitments have been made; declarations of high purpose have been uttered at national conferences and by representatives of the nursing home industry. But for all of that, long-term care for older Americans stands today as the most troubled, and troublesome, component of our entire health care system."

Later reforms, notably the Omnibus Budget Reconciliation Act of 1987 (OBRA-87), called for a certification and survey process that was focused more on patient care outcomes and patient rights and less on the infrastructure of care, but the medical model embedded in the delivery of conventional long-term care has persisted. While the living environment in nursing homes has been subject to rules and regulations, no one can be sure what it would have been like without those regulations. However, OBRA-87 also placed much emphasis on quality of life, with enhanced resident rights such as privacy, dignity, and autonomy. A clearer recognition and understanding of these rights may have been at least partially responsible for paving the way for the next stage of cultural and social change.

Stage V—Cultural and Social Change

Despite upgraded décor and furnishings in many facilities, people in need of long-term care continue to dread the prospect of being in a nursing home. Senator Moss had raised a challenging question: "Why should placement in a nursing home be the occasion for despair and desperation,

when it should be simply a sensible accommodation to need?" For years, quality improvement efforts had been directed toward medical and nursing care, and dietary, social, and activity programs, but little was done to address the problems of dependency, boredom, and loneliness among nursing home residents.

Recreation and activity programs make a difference for many nursing home residents, but physical and mental impairments prevent many others from active participation in these programs. Besides, most organized programs occupy people for only short periods during the day; for the bulk of the time the surroundings in typical nursing facilities provide little stimulation. In response to these conditions, some innovative steps are being undertaken to transform both the physical structure and the living environment in nursing homes. The next generation of facilities is likely to be designed around personal communities, rather than traditional wards and wings. The major movements now underway to brighten up nursing home environments are discussed in the remainder of this chapter.

EMERGING ALTERNATIVES TO THE MEDICAL MODEL

The emerging alternatives are by no means a substitute for the medical, nursing, and rehabilitation therapies most skilled care patients need. These alternatives promote an environment based on the philosophy of 'person-centered' or 'client-centered' care, in which care delivery is congruent with the values, needs, and preferences of care recipients (Eales et al. 2001). In **person-centered care**, health care professionals empower the residents to assert their rights and preferences. This empowerment is achieved through a bonding between residents and the caregivers who place supreme value on listening to the resident's preferences while offering professional advice and instruction on the risks and benefits of the choices the residents make. The resident's individual autonomy, the dignity of choice, and the freedom to take some risks are respected. The environment is built around friendly communities, private spaces, and family places in which each resident can live a life with the maximum possible independence and self-reliance. These personal communities are staffed by familiar caregivers who are there to help the residents find meaning, value, and joy. "These homes are filled with greenery and flowers, with

birds and fish and various furry and loveable friends, with baking and tasting and eating and sharing, with grandchildren and cousins and friends and neighbors" (Action Pact 2001). In such holistic philosophy of care, the environment is viewed as a "silent partner" in caregiving because it is a contributing factor to the healing process (Noell 1995).

Theoretical Foundations

Creation of enhanced or enriched environmental settings finds support in two complementary theories: biophilia framework and theory of thriving.

Biophilia Framework

E.O. Wilson, a biologist, coined the term **biophilia** for the human propensity to affiliate with other life forms. In short, it describes the human tendency to pay attention to, affiliate with, and respond positively to nature (Wilson 1984). People not only have an inborn biophiliac tendency to relate to animals and to natural settings, but people's relationship with nature is essential to their thriving. Plants, animals, water, and soil are the most common elements of the natural environment (Wohlwill 1983). Based on an integrative review of the literature, Jones and Haight (2002) reported consistent findings that interactions with the natural environment, which can be experienced both indoors and outdoors, produce beneficial effects in human beings, such as positive mood and mental restoration.

Theory of Thriving

Thriving means living life to the full. It is also a growth process that occurs as a result of humans interacting in a symbiotic relationship with their environments to enhance their physical, mental, social, and spiritual well-being. According to Haight and colleagues (2002), the integrative model of thriving includes three elements (1) the person, (2) the human environment comprising family, friends, caregivers, and others, and (3) the nonhuman environment comprising the physical and ecological surroundings of the person. Thriving occurs when the relationship among the three entities is mutually engaging, supportive, and harmonious. Conversely, a failure to thrive occurs when discordance exists among the person, the human environment, and the non-human environment. When thriving occurs, certain critical attributes are noticeable in the person: social connectedness, finding meaning in life, adaptation, and positive cognitive/affective function.

Applying the Theories

The two theories are applied within a holistic framework, in which the person or the patient is the central figure (Figure 6-2). Therefore, thriving is not entirely a function of external stimulus. Thriving also requires solitude, reflection, introspection, spiritual contemplation, study, and a sense of one's individuality and self-worth. But the environment must facilitate these inner pursuits by making the person feel secure, by allowing the individual to exercise autonomy, and by providing privacy, as discussed in Chapter 5. Also, external stimuli are not always to be equated with action and interaction with the external environment. Contemplation and inner reflection often occur in a passive relationship with serene natural surroundings. On the other hand, thriving also requires active engagement in meaningful social relationships, caring for live plants or animals, lending a helping hand to a fellow patient, playing with children, or working on hobbies such as gardening or woodworking. In its ultimate sense, thriving is achieved when a person feels a deep sense of belonging to and connection with the physical environment comprised of people and things, and also feels a closeness to a Supreme Being or the spiritual realm, in accordance with one's own belief system.

PRACTICAL MODELS OF ENHANCED ENVIRONMENTS

As discussed in Chapter 5, architectural designs such as the cluster arrangement and nested single rooms help create personal spaces and neighborhood communities, even in very large facilities. But more recent innovations in design go beyond cluster set-ups by establishing smaller cottage-like structures spread across a campus (Figure 6-3).

The Eden Alternative

Of all the various movements advocating cultural change in long-term care facilities, the Eden Alternative is perhaps the best known. In the early 1990s, Dr. William Thomas, while working as a physician in nursing homes, undertook a pilot project sponsored by the State of New York. Working with the staff in an 80-bed nursing home, which served mostly patients with dementia, Dr. Thomas developed some new ideas and a set

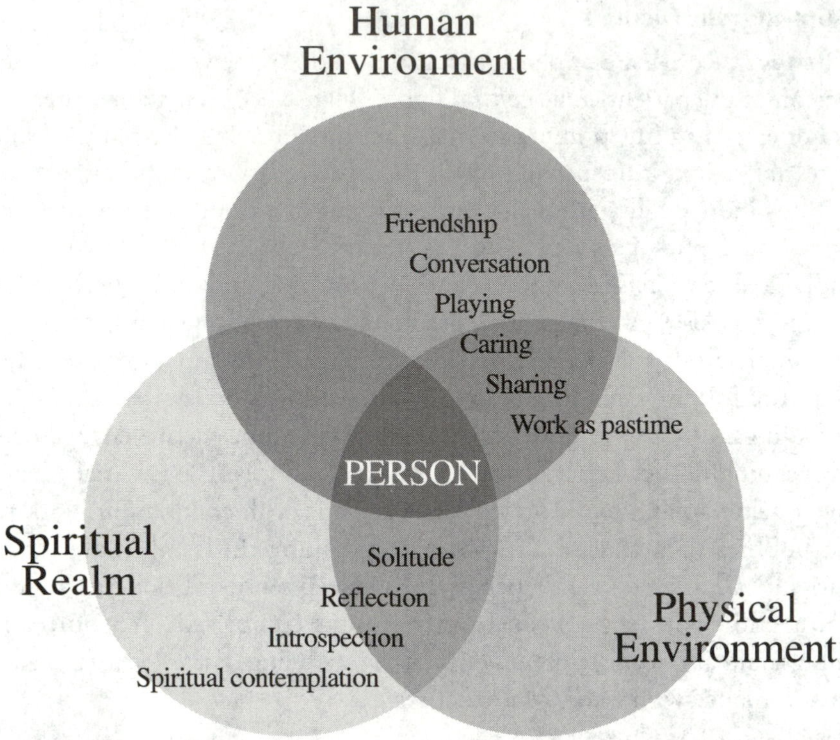

Human Environment

Friendship

Conversation

Playing

Caring

Sharing

Work as pastime

PERSON

Spiritual Realm

Solitude

Reflection

Introspection

Spiritual contemplation

Physical Environment

FIGURE 6-2 Holistic Environment for Thriving

of principles for creating a garden-like environment. As an advocate for change, Dr. Thomas explained:

> "I want an alternative to the institution. The best alternative I can think of is a garden. I believe when we make a place that's worthy of our elders, we make a place that enriches all of our lives—caregivers, family members, and elders alike. So the Eden Alternative provides a reinterpretation of the environment elders live in, going from an institution to a garden...There are kids running around and playing. There are dogs and cats and birds, and there are gardens and plants. I want people to think that this can't be a nursing home. Which it isn't—it's an alternative to a nursing home...The future of caregiving belongs to people and organizations who can dream new dreams about how to care for our elders" (McLeod 2002, 14–15).

The **Eden Alternative**, a trademark of its founding organization, entails viewing the surroundings in facilities as habitats for human beings rather than as facilities for the frail and elderly, as well as applying the lessons of nature in creating vibrant and vigorous settings. It is based on the

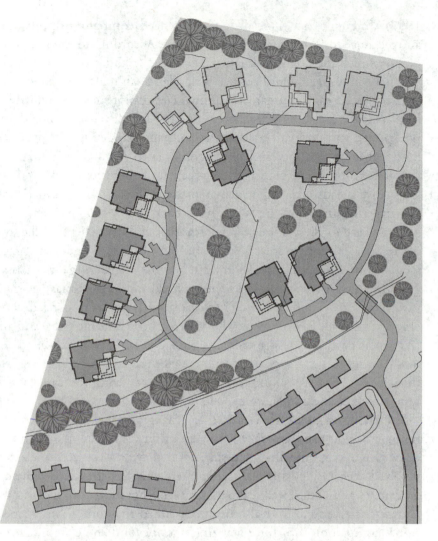

Source: The McCarty Company. Schematic Site Plan: Greenhouse Project, Methodist Senior Services, Tupelo, Mississippi. Reprinted with permission from the McCarty Company (courtesy of Stephen Ladd).

FIGURE 6-3 Overhead Perspective of Green Houses (small residential structures spread across a campus)

belief that the companionship of pets, the opportunity to give meaningful care to other living creatures, and the spontaneity that marks an enlivened environment have therapeutic values (The Eden Alternative 2002). One of the main objectives of the Eden Alternative is to banish from the lives of nursing home residents the loneliness, helplessness, and boredom that Dr. Thomas has called "the three plagues of nursing homes" (Bruck

1997). To counteract these ills, residents need companionship, variety, and a chance to feel needed (Stermer 1998). According to the ten principles on which the Eden Alternative is founded (Exhibit 6-1) the antidote to loneliness is meaningful contact with plants, animals, and children, as well as easy access to human and animal companionship; the remedy for helplessness is giving as well as receiving care; and the cure for boredom is unexpected and unpredictable interactions and happenings in surroundings that deliver variety and spontaneity (Eden Annual 2003). Among methods to build relationships between staff members and residents, alternative means of healing such as massage therapy and aromatherapy are suggested, based on the belief that a back-rub or foot-rub may eliminate the need for sleep-inducing medications, and the belief that the smell of lavender or peppermint can have a calming effect. A one-year demonstration project in a nursing home studied the effects of gentle massage given by nursing assistants who were trained by a licensed massage therapist. The study found that after 12 weeks of therapy pain scores declined among the 59 elderly residents who suffered from chronic pain, and anxiety scores declined among residents with dementia who exhibited anxious or agitated behaviors. Seventy-one percent of the caregivers reported that this type of massage improved their ability to communicate with the residents (Sansone and Schmitt 2000).

Edenizing is the expression used for changing a nursing home's environment and its processes of care delivery by implementing the Eden principles. For a long time, many nursing homes have, at least to some extent, involved their residents in nature-oriented activities such as pet therapy, gardening, and nature walks. Programs in collaboration with local schools and day care centers have also been developed to promote intergenerational companionship. But edenizing goes beyond these steps. From a management and operational perspective, edenizing requires five main components, all based on empowering the residents and staff (Bell 2002):

- A change in management practices in which administrators and department managers start treating their staff as they want the staff members to treat the elders. There is no room for any practices that devalue workers, most of whom are women who typically earn just a little above the federal minimum wage.
- A decentralized management approach in which decision-making is taken back to the elders and to the families and caregivers, and these stakeholders are given a voice in the elders' daily routine and life.

EXHIBIT 6–1

The Eden Alternative Principles

1. The three plagues of loneliness, helplessness and boredom account for the bulk of suffering among our Elders.

2. An Elder-centered community commits to creating a Human Habitat where life revolves around close and continuing contact with plants, animals and children. It is these relationships that provide the young and old alike with a pathway to a life worth living.

3. Loving companionship is the antidote to loneliness. Elders deserve easy access to human and animal companionship.

4. An Elder-centered community creates opportunity to give as well as receive care. This is the antidote to helplessness.

5. An Elder-centered community imbues daily life with variety and spontaneity by creating an environment in which unexpected and unpredictable interactions and happenings can take place. This is the antidote to boredom.

6. Meaningless activity corrodes the human spirit. The opportunity to do things that we find meaningful is essential to human health.

7. Medical treatment should be the servant of genuine human caring, never its master.

8. An Elder-centered community honors its Elders by de-emphasizing top-down bureaucratic authority, seeking instead to place the maximum possible decision-making authority into the hands of the Elders or into the hands of those closest to them.

9. Creating an Elder-centered community is a never-ending process. Human growth must never be separated from human life.

10. Wise leadership is the lifeblood of any struggle against the three plagues. For it, there can be no substitute.

Source: The Eden Alternative, http://www.edenalt.com

- Committees consisting of residents, families, and frontline care-givers make most of the decisions (Pope 2000).
- Surroundings rich in plants, animals, and children. Involving the residents in the care of plants and animals, and in interaction with children such as playing with them, helping them color, or reading them stories, enriches everyone's lives. A facility can have an onsite child day care center, providing opportunities to integrate child care with the care of the elderly. Children playing with toys in the facility's living room, or playing outdoors on a swing and slide set add to variety and spontaneity.
- Organizational commitment to human growth through relationships in which even the frailest and most demented elders can grow, and those providing companionship to the elders can grow as well.

Actions by a few states, such as North Carolina and South Carolina, to establish coalitions promoting the Eden Alternative have legitimized the concept by establishing partnerships with the respective state's regulatory and public health agencies. Voluntary Regional Coordinators have also been appointed in various locations across the country, under the auspices of the Eden organization, to promote education about the Eden Alternative and create a registry program to recognize organizations that make a commitment to change. On the other hand, widespread adoption of the Eden principles by individual nursing homes has failed to materialize; only 300 to 400 facilities (2% or less) nationwide have edenized to date.

Published literature on the actual outcomes of edenizing is scant, but one unpublished study of five nursing homes in Texas concluded that adopting the Eden Alternative had decreased behavioral incidents by 60%, formation of pressure sores by 57%, prevalence of bed confinement by 25%, and use of restraints by 18%. Positive outcomes were also reported on increased occupancy (11%), reduced employee absenteeism (48%), and decreased worker injuries (11%) [Cerquone 2001]. Some individual nursing homes have also reported decreases in staff turnover as a result of edenizing. On the other hand, a peer-reviewed published study that compared an edenized facility with a control (non-edenized) facility, using indicators of residents' well-being measured at baseline and a year later, reported that the Eden site had significantly greater proportions of residents who had fallen, residents who were experiencing nutritional problems, and those who required hypnotic drug prescriptions. However,

because of a number of uncontrolled variables in the study, the authors concluded that quantitative measures suggested no major effects of the Eden intervention, but anecdotal qualitative information indicated that an extended period of implementation of edenizing may yield positive changes (Coleman et al. 2002). In short, at this time, scientific evidence in favor of the Eden Alternative remains inconclusive.

Edenizing may pose some risks in the form of allergies, injuries, and illnesses. **Zoonosis** is the transmittal of infections from vertebrate animals to humans. Examples of zoonotic diseases include dermatophytosis, psittacosis, bartonellosis, toxocariasis, pasturellosis, Q fever, and leptospirosis (Guay 2001). However, potential problems can be managed with appropriate veterinary care and infection-control practices.

Proponents of the Eden Alternative explain that their approach is not a quick-fix for serious problems. Not every facility should embark on making such changes. Acceptance of the Eden Alternative by staff members and their training are necessary prerequisites because, right off the bat, questions come up about the staff's extra responsibilities of caring for the pets and cleaning up after them. Particularly in unionized facilities where union-management contracts prescribe tasks and duties of staff members, edenizing can be challenging. Costs of training and implementation may be another deterrent: In 2000, the costs to implement the Eden Alternative were estimated to be $30,000 over two years (Reese 2000). Also, the quality of life in long-term care facilities can be improved in ways other than edenizing.

Compliance with regulatory standards is often a concern for those who manage such facilities. But residents have choices, and the right to decide what they think is best for them. As long as the facility documents residents' choices, it will be in compliance with regulatory standards (Pope 2000). Changing an organization's culture takes time, effort, and leadership skills. Implementing the Eden principles can take an estimated three to five years (Hannan and Schaeffer 2003).

The Green House Project

The founder of the Eden Alternative had envisioned edenizing as a neverending process. But, perhaps because of the inherent difficulties in initiating and maintaining the necessary changes in large institutional settings, the Eden model has not been widely adopted (Rabig 2003). An outgrowth of the Eden Alternative, and also a brainchild of Dr. Thomas', the

Green House Project takes edenizing a step further by revolutionizing the way in which nursing home services are organized and delivered in small-scale settings.

In the New York state pilot project described earlier, Dr. Thomas experimented with restructuring the caregiving staff into permanent care teams designed to serve a particular "neighborhood" of elders according to those elders' special needs. The teams, consisting of nurses, social workers, housekeepers, dietary employees, and members of the activities staff, tried to adapt the traditional large-scale caregiving approach for smaller groups of residents. Each team participated in extensive training in communication and problem-solving, and some teams eventually became responsible for scheduling their own hours of work (Hannan and Schaeffer 2003). In the Green House model, these organizational ideas are applied to physically distinct small-neighborhood architectural units. Also, unlike edenizing a large institutional structure, the Green House model relies more on natural outdoor activities, such as watching and feeding birds and squirrels, and less on indoor pets because the small design of the buildings allows ready access to the outdoors (Rebig 2003).

The term **Green House** stands for architectural renderings of small freestanding facilities, each designed to house just six to ten residents who live together in a home-like setting (Figure 6-4). The freestanding units are called Green Houses, which are supported by the traditional organization of a skilled nursing facility, in which functions such as accounting, billing, medical records, purchasing, plant maintenance, professional nursing, and therapy are located (Rabig and Thomas 2003). A handful of such small-scale projects have begun, and the first one in Tupelo, Mississippi opened its doors in June 2003.

Each Green House has self-contained private rooms that include a commode, a sink, and a shower. To accommodate even the frailest elders, rooms are equipped with ceiling lifts for transferring. The lift operates on a ceiling track that runs from the bed to the bathroom sink and commode. In some instances, these lifts can be operated independently by the residents.

Residents can bring their own furniture and they can choose their room's décor. The residential units are connected by short hallways to a central living room, open kitchen, and dining area. Other amenities include a spa room, laundry room, alcove, and storage space. The small

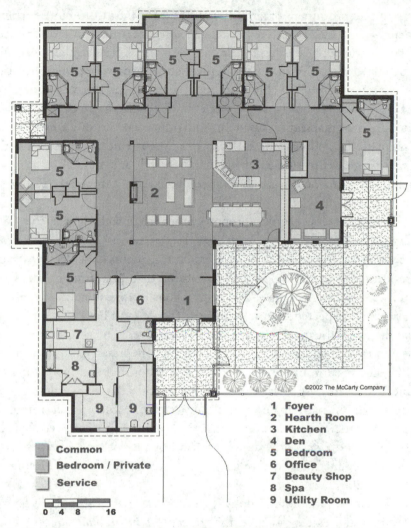

Source: The McCarty Company, Tupelo, Mississippi. Reprinted with permission from The McCarty Company (courtesy of Stephen Ladd).

FIGURE 6-4 10-Bed Skilled Nursing Green House (Methodist Senior Services, Tupelo, Mississippi).

size eliminates the need for nursing stations and medication carts. The nurse-call system is wireless, using silent pagers that can be activated from pendants worn by the residents (Rabig and Thomas 2003). In all aspects, the Green Houses fully comply with Life Safety Code and other building and safety standards covered in Chapter 5.

Another prominent organizational feature of the Green House arrangement is cross-trained and self-managed worker teams who are responsible for caring for the elders and their environment. A decentralized organizational structure eliminates the typical supervisor-subordinate relationships. Interdisciplinary clinical support teams (CSTs) that include physicians, nurses, therapists, social workers, dieticians, and others located in the support organization carry out individualized clinical assessment and care planning and visit the elders to meet their treatment needs. **Clinical practice guidelines** based on medical research and standards, as well as emergency protocols, are developed for use by caregivers (Rabig and Thomas 2003).

The Green House Project proposes other cultural changes, such as referring to the cross-trained workers as "elder assistants" instead of "nursing assistants" or "nurse aides," and referring to patients as "elders" instead of "residents," who are "welcomed into" rather than "admitted to" the Green Houses. Physicians, nurses, and other clinical professionals who visit the patients are expected to assume a "visitor's role" and behave as guests, giving the elders the maximum control possible over clinical information and decisions. Individual choices and preferences are preserved by allowing the elders the maximum possible latitude in establishing their own daily routines for sleep, rest, meals, personal care, and activities. Elders are also encouraged to participate in meal preparation, gardening, cleaning, and laundry work. Weekly joint meetings or "house discussions" between elder assistants and elders provide feedback on quality of care, identify unmet needs or concerns, and give input for household decisions (Rabig and Thomas 2003).

The Green House philosophy requires close relationships between staff members and elders based on the concept of *intentional community*, the intrinsic need shared by elders and caregivers to "come together" to form a bond and "live together" for a common purpose. For example, the concept is applied when assistants and elders sit around a large common dining table and together enjoy a family-style meal. The assistant may even help feed the patient sitting in the next chair. Even tube-fed patients may be brought to the dining table for sensory stimulation from the music, the chatter, and the aroma. The term *convivium* (from Latin, meaning "feast" or, more broadly, "living together") is used in Green Houses to describe the experience of a pleasurable dining experience in an enriched environment (Rabig 2003).

The Pioneer Network

The **Pioneer Network** began as a grassroots movement of caregivers, consumer advocates, and others who were concerned about the quality of life in even some of the finest conventional nursing homes. Beginning in 1997, nursing home professionals and advocates, referred to as "pioneers," began informal meetings to define common areas of endeavor and opportunities for bringing about a cultural change in nursing facilities. A few nursing home professionals, who had already experimented with some innovative approaches, were invited to share their experiences with various stakeholders, including regulators, nursing home administrators, directors of nursing, and social workers. Subsequently, regular meetings of these pioneers led to the formation in 2000 of a formal organization, named the Pioneer Network, an organization that had the aim of providing leadership to the grassroots movement. The group was established to promote enhanced and meaningful living for elders in all the various settings across the continuum of long-term care settings, such as in-home care, independent living, adult day-care, assisted-living, and skilled-nursing facilities. By sharing diverse care approaches, practices, principles, and values, the Pioneer Network has evolved into a growing national movement. The Network has continued to make some impact in the areas of education, in sharing information and ideas to form coalitions, and in advocacy to influence public policy (The Pioneer Network 2003). Regulators and policymakers in several states have formally recognized the work of this movement.

The Pioneer philosophy and goals are similar to those held by the Eden Alternative and the Green House Project; these approaches are viewed as practical ways to bring about cultural change in long-term care delivery. In the nursing facility, the frontline caregiver is recognized to be the primary vehicle of change, but the administrator's leadership is essential in bringing about a transformation in values and culture. Leadership in the nursing facility should be directed toward empowering the frontline workers through respect, training, and involvement in decision-making. Workers should be trained in clinical as well as relational skills (The Pioneer Network 2003).

Snoezelen

Derived from two Dutch words, **Snoezelen** literally means "to sniff and doze," and describes multisensory stimulation for the primary senses of touch, hearing, sight, smell, and taste through a combined effect of textured

objects, soft music, colored lighting, aromas, and favorite foods. The therapy, initially used for children with mental disabilities, has been employed for elderly patients with dementia, but it has been more widely used in Europe—particularly the Netherlands and England—than in the United States. An extensive review of published literature undertaken by Chitsey and colleagues (2002) concluded that multisensory stimulation made a significant improvement in the behavior, the affect, the social abilities, and the verbal skills of elderly patients. Some of the main studies of patients receiving Snoezelen therapy showed reduced psychological discomfort among Alzheimer's patients (Witucki and Twibell 1997); a significant decrease in the frequency of disruptive behavior among elderly patients with dementia (Robichaud et al. 1994; Holtkamp et al. 1997); and an increase in verbal and social skills and a decrease in boredom and inappropriate napping among noninstitutionalized elderly with dementia (Baker et al. 1997). Both empirical research and descriptive studies support the therapeutic and affective benefits of multisensory stimulation (Chitsey et al. 2002).

The Wellspring Model

Wellspring Innovative Solutions, Inc. is the outgrowth of an alliance of 11 nonprofit nursing homes in Wisconsin whose main mission has been to improve the well-being of residents and reduce staff turnover. The Wellspring Model was derived from published research on workforce issues and management practices, and on the effect of those issues and practices on the quality of patient care in nursing homes. Although this particular model does not specifically advocate transforming the physical surroundings, it is highly focused on empowering staff members. However, participating facilities in the consortium do have features such as innovative architectural designs, creative use of recreational programming to include community-dwelling residents, and integration of plants and pets into the nursing home environment and resident life (Reinhard and Stone 2001). More appropriately, other details on Wellspring are included in chapters 14 and 17.

CONCLUSION

History suggests that nursing facilities will continue to undergo change. Several national initiatives are in operation, leading nursing homes along

an evolutionary path in which quality of life factors will predominate in defining how the delivery of care is organized. But cultural change is expected to occur gradually. Although some advocates would like to see a rapid transformation of today's institutional model of large-scale patient care, that is unlikely to happen. But, as new facilities are built to replace old structures, as innovative models of organizing living arrangements and processes of care evolve, as research methods are employed to determine which innovations produce the best results cost-effectively, and as the American society is willing to make a substantial financial commitment to long-term care, we are likely to see, twenty or thirty years from now, nursing facilities that look radically different from the ones that exist today. Consumer preferences and pressure from advocacy groups, on the one hand, and, on the other hand, growing economic liabilities for future generations stemming from shifting demographics and unrelenting regulatory controls will, however, counteract each other as they shape the future of nursing home care.

DISCUSSION QUESTIONS

1. What do you think the living environment and quality-of-life features in nursing homes might have been like without the certification regulations and standards?
2. Besides the cultural and social change discussed in this chapter, what other factors, such as the financial and business aspects of the nursing home industry, may have to change to bring about the transformations envisioned by the Green House Project?
3. To what extent do you think administrators operating traditionally designed nursing facilities can adapt and innovate using the principles discussed in this chapter?
4. Discuss some methods the Pioneer Network can use to influence policymakers.

INTERNET RESOURCES FOR FURTHER LEARNING

Eden Alternative: Official website
   www.edenalt.com

The Greenhouse Project: Official website
   http://thegreenhouseproject.com/

Pioneer Network: Official website
   http://www.pioneernetwork.net/

The Wellspring Program: Official website
   http://www.wellspringis.org/

REFERENCES

Action Pact, Inc. 2001. Culture change. http://www.culturechangenow.com/culture_change/index.html.

Baker, R. et al. 1997. Snoezelen: Its long-term and short-term effects on older people with dementia. *British Journal of Occupational Therapy* 60, no. 5: 213–218.

Bell, D. 2002. And Thou Shalt Honor. Wiland-Bell Productions. **{Videotape}**

Brown, K.S. 2003. *LTC backwards and forwards.* ElderWeb. http://www.eldeweb. com/history/

Bruck, L. 1997. Welcome to Eden. *Nursing Homes Long Term Care Management* 46, no. 1: 28–33.

Cerquone, J. 2001. Administrating Eden. *Balance* 5, no. 6: 4–6.

Chitsey, A.M. 2002. Snoezelen: A multidisciplinary environmental intervention. *Journal of Gerontological Nursing* 28, no. 3: 41–49.

Coleman, M.T. et al. 2002. The Eden Alternative: Findings after 1 year of implementation. *Journal of Gerontology* 57A, no. 7: M422–M427.

Department of Health and Human Services. 1999. *Health, United States, 1999.* Hyattsville, MD: National Center for Health Statistics.

Eales, J., et al. 2001. Seniors' experiences of client-centered residential care. *Aging and Society* 21: 279–296.

The Eden Alternative. 2002. *What is Eden?* http://www.edenalt.com/about.htm

Eden Annual 2003. 2003. *Come Grow with Us,* ed. Jude Thomas. Printed by Chenango Union Printing.

Guay, D. 2001. Pet-assisted therapy in the nursing home setting: Potential for zoonosis. *American Journal of Infection Control* 29, no. 3: 178–186.

Haight, B.K., et al. 2002. Thriving: A life span theory. *Journal of Gerontological Nursing* 28, no. 3: 15–22.

Hannan, M., and K. Schaeffer. 2003. The Eden Alternative: More than just fuzzy props and potted plants. http://www.edenmidwest.com/about_eden.html

Holtkamp, C.C. et al. 1997. Effect of Snoezelen on the behavior of demented elderly. *Tijdschr Gerontology Geriatrics* 28, no. 3: 124–128.

Jones, M.M., and B.K. Haight. 2002. Environmental transformations: An integrative review. *Journal of Gerontological Nursing* 28, no. 3: 23–27.

McLeod, B.W. 2002. *And thou shalt honor: A caregiver's companion*. Emmaus, Pennsylvania: Rodale Press.www.rodalestore.com

Noell, E. 1995. Design in nursing homes: Environment as a silent partner in caregiving. *Generations* 19, no. 4: 14–19.

The Pioneer Network. 2003. History of the Pioneer Network. http://www.pioneernetwork.net/index/cfm/fuseaction/showHistory.cfm

Pope, P. 2000. Exploring the Garden of Eden alternative. http://www. morningsun. net/stories/121700/for_1217000007.shtml

Rabig, J. 2003. Personal conversation, September 25, 2003.

Rabig, J., and W. Thomas. 2003. The Green House project: An alternative model of elder care. Unpublished manuscript.

Ramsey County Minnesota. 2003. *Ramsey Nursing Home: History*. http://www.co.ramsey.mn.us/nh/history.asp

Reinhard, S., and R. Stone. 2001. *Promoting quality in nursing homes: The Wellspring model*. Monograph published by the Commonwealth Fund. www.cmwf.org.

Robichaud, L. et al. 1997. Efficacy of a sensory integration program on the behaviors of inpatients with dementia. *The American Journal of Occupational Therapy* 48, no. 4: 355–360.

Reese, D. 2000. Alternative lifestyle. *Contemporary Longterm Care* 23, no. 7: 38–42.

Sansone, P., and L. Schmitt. 2000. Providing tender touch massage to elderly nursing home residents: A demonstration project. *Geriatric Nursing* 21, no. 6: 303–308.

Stermer, M. 1998. Notes from an Eden alternative pioneer. *Nursing Homes Long Term Care Management* 47, no. 11: 35–36.

US Senate Special Committee on Aging. 1974. *Nursing Home Care in the United States: Failure in Public Policy*. Introductory Report of the Subcommittee on Long-Term Care, November 1974.

Wilson, E.O. 1984. *Biophilia: The Human Bond with Other Species*. Cambridge, MA: Harvard University Press.

Witucki, J.M., and R.S. Twibell. 1997. The effect of sensory stimulation activities on the psychological well being of patients with advanced Alzheimer's disease. *American Journal of Alzheimer's Disease* 12, no. 1: 10–15.

Wohlwill, J.F. 1983. The concept of nature: A psychologist's view. In *Behavior and The Natural Environment*, eds. I. Altman and J.F. Wohlwill, 5–37. New York: Plenum Press.

CHAPTER 7

Social Services, Admission, and Discharge

LEARNING MODULES

1. The nature of social-work practice.
2. Social services department. Staffing requirements. Qualifications for effective social work practice.
3. Key areas of skill competency. Practicing the skills of engagement, assessment, communication, interviewing, and documentation.
4. Understanding aging. Basic theories of aging. Inaccurate views of aging.
5. Roles and functions of the social worker. Ethics committee and its role.
6. The pre-admission inquiry process. Importance of a written plan. Intake interview, facility tour, and follow up.
7. Admission and orientation.
8. Role of discharge planning in the continuity-of-care model.
9. Resident council, its organization, and function. Social worker's facilitative role.
10. Family management. Family involvement and support.
11. End-of-life and hospice care.

The practice of social work in nursing facilities can be best characterized as an integrative and coordinating function that must deal effectively with client needs, problems, and issues that arise in the transactions among people within social systems. Because many complex social issues cannot be resolved in the best interest of everyone, the focus of social services is on the coping and adaptive capacities of individuals (Dubois and Miley 1999, 44). It may in some instances be possible to modify some aspects of a patient's immediate environment to facilitate coping and adaptation to the larger social environment. In other instances, conflicts must be resolved between what a patient or family wants and what the social environment can offer.

Effective social services also play a key role in linking the facility to its external environment. Besides the nursing home administrator, the social worker is an important representative of the facility who often plays an active role in forming exchange relationships with the external environment discussed in Chapters 1 and 2.

Social work is an essential component of long-term care from preadmission planning, through a patient's stay in the nursing facility, to the time of discharge. The roles and tasks associated with the social worker's position in a long-term care facility, and the use of skills necessary for carrying out those roles and tasks all take place in the context of a clear understanding of the aged and the aging process, which this chapter will also briefly address.

SOCIAL SERVICES DEPARTMENT

Staffing

In an average-sized facility of 100 to 120 beds, the social services department typically consists of one full-time social worker who holds the position of department head and reports to the nursing home administrator (see Figure II-1). Larger facilities generally have a director of social services who is in charge of one or more assistant social workers in the department. A facility of 120 beds or more may also have an additional position of director of admissions, admissions coordinator, or director of admissions and marketing who may report to the administrator or to the director of social services.

Federal regulations mandate a full-time social worker for every 120 residents. But apart from these minimum requirements, staffing considerations should be based on the overall scope of responsibilities assigned to the social services department. In very small facilities, which range between 30 and 50 beds, one full-time person may be given the responsibilities of both social work and activities. Supplemental part-time staff may be scheduled as needed. In facilities that have between 70 and 100 beds a full-time social worker may be assigned additional responsibilities such as marketing and public relations. Larger facilities may need additional positions in social services, admissions, or marketing. This chapter will address the core social-work roles and tasks. Activities and marketing functions will be discussed in the later chapters that are devoted to a more comprehensive coverage of these topics.

Qualifications

Qualifications of social workers are specified by state nursing home licensure regulations. Depending on what a state requires, social workers may or may not have to be licensed professionals. Typically, a bachelor's degree in social work (BSW) is the minimum academic preparation necessary. In addition to the bachelor's degree, individuals who have less than a specified amount of experience—which is typically one year—must receive regular consultation from someone who holds a master's degree in social work (MSW). Not all states require education in the social work field. Some states allow facilities to have the position of **social work designee**, a position filled by someone who has a related degree but not a BSW, in which case consultation from someone with an MSW will be required. Professionals with an academic degree in social work, however, are generally better prepared for the various roles and responsibilities of a social worker.

In addition to academic qualifications, social workers in a geriatric-care setting must have an understanding of the physical and psychosocial changes that accompany the aging process. They must understand the unique needs of the elderly and demonstrate a desire to work with the problems and issues confronting clients who need to be admitted to a nursing facility. They must be compassionate and considerate. They must have professional maturity and objectivity in addressing a diversity of issues. They must be knowledgeable of community resources and they

need to establish linkages with various external agencies in order to obtain needed services for patients and their families. Finally, trustworthiness is a necessary trait.

SKILLS AND COMPETENCIES

Kropf and Hutchison (1992) identified five specific skill areas for social workers working with the elderly:

- engagement skills
- assessment skills
- communication skills
- interviewing skills
- documentation skills

Engagement Skills

This skill is basic to all social-work practice because it entails recognizing client needs, demonstrating sensitivity and concern, and being committed to addressing client needs. Effective engagement with the elderly client is built on respect. Engagement requires building rapport with patients and their families.

Young adults tend to treat older adults as children, a process called **infantilization**. It is not uncommon for nursing home staff members to address patients by their first names, which may be taken as demeaning, even though the patient is not likely to openly protest about it. Similarly, addressing patients as "cutie," "sweetie," "baby," or "honey" is regarded as condescending. Patients are already dependant upon the caregivers; infantilization further strips away the patients' self-respect and dignity.

Deficiencies in human-relations skills can severely hamper a social worker's effectiveness. Skilled social workers can play an especially important role in training other staff members in effective ways to interact with the elderly, and social workers can periodically reinforce the need for appropriate staff-resident relations. Caregiving relationships are often characterized by **intimacy**, meaning closeness or proximity of the caregiver to the dependent elder; intimacy goes beyond mere familiarity (Agich 1995). Without conscious thought, intimacy can lead to infantilization and reinforce a resident's sense of dependency, which is the antithesis of autonomy.

Assessment Skills

Assessment in a care facility is akin to an exploratory study that forms the basis for decision-making and action (Coulshed 1991, 25). Assessment is a systematic investigation of all basic and special needs of the individual, including the patient's own perspective as well as that of his or her family or surrogates. Special attention is paid to the person's biophysical functioning in relation to psychological and social processes, such as the patient's attitudes about being in the nursing facility, economic needs, family support, and race or cultural issues. An initial assessment is generally quite comprehensive, but because needs change over time, assessment should be an ongoing process. The information gathered from the assessment is used to determine how the facility's resources and services will be deployed to best address the needs of the patient as well as the needs of family or surrogates. Such a plan of action takes into account any limitations in resources the nursing facility may have. When a facility is unable to furnish the resources necessary to address all the identified needs of a patient, services from outside the facility must be utilized or the patient should be moved to a more appropriate setting.

Communication Skills

Social workers need well-rounded communication skills, which include speaking, listening, writing, and presentation skills. Particular attention must be paid to language use with older adults. Use of technical jargon is commonplace among nursing home staff members, but such jargon should be avoided when communicating with clients and their families. For example, staff members should use the term "food service" instead of "dietary;" "recreation" instead of "activities;" and "safety device" instead of "restraint." Kropf and Hutchison (1992) make several practical suggestions to improve communication. Simple and straightforward language is the most effective method of verbal communication. A handshake or touch adds warmth to the communication process. Sitting in close proximity to an older client aids understanding of what is being said and is also taken as a sign of acceptance. Active listening, repeating, and feedback are essential techniques for communicating with the elderly to ensure understanding. Because hearing impairment is a common problem among nursing home clients, use of clear diction and a slow pace of talk-

ing are important. Another good strategy is to use the patients' names frequently, so they know that they are being addressed.

Interviewing Skills

Interviewing is commonly used for gathering facts about individual situations. As an interactive tool that is generally used when dealing with specific issues, interviewing involves communicating in a more focused way than usual. Effective interviewing generally requires some prior preparation, such as gathering background or other preliminary information that is used as the basis for further probing to obtain more pertinent and detailed information. When preparing for the interview the social worker needs to think through what specific questions to ask.

The actual interview requires a private and quiet place and adequate uninterrupted time. Effective interviewing employs the skills of engagement and communication just described. But it goes beyond a mere use of those skills. An interview should get to the main point of the issue and begin with a summary of the issue and the purpose of the interview. It is important to pose questions that get to facts and feelings. Questions posed accusingly or in a suspicious manner are likely to generate negative reactions. During the interview, particular attention must be paid to special cues that may require further probing. For example, the individual may try to dodge an issue or may be hesitant to respond to a question. A victim of abuse may be reluctant to discuss it because of embarrassment or for fear of retaliation. The interview should conclude with a summary that puts the total interview in perspective for the client, who should then be asked if any information has been misrepresented or omitted (Kropf and Hutchison 1992). The social worker should also explain what follow-up will take place.

Documentation Skills

Documentation often requires the use of prescribed forms and formats, but much of this work is now computerized. Documentation must be timely, accurate, complete, and descriptive but concise. In this manner, social-service documentation should provide a complete record of the patient's initial history, assessment, care planning, progress (or lack thereof), interventions, and discharge. A number of documents are also completed upon a patient's admission to the facility, as discussed later in this chapter.

KNOWLEDGE OF AGING AND THE ELDERLY

In geriatric facilities, the roles and functions of social services are performed by caregivers who understand aging and the special needs of the aged. Although an understanding of gerontology is essential for all staff members who work with the elderly, social workers typically make the first contact with families and patients when admission to a nursing facility becomes necessary. They must evaluate the need for nursing home care, provide information about the facility and its services, help the family reach a decision about admitting the patient, and make a referral to another agency if the nursing home is not suited to meet the patient's needs. After admission, the social worker must engage in an initial needs assessment, help the new patient adjust to the institution, and get involved in various social interventions as situations arise. Social workers are also called upon to assist other staff members in the facility or to provide staff training on issues pertaining to **gerontology**. Hence, this section provides a brief overview of aging and explores some erroneous views about aging and the elderly.

Understanding Aging

In our society, people are generally considered elderly or a "senior" when they are in their mid-sixties. At this age, people frequently take formal retirement from work, become eligible for Social Security and Medicare, and start paying more attention to some of the symptoms that naturally accompany advancing age. However, age itself merely provides a chronological context. Different people actually age differently. Attitudes toward one's own aging, and behaviors associated with the issues of aging, differ from person to person. From this perspective, the elderly are a very heterogeneous group. Categorizing every elderly person according to a stereotype is a gross error. The need to avoid such stereotyping is one reason that assessments, plans of care, and interventions require careful individualized attention. Attitudes and behaviors also differ among diverse cultural and ethnic groups. Family support, values and expectations, level of trust, and reaction to nursing home placement may be associated with a resident's cultural orientation.

Aging is loosely regarded as the culmination of a life cycle that started at birth. Although aging may be the final stage of life, this stage generally lasts a long time, and, as further changes occur, substages within this stage

manifest themselves. Hence, a person's background and history—upbringing, education, hobbies and interests, marriage, divorce, death of spouse, children, siblings, major illnesses, occupation, economic achievement, dysfunctions, and recent occurrences—provide meaningful information that should be used for planning strategies to help the individual cope, adapt to new circumstances, and get the best out of life despite current illness and declining physical functioning. Life changes and stressful life encounters affect the psychological well-being of the elderly. Factors associated with background and life changes can differ substantially according to one's culture and ethnicity.

During the past forty years or so, a number of theories have been proposed in an effort to understand behaviors associated with aging. Each theory has its limitations, and even together all these theories do not account for every possible situation. Of the several theories, three are considered most useful for their application in nursing home settings:

- activity theory
- continuity theory
- labeling theory

Activity theory

According to this theory, people in their old age seek to remain active. This theory counters the "rocking chair" stereotype, according to which the elderly are often visualized as sitting passively in a rocking chair and dozing off because of inactivity. Satisfaction in old age depends on a person's ability to substitute new roles and activities for those that the individual pursued during pre-retirement years. A career postal worker, for example, may enjoy distributing mail to other nursing home residents. Many elderly women still enjoy baking, cooking, knitting and other activities which should be incorporated into the facility's recreational planning. Although many residents find independence and life satisfaction by volunteering to do activities they had once enjoyed, it is also important to realize that not everyone wants to remain active, and that the notion of what constitutes satisfying activity generally differs from one person to another.

Continuity theory

The major assumption of this theory is that the experiences of one's earlier years prepare an individual to adapt to and cope with the demands of aging, which may help explain why some people adapt to new situations

better than others. Current behaviors of elderly individuals can be best understood by examining their behaviors in earlier stages of life, such as past habits, goals, preferences, hobbies, and leisure pursuits. Understanding the patient's past can enable facility personnel to assist the individual in adjusting to the new environment. This understanding can also help facility personnel think about ways in which routines can be made more flexible to accommodate certain past practices, which would help the person better adapt to a new setting.

Labeling theory

This theory helps one understand how a person's self-concept is molded by the labels others use for that person. It strikes at the negative stereotypes of the elderly, because the elderly may believe these stereotypes are true, and they may assimilate those stereotypes into their behavior. For example the belief that once people become old, they become dependent may actually promote dependency in elders (Harrigan and Farmer 1992).

Inaccurate Views of Aging

Myths and distorted views about aging encourage stereotyping, which results in treating the elderly in ways that are detrimental to their self-esteem, independence, and psychosocial as well as physical health. Prejudicial treatment of the elderly based on stereotypes is called **ageism**. Ignorance is the main cause of ageism, which creates barriers for adequate delivery of health care and social services to the elderly.

Certain changes, such as sensory decline in vision, hearing, tactile feeling, smelling, and tasting, occur naturally as a person ages. Sleep disorders may also become more common. But getting old does not necessarily mean becoming ill and disabled. Many biological and psychological changes that are commonly associated with aging actually start occurring at a much younger age. These changes do not take place uniformly in all people. Earlier life choices and unforeseen accidents have an effect on health in later years. Hence, chronological age is a poor indicator of health and vigor (Harrigan and Farmer 1992). Although some elders succumb to illness and disability and require assistance, most continue to live healthy and fulfilling lives. However, the risk of functional impairment increases with age as chronic conditions and comorbidities set in. But in spite of the heightened risk, only a small percentage of the elderly will require institutional care over a long period. Roughly 80 percent of the

elderly over the age of 65 have at least one chronic condition, but over 80 percent of the non-institutionalized elderly independently manage their activities of daily living (ADLs) (Newman and Newman 1987).

Old age does not necessarily mean that people lose the desire to remain physically attractive. Economic and physical constraints may interfere with one's ability to maintain proper grooming. Assuming that inactivity results from old age is also wrong. Because of sleep disorders, some elderly individuals may compensate for lack of sleep at night by taking naps during day, or they may fall asleep while sitting because of boredom and inactivity. Presuming that physical exertion is harmful for older people is also inaccurate. Within the parameters of physical limitations, most elderly people can engage in various types of physical activities under proper medical supervision. Although sexual functioning declines naturally, particularly in males, most elders retain the desire to express their sexuality.

Dementia and confusion do not naturally accompany aging. Even though only five percent of the elderly population has dementia that is severe enough to substantially hamper their independent functioning, many such patients require care in nursing facilities. According to one report, approximately 60% of patients in nursing homes have dementia at some level (Kaplan and Sadock 1988). Other temporary or permanent brain dysfunctions, referred to as organic brain disorders, include delirium. **Delirium** is a state of acute mental confusion which often manifests itself in the form of disorientation, incoherent speech, and physical agitation. Delirium is often caused by acute illness or toxicity. The condition is treatable, but a quick medical diagnosis is critical because the underlying causes can lead to a fatal outcome. Delirium can be mistaken for **dementia**, which is a chronic or progressive decline in mental functioning, but the underlying causes are rarely life-threatening.

Another area in which the elderly are quite heterogeneous is whether they are set in their ways or can learn new things. Many older adults can successfully adapt to changes and learn new skills, such as those demanded by new hobbies, crafts, or using the computer. Older people generally also have their long-term memory quite intact.

It is erroneous to think that the elderly like being dependent on others. To the contrary, older adults like to have control over their life decisions, and to the extent they can, they wish to take care of their own needs. Independence is closely related to self-esteem. A high level of dependency causes many patients in nursing facilities to have low self-esteem. The

concept of interdependence may provide a more appropriate way for addressing the needs of the elderly (Harrigan and Farmer 1992). **Interdependence** can be defined as a state of living together (symbiosis) in a mutually beneficial relationship. In most cases, people are in nursing homes because of impairments, and to that extent their dependent position cannot be helped. However, while being dependent in some ways, residents may be able to make a contribution to the community in other ways. A sense of being useful, competent, and needed must be preserved as much as possible. Interdependence often develops mutual bonds with other residents and pets in the nursing home.

Contrary to popular opinion, the elderly in America are not alienated, ignored, or abandoned by their families. Adult children and their elderly parents generally prefer to live separately. At the same time, most long-term care and assistance with activities of daily living are provided to elders by family members on an informal basis. The family continues to play a vital role in delaying or preventing institutionalization of elders. Community-based services, when available, are used to supplement family care as necessary. As a general rule, only when community-based care cannot adequately address an elder's needs is the elder admitted to a nursing facility. On the other hand, intergenerational conflicts in families do arise. Abuse and neglect, including verbal abuse and psychological mistreatment, exist at all socioeconomic levels of society and in all racial and ethnic groups (Harrigan and Farmer 1992).

SOCIAL SERVICE ROLES

The social service functions and roles discussed in this section paint a general portrait of what a social worker employed in a nursing facility does. The roles that a social worker plays highlight the importance of this position in a nursing facility. The various roles and functions can be classified into six main categories:

- Informational role
- Case manager role
- Coordination role
- Enabler role
- Intervention role
- Advocacy role

Informational Role

The social worker is generally the main source of information on several fronts: on the facility and its services; on eligibility for public financing and the services covered under programs such as Medicare and Medicaid; on resources and services available in the community and their suitability for a particular client; and on various issues related to long-term care. A social worker must acquire comprehensive knowledge in all these areas.

People who inquire about nursing home placement for a family member or acquaintance are often the primary recipients of information about the facility. But in many instances it is simply assumed that professionals in other community health care and social service agencies do not need to be educated about nursing home services. Such assumptions may, in the long run, be harmful to the facility. These assumptions may also be a disservice to the patients who could otherwise benefit from the facility's services but do not get referred to the facility because the agency that could have made a referral did not know about the facility or its services. As discussed in Chapter 2, taking information and educational resources to external agencies is one way in which exchange relationships are established. Similarly, the social worker should be involved with other community outreach programs described in Chapter 2.

Case-Manager Role

This role is also called the broker role, but the concept of case management is more straightforward. **Case management** is the process of matching client needs with available services that are likely to best address those needs. Case management encompasses assessment, a plan, follow-up, and reevaluation.

As a case manager, the social worker generally coordinates external resources to meet the total care needs of each patient. When a resident is admitted to a nursing facility, the facility takes on the responsibility of providing or procuring all appropriate services that the patient may need—a concept called **total care**. In the role of a case manager, the social worker must often coordinate personalized facility services according to each patient's needs. Services not provided by the facility are obtained from external sources. For example, a resident may require eyeglasses or dental care or may need a psychiatric evaluation. A referral for such services may require obtaining orders from a physician, involving family or

other responsible party, follow-up on financing, making an appointment with an appropriate professional, arranging transportation, and follow-up to ensure that the patient has actually received the service.

Coordination Role

The case manager role just discussed is closely linked to the social worker's role as a coordinator because successful case management depends on the social worker's ability to effectively coordinate a number of different types of services. However, the social worker's coordinator role goes beyond case management. Each admission and discharge requires careful coordination with both key staff members within the facility and with relevant parties outside the facility. The social worker is generally the facilitator of the resident council within the facility or a family support group sponsored by the facility. The social worker is also generally called upon to assist the facility administrator in sharing the facility's expertise with the community through well-coordinated programs on geriatric issues and financing for long-term care. An illustrative list of such outreach programs is included in Chapter 2.

Enabler Role

Although it is also referred to as the counseling role, giving advice and expressing personal opinions to patients or families are seldom appropriate in nursing home social work. The nature of social-work counseling is primarily based on helping patients help themselves. Hence, this role is more appropriately called the enabler role (Kropf and Hutchison 1992), in which the social worker functions as a facilitator.

New residents require adjustment to the new surroundings and the unfamiliar routines of the facility. The adjustment process and time required for adjustment varies from one patient to another. Social workers help residents adjust by frequently visiting them and by encouraging them to express their fears, anxieties, and feelings. The social worker can facilitate social adjustment by assessing compatibilities and introducing residents to other patients to encourage social bonding (Patchner and Patchner 1991). The resident's family also requires adjustment. Family members often carry feelings of guilt from putting a relative in a nursing home. There may be conflict among family members over the decision. The social worker can help family members explore their own feelings, clarify areas of disagreement, and confront the realities of the situation.

Intervention Role

The social worker is called upon to address a variety of problems that a nursing home patient may face. In most instances the patient has a conflict or lacks the ability to cope with his or her environment. Examples of this type of conflict include a patient repeatedly losing her eyeglasses or not having enough clothes to wear. The conflict may involve other people, such as a staff member or family. For instance, the family may find it too expensive to replace lost items and may not favor purchasing new eyeglasses or hearing aids. The family may blame the facility for losing items of clothing and decline to replace them, with the result that the patient has insufficient or inappropriate items to wear. There may be conflict between two roommates or between two residents who do not share a room or a dining table. Certain problems may call for the use of external resources, requiring the social worker to function as a case manager and coordinator. In conflict situations involving a staff member and a resident, the social worker may suggest ways to the staff member for minimizing or avoiding conflict. To address more common types of staff-resident conflicts, general staff training may be appropriate. Other types of conflict, arising from psychosocial problems or dementia, may require therapeutic intervention in the form of reality orientation, validation therapy, or sensory stimulation (Patchner and Patchner 1991). Activity personnel can assist with these therapies.

Advocacy Role

As an advocate, the social worker looks out for the best interests of the patient. It is the social worker's responsibility to inform patients of their rights (see Chapter 3). The social worker also monitors the enforcement of patient rights in the facility and educates the staff on the meaning and importance of patient rights. Many patients cannot express their desires and cannot determine on their own what is best for them. In the advocacy role, the social worker does not try to guess the patient's wishes or try to determine what is best for the patient. Rather, the social worker is responsible for bringing such issues to the attention of the administration and any other parties whose involvement may be necessary for decision-making and initiating action. For instance, a resident may have already lost two hearing aids and may be unable to express whether he or she needs a new one. The family may resist investing money in another hearing device. This patient needs someone to stand up as an advocate on his or her behalf.

Effectively managed nursing homes have ethics committees to address such issues. The social worker, along with other members of the professional staff, is a participant in such a committee. The social worker is responsible for bringing issues to the attention of the committee for decision and resolution. An **ethics committee** generally represents a number of professions and is therefore multidisciplinary. Such a committee usually includes the administrator, members of the nursing staff, a physician, social services, activity staff, clergy, an ethicist, and a legal representative. Depending on the issue, other experts such as a dietician or a therapist may also be included. Generally, family members are also invited to attend and to provide their input. A multidisciplinary forum allows for different insights and viewpoints. It relieves the social worker of the responsibility for making complex decisions independently. When the consequences of a decision turn out to be negative, blame cannot be assigned to one person. Finally, the decision of a committee is more likely to be accepted by individuals, such as family or staff members, whose action or support is necessary for carrying out that decision.

SOCIAL SERVICE TASKS

From the description of the six primary social service roles, it should be clear that social workers perform a variety of different tasks, which would be too numerous to enumerate. Most situations that require social-work intervention cannot be foreseen and must be dealt with as they arise. Yet some task-oriented functions are routine, and these social service functions can be clearly defined:

- pre-admission inquiry
- admission and orientation
- discharge planning

This section will examine the critical tasks required to handle inquiries, admission, and discharge planning.

Pre-Admission Inquiry

The social worker is generally the one to first meet a prospective client, unless the facility has a separate director of admissions, who would then be the one to take most inquiries. The information and case-manager roles discussed earlier best apply to the inquiry process. A prospective

client or a referral agency may call the facility and make arrangements for a family to visit the facility. In other instances, an inquirer may walk in unannounced. The facility must be prepared at all times to handle either situation promptly and professionally, because in today's competitive environment an inquiry delayed is an admission lost. Effective handling of an inquiry is an opportunity for the facility to "make a sale" if the facility offers the level of services to adequately care for the patient's needs. If the facility does not have adequate services, it must make a referral to another agency where more appropriate services may be available.

Handling an inquiry is akin to making a sale, but using a social-service approach. This approach requires the intake worker, who may be the social worker or the admissions coordinator, to function as an information disseminator and case manager. The focus is not simply on finding new patients for admission to the facility but also on determining the appropriateness of nursing home placement, given the patient's needs. If a community-based long-term care program or a residential institution is determined to be more suitable for a prospective client, the intake worker should make appropriate referrals. Establishing exchange partnerships with external agencies can result in two-way referrals, creating a win-win situation for both parties.

Written Procedure

The facility should have a written procedure for handling inquiries. The procedure should include a list, in descending order of preference, of back-up personnel in case the primary intake worker is not available. For instance, the list of personnel could start with the director of admissions and include the social worker, a second social worker (if the facility has one), the administrator (or an administrative staff member such as an assistant administrator, if the facility has one), the director of nursing, and the activity director.

The point here is that the facility should always have someone to provide complete information, regardless of whether the inquiry is initiated over the phone or in person. The procedure should include the main steps in handling inquiries, in which all personnel assigned to this task must be properly trained. The list of staff members should be available to the receptionist, so each inquiry can be appropriately directed, based on who is available at the time. The facility should also have a plan for handling inquiries after regular business hours and on weekends. For example,

many well-run nursing facilities designate a weekend manager. This role is carried out by the primary and secondary intake professionals mentioned earlier, who cover the role of weekend manager in rotation. An evening charge nurse or nurse supervisor should be trained to handle the occasional inquiry that may come in after regular business hours.

Initial interview

The facility should provide an office or other private area for the interview. This setting should be comfortable, inviting, and cheerfully decorated, but not to the point of being distracting. Handling an inquiry is an art, which is perfected with time and practice. An inquiry form in a checklist format can greatly facilitate the interview. Even if the intake process is computerized, making computer entries during the interview should be avoided.

The objective of the interview is to obtain essential information about the patient, starting with his or her name, age, gender, current location such as hospital or home, name of referring agency (if any), attending physician, when accommodation may be needed, diagnosis, ADL status, hobbies and interests, any special needs, and so forth. The inquiry form should also have space for the inquirer's name, relationship, phone number, and address. Even though all pertinent information is obtained at this time to make a judgment about the patient's needs, this is not a formal assessment, nor should an attempt be made at this juncture to make one.

Once the basic information has been obtained, the interview moves on to a discussion of the facility's services that can best meet the patient's needs, according to the best clinical judgment that can be made, given the information provided. If necessary, the intake worker can call the referral agency to seek further clarification. The intake worker should also call in the director of nursing, a specialized nurse, a therapist, or the dietician to provide additional expertise if specific issues arise during the interview. The facility should evaluate the case objectively. Admitting a patient and then not providing adequate services, because the facility is not equipped to handle the care that the patient's condition demands, would be a mistake.

Facility tour

Prospective clients seldom decline to tour the facility, but it can happen if the initial interview turns them off. This phase of the inquiry process consists of a guided tour, during which the inquiring party is accompanied by

the person who responds to the inquiry and conducts the interview. Well-managed facilities have written procedures for giving an effective guided tour. The written tour plan is also used for training staff members who may be called upon to conduct facility tours in the absence of the primary intake personnel.

The tour should include all the main amenities listed in Figure II-2. Some of the main areas of the facility to include in the tour are dining rooms, lounges and other social rooms such as a library, rehabilitation therapy room(s), barber/beauty parlor, and activity room and calendar. Facilities must have a large wall-size calendar of activities and events. In addition, safety features and practices, comfort factors, and privacy aspects of care should be emphasized in the conversation while touring the facility. The visitor must be able to observe and feel the caregiving environment to the extent it is possible without compromising the privacy of patients receiving care. For example, activity sessions and certain therapies, such as gait training, can be observed without compromising privacy. It is inappropriate to take visitors into occupied patient rooms unless permission to see their rooms has been obtained in advance. Some facilities set apart one or two furnished model rooms for visitors to see and to get some ideas about how a room may be personalized by bringing items such as small television sets, memorabilia, plants, personal furniture, and bed accessories. Visitors should not be taken inside the kitchen because it violates sanitation regulations.

Concluding Interview

The conclusion of a tour always brings the inquirer back to the place where the initial interview was conducted. The intake worker now continues to judge the client's reactions and provides an opportunity for questions and answers. At this point, financing should be discussed. If appropriate, the patient-accounts manager may join the conversation to provide any assistance with financing. For instance, the patient may be eligible for Medicare or Medicaid. An application may have to be made for Medicaid coverage. If the patient would come in under Medicare, an approximate length of stay and out-of-pocket costs should be discussed. Private pay rates should be furnished if that is appropriate. If the patient has private insurance or managed-care coverage, all necessary information on the coverage should be obtained. Bed availability, wait-list status, or a tentative date of admission can also be discussed at this time.

Information Packet

Before the prospective client leaves, he or she must receive an information packet, and the intake worker should briefly go over some of the materials contained in the packet. The information packet should be professionally designed and should contain all relevant information that may be needed for making a decision about placing someone in the facility. If the client has no further questions, the interview is concluded. The client should be courteously escorted to the main lobby and given a personal send-off.

Follow-up

When different personnel are involved in handling separate inquiries, all inquiries should be channeled to the person who has the primary responsibility for inquiry intake, such as the director of social services or the director of admissions. This individual should follow up on all inquiries, and the final disposition should be noted. If a prospective patient was considered an appropriate client for the facility but was not admitted, an attempt should be made to find out the reason why the facility was not selected. Inquiry dispositions should be periodically reviewed with the administrator. Over time, this information can be useful in identifying weak spots and taking appropriate measures to improve operational policies, procedures, and services.

Admission and Orientation

Nursing home admission trauma is common and affects most patients. But the social worker can take steps to minimize a patient's fear and anxiety. One source of anxiety for the patient, and of guilt for the family, is stereotyped and unpleasant images of nursing homes. Despite efforts made by industry leaders to change the gloomy portrayal of nursing homes, the effect of these images has not been overcome. Lingering negative perceptions require the industry to do more to change people's perceptions. The industry must remember, however, that people strongly prefer to stay at home for as long as possible, despite declining health and increasing disability.

Planning and Preparation

Once a family has decided to admit a family member to the facility, the social worker should make a personal visit, if possible, to meet the new patient at his or her current residence. The purpose of such a visit is to

attempt to allay unfounded fears that the new patient may have. A sizable number of patients are admitted to nursing facilities on a short-term basis for rehabilitation and convalescence. If that is the case, the fact that it will be a short-term stay must be emphasized to the patient, who otherwise may be thinking that admission to the facility may be his or her final living arrangement before death. If a long-term stay is contemplated, the social worker should emphasize the social and vibrant living environment of the facility and describe how the patient may become an active participant in that environment. Autonomy, privacy, and other features discussed in Chapter 5 should be highlighted. This is also an appropriate time for the social worker to discuss with the family which personal belongings may or may not be brought to the facility.

Any special instructions from the family should be passed on to the staff members who will be involved in the patient's care. Having a meeting with the staff on the nursing unit where the patient will be admitted is a good practice. Staff members can be better prepared if they know in advance the patient's requirements, such as assistance with specific ADLs, incontinence, patient's preferences, or other special needs.

Before admission, the patient's room must be given special attention to ensure that everything is in order. Paying attention to minute details is the key. For example, a corner of the room may need additional cleaning, a wall may need some touch-up paint, or a leaky faucet in the bathroom may need fixing. On the day of admission, a flower arrangement in the room is always a welcoming sign.

Admission Records

An important part of the admission process is ensuring that all pertinent medical records have been forwarded to the facility at the time of admission. If the patient is coming from the hospital or another nursing facility, the transfer of medical records is arranged with that institution. If the patient is coming from home or a residential facility, medical records must be obtained from the admitting physician's office. Records must include current physician's orders certifying the need for admission to the facility, and orders for medications, nursing treatments, rehabilitation therapies, therapeutic diets, etc.

By the day of admission, the social worker should also complete the admission paperwork. The resident or the responsible party should sign

an admissions agreement, which is a contract between the facility and the patient (or his or her representative). Another important document contains the rights and responsibilities of patients. The patient or the representative must sign this document to acknowledge that they have received it. Other documents should also be completed as required by regulations and facility policies. Generally, facilities have packets of admission forms prepared in advance to ensure that all paperwork gets completed. A monetary deposit may also be required. Besides the admission packet, the social worker completes a social history of the patient. The social history and assessment are incorporated into the patient's individualized plan of care (discussed in Chapter 8).

Orientation

The purpose of orientation is to help new residents adjust to the facility and its routines. On the first day, the new resident should be introduced to a handful of key staff members such as the unit's charge nurse, one or two nursing assistants, the recreational director, and the dietician or food service director. The administrator may also stop by for a welcoming handshake. If the admission takes place close to meal time, the family or friends who are accompanying the patient should be invited to dine with the patient in a private area. The patient may, however, express a preference to dine alone in the room or go to the dining room. In any event the patient's wishes should be respected. Every effort should be made to make the dining experience as pleasant as possible. During the first week, the social worker should contact the patient and staff regularly to find out how the patient is adjusting to his or her new surroundings. Communication with the family should also be maintained to ensure satisfaction with the services or to simply stay in touch. Such ongoing contact can prevent problems down the road, because it enables the facility to address minor issues as they arise. It also allays family's anxiety and projects a caring attitude.

An integral part of orientation is educating new residents about their rights and the decisions and choices they can make. Patients should be encouraged to participate in decision-making so that they do not fall into a pattern of "learned helplessness" because of their dependant position. Staff interactions should be supportive. Within their limitations, patients should be allowed to do for themselves as much as possible.

Discharge Planning

Discharge planning is more appropriately described as continuity-of-care planning (O'Hare 1988). Discharge planning falls within the social worker's case manager and coordination roles. According to the continuity-of-care model (Figure 7-1), discharge planning begins when a patient is admitted to the nursing facility. Upon admission, assessment and care planning are approached with discharge outcomes in mind. Discharge planning takes a multidisciplinary approach. Staff members from various disciplines, such as medical, nursing, dietary, rehabilitation, and social work, provide their input into the clinical and psychosocial progress made by the patient, their reevaluation of the patient's current status, and the patient's prognosis for discharge from the facility. Thus discharge planning becomes a continuous process as illustrated in Figure 7-1. The family should also be involved in discharge decisions. The social worker is primarily responsible for coordinating the process.

Financial considerations, such as coverage under Medicare, are also important. As discussed in Chapter 4, Medicare does not cover long-term stay in a skilled nursing facility. Length of stay depends on the patient's diagnosis, assessment, and rehabilitation potential. If additional length of

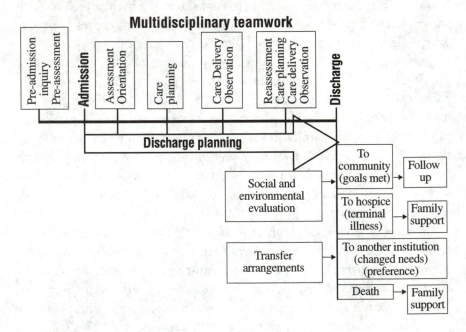

FIGURE 7-1 Continuity of Care Model

stay in the facility is necessary after Medicare benefits have been exhausted, the patient must pay privately or, if he or she is eligible, apply for Medicaid. Otherwise, the multidisciplinary team must prepare for the patient's discharge from the facility.

When discharge from the facility is determined to be in the best interest of the patient, the facility must plan for the actual discharge. Ensuring continuity of care after discharge is a primary consideration in the facility's decision about where the patient will be discharged to and what ongoing services the patient may still need. If a patient will go back to his or her home, the social worker will do a social evaluation to determine whether adequate support services will be available to the patient. An occupational therapist will perform a home evaluation to determine the extent to which the patient would be able to function independently in a safe environment. The occupational therapist may recommend adaptive equipment or home modification to enhance accessibility and may follow up to teach the patient adaptive skills. The facility may refer the patient to a home health agency, in which case the follow-up tasks are turned over to that agency. The key to successful discharge planning is to make arrangements so that all available resources are used to provide all the appropriate services that a patient needs after discharge. Follow-up is often essential to ensure that the arranged services are being delivered (Patchner and Patchner 1991).

RESIDENT COUNCIL

A **resident council** is an independent semi-formal body comprising all residents who are able to participate. The purpose of this forum is to empower the residents so they can have a say in the facility's operations. An active resident council in the nursing facility helps promote resident autonomy and gives the residents a sense of control. This council is also a means of promoting self-esteem among residents who are able to participate in decision-making concerning their own quality of life in the nursing home.

The social worker generally has the responsibility to assist the residents in organizing a council and to facilitate their regular meetings. For example, the social worker can assist the residents in electing council officers such as a president, a secretary, and a liaison for special events. Space should be designated where regular meetings can be held in privacy. Existence of the council should be publicized, and all new and long-term

residents who are able to participate should be encouraged to do so. Individual involvement, however, is totally voluntary. In some facilities, primary responsibility for the resident council is delegated to the Activity Director.

Because the resident council is a self-governing forum, the administrator and other staff members attend the meetings only when invited. However, the administrator or other staff members may ask the president for time when they can address the council on important issues and policies and provide follow-up reports on any previous concerns expressed or recommendations made by the council.

FAMILY MANAGEMENT

The family's decision-making role was discussed in Chapter 2. Once a patient has been placed in a nursing facility, the patient's family becomes a secondary client. Treating the patient's family as a client and addressing their emotional needs is generally important for the overall well-being of the patient, who is the primary client. Maintaining the patient's family ties becomes an important task of social work. The first step in this process is for the facility's administration to promote a policy of unrestricted visiting hours for family members.

Families often do not anticipate and prepare for placing a loved one in a nursing facility. In many instances, nursing-home admission is preceded by a family crisis such as the death of the patient's spouse (or that of some other informal caregiver), sudden hospitalization for some unforeseen complication, an accident (such as a fall that results in a hip fracture), or the relocation of adult children who may have been providing informal care. Such events can trigger rapid deterioration of a patient's physical health, mental health, or both. In such situations, families may show signs of desperation, frustration, anger, guilt, or conflict. Also, some families have had a history of internal dissension and resentment. Such dysfunctional family relationships can greatly complicate the staff's ability to adequately deal with the patient's needs, because family members may perpetuate disagreements and interference.

Greene (1982) advocates actively engaging the family in the preadmission inquiry process. Asking questions about the circumstances leading to the institutionalization, about family support and caring arrangements before admission, and about problems and stresses faced by

the family and their methods of coping with them can provide valuable insights into family dynamics. Involvement of all key family members in this exploratory process may help the family better cope with the "crisis of institutionalization," because they may have never discussed such issues, and such a discussion may help them to clarify what they want. The social worker's role in this process is to show acceptance and empathy and to provide a supportive atmosphere in which family members can express their true feelings, an atmosphere in which the social worker can help the family face reality.

During and after admission, reemphasizing the family's responsibility to stay involved is important provided, of course, that the relationship between the patient and the family has been positive. If a family is no longer involved in the patient's life, the patient may feel rejected by his or her family. Most families, fortunately, continue to visit, phone, write, and care for the patient following institutionalization.

The social worker's task becomes daunting indeed when bitterness and resentment have been, or remain present between the patient and family members. Trying appropriate interventions and setting reasonable goals and expectations become necessary to attempt mending dysfunctional family relationships, but only if these measures are in accord with the family's own wishes and their willingness to mend broken relationships (Greene 1982). Otherwise, facility staff members may have to accept the fact that tenuous family relationships exist, and that staff members should be prepared for occasional tensions between the staff and family. On such occasions, it is critical for the facility's staff to remain politely and pleasantly communicative with the family members.

The social worker can also assist families with making their visits with the patient more meaningful and enjoyable, especially when the patient is disoriented, confused, or bedridden. To keep the family involved, the facility can find ways to establish exchange relationships with family members. For instance, family members can become volunteers or informally adopt some patient who does not have a family. The nursing home can also help families by scheduling support group meetings and educational seminars. Programs and classes about visiting skills, processes of aging, institutionalization procedures, nursing home financing, facility policies, the relative merits of assistance and independence, roles and functions of different departments in the facility, volunteering opportunities, relationships with caregivers, and other topics can be very informa-

tive and productive. Such educational programs can also provide an opportunity for families to meet key staff members, some of whom they would otherwise never get to meet. These events help families better understand the challenges faced by the facility and they also help family members form more realistic expectations of what the facility can and cannot do. Family forums can also carry out an important advocacy role for the facility by expressing common concerns of the facility and family members. Although family members, on an individual basis, should be encouraged to express their dissatisfactions and complaints, educational seminars help focus on more productive issues. When creatively managed, these seminars can prevent family group sessions from turning into gripe sessions.

END-OF-LIFE AND HOSPICE CARE

Death is a reality in health care facilities. The association of nursing homes with death is an unfortunate stereotype. The truth is, however, that many long-term care patients will spend their final days in a nursing facility and will die there. But how a nursing home addresses end-of-life issues and how it provides appropriate services for dying patients is the important concern. Many patients will experience a natural death and pass away without any forewarning. Others may be terminally ill and may have, according to medical opinion, only a few months to live. Not all patients are likely to cope with terminal illness in the same manner. Some patients may express anger, others may become depressed, and some may show fear and anxiety. Family members may also express some of these emotions, or they may express guilt. As in other difficult circumstances, a multidisciplinary approach by the facility is likely to produce better outcomes in helping patients and their families cope with the issue of death.

Hospice care is an appropriate end-of-life service for many patients. However, the decision on whether to accept this alternative is left up to patients and their families. The multidisciplinary team, or someone functioning as the team's spokesperson, such as the social worker or the physician, is responsible for counseling the patient and family members about the hospice alternative. The patient must also give written consent that any attempts to cure terminal illness or active interventions to save life will not be pursued, if that is what the patient wants. Hospice services are

covered by Medicare, provided that life expectancy for the patient, based on medical judgment, is less than six months. Benefits under Medicare are quite generous; little or no out-of-pocket costs are usually incurred by the patient.

End-of-life care through a hospice can be provided at the nursing facility or in the patient's own home, or the hospice may be operating a small institution to which patients can be admitted. Regardless of the setting, **hospice** comprises a cluster of services to address the special needs of dying persons and their families. No heroic measures are taken to prolong life: Impending death is accepted as a given. From a medical standpoint, the emphasis is on **palliative care**, which has the objective of relieving pain and discomfort. Individual dignity and quality of life are emphasized. The patient's desires are respected, which may include suspending dietary restrictions, serving alcoholic beverages if the patient so desires, and changing established routines to accommodate the patient's wishes. It is not uncommon for patients to request spiritual counseling from a cleric of their choice or to request legal assistance handling wills and estates and finalizing funeral arrangements. These services are coordinated by the social worker. Another important aspect of hospice care is attention to the emotional needs of the patient's family, to help them cope with the expected departure of a loved one. Such assistance may continue in the form of bereavement counseling after the patient's death.

CONCLUSION

The diverse nature of social services emphasizes the need for social workers in nursing facilities who are well-trained in handling complex resident and family issues. The most critical social-service roles, according to the Institute of Medicine (2001, 27), include "linking people to a range of community resources and services, assisting in the resolution of family or financial problems, and arranging social and educational activities." In smaller facilities, social workers also handle inquiries and facilitate the admission and orientation process. However, many mid- to large-size facilities employ a director of admissions who is responsible for inquiry intake and marketing, which enables social workers to devote their energies to their core areas of responsibility.

DISCUSSION QUESTIONS

1. Provide examples of some situations in which the social worker will be required to use the skills of engagement, assessment, communication, and interviewing.
2. How can the three basic theories of aging discussed in this chapter be applied to promote individual autonomy of a patient residing in a nursing facility?
3. Describe some ways in which a nursing facility can promote interdependence to help residents feel useful and maintain their self-esteem.

INTERNET RESOURCES FOR FURTHER LEARNING

The American Hospice Foundation supports programs that serve the needs of terminally ill and grieving individuals of all ages.
www.americanhospice.org

The American Society on Aging is committed to enhancing the knowledge and skills of those working with older adults and their families.
www.asaging.org

The Hospice Association of America is a national trade organization representing more than 2,800 hospices and thousands of caregivers and volunteers who serve terminally ill patients and their families. The organization is the largest lobbying group for the hospice industry, advocating the industry's interests before Congress, regulatory agencies, other national organizations, the courts, the media, and the public.
www.hospice-america.org

The National Association of Social Workers is the largest organization of professional social workers in the world, dedicated to improving the professional growth and development of its members, to creating and maintaining professional standards, and to advancing sound social policies.
www.naswdc.org

The National Council on Aging (NCOA) is a private, nonprofit organization that provides information, training, technical assistance, advocacy, and

leadership in all aspects of aging services and issues. NCOA publications are available on topics such as lifelong learning, senior center services, adult day care, long-term care, financial issues, senior housing, rural issues, intergenerational programs, and volunteers in aging.
www.ncoa.org

The National Hospice Foundation is charitable organization whose mission is to broaden America's understanding of hospice care through research and education.
www.hospiceinfo.org

The National Hospice and Palliative Care Organization is the largest non-profit membership organization representing hospice and palliative care programs and professionals in the United States. The organization is committed to improving end-of-life care and expanding access to hospice care with the goal of profoundly enhancing quality of life for people dying in America and their loved ones.
www.nhpco.org

REFERENCES

Agich, G.J. 1995. Actual autonomy and long-term care decision making. In *Long-Term care Decisions: Ethical and Conceptual Dimensions*, eds. L.B. McCullough and N.L. Wilson, 113–136. Baltimore: Johns Hopkins University Press.

Coulshed, V. 1991. *Social Work Practice: An Introduction*. London: MacMillan.

Dubois, B. and K.K. Miley. 1999. *Social Work: An Empowering Profession*. 3rd ed. Boston: Allyn and Bacon.

Greene, R.R. 1982. Families and the nursing home social worker. *Social Work in Health Care* 7, no. 3: 57–67.

Harrigan, M.P. and R.L. Farmer. 1992. The myths and facts of aging. In *Gerontological Social Work: Knowledge, Service Settings, and Special Populations*, eds. R.L. Schneider and N.P. Kropf. Chicago: Nelson-Hall Publishers.

Institute of Medicine. 2001. *Improving The Quality of Long-Term Care*, eds. G.S. Wunderlich, and P.O. Kohler. Washington, DC: National Academy Press.

Kaplan, H.I. and B.J. Sadock. 1988. *Synopsis of Psychiatry*. 5th ed. Baltimore: Williams and Wilkins.

Kropf, N.P. and E.D. Hutchison. 1992. Effective practice with elderly clients. In *Gerontological Social Work: Knowledge, Service Settings, and Special Populations*, eds. R.L. Schneider and N.P. Kropf. Chicago: Nelson-Hall Publishers.

Newman, B.M. and P.A. Newman. 1987. *Development Through Life: A Psychosocial Approach*. Chicago: Dorsey Press.

O'Hare, P.A. 1988. An overview of discharge planning. In *Discharge Planning: Strategies for Assuring Continuity of Care*, eds. P.A. O'Hare and M.A. Terry. Rockville, MD: Aspen Publishers, Inc.

Patchner, M.A. and L.S. Patchner. 1991. Social work practice in nursing homes. In *Social Work Practice with the Elderly*, eds. M.J. Holosko and M.D. Feit. Toronto: Canadian Scholars' Press.

Medical Care, Nursing, and Rehabilitation

continues

6. Patient assessment, its objectives and approach. The resident assessment instrument (RAI). Care planning and progress charting.

7. Infection control. Main features of an infection control program.

8. Falls and their prevention. Pressure ulcers and their prevention.

9. Types of physical restraints. Risks of using restraints. When restraint use may be appropriate.

10. Urinary incontinence and the basic approach to managing incontinence. Toileting program. Urinary catheters and risks of infection.

11. Pharmacy consultation and its purpose. Storing drugs and recordkeeping. The emergency medication kit. Use and misuse of psychotropic drugs.

12. Rehabilitation and its objectives. Short-term restorative therapy. Cases when long-range therapy is necessary. Main types of restorative therapies. Examples of maintenance rehabilitation.

Nursing care forms the core of services provided in a long-term care facility. Nursing is also the largest department, employing about 70% of the nursing home staff. In a sense, almost all other services interface with nursing. But nursing's central role should not be interpreted as dominant over other functions. Administrative leadership and an integrative approach are essential to an organization in which other disciplines recognize nursing's central role, and each discipline provides adjunctive support. The best patient care can be delivered only when each discipline, including nursing, recognizes the interdependency between the various departments and services.

MEDICAL CARE

Attending Physicians

Each patient's individual care is under the general direction of an attending physician, chosen by the patient. Most attending physicians are gen-

eral or family practitioners. Often the patient has been under the care of a community-based physician for some time, and after being admitted to a nursing facility, may have the same physician follow up with medical care in the facility. Many physicians, however, avoid nursing home practice. In that case, the patient is given the option of selecting a physician from among those who make regular nursing home visits. But it is important to recognize that each patient has the right to receive care from his or her own physician, provided the physician is willing to comply with the facility's policies and regulatory standards. Time constraints, rigid regulatory requirements, negative perceptions of nursing homes, litigation, and inadequate reimbursement for their services are some of the main reasons why many physicians do not participate in nursing home care.

The medical services for long-term care patients differ quite substantially from hospital care which focuses on acute episodes, medical procedures, and surgical interventions. Medical care in a nursing facility is more akin to primary care office-based practice, except that the physician must make regular visits to the nursing facility instead of the patient going to the physician's clinic. Typically, physician visits are infrequent, generally occurring every thirty days or so, because most chronic conditions do not require frequent medical evaluation and treatment. Attending physicians diagnose medical problems and prescribe treatment and medications, but the actual treatment is rendered by nurses in accordance with the attending physician's orders. Nurses routinely monitor the patient's condition. Any substantial changes, non-response to treatment, or other negative observations are immediately relayed to the attending physician who then decides on the action to take. If a patient's condition changes for worse or some complication develops, most physicians require that the patient be transferred to a hospital.

Both physicians and nurses feel the need for shared communication to facilitate treatment decisions. Physicians typically must rely on nurses' skills. Nurses often express pride in their ability to judge clinical situations, report them to physicians by telephone, and get orders they need to give good care (Hanson et al. 2002).

Good patient care in nursing facilities is the product of teamwork in which an interdisciplinary (also called multidisciplinary) team of professionals is responsible for patient assessment, care planning, and delivery of clinical services. The attending physician should be a member of this

interdisciplinary team. Medical oversight by the physician is critical, but it must incorporate the input from other disciplines such as nursing, rehabilitation, social work, dietetics, recreational therapy, and pharmacy. Another important aspect of medical care in nursing facilities is involvement of the patient and family in the plan of treatment.

The attending physician also makes referrals when specialized services are needed. The referral may be for transfer to a hospital for acute episodes that the nursing facility is not equipped to handle. Other types of common referrals are to medical specialists such as cardiologists, nephrologists, and orthopedists. Nursing facilities generally provide the more common types of specialty services through contracts with independent practitioners such as podiatrists, dermatologists, and ophthalmologists who may do routine screenings and evaluations in addition to receiving sporadic referrals.

Medical Director

Nursing home regulations require the appointment of a licensed physician to function as the medical director. In all but a handful of large nursing homes, the administrator contracts with a community physician to fill the position on a part-time basis. In an average-sized 120-bed facility, the medical director can be expected to spend 2 to 4 hours per week (Krein 2003).

The medical director reports to the administrator but has an advisory relationship with the rest of the organization (see Figure II-1). Through regular communications with the medical director, the administrator can keep abreast of major patient care issues in the facility. On the other hand, by regularly communicating with the administrator, the medical director can remain in touch with administrative policies and management issues that may have a bearing on patient care services. The medical director also provides insights into the health care needs of the community and works with the administrator to address those needs.

In spite of the social and professional stigma that is sometimes associated with working in nursing homes, physicians report that caring for nursing home residents is gratifying and meaningful work. In a qualitative study conducted by medical students, physicians working in nursing homes reported that relationships with residents, families, and staff members; interesting and meaningful patient care; and autonomy were the most positive aspects of their role. Less desirable aspects included staff

turnover, difficult expectations, and administrative issues (Bern-Klug et al. 2003). This type of information about what physicians value about their work in nursing facilities can help administrators structure more desirable roles and attract more physicians to meet the growing demand in nursing homes.

Personal Traits and Qualifications

The medical director should be a team player with good interpersonal and conflict-resolution skills that will enable him or her to work effectively with the interdisciplinary team. He or she should have a flexible nature and be a good listener, with tolerance for addressing regulatory-compliance issues (Krein 2003).

Ideally, the medical director should be a geriatrician, but physicians who have this kind of specialization are rare. The next best choice is to have someone who has substantial experience in geriatric medicine or someone who has an interest in the field and is committed to acquiring the necessary knowledge and skills through continuing education. **Geriatrics** is a specialized area of medicine that deals with the special health problems faced by the elderly. Knowledge of geriatrics is essential for effectively treating a wide array of medical conditions in a diverse elderly population residing in nursing homes.

An important aspect of geriatric medicine focuses on managing chronic health problems and comorbidities that require simultaneous interventions. Comorbidities present special medical challenges in long-term care. For example, when congestive heart failure and chronic obstructive pulmonary disease are both present in the same patient, the treatment for one condition worsens the other (Peck 2001). Adverse drug interactions can occur, presenting serious consequences. It is also important to distinguish between changes that normally accompany aging and symptoms of illness that are treatable. Treatable medical conditions such as joint pain are sometimes trivialized as normal age-related problems. Similarly, delirium and dementia are not necessarily natural symptoms of old age, but may be manifestations of hypothyroidism, multiple emboli, fluid and electrolyte imbalance, or drug toxicity (Levenson 1985). Numerous other symptoms common in the elderly are frequently misdiagnosed and incorrectly treated. Other factors should also be taken into account. The elderly may show different responses to prescription drugs than younger people. Because the elderly may have reduced tolerance to

some drugs, inadvertant overdosage may be more likely in elderly patients than in younger ones. Hence, a judicious medical approach becomes necessary. Otherwise, **iatrogenic** problems, i.e., complications caused by medical treatment, are the likely results. Hydration and nutrition are of special concern when caring for the elderly patient. Multivitamins or special food supplements may have to be prescribed, particularly when regular food intake is inadequate. Certain organ functions may have declined, leading to impaired metabolism. Loss of skin turgor can lead to skin breakdown and development of pressure ulcers, which are often, although not always, preventable. Depression or other psychological disorders may accompany physical conditions. Dementia, delirium, and depression present symptoms that are quite similar, but each requires a different medical approach. Geriatric medicine also includes palliative care during terminal illness.

The American Medical Directors Association (AMDA) has developed the Curriculum on Geriatric Clinical Practice in Long Term Care to train attending physicians in both administrative and clinical management. AMDA also offers certification as a Certified Medical Director based on demonstrated competence in clinical medicine and medical direction/administrative medicine in long-term care. A number of residency programs in internal medicine and family practice also provide additional training in geriatric medicine. The American Board of Internal Medicine and the American Board of Family Practice confer a Certificate of Added Qualification in Geriatric Medicine on physicians who complete this training and pass the examination. However, only a few physicians hold such certification.

Functions

The medical director functions as a key consultant to the nursing facility on almost all aspects of patient care. Not uncommonly, the medical director is also the attending physician for most patients in a facility. As an attending physician, the medical director is in a position to obtain first-hand knowledge of the adequacy and appropriateness of clinical care provided to the patients and to become involved in consultations to improve quality of care for all residents. However, a medical director's involvement in the facility and the level of clinical oversight really depend on his or her qualifications and skills rather than how many patients he or she has in

the facility. In light of anti-kickback legislation (see Chapter 4), the medical director should be paid fair compensation for his or her administrative responsibilities. The medical director's involvement as an attending physician must be a completely separate practice as far as reimbursement and compensation are concerned.

The main functions of the medical director can be classified into four essential roles:

- Oversight
- Advisory
- Teaching
- Representative

Oversight Role

The medical director must help implement best practice standards. As the chief medical officer for the facility, the medical director helps ensure that clinical services meet or exceed established standards and also helps identify potential risks. Standards of care are defined in written policies and procedures. Some examples of clinical practices in which policies and procedures are necessary include infection-control practices; minimizing the use of indwelling catheters; techniques for handling catheters; obtaining urine and stool specimens; isolation practices; handling contaminated linen; preventing and treating pressure ulcers; disease-specific precautions (e.g., HIV and hepatitis); immunizations for residents and staff members; minimizing use of restraints; preventing falls; and investigating accidents or incidents. The medical director should also assist the facility with the oversight of infection-control surveillance, vaccination programs, efforts to reduce the risk of falls and use of restraints, adequacy of nutrition, hydration and skin-integrity programs, and quality-improvement analysis and processes (Krein 2003).

The medical director must also ensure that the facility's staff members follow the established policies and procedures. Regular rounds, observations, and attentiveness to any patient care concerns expressed by patients, staff members, and family members are generally the means of monitoring the adequacy of clinical care. Any breakdowns in the facility's skill capacity must be addressed with the administrator. Such breakdowns generally occur when the facility experiences turnover of key staff, or when it adds a new service.

Advisory Role

The medical director's advisory role directly stems from his or her effectiveness in carrying out the oversight role. Admission policies should be periodically reviewed to ensure that the facility has adequate skill capacity to deliver services to the types of patients being admitted. Similarly, other policies and procedures should be periodically reviewed to ensure that they remain current. The medical director also functions as an advisor to the various committees such as infection control committee, quality improvement committee, utilization review committee, medical records committee, pharmaceutical review committee, safety committee, and ethics committee. Most of these committees meet once a quarter, and for the sake of efficiency, meetings of the various committees are often combined. In case of an outbreak of infection, the medical director should work closely with the nursing staff in identifying the **pathogen**, preventing its spread, treating the affected patients and staff members, and, if necessary, reporting and coordinating recommended measures with the appropriate public health agency.

Teaching Role

The medical director plays an active role in staff training and can be very influential in establishing a professional and caring culture in the organization (Krein 2003). This role is often carried out informally during routine interactions with caregivers, or while making bedside rounds with nurses. Occasionally, the medical director may also be invited to make presentations in formal training sessions. Communicating with families and educating them about issues that are commonly misunderstood, and the medical director's participation in family seminars can help establish better relationships between the facility, patients, and families.

Representative Role

The medical director is the facility's representative to the medical community. During interactions with colleagues, he or she should function as the facility's advocate and as an expert on medical care issues in long-term care in general. Nursing facilities often have to address regulatory noncompliance issues related to the required frequency of visits and documentation with attending physicians. Even though noninterference with the practice of medicine is a well-recognized professional code of conduct, and physicians have as a result developed a high degree of autonomy, a medical director's collegial influence can go a long way in helping the

facility gain compliance from attending physicians. On the other hand, the medical director does have a responsibility to oversee that the delivery of medical care by other physicians is adequate and appropriate. In consultation with the administrator, he or she may have to take steps if attending physicians do not comply with basic standards of medical practice. One remedy is to advise and assist the patient in choosing another physician. Nursing facilities also feel the frustration when medical information often does not follow a patient when he or she moves from a hospital to the nursing home. The medical director should meet with the appropriate hospital personnel and create or obtain mutually agreed-upon transfer criteria and information-sharing protocols (Krein 2003).

NURSING DEPARTMENT

Nursing services are not only the central hub, but the department is also the largest in the facility, and the nursing staff generally has the most interaction with residents and their families. Organization of the nursing department is depicted in Figure II-1, but variations do exist.

Nursing Administration

The nursing department is headed by a director of nursing (DON). The DON is generally supported by an assistant DON (ADON), who may be responsible for staffing and also function as the In-service Director (director of training) in average-sized nursing homes. In larger facilities, an alternative to the ADON is to have a nursing supervisor on each shift—three supervisors covering the three shifts—in which case a separate in-service director's position would be necessary. If the facility operates a nursing assistant (nurse aide) training program, the in-service director must be a registered nurse (RN). Since resident assessment has become a critical driver of the Medicare prospective payment system (discussed in Chapter 4), most facilities of 120 beds and more also have a RN in the position of Resident Assessment Coordinator. This position, as well as the in-service director, may report to either the DON or the administrator.

Director of Nursing

The DON has a position of substantial responsibility. In most facilities, the position is second only to that of the administrator. Actually, the DON is often in charge of the facility when the administrator may be

temporarily absent. In larger nursing homes, where an assistant administrator may be employed, sometimes there is a direct chain of command
between the administrator and the DON, whereas the assistant administrator may have direct responsibility for the remaining departments.
Effectively-managed nursing facilities have a triad relationship between
the administrator, the medical director, and the DON, and this triad is
involved in making many top-level evaluations and decisions regarding
the facility's operation.

Skills, Qualifications, and Functions

The DON must be an RN, and the position requires a composite of clinical and management skills. However, DONs who have formal training in
both nursing and management are rare. Most acquire management skills
through experience, although management skill development through
continuing education, seminars, or college-level courses is highly recommended. On the clinical side, some DONs possess a bachelor's degree in
nursing, but many have nursing preparation through a two-year associate's degree or an RN diploma. A small number have master's degrees.
Although some have completed certification requirements in gerontology,
many have not. Regardless of their level of clinical preparation, however,
DONs—like other high-level clinical personnel—must know gerontology and geriatric care.

   The DON is not a direct caregiver, but mainly performs administrative
and supervisory functions, which at times can be quite challenging. The
main responsibilities of this position can be summarized under five main
categories:

- Staffing
- Training
- Patient care
- Policy
- Administration

Staffing

The DON is responsible for ensuring that the nursing units are adequately staffed and that the nursing personnel are adequately trained.
Staffing can pose some daunting challenges, because depending on labor-
market conditions, nurses may be in short supply. Recruiting and retaining qualified staff members is often difficult, and a typical facility experiences high turnover and absenteeism among nursing assistants. Staff

shortages coupled with the need to have adequate staff coverage 24 hours a day, 7 days a week present special challenges in staffing and scheduling. Large facilities often designate a full-time person to the tasks of recruiting and scheduling nursing assistants.

Training

The DON must ensure adequate levels of skill competency among the nursing staff. Needs for individual as well as group training should be evaluated periodically, and any deficiencies should be addressed through appropriate training programs. Many facilities also operate nursing assistant training programs. Regulations require that these programs be under the DON's general supervision. The DON, however, is not permitted to do the actual training, which should be delegated to a qualified nurse instructor. To provide well-rounded instruction, professionals from other disciplines such as the medical director, physical and occupational therapists, dietician, pharmacist, social worker, activities director, fire and safety expert, and nursing home administrator should also be included. The law prohibits states from approving nurse aide training programs at facilities found to have substandard quality of care or that have been subject to certain enforcement actions such as civil monetary penalties.

Patient Care

The responsibility for patient care actually begins at the time of preadmission inquiry (see Chapter 7). Particularly in non-routine cases, the DON should be included in the inquiry process to determine whether the facility is adequately prepared to provide the needed care demanded by a patient's condition. Subsequently, the DON may perform coordinating duties to ensure that the nursing unit is prepared for a new admission. The DON also oversees timely execution of patient assessments, development of an individualized plan of care (or care plan) for each patient, and the delivery of nursing care. The nursing staff looks to the DON for leadership and expertise when care-related problems arise. The DON also plays a vital coordinating role with attending physicians by facilitating timely visits and ensuring that they receive the necessary nursing support.

Policy

The DON is an active participant in the various patient care committees, such as infection control committee, quality improvement committee, utilization review committee, medical records committee, pharmaceutical

review committee, safety committee, and ethics committee. The DON's input into the policy and decision-making process is often indispensable. The DON generally provides information and data for evaluation and deliberation by the various committees. At a minimum, policies and procedures for nursing services must be established to comply with the state licensure regulations and Medicaid and Medicare certification requirements (summarized in Exhibit 3-2). However, this area of responsibility must extend beyond the minimum requirements with the objective of continuous improvement in the quality of patient care. The facility's nursing care policies, procedures, and practice guidelines constitute the standards of patient care delivery. They are compiled into a nursing policies and procedures manual, which is used as a reference and training resource for new staff members. This manual becomes a living document that is updated as policies and practices are revised.

Administration

The DON is responsible for the effective management of the nursing department. The DON is also involved in a variety of administrative tasks that free up the caregivers so that they can devote their time and energy to delivering patient care. Although, as a matter of routine, the DON is in the facility during regular business hours, some variation from routine is necessary so that the DON has some ongoing contact with the staff, patients, and families during evenings, nights, and weekends. Many families can visit the facility only during evenings or weekends. Therefore, charge nurses on the evening and weekend shifts should be trained to address family concerns. A communication system should be implemented so that family complaints and concerns regarding patient care are related to the DON. On the other hand, periodic availability of the DON during non-routine hours can lend support to the nursing staff, and contact with families can help resolve issues before they turn into bigger problems. Having a large staff, and a preponderance of licensed practical (vocational) nurses (LPNs/LVNs) in relation to RNs, the DON is frequently involved in ongoing training and consultation and in handling staff-related issues, such as disciplinary action for non-performance of duties.

Nursing Organization

A nursing facility's clinical structure, constituting nursing units and nursing stations, and the criteria for staffing were discussed in Chapter 5. The nurs-

ing units form the basis for establishing the organizational structure of the department, with each nursing unit headed by a charge nurse. Charge nurses report to the nursing supervisors, the ADON, or the DON, depending on how the nursing department is organized. In most facilities of moderate size, charge nurses report directly to the DON. Charge nurses are responsible for assessing patient needs and planning care, supervising staff on the unit, communicating with physicians and family members regarding patient care issues, and supervising patient care delivery.

The number of nurses on each nursing unit, skill mix of nurses (ratio of RNs to LPNs/LVNs), and the ratio of nursing assistants to patients on each shift, are dictated by the number of patients and the level of clinical care required by the patients (see details in Chapter 14). Most RNs working in long-term care are graduates of hospital-based diploma programs or 2-year associate degree (ADN) programs. RNs are generally responsible for patient assessment, care planning, and quality assessment. LPNs/LVNs are generally graduates of 1-year technical programs offered at community colleges or vocational technical schools. LPNs render treatments and administer medications. Several states allow the routine administration of medications by specially-trained medication aides (or medication technicians) under the general supervision of licensed nurses. Use of qualified medication aides or technicians can relieve nurses, enabling them to devote their time to other nursing care and monitoring functions.

Nursing assistants (nurse aides) are non-licensed **paraprofessionals** who provide most of the hands-on nursing care to residents. According to the nursing home reform legislation contained in the Omnibus Budget Reconciliation Act of 1987 (OBRA-87), nurse aides are required to be certified and are now commonly called certified nursing assistants (CNAs). To deliver effective care, CNAs must possess certain basic nursing skills that include taking vital signs such as temperature, pulse rate, and blood pressure; measuring height and weight; recognizing abnormal changes in body functions such as urine output and bowel function; reporting changes in patient's condition to the charge nurse; and documenting observations. CNAs also assist patients with their ADLs and personal care such as bathing, dressing, grooming, oral hygiene, eating assistance, hydration, transferring, positioning, turning, toileting assistance, cleaning up and drying after incontinence, and changing bed linens. CNAs also provide restorative nursing care such as range of motion exercises, bowel and bladder training, and use of assistive devices to promote

independence, although some facilities have specially trained rehab aides for restorative nursing care. CNAs are also required to meet the residents' mental health and social needs by responding to changes in behavior, providing family support, and caring for residents with dementia or other special needs, such as physical handicaps. The nature of these tasks requires CNAs to have appropriate training in how to communicate with residents and visiting family members. In addition, CNAs must be trained in infection-control practices, they must be prepared to use fire and safety procedures in case of an emergency, and they must understand how to preserve and promote the patients' rights to privacy, confidentiality, autonomy, dignity, and freedom from abuse and neglect.

PATIENT ASSESSMENT AND CARE PLANNING

Since 1998, a facility participating in the Medicare and Medicaid programs is required to conduct comprehensive resident assessments. The primary tool used in patient assessment is the Minimum Data Set (MDS) [See Appendix 4–I]. As discussed in Chapter 4, MDS data establish the basis for determining Medicare payments to the facility. In this chapter, the resident assessment instrument (RAI) is discussed from the patient care perspective. From this standpoint, assessment can be regarded as the first step in patient care planning and the delivery of patient care. **Assessment** is defined as the process through which health care professionals attempt to reliably characterize the patient's physical health, functional abilities, cognitive functioning, psychological state, social well-being, and past and current use of formal services (Kane 1995). Patient assessment serves two major purposes: (1) The process helps the facility staff learn about the resident's strengths, problems, and needs. These strengths and needs are subsequently addressed in the individualized plan of care for the resident. (2) It enables the staff to track important changes in the patient's overall status and to revise care plans accordingly.

Comprehensive patient assessment requires a multidisciplinary approach. Although the nursing department often coordinates and oversees the process, input from other disciplines such as social services, activities, dietary, and rehabilitation are also necessary. Included in the formal

assessment are history-and-physical information obtained from the admitting physician. The patient's and family's involvement in the assessment and care planning process have become increasingly more important, because they can furnish non-medical information vital to holistic care. The MDS also has a section on the patient's customary routines during the year prior to admission. This information is obtained from the patient or the family.

Resident Assessment Instrument

The RAI consists of a set of documents that streamline the assessment process. According to regulations, the RAI must be completed and/or coordinated by an RN who must sign and certify each assessment. The RAI has three components: Minimum Data Set (MDS), Resident Assessment Protocols (RAPs), and Utilization Guidelines. Utilization guidelines are instructions on when and how to use the RAI. The MDS incorporates a core set of screening, clinical, and functional status elements. An illustrative summary of the various sections of the MDS instrument appears in Exhibit 8-1. The full MDS instrument appears as Appendix 4-I.

Use of the MDS elements during the assessment process reveals some actual problems and also conditions that constitute risk factors for potential functional problems, which call for further evaluation. A **risk factor** is any attribute that is known to increase the likelihood of developing a disease or negative health condition in the future. Conditions that pose such potential risks are referred to as triggers. A **trigger** raises a "red flag" to alert the staff that a patient requires additional review and assessment. Examples of triggers include non-independence in functions such as bed mobility, transfer, walking, dressing, eating, or personal hygiene; impaired decision making; delirium; mood changes; and use of psychoactive medications. For each of the triggers, RAPs are used to carry out further assessment. There are 18 conditions that can trigger a RAP (see Exhibit 8-2). The multidisciplinary team reviews the trigger conditions to understand the nature of the problem from various perspectives and determines the causes specific to the resident. The team decides whether the trigger condition affects the resident's functional status or well-being and warrants a care plan intervention (Sullivan and Atlas 1998). The RAP document summarizes the most critical elements of the MDS, and the RAP information is used for developing the patient's plan of care. The assessment forms are made a part of the patient's medical record.

EXHIBIT 8-1

Assessment Sections of the Minimum Data Set (MDS 2.0) and Staff Members Responsible for Completing Each Section

Social Worker

Section A

- Identification information, such as name, gender, birth date, race/ethnicity, and Medicaid/Medicare information.
- Demographic information, such as prior living arrangements, prior occupation, education, language, conditions related to MR/DD, and customary routines (staying up late, daytime naps, activities, eating patterns, ADL patterns, and patterns of social involvement).

Section B

- Cognitive patterns, such as memory, ability to make decisions, and delirium.

Section C

- Communication/hearing patterns, such as speech, use of hearing aids, and ability to understand others.

Section E

- Mood and behavior patterns, such as depression, anxiety, wandering, and behaviors that are verbally or physically abusive

Section F

- Psychosocial well-being, such as social involvement, engaging in activities, social conflict, and past roles.

Section Q

- Discharge potential

Unit Charge Nurse

Section D

- Vision patterns, such as limitations, degree of impairment, and use of eyeglasses.

Section G

- Physical functioning, such as ADL dependence, ambulation, gait, range of motion, and functional rehabilitation potential.

continues

EXHIBIT 8–1 *continued*

Section H
- Continence issues, such as bowel or bladder incontinence, and elimination patterns

Section J
- Health conditions, such as weight, fluid intake, pain, shortness of breath, and recent accidents.

Section L
- Oral/dental status, such as dentures, condition of teeth and gums, and mouth care.

Section M
- Skin condition, such as presence of decubitus ulcers and their severity, skin problems (bruises, rashes, and tears), skin treatments (use of pressure relieving devices, ulcer or wound care, nutrition or hydration interventions, dressings, and use of ointments), and foot problems (corns, bunions, infection, or open lesions).

Section O
- Medications, such as prescription drugs, injections, and use of psychoactive medications.

Section P
- Special treatments and procedures, such as oxygen, dialysis, chemotherapy, tracheostomy, professional rehabilitation therapies, restorative care, and devices or restraints used.

Activity Staff

Section N
- Activity pursuit patterns, such as preferred activities, preferred location, and time spent in activities.

Dietician or Dietary Manager

Section K
- Oral/nutritional status, such as swallowing problems, height and weight, weight change, appetite, and nutritional approaches (tube feeding, mechanically altered diet, therapeutic diet, dietary supplements, etc.).

continues

EXHIBIT 8–1 *continued*

Medical Records

Section I
- Disease diagnoses, such as physical and neurological problems, infections, etc.

Plan of Care

Nursing facilities are mandated by regulations to prepare a comprehensive plan of care (or care plan) for each resident within seven days of completing the assessment. Based on the patient's limitations, strengths, and needs ascertained by the assessment process, the **plan of care** specifies approaches for addressing problems and needs by incorporating the

EXHIBIT 8–2

Trigger Conditions that Require Further Assessment Using Resident Assessment Protocols

Delirium
Cognitive loss or dementia
Visual function
Communication
Functional status (ADLs)
Urinary incontinence and use of indwelling catheter
Psychosocial well-being
Mood state
Behavioral problems
Activities
Falls
Nutritional status
Feeding tubes
Dehydration and fluid intake
Dental care
Pressure ulcers
Psychotropic medications
Physical restraints

patient's own strengths and potential for improvement, stipulating action by the staff, and establishing goals for progress to be achieved. A care plan is comprehensive. It must address the multiple issues faced by elderly patients. Because physical, psychosocial, emotional, and spiritual issues must be addressed in a holistic manner, care planning requires a multidisciplinary approach. The care planning team should include the unit charge nurse, social worker, activity staff, dietician or dietary manager, and rehabilitation staff. Input should be obtained from the attending physician and from direct care staff such as CNAs. The process should also involve the resident and family members. Care plans are generally reviewed and revised every 60 to 90 days or when a major change has occurred in the patient's condition. Previous goals and progress are evaluated. New problems and issues are addressed, and new goals are established. A professional staff member such as an RN or the social worker is assigned the responsibility to schedule care plan meetings and invite representatives from the various disciplines for their participation and input.

A plan of care is like a blueprint that guides the staff into providing routine interventions necessary for accomplishing clinical goals for a specific patient. It furnishes details on interventions such as nursing treatments, medications, special diets, rehabilitation therapies, participation in recreational activities, and restorative care. It also highlights the specific goals that each intervention is designed to accomplish. Interventions are planned after carefully considering what the patient can do or should be allowed to do for himself or herself, with the objective of promoting maximum independent functioning.

As the plan of care is carried out, each member of the multidisciplinary team adds progress notes to the patient's medical record. Progress made, or lack thereof, in achieving the established goals is evaluated over time and is carefully documented. The progress evaluations provide further guidance in establishing new goals, and in deciding which interventions should be discontinued, modified, or added.

INFECTION CONTROL

Infections are a common problem in health care settings, and the elderly in particular are predisposed to various types of infections. In nursing homes, most infections affect the urinary tract, respiratory tract, skin and soft tissues, or gastrointestinal tract (Ouslander et al. 1997). Complica-

tions resulting from infections constitute the main reason for transferring patients from a long-term care facility to an acute care hospital. Hence, preventing and containing infection should be a primary concern. Since overuse of antibiotics in recent years has rendered certain bacterial and viral strains resistant to drugs, treating some infections is presenting major medical challenges. Antibiotic-resistant microorganisms (AROs) are becoming common in nursing facilities. These microbes include methicillin-resistant *Staphylococcus aureus* (MRSA) and vancomycin-resistant enterococci (VRE), as well as strains of *Streptococcus pneumoniae*, *Pseudomonas* spp., *Neisseria gonorrhea*, *Salmonella* spp., and others (Sharbaugh 2003).

State and federal regulations require nursing facilities to implement infection-control programs. **Infection control** is a comprehensive program that is in essence a safety program. Its main goals are to protect the residents, the staff, and visitors from contracting infections while in the facility, and to prevent the transmission of infection. Generally, the task of surveillance and monitoring of infections is assigned to a registered nurse, such as the ADON. This individual is often called the **infection-control practitioner (ICP)**. But infection control is not merely a nursing responsibility. An effective program requires the involvement of all departments. In the following sections, the main features of an effective infection-control program are described:

- Policies and procedures
- Screening
- Infection control practices
- Surveillance
- Education
- Control of infectious outbreaks

Policies and Procedures

The facility should develop and update infection-control policies and procedures in consultation with the infection-control committee. The policies should cover areas such as admission and transfer of residents, employee health, immunizations, guidelines for visitors, housekeeping practices, laundry procedures, food preparation, food poisoning, procedures for cleaning and sterilizing equipment, isolation procedures, waste disposal, treatment of biohazardous waste, pest control, detection and

control of infection outbreaks, and staff education. Nursing practices such as caring for wounds, inserting catheters, and collecting urine specimens require sterile techniques, which should be outlined in written procedures.

Screening

Patient history and physical at the time of admission should be carefully reviewed for the presence of any infections or contagious disease. New tuberculosis (TB) cases occur more frequently among the elderly than among younger age groups, except those infected with the human immunodeficiency virus (HIV), and nursing home admission actually doubles a patient's risk of developing TB. Also, the TB case rate for nursing home employees is three times higher than the rate expected for other employed adults of similar age, race, and sex (Anonymous 1990). All patients admitted to nursing homes must be screened for TB in accordance with state health department guidelines. All staff members must have an initial physical examination at the time of employment and subsequent annual physicals to screen for any infectious diseases. If they have a documented positive tuberculin skin test (TST), a chest X-ray is necessary. Employees who show symptoms of transmissable infections, such as influenza or staphylococcus infection, should not come to work till they are declared safe to return.

General Infection-Control Practices

Asepsis, the absence of harmful microorganisms called pathogens, requires practicing clean procedures. The primary goal of asepsis is to prevent cross-contamination, that is, transferring pathogens from soiled surfaces to clean ones. Frequently washing hands with soap and clean water is among the most important aseptic practices but is often neglected. Hand hygiene should also incorporate hand **antisepsis**: removing or destroying microorganisms. Hand antisepsis can be achieved by using an alcohol-based hand rub, which is waterless, and therefore does not require a sink and paper towels. The microbe-killing action of an alcohol-based hand rub is twice as fast as that of traditional handwashing. Alcohol rubs have also been proven to be gentler on the hands than soap and water, because they contain emollients or moisturizers, which help the skin retain more of its natural water content, which soap and water often strip away (Hand hygiene 2001).

Other aseptic practices include washing food and utensils in the kitchen before cooking, cleaning food preparation surfaces, separating and properly handling clean and soiled linens, and removing trash using specific techniques. Infection-control training and practices are particularly important for nursing staff members, who are frequently exposed to soil and body wastes. They also provide patient care and touch clean surfaces. Without frequent handwashing in between clean and soiled contact, they can spread disease-causing pathogens. The environment should also be protected while transporting trash or soiled linens. All trash must be properly bagged and placed in sealed containers. Similarly, soiled linens should be placed in sealed containers when they are transported through the facility.

Isolation precautions constitute another important aspect of infection control. Two types of isolation precautions are used (Grubbs and Blasband 2000):

- Standard precautions
- Transmission-based precautions

Standard precautions (SPs), previously called universal precautions, are used when caring for all residents, regardless of whether or not they have an infectious disease. SPs are designed to protect caregivers from infection through exposure to blood, body fluids, and body substances. It is assumed that all body fluids are potentially infectious. The precautions include wearing gloves when touching body fluids, wearing gowns when the caregiver's clothing may come in contact with body fluids, and wearing masks and protective eye wear when body fluids may splash. SPs also include preventing injuries and infections from sharps, such as needles and blades, which must be disposed of in appropriately marked sharps-containers.

Transmission-based precautions are required during care for residents who may have a communicable disease. Transmission-based precautions are used in addition to standard precautions. The facility must establish procedures for visitors to report to the nursing station before visiting patients for whom transmission-based precautions are indicated.

Surveillance

Surveillance for **nosocomial** infections has been clearly established as a key element of all infection control programs (Stevenson 1999). This function is specifically delegated to the ICP. Surveillance is carried out by

collecting appropriate data on all infections in the facility, determining the rates of infection, identifying infection trends, isolating possible causes of infection, and implementing corrective measures. A strong surveillance program requires all nursing staff members to be vigilant and report all cases of infection. Surveillance may give early warning about the outbreak of an epidemic. It also provides valuable information to the infection control committee so that appropriate remedies may be proposed, such as changing certain policies, practices, or procedures.

Education

Ongoing education of staff and visitors about infection control is a critical preventive measure. All staff members in the facility should participate in infection-control training. These educational programs should be repeated often, particularly given the high staff turnover common in nursing homes.

Control of Infectious Outbreaks

An **epidemic** is defined as the excessive prevalence of a negative health condition in the facility. Epidemic outbreaks are noted by clustered cases of symptoms such as diarrhea, urinary tract infections, influenza, or scabies (Garibaldi et al. 1981). Influenza outbreaks, for example, can lead to substantial morbidity and mortality among the elderly when preventive measures are not rapidly deployed. Influenza outbreaks can be prevented by annually giving flu shots to residents and the staff.

Access to a laboratory must be available to do rapid antigen testing, and influenza antiviral medication must be available to control outbreaks. The DON-administrator-medical director triad should work together to isolate and address any outbreaks as swiftly as possible. The local health department is also typically involved in assisting the facility with a systematic approach to controlling infectious outbreaks.

SPECIAL AREAS OF NURSING CARE MANAGEMENT

Nursing care deals with numerous health conditions found in a diverse elderly population. Since the development of resident assessment protocols, certain trigger conditions must be targeted for further assessment

and care planning. This section deals with some of these areas that have special significance for nursing care management. The topics discussed in this section also have a great deal of relevance for improving the quality of patient care.

Falls and Fall Prevention

Injuries sustained from falls, and subsequent decline in the ability to carry out activities of daily living, are one reason why nursing home placement becomes necessary in the first place. In nursing homes, approximately 50% of the residents fall each year (Yarme and Yarme 2001), and an estimated 10% of falls result in serious injury (Tinetti 2003). Fall related injuries result in substantial legal liability for the nursing facility, as well as pain, suffering, loss of function, and death among residents. Among the elderly who are admitted to hospitals after falling, only about half remain alive a year later (Rubenstein et al. 1991). Experiencing a fall may induce a fear of falling again. Psychological factors such as anxiety and depression may follow.

Numerous factors, both intrinsic and extrinsic, may predispose older people to falls. Effects of certain drugs, cognitive impairment, visual impairment, and frailty caused by illness are some of the main intrinsic or medical factors (Downton 1992). Extrinsic factors are mostly environmental, such as poor lighting, wet floors, and loose objects. Preventing falls should be a major aim of the nursing staff, even though accurately predicting who would fall is very difficult, because so many factors are involved.

A fall prevention program begins with evaluating potential risks for falling (Figure 8-1). At a very basic level, a person with a history of falls is likely to fall again, but other risk factors may be discovered in a person who has never fallen before. Nursing interventions, such as working with new residents till they become properly oriented to where the bed is in relation to the chair and the bathroom, teaching residents how to safely navigate from the bed to the bathroom and back, strength training to improve gait and balance, and monitoring and supervision by the nursing staff, can all play a role in preventing falls. In collaboration with the nursing staff, the physical therapist should evaluate whether assistive devices are needed for safe ambulation. Staff members should monitor the patient's ability to use them properly during ambulation and transfer, and provide training as necessary. One study reported that almost half of the falls in nursing homes occur on the 3-11 shift. Adding one staff member

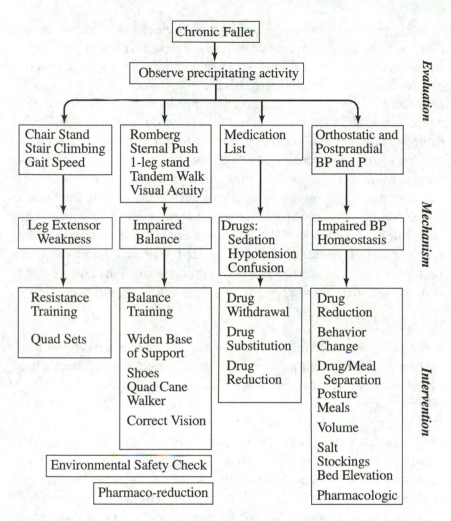

Source: Lipsitz, L.A., et al. 1997. Falls. In *Quality care in the nursing home*, eds. J.N. Morris et al., 258–277. St. Louis, MO: Mosby-Year Book, Inc. Reprinted with permission from Elsevier.

FIGURE 8-1 Key Components of the Clinical Evaluation of the Resident Who Falls Chronically

on this shift, repositioning room furniture, and adding a restorative activity program on the 3-11 shift curtailed the total number of falls by 38% and the total number of fractures by 50% (Hofmann et al. 2003). In some cases, it may be necessary to reduce or withdraw certain drugs that are potentially related to falls through their sedating, hypotensive, or cognitive effects (Lipsitz et al. 1997).

Safety of the environment is one of the key elements in fall prevention. Nursing facilities, as a rule, already have railings in hallways, grab bars in bathrooms, and other required safety adaptations. However, a program should be in place to routinely check these devices for proper mainte-nance and repairs. Janitorial procedures should be evaluated for resident safety during cleaning and mopping floors and during carpet vacuuming or floor buffing, when long electric cords running through hallways can become a tripping hazard. Bed height should be adjusted, or protective floor pads used, for those who may roll over and fall during sleep. For high-risk patients, it may be necessary to put the mattress on the floor. In patient rooms, a clearly visible passage should be ensured from the bed and chair to the bathroom. Patient incontinence can leave urine puddles, which may not be easy for other patients to detect. The nursing staff should be trained to observe such hazardous conditions and promptly clean up the affected areas.

Pressure Ulcers

A **pressure ulcer**, also called a pressure sore or decubitus ulcer, is a local-ized area of soft-tissue injury resulting from compression between a bony prominence and an external surface (Smith 1996). Pressure on the skin is normal when a person is sitting or lying down. With aging, however, the skin tissue develops reduced tolerance for pressure. Limited ability to change position while in bed or wheelchair that causes prolonged pressure against bony prominences, friction against wrinkled bed sheets or objects such as casts and braces, exposure to moisture from urine or feces, and poor nutrition, especially low calorie and protein intake, can all play a part in forming pressure ulcers. Neurological and cardiovascular disease can predispose the elderly to sores (Bennett 1992).

Once formed, pressure ulcers are slow to heal. They are also suscepti-ble to infections, a vulnerability that can lead to further complications such as permanent disability and even death (Bliss 1992). Therefore, prevention and early treatment are essential features of pressure ulcer management. Pressure ulcer prevention begins with proper nutrition and hydration. Basic care routines such as proper bed-making, position-ing the patient properly while sitting or lying down, use of pads and pil-lows to relieve pressure, repositioning at least once every two hours, keeping the patient clean and dry, and skin care are important in pre-venting pressure ulcers. At least once a day, skin should be systemati-

cally inspected in patients at risk. The skin should be cleansed at regular intervals and whenever it is soiled. Hot water and drying soaps should be avoided for skin care. To treat dry, flaky, scaly skin, optimum environmental humidity should be maintained and moisturizers used. Areas of redness over bony prominences should not be massaged or rubbed. Mobility through rehabilitation should be encouraged (Bergstrom 1997). Various types of pressure-relieving devices are also available, and should be used as necessary.

Pressure ulcers are categorized into four stages according to the depth of tissue destruction (Exhibit 8-3). Once developed, there can be rapid deterioration. Stage I is the beginning stage with a notable discoloration of the skin. This stage is actually not a true ulcer, because the skin is intact. However, a stage I pressure area increases the risk of additional ulcers by tenfold (Allman 1999), and stage I can be difficult to recognize in persons with dark skin (Dharmarajan and Ahmed 2003). At Stage IV, the most advanced stage, muscle or bone become exposed. Treatment is to be directed by the attending physician. Depending on their stage, treatment may include bed rest in a special pressure-relieving bed, use of anti-inflammatory drugs, antibiotics, special dressings called occlusive dress-

EXHIBIT 8-3

Pressure Ulcer Stages

Stage 1   A persistent area of skin redness (without a break in the skin) that does not disappear when pressure is relieved.

Stage 2   A partial thickness loss of skin layers that presents clinically as an abrasion, blister, or shallow crater.

Stage 3   A full thickness of skin is lost, exposing the subcutaneous tissues—presents as a deep crater with or without undermining adjacent tissue.

Stage 4   A full thickness of skin and subcutaneous tissue is lost, exposing muscle or bone.

Source: MDS 2.0, Centers for Medicare and Medicaid Services.

ings that keep tissue hydrated, whirlpool treatment, removal of dead tissue by surgical debridement, and skin grafting.

Use and Misuse of Physical Restraints

A **restraint** is a device that is used to restrict a person's freedom of movement (Grubbs and Blasband 2000). Examples of restraints include waist belts or chest jackets to prevent people from getting out of a chair or bed, geri-chairs with secured tray tables, bed siderails, roller bars for wheelchairs, mitts, and wrist ties. In the past, these restraints were in common use based on the widespread belief that restraining was necessary to keep patients from falling or otherwise hurting themselves. However, studies found that their value in promoting patient safety was at best marginal. Contrary to what was earlier believed, restraint use often caused injuries and resulted in negative physical and psychological outcomes. For example, between 1985 and 1995, 649 adverse events associated with bed siderails in hospitals and nursing homes were reported to the Food and Drug Administration (FDA), which regulates hospital beds as medical devices. One study based on the FDA database reported that during this period, there were 111 cases of entrapment in which the patient was found caught, trapped, entangled, or strangled by the rail while in bed. Of these cases, 65% resulted in death and 23% resulted in injuries (Todd and Ruhl 1997). In 1995, owing to increasing numbers of death and injury reports, the FDA issued a safety alert on hazards associated with bed siderails.

Formerly, restraints were also widely used to control behavioral disorders such as agitation and aggression. Often, the result was increased anger and further agitation because of frustration with restricted freedom. The use of various types of restraints was estimated to cause approximately 1 in every 1,000 deaths in nursing homes. When restraints are removed, quality of life and functional status improve; there does not appear to be an increase in serious falls, and serious injuries even decline (Palmer et al. 1999).

In contemporary nursing practice, use of restraints is seldom considered appropriate. When considered medically necessary, restraints should only be used temporarily, and under physician's orders and close supervision by the nursing staff. Otherwise, their use is illegal (see Chapter 3). Use of restraints should be considered only when alternative means to ensure safety have failed, because patients have the right to receive care in an environment that is least restrictive. When patients manifest agitation

or aggression, nursing professionals must first evaluate the underlying causes. For example, agitation may stem from depression or some other psychiatric disorder, in which case therapy should be directed toward the underlying disorder (Ouslander et al. 1997).

Urinary Incontinence and Catheters

It is estimated that over half of all nursing home residents are unable to control urination (Resnick and Baumann 1997). The starting point for addressing this problem is to maintain a bladder record over a period of five to seven days to determine the type and frequency of incontinence. A clinical evaluation and treatment of reversible causes is the next step. Reversible or transient causes include urinary tract infection, urinary retention, delirium, restricted mobility, atrophic vaginitis, urethritis, fecal impaction, and pharmaceuticals. Other serious conditions, such as bladder cancer, prostate cancer in men, stones or other types of blockage, may also lead to incontinence. Once reversible causes have been treated, therapeutic programs should be instituted as the next step. Developing toileting schedules has been a common approach. Some residents may require staff assistance for toileting every two hours; others can do quite well on a schedule of every 3 or 4 hours (Helping residents stay dry 2003). The schedule is based on the voiding patterns observed. Staff support with transfer and ambulation should be provided as necessary, and the resident should have easy access to the toilet or a portable commode. Low intensity exercise programs to strengthen the pelvic muscles can be combined with the toileting program.

Use of a catheter would be indicated when other measures fail to control incontinence. Condom catheters are used in men who have difficulty retaining urine. Indwelling catheters are used in both men and women when medically indicated and approved by the attending physician. However, some of the highest infection rates among nursing home residents are attributed to indwelling catheters.

PHARMACY CONSULTATION

A nursing facility is required by regulations to provide pharmaceutical services with consultation from a licensed pharmacist. The facility should have a written agreement with the pharmacist, who should also be an active member of the multidisciplinary team. The pharmacist assists the

facility in developing policies and procedures for the dispensing, storage, administration, review, discontinuation, and disposal of drugs. Pharmacy standards require a monthly review of drug regimen for each resident, and appropriate labeling and storage of drugs. As mentioned earlier, drug interactions and unexpected response to a given medication are special concerns in the medical care of the elderly. Hence, prescribing drugs requires careful monitoring in conjunction with changes in the patient's condition, results of laboratory tests, and use of any over-the-counter (non-prescribed) medications. State laws govern how medications are dispensed and labeled. Drugs should be stored in locked cabinets to which only authorized personnel should have access. Certain medications require proper refrigeration.

Specific policies and procedures govern the safeguarding and authorized use of controlled substances, which must be stored in a double-locked cabinet. Proper recordkeeping and verification are necessary to prevent unauthorized use. Nursing facilities must also maintain an emergency medication kit. The pharmaceutical review committee should determine its contents. In general, the emergency kit contains drugs needed during life threatening emergencies such as cardiac arrest, severe allergic reaction, or seizures. The drugs in the emergency kit are the responsibility of the pharmacist. They are often limited to a 72-hour supply. The kit is kept sealed (not locked), and records are kept whenever anything is used from the kit. The pharmacist is also responsible for ensuring that medication use is documented properly, and that no expired medications are used.

Use and Misuse of Psychotropic Drugs

Psychotropic (or psychoactive) drugs include antipsychotics, antidepressants, sedatives, and hypnotics. In the past, these drugs were overprescribed for nursing home residents. Some of these drugs were prescribed as 'chemical restraints' to sedate patients who were considered overly aggressive, disruptive, or assaultive. As a result of nursing home reform efforts, OBRA-87 contains specific rules for the use of psychotropic drugs in nursing facilities with the objective of reducing their use. For example, the legislation prescribes that antipsychotics can be used only when certain specified conditions have been documented. Less severe conditions for which these drugs should not be prescribed are also specified. Other requirements of the law include gradual dose reductions

unless such action is clinically contraindicated. Whenever appropriate, behavioral interventions should be tried first, such as modifying the environment and implementing staff approaches to care that would accommodate the resident's behavior to the largest degree possible. This is a broad requirement, which needs to be carefully evaluated when mental or behavioral problems are observed. For example, depression may be attributed to certain medications the patient may be on, in which case the nursing staff should work with the physician and the pharmacist to review the patient's drug regimen. If the depression is not severe enough, the patient may come out of it in a few days. In stead of rushing to seek pharmacological therapy, the nursing staff should carefully observe the resident's behavior, and maintain appropriate documentation. Nonpharmacologic approaches should also be tried in cases of anxiety, which is another common problem in nursing home residents. Interventions such as biofeedback, relaxation techniques, and participation in recreational programs may be useful for some residents (Ouslander et al. 1997). One study of 16 skilled nursing facilities in Wisconsin, involving 1,650 residents, demonstrated a significant overall decrease in the use of antipsychotic drugs. However, the change varied dramatically across facilities, from an 85 percent reduction to a 19 percent increase. Greater reductions were found in facilities with a resident-centered culture, a less severe case-mix, and a higher nurse-to-resident staffing ratio. The treatment culture was measured with a questionnaire for assessing nurses' beliefs and philosophies of care and their interactions with pharmacists and mental health workers (Svarstad et al. 2001).

REHABILITATION

In the geriatric context, **rehabilitation** can be defined as the process of delivering the minimal services that maintain the present or highest possible level of function (Osterweil 1990). Rehabilitation has three main objectives: (1) to restore functional status lost through disease, injury, or surgical intervention, (2) to maintain residual function, and prevent further decline, and (3) to help disabled individuals adapt to their functional deficits. In many instances, restoring an individual to his or her former functional status may not be possible. In that case, maintaining or maximizing remaining function would be the goal.

For nursing facilities, the overarching standard has been established by OBRA-87 regulations, according to which the facility must provide necessary services and appropriate treatments for residents to maintain or improve their functioning and range of motion. Restorative therapy is generally provided on a short-term basis immediately after the onset of a disability. It requires intensive therapeutic intervention. Examples of cases requiring short-term restorative therapy include orthopedic surgery, stroke, limb amputation, and prolonged illness. Frequently, the expected outcome of intensive short-term rehabilitation is to enable the patient to return to independent living. In other cases, especially when a patient must continue receiving long-term care because of other chronic needs, long-term rehabilitation is necessary after short-term restorative care has ceased.

Long-range therapeutic programs are necessary to maintain function and to prevent further disability. Such maintenance therapy is based on maximizing the use of remaining capacities. Certain capabilities cannot be recovered, but patients should be assisted to adapt to their deficits so that they can do for themselves as much as they possibly can in their activities of daily living.

Rehabilitation services are based on assessment and care planning by a multidisciplinary team comprising physician, physical therapy (PT), occupational therapy (OT), speech therapy (ST), nursing, dietary, social work, and recreational therapy. The attending physician must authorize all short-term rehabilitation treatments. Short-term treatments are carried out by professionally trained therapists, mainly, registered physical therapists (RPTs), physical therapy assistants (PTAs), registered occupational therapists (OTRs), certified occupational therapy assistants (COTAs), and speech-language pathologists (SLPs). Long-term maintenance therapy is carried out by paraprofessionals such as specially-trained restorative aides or certified nursing assistants.

Restorative Rehabilitation

The goal of restorative therapy is to help regain or improve functioning. It requires intense short-term rehabilitation treatments.

Physical therapy essentially focuses on evaluating and treating musculoskeletal disorder. Rehabilitation is geared toward improving ambulation, joint mobility, and balance; strength training; fitting and using artificial limbs; and training to use canes and walkers. Physical therapists (PTs) are also trained to give treatment modalities such as hot packs, cold

packs, massage, ultrasound, paraffin bath, electrical stimulation, compression therapy, and hydrotherapy. PTs can assist and train the nursing staff in techniques for preventing falls.

Occupational therapy specializes in the adaptive use of the upper extremities for performing various tasks. Its main focus is evaluating and treating functional impairments in the activities of daily living. This focus includes working on fine motor skills. Adaptive equipment may be prescribed. Splints and other support mechanisms may be tailor-made to facilitate the performance of daily tasks (Ramsdell 1990). Occupational therapists (OTs) also play a vital role in evaluating the independent living environment when the patient is scheduled for discharge to home.

Speech-language pathology encompasses evaluation and treatment of speech, language, and cognitive disorders. Speech-Language Pathologists (SLPs) treat several kinds of disorders such as **aphasia**, in which a person is not able to communicate at all; **dysarthria**, in which speech is slurred or unintelligible because of muscle weakness; or motor speech disorders such as apraxia, in which the tongue, lips, and vocal cords are unable to work together (Reynolds and Slott 1999). **Dysphagia**, or the inability to swallow, is another common problem SLPs are called upon to treat in nursing facilities. SLPs also work with patients with hearing loss to help them learn the use of amplification devices, lip-reading and other functional communication skills.

Maintenance Rehabilitation

Maintenance therapy has the goal of preserving the present level of function and preventing secondary complications. Such treatment is generally less intense and of longer duration than restorative therapy.

Ongoing long-term maintenance therapy, provided by paraprofessionals, is essential for promoting activity and circulation. Failure to do so can result in complications such as pressure ulcers, contractures, muscle atrophy, constipation, fecal impaction, and edema. Ambulation and range of motion are two common types of exercise programs. These programs often continue restorative treatments initiated by PTs and OTs.

CONCLUSION

Patient care is an important domain of practice in nursing home administration, because nursing care is the core of services in a skilled nursing facil-

ity. The administrator's leadership often plays a key role in setting the philosophy of care. An understanding of medical, nursing, and rehabilitation services is also necessary for decisions pertaining to resource allocation, staff development, hiring and retention, and other management functions.

DISCUSSION QUESTIONS

1. Discuss in what ways nursing plays a central role in a nursing facility. How can the centrality of nursing sometime result in conflict with other departments? As an administrator, how would you prevent such conflicts?
2. As a nursing home administrator, you are recruiting a new Medical Director. What are some of the main elements you should discuss during the interview?
3. What are some of the elements you think ought to be included in a contract between the facility and its Medical Director?
4. Refer to the organization chart in Figure II-1. Should the In-service Director report to the administrator or the DON? Present arguments, both pro and con.
5. Should the Resident Assessment Coordinator report to the administrator or the DON? Present arguments, both pro and con.
6. Sometimes there is a tendency for conflict and domineering attitudes to creep into multidisciplinary teams. As an administrator, how can you promote team spirit among the members of this group?

INTERNET RESOURCES FOR FURTHER LEARNING

The American Geriatrics Society is the premier professional organization of health care providers dedicated to improving the health and well-being of older adults.
www.americangeriatrics.org

American Medical Directors Association is the professional association of medical directors and physicians practicing in the long term care continuum, dedicated to excellence in patient care by providing education, advocacy, information, and professional development.
http://www.amda.com/

Centers for Disease Control and Prevention is the federal public health agency.
www.cdc.gov

Centers for Medicare and Medicaid Services. Information on MDS 3.0.
http://cms.hhs.gov/quality/mds30/

The Hartford Foundation: The Hartford Institute for Geriatric Nursing aims to improve the practice of geriatric nursing.
http://www.hartfordign.org/

National Association of Directors of Nursing Administration in Long Term Care: NADONA-LTC is a professional organization of directors and assistant directors of nursing in long term care. It has established standards of practice for directors of nursing, and also has a certification program for directors of nursing.
www.nadona.org

National Gerontological Nursing Association: NGNA, an organization of nurses specializing in care of older adults, informs the public on health issues affecting older people, supports education for nurses and other health care practitioners, and provides a forum to discuss topics such as nutrition in long-term care facilities and elder law for nurses. NGNA offers information on gerontological nursing and conducts nursing research related to older people.
www.ngna.org

National Institutes of Health: Information on HIV/AIDS treatment.
http://www.aidsinfo.nih.gov/

National Mental Health Association: The country's oldest and largest non-profit organization addressing all aspects of mental health and mental illness. It allows a search feature.
www.nmha.org

National Rehabilitation Information Center: NARIC, funded by the Department of Education, provides information on rehabilitation of people with physical or mental disabilities. Contact NARIC for database searches on all types of physical and mental disabilities, as well as referrals to local and national facilities and organizations.
www.naric.com

REFERENCES

Allman, R.M. 1999. Pressure ulcer. In *Principles of Geriatric Medicine and Gerontology*. 4th ed., eds. W.R. Hazzard, *et al*. New York: McGraw-Hill, 1577–1583.

Anonymous. 1990. Prevention and control of tuberculosis in facilities providing long-term care to the elderly: Recommendations of the Advisory Committee for Elimination of Tuberculosis. *Morbidity and Mortality Weekly Report* 39: 7–20.

Bennett, G.C.J. 1992. Pressure sores—aetiology and prevalence. In *Textbook of geriatric medicine and gerontology*. 4th ed., eds, J.C. Brocklehurst, R.C. Tallis, and H.M. Fillit. Edinburgh, U.K.: Churchill Livingstone.

Bergstrom, N.I. 1997. Strategies for preventing pressure ulcers. *Clinical Geriatric Medicine* 13, no. 3: 437–454.

Bern-Klug, M., et al. 2003. 'I get to spend time with my patients': Nursing home physicians discuss their role. *Journal of the American Medical Directors Association* 4, no. 3: 145–151.

Bliss, M.R. 1992. Pressure sore management and prevention. In *Textbook of geriatric medicine and gerontology*. 4th ed., eds, J.C. Brocklehurst, R.C. Tallis, H.M. Fillit Edinburgh, U.K.: Churchill Livingstone.

Dharmarajan, T.S., and S. Ahmed. 2003. The growing problem of pressure ulcers. *Postgraduate Medicine* 113, no. 5: 77–83.

Downton, J. 1992. Falls in the elderly. In *Textbook of geriatric medicine and gerontology*. 4th ed., eds, J.C. Brocklehurst, R.C. Tallis, H.M. Fillit. Edinburgh, U.K.: Churchill Livingstone.

Garibaldi, R.A., S. Brodine, and S. Matsumiya. 1981. Infections among patients in nursing homes: Policies, prevalence, and problems. *New England Journal of Medicine* 305: 731–735.

Grubbs, P. and B. Blasband. 2000. *The long-term care nursing assistant*. Upper Saddle River, NJ: Prentice-Hall, Inc.

Hand hygiene. 2001. Yale-New Haven Hospital, Quality Improvement Support Services. http://info.med.yale.edu/ynhh/infection/precautions/handhygiene.html

Hanson, L.C., et al. 2002. As individual as death itself: A focus group study of terminal care in nursing homes. *Journal of Palliative Medicine* 5, no. 1: 117–125.

Helping residents stay dry. An interview with Mary H. Palmer, Ph.D. *Nursing Homes Long Term Care Management* 52, no. 6: 70–72.

Hofmann, M.T., et al. 2003. Decreasing the incidence of falls in the nursing home in a cost-conscious environment: a pilot study. *Journal of the American Medical Directors Association* 4, no. 2: 95–97.

Kane, R.A. 1995. Decision making, care plans, and life plans in long-term care: Can case managers take account of clients' values and preferences? In *Long-*

term care decisions: Ethical and conceptual dimensions, eds, L.B. McCullough and N.L. Wilson. Baltimore: The Johns Hopkins University Press.

Krein, K. 2003. Choosing a medical director: One size does not fit all. *Nursing Homes Long Term Care Management* 52, no. 4: 15–21.

Levenson, S.A. 1985. The physician. In *Care of the elderly: A health team approach,* ed, G.H. Maguire. Boston: Little, Brown and Company.

Lipsitz, L.A., et al. 1997. Falls. In *Quality care in the nursing home,* eds. J.N. Morris et al., 258-277. St. Louis, MO: Mosby-Year Book, Inc.

Osterweil, D. 1990. Geriatric rehabilitation in the long-term care institutional setting. In *Geriatric Rehabilitation,* eds, B. Kemp, K. Brummel-Smith, and J.W. Ramsdell. Boston: College-Hill Press.

Ouslander, J.G., D. Osterweil, and J. Morley. 1997. *Medical care in the nursing home.* 2nd ed. New York: McGraw-Hill.

Palmer, L., et al. 1999. Reducing inappropriate restraint use in Colorado's long-term care facilities. *Joint Commission Journal on Quality Improvement* 25, no. 2: 78–94.

Peck, R.L. 2001. Perspectives. *Nursing Homes Long Term Care Management* 50, 2: 36–38.

Ramsdell, J.W. 1990. A rehabilitation orientation in the workup of general medical problems. In *Geriatric Rehabilitation,* eds, B. Kemp, K. Brummel-Smith, and J.W. Ramsdell. Boston: College-Hill Press.

Resnick, N., and M. Baumann. 1997. In *Quality care in the nursing home,* eds. J.N. Morris et al., 258-277. St. Louis, MO: Mosby-Year Book, Inc.

Reynolds, C., and S. Slott. 1999. Geriatric speech pathologist. In *Geriatric Rehabilitation Manual,* ed., T.L. Kauffman. New York: Churchill Livingstone.

Rubenstein, L.Z., A.S. Robbins, and K.R. Josephson. 1991. Falls in the nursing home setting: Causes and preventive approaches. In *Advances in long-term care, volume 1,* eds, P.R. Katz, R.L. Kane, and M.D. Mezey. New York: Springer Publishing Company.

Sharbaugh, R.J. 2003. When drugs don't kill bugs. *Nursing Homes Long Term Care Management* 52, no. 5: 70–72.

Smith, D.M. 1996. Pressure ulcers. In *Medical care of the nursing home resident,* eds, R.W. Besdine and L.Z. Rubenstein. Philadelphia: American College of Physicians.

Stevenson, K.B. 1999. Regional data set of infection rates for long-term care facilities: Description of a valuable benchmarking tool. *American Journal of Infection Control* 27, no. 1: 20–26.

Sullivan, C.F., and C. Atlas. 1998. *Health care food service systems management.* Gaithersburg, MD: Aspen Publishers, Inc.

Svarstad, B.L., et al. 2001. Variations in the treatment culture of nursing homes and responses to regulations to reduce drug use. *Psychiatric Services : A journal of the American Psychiatric Association* 52, no. 5: 666–672.

Tinetti, M.E. 2003. Preventing falls in elderly persons. *The New England Journal of Medicine* 348, no. 1: 42–49.

Todd, J.F., and C.E. Ruhl. 1997. Injury and death associated with hospital bed side-rails: Reports to the US Food and Drug Administration. *American Journal of Public Health* 87, no. 10: 1675–1977.

Yarme, J., and H. Yarme. 2001. Flooring and safety. *Nursing Homes Long Term Care Management* 50, no. 10: 82–83.

CHAPTER 9

Recreation and Activities

LEARNING MODULES

1. Meaning and purpose of activities. Differences between activities, social services, and rehabilitation.
2. The activity department: staffing and qualifications. Certification of activity professionals.
3. Skills, competencies, and traits of successful activity professionals. Assessment of activity pursuit patterns as the basis for individualized programming.
4. Basic considerations in program development: participants' age and type of disability, space and time factors, supplies and equipment, staff resources and community resources.
5. Program development for meeting a variety of common needs that include physical, cognitive, social, affective, awareness, and spiritual needs.
6. Other programming considerations: Scheduling, active and passive stimulation from socializing, and intergenerational appeal.
7. Special programs for stimulating cognitive functioning. Special needs of dementia patients. Multisensory stimulation.

continues

8. Planning and implementing the activity program
9. Purpose, goals, and process of program evaluation
10. Roles, recruitment, and retention of volunteers

In this chapter, the term **activity** means active or passive involvement of patients in any activities, outside the activities of daily living (ADLs), that provide meaning and personal enrichment. These activities are pursued by an individual for the purpose of obtaining a sense of well-being. Purposeful activities also build self-esteem and give pleasure, comfort, personal fulfillment, and emotional independence (Perschbacher 1993). Finally, activities should also promote physical and mental fitness, a sense of accomplishment, as well as social and spiritual fulfillment.

Meaningful activities involve more than just games and outings. "Activities should do more than produce an occasional bright spot of entertainment in an otherwise dull existence; activities must help people learn new information, skills, or behaviors or improve their feelings of self-worth..." (Carroll et al. 1978). A well-rounded activity program addresses the physical, mental, social, and spiritual aspects of health. Hence, activity programming must be designed with the objectives of enriching the lives of residents and promoting holistic health.

The purposes and roles of activities programming must be distinguished from the purposes and roles of social work (see Chapter 7) and rehabilitation therapies (see Chapter 8), although the goals pursued by each of these disciplines generally overlap. For instance, maximizing independent functioning, promoting self-esteem, meeting psycho-social needs, and enhancing quality of life are the overarching goals pursued by all three disciplines. Yet, there are two main differences: (1) Each is a specialized discipline that addresses patient care issues that other disciplines do not address, and (2) the approach used for achieving the common goals just mentioned is different in each discipline. Therapeutic recreation is the primary approach used in activity programming, which is quite distinct from the other two disciplines: Social services focus mainly on coping and social adaptation; rehabilitation therapies employ a clinical approach to specific functional deficits, mainly by using established therapeutic modalities. By their nature, social services and rehabilitation are intervention-oriented. They deal with problems and issues that are clearly defined. In activities, inter-

vention may be used, but only to a limited degree. Among the three disciplines, recreational activities also allow the greatest degree of latitude for residents to pursue their own interests.

For the most part, activities are program-oriented rather than intervention-oriented. **Program orientation** means that programs are structured with the needs of various residents taken into consideration, but residents' participation is voluntary. Compared to intervention-oriented therapies, participation in activities allows the resident a much greater degree of voluntary choice, personal control, autonomy, and self-confidence. **Intervention orientation** respects autonomy and choice to a degree, but participation is nonvoluntary unless the patient signs a release refusing treatment.

Activities must offer a wide variety of programs that enable individuals to pursue their personal interests and to develop new interests, with the objective of finding meaning and purpose in life despite chronic illness, frailty, and functional impairment. Social adaptation and maintenance rehabilitation are often by-products of activities, although they may not be specifically pursued. Activities allow residents freedom of expression, which, from a holistic viewpoint, adds a necessary dimension to nursing home services that no other discipline in the facility can furnish. Achieving self-fulfillment by engaging in meaningful recreational diversions adds necessary balance and a sense of control to the lives of residents in an otherwise restricted environment. Because personal interests can vary substantially across the resident population in a nursing facility, activity programming presents special challenges in creativity and resourcefulness.

ACTIVITY DEPARTMENT

Staffing

Each state specifies the staffing levels and required qualifications for activity personnel, but clear-cut guidelines are generally lacking. Because of the unique nature of activities, a facility needs a separate activities department headed by an Activity Director or Activity Coordinator. The director or coordinator reports to the administrator. In small facilities that range between 30 and 50 beds, one full-time person may be assigned the responsibilities of both social work and activities. However, to the extent

possible, the administrator should try to have separate departments for these two services; otherwise, the effectiveness of both services is likely to be compromised. In facilities with more than 50 beds, a full-time activity director is generally needed. Additional personnel are generally necessary in facilities with more than 100 beds. Part-time activity assistants may be used to fill in as needed.

Qualifications

The Omnibus Budget Reconciliation Act of 1987 (OBRA-87) mandates that activity programs be directed by qualified professionals. Federal regulations do not specify the qualifications, but activity professionals certified by the National Certification Council for Activity Professionals (NCCAP) automatically satisfy federal requirements. NCCAP offers three levels of certification: Activity Director Certified (ADC), Activity Assistant Certified (AAC), and Activity Consultant Certified (ACC). Certification at each level depends on academic qualifications, experience, and continuing education.

Directors may also meet OBRA-87 requirements by satisfying the licensure or registration requirements specified by their state. Directors who do not meet the qualifications specified by the state are required to have regular consultation from an outside qualified activities consultant. The consultant's role is to train the activity staff, evaluate existing programs, make recommendations for program enhancement, assist in implementing new programs, and ensure that all requirements mandated by federal and state regulations are met (Tedrick and Green 1995).

SKILLS AND COMPETENCIES

Activity staff members are key participants on the multidisciplinary team discussed in previous chapters. As such, they contribute to resident assessment, care planning, and documentation in the patient's medical record. Hence, activities programming requires a therapeutic perspective. These requirements of the position must be carefully evaluated when activity professionals are recruited and trained.

Many of the general skills that activities specialists need for effective performance are very similar to those necessary for social workers discussed in Chapter 7. For instance, the same skills of engagement, assessment, communication, and documentation are necessary for activity directors.

They must also have knowledge of aging and the elderly (see Chapter 7). Indeed, these skills can actually improve the performance of any professional who needs to interact with nursing home patients as a care provider.

Assessment is the cornerstone of activity programming. The Minimum Data Set (MDS) contains a special section for assessing activity pursuit patterns. The five elements of activity pursuit patterns are times during which a resident is awake, average time involved in activities, preferred activity settings, general activity preferences, and preferences for change in daily routines (Exhibit 9-1). This section should be completed within the context of all other relevant information contained in the MDS. Assessment yields valuable information on the needs and desires of each resident, and forms the basis for planning and developing appropriate programs. Similar to other members of the multidisciplinary team, activity professionals also have responsibilities for care planning and documentation of patients' activity goals and progress.

Activity professionals also need to have special skills of engagement and communication with the residents and family members. For example, during assessment, vital information must be obtained from both the residents and their family members, the latter being the key providers of information in case of residents who are cognitively impaired. Motivating the elderly to participate in activities is one of the special challenges for activity professionals. Because motivation varies from person to person, getting to know each individual resident's needs, interests, and abilities is essential (Hastings 1981).

Friendliness, cheerfulness, and a pleasant disposition are special personality traits administrators should try to cultivate in activity personnel. Activity professionals must be innovative in designing appropriate activities to meet individual needs; resourceful in engaging family members and volunteers to enhance the activity programming; skilled in planning and coordinating a wide variety of programs; and able to evaluate the effectiveness of the different programs.

PROGRAM DEVELOPMENT

Understanding a number of factors clearly is essential for developing effective activity programming. The various factors discussed in this section should be evaluated carefully, to generate ideas that can add variety, novelty, appeal, and meaning to resident activities.

Activity Pursuit Patterns

Intent: To record the amount and types of interests and activities that the resident currently pursues, as well as activities the resident would like to pursue that are not currently available at the facility.

Definition: Activity pursuits. Refers to any activity other than ADLs that a resident pursues in order to enhance a sense of well-being. These include activities that provide increased self-esteem, pleasure, comfort, education, creativity, success, and financial or emotional independence.

1. Time Awake

Intent: To identify those periods of a typical day (over the last seven days) when the resident was awake all or most of the time (i.e., no more than one hour nap during any such period). For care planning purposes this information can be used in at least two ways:

- The resident who is awake most of the time could be encouraged to become more mentally, physically, and/or socially involved in activities (solitary or group).
- The resident who naps a lot may be bored or depressed and could possibly benefit from greater activity involvement.

Process: Consult with direct care staff, the resident, and the resident's family.

2. Average Time Involved in Activities

Intent: To determine the proportion of available time that the resident was actually involved in activity pursuits as an indication of his or her overall activity-involvement pattern. This time refers to free time when the resident

continues

EXHIBIT 9-1

EXHIBIT 9–1 *continued*

was awake and was not involved in receiving nursing care, treatments, or engaged in ADL activities and could have been involved in activity pursuits and Therapeutic Recreation.

Process: Consult with direct care staff, activities staff members, the resident, and the resident's family. Ask about time involved in different activity pursuits.

3. Preferred Activity Settings

Intent: To determine activity circumstances/settings that the resident prefers, including (though not limited to) circumstances in which the resident is at ease.

Process: Ask the resident, family, direct care staff, and activities staff about the resident's preferences. Staff's knowledge of observed behavior can be helpful, but only provides part of the answer. Do not limit preference list to areas to which the resident now has access, but try to expand the range of possibilities for the resident.

Example

Ask the resident, "Do you like to go outdoors? Outside the facility (to a mall)? To events downstairs?" Ask staff members to identify settings that resident frequents or where he or she appears to be most at ease.

---

4. General Activity Preferences (adapted to resident's current abilities)

Intent: Determine which activities of those listed the resident would prefer to participate in (independently or with others). Choice should not be limited by whether or not the activity is currently available to the resident, or whether the resident currently engages in the activity.

continues

EXHIBIT 9–1 *continued*

Definition: **Exercise/sports** — Includes any type of physical activity such as dancing, weight training, yoga, walking, sports (e.g., bowling, croquet, golf, or watching sports).

Music — Includes listening to music or being involved in making music (singing, playing piano, etc.)

Reading/writing — Reading can be independent or done in a group setting where a leader reads aloud to the group or the group listens to "talking books." Writing can be solitary (e.g., letter-writing or poetry writing) or done as part of a group program (e.g., recording oral histories). Or a volunteer can record the thoughts of a blind, hemiplegic, or apraxic resident in a letter or journal.

Spiritual/religious activities — Includes participating in religious services as well as watching them on television or listening to them on the radio.

Gardening or plants — Includes tending one's own or other plants, participating in garden club activities, regularly watching a television program or video about gardening.

Talking or conversing — Includes talking and listening to social conversations and discussions with family, friends, other residents, or staff. May occur individually, in groups, or on the telephone; may occur informally or in structured situations.

Helping others — Includes helping other residents or staff, being a good listener, assisting with unit routines, etc.

Process: Consult with the resident, the resident's family, activities staff members, and nurse assistants. Explain to the resident that you are interested in hearing about what he or she likes to do or would be interested in trying. Remind the resident that a discussion of his or her

continues

EXHIBIT 9–1 *continued*

likes and dislikes should not be limited by perception of current abilities or disabilities. Explain that many activity pursuits are adaptable to the resident's capabilities. For example, if a resident says that he used to love to read and misses it now that he is unable to see small print, explain about the availability of taped books or large print editions.

For residents with dementia or aphasia, ask family members about resident's former interests. A former love of music can be incorporated into the care plan (e.g., bedside audiotapes, sing-a-longs). Also observe the resident in current activities. If the resident appears content during an activity (e.g., smiling, clapping during a music program) check the item on the form.

5. Prefers Change in Daily Routine

Intent: To determine if the resident has an interest in pursuing activities not offered at the facility (or on the nursing unit), or not made available to the resident. This includes situations in which an activity is provided but the resident would like to have other choices in carrying out the activity (e.g., the resident would like to watch the news on TV rather than the game shows and soap operas preferred by the majority of residents; or the resident would like a Methodist service rather than the Baptist service provided for the majority of residents). Residents who resist attendance/involvement in activities offered at the facility are also included in this category in order to determine possible reasons for their lack of involvement.

Process: Review how the resident spends the day. Ask the resident if there are things he or she would enjoy doing (or used to enjoy doing) that are not currently available

continues

EXHIBIT 9–1 *continued*

or, if available, are not "right" for him or her in their current format. If the resident is unable to answer, ask the same question of a close family member, friend, activity professional, or nurse assistant. Would the resident prefer slight or major changes in daily routines, or is everything OK?

Source: Adapted from Centers for Medicare and Medicaid Services, MDS Manual.

Basic Considerations

Programming requires developing and carrying out a meaningful plan. **Programming** means structured methods of delivering needed services. Planning an effective program requires that the activity professional consider the kind of service to deliver, the manner in which it will be delivered, and its anticipated effect on the residents involved (Lanza 1997).

Six basic considerations are valuable in developing a well-rounded activity program (Greenblatt 1988; Lanza 1997):

(1) **Age of participants**. Nursing facilities are likely to have substantial age differences among residents, and individual interests often vary according to a person's age group.

(2) **Nature and extent of disabilities**. Disabilities must be assessed, because active participation requires a certain level of functioning. Certain activities are suitable for passive participation by those who may be unable to have active involvement. Abilities and skills required for participation may be limited by disorders in any of the three behavioral arenas (Greenblatt 1988):

- Sensory-motor skills are affected by poor ambulation, strength, range of motion, vision, or hearing.
- Cognitive functioning is affected by disorders such as inability to recognize, store, or retrieve information; make judgments; or maintain attention span.
- Affective functioning is impaired by depression, anxiety, anger, agitation, fear, or frustration.

Activity planning must consider the needs of residents who possess functional limitations in any of these areas. Also, any medical

contraindications must be carefully considered. For example, patients with serious cardiovascular conditions, asthma, or respiratory problems may require medical clearance for participation in certain types of activities. Use of certain medications produce side effects, such as dizziness, drowsiness, and sensitivity to sunlight, that require necessary precautions, such as assisting residents on certain medications to move slowly or using sunscreen for outdoor activities. Regardless of the type of limitation, therapeutic activities should use patients' unaffected capabilities; otherwise, functional loss in these remaining areas is likely to occur. This additional functional loss, called **secondary disability**, can be reversed or prevented. For example, an elderly person with the primary condition of hearing loss may tend to isolate himself, which can lead to deterioration of other types of functional capabilities (Greenblatt 1988).

(3) **Space and time**. Availability of space is an important consideration, especially for group programs. Certain individual pursuits such as knitting, crocheting, reading, drawing, painting, or listening to music can be effectively carried out in the patient's own room. However, most facilities have limited space for group activities. An activity room is often provided in medium-size and large facilities. This room is generally equipped for crafts, cooking, and baking and can accommodate small- to medium-size groups. Large facilities may also have a chapel for religious services. Other activities generally require some ingenuity in adapting existing common spaces. For example, dining rooms, day rooms, lounges, lobby areas, open spaces near nursing stations, and alcoves can, with some improvisation, all be used for different activities, even though they may not be ideal. Use of common areas for activities requires proper planning and coordination to minimize interference with other services that must also be carried out. For instance, activities should not interfere with the use of dining areas for meals. Only a limited number of programs can be effectively conducted at a given time so that space is also available for individual leisure or private visiting. When weather conditions permit it, outdoor spaces such as patios, gazebos, and balconies should be used for certain types of activities. Outdoor gardening, tending to flowers and shrubs, and bird-feeding are also therapeutic for many residents.

Activity schedules should take into account possible conflict with meal times and nursing care routines. Structured activities should be scheduled to take place when patients are likely to be inactive and bored. At the same time, residents should be given the choice to engage in individual pursuits. Activities should also be planned for evenings and weekends. The length of each program will depend on the physical and mental endurance of participants.

(4) **Supplies and equipment**. Reusable supplies and equipment are acquired over time. Simple, inexpensive equipment is generally quite sufficient for most activities. Additional needs can be met by seeking donations or purchasing things in good condition at garage sales. Any remaining needs should be met by allocating adequate financial resources in the annual budget. In most facilities, a multi-purpose, folding mobile cart is an important piece of equipment for bringing games, crafts, magazines, books, and other items to residents in their rooms, particularly those who are room-bound. The same cart can be used for serving refreshments and distributing items at parties and other large gatherings (Hastings 1981). Some equipment commonly used for activity programs includes folding tables and chairs, adjustable over-the-bed tables for use with wheelchairs, movie projectors, slide projectors, portable screens, compact disk and cassette players, VCR equipment, movable organs or pianos, cameras, radios, woodworking tools, garden tools, ceramic kilns, cooking utensils, microwave ovens, ice cream makers, popcorn makers, barbecue grills, Christmas ornaments and other festival or seasonal decorations, and a variety of games, puzzles, and large-print books. Use of the computer for information and fun has become increasingly popular.

(5) **Staff**. Creativity and resourcefulness are actually more basic requirements than supplies, equipment, or space (Lanza 1997). Staffing considerations also should not be ignored. The number of staff members, and their qualifications, training, experience, and personality traits, are key factors in developing and implementing quality programs. Building strong volunteer support is often necessary to supplement staffing in the activity department, because additional hands are often needed for programs such as parties,

shows, and outings. Involvement of families can also be successfully pursued, because many of the residents' family members are retired but in good health, and family and friends often would like to stay involved in the lives of their loved ones. The activity director should work closely with the social worker to identify families who are likely to become volunteers at some point.

(6) **Community resources**. Maintaining a link with the outside community is vital to enhancing the residents' quality of life. This consideration is one reason why exchange relationships with the local community must be actively pursued (see Chapter 2). The administrator plays a critical leadership role in initiating and nurturing external contacts, but key department managers in the facility such as the social worker, director of nursing, activity director, and any staff member holding a liaison position (such as a marketing director) must continue to strengthen the relationships with external agencies. Local religious establishments, clerical associations, schools, Boy Scouts, Girl Scouts, non-profit social-service agencies, businesses, libraries, shopping malls, and many other types of organizations and establishments can support the facility's activity programs by offering their resources. Using community resources does not always mean bringing the resources into the facility. Community resources are also used when residents are taken for outings. For example, a trip to the mall may require making advance arrangements to accommodate a relatively large group of residents at the ice-cream parlor, or a group visit to a department store would require some coordinating so that residents could be taken at an appropriate time to look at preselected merchandise-display areas.

Meeting a Variety of Needs

Federal guidelines require that activity programming be multifaceted. Programs must incorporate each individual resident's needs. Programs should also provide "stimulation or solace; promote physical, cognitive and/or emotional health; enhance to the extent practicable each resident's self-respect by providing, for example, activities that allow for self-expression, personal responsibility and choice" (Lanza 1997).

Multifaceted programming must cover the following major needs (Lanza 1997):

- physical
- cognitive and educational
- social
- affective
- integration or awareness
- spiritual

Physical needs require some activities that provide exercise, movement, and general physical stimulation of the body parts. Programs such as dance therapy, exercise programs, and walking outdoors specifically address physical needs. Exercises and sports programs often require simulation. For example, a balloon volleyball, in which residents toss the balloon among themselves while seated in a circle, can simulate the real game.

Cognitive and educational needs demand programs designed to stimulate the mind and promote learning. Word games, games such as Trivial Pursuit, discussions of current events, and book reviews are activities that fall into this group. Nursing facilities must also provide residents with computers, Internet access, and other self-directed pastimes.

Social needs call for activities that provide opportunities for interaction and companionship with others. Examples of such programs include parties, functions, room visits, sing-alongs, and birthday parties and other celebrations.

Affective needs require activities that enable residents to express feelings, emotions, and creativity. Art therapy, music therapy, touch therapy, pet therapy, bird-feeding, entertainment, and other types of programs that provide sensory stimulation and foster reminiscence are some examples. Entertainment programs require resourcefulness and planning. Movies are a common form of entertainment, but a resourceful activity director can arrange for a variety of other things, such as puppet shows, fashion parades, magic shows, live bands, chamber music, plays and skits, and cooking demonstrations. Some residents may be interested in journal-writing to reminisce their past.

Integration or awareness needs call for participation in programs that can help build self-esteem. Examples of such programs include roles in which the resident is needed by others, such as mail delivery, folding linens in the laundry, participation in resident council, acting as surrogate grandparents to children from the local day-care center, and telling stories to children.

Spiritual needs are answered, in the lives of many elderly residents, by religious and spiritual pursuits considered important in their lives for achieving personal satisfaction, well-being, self-realization, and as a means of coping with stressful situations. Private devotions, quiet meditation, reading, and congregational religious programs brought in by local churches and synagogues are examples of activities in which many elders like to engage to find personal fulfillment and peace.

Scheduling

High-quality activity programming calls for a variety of scheduling patterns. As a rule of thumb, scheduling should attempt to mirror the residents' usual patterns of rest and recreation before they were institutionalized. In this regard, Greenblatt (1988) proposes that holidays, to the extent possible, should be celebrated on the days they actually occur. Crafts and hobbies ought to be pursued in late morning before lunch; the elderly often take naps or just rest after lunch. Parties normally take place in late afternoon or evening. Residents like to have leisure time after dinner, which is generally over by 6:30 p.m., and on weekends when no showers are scheduled and family visits are common. On the other hand, it is also an irony that activity programming is frequently curtailed during periods when the residents have the most leisure time available; this lack of scheduled activity results in boredom, frustration, agitation, and functional decline. Hence, scheduling activities in general is challenging, and providing regular programs in the evenings and on weekends and holidays is particularly challenging. As a rule of thumb, some morning activities should be offered starting at around 10:00 a.m.; then afternoon activities, starting at around 2:30 p.m.; and evening activities, starting at around 7:00 p.m. Within these guidelines, however, residents' own preferences for activity times should be accommodated (Lanza 1997).

Socializing

A variety of activities suitable for individual participation, or for participation in small and large groups, must be planned to accommodate each resident's personal preferences. Residents can get active and passive stimulation during individual activities as well as in large group activities. Residents who cannot actively participate can simply be passive "bystanders," and receive stimulation from listening and watching other active participants. Some residents are intimidated by small-group settings, in

which more active participation is generally required, whereas others may not like being in large groups. Small groups often form spontaneously as friendships between two or among more people develop. The activity staff can help such groups find something meaningful to do together.

Intergenerational Appeal

Children's interactions with the elderly have universal appeal. Eyes brighten up, smiles begin to form, and muffled laughter is often heard when the elderly are exposed to little children. Children also get a special sense of fulfillment when they can sit in an older person's lap, tell a tale, show the elder their favorite toy, or ask the elder some question. Every nursing home should explore ways to facilitate intergenerational contact. By working with local schools, child day-care centers, and parents many facilities across the country have developed formal programs that allow small children to make regular visits to nursing homes and to participate in nursing-home activities.

Cognitive Functioning

In contrast to most other types of activity programming, therapeutic services for cognitive disorders generally require an intervention approach. Using such an approach means that voluntary choice and personal control do not play as much of a role as they do in most program-oriented approaches, because in many instances residents who need therapeutic services are unable to express their wishes. However, the patients' past practices and habits are taken into account to develop appropriate interventions. This section categorizes activities that are specifically designed for sensory and cognitive stimulation. A variety of programs are appropriate for individual as well as group interaction, including:

- sensory stimulation
- reality orientation
- reminiscence

Sensory stimulation can benefit residents who have cognitive, visual, or hearing impairments, or those who are bed-ridden or comatose and are likely to undergo sensory deprivation over time. Sensory deprivation speeds up degenerative changes in mind and body and accelerates the loss of functional cells in the central nervous system. This loss can lead to sec-

ondary physical and psychological abnormalities (Oster 1976). A patient's perception and alertness can be improved by eliciting responses to stimuli in the five sensory areas: vision, hearing, smell, taste, and touch. Use of objects with bright colors, lighted objects, music therapy, aroma therapy, and pet therapy are means of providing sensory stimulation.

Reality orientation using simple, straightforward, factual information on a regular basis can help residents with substantial cognitive disabilities remain oriented and communicative. Facts such as the resident's name, the name of the facility where the patient is residing, the day, the date, and the season are presented to the resident one at a time, and the resident is encouraged to verbalize the information. Use of calendars, clocks, pictures, and information boards are used as aids (Buettner and Martin 1995; Lanza 1997).

Reminiscence—remembering, and in some way reliving, past experiences—is important for emotional well-being. Engaging in certain activities can help bring back "the good old days." Such activities for residents include singing or listening to old-time songs, seeing clips of old TV shows, watching old movies, going through photo albums, or discussing memorabilia from a certain era. Reminiscence differs from **validation therapy**, in which people, particularly those with dementia, may actually believe that they are living in the past, and this belief is accepted and validated by the staff members working with the patient.

Special Needs of Dementia Patients

Patients with dementia present special challenges. Wandering, soliloquizing, repetitive yelling, crying, or staring are some of the commonly observed behaviors in patients with dementia. Some patients may display social withdrawal symptoms. Generally, these residents possess a lot of nervous energy that must be channeled into more constructive outlets. Otherwise, a noisy and chaotic environment can provoke a sense of bewilderment and anxiety in such patients, which, in turn, reinforces disruptive patterns of behavior, such as combativeness and other aggressive manifestations.

Under a grant from the New York State Department of Health, one facility discovered that a small-group program may best address the needs of dementia patients. This model proposes a staff-to-resident ratio of 1:8, particularly when patients with mid-stage dementia are involved (Hutson and Hewner 2001). Focusing on the residents' cognitive and affective

needs is critical. The small-group program requires cross-trained staff teams consisting of social workers, activity assistants, and certified nursing assistants. One staff member works with a small group of 6 to 10 residents at a time, and practitioners of the three disciplines rotate among the small groups. Group composition is roughly homogeneous; for example, wanderers are in one group, and patients displaying disruptive behaviors are in another group (Hutson and Hewner 2001).

The day often begins for women with grooming and makeup that involves personal touch. Men are in a separate group, in which staff members engage them to talk about the news or sports. These activities allow residents to reminisce and do something with which they are familiar. Staff members take the time to listen, and they provide physical contact, such as hugs and holding hands. They use gentle touches as aids to communication and as reassurances that someone is present and listening. Wandering residents are taken for walks, both indoors and outdoors, and they are asked to hold hands with one another to feel connected and safe (Hutson and Hewner 2001).

Dementia patients can also be involved in constructive activities, such as folding towels. Cognitive activities, such as matching painted rocks with colors painted inside an egg carton, can also be employed. Other activities meet the residents' affective needs. For example, soothing music often elevates mood and counters social withdrawal and depression (Humphrey 2000).

Multisensory stimulation (MSS, also called Snoezelen—see Chapter 6) has become increasingly popular in European countries. MSS procedures have not been standardized, but Baker and colleagues (2001) propose that three main characteristics differentiate MSS from other therapies:

- Visual, auditory, tactile and olfactory stimulation is offered to patients, often in a specially designed room (sometimes called a Snoezelen room), using a variety of lights, soft music, aromas, and tactile objects.
- Staff work one-on-one with patients, adopting a non-directive, enabling approach in which they follow the patients' lead. Patients are encouraged to engage with sensory stimuli of their choice.
- Stimuli used are non-sequential and unpatterned, experienced moment by moment without relying on short-term memory to link

them to previous events. They present few specific attentional or intellectual demands on the patient with dementia.

The effectiveness of MSS with dementia patients is currently being investigated, but preliminary results show some promise. For example, one preliminary study by Chung and colleagues (2002) found that, during MSS sessions, dementia patients presented fewer apathetic, restless, disruptive, and repetitive behaviors than patients who did not undergo such therapy. On the other hand, in another study, MSS was found to be no more effective than regular activity programs in changing the behavior, mood, or cognition of patients with dementia (Baker et al. 2003).

PROGRAM PLANNING AND IMPLEMENTATION

The number and types of activity programs are limited only by the resources that a facility is able to provide and by the knowledge, creativity, and resourcefulness of its activity staff. However, the activity director should work within these constraints and plan programs that provide the greatest variety of activities in accordance with the interests of most residents, yet no one's needs should be left out. In essence, the special challenge for activity professionals is to create maximum recreational opportunities for each resident and appropriate interventions for those who lack the ability to choose. Implementation requires three stages:

- identifying suitable programs by evaluating the numerous factors just discussed in the various sections on program development
- planning programs by selecting and scheduling specific activities
- conducting each activity in accordance with the plan

Identifying Suitable Programs

Identification of appropriate programs begins with resident assessment. The next step after resident assessment requires compiling information on individual interests and needs and putting them into a composite profile. An interest checklist (Lanza 1997) can be developed to facilitate this task. Such a checklist can be easily created using a standard spreadsheet program such as Excel or Quattro Pro, in which a horizontal row can be assigned to each resident and the vertical columns can be marked with

various interests such as art, baking, dancing, fishing, reading, etc. Columns can also be used for the degree of social activity preferred. The computer spreadsheet enables the activity director to produce useful summaries of the data. The summaries can be very effective in planning the range of programs without leaving out any resident. This information can be easily updated on a regular basis as the facility's population changes over time. Lanza (1997) also recommends developing a risk awareness profile, which can also be maintained on a computer spreadsheet. Risk awareness profiles are based on residents' functional limitations as well as cautionary information about things such as allergies, or other health conditions or treatments that may require staff members to observe certain precautions, as in case of drug side effects.

Planning Programs

The step described above is likely to identify a large number of programs suitable for the facility's residents. However, specific programs should be selected on the basis of various considerations such as space, equipment, staffing, and availability of community resources. Activities that would meet the common needs of most residents become the core activity programs. Additional activities should be planned to accommodate the special needs and interests of the remaining residents. A policies and procedures manual for activities should include a variety of choices, to help select and plan appropriate programs. Much like a recipe book, the procedures section of the manual should list the "ingredients" for various activities, such as the name and description of each activity, the resources the activity requires, the amount of time it takes, the functions of the staff involved in carrying it out, and the type of resident for whom the activity is appropriate.

Activity calendars provide the most effective means for planning. A master calendar is prepared to earmark the main activities for an entire year. This calendar helps the activity staff plan and prepare for major events, special celebrations, and seasonal festivities well in advance. The master calendar is also used to identify programs of wide appeal that would be offered on a regular basis, and programs for which some lead-time is necessary.

A tentative weekly calendar of activities, showing the time and place for each activity, should be circulated among department heads, key nursing staff, and the administrator a couple of weeks in advance. This review

helps to address any potential conflicts and allows for sufficient time to finalize the weekly calendar. The final weekly calendar should be sent to all key departments and personnel a few days in advance, but it should not be posted until Monday morning; otherwise it is likely to be mistaken for the current week's calendar by residents and families.

The first order of business for the activity director each Monday morning is to announce over the public address system the activity schedule for that week. A large, wall-size activity calendar must be prominently displayed at one or more designated locations within the facility. An activity calendar with well-planned programs listed on it is also an asset in marketing the facility to prospective clients during the facility tour. During the pre-admission inquiry process, a stop at the posted activity calendar and some comments by the tour-giver on the variety and substance of the activities must be part of the facility tour.

No clear guidelines exist regarding the number of programs that should be offered. The key is to find the right balance between quantity and quality. A full schedule with a number of large group activities may not be effective in meeting the needs of some patients. The greatest benefit to residents may come from having fewer activities but activities that are of high quality and truly meet residents' needs (Carroll et al. 1978). At the other extreme, a schedule with very few activities is also undesirable, because it would lack variety and would leave residents with large blocks of time with not much to do.

In planning time for activities, Carroll and colleagues (1978) suggested that each full-time staff member should spend approximately 25 hours per week actually conducting activities and devote the remainder to planning, documentation, and attending meetings. Twenty-five hours of programming per full-time staff member allows for 12 or 13 separate group activities per week. Synergies can be added by using volunteers to complement staffing, which is often short-handed. Realistic amounts of time should be allowed to setup the activity location, to prepare materials and equipment, to transport non-ambulatory residents to and from the activity location, and to return the area to its original set-up.

Nursing staff members generally help with transportation. Cooperation from nurses is also needed for dressing residents appropriately, helping residents to use the toilet before activities, and dispensing medications and treatments in a way that will not interfere with the resident's ability to participate in activity programs. Hence, nursing schedules are often an impor-

tant consideration in activity planning. The dietary staff may be involved when refreshments are a part of the activity. Housekeeping and maintenance staff members are needed for special set-ups that require moving and arranging furniture and cleaning up after activities (Carroll et al. 1978).

Conducting Activities

The actual implementation of an activity is greatly facilitated by how well a program is planned. Execution of most routine programs simply requires bringing together the planned resources. But for larger programs such as parties, functions, and outings, efforts and resources must be coordinated, and follow-up is necessary to make sure that everything proceeds smoothly. Each program should be carried out in accordance with the plan, while allowing for any unforeseen circumstances that may occur. Whenever possible, if a planned program must be canceled an appropriate substitute activity should be provided in accordance with a contingency plan. Hence, some back-up programs that can be carried out on short notice are necessary.

PROGRAM EVALUATION

Program evaluation is the process of systematically appraising a program to determine whether expected results are being achieved. Evaluating activity programming is a necessary prerequisite for improving the quality of a program. New and improved programs can be created only if the effectiveness of current programs can be objectively evaluated. When the evaluation validates the effectiveness of programs that staffers have helped create, staff morale is improved. On the other hand, evaluation should not be used to criticize or penalize activity personnel.

For effective evaluation, program goals and expected results must be established at the planning stage: programs should be planned with certain outcomes in mind. Determining whether or not the expected outcomes are achieved is the focus of program evaluation. The primary focus should be to determine whether residents' needs are being met. When desired outcomes are not achieved program directors must try to discover the reasons why these goal were not reached. An outside activity consultant may be employed to either do the program evaluation or to train the activity staff on how to do the evaluation.

The process of program evaluation involves continuous and systematic collection of relevant data. Because resource inputs such as staff time for activities are generally fixed, data collection pertains mainly to the outcomes. To collect outcome data, two main records should be kept: First, an accurate attendance record should be maintained for each activity. A computer spreadsheet can greatly facilitate this type of record-keeping. The data should reflect each resident's participation by the specific program he or she attends, how many times the resident attended each program. These attendance data would yield two critical pieces of information: which programs are the most popular, and the level of participation for each resident.

The second type of record involves qualitative information on the goals and progress of the program in relation to the goals planned for each resident in the care plan. This information is directly related to the assessment, care planning, and progress of the resident and can greatly facilitate documentation in each patient's medical record. When these two types of records are analyzed for each patient, it will be clear how well the activity programming is addressing each patient's individual needs, and what changes may be necessary when certain needs are not met.

VOLUNTEER SUPPORT

The activity director generally is responsible for developing and coordinating the facility's volunteer program. With proper training and supervision, volunteers from the local community can provide valuable assistance in a number of non-technical areas in which staff resources are often scarce. Hence, volunteer support is a critical adjunct to staff efforts to augment services and to improve the quality of life for the residents. Because most volunteers have regular and frequent contact with the facility, they establish an important link between the facility and the local community. Such an exchange is very meaningful within the open system context discussed earlier in the book.

Volunteer roles are not just confined to helping with activity programs. Depending on personal interests, volunteers may complement the efforts of the staff by passing meal trays during lunch or dinner, pouring water, sweeping up the dining room after dinner, tuning up wheelchairs, and other such tasks. Volunteers may also assist with shopping and other chores for patients, or provide transportation for outings.

Some key factors in recruiting and retaining volunteers are described below.

- A facility that has successfully established exchange relationships with the community is likely to have an easier time finding people interested in volunteering than facilities that have not formed such exchanges. However, recruitment efforts must be ongoing.

- People most likely to volunteer are retirees, homemakers without small children to take care of, and young adults in school. Various avenues can be pursued for recruiting interested people from these three groups. As mentioned earlier, some family members are also potential recruits for volunteering. Involvement by family members in activities can be a successful avenue for a facility to build positive relationships with families.

- A facility's advertising budget is generally small, and advertising may not be a very effective avenue for recruiting volunteers. Other methods, such as contacting potential volunteers directly, visiting local schools and discussing after-school opportunities, using current volunteers to recruit others, offering incentives, or sponsoring a volunteer recruitment day in collaboration with other service agencies, are some of the more effective means.

- Volunteers' availability, skills, and interests should be matched with the needs of the residents. The facility may state what its most critical needs are, but it should not pressure any volunteer into filling a certain role. The desired area of service should be chosen by each volunteer.

- Volunteers must be carefully selected using a formal process that should include filling out an application, screening, interviewing, and reference checks. Orientation and training must follow.

- Maintain a log book for recording the time each volunteer spends in the facility.

- Praise and recognition are paramount. Apart from providing the opportunity for personal gratification that the volunteer derives from helping others, recognizing the volunteer's work is the only way that the facility compensates volunteers for their efforts. Effectively managed facilities have an annual dinner and award ceremony exclusively for volunteers. Letting volunteers have meals at the facility at subsidized prices or for free, depending on the tasks they perform while they are in the facility, is also a good policy.

CONCLUSION

Activity programming is not simply a matter of putting together some recreational programs to comply with regulatory requirements; this programming requires a great deal of skill and resourcefulness. Activity programs must strike a balance between quantity and quality. Through evaluation, the effectiveness of each program must be established, and changes must be made accordingly. Activity programming should assess the needs of each resident and develop suitable programs so that no resident is left out. The biggest challenge for those who oversee activity programs in a facility is to make sure that those programs meet the needs of individual residents regardless of their physical, mental, social, or emotional status.

DISCUSSION QUESTIONS

1. As a nursing home administrator, how would you determine whether or not you have an effectively-run activity program in your facility?
2. What type of policies are appropriate for residents' participation in religious activities in nursing homes that are affiliated with religious organizations? What type of policies for religious activities are appropriate for residents in nursing homes that do not have such religious affiliations?

INTERNET RESOURCES FOR FURTHER LEARNING

The National Association of Activity Professionals is the only national group that represents activity professionals in geriatric settings exclusively. www.thenaap.com

The National Certification Council for Activity Professionals is one of the certifying bodies recognized by federal law and is the only national organization that exclusively certifies activity professionals who work with the elderly. www.nccap.org

REFERENCES

Baker, R., et al. 2001. A randomized controlled trial of the effects of multi-sensory stimulation (MSS) for people with dementia. *British Journal of Clinical Psychology* 40, no. 1: 81–96.

Baker, R., et al. 2003. Effects of multi-sensory stimulation for people with dementia. *Journal of Advanced Nursing* 43, no. 5: 465–477.

Buettner, L., and S.L. Martin. 1995. *Therapeutic Recreation in the Nursing Home.* State College, PA: Venture Publishing, Inc.

Carroll, K., et al. 1978. *Therapeutic Activities Programming with the Elderly.* Minneapolis: Ebenezer Center for Aging and Human Development.

Chung, J.C., et al. 2002. Snoezelen for dementia. *Chochrane Database of Systematic Reviews* [electronic resource] 2002 (4): pp. CD003152.

Greenblatt, F.S. 1988. *Therapeutic Recreation for Long-Term Care Facilities.* New York: Human Sciences Press, Inc.

Hastings, L.E. 1981. *Complete Handbook of Activities and Recreational Programs for Nursing Homes.* Englewood Cliffs, NJ: Prentice-Hall, Inc.

Humphrey, M.A. 2000. Alzheimer's disease meets the 'Mozart effect.' *Nursing Homes Long Term Care Management* 49, no. 6: 50–51.

Hutson, J.A., and S.J. Hewner. 2001. Activities 'plus' improve Alzheimer's care. *Nursing Homes Long Term Care Management* 50, no. 6: 52–55.

Lanza, S.E. 1997. *Essentials for the Activity Professional in Long-Term Care.* Albany, NY: Delmar Publishers.

Oster, C. 1976. Sensory deprivation in geriatric patients. *Journal of the American Geriatrics Society* 24, no. 10: 461–464.

Perschbacher, R. 1993. *Assessment: The Cornerstone of Activity Programs.* State College, PA: Venture Publishing, Inc.

Tedrick, T., and E.R. Green. 1995. *Activity Experiences and Programming within Long-Term Care.* State College, PA: Venture Publishing, Inc.

CHAPTER 10

Dietary Services

LEARNING MODULES

1. Purpose and broad objectives of dietary services.
2. The dietary department and its organization. Responsibilities and qualifications of the dietary manager and other food-service staff members. Need for consultation, and the role of consultant dietician.
3. Nutritional screening, assessment, and care planning.
4. Policies on meal plans, menu cycle, and seasonal menu variations.
5. Factors to be considered for menu development.
6. Importance of standardized recipes and portions. Main contents of a recipe.
7. Selecting food vendors and establishing contracts. Food ordering schedules and food order planning.
8. Types of dietary supplies. Reusable and disposable service supplies.
9. Receiving procedures. Proper food storage methods. Temperature control in dry-food storage areas, refrigerators, and freezers.

continues

10. Maintaining adequate food inventories. Methods of inventory control. Calculating food costs. Inventory rotation. Minimizing waste and pilferage.

11. Preparation planning and food preparation methods. Advantages and disadvantages of the three main types of meal production methods.

12. Types of therapeutic or modified diets. Food intake, plate waste, and the need for light snacks.

13. Enteral and parenteral nutrition. Methods of intensive nutrition delivery.

14. Centralized and decentralized methods of food service. Modified tray service. Portion control and accuracy checking methods. Food transportation methods. Observing the dining experience.

15. Food safety and sanitation practices. Proper holding and storage of cooked food. Proper dishwashing and sanitizing procedures.

The dietary operation in a nursing facility comprises clinical food services whose main objective is to provide individualized total nutritional care for each patient. A person's state of health, any eating disorders, and psychological factors are taken into account for planning and preparing meals that must have the appearance and taste of regular food to the extent it is practicable. In many nursing facilities the dietary department is also responsible for preparing meals for the staff, visitors, and volunteers. In most cases, preparing food separately for residents, staff members, and guests is impractical. Hence, the basic menu should be designed to meet the needs of all these groups. The dietary department is generally also responsible for making refreshments or special preparations for certain activities such as parties and functions. Some large facilities may also have contracts to prepare meals for the local Meals-On-Wheels program.

Food has universal appeal as a necessity for physical sustenance, as a means of sensory gratification, and as an agent for creating social interaction. These three major aspects of food provide the basic principles that guide food preparation and service in nursing facilities. For patients who have special dietary needs, food intake must also serve a therapeutic pur-

pose. Loss of appetite, inability to feed oneself, problems with chewing, swallowing difficulties, and inadequate nutrition are some common problems among nursing home residents. Other dietetic needs are related to diseases such as diabetes, heart conditions, or liver disease. To meet these special dietetic needs and to address these common problems dietary services in nursing facilities have to combine the functions of food service and dietetics.

DIETARY DEPARTMENT

Supervision

After nursing services, dietary is the second largest department in a nursing facility. The department is managed by a full-time food-service director, also known as dietary manager, who reports to the administrator. The dietary manager has both management and clinical responsibilities. This individual is responsible for staffing functions that include hiring, training, and scheduling; purchasing food and supplies; inventory management; and managing the food preparation and food service within the departmental budget. The dietary manager supervises all aspects of dietary operations such as food storage, food production and preparation of therapeutic diets, meal service, dish washing, and sanitation. Clinical responsibilities of this position include nutritional screening, assessment, care planning, diet planning, and documenting progress notes under the general direction of a clinical dietician.

Large facilities require one or more assistant food-service managers. Dietary managers and assistants should supervise the preparation and service of all meals and share clinical responsibilities. Supervision should also be provided on weekends and holidays, particularly when special meals are planned and when the facility is likely to have more than the usual number of visitors, some of whom may have a meal with the residents they may be visiting.

State regulations specify the qualifications required for the position of dietary manager. A registered dietician (RD) fulfills the requirements for this position in all states. However, RDs are difficult to recruit in nursing facilities. Only some very large facilities can generally afford to have a full-time RD. The two most common choices for filling the dietary manager's position are a registered dietetic technician (DTR) who holds an asso-

ciate's degree in general dietetics from a program approved by the American Dietetic Association (ADA) or a certified dietary manager who has completed the requirements for certification by the Dietary Managers' Association (DMA).

A DTR often works in partnership with a registered dietitian to screen, evaluate and educate patients. In addition to a two-year associate's degree from an ADA approved dietetics program located in an accredited college or university, DTRs also must have had supervised practical experience in dietary services, and they must pass a nationwide examination and take continuing education courses throughout their careers. Both RDs and DTRs are certified by the Commission on Dietetic Registration.

Food-Service Assistants

The functional organization of the dietary department has three main categories of food-service workers who perform a number of functions in the main kitchen under the general direction of the dietary manager, and assistant food service manager, if the facility has the latter position. Food-service workers include cooks, cook's helpers, and dietary aides (see Figure II-1). Cooks and their helpers are responsible for food preparation according to preplanned menus and standard recipes. Cooks prepare the main dishes (also known as entrées) and are responsible for portion control. Cook's helpers may assist with the preparation of main dishes, but their main job is to prepare side dishes, such as potatoes, pasta, vegetables, and salads. Dietary aides are responsible for food-service duties at the tray line and for clean-up and dish washing. Cross-training these employees is often necessary, especially to allow cook's helpers and dietary aides to perform more skilled functions when they must fill in for cooks and helpers because of sickness, and other instances when cooks and helpers need time off.

During meal service, as a general rule, certified nursing assistants (CNAs), preferably with additional help from volunteers, pick up meal trays at the end of the kitchen tray line and serve patients in the dining room. Trays are also served from carts transported to any auxiliary dining rooms located in other sections of the facility. CNAs are also responsible for collecting trays and dishes after each meal, and for bringing them to the dishwashing area.

Dietary aides operate the dishwasher and clean cooking utensils. Some large facilities have a position of night cleaner who comes in after the

kitchen has been closed to thoroughly clean floors, equipment, and other cooking, service, and storage areas.

Dietary Consultation

Therapeutic functions, which include menu planning based on nutritional guidelines, are under the direction of a registered dietician (RD). Dieticians are registered by the ADA. Full-time dieticians are rarely employed in nursing homes, although some facilities may be able to recruit a part-time dietician. However, regulations require the services of a dietary consultant, who works under contract only when a facility does not employ its own full- or part-time dietician. Multifacility chains are likely to have one or more clinical RDs in a corporate-level position who provide(s) consultation to the facilities operated by the chain. The extent and frequency of consultation is specified by nursing home regulations in each state. The consultant dietician must have active involvement in planning menus, developing recipes, ensuring the nutritional adequacy of food served, and assessing nutrition-related resident problems, such as weight loss or feeding problems. The consultant dietician must also review dietary assessment and care plans, determine equipment needs, review dietary policies and procedures, and make recommendations for sanitary and safe food preparation and storage practices.

After each consultation, the dietician must furnish the dietary manager a written report, and the administrator should receive a copy of this report. The administrator should also have periodic face-to-face meetings with the dietician to remain involved with any issues or concerns. The consultant dietician should also meet with charge nurses to address specific patient problems and consult regularly with the director of nursing. Diet and nutritional issues should also be discussed with the patient's attending physician.

NUTRITIONAL ASSESSMENT

Screening

Nutritional status of the patient is a critical aspect of holistic care, and determining a patient's nutritional needs begins with nutritional screening. The purpose of **nutritional screening** is to identify patients who may be at risk for nutritional problems. Examples of at-risk patients include

those who sustain weight loss, those on therapeutic diets, and those who either cannot take food by mouth or have difficulty eating. Nutritional screening relies on the physician's diet orders and on a comprehensive screening by the dietician. The Minimum Data Set (MDS) is the primary instrument used for screening. When the screening process yields certain triggers (conditions that pose potential health risks), further review and assessment are indicated. According to the MDS instrument, nutritional risk is indicated by one or more of five triggers: poor nutritional status, presence of feeding tubes, dedydration or a need for fluid maintenance, dental care, and pressure ulcers.

Assessment and Plan of Care

When a patient is found to be at risk, according to MDS triggers, further review and an in-depth assessment should be carried out by the clinical dietician. This follow-up assessment is done using the Resident Assessment Protocols (RAPs), as discussed in Chapter 8. The multidisciplinary team assesses each triggered condition to determine the type of care-plan intervention that may be necessary. The RAPs assist in clinical decision-making and serve as a link between assessment and plan of care (Sullivan and Atlas 1998). All nutritional interventions should be monitored, evaluated, and documented in the patient's medical records.

MENU PLANNING

The menu is central to the food-service operations because it determines how the resources of the department will be used. Hence, menu planning is a major function which is carried out with the assistance of the clinical dietician.

In multifacility chains, the menu-planning function is generally centralized at the corporate office. Standardized menus and recipes are developed for use by affiliated facilities. In this situation, corporations must allow their individual facilities some flexibility for variation to accommodate local tastes. Too rigid a system is likely to result in patient dissatisfaction. In non-chain affiliated independent facilities, the consulting dietician helps the dietary manager develop appropriate menus for the facility.

Meal Plans

Three considerations are fundamental to menu planning. First, menu planning requires a policy on the number of meals to be served per day. The daily nutrient intake should be distributed in a balanced fashion over the number of meals served (Mahaffey et al. 1981). Another factor is choice. A facility may or may not offer a choice for entrées. A third planning consideration is the meal service hours.

Traditional Three-Meal Plan

Nursing facilities typically follow a three-meal plan consisting of breakfast, lunch, and dinner (also known as supper). Federal and state regulations specify the maximum time lapse between dinner served one night and breakfast the following morning. A maximum time lapse of 14 hours is the common standard. Regulations also generally require that residents be offered a light bedtime snack, such as crackers, cheese, cookies, ice cream, milk, fruit, or juice. Typically, under the three-meal plan, breakfast is served between 7:30 and 8:30 a.m., lunch at 11:00 to 12:30 p.m., and dinner at 5:30 to 6:30 p.m.

Modified Five-Meal Plan

In recent years, a modified meal plan with five daily meals has come into vogue, and this plan has received enthusiastic acceptance from both residents and caregivers. The modified plan gives residents choice and flexibility with their daily lives. The extended meal-service hours of a modified plan give residents greater access to meals with less disruption of their preferred daily routines. In contrast, under the conventional meal plan, residents need to be up, toileted, and dressed for the scheduled breakfast service. The mornings become the busiest and the most rushed time for the nursing staff, and many patients resist having to get up early in the morning and to be hurried through daily hygiene chores.

Under the modified five-meal plan, a continental breakfast consisting of items such as rolls, muffins, yogurt, egg custard, juice, and coffee is served at 7:30 a.m. Residents can sleep in if they do not wish to be up that early. By the time a more substantial brunch is served from around 10:30 to 11:30 a.m. almost all residents are up and around. The other three meals include a lunchtime snack consisting of beverages and high calorie items served from 1:30 to 2:00 p.m.; a regular dinner at around 6:00 p.m.; and a late evening snack before bedtime.

Choice of multiple small meals during the day can lead to greater client satisfaction as well as greater nutritional intake. In a study evaluating family members' preferences for a range of treatment alternatives designed to improve nursing home residents' oral food and fluid intake, three nutritional interventions were rated as the most desirable: improving food quality, providing feeding assistance, and making multiple small meals and snacks available throughout the day (Simmons et al. 2003).

Selective and Nonselective Menus

Nonselective menus are the most common in nursing homes. One main item is specified for each of the three meals. The main item is served unless the patient has clearly indicated preferences that conflict with what is on the menu. Even when facility policy is to offer a nonselective menu, regulations state that an alternate food item of equal nutritional value be made available to accommodate individual preferences. Upscale facilities, with a high proportion of private-pay residents, typically offer a **selective menu** that gives a choice of two entrées from which each resident can make a selection. A full selective menu also generally offers two choices of vegetables and desserts. Offering a selective menu can lower plate waste (food left unconsumed), increase personal satisfaction, and still be accommodated within the food budget. To accomplish this goal, Puckett and Miller (1988) proposed pairing an expensive entrée with an inexpensive one to offset costs. However, a selective menu is likely to require some additional staff time and is more expensive to produce than a nonselective menu. Another alternative to a selective menu is a buffet offering a variety of food choices. A buffet can also be used as an alternative to a five-meal plan, straddling the hours of the brunch and light lunch services, and offering greater mealtime flexibility to residents.

Menu Cycle

Dietary policies and procedures should specify the length of time for menu rotation. A set of menus is developed to cover a pre-defined period during which the main items on the menus are not repeated. At the end of this period, the same daily menus are repeated in the same order. A three- to four-week length of time is quite adequate for the menu cycle. Different cycle menus can be created to go with changing seasons. For example, hot soups are more popular in winter, whereas cold-cuts and salads go well in summer. Cycle menus do not have to be rigid. There should

be flexibility to include festive menus for holidays and other social occasions. Special ethnic themes, such as Chinese, Italian, or Hawaiian, can also be incorporated to break the monotony of regular meal service, especially when special menus are coordinated with social activities promoting some ethnic theme. An outdoor barbecue in summer or a picnic in early fall also add variety to the menu and provide a non-routine social setting.

Menu Development

Once a meal plan and a menu cycle have been established, the clinical dietician and the dietary manager should work together in selecting appropriate main and side dishes for each meal. Several factors should be considered when selecting menu items:

- residents' preferences
- nutritional value of the items
- appearance and palatability
- cost
- facility resources and capabilities
- adherence to Dietary Reference Intakes
- emergency menus

Food preferences are based on cultural, geographic, and religious traditions. Items selected for the menu should appeal to as many residents as possible.

Nutritional adequacy should be ensured by including a variety of foods from the five major food groups shown in Figure 10-1. The five major food groups are milk and milk products; meat, fish, poultry, and eggs; fruits; vegetables; and grains and starches such as bread, rice, pasta, and potatoes. Legumes, nuts, and soy products must be included in meals as appropriate meat substitutes to furnish adequate proteins for vegetarians. Unless a resident has special nutritional requirements, a balanced combination of foods can meet the nutritional needs of most people. Several years ago, Zaccarelli and Maggiore (1972) proposed ten groups from which foods should be selected every day: leafy, green, and yellow vegetables; citrus fruit and tomato; potatoes and sweet potatoes; other vegetables and fruits; milk, cheese, and ice cream; meat, poultry, and fish; eggs (3 to 5 a week); flour, cereal, and baked goods; fats and oils; and sugar, syrups, and preserves. In addition to the 10 groups, dry beans, dry peas, or nuts should be included at least once a week.

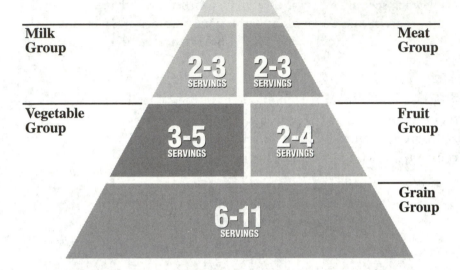

Fats, Oils and Sweets
USE SPARINGLY

Milk
Group

Meat
Group

2-3
SERVINGS

2-3
SERVINGS

Vegetable
Group

Fruit
Group

3-5
SERVINGS

2-4
SERVINGS

Grain
Group

6-11
SERVINGS

Notes: The pyramid is a guide for the daily servings of foods chosen from each of the five categories illustrated below the tip of the pyramid. The small tip shows fats, oils, and sweets. These are foods such as salad dressings and oils, cream, butter, margarine, sugars, soft drinks, candies, and sweet desserts. These foods provide calories, but little else nutritionally, and should be used sparingly. On the next level of the Food Guide Pyramid are two groups of foods that come mostly from animals: milk, yogurt, cheese; and meat, poultry, fish, dry beans, eggs, and nuts. These foods are for protein, calcium, iron, and zinc. The next level includes foods that come from plants—vegetables and fruits. Most people need to eat more of these foods for the vitamins, minerals, and fiber they supply. At the base of the pyramid are breads, cereals, rice, and pasta—all foods from grains. You need the servings of these foods each day.

Source: U.S. Department of Agriculture and the U.S. Department of Health and Human Services.

FIGURE 10-1 The Food Guide Pyramid

Pleasing combinations of food items should be included on the menu by varying color, flavor, texture, shape, consistency, and method of preparation (Graves and Stewart 1985). Food served to the residents must be both palatable and attractive.

One of the most challenging aspects of menu planning is to keep the cost of food to a minimum without compromising quality. The dietary department is generally allowed a per-patient-day (PPD) cost for the raw food budget. The daily raw food budget will be a dollar amount calculated as:

Daily raw food budget = PPD cost × census (number of patients)

To stay within the budgeted allowance, the daily food cost allowance should first be allocated to each meal and food category. Then the cost of each item on the menu should be calculated (Sullivan and Atlas 1998). Lunch is generally the most expensive of the three meals, followed by dinner and then by breakfast. The cost of bedtime snacks must also come out of the food budget.

Preparation methods, time required for food preparation, skills of the kitchen staff, storage space, serving temperatures, and type of kitchen equipment are things to consider when planning a menu. In other words, facility resources and capabilities must be taken into account.

Before the menus are finalized, their nutrient content must be evaluated to comply with the Dietary Reference Intakes (DRI). The DRI consist of two sets of values, called Recommended Dietary Allowances (RDAs) and Adequate Intake (AI). Both these sets of values establish levels of calories and nutrients such as proteins, vitamins, and minerals. DRIs establish not only recommended daily intakes necessary to help maintain health, but also tolerable upper intake limits to help avoid any potential harm from excessive intake. AI suggests nutritional adequacy when not enough scientific evidence exists to establish an RDA. The DRIs have been compiled by the Food and Nutrition Board of the Institute of Medicine at the National Academy of Sciences.

In addition to the menus included in the regular menu cycle, the facility's dietary policies and procedures should specify menus for emergency situations such as when the facility has a prolonged power failure, or when the dietary department may have to be operated on a skeletal crew because of emergencies such as snowstorms, floods, or other natural events that prevent most of the scheduled staff to get to work. Under these conditions, preparing the regular menu would be impractical. Emergency menus require the use of canned, preserved, packaged, and precooked food items. The facility must also make prior arrangements for procuring bottled water in case of an emergency.

Standardized Recipes and Portions

The menu functions as the "road map" for dietary operations, and standard recipes provide the "directions" on the road map. A standard recipe is a blueprint for food preparation and is essential for controlling food

costs. Recipes are designed and tested so that a consistent product—with known quality, quantity, and taste—will be produced. Standard recipes will also yield consistent costs, predictable labor hours, and nutritional value (Ninemeier 1985). Each recipe must provide details on the specific raw ingredients and their quantity, method of preparing, utensils and equipment needed, method and temperature for cooking, amount of time needed for preparation and cooking, total yield, number of portions, size of each portion, temperature for serving, and any other pertinent information. Recipes based on 100 portions can be easily adapted to serve any number of people. Recipes are commonly printed on plastic-coated recipe cards so that they can be easily filed and retrieved when needed.

PURCHASING FOOD AND SUPPLIES

Vendor Arrangements

The facility should make arrangements with reputable food vendors to procure dry goods, frozen foods, fresh produce, and dairy products. Several vendors should be asked for competitive bidding based on written specifications. Reliability, regular delivery schedule, consistent quality, and price are important considerations when selecting the vendors. Depending on the location of their facilities, multifacility chains often have a great deal of purchasing power to select the vendors that their affiliated facilities are required to use. Independent facilities and small chains can explore the possibilities of participating in cooperative or group-purchasing arrangements that can give even small facilities some buying power. Food vendors have different grades of products to meet the needs of a variety of customers. For instance, quality can vary according to brand, grade, size, thickness, weight, or count. Because of these variations, a facility ought to have written specifications for the food it buys as part of its contracts with vendors. Prices are also negotiated in advance but are subject to change with sufficient advance notice by the vendor.

Food Ordering

The planned menu and recipes provide the basis for food purchasing. However, careful planning is necessary to ensure that the needed food

items will be available in time for food production. Size of the order is governed by the patient census, anticipated number of guest meals, and, if the facility serves them, volunteer and staff meals. In essence, the number of portions to be served must be carefully forecasted, and the time lapse between food preparation and delivery must be taken into account. The frequency of delivery depends on the vendor's delivery schedule, the type of food item delivered, and the facility's storage capacity. Puckett and Miller (1988) suggest these steps for economical food delivery:

- frozen food: weekly or semi-monthly
- chilled meat, fish, and poultry: twice a week
- fresh produce: once or twice a week
- canned goods and staples: weekly, semi-monthly, or monthly
- fresh dairy items, breads, and baked goods: daily or every other day
- butter, eggs, and cheese: weekly

Dietary Supplies

Supplies used in the dietary department can be classified into three main categories: supplies used in the kitchen for food production, such as aluminum foils, plastic wraps, and storage bags; supplies used for serving meals; and chemicals and supplies for dishwashing and cleaning. Service supplies can be categorized as reusable or disposable. Such supplies include trays, dinnerware, tableware, hollowware, glassware, and disposable paper, plastic, and styrofoam products.

Reusable supplies come in a variety of materials, such as rubber, plastic, fiberglass, and other materials, such as vitrified china, which is designed for both durability and attractiveness. Stainless steel cutlery resists tarnish, is durable, and is easy to clean. Some disposables are used on a regular basis when needed, but they should mostly be kept on hand for emergency use. An adequate amount of disposable plates, cups, and cutlery should be kept in stock to be used when a power outage occurs or when the dishwashing equipment is out of order. Regular use of disposables in the long run is quite expensive, yet it comes across as "cheap" to residents and visitors and diminishes the aesthetical appeal of the dining experience. Table cloths, cloth napkins, and table center pieces, used at least for the main meal, add to the quality of the dining experience.

FOOD STORAGE AND INVENTORY

Receiving

The dietary department should have effective control procedures to ensure that the food and supplies delivered by vendors match the quality and quantity of items ordered. Dietary policies should assign the job of receiving to authorized personnel, and receiving responsibilities and procedures should be clearly described. Two receiving methods are commonly used (Puckett and Miller 1988):

- invoiced receiving
- blind receiving

Invoice receiving is a method in which the items delivered are checked against the original order. The focus is on finding any discrepancies between what was ordered and what is received. Shortages, substitutions, deviations from quality specifications, and any rejections should be carefully noted by the receiver.

Blind receiving is a method in which the original order shows the specific items but not the quantities. The quantities of the items received are recorded by the person checking the order. This method is more reliable than invoice receiving, because the receiver may fail to do accurate comparisons when using the invoice receiving method. In either case, the facility should use its own ordering record rather than the supplier's delivery invoice to ensure that all items received are exactly as they were ordered.

Storage

The facility should have adequate, secure, and sanitary space for storage of various food items at their proper temperatures. Three types of food storage space are necessary: dry storage, refrigeration, and freeze storage.

The dry storeroom must be clean, cool, and dry. It should also have adequate ventilation and lighting. The recommended temperature range for dry food storage is between 50° F and 70° F (Puckett and Miller 1988). All food must be on shelves or kept above the floor on dollies or pallets, which should be six to twelve inches above the floor, depending on state regulations. Off-the-floor storage makes it possible to keep the entire floor area clean.

Refrigerator temperatures should be maintained at 40° F or lower. To prevent cross contamination, raw meat should be separated from other foods, and should be stored on the bottom shelves so meat juices do not drip on other foods.

Frozen foods should be kept at 0° F or below. Refrigerators and freezers should be equipped with functioning thermometers. A temperature log should be maintained to record regular temperature readings for refrigerators and freezers. Any malfunctions should be reported to the maintenance department for prompt rectification. Chemicals and cleaning supplies should be stored in a separate area away from food and other dietary supplies.

Inventory Control

Determining how large a food inventory should be on hand at any given time depends on two main factors: immediate needs and contingency needs.

Adequate quantities of food supplies required for the menus must be available when needed. A sufficient stock of food must be on hand at all times to prepare meals for the next four to seven days, depending on the ordering cycle.

In accordance with the policy on emergency menus, adequate non-perishable food items must be held in stock to last for three to four days. State regulations may also specify how many days' worth of food inventory and non-perishable emergency food supplies must be maintained.

There are two methods of inventory control. A **perpetual inventory system** is a continuous record of the quantity on hand for each item at any given time. In large dietary operations, a separate card is maintained for each item. The card has four columns for recording purchases, amounts used, and amount remaining on hand:

*Amount on hand = Amount on hand shown on the previous line
+ Purchases − Amount withdrawn*

The main advantage of this system is that it provides a running balance of quantities remaining on shelves, which can be checked at any time by taking a physical inventory. The second method of inventory control, **physical inventory system**, calls for actually counting each item in storage, this inventory is generally undertaken once a month.

The perpetual inventory indicates the amount that should be on hand. The physical inventory gives an accurate count of what is actually on hand. Discrepancies may suggest either pilferage or errors in recording data (Sullivan and Atlas 1998). The perpetual inventory system is time-consuming because quantities must be recorded each time items are added or withdrawn. For small institutions, it may not be worth the extra time and effort, although such institutions should control the costs of expensive items by using a simplified perpetual inventory system. However, all facilities should at least take a monthly physical inventory to accurately determine the food cost, which is calculated as follows:

(a) Cost of physical inventory at the end of the previous month

$$+$$

(b) Cost of all food invoices (food purchased) during the current month

$$-$$

(c) Cost of physical inventory at the end of the month

$$=$$

(d) Total gross food cost for the month [(a) + (b) − (c)]

$$-$$

(e) Cost of meals served to non-patients:

$$\frac{(d)}{\text{Total number of meals served}} \times \text{number of nonpatient meals served}$$

$$=$$

(f) Net patient food cost for the month [(d) − (e)]
(g) Food cost per patient day (PPD):

$$\frac{(f)}{\text{number of patients days for the month}}$$

Note: Patient days and PPD costs are described in Chapter 16

Rotating the inventory is another aspect of inventory control. The **first-in first-out** system, abbreviated as FIFO, requires that all products be dated when received. Secondly, newly received products should be stored at the back of the shelves; products already on the shelf should be moved to the front. When products are needed for food preparation, they should be picked from the front. This system ensures that older products are used first.

A high food cost does not necessarily indicate that the food being served is of high quality. The dietary manager must always be conscious of food waste and the potential for pilferage. Periodic monitoring of receiving procedures and regular checks of receiving and storage areas can reveal problems that may otherwise go unnoticed. Food in poor condition may have to be discarded, but the department must have a strict policy that no food is to be discarded without specific approval from the dietary manager. Ordering foods not called for by the menus, ordering in excessive quantities, and overproduction are other practices that often lead to waste and higher food cost than what is necessary. Theft and pilferage may be occurring that may go unobserved; the dietary manager should do occasional spot checks to reconcile invoiced and received items. Also, designating one or two individuals to be responsible for receiving and storage can help pinpoint any discrepancies.

FOOD PREPARATION

Preparation Planning

Menu planning, standard recipes, food purchasing, storage, and inventory management are the essential prerequisites for food production in a facility. But food production itself requires planning ahead. For instance, frozen meats must be thawed in the refrigerator three to four days in advance so that they are available for cooking on the day they are on the menu. Some food items require full or partial cooking on the day before the menu is to be served. However, in spite of the best planning efforts, some deviation from the menu may sometimes become necessary. For example, an item needed for the menu is not received on time, or the quantity of raw ingredients is not sufficient. In such cases occasional substitutions become necessary and the facility must make contingency plans, because the need for substitutions generally crops up at the last moment. Menu substitutions should match the nutritive value of the food item replaced, and all substitutions should be properly documented.

Preparation Methods

Three basic types of food preparation methods are commonly used in health care institutions (Puckett and Miller 1988). Each method has its

advantages and disadvantages, which should be carefully evaluated during menu planning. The food-service objectives of each nursing facility will determine the right blend of these methods:

- cook-and-serve
- cook-and-chill or freeze
- assemble-and-serve

Cook-and-Serve Method

The cook-and-serve method is the traditional approach to food production, in which most menu items are prepared primarily from raw ingredients on the day they are to be served. After cooking, the food is kept hot or cold until serving time. Cook-and-serve requires a relatively large inventory and more labor than the other two methods. Another disadvantage is the limited time the staff generally has to get the food ready for serving. Greater control over quality is one of the main advantages. Food cooked from scratch has the "home cooked" appeal. Use of seasonal fresh produce makes food even more appealing. Home-style cooking can be marketed to prospective clients as an added value. Some facilities prepare fresh bakery items, such as breads and pies, on a daily basis. The pleasant aroma of freshly baked goods permeating throughout the facility appeals to most people, and it adds to the homelike atmosphere. This aroma can be easily achieved by using premixed products, which are widely available in dry or frozen form.

Cook-and-Chill or Freeze Method

Chilling or freezing after cooking requires two stages of heating: initial cooking and reheating before serving. The cooking stage can be done up to 6 weeks in advance for cook-and-chill items, and earlier for cook-and-freeze items.

In the cook-and-chill method, the food is first completely cooked. It is then rapidly chilled to between 32° F and 40° F, using an ice bath or blast chiller. Typically, complete chilling is accomplished in 90 minutes to two hours, using special cook-chill equipment. It is critical to maintain the specified temperature range during storage until the food is ready to be served, when it is reheated to a temperature of 150° F.

The cook-chill and cook-freeze methods are similar in all respects except that the latter method involves freezing the food to 0° F or below,

instead of chilling. The equipment is also similar, except that cook-freeze requires a fast-freezing unit which increases the cost of the equipment. Quick freeze also requires additional packaging which adds to the cost. One major advantage of cook-and-freeze items is that they can be kept on hand for contingency use or be used during a subsequent menu cycle.

Incorporating these methods is also helpful when selective menus are offered. Menus can be planned in such a way that low labor productivity (slack time) on certain days can be used to prepare additional items to be served on a later day. Another major advantage is that chilled or frozen foods are less perishable and retain nutrients longer than foods cooked and held at serving temperatures for relatively long periods in the cook-and-serve systems. One major drawback is that not all chilled and frozen foods can be successfully prepared without extensively modifying the ingredients or recipes. Certain foods lose their flavor or texture after freezing. Also, staff must be skilled in exercising strict temperature controls for precooking, quick chilling or freezing, and reheating in order to prevent bacterial growth. Limited refrigeration and freezer space presents additional obstacles.

Assemble-and-Serve Method

This method is also called the "convenience system" because only minimal food preparation is necessary. The foods are commercially prepared and packaged. Depending on how they will be used on the menu, a variety of prepared products can be purchased in fresh, frozen, canned, or dehydrated forms. Menu variety is often greater in assemble-and-serve systems than in most cook-and-serve systems. But inconsistent quality and greater up-front expense are the main drawbacks. Despite its advantages, the higher cost of assemble-and-serve products cannot be justified unless it reduces labor costs.

THERAPEUTIC DIETS AND NOURISHMENTS

A regular well-balanced diet is the most appropriate diet for most elderly patients. Certain medical conditions, however, necessitate diet modification or supplementation. Nutritional needs can also be altered by disease, stress, and drugs. The need for modified diets or food supplements should be evaluated by the dietician, nurses, and the patient's attending physician.

Modified Diets

Therapeutic diets are commonly referred to as modified diets because, in most instances, only minor modifications of the regular menus are necessary. For instance, a mechanical soft diet is produced by simply grounding or chopping the food so it requires minimum chewing. For a puréed diet, the regular food is pulverized to a puréed consistency, using a food processor. These are the simplest types of therapeutic diets.

Restricted diets are also relatively simple modifications of regular menu items, and these diets generally require restricting or eliminating certain condiments. For example, in a sodium-restricted diet, salt and processed foods that may have a high salt content are restricted. In a bland diet, irritants such as caffeine and spices are left out. A low-cholesterol diet requires restricting foods rich in saturated fats.

More complex diets than those just described call for substituting certain items on the regular menu and may need nutrients to be balanced. Examples include low-fiber and high-fiber diets in which appropriate foods must be added or eliminated from the diet. A diabetic diet requires a careful balance of carbohydrates, proteins, and fats, and sugar substitutes are used in place of natural sugars. High-carbohydrate and high-protein diets also must be carefully balanced. Clear-liquid and full-liquid diets are based on a judicious selection of appropriate liquids such as clear broths and gelatin-based products. Certain food allergies or food intolerances also call for appropriate substitutions.

Maintaining nutritional content and ensuring the patient's acceptance of the diet are the biggest challenges in preparing special diets. It can be argued that overly rigid enforcement of a dietary regimen may not be in a patient's best interest if the patient will not consume the food and will remain unhappy. Imposing severe restrictions may lead to stress, anger, anxiety, or depression (Robinson and Leif 2001). Such issues should be resolved by the multidisciplinary team, in consultation with the patient's attending physician. In recommending therapeutic diets, the potential benefits must be evaluated against the possible detriments to optimal food intake and the disruption in the resident's quality of life (Gerwick 1992). The patient is responsible for following the recommended nutrition care plan, but also has the right to refuse medical treatment, including a therapeutic diet. But if the resident refuses to follow the nutrition care plan, he or she bears the responsibility for any adverse consequences. However, such incidents must be addressed in care-plan meetings and carefully doc-

umented in the patient's medical record; this record ought to include what efforts the staff may have made to try and persuade the patient to follow the dietary regimen.

Nourishments

Nourishments consist of light foods that are served in between the main meals, generally two to three hours after a regular meal. A nourishing snack must be offered to all patients before bedtime, although many patients do not desire it. During the day, however, most patients do not require additional snacks if they have adequate food intake. Snacks may actually diminish a person's appetite for consuming the regular meals. Yet some patients may not be consuming the regular meals properly. Depression, certain medications, and difficulty in chewing or swallowing may curtail a person's appetite.

Food-intake problems are also related to a decline in self-feeding skills or improper positioning while eating. Such problems should be evaluated by an occupational therapist (OTR) who may recommend proper positioning or adaptive tableware to improve a patient's self-feeding skills. Problems related to swallowing should be addressed by a speech-language pathologist.

Food intake and plate waste must be documented for each patient. The multidisciplinary team should also evaluate any food acceptance problems. Refusal of food should be addressed with the resident. Simply reevaluating a patient's likes and dislikes and providing appropriate substitutes may solve food acceptance problems. Only when regular food intake becomes a chronic issue, particularly when adverse health problems such as weight loss are observed, should the need for supplemental nourishments be addressed with the dietician and with the patient's attending physician. Widespread plate waste among residents often indicates poor choice of foods for the resident population or preparation methods that most people do not like. In such cases, menus must be revised. Such issues can be best addressed through the resident council and call for prompt action before the meals become a pervasive cause for discontentment.

INTENSIVE NUTRITION

Intensive nutrition support, commonly called tube feeding, may be necessary for patients who are unable to maintain adequate food intake with either a regular or a modified diet. Conditions that might require tube

feeding include protein-energy malnutrition, liver or kidney failure, coma, or dysphagia, the inability to chew or swallow because of stroke, brain tumor, or head injury. Patients who are receiving radiation therapy or chemotherapy treatments for cancer may also be candidates for tube feedings (Edgren 2003).

Enteral and parenteral nutrition are two types of intensive feeding methods, and which one is used depends on the patient's condition The dietician, nurses, and the attending physician determine what the patient's medical needs are, and they also determine the appropriate method of nutrient delivery. Although the care and monitoring of feeding tubes is a nursing responsibility and not something overseen by the dietary staff, intensive nutrition is discussed here because it is an integral part of meeting patients' total nutritional needs.

The cost of enteral and parenteral formulas is generally not regarded as a food expense. This cost is best classified as a separate line item on the budget, either under the nursing department or under the dietary department. To correctly calculate the regular food cost, the number of patient days incurred by patients receiving intensive nutrition should be subtracted from the total number of patient days.

Enteral Feeding

Enteral feeding is a method of delivering liquid food directly into the stomach. Commercially prepared liquid formulas are used according to the patient's nutritional needs, and either a small bedside pump controls the amount of liquid to be delivered or the feeding is allowed to drip naturally into the tube. In other instances, puréed or liquefied foods may be used, requiring special preparation by the dietary department.

Enteral feeding is a safe method of providing nutrients to patients who have a normally functioning gastrointestinal system, but who cannot eat normally. Depending on the patient's medical needs, tube feeding may be necessary for only a short time, or permanently. Enteral feeding may be used as the sole source of nutrition or as a supplement to inadequate oral intake.

There are two common methods of enteral feeding: A **nasogastric (NG) tube** passes through the nasal openings, down the esophagus, and into the stomach; a **gastrostomy (G) tube** passes through a surgical opening in the abdomen and into the stomach.

Other less common tube-feeding methods include those that use **naso-duodenal**, **esophagostomy**, and **jejunostomy** tubes. A **nasoduodenal tube** passes through the patient's nose and goes down into the duodenum, the first part of the small intestine, thus bypassing the stomach. This method is particularly indicated for patients who have an abnormally functioning pylorus (the opening between the stomach and the duodenum); problems with aspirating stomach contents into the lung (which can cause lung damage or pneumonia); or delayed gastric emptying. An **esophagostomy tube** is a small tube that enters a surgical incision on the side of the neck and is generally removed after each feeding. The tube allows food to enter the esophagus, bypassing the mouth, and then flow down into the stomach. Esophagostomy tubes are particularly indicated for patients who cannot swallow. A **jejunostomy (J) tube** is a surgically placed tube that enters the small intestine from an opening in the belly.

Although nutritional formulas are generally prescribed for the tube-feeding methods just discussed, flavored enteral formulas can also be used as oral supplements for patients who may not be eating enough to get balanced nutrition. Specialized oral supplements have been formulated to meet almost any type of special nutritional requirement. Examples include nutritionally complete puddings, calorically dense supplements, or protein supplements (Gerwick 1992).

Parenteral Feeding

Parenteral nutrition is a method of delivering balanced nutrition directly into the bloodstream, a method used when the gastrointestinal tract is not functioning properly. A special liquid formulation, called total parenteral nutrition (TPN), is infused into the bloodstream by inserting a catheter in a central or peripheral vein (Robinson and Leif 2001), and the process must be carefully monitored by licensed nurses.

FOOD SERVICE

Centralized and Decentralized Systems

Tray service is the most common method of serving food to residents in nursing facilities. Most facilities use the system called **centralized meal service** in which all trays are assembled at the kitchen service line. At meal time, the food-service station is staffed by several people in order to min-

imize the serving time. Another system that may be appropriate for some facilities is **decentralized meal service**, in which food produced in the main kitchen is transported in bulk to various smaller dining locations where the food is portioned and served. For example, the cluster architectural design with decentralized dining rooms (see Chapter 5) requires this type of food service. The service can be modified if the serving location has an auxiliary kitchen, which can be furnished with salad, beverages, and bread. In this case, the main dish and vegetables are prepared in the facility's central kitchen, and food is transported in bulk to individual dining areas. The food is kept hot on steam tables from where it is dished out on plates and served family-style, eliminating tray service (Noell 1995). Even when tray service is used, some facilities have improvised family-style dining by taking the plates off the trays while serving. Thus, instead of putting a tray in front of the resident, food and beverages are placed before the resident in individual plates and containers.

Portioning food in the residents' dining room (as opposed to the kitchen) simulates a homelike atmosphere and thereby encourages increased food consumption, which can contribute to residents' improved nutritional status. There can be positive nutritional and clinical consequences of changing from a centralized food-delivery system to decentralized bulk-food portioning. One study reported a significant increase in the average food consumption of residents after a bulk food portioning system was introduced in a facility. Mean energy intakes rose from 1,555 to 1,924 calories (kcal) per day and intake of most nutrients also increased (Shatenstein and Ferland 2000). However, before implementing a decentralized bulk-food service, decision-makers should take into consideration concerns of employees who may experience frustration because of increased demands on their time, as one Canadian study pointed out (Shatenstein et al. 2001).

Noell (1995) reported that serving meals in decentralized dining rooms in "neighborhood" family-style settings improved resident intake of food and fluids. It also resulted in cost savings by reducing waste and by curtailing the need to provide nutritional supplements because of low food intake. Hence, evaluating the cost-benefit aspects of these alternative service methods is necessary. For example, cost savings from reductions in the use of nutritional supplements or an increased facility census because of better perceived value by prospective clients may compensate for increased spending on family-style table service.

Food-Service Station

The food-service station is a food-holding and food-assembly area. As each tray is assembled, a non-powered conveyor system moves the trays on rollers from the serving area to a platform where they are picked up by the serving staff.

In efficient kitchen design, the food-service station is located between the food production and food pick-up areas. Cooked food is transferred from the cooking area to the service station where all foods are maintained at appropriate temperatures and assembled for service to patients. Any cold food is put on the plate first, and then the plate is moved to the hot section where hot food is dished out from a steam table. Infrared lamps are also used to keep certain foods hot. Holding wells in the steam table are replenished as needed. The recommended holding and serving temperatures are $\leq 45°$ F for cold foods, and $\geq 140°$ F for hot items. Clean thermometers must be available at the serving station to periodically monitor food temperatures during meal service. The holding equipment is not meant for reheating food, only to maintain food at the right serving temperature.

All food-service employees must be trained in portion control. Standardized recipes establish the size of portion to be served for each food item. Measuring scoops, ladles, serving spoons, food-weighing scales, and other serving equipment are essential for portioning food. Some food items are prepared in predetermined portions, which makes service both quicker and easier.

Accuracy

Individual trays are assembled using a diet card or diet ticket. Diet tickets are now generated by computerized systems, whereas diet cards are used in the manual system. A separate diet card is maintained for each patient, and it is updated to reflect any changes. To minimize diet errors, a trained individual must work at the end of the tray line as a checker. The checker is responsible for ensuring that the food items on the patient tray are what should be on the tray in accordance with the diet orders, individual preferences, and any contraindications noted on the patient's diet card.

Food Transportation Systems

In larger facilities, if centralized tray service is used, food often must be transported from the kitchen to auxiliary dining rooms located away from the

main kitchen and dining areas. In this case, food is dished out in the main kitchen where the diet cards are maintained. The trays are loaded onto enclosed carts, which are transported to auxiliary dining areas. The challenge is to maintain foods at their right serving temperatures. To facilitate this goal, a variety of food-transportation systems are available. Heated pellets have been in use for a long time. A pellet is a metal plate that requires heating in a pellet dispenser before the food plate is placed on the heated pellet. The pellet system requires removing the hot pellet before serving the tray to prevent burns to residents. To overcome these drawbacks, insulated trays with hot and cold compartments can be used, and they have been available for some time. With either the pellet system or the insulated-tray system, basic transportation carts are used. These carts do not have heat or refrigeration-maintenance systems.

Carts with temperature controls are equipped with heat and refrigeration mechanisms. Specially designed split trays can slide into a cart that has hot and cold sections. In this system, half the tray is held in a heated compartment and the other half in a refrigerated compartment. All hot foods are placed on one side of the tray, and cold foods are placed on the other side of the tray. A major drawback of all food transportation carts is the difficulty of maneuvering them because of their heavy weight (Greathouse and Gregoire 1997).

Finally, specialized trays can be used with rethermalization carts. The trays have special cut-out areas for entrée, soup, and vegetable dishes so that, when the trays are loaded onto the rethermalization carts, the dishes make contact with the conduction heat element in the cart (Greathouse and Gregoire 1997).

When properly used, all of these systems can work quite satisfactorily. But each system has its own advantages and disadvantages that must be carefully evaluated by the administrator and the dietary manager when deciding on which system to use.

The Dining Experience

Dining plays a critical role in a resident's quality of life because most residents look forward to mealtime. A satisfying experience can also improve clinical outcomes through better nutrient intake. Jackson (2003) asserted that dieticians and food-service managers who routinely circulate in dining rooms during mealtime can gather a wealth of information by simply

observing and talking to residents. Such observation can reveal, among other things, which menu items are well-accepted, whether the food presentation is attractive, whether personal food preferences are respected, whether diet orders are being followed, and whether portion control standards are adhered to. Routine observation of dining rooms may also bring other problems to light that may require a change in care plans. Similarly, the nursing staff should ensure that patients who are eating are positioned properly. Inappropriately positioned patients can aspirate, experience difficulty eating, or get tired and frustrated (Jackson 2003).

FOOD SAFETY AND SANITATION

Promoting food safety and preventing food-borne illnesses are of critical importance in nursing facilities. Compared to the general population, residents in nursing homes are likely to be more susceptible to illness and may exhibit more severe adverse outcomes when they are ill. An outbreak of disease can place severe burdens on the nursing home staff and result in much adverse publicity in the community. Therefore, all staff members involved with the handling, cooking, and service of food must receive training in food sanitation and safety. Hygienic practices, such as handwashing, cleaning and sanitizing equipment and food-preparation surfaces, and washing fresh produce and all types of meats before use must be enforced by management. All staff members must wear appropriate head covering. The dietary department must also have written policies on food safety, and the staff must be trained on the proper storage and use of cleaning chemicals.

Food-borne illnesses can result when food is contaminated by bacteria, viruses, parasites, or chemicals. Bacterial infection is the most common cause of food-borne illness because bacteria can easily grow and produce toxins in foods. Almost half of all bacterial outbreaks (incidents involving two or more single cases) are the result of cross-contamination (Cody 1997). Common examples of cross-contamination sources include using the same knife or cutting surface to prepare raw and cooked foods, using a contaminated sink for thawing frozen food, and unsanitary food handling. Flies, cockroaches, and rodents can transmit pathogens (disease-causing organisms) to food. Therefore, pest control by a reputable firm is an essential part of food sanitation.

Maintaining proper food-holding temperatures is critical, because bacteria thrive best at temperatures between 45° F and 140° F, the range regarded as the "danger temperature zone." In general, food should not be held at room temperature for longer than two hours. Simply reheating food that has been left out for that long may not destroy pathogens if they are present (Cody 1997). Another frequent cause of temperature-related food-borne disease is improper cooling when cooked food requires storage. Potentially hazardous foods must be cooled from 140° F to 70° F within two hours, and from 70° F to 41° F or below within four hours (Gregoire and Nettles 1997). Potentially hazardous foods are defined by the Food and Drug Administration in *Food Code*, 1995. These foods include any food that consists in whole or in part of milk or milk products, eggs, meat, poultry, fish, shellfish, or other ingredients in a form capable of supporting rapid and progressive growth of infection- or toxin-producing microorganisms. Most harmful organisms, especially the most common disease-producing ones, such as salmonellae and clostridium botulinum, are destroyed by heat. Therefore, cooking food to an internal temperature of 165° F is essential. Internal temperatures must be checked using a probe thermometer. Other pathogens, such as staphylococcus aureus, are not destroyed by ordinary cooking. Therefore, practice of food hygiene by all staff members is essential.

Proper dishwashing procedures for cleaning and sanitizing tableware and kitchenware are also critical. A three-compartment sink for cleaning, rinsing, and sanitizing is recommended for hand-washing utensils and equipment. Sanitizing can be achieved by immersion in hot water (170° F) or by using chlorine or iodine at recommended strengths. The recommended temperatures for mechanical dishwashing are 140° F for wash, 160° F for rinse, and 180° F for final rinse and sanitizing (Sullivan and Atlas 1998). Dishes and utensils should be left on racks to air-dry. Wiping with cloths can result in cross-contamination.

CONCLUSION

Dietary standards and methods play a critical role not only in meeting the residents' total nutritional needs but also in the facility's marketing strategy (discussed in Chapter 15). Food service is one area in which even the most effectively run facilities may have difficulties satisfying all residents. Even though a 100% satisfaction rate may be an unreasonable

objective, the administrator must constantly strive to achieve this lofty goal through personal involvement and leadership. Effective administrators routinely observe food storage and preparation areas, food handling, food service, and dining. They take the time to talk to residents and family members about the quality of food being served, and promptly address any concerns. They also make it a practice to eat the same meals that are being served to the residents to experience first-hand the taste, flavor, potion size, and temperature of the food that the facility serves to its residents.

DISCUSSION QUESTIONS

1. What are the main advantages of an extended-meal plan? What are the main disadvantages?
2. What can the administrator of a nursing facility do to minimize pilferage of assets such as supplies and food?
3. Discuss some factors to evaluate in determining the costs and benefits of providing family-style meal service in a nursing facility.
4. Discuss some ways in which the administrator can have continuous involvement in striving toward the goal of 100% client satisfaction with the food the facility serves.

INTERNET RESOURCES FOR FURTHER LEARNING

The American Dietetic Association (ADA) is the nation's largest organization of food and nutrition professionals. The ADA's Commission on Accreditation for Dietetics Education (CADE) is recognized by the Council on Higher Education Accreditation and the United States Department of Education as the accrediting agency for education programs that prepare dietetics professionals.
http://www.eatright.org

The Commission on Dietetic Registration (CDR) has the sole and independent authority in all matters pertaining to certification of registered dieticians and registered dietetic technicians.
http://www.cdrnet.org

The Dietary Managers Association (DMA) is a national nonprofit association and is the premier resource for food-service managers, directors, and those aspiring to careers in food-service management.
http://www.dmaonline.org

Nutrition Index. Published by Columbia University Health Services, the Index includes detailed information on the nutritional requirements of the elderly, assessment of nutritional status, common nutritional problems of older adults, dietary intervention, etc.
http://cpmcnet.columbia.edu/dept/dental/Dental_Educational_Software/Gerontology_and_Geriatric_Dentistry/nutrition/nutrition_index.html

U.S. Department of Agriculture: Food and Nutrition Information Center.
http://www.nal.usda.gov/fnic/etext/000105.html

REFERENCES

Cody, M.M. 1997. Current issues in food safety. In *Nutrition and Food Services for Integrated Health Care: A Handbook for Leaders,* ed. R. Jackson. Gaithersburg, MD: Aspen Publishers, Inc.

Edgren, A.R. 2003. Tube feedings. *Gale Encyclopedia of Medicine.* LookSmart, Ltd. http://www.findarticles.com/cf_dls/g2601/0014/2601001406/p1/article.jhtml

Gerwick, C.L. 1992. *Nutrition Care in Nursing Facilities.* 2nd ed. Chicago: The American Dietetic Association.

Graves, N., and S. Stewart. 1985. Patient/client services: Provide food services. In *Man-aging Food-Service Operations: A Systems Approach for Healthcare and Institutions,* ed., J.D. Ninemeier. West Lafayette, Indiana: Purdue Research Foundation.

Greathouse, K.R., and M.B. Gregoire. 1997. Options in meal assembly, delivery, and service. In *Nutrition and Food Services for Integrated Health Care: A Handbook for Leaders,* ed., R. Jackson. Gaithersburg, MD: Aspen Publishers, Inc.

Gregoire, M.B., and M.F. Nettles. 1997. Alternative food production systems. In *Nutrition and Food Services for Integrated Health Care: A Handbook for Leaders,* ed., R. Jackson. Gaithersburg, MD: Aspen Publishers, Inc.

Jackson, R. 2003. The dining experience: Making it pleasurable for long-term care residents. *Health Care Food and Nutrition Focus* 20, no. 1: 1–4.

Mahaffey, M.J., M.E. Mennes, and B.B. Miller. 1981. *Food Service Manual for Health Care Institutions.* Chicago: American Hospital Association.

Ninemeier, J.D. 1985. *Managing Food-Service Operations: A Systems Approach for Healthcare and Institutions.* West Lafayette, Indiana: Purdue Research Foundation.

Noell, E. 1995. Design in nursing homes: Environment as a silent partner in caregiving. *Generations* 19, no. 4: 14–19.

Puckett, R.P., and B.B. Miller. 1988. *Food Service Manual for Health Care Institutions.* Chicago: American Hospital Publishing, Inc.

Robinson, G.E., and B.J. Leif. 2001. *Nutrition Management and Restorative Dining for Older Adults.* Chicago: American Dietetic Association.

Shatenstein, B., et al. 2001. Employee reactions to the introduction of a bulk food distribution system in a nursing home. *Canadian Journal of Dietetic Practice and Research* 62, no. 1: 18–25.

Shatenstein, B., and G. Ferland. 2000. Absence of nutritional or clinical consequences of decentralized bulk food portioning in elderly nursing home residents with dementia in Montreal. *Journal of the American Dietetic Association* 100, no. 11: 1354–1360.

Simmons, S.F., et al. 2003. Family members' preferences for nutrition interventions to improve nursing home residents' oral food and fluid intake. *Journal of the American Geriatrics Society* 51, no. 1: 69–74.

Sullivan, C.F., and C. Atlas. 1998. *Health Care Food Service Systems Management.* Gaithersburg, MD: Aspen Publishers, Inc.

Zaccarelli, H.E., and J. Maggiore. 1972. *Nursing Home Menu Planning Food Purchasing, Management.* Chicago: Cahners Publishing Co., Inc.

CHAPTER 11

Plant and Environmental Services

LEARNING MODULES

1. The nature, purpose, and broad objectives of environmental services.
2. Organization of maintenance, housekeeping, laundry, security, and safety functions.
3. Maintenance operation. Arranging for urgent service calls. Implementing a system for handling routine repairs.
4. Preventive maintenance: what it is, its goals, and three main functions. Implementing a preventive maintenance program consisting of daily, weekly, and rotating tasks.
5. Routine and non-routine maintenance contracts.
6. Housekeeping operation. Daily and weekly schedules, and reconditioning tasks. Sanitizing and infection-control procedures.
7. Laundry operation. Microbicidal washing and use of standard precautions. Linen inventory and control procedures using par levels.
8. Physical and procedural security. Protecting supplies, materials, and movable capital assets. Access control.
9. Fire and disaster planning. Fire safety steps and evacuation procedures. Fire and disaster simulation drills.

continues

10. Management of general and hazardous wastes.
11. Environmental safety.

The main function of plant and environmental services in any facility is to maintain the physical plant structures, support the clinical and socio-residential structures, and promote a safe environment in the nursing facility. Plant and environmental services are organized with two main objectives in mind: maintaining and protecting the structures so they continue to function in the most effective and efficient manner while providing a clean, comfortable, and safe environment; and protecting people who live and work in these structures against the threat of bodily harm. Plant and environmental services play a critical role in enhancing the socio-residential component that creates a total living environment (see Chapter 5). Optimized clinical care is an indirect outcome of effective plant and environmental services.

Complete environmental support is necessary, not only for patients but for staff members and visitors as well. Griffith (1995) suggested that the environmental support system provides all the services of a hotel, but with narrower tolerances. Compared to hotels, environmental services in health care facilities require narrower tolerances for temperature and humidity controls, air quality, cleanliness, waste removal, and environmental safety. Environmental services should also support the aesthetic appeal of the facility's exterior.

Environmental services can be classified into housekeeping, maintenance, laundry, security, and safety functions. The main environmental functions include cleaning all spaces; removing trash; controlling pests; performing general maintenance and repairs on the building and all of its components; ensuring an adequate supply of clean linens; enhancing the external appearance of grounds and building; having adequate security so that patients, visitors, and staff members feel safe in and around the building; preventing property loss and pilferage; safety against potential fires and disasters; and preventing accidents.

ORGANIZATION OF ENVIRONMENTAL SERVICES

The organization of environmental services departments varies according to the size of the facility and the skill levels of the supervisory personnel working in the environmental services departments.

Maintenance Department

In most facilities, maintenance is a separate department, even though it may be staffed by just one or two people. An average-sized facility of 100 beds needs one full-time person responsible for all maintenance and repairs. A half-time person may be added for each additional 50 to 60 beds. Staffing for maintenance will vary according to how much of the routine work, such as groundskeeping, is contracted out. For the winter season, snow removal is generally contracted out especially if the facility has large parking areas and walkways. Many facilities add short-term staff during summer to do their own groundskeeping whereas others outsource this service. Large facilities may find it cost-effective to have a painter on staff. As a rule of thumb, every patient room and private bathroom should be completely repainted once every two to three years. Some areas of the building may require more frequent painting than others. Touch-up painting to keep walls free of scuff marks is an ongoing function.

In a typical nursing home, the maintenance department is headed by a maintenance mechanic (usually called "maintenance man") although the position is formally referred to as Maintenance Supervisor. This individual must be multi-talented and need not have special skills in any particular craft. This individual should be able to handle simple plumbing, heating, ventilation, air conditioning, and electrical problems. Apart from handling routine repair jobs, the maintenance supervisor is responsible for an ongoing preventive maintenance program in the facility. Other than minor troubleshooting and repairs, mechanical system breakdowns are restored by calling outside service contractors (Magee 1988). By working alongside these external tradesmen, the maintenance supervisor can develop substantial skills in handling more than just basic problems.

Housekeeping and Laundry Departments

Housekeeping and laundry departments are generally headed by one supervisor. In facilities that operate their own laundries, housekeeping and laundry are considered two separate departments even though they may have a common supervisor. Depending on the size and layout of the facility, the person heading housekeeping and laundry operations may be a working supervisor; he or she may take on routine cleaning assignments for certain sections of the building, or may perform specific tasks such as floor polishing. A position strictly confined to supervisory duties may be necessary only when the number of beds exceeds 150, provided that the facility operates its

own in-house laundry. The other option for management is to have separate working supervisors for housekeeping and laundry.

The facility should determine the number of housekeepers needed according to the square footage, the layout of the facility, and the number of resident rooms. Adequate weekend coverage is also essential, and a skeleton crew should cover the evenings to finish clean-up chores after dinner and attend to any other sanitation needs in the facility. Most facilities also require janitorial staff for routine floor and carpet maintenance and for handling other heavy work such as window-washing and moving furniture.

The laundry requires personnel in two categories: sorting and washing soiled laundry and drying and folding clean laundry. Separating these two functions is essential to prevent cross-contamination.

The maintenance supervisor and the supervisor of housekeeping and laundry departments report to the administrator (Figure II-1) and are considered heads of departments. In large facilities, these supervisors may report to the assistant administrator if such a position exists.

Security and Safety Functions

In many locations, security has become a growing concern for facilities. Except for some very large retirement-living and nursing-care complexes, a typical nursing facility does not have a security department. In fact, most facilities do not employ any security personnel. Nevertheless, the security function is essential. In the absence of a designated person being in charge of security, the responsibility for security falls on the administrator's shoulders.

Safety specifically means fire and disaster preparation and accident prevention. Some aspects of safety and physical security (discussed later) can be delegated to the maintenance supervisor. Accident prevention, on the other hand, requires leadership from the administrator but is the responsibility of everyone working in the facility.

MAINTENANCE OPERATION

The main operations in the maintenance department can be classified into four areas: urgent service calls; routine repairs; preventive maintenance; and contract work.

Urgent Service Calls

Because emergencies arise without warning, unexpected breakdown of critical mechanical systems, components, or equipment can severely disrupt vital services, compromise patient safety, or result in loss of property. For example, a breakdown of the heating system in the middle of winter will severely disrupt patient care and threaten the safety of patients. Failure of the food-storage freezer can result in the loss of hundreds or even thousands of dollars worth of food. Such breakdowns or a failure of the facility's emergency systems, such as fire alarms, fire suppression system, or emergency power generator, must be attended to immediately.

Along with the administrator, the director of nursing (DON) and the maintenance supervisor are on call 24 hours a day, 7 days a week. If by chance the maintenance supervisor is not available during an emergency, the administrator should be notified so that an outside firm can be called to deal with the situation. Similar authority should be given to the DON and also to the dietary manager in case urgent attention is needed for any dietary equipment.

Routine Repairs

Routine repair work is organized by instituting a system in which all routine requests for repairs are submitted on a work-order slip. Each department and each nursing station keeps a box where their work orders are placed. The orders are picked up daily by the maintenance supervisor, who makes a round of the building to observe anything that may require prompt attention. The work orders are prioritized to plan the day's work. Other routine tasks such as lawn care should be included in a weekly schedule. Local trips to purchase needed supplies and parts should also be planned to minimize the number of trips away from the facility. With proper planning, no more than one trip should be necessary each week.

A work-order system generally works well for reporting problems that hinder staff members' ability to do their jobs, or to address complaints from residents and family members. However, this system misses many other problems, and those problems go unreported. To address unreported concerns, the facility needs a preventive maintenance program.

Preventive Maintenance

Preventive maintenance is the term used for routine inspections and performance of certain tasks that are planned in advance and are carried out to prevent unexpected equipment failures (Niebel 1985). Over the long run, a good preventive maintenance program is cost-effective because it prevents costly breakdowns, delays the need to replace equipment that may otherwise wear out prematurely, and minimizes disruption of vital services. Appropriate training is needed to set up and manage a well-designed preventive maintenance program. All equipment must be periodically checked for smooth operation. Coils and motors require periodic cleaning. In accordance with the manufacturer's recommendations, equipment may also require periodic lubrication, filter changes, or inspection and replacement of components that show signs of wear and tear. If the maintenance supervisor does not possess the necessary training and skills to perform this maintenance, the administrator may outsource preventive maintenance work to a private independent firm. At the very least, however, the facility must have a basic preventive maintenance program that includes three main preventive functions:

- weekly checks
- revolving inspections
- ongoing upkeep

Weekly Checks

Weekly checks are necessary to ensure that all emergency systems are operating. A log of these tests must be maintained. Emergency systems include the fire alarms, automatic fire doors, smoke detectors, and emergency power generators. The Life Safety Code (see Chapter 5) requires testing the fire alarm system monthly, but many facilities do this check weekly.

Revolving Inspections

A plan must be instituted by the facility to ensure that every day, in accordance with a rotating schedule, a different specified section of the building interior and exterior is closely inspected. The goal should be to conduct a revolving inspection so that all patient rooms, bathrooms, utility rooms, kitchen, laundry, mechanical rooms, and all other areas receive a close inspection once every four to six weeks. The administrator can monitor this schedule by requiring that the maintenance department keep a

written log and provide a report to the administrator as inspections are completed in each area of the building. Such inspections often reveal irregularities that do not get reported through the routine work-order system. Repair problems that frequently go unreported include leaky faucets; leaks at the bottom of toilet bowls; windows that do not close or lock; doors that do not completely shut; missing ceiling tiles; ventilation or exhaust problems in bathrooms, kitchen, laundry, or utility areas; scuffed walls in need of painting or repair to the wallcovering; and curtains and window coverings in disrepair. The administrator should do periodic spot checks to see whether a revolving inspection program is being followed.

During the detailed inspections, the maintenance supervisor should look for safety problems such as missing fire extinguishers, torn or buckled carpeting, non-functional patient call systems, missing floor tiles, and burned-out light bulbs. Sanitation problems may be noticed near the garbage dumpster, which can attract vermin and other scavengers. Broken screens or missing exterior screen doors may allow flies to enter food preparation areas. Signs of pest activity, such as droppings, may be noticed in the kitchen, food storage areas, or patient rooms. Outside the building, lights may be missing, the parking lot may be in need of cleaning, cracks in pavement may require sealing, or bushes may require trimming.

Ongoing Upkeep

Ongoing maintenance of a facility's internal and external appearance is also an important part of preventive maintenance. Damage to walls caused by wheelchairs and other equipment is a common occurrence. However, effectively managed facilities set themselves apart from others by instituting a daily touch-up painting program. When undertaken on a daily basis, touch-up painting only requires a fraction of the time it would take to paint large sections of the building that have been left unattended. Wallcoverings should be cleaned and repaired periodically and replaced when they are heavily worn or faded. The parking lot also needs daily attention, in order to pick up loose trash and cigarette butts. Effectively managed facilities maintain attractive lawns, have some basic landscaping, and plant seasonal flowers to present an inviting appearance.

Contract Work

The need for contracting is unavoidable, but the maintenance supervisor should oversee the work of outside contractors to ensure that the agreed-

upon work is completed satisfactorily. Professional completion of work includes any clean-up and removal of debris after a job is finished.

Some contracts for services that are performed on a regular basis, called **routine contracts**, are generally executed annually. Routine contracts include agreements covering pest control, waste removal, snow removal, lawn care, annual inspection of emergency equipment, inspection and maintenance of elevators, and expert preventive maintenance. Routine contracting is undertaken by the administrator, in consultation with the maintenance supervisor. As a matter of policy, no contract should exceed one year. This limit allows the administrator to review each year the quality of services performed and to compare the prices of a contractor's competitors before renewing an existing contract or going with a new one.

Non-routine contracts include open-call contracts and job-unit contracts. **Open-call contracts** are established with preferred contractors to provide services on an as-needed basis. Contracts for heating and cooling, plumbing, and electrical work are the most common types of open-call contracts. This type of contracting eliminates the time and administrative effort required in setting up a separate contract each time the need for services arises (Heintzelman 1987). By making a commitment to use the same contractor on an open-call basis, the facility can often negotiate discounted service fees.

A second type of non-routine arrangement is called **job-unit contracting**. In this case, a separate contract is established each time a need arises for contracted services (Heintzelman 1987). The contract automatically terminates when the specified work has been completed and paid for. Job-unit contracting is appropriate for jobs that must be done only infrequently, are planned ahead of time, and generally involve substantial capital outlays. Examples include renovation projects, roof repair or replacement, installation of major equipment, and major landscaping.

HOUSEKEEPING OPERATION

The housekeeping department is responsible for maintaining a sanitary, pleasant, and safe environment in the facility. The department must develop policies and procedures for cleaning, sanitizing, infection control, and safety. Unlike hotels and motels, the housekeeping staff in nursing facilities must not handle either clean or soiled linens. The tasks of bed-

making, replacing clean linens in patient rooms, and removing soiled linens are assigned to nursing assistants.

Cleaning, Reconditioning, and Floor Care

Housekeeping jobs can be classified as daily cleaning, weekly cleaning, reconditioning, and floor care. **Daily cleaning** consists of routine procedures for cleaning, sweeping, mopping, and vacuuming all patient-care and public areas in the facility. **Weekly cleaning** tasks include dusting furniture and fixtures, cleaning baseboards, paying attention to floor edges and corners, polishing bathroom fixtures, cleaning draperies and cubicle curtains, and other heavy-duty tasks. The housekeeping supervisor should develop a rotating schedule so that all areas of the building receive weekly heavy-duty cleaning. To accomplish this goal, certain sections of the building are included in the daily cleaning schedules to receive the weekly heavy-duty attention. On weekends many facilities have reduced staffing to perform the daily tasks; in that case weekly tasks are covered using a five-day rotating schedule.

Reconditioning involves thorough cleaning of certain areas, particularly patient rooms. Reconditioning is always performed after a patient has been discharged and involves tasks such as cleaning and sanitizing the bed and mattress. All patient rooms should receive reconditioning attention on a rotating basis every five to six weeks. Floor care generally is assigned to custodians who are responsible for stripping, waxing, and polishing floors and for shampooing carpets.

Sanitizing

The term **sanitizing** describes a process that results in a reduction of microbes to relatively safe levels on an inanimate object (Belkin 2003). Sanitizing requires the appropriate use of disinfectants approved by the U.S. Environmental Protection Agency (EPA), which oversees the registration of anti-microbial products. A list of registered antimicrobials is available at the EPA's website. The listed categories include sterilants, tuberculocides, anti-HIV products, and anti-HBV (hepatitis B virus) products. A fresh solution of diluted household bleach (one part bleach to ten parts water) made up every 24 hours is also considered appropriate to disinfect environmental surfaces and decontaminate sites. Contact time for bleach solution is generally considered to be the time it takes the prod-

uct to air-dry. Rinsing is necessary after sanitizing with 1:10 bleach solution.

The housekeeping supervisor should periodically determine if the housekeeping procedures are effective on a microbiological level. Such an evaluation is done by taking periodic cultures from various surfaces for bacterial colony counts.

Infection Control

The housekeeping staff plays a vital role in controlling infections in the facility by following sanitary practices that can prevent the spread of microorganisms. Disease-causing pathogens can spread through dust particles, air particles, and surface contact. Properly cleaning and disinfecting floors and other surfaces is a means of infection control. But housekeeping practices employed while performing daily tasks are equally important. For instance, a housekeeper who gives a quick shake to a dust rag after using it to dust furniture is spreading germs through the air. Hence, plain dry sweeping, for example, has no place in health care housekeeping practices because it can disseminate microorganisms in the air; chemically treated disposable dust cloths should be used for preliminary cleaning before wet mopping. Dry vacuums used for carpeted areas should have effective microbial filters to avoid disseminating bacteria from the vacuum exhaust. Wet-mopping should employ a double-bucket technique, with one bucket for cleaning with a disinfectant solution and the other for rinsing the mop (Vesley and Greene 1973). Frequently changing the mop-water is also necessary for minimizing the spread of microorganisms along the floors. Hand-washing is critical when contact is made with clean surfaces after touching soiled objects or surfaces.

LAUNDRY OPERATION

The nursing-home laundry department is responsible for the processing, distribution, and storage of washable linens, garments, and other such items (Goldberg and Buttaro 1990). The basic laundry tasks include sorting, washing, drying, folding, storing, and delivering. Soiled linens are brought to the laundry by nursing assistants, or bags of soiled laundry are conveyed to the laundry down a laundry chute. Clean linen is delivered to the patient-care areas by the laundry staff. Nursing-home laundries gener-

also specify that after certain hours no employee can go outside the building unaccompanied.

Many facilities provide employee lockers for safeguarding personal effects such as purses and cash. Most facilities also have resident policies that discourage keeping valuables, such as expensive jewelry, or more than minimal amounts of cash on one's person or in the room. A variety of monitoring systems are available to prevent unnoticed wandering by residents who may be particularly vulnerable because of dementia or confusion. In many locations, local or state codes allow installation of a delayed opening system on fire exit doors. With these devices the doors will not open for a set time, usually 15 seconds, when someone tries to open a fire exit door. During the delay period an alarm sounds to alert the staff on duty (Sells 2000). This short delay, along with the sound of the alarm, may be sufficient to dissuade a patient who may be attempting to exit unnoticed.

Periodically, the administrator should undertake a security audit. In this audit, all physical security measures and potential lapses should be closely examined. A comprehensive audit must be undertaken any time a significant security incident occurs or a problem that could have resulted in an incident is reported. A security audit would be undertaken in addition to a thorough investigation and documentation of any actual incidents. The purpose of an audit is to prevent recurrence of an incident or prevent the occurrence of a non-related incident. All security audits and corrective actions resulting from such audits should be documented.

Procedural Security

Procedural security is achieved by developing, implementing, and monitoring internal control systems. Three different systems are needed to protect the facility's assets:

- a system for ordering, receiving, storing, and inventorying all supplies and materials
- a tagging and inventory system for all movable capital assets
- a key-control system that restricts access to various storage and office areas

Supplies and Materials

In addition to the systems for food and dietary supplies discussed in Chapter 10, the facility must have a central system for ordering, receiving,

ally do not do ironing and mending. Widespread use of no-iron linens has eliminated the need for ironing. An alternative to operating an on-site laundry is to have a contract with a commercial laundry service. For small facilities in particular, it may not be cost-effective to operate an on-site laundry.

Microbicidal Washing

The microbicidal (killing of microbes) action of the normal laundering process is affected by several physical and chemical factors. Soaps or detergents loosen soil and also have some microbicidal properties. Hot water provides an effective means of destroying microorganisms. A temperature of at least 160° F for a minimum of 25 minutes is commonly recommended for hot-water washing of laundry. Chlorine bleach in the wash provides an extra margin of safety (Office of Health and Safety 2002). The last action performed during the washing process is to add a mild acid to neutralize any alkalinity in the water supply, soap, or detergent. Detergents that can reduce microbial contamination at lower water temperatures are now available. Instead of the microbicidal action of hot water, low-temperature laundry cycles rely heavily on the presence of bleach to reduce levels of microbial contamination.

Standard Precautions

Nursing facilities must follow **standard precautions** (discussed in Chapter 8) when handling all soiled laundry. Standard precautions constitute a system of barrier precautions to be used by all personnel when handling items that may contain blood, body fluids, secretions, and excretions, regardless of the patient's diagnosis. Laundry workers should use gloves, gowns, and masks when sorting and washing linens. Laundry should be handled as little as possible and with minimal agitation. To avoid punctures from improperly discarded syringes, personnel should hold laundry bags and linens away from the body and avoid squeezing when transporting them. Using normal washing cycles, according to the laundry detergent manufacturer's recommendations, should be quite sufficient for thorough washing. However, patient linens should be washed separately from kitchen laundry and patients' personal clothing. As mentioned earlier, soiled-laundry sorting and clean-linen processing must be separated. A separate room, equipped with negative-pressure ventilation,

is best for the sorting process. The negative pressure allows air to move from a clean to a soiled area, and not vice versa, and is designed to prevent movement of airborne particles from the soiled area to the clean linen processing area (Vesley 1973).

Linen Inventory

A system of linen inventory is essential for control purposes. This system requires a secured linen-storage room to which only authorized personnel have access. The main institutional linens include bed sheets, bath towels, hand towels, and wash cloths. After washing, drying, and folding, all institutional linens are stored in the linen room. Patients' personal clothes are delivered to their individual rooms. The nursing facility must have enough quantities of linens so that after washing all linens get a chance to "rest" for at least 24 hours before being put into service again. Adequate linen quantities are also required to meet all patient-care needs over the weekend when the laundry operation is generally shut down. Goldberg and Buttaro (1990) proposed a stratified inventory system that assumes that for every piece of linen in use, four others are being processed or are in storage. Under such a system, the linen inventory should consist of the number of items used daily multiplied by five. The resulting number is called the **par level**.

A certain amount of linen loss is to be expected. Such losses can result from wear and tear as well as pilferage. An inventory-control system is used to find out the extent of loss and to determine the quantities of linen that should be purchased to replenish the stock to par levels. A running linen inventory record includes the following entries:

Initial inventory (quantity on hand at the beginning of the period after the last physical inventory was taken)
+ Purchases
− Discards (frayed or heavily stained linens taken out of circulation)
= Closing inventory

The facility should take a physical inventory of linens once every three or four months to compare the actual linen count to the closing inventory. The difference shows how much linen is being lost that must be replenished to maintain the par levels. See Chapter 16 and Exhibit 16-7 for more information about inventory control.

SECURITY OPERATION

Rowland and Rowland (1984) pointed to two basic facets of security: physical and procedural. **Physical security** concerns protecting the facility against intrusion from the outside, protecting patients who may be inclined to wander away without the ability to get back safely, and protecting against theft. **Procedural security** involves control systems to prevent internal theft and pilferage of supplies and materials.

Physical Security

Physical security encompasses three main areas: Protecting people against bodily harm by intruders from the outside, protecting residents from wandering out and getting injured, and protecting the property of both residents and the facility against theft. Physical security generally requires integrating a variety of protective measures, including control of the facility's parameter, intrusion alarms, lock-up procedures, and electronic surveillance. Installing and maintaining security systems and hiring security personnel can be quite expensive. However, some minimal equipment installed in strategic locations may be necessary. Undertaking risk-assessment and cost-benefit evaluation are essential before a large investment is committed for security. Potential costs to the facility include restitution to the party harmed, legal action against the facility, and loss to the facility's image if a resident or staff member is harmed and the injury is attributed to lax security. The probability of such losses should be taken into account in doing a cost-benefit evaluation.

The administrator should work with the local law-enforcement agencies to evaluate security needs. Following their recommendations, the administrator can then work with two or three reputable security firms to obtain recommendations and bids for appropriate security technology. At a minimum, the facility must ensure that all parking areas and the building's exterior are adequately lit. The administrator should also arrange with local law enforcement to have the facility on routine police patrol. A high-visibility patrol is one of the best deterrents against crime (Sells 2000).

All facilities must have policies specifying who is responsible for locking up designated entrances after specified hours in the evening and for locking up the remaining entrances for the night. Self-locking time devices can be installed to minimize human error. Security policies ma

storing, and controlling the inventory for all supplies and materials. The administrator should be aware that even though the food service director and his or her assistants have the responsibility for controlling dietary products, the supervisors may themselves be involved in theft. This consideration does not automatically imply guilt, but it should increase awareness of the possibility of theft by supervisors, especially when the actual food cost exceeds the menu cost. Pre-costing menus establishes the expected food cost. When the actual food cost substantially exceeds or routinely exceeds the expected cost, the administrator should first look into the methods being used for inventorying food and calculating the food cost before investigating probable breaches of security. Other supplies and materials that may be vulnerable to theft, such as linens, cleaning chemicals, maintenance tools and equipment, and medical supplies also require appropriate procedural controls. Large facilities may have a central storeroom with a stock clerk responsible for all items other than food. In most facilities, however, each department head has the responsibility for ordering and maintaining supplies used by the department. In this case, each department manager must exercise adequate controls over the supplies and materials by using inventory systems to minimize theft.

Movable Capital Assets

A tagging and inventory system is used to identify and control all movable capital assets, such as television sets, cameras, computers, office equipment, and medical equipment. Permanent non-detachable metal tags with the facility's name and an item number should be affixed to all movable assets. A record, which can be easily computerized, should identify each item, its tag number, location, date of acquisition, and cost. This record should also bear the date of retirement after an item has been retired from service. An annual or biannual inventory should verify that each item still in service is actually present in the facility.

Access Control

Access to various parts of the building is controlled by establishing a centralized system to regulate distribution of keys to authorized personnel only. This function is best controlled by the administrator or assistant administrator. Working with a master locksmith, the facility should plan and implement a hierarchical system of grand master keys, master keys, submaster keys, and individual keys. The system allows various personnel

to have access to one or more locked areas, using no more than two keys. For instance, the administrator and the assistant administrator can have access to all secured areas using the grand master key. A submaster key may allow the DON to have access to all secured areas except food storage and maintenance areas.

Records must be kept to account for every key issued. Keys must be retrieved and accounted for as personnel leave their positions. Appropriately maintained key-inventory records can help track missing keys. When keys are missing, a decision can be made whether to rekey or change the locks in certain areas of the building. Establishing a key-control system initially requires rekeying all locks in the building, something that can be quite expensive. First, a cost-benefit evaluation of a key control system should be made. Second, if a decision is made to implement the key-control system the system must be maintained. A facility can quickly lose most of the benefits of such a system and its investment in it if the system is allowed to break down. "Do not duplicate" should be engraved on all keys as a deterrent against unauthorized duplication. It is not known to what extent nursing homes may be using electronic key or pass systems. At any rate, installation and maintenance of such systems would be quite expensive.

FIRE AND DISASTER PLANNING

All facilities must have fire and disaster plans, and the staff must be adequately trained to calmly and effectively react in the unlikely event of a fire, a natural disaster, or a terrorism threat. Routine maintenance of fire-safety equipment was discussed earlier; the facility must also have a written fire safety plan and an emergency evacuation plan. Written plans must also outline procedures to be followed during a disaster such as a tornado, hurricane, earthquake, flood, or snow blizzard. These plans are best developed and rehearsed in conjunction with the local fire department and other civil defense agencies. The plans must address the individual characteristics of the particular facility and take into account the availability of local resources and the response time of emergency services to deal with events in which the safety of residents is paramount.

Fire Safety Steps

All staff members must receive training in basic sequential fire-protection steps represented by the acronym RACE (Kavaler and Spiegel 1997):

R—Rescue and remove anyone in immediate danger.

A—Alarm everyone by activating the nearest fire alarm.

C—Confine and contain the fire and smoke by closing all doors and windows.

E—Extinguish the fire with portable extinguishers, wet sheets, and blankets.

The most critical step in fire protection is to activate the fire alarm. This step is vital because the fire department must be notified immediately when fire is suspected. The Life Safety Code requires that the fire-alarm system be connected to an outside agency, such as a fire-security company, that will transmit the alarm to the nearest fire department. Pulling the fire alarm is the quickest way to summon the fire brigade to the facility. When the alarm box is activated a fire alarm goes off within the facility, and all fire doors close automatically.

The facility's fire safety protocols should also include a pre-established code word, such as "Doctor Red" or "Code 99." The code should be used, to alert all staff members in case of a fire; the alert is generally given by announcing the code over the intercom system. Also, the real danger from a fire is usually not the flames, but smoke that can travel quickly to areas far from the fire. Smoke inhalation is the major cause of death during a fire. Hence, closing doors and windows and using wet towels to cover any open spaces between the doors and the floor must be given top priority after patients in immediate danger have been evacuated and the fire alarm has been activated. The staff should start closing doors and windows throughout the facility as soon as the code word is announced. In all emergency situations, the staff must remain calm and reassure patients and visitors that appropriate procedures are being followed.

Fire-safety procedures should clearly designate the person who takes charge when a fire or suspected fire is discovered. Generally, the administrator, the DON (in the administrator's absence), or a charge nurse (on the night shift) will ascertain whether smoke or fire is present anywhere in the facility. Once the presence of fire is confirmed, a phone call should also be made to the local fire department to confirm that there is a fire. A staff person should be posted at the front entrance of the facility to direct the fire department personnel to the location of the fire in the building, while the person in charge of fire safety directs staff members to secure all patients and follow the RACE steps.

On the other hand, when no smoke or fire is detected, notice of a false alarm should be relayed by telephone to confirm that there is no fire, because an alarm would have been previously relayed if a fire alarm was activated. In most instances, however, the fire brigade is already on its way by the time the person in charge of fire safety has confirmed the state of "all clear." In this case, the individual should meet the fire brigade at the front entrance and explain the situation. Some fire personnel may still want to go through the building and ensure complete safety before leaving the premises.

Emergency Evacuation

Evacuation is the removal of patients and vital equipment from an unsafe area to a safe area during a fire or other emergency situation (Tweedy 1997). Evacuation plans should cover both partial and total evacuation of patients. When a fire alarm is activated, automatic closure of fire doors segregates the point of origin of the fire from other areas on the same floor. Because fire doors provide a barrier against smoke and flames, a **safety zone** is created beyond the fire doors away from the point of origin of the fire (Figure 11-1). A **partial evacuation** consists of moving patients from the area of fire to a neighboring safety zone. **Total evacuation** consists of removing patients and vital equipment from an entire wing or floor, or evacuating the entire building. Bed-bound patients should be removed on stretchers because rolling beds into the hallways can quickly

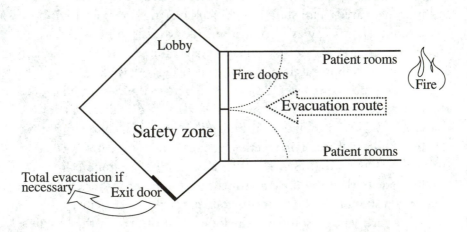

FIGURE 11-1 Partial Evacuation to a Safety Zone or Total Evacuation during a Fire Emergency

clog vital evacuation routes. Non-ambulatory patients who are not bed-bound can be rolled out in wheelchairs. Ambulatory patients should be led as a group, holding each other's hands. A staff member should lead such a human chain, with another staff member following the chain. After patients have been moved to a safety zone, they must remain under staff supervision. In the event of a total evacuation, the facility must make prior arrangements for temporary shelter for residents in a local school, hospital, or Red Cross center. Evacuation plans should include protecting and transferring medical records, continuing critical medical care services, and maintaining vital functions such as providing food, water, and clean linens.

Simulation Drills

The facility must conduct regular fire drills on all shifts. In most states, regulations require that the facility conduct an unannounced fire drill on each shift once a quarter. Because of staff turnover, however, more frequent fire drills are recommended. The facility's staff members are not expected to function as firefighters, but they must know how to operate a portable fire extinguisher. The staff members' main role is to contain any immediate danger and minimize the spread of fire till the fire brigade gets to the scene, at which point the firefighters will take over. A disaster-simulation drill is necessary once a year to rehearse the response of key staff members and the response of the local civil-defense teams. All fire drills and disaster-simulation drills must be documented, and training should follow to address areas of weak response. Simulation drills are also used to educate the staff about the importance of remaining calm and thinking clearly during unexpected emergencies.

WASTE MANAGEMENT

General Waste

As much as 90% or more of the waste produced by nursing-care facilities is regarded as "non-risk" general waste, which is comparable to domestic garbage and can be safely disposed of by contracting with a reputable waste-removal company. A dumpster of sufficient size is essential, so that trash does not overflow at any time. The dumpster must be a covered container, and it must remain covered after each use. No loose trash should

be thrown into the container; all garbage and waste must be appropriately bagged. The ground around the dumpster should be kept clean at all times. This function is generally the responsibility of the maintenance department.

Hazardous Waste

The facility must have policies and procedures in effect for the safe handling, removal, and disposal of all wastes regarded as hazardous. The most common types of hazardous waste can be classified as infectious wastes, pathological wastes, and sharps. **Infectious waste** can come from patients who have been isolated for infections, dressings from infected wounds, human excreta, or laboratory cultures. **Pathological waste** contains blood and body fluids. It includes stoma bags, incontinence pads, and protective gloves and masks used by staff members. **Sharps** can be any objects that can cut or puncture, such as needles, blades, broken glass, and nails.

Hazardous waste should not be deposited in the regular dumpster used for general waste. Safe handling requires caution to avoid injury from sharps and to prevent cross-contamination from infectious and pathological waste. Special puncture-proof containers are used for all sharps. Infectious and pathological waste is bagged in clearly marked or color-coded heavy-duty plastic bags that are also leak-proof. Unlike most hospitals, nursing facilities generally do not have on-site disposal or incineration facilities because of the costs involved. Contracts must therefore be established with qualified waste carriers for the regular removal and disposal of all hazardous wastes. Any storage of waste before collection for off-site disposal should be in a secure location designated for the purpose (Prüss et al. 1999).

ENVIRONMENTAL SAFETY

Safety is one of the primary elements to be incorporated in the various environmental policies and procedures discussed in this chapter. Personnel working in a facility's environmental services departments need specific training in safe work habits and in monitoring the environment for safety. For instance, monitoring hot water in patient rooms and bathrooms is a critical aspect of safety that prevents scalding. As a general rule, hot-water temperature in these areas should not exceed 110° Fahrenheit. Hot-water supply to patient areas and public areas is equipped with ther-

mostatically controlled mixing valves to keep the water temperature from rising above the specified limits. The maintenance supervisor must pay particular attention to this area and record daily temperature readings to ensure safety. On the other hand, adequate supply of water that is hot enough for washing and sanitizing in the kitchen and laundry is equally important. Because the hot-water temperatures required for patient care areas and for sanitizing functions differ substantially, a common practice is to have separate hot-water systems and booster heaters that are locally mounted on sanitizing equipment to achieve the desired results.

Maintenance and housekeeping personnel must pay close attention to their equipment. If equipment is left unattended it presents a hazard. Floor-cleaning and polishing chemicals should be non-skid. Safety signs must be used while mopping floors. Mopping the hallways lengthwise, doing one half of the hall at a time, leaves the other half for safe passage through the hallways. Furniture and equipment must be kept away from traffic paths and exits. Various electrical gadgets are operated with long cords, which should be kept along the baseboards and not cross the hall-way. Heavy housekeeping trucks, food-transportation carts, and linen carts can cause serious injury. They often block the operator's view and require caution, especially when turning blind corners. Strategically placed mirrors can help staff members using these carts to see people around the corner and use caution to prevent injuries.

CONCLUSION

Plant and environmental services play a major adjunct role in facilitating the processes of clinical care. To fulfill this role effectively, these adjunct departments must dovetail their efforts with the clinical departments of nursing, activities, and rehabilitation. For example, therapy rooms must be cleaned early in the morning before therapy sessions begin. Schedules for delivering clean linens to patient care areas must be established with input from the nursing department. The heads of the activity and house-keeping departments should have weekly discussions about areas that must be prepared in advance of scheduled activities. The administrator must oversee the protocols for safety, security, and preparedness for fire and disasters, along with ensuring that all staff members are adequately trained in these areas.

DISCUSSION QUESTIONS

1. What would be some of the important clauses to include in (a) routine contracts, (b) open-call contracts, and (3) job unit contracts?
2. What may be some of the reasons for not allowing the housekeeping staff in nursing facilities to handle either clean or soiled linens, unlike hotel and motel operations?
3. Discuss how certain environmental standards in the facility can be effectively used to convey value to potential clients.

INTERNET RESOURCES FOR FURTHER LEARNING

National Fire Protection Association: A nonprofit international agency whose mission is to reduce fire and other hazards by providing and advocating scientifically-based consensus codes and standards, research, training and education.
http://www.nfpa.org/catalog/home/index.asp

U.S. Environmental Protection Agency: Provides information on antimicrobial products.
http://www.epa.gov/oppad001/

REFERENCES

Belkin, N.L. 2003. Disinfecting versus sanitizing. *Health Facilities Management* 16, no. 11: 34–36.

Goldberg, A.J., and R.A. Buttaro. 1990. *Hospital Departmental Profiles.* 3rd ed. Chicago: American Hospital Publishing, Inc.

Griffith, J.R. 1995. *The Well-Managed Health Care Organization.* 3rd ed. Ann Arbor, MI: AUPHA Press/Health Administration Press.

Heintzelman, J.E. 1987. The *Complete Handbook of Maintenance Management.* Englewood Cliffs, NJ: Prentice-Hall, Inc.

Kavaler, F., and A.D. Spiegel. 1997. Assuring safety and security in health care institutions. In *Risk Management in Health Care Institutions: A Strategic Approach, eds.* F. Kavaler and A.D. Spiegel. Boston: Jones and Bartlett Publishers.

Magee, G.H. 1988. *Facilities Maintenance Management.* Kingston, MA: R.S. Means Company, Inc.

Office of Health and Safety, Centers for Disease Control and Prevention. 2002. Guidelines for laundry in health care facilities. http://www.cdc.gov/od/ohs/biosfty/laundry.htm

Prüss, A., E. Giroult, and P. Rushbrook. 1999. *Safe Management of Wastes from Health-Care Activities.* Geneva: World Health Organization.

Rowland, H.S., and B.L. Rowland. 1984. *Hospital Management: A Guide to Departments.* Rockville, Maryland: Aspen Systems Corporation.

Sells, D.H. 2000. *Security in the Healthcare Environment.* Gaithersburg, MD: Aspen Publishers, Inc.

Tweedy, J.T. 1997. *Healthcare Hazard Control and Safety Management.* Boca Raton, FL: Lewis Publishers.

Vesley, D. 1973. Selected topics in environmental health. In *Environmental Health and Safety in Health-Care Facilities*, eds., R.G. Bond, G.S. Michaelsen, and R.L. DeRoos. New York: Macmillan Publishing Co., Inc.

Vesley, D., and V.W. Greene. 1973. Sterilization, disinfection, and cleaning techniques. In *Environmental Health and Safety in Health-Care Facilities*, eds., R.G. Bond, G.S. Michaelsen, and R.L. DeRoos. New York: Macmillan Publishing Co., Inc.

CHAPTER 12

Administrative and Information Systems

LEARNING MODULES

1. Business office core functions. Staffing the front office.
2. Reception functions. Protocols for welcoming visitors and answering the telephone. Routine secretarial and clerical functions.
3. Accounting and bookkeeping functions.
4. Payroll regulations and policies governing employee classification, work hours, pay systems, compensation, overtime pay, and payroll withholdings.
5. Processing accounts payable. Controlling petty cash.
6. Billing, accounts receivable, and collection procedures.
7. Patient trust fund. The facility's obligations and resident rights to manage their financial affairs. How to establish and manage a patient trust fund.
8. Handling cash receipts and deposits.
9. Medical records staffing and functions.
10. Maintaining and auditing medical records. Content and purpose of medical records. Confidentiality: access, use, release of information. Privacy provisions of HIPAA 1996.
11. Information systems: purpose, integration, and security.
12. Information system development and vendor selection.

Administrative and information systems are necessary for the effective support of the management and clinical functions within the facility. In a hospital, these support functions are generally segregated into several departments; however, in nursing facilities, they are generally consolidated in one department. The business office generally combines reception, secretarial, clerical, and bookkeeping functions. These four functions form the business office core, which closely interfaces with the work of the administrator. The medical records office is typically a separate administrative function under the supervision of the director of nursing (see Figure II-1).

Multifacility chain operations as well as hospital-based operations centralize most accounting and finance functions at their corporate offices, but the corporate office relies on the facility's business office for vital inputs needed to prepare financial and management reports. Stand-alone facilities often contract with an accounting firm to carry out most accounting and finance functions. Large facilities may extend the core business functions into additional areas such as materials management, whereas most small- to medium-sized nursing homes combine the materials-management function with that of medical records.

THE BUSINESS OFFICE

The business office forms the key administrative core of the facility. Visitors, patients, family members, and employees have frequent contact with the business office. Facilities with 80 or more beds have a front desk staffed by a receptionist, and an adjoining office occupied by a bookkeeper. In most facilities, the receptionist also performs secretarial and clerical duties. Large facilities may have a lot of traffic at the front desk and may receive a large number of telephone calls. In that situation, the receptionist may devote most of his or her time to reception functions. The number of bookkeepers needed by the facility depends on two factors: the size of the facility and the business and accounting functions performed at the facility.

The business office is supervised by a business-office manager who is a department head that reports to the administrator. This individual also handles the facility's bookkeeping. Even though the business office is open five days a week during regular business hours, facilities with 100 to

120 beds or more should have a receptionist for evenings and weekends. In smaller operations, telephone-answering duties are taken over by a designated nursing station when the business office is closed.

Regulations do not mandate specific qualifications for the employees who staff the business office. Finding qualified people who possess the necessary combination of receptionist, secretarial, and clerical skills is not always easy. Nevertheless, every effort should be made to staff the front office with personnel who can display a pleasant demeanor in person as well as on the telephone and also have the mental capacity to carry out clerical and secretarial duties in an atmosphere in which frequent interruptions and distractions are common.

Bookkeepers must be skilled in basic accounting functions. However, bookkeepers also have regular interactions with patients and families, so they must have a good combination of bookkeeping skills and people-skills. The bookkeepers also generally relieve the receptionist for lunch and break time, sickness, and vacations by doing the receptionist's job at those times. Cross-training may also enable a facility to use other personnel, such as the medical records clerk, to cover the reception desk for brief durations.

RECEPTION FUNCTIONS

To most first-time visitors, the front office provides a window into the facility. With their first contact, many people form lasting opinions about the rest of the operation and its services. A smile, a warm greeting, an offer of assistance, and an eagerness to meet people's needs create a positive impression. A warm human touch can have a soothing effect in calming down people's anxiety, anger, frustration, and other negative emotions.

Effectively managed facilities have written protocols for interacting with visitors and assisting telephone callers. Some administrators may regard it as petty, but standardized procedures are vital for consistent quality and for staff training. Adhering to well-formulated protocols helps the facility project a professional image.

Every visitor to the facility must be made to feel welcome. The receptionist must interrupt whatever he or she is doing and attend to the visitor. Once greeted, the visitors should be asked how they could be assisted. Knowledge of the facility, the location of resident rooms, the key func-

tions of the different departments, the names of residents, and knowledge of some of the residents' routines and habits can all play an essential role in directing visitors appropriately. The receptionist's length of employment and experience with the facility can pay rich dividends here. The front office must maintain an updated roster of residents, along with their room numbers.

Effectively-managed facilities maintain a notification system for the receptionist to know when certain key personnel are out of the facility or in meetings. A small board with the names of all key personnel can be easily updated to avoid embarrassing moments when a visitor may be kept waiting for someone who is eventually found to be unavailable. As stated in chapter 7, the facility must have a written plan for handling inquiries for potential admissions. The receptionist is not responsible for providing detailed information about the facility and its services. But the facility must have protocols in place, so the receptionist knows who is available at any given time to attend to a walk-in or telephone inquiry.

The receptionist should also know when certain activities are taking place in the facility, and which residents may be out of the facility, as for an outing or a shopping trip. Some acquaintance with residents is also important. Just imagine how awkward it could be when a church pastor comes to visit a particular resident, but because the receptionist does not know who that resident is the pastor is directed to the resident's room while the resident is sitting right there in the front lobby.

Having a written telephone-answering protocol is another hallmark of an effectively managed facility. A telephone call must be answered within the first three to four rings. When more calls than one come in at the same time, keeping the caller on hold for several minutes after saying "Can you hold, please?" or "one moment, please," is inappropriate. The bookkeeper(s), and other personnel if necessary, should assist the receptionist when the switchboard gets busy. Once the call is picked up, the recommended protocol is an appropriate greeting followed by the name of the facility, followed by "how may I help you." The call should then be directed promptly to the appropriate individual. Depending on the facility's protocols, the call may be directed to another individual (in case of an inquiry or other important matter), the person may be paged, or a message may be taken. In many facilities, key staff members now have portable pagers to minimize use of the intercom system.

SECRETARIAL
AND CLERICAL FUNCTIONS

Depending on the facility's size, the receptionist may be assigned additional duties, such as clerical work, minor bookkeeping tasks, filing, faxing, handling mail, and photocopying. Use of computers has eliminated the need to use typewriters for correspondence, which allows the administrator and department heads to type their own letters using a word-processing program. At the administrator's discretion, the receptionist may be responsible for handling the patient trust fund, or this task may be assigned to the bookkeeper. Clerical and bookkeeping functions that are often assigned to the receptionist include processing employee time-cards for payroll and processing vendor invoices for accounts payable. As stated earlier, size of the facility is a key factor that determines the extent to which clerical functions can be handled effectively by the receptionist.

ACCOUNTING
AND BOOKKEEPING FUNCTIONS

The main accounting and bookkeeping functions include payroll, accounts payable, the petty-cash fund, billing for patient services, accounts receivable, the patient trust fund, and cash deposits. As stated earlier, some of the more basic functions may be delegated to the receptionist. In large facilities, however, almost all of these functions are handled by the bookkeeping personnel. Trained bookkeepers may also be able to perform more advanced accounting functions, such as posting to the general ledger, doing payroll accounting and processing payroll checks, processing payable checks for vendors, and doing quarterly tax forms. Most free-standing facilities, however, contract with an accounting firm to handle all accounting transactions, prepare financial statements, and prepare managerial reports. For nursing homes affiliated with a hospital or multifacility corporation, these functions are generally centralized at the corporate office, and the costs are passed on to the facility in the form of management fees. Nevertheless, for chain-affiliated facilities, centralized accounting functions are more cost-efficient than outsourcing these functions to an accounting firm.

Payroll and Compensation

Payroll accounting comprises three main activities: determining gross wages, deducting payroll withholdings, and calculating payroll-based contributions made by the employer on behalf of the employee. The actual pay employees receive is gross wages minus the withholdings. Payroll-based employer contributions are regarded as benefits. An example of these contributions is the employer's payment of one-half of the social-security and Medicare taxes paid by the employer on behalf of each employee.

Employees are paid on the basis of their rates of pay and the hours they work. The Fair Labor Standards Act (FLSA) requires employers to maintain accurate payroll records that include certain identifying information about each employee, along with data about the hours worked and wages earned. The administrator should authorize the initial rate of pay when an employee is first put on the payroll. For later changes in the established rate of pay, controls requiring proper authorizations for changes in the rate of pay must be instituted to prevent any irregularities. The number of hours worked must be calculated in strict accordance with established payroll policy.

This section is intended to provide only an overview of the main FLSA requirements. The Wage and Hour Division of the U.S. Department of Labor is responsible for administering and enforcing federal labor laws.

Exempt and Non-Exempt Employees

Under FLSA, all employees must be classified as either exempt or nonexempt (Jacksack 1998). **Nonexempt employees** are paid an hourly rate, which must at least equal the minimum wage established under law. Nonexempt employees are also entitled to overtime pay.

Exempt employees are most often salaried and are exempt from the overtime provisions of the law. However, to be classified as exempt, an employee must meet other criteria in addition to being salaried. As a general rule, exempt employees can fall into three categories: executive, administrative, and professional. These classifications cannot be used arbitrarily with the intent of classifying certain employees as exempt. Executive employees must perform managerial functions at least 50 percent of the time (Jacksack 1998), and both executive and administrative personnel must have the latitude to exercise discretion and independent judgment in carrying out their responsibilities. Administrative work can

also include assisting an executive, working on special assignments, or performing work related directly to management policies. To be categorized as professionals, employees must belong to a learned profession with recognized status, as defined by law. For example, registered nurses may meet the requirements for learned professional exemption under the law, but licensed practical (vocational) nurses do not meet the legal requirement. To determine which positions in the nursing facility should be classified as exempt, legal advice may be necessary. As a general rule, most department-head positions in nursing homes are unlikely to be classified as exempt, the director of nursing being one notable exception.

Most employees in a nursing facility are nonexempt and are typically paid an hourly wage. The payroll system should distinguish between salaried and non-salaried nonexempt workers. Salaried employees earn a fixed amount each pay period. Non-salaried employees are issued time cards for each pay period and are required to punch a time-clock that records the times when an employee came in to work ("clocked-in") and when the employee left work ("clocked-out").

Work Time and Compensation Policies

Compensation for work is governed by federal and state wage-and-hour laws. The facility should establish its own payroll policy in full compliance with the law.

Facility policy should specify the amount of time allowed as incidental or preparation time. For instance, at the change of shift, many workers need to clock-in or clock-out at the same time, but generally some waiting time is involved, because they cannot all use the time-clock simultaneously; this time could be considered incidental or preparation time. Employees may also use lockers and wash-up facilities before and after work. The facility should determine a reasonable non-paid incidental time, such as ten minutes before a shift begins and ten minutes after a shift ends. Even though such extra minutes are recorded on the time card, the incidental time is not generally compensated; at least the law does not require that this time be paid. Employees have to be compensated for break and rest periods of up to twenty minutes, but they do not have to be paid for meal time that lasts at least 30 minutes, and most organizations do not pay for this meal time. Keep in mind, however, that to avoid paying employees for meal time, those employees must be completely

relieved of all duties and be free to leave their work stations during their meal breaks (Jacksack 1998). It is particularly important to monitor meal breaks in facilities experiencing staff shortages and in facilities where well-meaning employees may have a tendency to "grab a quick bite" at the work station itself in order to minimize interruptions in patient care. If this is the case, the law requires that the employee be compensated for meal time. Payment for sick time, holidays, vacations, and personal time are governed by the facility's personnel policies.

The facility must compensate nonexempt employees for all work and work-related activities required by the facility. Compensable work includes orientation, training, and in-service education that an employee may be required to have.

Overtime Compensation

A workweek, which can begin on any day of the week, is seven consecutive 24-hour periods or 168 consecutive hours. Federal law mandates that nonexempt workers be paid overtime for any hours worked in excess of 40 hours in a work week. Although the 40-hour week is generally the standard for determining overtime, FLSA permits employers to enter into agreements with employees whereby a work period of 14 consecutive days (instead of seven) may be established. Commonly known as the 8-80 rule, this alternative requires paying overtime for any hours in excess of 8 hours in any one day or for any hours in excess of 80 hours during the 14-day work period (Pozgar 1992). Management has the option to decide whether to apply the 8-80 rule, which it can do, if it wants, for just one class of employees such as nurses.

Overtime must be paid at the rate of time-and-a-half the regular rate of pay. Even when overtime is not authorized, if an employee has incurred it, it must be paid. According to the new "white collar" overtime exemption (Fair Pay) rules issued by the Wage and Hour Division in April 2004, workers earning less than $23,660 per year will be automatically eligible for overtime pay even if such employees could be classified as exempt.

Nonexempt employees cannot be given compensatory time off in lieu of overtime. Such a practice is illegal. It is not illegal, however, in the case of exempt employees. The law does not require employers to pay more than an employee's established rate of pay for working the evening shift, night shift, or weekends. However, many facilities have established extra pay for late shifts, weekends, and holidays.

Payroll Withholdings

Employers are legally required to withhold taxes from their employees' pay and to deposit the withheld amounts with the appropriate tax agencies (Jacksack 1998). Taxes normally withheld from employee paychecks include federal, state, and local income taxes. Employers who fail to withhold and deposit taxes in a timely manner are subject to severe penalties and interest charges (Seawell 1992). Under the Federal Insurance Contributions Act (FICA), employers must also withhold half of the Social Security and Medicare taxes from the employees' paychecks. The other half of these FICA taxes is to be paid by the employer. Employers must also pay Federal Unemployment Taxes (FUTA) on behalf of the employees. In most states, the employer must also pay a state unemployment tax. These taxes are based on taxable wages paid to employees. In some states, employers are required to pay a disability insurance tax for workers' compensation. Most states, however, allow the employer to cover workers' compensation through private insurance purchased from a commercial insurance company (Seawell 1992).

Payroll withholdings from employee paychecks for income taxes and FICA are compulsory. The employer may also be required to withhold union dues for employees who belong to a trade union. Wage garnishment is another type of compulsory withholding. A **wage garnishment** is any legal or equitable procedure through which some portion of an employee's earnings must be withheld by an employer to pay a debt incurred by the employee. Most garnishments are made by court order with which employers must comply. Other types of legal or equitable procedures include levies by the Internal Revenue Service (IRS) or a state tax-collection agency for unpaid taxes and federal-agency administrative garnishments for non-tax debts owed to the federal government.

There may be other withholdings that are voluntary, and these usually require the employee's written consent. Voluntary withholdings include the employee's portion of health insurance and life insurance premiums, employee contribution into a retirement plan, dental plan premiums, and premiums for other types of insurance, such as accident and disability.

Accounts Payable

Accounts payable is the accounting term for money owed to vendors from whom goods, supplies, and services have been purchased on credit. With the exception of minor and non-routine purchases, most goods and

services are purchased on a non-cash basis. An invoice showing the amount due generally accompanies the goods at the time they are delivered to the facility. Other vendors deliver the products and then separately mail the invoice. Service vendors also provide their services and issue an invoice later.

A common practice among most vendors is to extend credit for 30 days. Utility companies for telephone, gas, electricity, water, and sewer may allow less than 30 days for full payment of the amounts due. Payments are generally made by check and are recorded in the general ledger, which is maintained on a computer-based accounting system. As each invoice is paid, it is indelibly stamped or perforated "PAID" to prevent double payment (Seawell 1992). All invoices must be authorized by the appropriate department heads before they are paid. Department heads must carefully check to ensure that the items on the invoice were actually received and note any discrepancies.

Petty-Cash Fund

As a general rule, all purchases must be paid for by check through the accounts-payable system. In some situations, however, payment by check is impractical. To pay for certain cash purchases and other small incidental expenses, every facility must maintain a petty-cash fund. The facility should establish a policy on the imprest amount, and on the maximum amount per disbursement that the business office can incur without requiring authorization from the administrator. The **imprest amount** is a fixed amount, such as $400 or $500, and this amount, replenished periodically, depends on the facility's petty-cash needs. Petty cash is maintained in a locked box or drawer.

Each disbursement from the petty cash fund requires completion of a petty cash voucher, to which any supporting documentation, such as a sales receipt from a store, is attached. The voucher is signed by the person receiving the money. Under the imprest system, the cash and the amounts shown on the vouchers must always add up to the imprest amount. This system allows the administrator to periodically check the petty-cash fund. When the amount of cash drops below a predetermined level, the vouchers are removed and totaled. Cash equaling this total is added to the petty cash fund. At that point, the petty cash fund should equal the imprest amount. Inconsequential shortages may occur because of errors, but substantial or frequent shortages may indicate mishandling of funds.

Billing, Accounts Receivable, and Collection

Just as the nursing facility receives products and services from outside vendors and does not pay cash for them right away, similarly it provides services to patients but does not get paid for those services immediately. The facility, however, has the legal right to receive money at a future date. The amounts that remain to be collected by the facility for services already rendered are called **accounts receivable**.

The facility must bill the respective payers such as Medicare, Medicaid, private insurance companies, or individual private parties responsible for paying. Bills are prepared and sent to the payers once a month. Medicaid and Medicare bills, called **claims**, are submitted electronically.

The billing system should be set up so each patient is accurately classified according to pay type. It is particularly important to keep track of changes in pay status, when a patient's payment status switches from one pay-type to another, such as from Medicare to Medicaid, or from Medicare to private-pay. The billing system must also separate the copayment and any other amounts that must be collected from the patient from the amount to be billed to third-party payers.

The basis for daily charges is the **midnight census report**, which is prepared each night by the charge nurse on duty and verified by the DON. The midnight census report verifies the presence of each person who was an inpatient in the facility on that day. On a daily basis, the bookkeeper should match patients in the billing system against the midnight census report. The report must be reconciled daily because, from time to time, a facility may have patients on **bed-hold**, which happens when patients are temporarily away (to a hospital, or with family), but their beds are being held for them and must be paid for.

The daily charge, or the *per diem* rate, covers room, board, nursing care, and other routine services. Depending on the payer, other services may or may not be covered by the *per diem* rate. Any services or supplies not covered by the *per diem* rate must be billed separately. All services and supplies must be itemized and billed when a patient is a private-pay patient. To accomplish this task, nursing must have a system to identify and charge for all supplies used by each individual patient. Recording these ancillary charges requires cooperation from the nursing staff, who must be adequately trained on how the system works. The business office must also receive charge tickets from independent contractors, such as barbers and beauticians, that provide personal services to patients.

On a daily basis, the various patient charges as well as all payments received are posted to each patient's ledger account. These ledger accounts are used to prepare a monthly accounts-receivable **aging report**, which is a managerial report. Also known as an aging schedule, this report provides a detailed account-by-account analysis of outstanding balances on unpaid patient accounts. It also shows account balances classified by "age" groups according to the number of days a given balance has been outstanding (Seawell 1992). For instance, each account shows the receivable balance under columns for 0-30 days, which is considered "current;" 31-90 days past due; 91-120 days past due; and over 120 days past due, as shown in Exhibit 16-8. The older an unpaid account gets, the less likely it is to be collected.

Third-party claims are often rejected because of billing errors. The only way such accounts can be collected is by rectifying the errors and resubmitting corrected claims. To collect past-due balances owed by private individuals, the facility must have collection policies and procedures.

The following guidelines can be used by facilities to formulate their own collection policies: Accounts receivable are considered current during the first thirty days. However, even before an account balance gets to be 30 days old, a telephone call should be made to the party responsible for paying the private portion of the bill. The objective of this call is to remind the individual that the payment is due and to tell the payer what is the exact amount of the balance due. The caller should also ask when payment might be expected and try to reach an agreement with the payer on a payment date that is no later than one week after the phone call. A week later, a second call should be made if payment has still not been received. The caller should now try to find out if there is a reason why payment was not made and whether there is some problem with the bill and the amount due. Again, the caller should try to obtain some form of a promise to pay (Frew and Frew 1982). A friendly tone must be maintained by the facility's representative during these telephone conversations. The administrator should institute a mechanism that enables the staff to conduct timely follow-ups and maintain documentation on each conversation. Detailed notes are helpful for any subsequent follow-up. Generally, when an account is in arrears for 45 days or more, a letter should be mailed to the party responsible for paying the bill. The letter should contain a polite request for payment in a manner that is firm but does not present an ultimatum (Frew and Frew 1982). Any subsequent letters should still be polite but should contain a stronger tone including

a warning that use of a collection agency may be required if the balance is not paid by a given date. By the 90th day of being past due, an account should be turned over to a collection agency.

Patient Trust Fund

Residents of a nursing home may ask the facility to manage their funds. When asked to do so, the nursing home is obligated to establish a patient trust fund. The facility should also inform residents and their families that they have the option to use the patient trust fund. Nursing home regulations, however, allow residents to retain the right to manage their own financial affairs. Residents who choose to manage their own money cannot be required by the nursing facility to deposit funds in the patient trust account managed by the facility.

Most state laws have established limits on the maximum amount a facility is required to manage for each resident. Under Michigan law, for example, a nursing home must hold and manage up to $5,000 for each resident. A facility cannot refuse to handle funds of less than $5,000, although it may refuse to handle funds that exceed that amount.

Medicare and Medicaid certification regulations mandate that nursing homes deposit into an interest-bearing account all individual patient funds exceeding $50. Up to $50 per resident may be held in a non-interest bearing account or petty-cash fund held at the facility. Depending on state law, the requirements may vary for non-certified facilities that admit only private-pay patients. The facility is not allowed to charge Medicare and Medicaid patients any fee for managing the trust fund.

Patient funds are in a demand trust with the facility, which means that the funds are available to the patient upon request (Abramovice 1988). In addition, the money can only be spent by the facility with specific permission from the patient or from someone authorized by the patient. To manage the patient trust fund, the facility should:

- Open an interest-bearing account; this account must be separate from the facility's own bank account.
- Maintain a petty cash system that is separate from the facility's own petty cash fund. Patients must have access to their funds during normal office hours.
- Implement a cash-receipt or cash-ledger system to record each transaction. The records should include the patient's name, account

number, amount of cash withdrawn or deposited, and the purpose for which funds were withdrawn (such as cash, telephone bill, purchase of clothing, etc.). The signature of the patient or the patient's authorized representative should be required for each transaction unless there is an invoice bearing the patient's name to support the disbursement of funds.

- As a safeguard against misuse of funds, balances must be reconciled each month by someone other than the person responsible for maintaining the fund.

- Regulations require the facility to provide the patient or the authorized person a statement at least once every quarter. The quarterly statement should include at a minimum the balance at the beginning of the period, current balance, amount of interest earned, total deposits and withdrawals, and detailed information on each transaction.

- The full balance of funds belonging to a patient must be returned promptly after a patient has been discharged from the facility. After a patient's death a written statement must be sent to the administrator of the resident's estate.

- The facility must notify Medicare and Medicaid residents when the funds attain a level within $200 of the resource limit for the Supplemental Security Income (SSI) or Medicaid. Such residents must be informed that if they go over the SSI or Medicaid resource limits, they may lose eligibility for the SSI and Medicaid programs.

- The facility is required by law to purchase a surety bond or provide evidence of self-insurance, such as facility funds that are irrevocably set aside for repaying the residents in case of loss.

Cash Receipts and Deposits

Control of cash receipts is a critical function. All cash and checks must be recorded on a cash-receipt voucher that shows the exact amount received. Actual cash received must be kept separate from any other cash funds such as the petty cash fund or the patient trust fund. No cash disbursement should ever be made out of cash receipts (Seawell 1992). Cash and checks must be deposited into the facility's bank account daily. The bank deposit slip should be reconciled against the cash-receipt vouchers, which are then used for posting credits to the respective patients' ledger accounts. The ledger account for each patient shows the debits or amounts initially owed, credits or amounts paid, and the accounts receivable due.

MEDICAL RECORDS

Staffing

Depending on the size of the facility, medical record services are staffed by a full- or part-time individual. Certification as a medical records administrator (RHIA) or technician (RHIT), conferred by the American Health Information Management Association (AHIMA), is a necessary qualification for a hospital's medical records personnel. Certification is based on academic qualifications and an examination. RHIA certification requires a bachelor's degree from a college or university program in health-information administration that is accredited either by AHIMA or by the Commission on Accreditation of Allied Health Education Programs (CAAHEP). RHIT certification requires an associate's degree from an accredited academic institution. However, only large facilities may be able to employ a registered health-information administrator (RHIA) or a registered health information technician (RHIT). Most facilities designate a clerical person with some appropriate experience to handle medical records and contract with a duly certified medical-records consultant who provides routine oversight.

Functions

The medical-records clerk must ensure that medical records are completed within a reasonable time. When a resident is first admitted a new chart for that resident is opened by the medical-records clerk. In case of a readmission, the previously closed record is reactivated. Open records are maintained at the nursing station responsible for the care of the patient. The medical-records clerk is responsible for ensuring that the records are maintained in an organized manner in accordance with current laws and accepted professional standards. Quality is ensured by auditing records according to an audit schedule. Upon discharge, the patient's clinical record is closed and moved to the medical-records office. Before the closed records are filed away, they are reviewed for completeness and compliance with regulations and the facility's policies.

Standardized methods exist for systematizing, indexing, and filing medical records. The medical-records clerk is responsible for the safekeeping, confidentiality, and retrieval of stored records. Medical records on patients who have been in the facility for a long time can become quite bulky. Such records can be thinned in accordance with the facility's policies and regu-

latory provisions. However, clinical medical records in nursing homes are increasingly being computerized, although the progress is slow.

Medical Record Content

A nursing facility is required by law to maintain individual medical records on each patient. The record contains all significant information on the care of the patient from admission to final discharge. Thus, it becomes a permanent and comprehensive historical record of the patient's medical condition, the course of treatment and specific services delivered during the patient's stay in the facility, and the clinical outcomes. The facility's medical records should contain only original notes and reports. Records sent from another facility are retained in a file but are not considered a legal part of the medical record (Burger et al. 1986). However, when a patient is transferred from the hospital to a skilled nursing facility, a summary of the acute-care stay should be part of the nursing home records. The instructions and orders for skilled care must also be entered into the health record as the patient's care continues (Kiger 2003). Timeliness, objectivity, accuracy, and brevity without the sacrifice of essential facts are the hallmarks of effective medical recording (Bruce 1988).

The medical record includes a patient's identifying information as well as the patient's clinical information. The patient's identifying information includes name, address, gender, date of birth, social security number, Medicare and/or Medicaid claim number, marital status, name and contact information on next of kin, race and ethnicity, and religious preference. Clinical information includes records of medical and social history, physical examinations, principal diagnoses, results of the initial assessment and any subsequent reassessments, informed consent and advance directives (see Chapter 3), plan of care, treatments prescribed, diet plan, therapeutic procedures carried out, and medications administered. Also included in the clinical information are records of laboratory test results, clinical observations, response to treatment, any change in condition and action taken, any incidents or accidents, any treatment errors and action taken, any adverse reaction to medications, any use of restraints and psychotropic drugs, and discharge summary. All physicians' orders must be signed and dated by the attending physician.

Typically, medical records are arranged in chronological sequence and divided into sections by the source of documentation. Thus, typical sec-

tions include sections for physicians' notes, clinical laboratory, social services, nurses' notes, and dietary records. Another method uses an integrated format in which physicians and other health care professionals enter all progress notes in chronological order on one form, rather than in separate sections. This format promotes interdisciplinary collaboration as each discipline can easily see documentation furnished by others (Kiger 2003).

State laws dictate the length of time for which medical records must be stored. The length of time for retaining medical records should also take into consideration the **statute of limitations**, a period prescribed by law within which a legal action can be taken, which varies from one state to another (Bruce 1988).

Purpose of Medical Records

Maintaining complete medical records is critical from several different perspectives:

- coordinating interdisciplinary care
- ensuring continuity of care
- documenting compliance and medical necessity
- providing data to improve care
- recording services rendered

The primary purpose of medical records is to assist caregivers in coordinating services provided to a patient. Individual medical records provide all relevant information on each patient in one place to a diverse group of caregivers. These records help the interdisciplinary caregivers coordinate their efforts.

From the patient's standpoint, the medical record ensures continuity of care because it provides vital information needed by all caregivers. Each caregiver can also see what staff members from the other disciplines may be doing to address patient needs.

Medical records provide documentary evidence of actual care rendered. Regulators and third-party payers rely on the medical records as a basis for determining compliance with requirements. The documentation also forms the basis for payment for services delivered and for evaluating whether the services provided were clinically necessary.

Medical records provide vital information for improving quality and for research.

Attorneys pursuing malpractice cases rely on the medical records to determine whether there were any lapses in care. As part of a facility's defense during litigation proceedings, timely, complete, and accurate medical records are necessary to demonstrate that all reasonable and necessary care was provided. It is important for nursing home administrators to become familiar with the system of medical records used in their facilities. Administrators should review these records as part of their investigation when allegations of lapses in care are made by family members, regulators, or others. Common abbreviations used in patient documentation are listed in Appendix 12-I.

Confidentiality

Protecting the confidentiality of information contained in the medical records is a legal and ethical requirement. A patient has the right to privacy even though he or she does not have the property right to medical records; the facility retains ownership of the record, but the information contained in it belongs to the patient. To protect the records from unauthorized disclosure and use, policies and procedures are necessary to define who has access to medical records and for what purpose the records will be used. At a minimum, these security concerns mean that access to records must be restricted to only those staff members whose responsibilities require them to have this information. Medical-records policies should also cover areas such as release of information, written authorization for release, and disposal of records.

Clearly, sharing a patient's confidential information is necessary among health care professionals involved in the care of that patient. Also, sharing information between health care institutions and providers is necessary for continuity of treatment, particularly when a patient is transferred from one facility to another. With a patient's written authorization medical records may also be released to other parties such as insurance companies, managed care organizations, or the patient's attorney. As a general rule, releasing individual medical information for any purpose other than patient care should only be done with the patient's express written consent. In addition, the patient's authorization must be made with informed consent; the patient must be aware, in a general way, what information will be released and what use will be made of the information. The information released should be strictly limited to that required to fulfill the purpose of the authorization. Authorizations should be retained as a part of the official medical record (Huffman 1990).

Generally, patients have the right of access to their own medical records, but there are some exceptions. Access may not be allowed to minors or to those deemed legally incompetent. When the attending physician makes specific restrictions that access could be detrimental to the patient, access to records may not be allowed (Texas Health Information Management Association 1994).

The Health Insurance Portability and Accountability Act (HIPAA) of 1996 (called the Privacy Rule) requires health care organizations to develop a comprehensive set of policies and procedures that address how patient information is used and disclosed (see Exhibit 3-4). The law applies to health care providers who conduct certain transactions electronically and is designed to protect individually identifiable information on patients. The law requires providers to take reasonable steps to limit the use of, the disclosure of, and the requests for protected health information to the minimum necessary to accomplish the intended purpose, unless the disclosure is for the purposes of medical treatment or is in accordance with the patient's authorization. On the other hand, the Privacy Rule is not intended to impede customary disclosure of records and essential communications among caregivers. However, the facility must have in place reasonable safeguards to protect an individual's privacy. A notice of the facility's privacy practices should be posted, individual copies of this notice should be included in the admissions paperwork, and signatures for the receipt of this notice should be obtained.

INFORMATION SYSTEMS

Information systems are computer-based applications used for transforming raw data into information that can be used in a variety of ways to improve operational efficiencies and the quality of services. Data themselves do not constitute information. Discrete data become information only when the data have been accurately recorded, organized, processed, interpreted, and used. Large quantities of data can be processed by computers to produce summaries and reports that can help employees do their jobs more effectively, and help managers make decisions for improving the operations. Examples include information on patient case-mix, effectiveness of clinical interventions, costs for taking care of different categories of patients, budgetary variances, and marketing. Meaningful information can facilitate instituting managerial controls, making timely decisions, making quality assessments, and delivering improved patient care.

During the 1970s and 1980s, information systems were used primarily to automate and speed up the financial accounting functions such as billings and receivables, payroll, payables, and budgeting. These systems were also used to speed up preparation of financial statements such as income statements and balance sheets. Basic financial information systems were expanded to produce routine management reports to facilitate operational controls. Such reports included summaries of payables to help management identify unauthorized payments to vendors. Different types of reports also help management to study labor-hour use and overtime in order to control labor costs; to monitor aging of accounts receivables to identify and collect past due accounts; and to control costs using budget variances. Illustrations of these reports are included in Chapter 16.

Since the 1990s, information-system applications have been expanded into clinical areas such as patient assessment, care-planning, progress notes, and quality improvement. Related applications include other internal functions such as staff scheduling, menu planning and food ordering, inventory management, activity planning, and preventive maintenance scheduling. Information systems can also be used to manage the facility's marketing program and to keep track of inquiries, follow-up, and admissions generated from inquiries. Finally, electronic communications by e-mail and messaging have become commonplace because of their superior efficiency.

Integrated Networks

Griffith (1995) suggested that not every computer application is part of an information system. An application becomes part of an information system when the information is integrated to provide immediate electronic access. Integrated information systems go a step beyond the functions described in the previous section. These systems are designed to integrate multiple functions and provide multiple users access to the same information. Several examples can be given to illustrate how integrated information systems can support more efficient management planning and decision-making:

Staffing: Integrated systems can enable the facility to incorporate absenteeism and turnover patterns into staff scheduling to minimize understaffing. Staff turnover patterns can be projected to determine future hiring and training needs. Clinical information can be incorporated to determine the appropriate staffing levels and skill-mix needed in

accordance with the overall patient acuity levels represented by the facility's case-mix. Using this information, the system can produce staff schedules. Chapter 14 includes the working details on nursing staff planning using patient case-mix and staff skill-mix.

Capital budgeting: Preventive maintenance and repair history can be used for forecasting future capital needs for equipment replacement. Such information can help the administrator decide at what point it makes better financial sense to replace equipment than to repair it.

Quality improvement: Data pertaining to a variety of clinical outcomes, such as infections, falls, and medication errors, can be analyzed to better understand their causes and to propose actions for minimizing negative outcomes. Standardized clinical practice guidelines can be integrated with assessment and care plans to improve care delivery. **Clinical practice guidelines** are protocols based on research and expert opinion for patient care delivery in specifically identified areas needing clinical intervention, such as falls reduction, pain management, prevention of pressure ulcers, and incontinence care. Development and use of these guidelines are an important step toward ensuring high-quality nursing home care.

Operational budgeting: Historical data on census patterns, associated revenues, and costs can be automatically retrieved to project future budget needs.

Marketing: Data on inquiries, follow-up, and admissions can be analyzed to determine the type of patients the facility is admitting in terms of pay types and acuity levels. The system can also help identify the major sources of referral and determine why certain patients may have selected other facilities.

National data: Comparison of a facility's operations with state and national benchmarks will become increasingly common. To some extent, national databases compiled by the Centers for Medicare and Medicaid Services (CMS) are already being used by consumers, consumer advocates, providers, and researchers. Integrated care will be the next step. Centralized data from the Resident Assessment Instrument (RAI—see Chapter 8), for example, may help one day to coordinate long-term care services along the continuum of care that would include home care, custodial care, skilled nursing care, and mental health services. The On-line Survey Certification and Reporting (OSCAR) system is a national database of certification deficiencies and other information collected during facility surveys. One important use of this database is in providing benchmarks on survey defi-

ciencies. For example, CMS now makes available on its Website detailed information on survey results and staffing for every certified nursing home in the U.S. The program, called Nursing Home Compare, reports the date of inspection, the standard that was not met, when the deficiency was corrected, level of harm ranging from least to most, and how many residents were affected. Exhibit 12-1 provides an illustration of survey deficiencies reported in Nursing Home Compare. Exhibit 12-2 provides an illustration of how nursing staff hours are reported.

Posting data daily enables management to have access to timely information that is essential for taking quick corrective action when necessary. Sophisticated software programs can also provide information such as the cost of producing a particular type of service. Such information is necessary for contract negotiations with managed care or VA entities and can also be used for evaluating payoffs from interventions such as new quality initiatives. The efficiency of self-managed work teams (discussed in Chapter 14) can be greatly enhanced by integrated networks because worker teams assume a variety of decision-making and problem-solving responsibilities that are left to management in traditional work settings. Such systems need careful designing because both information shortfalls (too little information) and information overload (excessive information) can prevent the effectiveness of work teams. The quality of information systems has a direct effect on processes and procedures, and on the use of resources (Yeatts and Hyten 1998).

Security Issues

Integrated information networks are fast becoming indispensable, but they also provide critical challenges to the maintenance of security and confidentiality. Administrators must grapple with the critical question of who should have access to what information on the network. For instance, the facility's financial information should not be accessible to everyone who uses a computer terminal in the facility. The system must also have adequate safeguards to prevent tampering with existing data. Some high-profile cases of break-ins by external hackers into computer systems of major U.S. corporations and the government further highlight the need for adequate security measures. Other security issues pertain to the physical security of the equipment. For instance, having back-up records, in case a system is destroyed in a disaster or is vandalized, is essential.

EXHIBIT 12–1

Survey Deficiency Reporting by Medicare

Facility X
Date of inspection: 08/05/2003

1. Give residents proper treatment to prevent new bed (pressure) sores or heal existing bed sores.
   Date of Correction: 01/03/2003
   2 = Minimal harm or potential for actual harm

   Residents Affected: Few   1 **2** 3 4

2. Make sure each resident is being watched and has assistance devices when needed, to prevent accidents.
   Date of Correction: 01/03/2003
   2 = Minimal harm or potential for actual harm

   Residents Affected: Few   1 **2** 3 4

3. Store, cook, and give out food in a safe and clean way.
   Date of Correction: 01/03/2003
   1 = Potential for minimal harm

   Residents Affected: Many   **1** 2 3 4

4. Make sure that the nursing home area is free of dangers that cause accidents.
   Date of Correction: 01/03/2003
   3 = Actual harm

   Residents Affected: Few   1 2 **3** 4

5. Get rid of garbage properly.
   Date of Correction: 09/04/2003
   1= Potential for minimal harm

   Residents Affected: Many   **1** 2 3 4

Source: Nursing Home Compare

EXHIBIT 12-2

Nursing Staff Hours Per Resident Per Day

	Facility X	State Average	National Average
Number of Residents	129	77.9	89
RN Hours per Resident per Day*	0.39	0.7	0.7
LPN/LVN Hours per Resident per Day*	0.72	0.9	0.8
CNA Hours per Resident per Day*	1.64	2.1	2.4
Total Number of Nursing Staff Hours per Resident per Day*	2.75	3.7	3.9

*Hours per resident per day is the average daily work (in hours) given by the entire group of nurses or nursing assistants divided by total number of residents. The amount of care given to each resident varies.
Source: Nursing Home Compare

System Development

Most nursing facilities do not have the resources to employ personnel skilled in information technology, often because the facilities are not large enough. In most cases, facilities must rely solely on outside vendors to meet the needs of their information systems. Numerous vendors specialize in hardware, software, and set-up of local-application networks (LANs) within the facility. Because a turn-key system can be quite expensive, a decision to upgrade existing systems should not be undertaken without careful study and planning. The administrator must first define the objectives of the system in terms of what the system should be able to accomplish. These objectives must specify the level of integration a proposed information system must achieve. Current capabilities should then be evaluated in conjunction with these desired objectives. In some cases, certain upgrades may enable the facility to reach its objectives. In other instances, replacing the existing system may be the best alternative.

Several reputable vendors should be invited to evaluate the current systems and desired objectives and to submit detailed written proposals along with costs. The facility may not be able to purchase a fully integrated system immediately. In that situation, feasibility of future upgrades should be discussed. In any case, making a firm commitment is not advisable without a test run to ensure that the system would indeed accomplish what the facility desires. Finding out what kind of ongoing support and training the vendor provides, and how often the vendor upgrades prod-

ucts to meet changing needs and improve informational efficiency, is also critical. Another important consideration is the system's compatibility with Medicare and Medicaid billing and with clinical data requirements. For instance, the system should enable electronic billings as well as electronic transmission of patient-assessment information. Finally, the system must comply with all applicable laws and regulations.

CONCLUSION

As in other health care settings, nursing homes are moving toward fully automated systems for administrative and clinical records. Information systems were initially designed to facilitate routine processes such as payroll and billings. Increasingly, however, clinical and administrative systems are being integrated to produce sophisticated reports that provide timely information on quality indicators, costs, and other data important for decision making. At some point paperless electronic systems may become the norm. In the meantime, however, privacy and security issues remain to be addressed.

DISCUSSION AND APPLICATION QUESTIONS

1. Why is it important that the petty-cash and patient trust fund be reconciled each month, and that reconciliation be done by someone other than the person responsible for maintaining the funds?
2. A nursing facility's 14-day pay period starts on a Sunday and ends on a Saturday. The following data come from an employee's timecard:

1st week

Sunday	Time in	5:46 a.m.	0.5 hours lunch	Time out	2:35 p.m.
Monday	Time in	5:52 a.m.	0.5 hours lunch	Time out	2:36 p.m.
Tuesday	Blank				
Wednesday	Time in	1:57 p.m.		Time out	3:02 p.m.
Thursday	Time in	5:45 a.m.	0.5 hours lunch	Time out	2:43 p.m.
Friday	Time in	5:56 a.m.	0.5 hours lunch	Time out	3:36 p.m.
Saturday	Time in	6:20 a.m.	0.5 hours lunch	Time out	2:39 p.m.

2nd week

Total hours worked = 39

If the pay rate is $11.36 an hour, the employee should be paid for how many hours for this pay period? What is the gross amount (without deductions) for this pay period?

INTERNET RESOURCES FOR FURTHER LEARNING

American Health Information Management Association (AHIMA): Professional association for health information administrators and health information technicians. The organization also certifies coding associates and specialists and offers certifications in health care privacy and security. http://www.ahima.org/certification/

Nursing Home Compare is accessible through the main Medicare Website http://www.medicare.gov

U.S. Department of Labor. This website provides comprehensive information on the various aspects of the Fair Labor Standards Act, and other payroll and workplace issues such as unemployment compensation. It also provides links to other department agencies such as OSHA. http://www.dol.gov/

REFERENCES

Abramovice, B. 1988. *Long Term Care Administration*. New York: The Haworth Press.

Bruce, J.A.C. 1988. *Privacy and Confidentiality of Health Care Information*. 2nd ed. Chicago: American Hospital Publishing, Inc.

Burger, S.G., B.H.S. Miller, and B.F. Mauney. 1986. *A Guide to Management and Supervision in Nursing Homes*. Springfield, IL: Charles C. Thomas Publisher.

Frew, M.A., and D.R. Frew. 1982. *Medical Office Administrative Procedures*. Philadelphia: F.A. Davis Company.

Griffith, J.R. 1995. *The Well-Managed Health Care Organization*. 3rd ed. Ann Arbor, MI: UPHA Press/Health Administration Press.

Huffman, E.K. 1990. *Medical Record Management*. 9th ed. Berwyn, Illinois: Physicians' Record Company.

Jacksack, S.M. 1998. *Start, Run, and Grow a Successful Small Business*. Riverwoods, IL: CCH Incorporated.

Kiger, L.S. 2003. Content and structure of the medical record. In *Health Information Management: Principles and Organizations for Health Information*

Services (5th ed.), ed. M.A. Skurka, 19–44. San Francisco: Jossey-Bass/John Wiley & Sons, Inc.

Pozgar, G.D. 1992. *Long-Term Care and the Law: A Legal Guide for Health Care Professionals*. Gaithersburg, Maryland: Aspen Publishers, Inc.

Seawell, L.V. 1992. *Introduction to Hospital Accounting*. 3rd ed. Dubuque, Iowa: Kendall/Hunt Publishing Company.

Texas Health Information Management Association. 1994. *Health Record Information Manual*. Texas Health Information Management Association.

Yeatts, D.E., and C. Hyten. 1998. *High-Performing Self-Managed Work Teams*. Thousand Oaks, CA: Sage Publications, Inc.

APPENDIX
12-1

Appendix 12-1 Common abbreviations used in patient documentation

act	before meals
ad lib.	as desired
AMA	against medical advice
A&O	alert and oriented
aq	water
ASS:	assessment
ATC	around the clock
B	both
B&B	bowel and bladder
b.i.d.	twice daily
bin	twice a night
b.i.w.	twice a week
BKA	below knee amputation
BM	bowel movement
BP	blood pressure
BR	bed rest
B.R.	bathroom
b.t.	bedtime
BTW M	between meals
BUE	both upper extremities
CBR	complete bed rest
CHO	carbohydrate
chr	chronic
c/o	complains of
COPD	chronic obstructive pulmonary disease
ct.	count
CV	cardiovascular
CVA	cardiovascular accident
CXR	chest x-ray
d/c	discharged
d.c.	discontinued

Appendix 12-1 continued

decub	decubitus
def	deformity
D.F.A.	difficulty falling asleep
Diab	diabetic
DOB	date of birth
Dx	diagnosis
ELOS	estimated length of stay
end	endurance
ESRD	end stage renal disease
et	and
ETOH	alcohol
EXP	expired
FAM	family
F.B.	foreign body
FBS	fasting blood sugar
Fe	Iron
flds	fluids
Fx	fracture
gt.	drop
gtt.	drops
HBP	high blood pressure
HL	hearing loss
H&P	history and physical
hr	hour
h.s.	at bedtime
Hx	history
I&O	intake and output
IV	intravenous
K	potassium
LBP	lower back pain
lf	left
lg	large
MB	mix well
MI	myocardial infarction
M/S	mental status
NA	not applicable
N/A	no authorization
Na	sodium
NGT	nasogastric tube

Appendix 12-1 continued

NKA	no known allergies
noct	at night
NPO	nothing by mouth
NSC	no significant change
OBS	organic brain syndrome
o.d.	once a day
om	every morning
on	every night
OOB	out of bed
os	mouth
p	after
pc	after meals
PN	pneumonia
po	by mouth
p.p.	after meals
p.r.n.	whenever necessary
pt	patient
PTA	prior to admission
pvt.	private
q	every or each
qam	every morning
qd	every day
qh	every hour
qhs	every bedtime
ql	as much as desired
qn	every night
qod	every other day
q/s	every shift
qw	once a week
ROM	range of motion
Rx	prescription, treatment
SHx	social history
si/sx	signs/symptoms
S/O	standing order
SOS	only if necessary
ss	one-half
Stat	at once
T	temperature
TB	tuberculosis

Appendix 12-1 continued

TF	tube feeding
Tid	three times daily
Tin	three times a night
Tiw	three times a week
T/O	telephone order
T&P	turn and position
TPN	total parenteral nutrition
TPR	temperature, pulse, and respiration
ung	ointment
URI	upper respiratory infection
UTI	urinary tract infection
VS	vital signs
w/	with
W/C	wheelchair
w/o	without
X3	oriented to time, person, and place

PART III

Effective Management and Strategic Action

The structure, processes, and functions discussed in Part II must be effectively managed to create internal organizational strengths. A nursing facility administrator generally inherits both the physical and the human infrastructure when he or she is appointed to take charge of a facility. By effectively managing available resources, the administrator's main objective should be to create maximum value for the patients, the staff, the corporation, and the community. In a nutshell, creating value is the main purpose for which managers are hired. This value creation builds internal organizational strengths needed for accomplishing the organization's strategic objectives, especially when changes in the external environment pose new challenges.

The nursing home administrator accomplishes the facility's objectives by undertaking three main courses of action:

- Directing and supporting the department heads responsible for the major organizational functions discussed in Part II.
- Performing the executive function and key management functions of human resource management, marketing and public relations, financial management, and quality management. This section of the book is devoted to these areas of facility management.

- Carrying out the directives from the governing board or corporate officers.

By overseeing and coordinating the efforts of the operational departments of the facility, the administrator creates an environment in which the multidisciplinary approach to patient care becomes a reality. Providing supportive leadership and direction to the department heads also fosters a work environment in which concerns about the patients' quality of life are paramount, and improvement of clinical quality becomes a major priority. The administrator becomes responsible for the executive and management functions because, with few exceptions, most facilities do not have separate positions of human resource manager, financial officer, marketing director, and quality-assurance coordinator. Thus, a typical nursing home administrator wears several different hats. Governing boards and corporate officers exercise varying degrees of control over the facility and allow varying degrees of autonomy to the administrator. But, regardless of the extent of autonomy, a typical nursing facility administrator is expected to take personal responsibility for the management roles described in the five chapters contained in this section.

CHAPTER 13

Effective Management and Leadership

LEARNING MODULES

1. Three types of executive roles, how they differ, and how they can vary according to the corporate structure.
2. Effective management as a skillful juggling act between managing a business, managing work and workers, and managing the facility in community and society. A model for effective nursing home management.
3. The meaning and purpose of leadership. Attitudes about people and their relationship to leadership styles. Leadership approaches based on task-orientation and person-orientation. Contemporary situational approach to leadership.
4. Implications and application of leadership theories. Link between leadership and strategic thinking.
5. The purpose and role of bureaucracy in effective management. Organizational structure, monitoring, and control as essential elements of bureaucracy. The need to balance leadership and bureaucracy for effective management.
6. Management tools: vision, mission, and values.

continues

7. Management tools: decision-making and strategic analysis.
8. Management tools: effective meetings and conflict management.
9. Management tools: relationship with superiors.
10. Management tools: risk management.

By nature, a nursing facility is a lean organization with a relatively flat hierarchy (see Figure II-1). The layers of management found in many other types of organizations are mostly absent from the organizational structure of a typical nursing facility. A flat structure implies that the nursing home administrator (NHA) has a broader span of administrative responsibilities compared to other types of organizations with a tall hierarchical structure. Administrative responsibilities refer to the day-to-day internal management of the organization. Because numerous decisions must be made for delivering services effectively, the NHA must be closely involved in internal operational details. Hence the NHA must acquire a certain level of expertise in the various departmental functions and processes covered in Part II of this book.

The NHA may also have executive responsibilities, particularly when a nursing facility is managed according to the open system model presented in Chapter 1. The executive responsibilities vary according to the three types of roles discussed in this chapter. However, regardless of the level of responsibility, the administrator must provide leadership and direction to the facility's staff.

The NHA must also adhere to certain policy guidelines in managing the facility. Nursing home policies are largely derived from various laws and regulations. Incorporating laws and regulations into operational policies is a major step toward ensuring compliance with these laws and regulations. In each department, policies and procedures must be revised as new regulations come out and as more effective procedures to deliver services become known. Other operational policies describe the organization's procedures for how certain things must be done. These policies often reflect corporate philosophy and values.

THE EXECUTIVE ROLES

There are three distinct executive roles that characterize the position of a nursing home administrator (NHA):

- the chief executive officer (CEO) role
- the chief operating officer (COO) role
- the administrative officer role.

Although the position encompasses all three roles, which one is predominant depends on the degree of decision-making autonomy given to the administrator by the governing board. The degree of autonomy determines how much authority the administrator will have in the formulation of long-range strategies, major planning decisions, facility policy, and budgets (Figure 13-1). When the administrator is given relatively little autonomy, the governing board exercises a high degree of control over major decisions and the facility's future direction. Low autonomy also suggests that the administrative focus will be primarily on internal operations, and the facility would function mainly as a closed system as opposed to an open system (see Chapter 1).

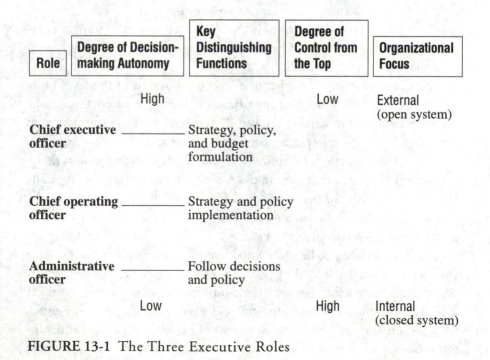

FIGURE 13-1 The Three Executive Roles

Sometimes, a facility's ownership or affiliation may determine how much autonomy the administrator will be given. An owner/administrator who owns the nursing home and also manages it generally functions like the CEO of a small company. In other situations, the owner(s) may have little involvement in the facility's operations and may delegate complete decision-making authority to a CEO administrator appointed to manage the facility. In multifacility corporations, the governing board is mainly composed of corporate officers who generally retain executive authority. But if the corporate officers delegate sufficient responsibility and authority to the administrator, that administrator is likely to adopt the role of a COO. Nearly all nursing facility administrators function in this capacity.

The Roles of CEO and COO

The main difference between the CEO and the COO roles lies in strategy formulation, which is characterized primarily by having the authority to make long-range decisions and to commit resources over a relatively long period in response to major demands from the external environment. In contrast to the CEO role, the COO's role emphasizes strategy implementation, which is to carry out decisions and commitments made by corporate officers. In this sense, the COO role has an internal (implementation) focus, whereas the CEO role has mainly an external (formulation) focus (Griffith and White 2002).

The nursing facility administrator who is employed in the COO role will perform a linking or exchange function with the external environment (as described in Chapters 1 and 2) and relay critical information to superiors, but any strategic decisions are made at the corporate office, where the CEO role is carried out. However, effective organizations invite the administrator to participate in discussions and to help formulate strategy. The administrator is often more knowledgeable than corporate officers about trends and changes occurring within the first three levels of environmental proximity (see Figure 1-4). Corporate officers, on the other hand, are likely to be more knowledgeable about shifts taking place within level four, the secondary proximity (see Chapter 1). Hence, a strategy-making partnership between the administrator and corporate officers is likely to result in effective long-range decisions about the future direction of a nursing facility. Other key areas of decision-making that distinguish between the roles of CEO and COO are the responsibilities these

administrators have in formulating broad administrative policies and in planning annual budgets. The two roles differ according to the degree of involvement the administrator has in formulating the facility's operational policies and establishing its annual budget.

The Administrative Officer Role

A third type of role that could predominate in the administrator's position is akin to that of an administrative officer. Of the three different role types described here, the administrative-officer role gives the least decision-making authority to the administrator who, for the most part, is expected to carry out the decisions, policies, or specific directives handed down by the corporate officers. The administrator's position is highly structured, and the corporate officers exercise tighter controls over the facility's operations than they do over facilities with administrators who perform the roles of CEO or COO.

THE EFFECTIVE ADMINISTRATOR

Effective NHAs come in all shapes and sizes; the only thing they have in common is the ability to get things done (Drucker 1985). Regardless of the executive role assigned by the parent corporation or governing board, the administrator should function as the general manager of a nursing facility. Without effective management, a nursing facility can quickly fall into chaos. Applying the manager's tasks described by Drucker (1974) to the NHA position, the administrator must find the right balance between three management domains:

- managing a business
- managing work and workers
- managing the facility in community and society

A balance among the three is necessary because "a decision or action that satisfies a need in one of these functions by weakening performance in another weakens the whole enterprise" (Drucker 1974, p. 398). Thus, effective management becomes a skillful juggling act; it requires expertise in various management disciplines and employs the open system approach. Figure 13-2 provides a full model of effective nursing home management.

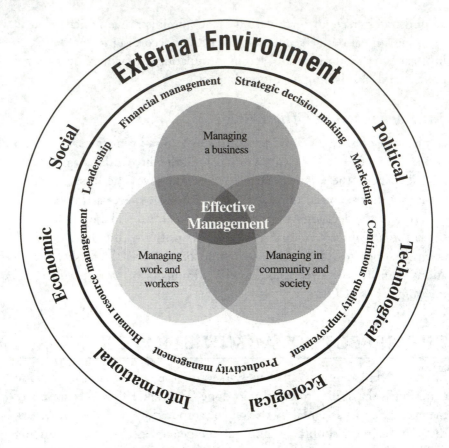

FIGURE 13-2 A Model for Effective Nursing Home Management

Managing a Business

Here, the term "business" is used in the sense of economic performance (Drucker 1974), which is not confined to for-profit operations only. The essence of business management lies in using resources in a manner that adds value, that is, worth as perceived by the facility's key stakeholders. By adding value, an organization produces a far greater good for the consumers of services, for the employees, and for society at large than what is inherently contained in the resources themselves. In this broad sense, the term "business" is also applied to non-profit and public (government-owned) entities. The added value that society expects from a nursing facility is affordable patient care that meets certain generally agreed-upon standards of quality. Even though what is "affordable" and what

constitutes "agreed-upon standards of quality" are not clearly defined, taken together these terms mean that a nursing facility must satisfy the patients, their families, and the payers. Because the payers include those who pay the facility directly on a private-pay basis or those who pay premiums to purchase private long-term care insurance, as well as government payers—mainly Medicare and Medicaid—who pay indirectly out of taxes levied on citizens, society as a whole has expectations that nursing facilities achieve the twin goals of affordability and quality. These expectations from both the consumer and the larger society hold true regardless of whether a facility's ownership structure is for-profit, nonprofit, or public.

Managing Work and Workers

One of the essential functions of management is to make work productive (Drucker 1974). Here the term **productivity** is equivalent to value creation. Productivity incorporates quality as a major output that results from the use of resources over which management has control. Productivity maximizes quality for each unit of resources used in delivering health care. Thus, effective management aims to deliver quality at an affordable cost.

In order to make work productive, managers must first understand what work needs to be done and how to organize it. The entire Part II of this book is devoted to understanding and organizing various tasks necessary for effective patient-care delivery. All departments in a nursing home either provide direct hands-on patient care or provide essential support services, without which quality cannot be achieved and maintained. To deliver services effectively, organizing work and workers into functional departments and positions, as illustrated in Figure II-1, is the first step. As discussed in previous chapters, a nursing home's size is an important factor to consider how the various functions are organized.

A second and often a more difficult task in achieving productivity is building a cooperative spirit among the workers through leadership and motivation. This second task is difficult because every worker in the organization "is a unique individual, and treatment that will work effectively with one may prove disastrous when meted out to another" (McCarthy 1978, p. 37). The challenge for the effective administrator lies in creating a workplace environment in which each person contributes his or her best efforts toward goals that are important to management. The

effective administrator understands that if work and workers are misman-
aged, organizational performance will suffer no matter how good the
administrator may be in managing the business side of the operation
(Drucker 1974). To increase productivity, an organization must create
value for its employees. Because employees constitute a major resource
input, the rewards they receive in the form of wages, benefits, personal
satisfaction, self-esteem, and individual development must at least be
commensurate with what they bring to the organization.

Managing the Facility in Community and Society

In Drucker's words, "None of our institutions exists by itself and is an end
in itself. Every one is an organ of society and exists for the sake of society . . .
Institutions must be part of the community . . . Mismanaging social
impacts eventually will destroy society's support for the enterprise and
with it the enterprise as well" (Drucker 1974, p. 41–43). From this perspective, the effective administrator must frequently evaluate whether the
facility is making positive strides in connecting with the community and
whether it is adequately discharging its responsibility toward society.
Much of the Part I of this book is devoted to helping the administrator
understand this key managerial responsibility.

APPROACH TO EFFECTIVE MANAGEMENT

Having explained the model for effective management, this section discusses the approach necessary for carrying out the three main tasks presented in the previous section. The approach is based on a good foundation of leadership and bureaucracy. These two terms distinguish between
two separate concepts that many authors call leadership and management.

Leadership

The Meaning and Purpose of Leadership

Leadership can be defined as influencing people to act for certain goals
that represent the values and motivations—wants, needs, aspirations, and
expectations—of both leaders and followers (Burns 1998). Although it

can have many different meanings, Northouse (2001, 3) concluded that four main components are central to leadership:

- Leadership is a process that requires continuity. It is also interactive and involves give-and-take between the leader and followers.
- Leadership affects the followers. The essence of leadership is to influence others.
- Leadership occurs within a group or "people" context. Leadership finds its meaning in relation to other people because the need for leadership dissipates when there are no people to be led. Leaders use their influence to direct people toward a common purpose.
- Leadership involves goal attainment. Leaders direct their energies toward individuals who are trying to achieve something together.

The following words on leadership have been ascribed to the Chinese philosopher Lao Tse, who lived in the 5th century B.C.:

A leader is best when people barely know that he exists,
Not so good when people obey and acclaim him,
Worst when they despise him.
Fail to honor people, they fail to honor you.
But, of a good leader, who talks little,
When his work is done, his aim fulfilled,
They will say, "We did it ourselves."

The entire process of leadership is people-focused. Hence, "the signs of outstanding leadership appear primarily among the followers. Are the followers reaching their potential? Are they learning? Are they devoted to serving? Do they achieve the desired results" (DePree 1998, p. 130)?

Leadership Attitudes and Styles

In management theory, much has been written about leadership styles that explain how leaders think and act when managing workers. Leaders' behaviors emanate from their general attitudes and assumptions about workers. To explain management behavior, Douglas McGregor (1906–1964) proposed two models known as Theory X and Theory Y, which present two contrasting assumptions leaders make about workers. According to Theory X, leaders assume that:

- Workers are lazy
- They dislike work and responsibility

- They will avoid work if not closely supervised
- They are indifferent to organizational needs and goals

Traditional leadership was based on theory X and thus focused on monitoring and controlling people in the organization in an effort to make them obey management's orders or face negative consequences. Theory X assumptions lead to task-oriented behaviors on the part of leaders, as opposed to relationship-oriented behaviors; such leaders will have a tendency to adopt a directive style (Figure 13-3). Directive leadership can be characterized as take-charge, one-directional, and single-handed decision-making by the leader. Directive leadership involves giving orders, establishing goals and methods of evaluation, setting time lines, defining roles, and establishing methods and processes for achieving the organization's goals (Northouse 2001, 57).

In what McGregor called Theory Y, leaders have the opposite attitudes toward workers:

- Workers want to take responsibility
- They like challenging work
- They desire opportunities for personal development
- They want to help achieve organizational goals

Leaders who espouse a Theory Y perspective are likely to adopt relationship-oriented behaviors and will be inclined to use a participative or a delegative style of leadership (Figure 13-3). This relationship orientation results in supportive behaviors in which open communications, listening, praising, asking for input, and giving feedback are important (Northouse 2001, 58). The main characteristic of participative style is involving other people in decision making and giving their ideas due consideration. The

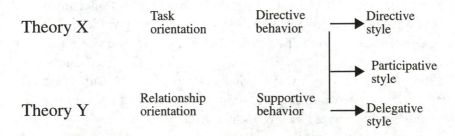

FIGURE 13-3 Relationship between Leadership Attitudes, Behaviors, and Styles

leader may present ideas and invite feedback from workers, or solicit new ideas from staff members. In the delegative style, leaders derive considerable satisfaction from giving decision-making responsibilities to their staffs (Brody 2000).

In the mid-20th century, several independent research studies resulted in two-dimensional models of leadership comprising task-orientation (also called production-orientation, or initiating structure, depending on the source) on one end of a continuum, and relationship-orientation (also called person-orientation, or consideration, depending on the source) at the other end. The main contribution of the two-dimensional theory has been in highlighting that leadership is not necessarily a dichotomous phenomenon, and that leaders could be oriented toward both tasks and people. Accordingly, Blake and Mouton (1964) proposed a managerial grid in which each leader could be rated on both task-orientation and person-orientation and be classified into one of five leadership styles (Figure 13-4):

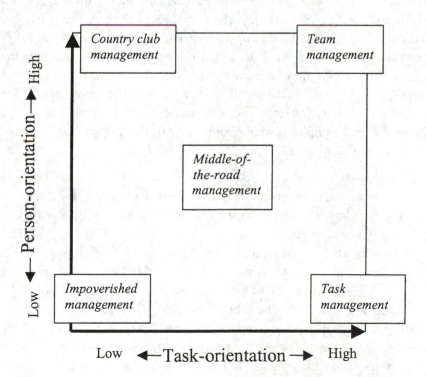

FIGURE 13-4 Blake and Mouton's Managerial Grid and Leadership Styles

Impoverished management. Characterized by low task-orientation and low person-orientation, these leaders remain hands-off and aloof.

Task management. These leaders are highly task-oriented. They are mainly concerned with getting work done and have minimal concern for people.

Country-club management. These leaders rate very high on person-orientation. They are concerned mainly with creating a pleasant and harmonious working environment and have little concern for accomplishing tasks.

Team management. These leaders value their workers and solicit their participation in goal-setting, decision-making, and task accomplishment.

Middle-of-the-road management. These leaders seek the middle ground and try to balance productivity with worker satisfaction.

Contemporary management theories recognize that leadership styles must fit the situation. Different situations demand different styles, and to be effective, leaders must change their styles according to the situation. Conceptually, this situational approach is similar to Blake and Mouton's managerial grid model. Instead of using task-orientation and person-orientation, the two dimensions in the situational model are directive and supportive behaviors. A leader will apply an appropriate measure of each as dictated by the competence and commitment of each worker or group. Situational leadership thus matches the style to the development level of subordinates (Northouse 2001, 57, 58) [Figure 13-5]:

Directing style, characterized by high directive-low supportive behavior, is appropriate when the development level of a subordinate or group is low. The leader focuses on giving specific instructions and engages in close supervision.

Coaching style, characterized by high directive-high supportive behavior, is useful when the development level of a subordinate or group is moderate to low. The style requires focusing on goals while soliciting input from the subordinate and giving encouragement.

Supporting style, characterized by low directive-high supportive behavior, is useful when the development level of a subordinate or group is moderate to high. In this approach, the leader uses supportive behaviors that bring out the employee's skills. The subordinate is given flexibility in routine decisions, and the leader is available for

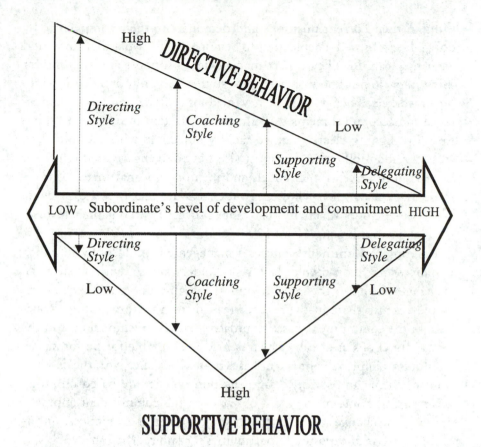

FIGURE 13-5 Situational Leadership Model

consultation as needed. Listening, praising, asking for input, and giving feedback are commonly employed.

Delegating style is characterized by low directive-low supportive behavior. The delegating leader lessens his or her involvement in planning, control, and goal clarification. Once agreement is reached on what must be done, the subordinate or group takes responsibility for getting the job done.

Implications of Leadership Theories

Today, success in achieving high performance depends on building a deep sense of commitment among employees, not obedience extracted by threats. A basic premise of leadership is the belief that most people want to achieve success in their own careers: They want to accomplish some-

thing in their current positions and demonstrate their competence by doing their jobs well. People want to be respected for what they know and what they can do. They expect management's support and training for things they do not know or cannot do so they can grow and develop into better workers. They want to be rewarded for their demonstrated competence and accomplishments. An effective leader taps into people's aspirations by aligning clearly defined facility objectives with the followers' areas of responsibility. Leaders must direct but also engage their followers. Leaders must serve as role models and mentors, not martinets. "Leaders must try to make their fellow constituents aware that they are all stakeholders in a conjoint activity that cannot succeed without their involvement and commitment" (Gini 1998).

Building commitment requires a management philosophy in which employees are considered key stakeholders along with customers, exchange partners, the public, and the regulators. As stakeholders, employees also share in the rewards reaped from the organization's success. In the commitment-based approach each organizational unit in the facility functions as a team which is held accountable for performance. Continuous improvement is emphasized, in accordance with the expectations of clients and society. Compensation policies are based on group achievement. Some of the main obstacles to the commitment approach are the slow change in management philosophies and practices, uncertainty, and fear of exposure to possibilities for failure (Walton 1992).

Leadership and Strategic Thinking

As a leader, the administrator sets a direction for the entire facility. Setting a direction means aligning internal organizational resources with the demands of the external environment (Figure 13-2). Setting a direction also means anticipating how those demands may change in the future and preparing changes that can be foreseen. This flexibility is what strategic thinking is all about. The desired direction is articulated in an expressed long-range vision and in strategic objectives. Vision and strategic objectives describe a facility "in terms of what it should become over the long term and articulate a feasible way of achieving this goal" (Kotter 1992, p. 104). Nothing mystical is involved in developing a good business direction. Visions and strategies do not have to be brilliantly innovative; they do, generally, have an almost mundane quality, usually consisting of ideas that are already well known. What is sometimes new is the particular combination or pattern of these ideas

(Kotter 1992). Finally, visions and strategies have to be realistic. For example, when a facility that has been a struggling competitor suddenly envisions becoming number one it is espousing a pipe dream, not a vision.

As a first step toward their accomplishment, the vision and objectives must be clearly defined and communicated to the department heads and other key personnel. These key staff members should be included in charting out a course for accomplishing the vision and objectives. The planned course must specify exactly what each department is expected to achieve in order for the facility to realize the vision and objectives.

Bureaucracy

Bureaucracy is generally viewed in a pejorative way. People often think of a bureaucracy as an organization that is impersonal, inflexible, unwieldy, and inefficient. People think of bureaucrats as managers who are unresponsive to clients, impose excessive controls, and use power without being held accountable for its effects. Hence, it may come as a surprise that bureaucracy is actually an essential ingredient for effective management. The characteristics just stated have become unfortunate stereotypes. In fact, bureaucracy is essential to instill order and discipline in an organization that may otherwise become chaotic. Bureaucracy minimizes ambiguity and is necessary for monitoring and control purposes. But bureaucracy focuses on controlling the structures and processes described in Part II, not on controlling or manipulating people. Well-managed bureaucracies create interdependent relationships within an organization by emphasizing the performance of all parts and all members of the system. These systems are also necessary for measuring and improving quality (Ross et al. 2002, 232).

Emphasis on vision and strategy in the previous section may create the impression that an effective administrator must constantly change things around within the facility. But an obsession with change is dysfunctional. Even an otherwise fitting response to a stimulus in the external environment should not be pursued if it puts the stability of the organization in serious jeopardy. Effective management is not so much to promote change as to know when to do so. The trick is to manage within a given strategic orientation most of the time, yet be able to pick out the occasional discontinuity that really matters (Mintzberg 1989). Thus, a response to external change is essential; however, effective management is mainly about managing stability and making the organization as effective as possible in doing what it is designed to do. In a nutshell, it is about finding what works and

doing it well. Consistently pursuing this objective institutionalizes excellence and places the organization in an enviable position to respond to well-studied change when change is necessary to enhance value.

Stability begins with a formal structure of authority and responsibility. The formal structure is depicted in an organizational chart, which illustrates the lines of authority commonly referred to as the chain of command (see Figure II-1). An organizational chart should include every position in the facility to show where employees can go when they need answers. Within the formal structure, members are granted authority over certain functions, held accountable for certain results, and given incentives for achieving those results (Griffith and White 2002). Part II of this book provides an overview of the formal structures and functions necessary for effective delivery of services to nursing-home clients. The primary task of the administrator is to ensure that these structures function smoothly as a coordinated system and deliver services according to pre-established expectations and standards. This task is what the monitoring and control functions of management should accomplish.

Smooth operation of the system requires that goals are explicitly formulated, rules are followed, policies guide action, and procedures facilitate task performance. Formulating goals, rules, policies, and procedures is a management responsibility. These elements should be designed to promote discipline, consistency, reliability, predictability, stability, and efficiency. Ongoing training and developing a culture of excellence instill stability and consistency that clients and exchange partners can rely on. In this manner, what the various departments of a facility do becomes routine and standardized. The managerial challenge is to maintain consistency by monitoring compliance with the formulated goals, rules, policies, and procedures. Managers must evaluate operations and improve processes to maintain standardized routines.

The formal structures discussed here do not effectively perform on their own. They need management and direction; clarification of ambiguities; mediation and harmonizing when conflicts arise; adjustment if certain roles falter because of absenteeism, turnover, and planned absences; and routine performance of administrative tasks discussed in subsequent chapters.

Balance Between Leadership and Bureaucracy

Both leadership and bureaucracy are essential for effectively managing a long-term care facility. Bureaucracy provides the framework within which

the administrator exercises leadership. It was stated earlier that a critical challenge for effective management lies in creating a workplace environment in which all staff members contribute their best efforts toward organizational goals. A balance between leadership and bureaucracy is necessary for meeting this challenge. Some key ideas on creating a productive environment have been discussed earlier. Kelley (1998) offers additional practical thoughts on how to create environments in which exemplary followers are likely to flourish:

- Remove roadblocks to productivity by shielding the followers from excessive bureaucratic demands that may interfere with getting real work done. Workers must fill out papers and reports and attend meetings, but such demands can be overdone.
- Workers should be left alone to do their jobs and kept free of constant interruptions from administration. Facility administrators can keep their fingers on the pulse but also promote self-management, because most workers want to manage themselves.
- Participative management is fine, but most workers want to be involved only in decisions that affect them. Above all, exemplary workers are not interested in knowing the trivia about the leaders' jobs or their personal lives.
- Although workers want to manage themselves, the administrator must make sure that the various departments' efforts come together. An important aspect of administrative responsibility is to fill any chasms between departments and to promote interdependencies that will enhance the value of the services delivered.
- People are interested in knowing what outcomes their efforts have produced. Similarly, the value added by the synergistic use of interdependencies should be disclosed to workers to promote ongoing cooperation between departments.

TOOLS FOR EFFECTIVE MANAGEMENT

Leadership and bureaucracy provide the foundations for effective management. In this section, some of the main tools of effective management are discussed. These tools provide the necessary means for planning, for converting plans into actions, and for day-to-day administration of the facility.

Vision and Mission

How does the administrator, and for that matter the other members of the organization, know that a certain course is indeed the right direction for a nursing facility? Leadership itself must be channeled toward achieving certain purposes, which should be clearly defined in formal statements. Operating an organization without a clearly defined vision and mission is like navigating in the open seas without a compass.

The vision and mission comprise an organization's guiding philosophy (Collins and Porras 1998). Although much has been written about vision and mission, a lack of clarity still persists about what they are. In terms of focus, a vision is about the organization, whereas a mission is about key stakeholders, particularly the customers and the community. The purpose of a **vision** is to clarify what an organization should become. This vision is a compelling picture of how an organization will look and function when its main objectives are achieved (Ciampa and Watkins 1999). Organizational vision often starts with the administrator, but it remains fluid and dynamic. Interactions with the facility's staff, families, corporate officers, and external stakeholders bring in additional inputs for refining and clarifying the vision.

The **mission** is derived from and is closely connected to the vision. However, the mission emphasizes the benefits that would accrue to patients and their families, employees, and the community as the organization goes about the business of achieving its vision. An organization's mission defines its basic purpose and enunciates why the organization exists. A nursing home's mission statement should incorporate its distinct competencies, its clients' needs, and its relationship to the community. Exhibit 13-1 provides an example of a mission statement.

Accomplishing the vision and mission is not just a leadership activity. Organizational purposes and direction must be widely shared within the organization. A turning point occurs when the staff begin to share the vision of what can be accomplished and to put their energies behind it (Ross et al. 2002, 49).

Values

The way in which the members of a facility collectively think about what they do, and how they relate to patients, families, and coworkers, is based on certain beliefs and assumptions. Individuals have personal beliefs and

EXHIBIT 13-1

Example of a Mission Statement

We pledge uncompromising dedication to excellence in helping older adults grow in spirit, live with a sense of fulfillment, experience dignity, and meet the challenges of their changing lives.

We aspire to be consistent in our quality of care, distinctive in our approach, outstanding in performance, and to provide leadership in the field of service to older adults.

We welcome others who will join us in pursuit of our mission.

values, which guide their thinking and behaviors in various social settings, including work. Such individual beliefs and values are likely to permeate the workplace in a sort of conflicting network unless the administrator clearly defines and communicates the core values on which the facility will base all its decisions, judgments, and actions.

Values constitute principles and ideologies "held sacred" by an organization. Organizational values underscore the moral principles by which the organization will be governed as it goes about the business of realizing its vision and mission. Once the values have been defined and communicated, they are viewed by the stakeholders as standards that define the attitudes and philosophies according to which the members of the organization can be expected to behave. Administrators and corporate officers should develop a set of values that are relevant to the institutional delivery of long-term care. These values should be communicated to all members of the organization, and, more importantly, should be espoused in routine conduct and decisions. As examples, some of the relevant core values are:

- Respect: How administration and staff members are expected to treat coworkers, clients, and other stakeholders.
- Honesty: How administration and staff members will conduct their affairs so that their ethics are beyond reproach.
- Openness: What information the stakeholders can expect facility administration to share with them.
- Fairness: How administration and staff members will conduct their affairs to promote equality and justice.

- Quality: How quality is defined, and how it will be incorporated into the services provided.
- Economic gain: Articulation of why profits are important, and how the rewards of success will be shared with relevant stakeholders.

When these values are clearly defined, communicated, and integrated into decision-making and actions they become, over time, the main driving force of an organization's culture.

Organizational values also play a vital role in hiring key members of staff. Besides considering a potential jobseeker's qualifications and other desired characteristics, the jobseeker's values should match those of the facility. Dissonance occurs when employees' values are incompatible with those of the organization, and this mismatch creates cultural discord. A discord in values can eventually lead to dissatisfaction and turnover, which in turn create organizational instability (Singh and Schwab 1998). There can be substantial difference in core values among facilities operated under for-profit, non-profit, and public ownerships. Recent business literature affirms that matching of values is a critical factor in achieving organizational success. For example, studies by Fernández and Hogan (2002) concluded that "the most effective CEOs were those whose values were most like those of the firm, rather than those who had the greatest knowledge of the firm's industry (p. 26)." The lesson here is that governing boards must take into account a candidate's core values when hiring NHAs. Similarly, candidates seeking NHA positions should try to discover the organization's values by asking appropriate questions during the job interview, and evaluate the organization's values against their own values to see whether a good match exists.

Decision Making

Decisions are made by people at all levels in an organization, and decisions made at lower ranks are not necessarily less important than those made by the NHA. Decisions made at lower levels can have a major effect on whether a facility meets its objectives in delivering the desired quality of patient care. The main differences between decisions made by lower-level employees and those made by the administrator are in the quantity and complexity of decisions, in their strategic or tactical significance, and in the processes used for making them. One of the administrator's major responsibilities is to make decisions that are in the best interest of the

facility and its main stakeholders. These decisions often require the context of the "big picture," which keeps in view the entire facility, its relationships between departments, its relationship between the facility and the corporation, and its relationship between the facility and its stakeholders. Decisions at lower levels are routine and are guided by goals, rules, policies, and procedures established within the bureaucracy to facilitate decision-making. When the goals, rules, policies, and procedures are aligned with the facility's vision and mission and encompass its organizational values, the facility has taken the first major step toward achieving desired decision-making by workers at lower ranks in the facility. Desired decisions are those that contribute to accomplishing the facility's goals, vision, and mission. The second major step is for the administrator to provide leadership. The third step is monitoring compliance with the goals, rules, policies, and procedures.

Decision-making is commonly defined as choosing from among different alternatives. Problem-solving also requires decision-making although not all decisions involve problem-solving. The alternatives a decision-maker considers must be relevant to actions needed to accomplish certain desired objectives. Deciding on what objectives ought to be achieved by the facility is a primary managerial responsibility. Next, the administrator "makes the objectives effective by communicating them to the people whose performance is needed to attain them" (Drucker 1974, p. 400). The processes followed by executives for setting objectives, for exploring different alternatives for achieving the objectives, and for selecting from among stated alternatives often involve a rather complex interplay of facts, opinions, judgments, and dissenting views, as well as consensus. These factors are carefully weighed by the administrator to arrive at a decision. In some cases it may be important to seek consensus. In other instances the administrator would encourage people's input but make the final decision. Regardless of how the final decision is made, suggestions about possible alternatives as well as information and opinions provided by participants are valuable. An explanation of how and why a particular decision was made may help people understand that their thoughts and views were valued.

The administrator should always be aware that the decision-making process may be tainted with personal biases. Personal biases are not always easy to acknowledge. People's opinions and judgments incorporate biases that may emanate from their own value systems, past experiences, likes and dislikes, and emotions.

Intuition generally plays a role in decision-making, because few ideas are subject to factual analysis. Informed opinions and judgments must therefore be taken into account. On the other hand, data-driven decision-making can help reevaluate old assumptions or challenge conventional wisdom. Certain decisions require analysis of facts, such as a careful recounting of events as they had occurred, official interpretation of a regulation, information on what competitors are doing, or data on the facility's financial performance. Whereas organizational bureaucracy supports conventional decision-making, sometimes organizations must stray from the norms and look for the "wild card" when making decisions on key issues. The wild card is the instinct for the right time to act—or not to act—in spite of data that indicate the contrary. Taking some risk and acting according to unconventional approaches can stimulate organizational innovation (Ross et al. 2002, 235).

The principal criterion for weighing alternatives is the consequences a particular course of action is likely to produce. Another key factor that must be considered while evaluating alternatives is the feasibility of implementation. Sometimes the best alternative has to be rejected because resources needed for its implementation are not available, or that it may be too costly to implement, or that it may not fit the schedule for action.

Once a decision has been made, it must be implemented. Finally, its progress and outcomes must be evaluated to determine whether the desired objective is being reached. Figure 13-6 presents a general model for decision-making and problem-solving. Rational decision-making, as opposed to intuitive decision-making, is a systematic process that begins with carefully evaluating the status of a given situation and articulating what is desired. Objectives are set in terms of what must be achieved. Generally, all possible alternatives are considered and examined for their feasibility in achieving an objective with present resources at minimal cost. Sometimes, additional resources are necessary for achieving an objective. The chosen alternative is implemented by clarifying what steps will be taken, who will do what, and deciding on how progress will be monitored. Managerial **control** involves monitoring progress, evaluating results against the objective, assessing deviations, and taking corrective action.

Strategic Analysis

A **strategy** is a decision that defines the nursing facility's future direction in response to changes in the external environment. Undertaking a major

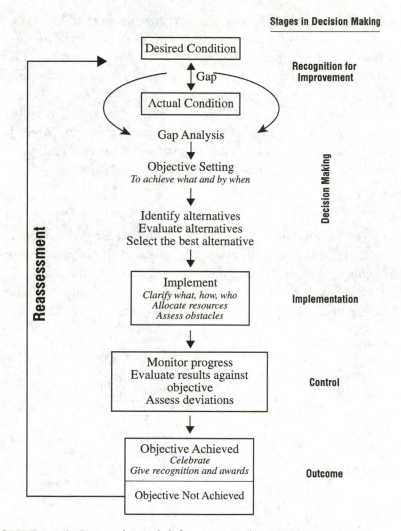

FIGURE 13-6 General Model for Rational Decision-making/ Problem-solving

renovation project, starting an adult day-care center in the facility or discontinuing an existing one, expanding into residential care, acquiring another nursing facility, and decertifying a section of the facility from participation in Medicare/ Medicaid in order to concentrate on private-pay clients are all examples of strategy. Clearly, all such decisions are associated with varying degrees of risk.

Strategy development requires analyzing and visualizing the external environment with the aim of recognizing threats and opportunities for

the organization. A SWOT (or TOWS) framework (Figure 13-7) is a useful tool that allows a simultaneous evaluation of the facility's internal strengths (S) and weaknesses (W) against external opportunities (O) and threats (T). Compared to a weak organization, a strong organization is better equipped to take advantage of new opportunities and confront evolving threats. For example, an organization that is struggling to improve its mediocre quality of services or has other internal operational problems should not consider new opportunities for expanding current operations or launching a new service.

Effective Meetings

Meetings are an essential tool for management because they promote participation and personal interaction. Open-ended discussion of issues is often richer and more creative than isolated thought and action (Ware 1992). Meetings can be a valuable tool when important information must be disseminated to people, particularly when personal interaction such as

Internal

	Strengths	Weaknesses
Opportunities	*Evaluate opportunities to pursue*	*Strengthen internal operations to prepare for future opportunities*
Threats	*Evaluate threats and develop action plan to minimize their impact*	*Strengthen internal operations to overcome current and potential threats*

FIGURE 13-7 The SWOT (TOWS) Framework for Strategic Analysis and Action

asking questions by the recipients of information or gauging people's reactions are important to managers. Announcement of some change that may have a significant effect on others is better handled in a meeting than it is through written communication. Sometimes information is personally conveyed because of its symbolic value, such as achievement of a major goal by the facility. Similarly, a meeting can be an effective avenue for reinforcing the organization's essential values, mission, and broad organizational objectives (Brody 2000, 250).

Meetings are also essential when input from others is considered vital for decision-making or problem-solving. Such meetings may be either for the purpose of information exchange or for actually making a group decision. Problem-solving meetings provide an opportunity to combine the knowledge and skills of several people at once, and participants are selected on the basis of their potential for contributions (Brody 2000). Generally, information exchange and problem-solving should not be combined in the same meeting (Ware 1992). Other meetings may be routine; in such meetings "keeping in touch" on a regular basis is valued by the participants. Department-head meetings generally fall in this latter category, although they are also used for keeping members abreast of any changes, discussion of operational issues, and information exchange.

Whenever people get together as a group, some socializing and casual exchanges occur naturally. On the other hand, meetings must also accomplish their predefined purpose. This purpose may be clear to the administrator, but it must also be communicated to the participants well before the meeting. Open-ended meetings often have a tendency to drift along almost endlessly without accomplishing much of anything. Even informal meetings can be given a sense of direction by having an agenda, which may or may not be formally written. An agenda helps the administrator focus on the meeting's purpose, and it provides a plan that helps sort out relevant and irrelevant topics during the discussions. Another effective technique is to distribute ahead of time an annotated meeting agenda called a docket. A **docket** differs from an ordinary agenda in that the docket lists not only the items to be discussed but also provides pertinent explanations and details for each item. By saving time, a docket can be effectively used to cover a number of items in a short time (Brody 2000).

Irrelevant topics may slip in during a meeting. The administrator should patiently listen to see if the discussion has relevance to the meeting and may even ask about how the topic is related to the main issues under

discussion. If the topic is not relevant, the administrator must tactfully steer participants back to the main topic.

Every meeting with a clear purpose behind it needs some preparation. Planning an agenda is the first step. Along with communicating the purpose of the meeting to the participants, the participants should also be asked if they wish to place anything on the docket. Once the agenda is established, preparation for a meeting requires collecting relevant information. The administrator should also think about how the information will be communicated, whether it will be communicated verbally, on a flip chart or chalkboard, in a handout, or using Powerpoint. If information from other participants is required, they should be notified ahead of time and clearly advised as to what exactly they should bring to the meeting. At other times, it may be necessary for all participants to review certain information before they come to the meeting. In that case, the materials should be delivered to participants well before the meeting so they have a chance to prepare.

Before a meeting ends, clarifying what happens next is important. All items requiring follow-up should be reviewed. If certain individuals have responsibility for following up on something, that responsibility should be clarified along with any time schedules by which certain actions ought to be taken. If a follow-up meeting is necessary, it should be scheduled there and then (Ware 1992).

The administrator is also likely to be involved in meetings with external stakeholders. In such meetings, the administrator should keep in mind a clear purpose but be willing and open to new ideas and face reality, ask questions, and explain value, provided that the facility can deliver value. In seeking to establish new linkages with external stakeholders, the first contact is usually exploratory. The purpose of the first contact is often to exchange information and ideas with the objective of finding some common ground that will provide the basis for establishing a win-win relationship for both the facility and the external stakeholders. Based on the initial findings, further exchanges are made if both parties see the potential for engaging in a more formal relationship of mutual benefit.

Conflict Management

Conflict is unpleasant, but it is an unavoidable aspect of an organization. Conflict is often dysfunctional to the organization, but it can also be

functional if it stimulates innovation and adaptability. Conflict can be psychologically healthy for people when it enables them to vent frustrations in a constructive manner. Conflict in society may initiate conditions for social change by challenging the status quo (Hatch 1997). However, conflict taken to its extreme can result in unwanted hostilities, violence, or other destructive behavior. According to modern organizational theory, too little conflict can lead to unhealthy conformance, poor decision-making, and stagnation, whereas too much conflict can lead to uncooperative behavior, loss of productivity, turf battles, and sabotage.

An understanding of conflict can be used as a managerial tool to assess how strongly certain people may feel about an issue, to discern individual personalities and dispositions, to evaluate relationships among people, and to gauge territorialism and power struggles. Evaluating conflict may lead to reevaluating certain work rules. Such evaluation may justify a change in current rules, or it may reveal the need for further clarification on why the rule is important. Conflict may expose certain problems that may otherwise go unnoticed, such as a chronic shortage of staff or a chronic shortage of certain supplies or equipment. An investigation may show that the current supplier frequently backlogs needed items, or that the maintenance department is far behind in keeping up with repairs. Evaluating conflict may also help administrators understand their own leadership styles, which may prompt them to change the way they handle their interpersonal relationships.

Conflict resolution and administrative intervention become necessary when conflict may create disorder or pose a threat to the achievement of organizational goals. However, no one best way has been devised to manage interpersonal conflict. The administrator may be involved as an adversary, as would occur when a family member barges into the office very upset about some service-related issue. In other situations, the administrator may act as a third party to mediate differences between two or more individuals, as when an angry employee comes in all upset about a supervisor "playing favorites." In almost all situations, the administrator must keep strong personal feelings under control and remain objective.

Listening attentively is often the first step in resolving a conflict. The administrator must first understand the nature of the conflict and get perspectives from all sides. Administrators must keep in mind that in many situations people are not expecting immediate action. Further investigation, fact-gathering, and getting the "other side of the story" are often

necessary before committing to a decision when mediating conflicts between others. Also, when emotions are high, a "cooling off" period often gives time to reevaluate the situation from a fresh perspective. In other situations, accommodation or capitulation may make sense by giving one side what it wants, particularly when that side is right.

Other strategies for resolution of conflicts include negotiation, keeping the conflict controlled within certain boundaries, and constructive confrontation (Ware and Barnes 1992):

- Negotiation can be used if a compromise is more desirable than outcomes realized without a compromise. Negotiation can provide a win-win outcome especially when the pursuit of opposing goals by the two sides would be counterproductive.
- Adversarial relationships may be controlled by separating two individuals, such as assigning the two adversaries to work on different units or on different shifts. If the two must work together because such a separation is not practical, control over their conflict ought to be exercised by adopting clear guidelines of behavior and following through with an impartial attitude.
- Constructive confrontation is a strategy that begins not with a confrontation but with an attempt by each party to explore and understand the other party's feelings and perceptions. As such, constructive confrontation may result in a new definition of what the problem was initially perceived to be, and it may forge new motives for seeking a common solution (Ware and Barnes 1992).

When the administrator is one of the parties involved in a conflict, he or she can retain control of a confrontational situation by focusing on the problem and issues and not engaging in personal attacks even when the other party may initiate such confrontation. Depending on the nature of the conflict, the administrator may withdraw or remain neutral. Capitulation or "giving in" may also be a good idea if the NHA considers the issue of conflict to be relatively minor, or when the other side has more power than the NHA does.

Relationship with Superiors

Management textbooks almost always ignore the important aspect of "managing the boss." In this context, the term "boss" may mean the board

of directors, the owner(s), or a corporate supervisor. Administrators who are otherwise very capable of managing subordinates and establishing exchange relationships with the stakeholders often ignore this aspect of management. Administrators can have unrealistic assumptions and expectations about the nature of the boss-subordinate relationship, which can lead to conflict in which both the administrator and the facility can end up losing. Managing the relationship with corporate officers becomes even more critical in large multifacility corporations in which the administrator is often distanced from the corporate office.

The boss-subordinate relationship is based on mutual dependence. The boss needs the administrator's help and cooperation, and the administrator needs the same from his or her boss. According to suggestions by Gabarro and Kotter (1992), the corporate boss can play a critical role in linking the NHA to the rest of the organization, in making sure the NHA's priorities are consistent with organizational goals, in securing the resources the NHA needs to perform well, and in providing inside information about corporate thinking, culture, and values. Administrators make a mistake when they consider themselves as self-sufficient, no matter how well they may be qualified in terms of education and experience.

The first step in managing the boss-subordinate relationship is to understand the boss's management style, strengths, weaknesses, preferred means of communication, priorities, and need for information about facility operations. The administrator should seek out information about his or her boss's goals, problems, and pressures, and pay attention to clues in the boss's behavior. Some bosses prefer to be more closely involved in the facility's operations than others. Such bosses may want the administrator to frequently touch base with them. Others do not want to be closely involved but would like to be kept apprised of important problems or changes. The administrator should also understand his or her own needs, strengths, weaknesses, and personal styles (Gabarro and Kotter 1992).

The potential for conflict often exists. The administrator may make a decision or proceed with some action only to be thwarted by his or her boss. Often, the reality is that bosses have their own pressures and concerns that are sometimes at odds with the wishes of the administrator. Depending on their own personalities and predispositions, some administrators may become resentful (a counterdependent behavior) and at some point may even become openly rebellious; others may submissively comply (an overdependent behavior). In both instances the administrator can

provide more information than the parties in conflict have at the beginning. In some instances, the boss's mind may change. In other situations, a compromise may be reached. At the very least, the administrator may gain insights into the boss's thinking regardless of the outcome.

The second critical step for the administrator in managing the boss-subordinate relationship is to understand mutual expectations. The boss may not always be straightforward in expressing what his expectations are. Questions asked during face-to-face meetings may lend important clues to the administrator about the boss's expectations. The administrator can pose questions such as "Am I providing you all key information you need?", "Do you have any particular comments on this?", "How often should I do this?", "Do I need to check back with you on this?", and "How important is this to you?".

Gabarro and Kotter (1992) suggested that managers often underestimate what their bosses need to know. Keeping the boss informed is an important rule to follow. Few things are more disabling to bosses than administrators on whom they cannot depend or administrators they cannot trust. Inconsistent behavior and unreliability can erode an administrator's credibility very quickly. Shading the truth a little, or playing down problems and concerns, is a bad idea. Such behavior can at some point create surprise problems, when the boss is likely to ask, "Why did you not tell me about this earlier?"

Finally, the administrator should discuss needs for help, guidance, and support with the boss. There should be open discussions about issues that could potentially turn into major concerns. It is all right for the administrator to acknowledge, "I really don't know how to address this. I need some help."

Risk Management

The health care delivery environment has been characterized by an upsurge in malpractice lawsuits. Regardless of the outcome, legal action against a facility is costly for the facility when the direct costs of defense and indirect costs from loss of reputation are factored in. Considering such undesirable consequences, risk management has become a critical domain of nursing home administration. **Risk management** means identifying, analyzing, and reducing or preventing risks (Becker 2001). For an administrator, the primary focus of risk management is on risks affecting patients and patient care, but a risk-management program should also

include consideration of the risks to employees, contracted staff, visitors, and facility assets.

Written policies, procedures, and practices are the first line of defense against potential risks. Such policies should address informed consent, handling of disruptive patients, patient transfers, restraint use, confidentiality, and other concerns discussed in previous chapters. Policies must also cover routine practices to be followed in the delivery of services by each department of the facility. Ongoing training of the staff and monitoring the staff's work are necessary for compliance with established policies.

Risk identification involves collecting information about all incidents. An **incident** is any unexpected negative occurrence involving a patient, employee, or visitor. Patient-care occurrences, and all other events that present potential loss to the facility must be investigated. Meticulously documenting patient care assessments, care plans, and progress notes is also essential. Similarly, adverse clinical outcomes, accidents and incidents, errors in treatment, and complaints from patients or family members must be carefully documented. Documentation should include what was done in each situation. Risk identification also requires looking for early warning signs that may appear in security reports, quality improvement studies, licensure and certification inspections, and client complaints (Kavaler and Spiegel 1997).

Incidents must be reported, and the facility must have policies and procedures in place so that anyone can report all incidents, regardless of how small they may be. The staff should receive training on how to document incidents, which may involve patients, staff members, or visitors. The language used in documentation should be accurate, objective, and factual; it should avoid opinions, confessions, or accusations. Inconsistent explanations or remarks to patients or families by different members of staff should be avoided. One person should be designated to handle questions from patients, family members, staff members, and external parties (Becker 2001). Potential as well as actual lawsuits should be reported to the insurance carrier.

CONCLUSION

Effectively managing a nursing facility is a complex undertaking because it involves a wide spectrum of responsibilities and actions requiring careful balancing in accordance with the varied organizational needs. Leadership and

management skills must be constantly developed and refined in conjunction with frequent self-evaluation. But in spite of an ongoing commitment toward self-improvement, the administrator will no doubt encounter new and unforeseen challenges. The various skills and tools discussed in this chapter provide a basic foundation for effective management, but they must be practiced along with common sense and personal judgment. Taking risks based on well-informed decisions is part of the process in executive development. Successful executives also recognize their own weaknesses but are resourceful in finding help and using strengths that others, either within or outside the organization, may possess. Above all, successful executives keep their organization's vision, mission, values, and major goals in clear sight, and focus on actions that are consistent with the objectives outlined in them.

DISCUSSION AND APPLICATION QUESTIONS

1. Achieving the right balance among what Drucker described as managing a business, managing work and workers, and managing the facility in community and society will vary from one facility to another. As the NHA of a nursing home, how would you decide which area should be given more emphasis than the others?
2. It can be said that the main objective of the NHA's position is to create value. Provide some examples of how the NHA can create value.
3. Is Theory Y better than Theory X?
4. Which of the five leadership styles proposed by Blake and Mouton is likely to be most effective in nursing home administration?
5. Critically evaluate the mission statement in Exhibit 13-1.
6. You are the administrator of a skilled nursing facility. You open an envelope left in your mailbox and learn that your director of nursing (DON) is resigning, giving you a one-month notice. You have tried to persuade the DON to stay, but her decision is final. Employ the decision-making model in Figure 13-6 to address this situation.

REFERENCES

Becker, S. 2001. *Health Care Law: A Practical Guide.* 2nd ed. Newark, NJ: Matthew Bender & Company Inc.

Blake, R.S., and J.S. Mouton. 1964. *The Managerial Grid*. Houston: Gulf Publishing.

Brody, R. 2000. *Effectively Managing Human Service Organizations*. 2nd ed. Thousand Oaks, CA: Sage Publications, Inc.

Burns, J.M. 1998. Transactional and transforming leadership. In *Leading Organizations: Perspectives for a New Era*, ed. G.R. Hickman, 133–134. Thousand Oaks, CA: Sage Publications, Inc.

Ciampa, D., and M. Watkins. 1999. *Right from the Start: Taking Charge in a New Leadership Role*. Boston: Harvard Business School Press.

Collins, J.C., and J.I. Porras. 1998. Organizational vision and visionary organizations. In *Leading Organizations: Perspectives for a New Era*, ed. G.R. Hickman. Thousand Oaks, CA: Sage Publications, Inc.

DePree, M. 1998. What is leadership? In *Leading Organizations: Perspectives for a New Era,* ed. G.R. Hickman, 130–132. Thousand Oaks, CA: Sage Publications, Inc.

Drucker, P.F. 1974. *Management: Tasks, Responsibilities, Practices*. New York: Harper & Row Publishers.

Drucker, P.F. 1985. *The Effective Executive*. New York: Harper & Row Publishers.

Fernández, J.E., and R.T. Hogan. 2002. Values-based leadership. *The Journal for Quality and Participation* 25, no. 4: 25–27.

Gabarro, J.J., and J.P. Kotter. 1992. Managing your boss. In *Managing People and Organizations*. Readings selected by J.J. Gabarro. Boston: Harvard Business School Publications.

Gini, A. 1998. Moral leadership and business ethics. In *Leading Organizations: Perspectives for a New Era*, ed. G.R. Hickman, 360–371. Thousand Oaks, CA: Sage Publications, Inc.

Griffith, J.R. and K.R. White. 2002. *The Well-Managed Healthcare Organization*. 5th ed. Chicago: AUPHA Press/Health Administration Press.

Hatch, M.J. 1997. *Organization Theory: Modern, Symbolic, and Postmodern Perspectives*. New York: Oxford University Press.

Kavaler, F., and A.D. Spiegel. 1997. Risk management dynamics. In *Risk Management in Health Care Institutions: A Strategic Approach*, eds. F. Kavaler and A.D. Spiegel. Sudbury, Massachusetts: Jones and Bartlett Publishers.

Kelley, R.E. 1998. Leadership secrets from exemplary followers. In *Leading Organizations: Perspectives for a New Era*, ed. G.R. Hickman. Thousand Oaks, CA: Sage Publications, Inc.

Kotter, J.P. 1992. What leaders really do. In *Managing People and Organizations*. Readings selected by J.J. Gabarro. Boston: Harvard Business School Publications.

McCarthy, J.J. 1978. *Why Managers Fail, and What to Do About It*. New York: McGraw-Hill Publications Company.

Mintzberg, H. 1989. *Mintzberg on Management: Inside Our Strange World of Organizations*. New York: The Free Press.

Northouse, P.G. 2001. *Leadership: Theory and Practice*. 2nd ed. Thousand Oaks, CA: Sage Publications, Inc.

Ross, A., et al. 2002. *Leadership for the Future: Core Competencies in Healthcare.* Chicago: Health Administration Press/Washington, DC: AUPHA Press.

Singh, D.A., and R.C. Schwab. 1998. Retention of administrators in nursing homes: What can management do? *The Gerontologist* 38 (3): 362–369.

Walton, R.E. 1992. From control to commitment in the workplace. In *Managing People and Organizations.* Readings selected by J.J. Gabarro. Boston: Harvard Business School Publications.

Ware, J. 1992. How to run a meeting. In *Managing People and Organizations.* Readings selected by J.J. Gabarro. Boston: Harvard Business School Publications.

Ware, J., and L.B. Barnes. 1992. Managing interpersonal conflict. In *Managing People and Organizations.* Readings selected by J.J. Gabarro. Boston: Harvard Business School Publications.

CHAPTER 14

Effective Human Resource and Staff Development

LEARNING MODULES

1. The human resource function, its importance, and its relationship to effective management and leadership. Designation of responsibility for the human resource function.
2. Goals and main functions of human resource management. Importance of staff motivation and satisfaction. Human resource challenges in long-term care management.
3. Determining staffing levels using skill mix, volume factor, and weighting factor.
4. Estimating hours spent in direct patient care, clinical support, and documentation. Developing relative values to determine skill mix and total hours in nursing. Using relative values to determine weighted census. Developing alternative staffing patterns. Factors to be incorporated in staffing schedules.
5. Creative methods for recruiting staff. Monetary and non-monetary incentives for attracting employees.
6. Staff license, certification, and registration, and record-keeping requirements. State CNA registries.

continues

7. Monitoring turnover and absenteeism. Managing turnover and absenteeism through leadership stability; selection, orientation, and mentoring; a sense of social community; and administrative support.

8. A well-rounded approach to staff development and training. Performance appraisal and its relationship to staff development. Use and misuse of management by objectives (MBO).

9. Self-managed work teams (SMWT); what they are and how they function. Benefits of high-performing SMWTs. Factors contributing to effectively functioning SMWTs. The Green House and Wellspring models of staff empowerment.

10. Counseling, disciplining, and terminating as progressive steps. Management's approach to counseling. Common disciplinary problems. Key factors to guide fair action on the part of managers. Steps in progressive disciplining. The appeals system. Handling terminations appropriately.

11. The legal basis for unionization. Employee rights. Reasons why employees may unionize. The process leading up to an election for representation. Management's rights and permissible actions during a unionization campaign. Unfair labor practices during a campaign and associated consequences.

12. Collective bargaining. Union contract and management's rights. The grievance procedure and arbitration.

13. Strikes and picketing. A union's legal obligations before a strike. Management's rights during an economic strike. What striking workers cannot do.

14. Employment discrimination. Employment-at-will doctrine and its application. Equal employment opportunity and the Civil Rights Act. Types of discrimination: pregnancy, age, pay, disability, family needs, and harassment.

An organization is a collection of people working together to achieve a common purpose within a formal structure. A simple, yet sometimes overlooked, fact is that organizations function as they do because of the people employed by the organization. The most important asset of a

nursing facility is its staff. An organization with a superior workforce undeniably gains a competitive advantage in the marketplace, because a superior workforce lends internal strengths to an organization for meeting competitive threats and for exploiting new opportunities presented by changes in the external environment. Therefore, effectively managing human resources is a vital aspect of nursing facility management.

An effective workforce brings value to the organization, and management must determine how the potential of this value is tapped. The primary objective of effective management is to transfer this value to the patients in the form of high-quality care and to the organization in the form of cost-efficiency. Other assets, such as buildings, equipment, and supplies are also essential. But a nursing facility's success in accomplishing its goals depends to a large extent on human dynamics. Effective leadership and management, discussed in Chapter 13, are crucial for influencing and shaping human behaviors. But the dynamics are also influenced by the number of staff members and the quality of the staff, along with the facility's training and development opportunities, fair compensation, grievance practices, performance appraisal, termination practices, and employment policies that govern the exchange relationship between the facility and its employees. Hence, human resource management is critical for achieving organizational goals.

Human resource management is also known by other terms, such as "personnel management" or "employee relations." It can be defined as the organizational function of planning for human resource needs, recruitment, selection, compensation, development, evaluation, and handling of grievances and labor relations (Boone and Kurtz 1984). Large nursing homes generally have a designated position, such as a human resource director, to handle human-resource functions; the responsibility may also be assigned to the assistant administrator. In most facilities, however, the administrator assumes these responsibilities; in facilities affiliated with a hospital or a multi-facility chain, the administrator receives some human-resource support from the corporate office. Some human-resource responsibilities may be delegated to the nursing department, especially the responsibility for hiring and training licensed nurses and certified nursing assistants (CNAs). Other department heads who supervise employees, such as the food-service director, business-office manager, and activity director also have some degree of responsibility in hiring, evaluating, training, and disciplining

staff members. The administrator should make sure that these managers are adequately trained in human-resource functions.

GOALS, MAIN FUNCTIONS, AND CHALLENGES

Human-Resource Goals

The primary goal of human-resource management is to maintain desired staffing levels by having a well-qualified and stable workforce. However, this goal cannot be achieved through some mere mechanical or bureaucratic procedure. Effective leadership as well as sound human resource policies and practices play a key role. Griffith (1995) proposed that success in attracting and retaining employees tends to be self-sustaining; organizations with a satisfied and well-qualified staff are able to attract capable and enthusiastic people. Although such an ideal may never be fully achieved, sustained and purposeful leadership on the part of any facility can ensure that it has a stable and qualified workforce over time.

Human-Resource Functions

Building a desirable and stable workforce is achieved by recruiting qualified employees when needed, improving the skills of employees, increasing satisfaction among staff members, and retaining employees who perform well. Accordingly, De Cenzo and Robbins (1996) classify human-resource management into four main functions:

- **Staffing:** recruitment of qualified staff members; planning staffing levels in accordance with patient needs; and scheduling to maintain adequate staffing, while taking into account employees' needs for time off.
- **Training and development**: orientation of newly hired staff members; ongoing coaching and mentoring by senior staff members and supervisors; formal training to maintain and advance skill levels; and developing staff members for career advancement.
- **Motivation:** addressing the issues of job performance; job satisfaction; and labor relations.
- **Maintenance function**: building employee commitment; reducing absenteeism and turnover; and retaining productive employees.

Effectively managed nursing facilities aim at achieving a high level of motivation and satisfaction among their staff members. Many employees in the nursing home come into frequent contact with patients, family members, and visitors, so employees have an unusual degree of influence over these stakeholders. "What they say and do for patients and visitors will have more influence on competitive standing than any media campaign the organization might contemplate" (Griffith 1995, p. 662). No wonder staff satisfaction is an important predictor of customer satisfaction! Therefore, an effectively managed nursing facility should market itself to its staff almost as much as it markets itself to its clients and the community.

Human-Resource Challenges

Managing human resources is a complex task. First, almost every aspect of human-resource management is governed by complex labor laws. The main laws are discussed later in this chapter. Nursing facilities must also comply with regulations mandating minimum levels of staffing and licensing, and, in some cases, certification for staff categories. Experts believe that staffing levels in some facilities are not sufficient to meet the minimum needs of residents for provision of quality of care, quality of life, and rehabilitation (Institute of Medicine 2001).

The second human-resource challenge faced by long-term care facilities is the unprecedented upsurge in union-organizing activity and, sometimes, union militancy. Although unionization in most private sector industries has steadily declined for several years, the health-care sector has been one exception: In the early- to mid-1990s, unions prevailed in only about 50% of the elections to unionize health care facilities. By 1999, unions were able to win 68% of the elections in long-term care facilities (Lyncheski 2002).

A third challenge comes from the nature of workforce. Nursing facilities employ predominantly unskilled or semi-skilled workers. Most nursing-home employees are nursing assistants, housekeepers, laundry workers, and dietary aides. To recruit these staff members, long-term care facilities compete against fast-food restaurants, discount stores, hotels, motels, and hospitals. Local hospitals and other health-service agencies also present substantial competition for skilled employees such as nurses, social workers, and therapists. Such skilled employees often prefer to work for hospitals and for other agencies in which pay, benefits, and opportunities for

training and career growth are better than in nursing facilities. Nursing-home employees are predominantly female, which requires a particular sensitivity on the part of a facility's administration to the needs of female employees, because their needs are often intertwined with those of their families. Also, in most regions of the country, the workforce is becoming more diverse because of an increasing proportion of minority workers. Diversity presents special challenges, because various cultural characteristics, such as language, customs, and beliefs affect how workers relate to patients, family members, fellow employees, and supervisors.

HUMAN-RESOURCE PLANNING

Nursing facilities are often plagued with staff shortages. One factor that exacerbates this problem is haphazard planning. In the human resource context, the planning function can be defined as the process of systematically reviewing human-resource requirements to ensure that the desired number of employees, with the required skills, is available when needed (Mondy and Noe 1993).

Determining Staffing Levels

Staffing levels have two main components. The first is number of staff members, such as total nursing staff or total dietary staff. The total staff can be expressed in terms of either as full-time equivalents (FTEs) or as staff hours. FTEs express staffing levels as number of staff members; staff hours express staffing levels as number of hours worked. The second component of staffing is referred to as skill-mix. **Skill-mix** is the ratio of staff members with a particular skill type to the total staff in a unit or department. The ratio of registered nurses (RNs) to the total nursing staff on a nursing care unit is an example of skill-mix. The skill-mix on a nursing care unit increases as the number of RNs or LPNs increases in relation to the total nursing staff on that unit. Similarly, the ratio of cooks to the total dietary staff is an indicator of skill-mix in the dietary department.

In general, staffing levels are determined by two basic factors: a volume factor, and a weighting factor. The **volume factor** incorporates measures such as number of patients to care for, number of meals to prepare and serve, number of rooms to clean, and pounds of laundry to

process. The **weighting factor** is associated with measures of the intensity of resource use. As an example, for nursing care, patients could be classified into three broad categories to determine resource use: light care, intermediate care, and heavy care. In the dietary department, preparing each meal—breakfast, lunch, and dinner—requires different levels of resource consumption. Both the volume factor and the weighting factor should be used conjointly to determine the total staff level and the skill mix required. Application of these concepts is illustrated in the next section.

Nursing-Staff Planning

The biggest staffing challenge lies in the nursing department. Conceptually, a facility's goal is to determine staffing levels in terms of both staff hours and skill mix that are adequate to meet the patients' clinical needs. Matching staffing to patient needs should be accomplished using a systematic approach in which three separate components of nursing tasks—direct patient care, clinical support, and documentation—should be evaluated. Over time, increasing regulatory mandates have required licensed nurses to spend more and more time on documentation which can take time away from patient care and support of nursing assistants. Determining the need for staff resources in each of the three components of nursing care is not very easy, but it can be done by doing a time study on a patient sample that represents the facility's patient population.

Nursing staff planning is a three step process:

(1) Do a time study on a patient sample to determine the staff hours necessary to care for the needs of each patient.
(2) Use the skill mix employed to calculate weights. Establish acuity categories. Determine weighting factors or relative values to reflect the relative difference in resource use between the acuity categories.
(3) Use weighted census to determine staffing patterns.

Time Study

The first step in a time study is to list all the tasks to be performed in the three task categories (described in the previous section) for each patient in the sample. Tasks related to direct patient care and documentation are relatively easy to identify. Clinical support can include a variety of items such as nurse interaction with CNAs; communication with physicians, families,

or staff members in other departments; supervision of clinical tasks; and interventions during meal service.

In the second step, estimates of the amount of time spent for each task will be noted in a log for each staff category, such as RN, LPN, and CNA. A log is maintained for each patient. Compiling this information for each shift is necessary, because tasks vary among the three shifts. Similarly, weekend tasks may differ somewhat from tasks performed on weekdays. One week's data is generally sufficient for estimating the time spent in the three task categories. In Exhibit 14-1, the logged hours for the three task categories have been combined, and average daily hours spent on each patient have been calculated for time spent by RNs, LPNs, and CNAs.

Calculating Weights and Relative Values

The average time spent on each patient by RNs, LPNs, and CNAs is used to calculate weights. These weights are used as a guide to classify patients according to staff resource use. Administrators can either use their judgment to decide on the number of acuity levels, or simple quantitative techniques can be used, as described later. Finally, weighting factors, or **relative values**, are extracted by using average weights for each acuity category.

Exhibit 14-1 illustrates how the weighting factors (relative values) are established using a sample of 21 patients. This sample includes three patients from each of the seven basic RUG-III categories associated with MDS assessment (see Chapter 4). The "average hours spent per day" column shows the time spent on each sampled resident by each staff category—RN, LPN, and CNA—in performing the tasks of direct patient care, clinical support, and documentation on an average day. In this example, a statistical technique called "squares about the mean" is used to establish three patient acuity levels. Those familiar with basic statistics will recognize the formula used for calculating a standard deviation (calculating the squares about the mean is the first step used for arriving at the standard deviation):

$$\text{Square about the mean} = (x_i - \bar{x})^2$$
$$\text{Where } x_i = \text{ the } i^{th} \text{ value, and } \bar{x} = \text{ the mean of all values}$$

The weighting factors (relative values) show the relationship among the acuity levels in terms of resource requirements. In Exhibit 14-1, for instance, the three acuity levels have relative values of 1.0 for category I, 1.31 for category II, and 1.75 for category III. It means that category II,

EXHIBIT 14-1

Patient sample for extracting weighting factors (this example is illustrative only)

Patient	Average Hours Spent per day RN	LPN	CNA	(1) Hours	(2) Total to total	(3) % Nurse time factor	(4) CNA % factor	(5) Nurse Weights	(6) Acuity Categories	(7) Average Weights	(8) Weighting Factors (relative values)	(9) Squares About the Mean
1	0.1	0.4	1.4	1.9	26.3%	1.00	1.05	1.05	I	1.06	1.00	0.2
2	0.1	0.4	1.4	1.9	26.3%	1.00	1.05	1.05	I	1.06	1.00	0.2
3	0.1	0.4	1.5	2.0	25.0%	1.07	1.00	1.07	I	1.06	1.00	0.1
4	0.1	0.4	1.5	2.0	25.0%	1.07	1.00	1.07	I	1.06	1.00	0.1
5	0.2	0.4	1.5	2.1	28.6%	1.07	1.14	1.22	II	1.39	1.31	0.0
6	0.2	0.4	1.5	2.1	28.6%	1.07	1.14	1.22	II	1.39	1.31	0.0
7	0.2	0.4	1.6	2.2	27.3%	1.14	1.09	1.25	II	1.39	1.31	0.0
8	0.2	0.4	1.6	2.2	27.3%	1.14	1.09	1.25	II	1.39	1.31	0.0
9	0.2	0.4	1.6	2.2	27.3%	1.14	1.09	1.25	II	1.39	1.31	0.0
10	0.2	0.5	1.6	2.3	30.4%	1.14	1.22	1.39	II	1.39	1.31	0.0
11	0.2	0.5	1.6	2.3	30.4%	1.14	1.22	1.39	II	1.39	1.31	0.0
12	0.2	0.5	1.6	2.3	30.4%	1.14	1.22	1.39	II	1.39	1.31	0.0
13	0.3	0.5	1.7	2.5	32.0%	1.21	1.28	1.55	II	1.39	1.31	0.0
14	0.3	0.5	1.7	2.5	32.0%	1.21	1.28	1.55	II	1.39	1.31	0.0
15	0.3	0.5	1.7	2.5	32.0%	1.21	1.28	1.55	II	1.39	1.31	0.0

continues

EXHIBIT 14–1 *continued*

Patient	Average Hours Spent per day			Hours	Total Hours to total	% Nurse time factor	CNA % factor	Nurse Weights	Acuity Categories	Average Weights	Weighting Factors (relative values)	Squares About the Mean
	RN	LPN	CNA	(1)	(2)	(3)	(4)	(5)	(6)	(7)	(8)	(9)
16	0.3	0.5	1.9	2.7	29.6%	1.36	1.19	1.61	II	1.39	1.31	0.0
17	0.3	0.6	1.9	2.8	32.1%	1.36	1.29	1.74	III	1.86	1.75	0.1
18	0.4	0.6	1.9	2.9	34.5%	1.36	1.38	1.87	III	1.86	1.75	0.2
19	0.4	0.6	1.9	2.9	34.5%	1.36	1.38	1.87	III	1.86	1.75	0.2
20	0.4	0.6	2.0	3.0	33.3%	1.43	1.33	1.90	III	1.86	1.75	0.2
21	0.4	0.6	2.0	3.0	33.3%	1.43	1.33	1.90	III	1.86	1.75	0.2

(1) Sum of RN, LPN, and CNA hours for all tasks performed during an average day

(2) ((RN + LPN hours) / Total hours in "1") × 100

(3) For each patient, CNA hours are divided by the minimum CNA hours (1.4)

(4) For each patient, nurse % is divided by the smallest % figure (25.0)

(5) Multiply columns (3) and (4)

(6) Decide on the number of acuity categories based on weights. In this example, a simple statistical tool called 'squares about the mean' is used (column 9).

(7) Average of the weights (5) for each of the acuity categories (6)

(8) The first acuity category is assigned a weight of "1." The remaining two weighting factors are calculated in relation to the first category, using average weights (7). For example, the weighting factor for Acuity Category II = 1.39/1.06 = 1.31; for Acuity Category III, it is 1.86/1.06 = 1.75

(9) The 'squares about the mean' are the squared deviations of values in (5) from the mean (arithmetical average) of these values. In this case the mean is calculated to be 1.44. For example, the 'square about the mean' for patient 18 = $(1.87 - 1.44)^2 = .1849$ (rounded to one decimal point). Notice that the weights for patients 5 through 16 are closest to the mean, and are classified into category II. The other two categories are farther away from the mean."

462

on the average, requires 31% more hours of staffing than category I, and category III requires 75% more staffing than category I. Both categories II and III show staffing needs in relation to category I, which is the base category.

Weighted Patient Census and Staffing Patterns

Relative values are necessary for designing a staffing plan. The other factor needed for designing a staffing plan is case volume, which, in a nursing facility, is the patient census. Exhibit 14-2 illustrates how the patient census on a given nursing unit, or in the entire facility, may be used to formulate a staffing plan by first assigning each patient to one of the acuity categories based on patient assessment. The weighting factors are used to convert the raw census into a weighted patient census that reflects the patients' clinical acuity on which the staffing patterns are based. Notice how a raw census of 36 is equivalent to 50.3 patients after the weighting factors have been applied to the raw census. Staff planning should be based on the weighted patient census. Notice that two staffing patterns have emerged. In both models, the total staff hours are the same (128 hours or 16 FTEs per day), but model I has a higher skill-mix, as indicated by the percentage of nurse time to total hours. The choice between pattern I and pattern II will be driven by tradeoffs between economic constraints and quality expectations. Pattern I will be the model of choice if quality must supersede economic concerns, whereas pattern II will be used when cost constraints are more important. The higher skill-mix in pattern I will result in higher costs for direct labor and benefits. In this example, total hours in each staff category assume 8-hour shifts. Some facilities use 7.5-hour shifts for CNAs. Differences in shift lengths, however, should not change the total number of hours needed to provide an adequate level of services.

Scheduling

Scheduling can be viewed as the final step in human-resource planning. Before scheduling can be undertaken, the staffing model appropriate for the facility's goals should be established, as described in the previous section. Available personnel in each staff category are then assigned to fill the time slots for each of the three shifts for all seven days of the week. For example, if the facility decides to use staffing pattern II (Exhibit 14-2), staff coverage per shift will be like that shown in Table 14-1.

EXHIBIT 14–2 Daily staffing pattern for Nursing Unit B (40 beds) (this example is illustrative only)

Acuity categories	Expected raw census	Weighting factors	Weighted census (1)	Average hours per patient RN (2)	Average hours per patient LPN (2)	Average hours per patient CNA (2)	Total Hours	% Nurse time to total	Total hrs to wt census
I	7	1	7.0	0.10	0.40	1.45			
II	17	1.31	22.3	0.23	0.46	1.63			
III	12	1.75	21.0	0.38	0.60	1.94			
			Total hours for each staff category						
Totals (3)	36		50.3	14	26	87	127	31.2%	2.52
Staffing pattern I				16	32	80.00	128.00	37.5%	2.55
Staffing pattern II				16	24	88.00	128.00	31.3%	2.55

(1) Multiply raw census by the weighting factors (from Exhibit 14-1)
(2) Average hours for each acuity category (from Exhibit 14-1)
(3) The total RN, LPN, and CNA hours are based on average hours per patient for the weighted census in each category
For example, total RN hours = $(7 \times .10) + (22.3 \times .23) + (21 \times .38) = 13.9$ (rounded to 14)
Staffing patterns assume 8 hour increments
In staffing pattern I, the 26 LPN hours have been rounded up. Skill mix: RN 12.5%, LPN 25%, CNA 62.5%
In staffing pattern II, the 26 LPN hours have been rounded down. Skill mix: RN 12.5%, LPN 19%, CNA 69%
Total staff hours (128) = 16 FTE (128/8)

Table 14–1 Daily Staffing Schedule Based on Staffing Pattern II in Exhibit 14-2

	RN	LPN	CNA
Day shift (number of staff members)	1	1	6
Evening shift	1	1	3
Night shift	0	1	2
Total staff per day	2	3	11
Total hours per day	16	24	88

Note: The facility may stagger the shifts to provide CNA coverage during peak times. For example, one CNA could begin work at 10 am, providing one extra staff member during the evening meal.

Filling all slots in the schedule depends on having a sufficient number of full-time and part-time employees on the payroll. A second factor in filling the slots is scheduled personal time off for employees. Unscheduled time off for employees is the third factor that planners must take into account. Even when all the slots in the schedule are filled, actual shortages in staffing occur because of absenteeism, which is a substantial problem in many nursing homes. Shortages in staffing also occur when people leave their positions without giving advance notice, or when the facility is unable to fill vacant positions.

Because some of these variables are beyond management's control, scheduling can pose substantial challenges. If a facility has serious absenteeism and turnover problems, it should try to schedule extra staff in addition to what a full schedule calls for, because the facility anticipates that some employees on the schedule are not going to show up for work. On occasion, this approach will result in overstaffing, but, more frequently, it will offset shortages arising from severe absenteeism or turnover. From an economic perspective, the additional net costs of overstaffing, if any, should be relatively small, because such scheduling would reduce overtime costs and the use of temporary staffing agencies. The payoffs of extra scheduling are high in terms of consistency, quality of patient care, and staff satisfaction. A fourth factor to be incorporated in scheduling is the amount of training and orientation the staff should receive. Staff planning, discussed in the previous section, is to schedule actual hands-on caregiving; training and orientation hours are scheduled separately.

STAFF RECRUITMENT AND RETENTION

Recruitment and retention of staff go hand-in-hand with staff planning. Effectively managed facilities measure turnover and absenteeism rates on a regular basis. These measures are useful in projecting future staffing needs. They help management gauge the outcomes of any new programs or policies and also provide an ongoing measure of staff satisfaction. Adverse trends, for example, may indicate the presence of underlying problems that need probing and investigation.

Creative Recruitment

In many labor markets, the long-term care industry faces staff shortages because the demand for qualified staff members is greater than the supply. Some actions that may help nursing homes overcome such imbalances include creative recruiting, compensation incentives, and training programs (Caruth and Handlogten 1997). Creativity often involves a more effective use of recruitment resources that already exist. For example, a facility's current employees, local schools and colleges, churches, neighborhood newspapers, and partnership and frequent contact with the local employment agency can be effective resources for staff recruitment. Other creative approaches may include a job fair or open house at the facility in which facility personnel are available to explain various job opportunities.

Nursing-assistant certification programs are organized by many facilities to attract candidates who otherwise would be unemployable for lack of marketable skills. Other avenues for training include tuition assistance and continuing education for promising employees and financial assistance and scholarships for students currently enrolled in nursing programs. A facility can also provide opportunities for internships to students in nursing and other disciplines. Interns may be paid a stipend that serves as a token of appreciation for the work interns perform as part of their training. Such direct investments in training, consistently undertaken, can help alleviate future staff shortages by providing a steady stream of qualified workers.

Compensation should match market rates of pay. Paying a high premium over market rates can trigger a bidding war, which can raise hiring salaries to artificially high levels and can send ripple effects throughout the organization or through the local long-term care industry. Hence, during periods of critical shortages, many organizations use sign-on

bonuses, because they can be discontinued at any time without creating negative economic effects for the rest of the organization. Other forms of non-monetary rewards can appeal to many people. Four-day work weeks, flexible working hours, and on-site child care are attractive incentives (Caruth and Handlogten 1997). Market rates of pay apply mainly to starting wages. Once employees are on the job, additional perks (discussed later in this chapter) can be used to reward them for personal development, job performance, and supplementary responsibilities.

Staff Licensure, Certification, and Registration

Recruiting RNs, LPNs (or LVNs), and CNAs requires compliance with regulatory mandates. RNs and LPNs must be licensed by the state in which they wish to practice. The nursing facility must verify current licensure status of all its RNs and LPNs and must maintain a copy of the license in each employee's personnel record. Similar documentation must be maintained for all other licensed staff members—such as therapists and therapy assistants—regardless of whether these workers are directly employed by the facility or are on contract through an agency.

CNAs must have current certification, which is earned through a state's standardized nurse-aide training and competency evaluation program as mandated by the Omnibus Budget Reconciliation Act of 1987 (OBRA-87). The objective of this mandate is to establish minimum qualifications for nurse aides and to evaluate whether a person possesses basic competencies to work as a nurse aide in a long-term care facility. Even though nurse aides are not required to have a state license, the effect of this legislation is the same as if there were such a requirement.

CNA training programs are offered by nursing facilities, community colleges, and the American Red Cross. Certification is conferred by the state's nurse-aide registry after an applicant passes an examination. The state's nurse-aide registries enable facilities to verify the certification status of a nurse aide. The registry also provides information on resident abuse, neglect, or misappropriation of personal property in which an aide may have been involved. Before employing a CNA, a facility is required to contact the registries in all states in which the individual is believed to have worked. Non-certified nurse aides employed in permanent positions have a four-month window during which they must receive the required training and receive certification. Laws in many states also require criminal background checks and drug testing when a nursing staff member is

hired. Legislative proposals have been made for mandating a national information-sharing registry on all long-term care workers.

Managing Turnover and Absenteeism

Most nursing homes have a relatively small core of very stable and dedicated staff members. But most facilities are also plagued by enormous rates of turnover, which generally exceed those in other industries. Despite efforts to understand why turnover is so common, and despite efforts to slow down the speed at which the exit door revolves, staff turnover remains one of the most daunting problems for the nursing home industry. No single approach exists for increasing staff retention, and piecemeal efforts to address the issue have produced little success to date. This section provides a comprehensive approach that requires coordinated support from governing boards, administrators, and key department heads to carry out a successful campaign against high turnover of staff.

Measuring Turnover and Its Costs

Turnover and retention are flip sides of the same coin, that is, increased staff retention translates into lower rates of turnover. Turnover in a facility can be calculated by using the following formula, which can be applied to a particular position, or to the entire staff:

$$\text{Turnover rate (\%)} = \frac{\textit{Number of separations per time period*}}{\textit{Average number of employees during the same period}} \times 100$$

Any period can be used, but a year is the most common. However, keeping track of turnover for each month or for each quarter can help administrators better understand the trends.

$$\text{Functional turnover rate (\%)} = \frac{\begin{array}{c}\textit{Number of separations of employees}\\ \textit{who would not}\\ \textit{be rehired}\end{array}}{\textit{Average number of employees}} \times 100$$

$$\text{Dysfunctional turnover rate (\%)} = \frac{\begin{array}{c}\textit{Number of separations of employees}\\ \textit{who would be rehired}\end{array}}{\textit{Average number of employees}} \times 100$$

Turnover is expensive. The two major costs directly associated with turnover are replacement costs and training costs for the new worker. A

rough estimate of these direct costs is two to three times the monthly salary of the departing employee (Sherman et al. 1998). Additional indirect costs include overtime paid to cover vacant positions, temporary staffing-agency fees, management time used to find replacements, low productivity before employees quit, and low morale among staff members.

Measuring and Managing Absenteeism

Absenteeism and turnover are twin problems. Lower rates of absenteeism, for instance, are associated with higher seniority on the job (Cohen-Mansfield and Rosenthal 1989). Some absenteeism occurs because of legitimate reasons such as sickness. Much of it, however, is associated with apathy, low morale, and a low sense of self-worth among the workers.

Maintaining records on individual absenteeism is essential, and so is keeping track of absenteeism rates for the purpose of staff planning and scheduling, as discussed earlier. Absenteeism rates are calculated as follows:

$$Absenteeism\ rate\ (\%) = \frac{Number\ of\ workdays\ missed\ per\ time\ period}{Average\ number\ of\ employees \times number\ of\ workdays\ in\ the\ same\ time\ period} \times 100$$

Absenteeism is managed by having written policies, which should include a distinction between what the facility considers an excused absence or an unexcused absence, and a statement on what level of absenteeism is considered excessive. Policies should also outline the consequences employees will bear when their absenteeism is excessive. Absenteeism should be addressed both individually and for the organization as a whole: At an individual level, a counseling session should be held between the employee and the supervisor to seek out the underlying problems and determine how management may be able to assist the employee to overcome those problems. Additional key areas discussed in the next section can also help minimize absenteeism.

Managing Turnover

Leadership Stability

Unfortunately, with few exceptions, turnover permeates the typical facility from top to bottom. At the industry level, turnover among nursing home administrators (NHAs) has been estimated to be at least 40%, with the median length of employment at a facility just over 2-years (Singh and Schwab 1998). A study of this turnover phenomenon suggested that there

actually may be a bidding war among nursing facilities in an attempt to attract qualified administrators, as indicated by the relatively large proportion of administrators voluntarily leaving their positions after relatively short tenures (average length, 1.3 years) to pursue opportunities for promotions that offer more responsibility, better pay, etc. (Singh and Schwab 2000). This phenomenon implies that administrators who possess the qualifications facilities seek are in short supply. This type of instability at the top keeps the entire organization in a state of flux because leadership and strategic direction are interrupted, employees feel the stress of frequent change of leadership, and many other disruptions occur. Similarly, in the nursing department, it has been demonstrated that turnover among RNs may be linked to turnover among nursing assistants (Brannon et al. 2002). Hence, stability of key leadership positions is one goal nursing facilities must address.

Selection, Orientation, and Mentoring

From the administrator's standpoint, attention to recruitment practices may be the first step in reducing staff turnover. Many people who apply for jobs in nursing homes do indeed have a desire to help the elderly, but they soon become discouraged and disenchanted. As a result, much of the turnover in health care facilities occurs within the first 90 days of employment. Lescoe-Long (2000) cites two main reasons for this phenomenon: First, the job turns out to be different than what the employee had expected it to be; perhaps the job was made to appear more glamorous than it truly is. Second, employees feel abandoned after the first few days of employment, and they lack skills to cope with many of the demands of the new job. The first of these two reasons points to the need for a more in-depth selection process, in which the facility should try to explore the potential employee's expectations in relation to the realities of what the job entails. The second reason underscores the importance of developing coping skills. Technical training, such as a nursing-assistant certification program, focuses mainly on how to perform certain job-related functions correctly. Even though such training is essential, it does not prepare workers to handle nonroutine and stressful situations. For example, unexpected verbal or physical abuse from a patient or sudden criticism from a family member can leave the employee bewildered and overwhelmed. A new job that already places heavy responsibility for meeting certain standards of care often becomes frustrating when the employee confronts unexpected

situations but does not know how to deal with those situations. For an employee to face consistent staffing shortages and have to pick up the slack is also demoralizing. Such experiences leave the employee feeling disillusioned, powerless, and incompetent for the position.

To overcome early burnout among new employees, a peer-mentoring program can be instituted by identifying, training, and rewarding experienced nursing assistants who are committed to helping new caregivers learn the ropes. Besides helping retain new staff members, such a program cultivates teamwork and enhances understanding of roles and expectations (Hoffman 2001). Also called the "buddy system," it makes peer resources available to help new employees fit in and to avoid frustration during the most critical period of employment. The new employee generally starts in such a program by observing and following the "buddy," an experienced nursing assistant. The new employee then starts working independently while still in frequent contact with the buddy, and the new employee receives ongoing support from the buddy. A buddy's duties should be clearly outlined; these duties can include explaining how to use the organization's systems, such as developmental resources and personnel resources. A variation of the buddy system can be used in the preselection process; a job candidate is given the opportunity to spend time informally with a current employee so that the candidate can find out first-hand what the job actually entails ("Buddy system can lower turnover, raise morale" 2002).

Social Community

An atmosphere of social support and a sense of belonging is highly conducive to staff retention. The social approach to staff retention views a nursing facility as a community in itself. The organizational culture promotes the feeling of belonging to a family in which people care for each other. Even though the family touch is likely to diminish in inverse proportion to the facility's size, the administration can place increased emphasis on a more flexible, people-centered, participatory, and nurturing atmosphere for both staff members and residents.

The philosophy of social support can be reinforced by policies and practices that promote the workers' ability to meet their social obligations. Examples include flexible scheduling, child care, and access to health care when needed. Furthermore, administration makes an effort to learn about each individual's needs and goals. Based on the findings,

career paths can be created for growth-oriented individuals. Some employees may be recognized for their skills in training others and groomed for becoming peer-mentors. Others may be able to provide insights into process improvement such as safety enhancement, disaster planning, or quality assurance. In nursing facilities, which typically have few opportunities for career growth, employee contribution to the activities just mentioned—self-development and achievement—must also be rewarded. Hoffman (2001) observed that increased compensation by itself would not slow turnover but that increased compensation tied to professional development can be very effective in promoting self-worth and thus slowing turnover.

Administrative Support

Other ways to reduce turnover include supporting the staff with adequate resources. Chronic staff shortages and unreasonably heavy workloads promote the feeling that management does not care, and so do a deficient staff skill-mix that does not take into account the heavier staffing weights called for by the levels of clinical acuity. A shortage of physical resources, such as equipment and supplies helps to reinforce this feeling. Despite what administrators might say about quality standards, workers are quick to perceive inconsistencies when resources are inadequate. Employees do not feel that they ought to be the ones to pay the price for inadequate resources in the form of higher stress and personal dissatisfaction. In multifacility chains, administrators often assign blame to the corporate office and try to portray the governing body as the villain in the eyes of the staff. In most instances, however, governing bodies remain unconvinced with a mere request for additional resources; they want data and analysis to justify the need for additional resources. The point here is that the ultimate responsibility for resource allocation remains largely with the administrator, but the governing board also must develop a more realistic understanding of the challenges of patient care.

STAFF DEVELOPMENT AND PERFORMANCE APPRAISAL

Job performance, training, and personal development are closely related. One of the primary goals of managing human resources should be em-

ployees' personal development. Such development entails more than building technical skills; it also entails preparing individuals to function responsibly in the nursing home community and in society. The programs of performance evaluation and training should be designed to promote this objective.

Staff Development

Staff development typically means training staff members to enhance their knowledge and expertise. Enhancing staff knowledge and expertise is without doubt an important goal of staff development, because it plays a critical role in building internal organizational strengths that a facility needs in a competitive environment. However, the goals of staff development must be extended beyond improving basic skills needed for the performance of routine functions. The overarching goal of staff development should be to make employees productive citizens of the organization and of society. Approaching staff development from this broad perspective can pay rich dividends in better quality, improved morale, and higher commitment.

Training should first and foremost focus on the worker's immediate job. As mentioned earlier, training and job orientation should help the employees improve not only their technical skills but also the coping skills that can help them deal with difficult situations. But in the broader context discussed here, training should connect the employees not only to their jobs, it should also assimilate them into the organization's community. Hence, training should enable employees to get a clear understanding of the organization's vision, mission, and values. New employees in particular should receive appropriate training in the facility's rules, policies, and procedures. Training should also include other key areas such as patient relations, family relations, teamwork, stress management, conflict resolution, work safety, and quality management. Finally, training should help people become responsible citizens of society. This last element may not appear at first to be work related, but it is. Employees who act responsibly in their social and home lives are also likely to be responsible and committed at work. Administrators know all too well that their employees' personal problems frequently become work problems. Nursing home employees predominantly come from low socio-economic backgrounds. Many have low self-esteem and lack the skills they need to address social and personal conflicts. For many employees balancing their home lives with the demands of the job is a daily struggle. Money management, family budget-

ing, problem solving, child care, nutrition, and wellness are only a few areas in which most staff members can benefit from training. Staff development in most nursing home organizations lacks the well-rounded approach it takes to build a stable and productive work environment.

Performance Appraisal

Instead of being a judgmental and punitive tool, the performance appraisal process should focus on staff development. Achieving this objective requires the participation of both the employee and the supervisor who does the evaluation. If both employees and supervisors understand the facility's philosophy of staff development and its relationship to performance evaluation, the process will not be as difficult for both parties as it often turns out to be.

Performance appraisal is a part of **management by objectives** (MBO). Simply put, MBO is based on a joint agreement between supervisors and employees on what specific and measurable objectives will be accomplished over a given time, and at the end of that time, the supervisors evaluate individual employees according to whether they have accomplished these objectives (Bounds and Woods 1998).

Most people would readily agree that MBO makes intuitive sense. What is often lacking, however, is the awareness of the linkage of employee performance to employee development; this linkage is a management responsibility. The point made here is that employee performance is a joint responsibility of supervisors and their employees, and both must be jointly held accountable for improving performance. On further thought, it should become clear that all supervisors in the chain of command, including the administrator, have some degree of responsibility for performance (or lack thereof) at even the lowest level of the organizational hierarchy.

For this MBO approach to work, several prerequisites are necessary:

- All employees in the organization must understand clearly what is expected from them individually, commensurate with their qualifications and level of expertise. It requires abandoning the "one-size-fits-all" approach.
- Objectives must be set, such as how many patients the employee is responsible for, and what outcomes of care would be expected. The objectives ought to incorporate an assessment of skills and of the

employee's ability to adapt to the facility's policies, procedures, values, schedules, and routines.

- Individual training needs, as well as needs for further orientation, should be governed by the assessments already mentioned. This measure would result in training programs that match individual needs.
- Personal development based on training and ensuing performance of employees are periodically assessed as a joint undertaking by employees and supervisors, including peer-mentors.
- Rewards are associated with participation in training, evidence of personal development, and objective measures of performance.
- Rewards for peer-mentors and supervisors are based on their achievements in staff development.

One problem with MBO is its potential for misuse by management when management's focus is on punishing individual employees instead of on using MBO for development purposes. According to W. Edwards Deming, the esteemed marketing guru, MBO and individual work quotas promote short-cuts in quality because individuals work to meet quotas rather than engage in continuous quality improvement. The commitment-based approach discussed in Chapter 13 places accountability for task accomplishment and quality on teams rather than on individuals. According to Deming's philosophy, performance evaluation and rewards would be implemented at the group rather than at the individual level.

SELF-MANAGED WORK TEAMS

In **self-managed work teams** (SMWTs)—also called self-directed work teams—a group of employees, the "team," are together responsible for performing a range of tasks that include scheduling, planning, and monitoring the team's performance. Members of a SMWT routinely work together to perform all daily tasks, and they routinely depend on each other to get the tasks accomplished and to make management decisions related to their work (Yeatts and Seward 2000). As an example, in the traditional staffing models presented in Table 14-1, each CNA will be assigned 6 patients on the day shift, 12 patients on the evening shift, and 18 patients on the night shift (because the staffing pattern is for 36 patients—see Exhibit 14-2). In the SMWT model, all 6 CNAs on the day shift will form one team who will be

responsible to render care to all 36 residents. As shifts change, the teams can develop information-sharing and coordination activities for continuity of care. Team members also decide who would serve which residents and what specific services should be provided to each resident (Yeatts and Seward 2000). Because SMWTs are given the authority to make all or most decisions related to their work, the process results in an enriched work environment and staff empowerment (Yeatts and Hyten 1998, 17). Preliminary research shows that this kind of empowerment leads to higher job satisfaction and lower turnover. When midlevel managers, such as unit charge nurses, are receptive to advice and input from CNAs and involve them in care planning and group problem solving, turnover rates are reduced, possibly because of an enriched work environment in which workers take responsibility for, and feel in control of, patient care (Banaszak-Holl and Himes 1996). Also, the quality of services is positively affected when team members are able to discuss resident desires and needs among themselves (Yeatts and Seward 2000). Communication links between employees and supervisors are kept open in a work environment with SMWTs.

The use of SMWTs in nursing homes is rare. However, in the emerging models of care that reflect cultural change (discussed in Chapter 6), such teams play a pivotal role. The Green House model, for example, relies on cross-trained, self-managed worker teams who are responsible for providing all basic and routine services to all elders. The teams are also responsible for the environment in each Green House. In this model, the typical supervisor-subordinate relationships are minimized because the workers make team decisions and the teams manage themselves in carrying out all routine tasks and responsibilities.

Another innovative model based on staff development and empowerment is the Wellspring Model created by Wellspring Innovative Solutions, Inc. Implemented in 1994, the Wellspring Model has been used by an alliance of 11 nonprofit nursing homes in Wisconsin. The consortium of 11 facilities pooled their resources to employ a geriatric nurse practitioner (GNP) and to pay for staff training and data analysis. The GNP is involved in clinical training, support, and reinforcement in all facilities, and the management staff learns to adopt a coaching and mentoring style. For example, a nurse coordinator in each facility provides coaching in implementing clinical modules. Staff is permanently

assigned to teams responsible for rendering care to the same residents, an approach that fosters collaboration (Manard 2002). All employees participate in decisions that affect their work and the care of residents they serve. Permanent resident assignments enable the staff to get to know the residents with whom they work on a daily basis. Some of these facilities have also turned over staff scheduling to the teams (Reinhard and Stone 2001).

Yeatts and Hyten (1998) recommend paying attention to several general rules that are important for SMWTs to function effectively:

- **Establishing a team charter**. The purpose of the team charter is to clarify the team's overall purpose and to establish some ground rules for making decisions. The rules are established with substantial input from team members as well as management.
- **Goals and priorities**. These are established by team members with support from management. The goals should be clear, challenging, and measurable.
- **Work responsibilities and training**. SMWTs are able to match the team members' talents and preferences to the tasks to be performed; this practice has positive effects on the team's performance. This type of matching results in a more specific allocation of responsibilities for individual team members and allows for accountability. The matching process also helps identify the specific areas in which further training is necessary. For example, the entire team may need training in decision-making, or a particular team member may need training in rendering maintenance-rehabilitation therapies.
- **Team leader**. The teams determine who will be the team leader. Team leaders rotate within each group as other team members are given the opportunity to take on the role of a team leader. Some teams may require all members to rotate, whereas others have an election that includes only those who are interested in the position.
- **Work procedures and problems**. Team members identify the most appropriate procedures and find effective solutions to work-related problems. When goals are based on measurable criteria, performance can be effectively monitored. By monitoring their own performance, SMWTs tend to take ownership of any performance problems and take action to improve performance.

COUNSELING, DISCIPLINING, AND TERMINATING

The three steps discussed in this section are progressive or sequential, and are undertaken when problems surface in conjunction with employee performance and work-related behaviors. Subsequent steps in the disciplinary process become unnecessary when performance or behaviors improve. But the probability of salvaging an employee becomes increasingly small as the process continues (Figure 14-1).

Counseling

Counseling entails an informal discussion between the employee and the supervisor when an employee needs to make improvement. Almost all employees at one point or another require some type of counseling. Counseling is a mild form of attention-getter that is devoid of any kind of threat to an individual's sense of job security. Expressions such as, "I have been through this myself," or "It is not uncommon for new employees to face this," or "It generally takes some time to get this right, but let's keep working at it," or "It can be serious, so let's focus on this some more," are commonly used by supervisors to address issues realistically and constructively and yet address those issues in a context that puts the employee at ease. Counseling is closely related to coaching, but it focuses on excep-

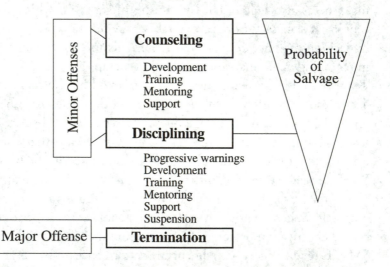

FIGURE 14-1 Progressive Corrective Steps and the Probability of Salvage

tions, that is, on behaviors that fall outside the bounds of acceptable job performance. Even though some "hand-holding" may be involved, the goal of counseling is to help employees "take responsibility for and manage their own decision-making" (Bolton 1997, p. 212). However, at this stage, the manager must identify the need for further development and training and find ways to provide those for the employee. Achieving these goals in a non-threatening way requires tact and skill on the part of the manager.

Disciplining

Disciplining involves a more formal approach to work-related problems than counseling. Management's right to discipline others first assumes that the managers themselves have exercised self-discipline and have set the right example for their staff. Starting with the administrator, the department heads and nursing supervisors should set an example before they can expect their employees to engage in positive behaviors. Otherwise, disciplining becomes hypocritical, and employees can see through any double standards.

All of the management actions and approaches discussed in this chapter so far are, in one form or another, related to staff development. A facility's staff development efforts can be regarded as successful when most of its staff members employ self-discipline by adhering to rules and standards of acceptable behavior. But a few employees will not take on the responsibility of self-discipline. Such employees will require some form of extrinsic disciplinary action (De Cenzo and Robbins 1996).

Common disciplinary problems identified by managers can be classified into four categories (Sherman et al. 1998): (1) attendance and tardiness problems, (2) dishonesty, (3) substandard work performance, and (4) behavioral problems, such as violation of rules. Failure to take disciplinary action only compounds a problem that eventually has to be dealt with. By then, inaction will have already done some damage to group morale. Inaction also implies that employee behaviors and work performance have been acceptable.

Fairness should be the primary guiding principle in any type of disciplinary action. Fairness requires that managers take into consideration some key factors to guide their practices (De Cenzo and Robbins 1996):

Seriousness of the problem. For example, dishonesty is more serious than occasional tardiness.

Duration and frequency. For example, repeat offenses are more serious than a first occurrence. Discipline should take into account the employee's past work record.

Extenuating circumstances. For example, automobile breakdown on the way to work may be a legitimate excuse for tardiness or absence.

Orientation, training, and counseling. For example, the extent to which an employee may have received assistance in adapting to the organization should be reviewed before that employee is disciplined. Disciplining should also be used as an opportunity to assess the need for additional training.

Employee's viewpoint. Before any action is taken, the employee must be given the opportunity to explain his or her position. The employee may not have been aware of the existence of a particular rule. In some situations, an investigation may be necessary to determine whether the employee was at fault.

Fairness. Fairness demands that all discussions and actions pertaining to disciplining be carried out in private. In effective management practices, humiliating someone in front of other people is never acceptable.

Once disciplinary action has been deemed necessary, the approach to disciplining should be positive and progressive. A positive approach requires emphasis on the corrective, rather than punitive, nature of disciplinary action. This emphasis does not mean, however, that punishment can never be a part of disciplinary action. It means that punishment may be employed with the objective of correcting behavior; otherwise it may lead to adversarial relationships between employees and their supervisors. Sherman et al. (1998) suggested that in positive disciplining, the total responsibility for correcting a problem is placed on the employee. Although the supervisor and the employee engage in joint discussion and problem solving, nothing is imposed by management; all solutions and affirmations are jointly reached.

As a matter of general practice, disciplining should be progressive. Progressive action may be bypassed only for the most serious offenses. **Progressive discipline** evolves through four main stages:

Verbal warning. Even though the warning itself is verbal, it is documented in the employee's personnel record.

Written warning. The written warning should document the problem, what the employee needs to do to demonstrate that the problem has been corrected, and further disciplinary action that will ensue if the problem remains uncorrected within a specified period. All warnings should be discussed with the employee, and the employee should be asked to sign the disciplinary document.

Final written warning or suspension without pay. At this point, documentation should be made that states that if the problem remains uncorrected for a specified length of time dismissal will follow.

Dismissal. Termination from employment becomes necessary when agreed-upon results are not demonstrated.

To keep the system fair and balanced, facility administrators should consider instituting an appeals system, like those used successfully in other industries, to resolve any disagreements between employees and supervisors over disciplinary matters. An appeals system that is likely to be most trusted by employees consists of a committee composed of an equal number of employee representatives and management staff. A small committee of no more than four to six members is recommended. The committee renders decisions, either upholding or rescinding a particular disciplinary action, based on reviewing facility policies, examining the evidence, and separately hearing the supervisor and the employee (McCabe 1988).

Terminating

Terminating employment is generally the final step in a progressive disciplining approach when all efforts and opportunities fail to bring about the desired behavior. If progressive disciplining is followed, there should be adequate documentation in the employee's personnel record on which the decision to terminate would be based. At times, however, termination becomes necessary for a serious one-time offense such as theft, patient abuse, deliberate destruction of facility property, or using alcohol or illegal drugs on the premises.

Regardless of how serious the offense, terminating an employee on the spot, or proclaiming "you are fired," is never a good idea. Such an action often raises questions about objectivity and perceived fairness. The employee may disagree with an allegation, and yet management may not want the employee to continue on the job while serious questions remain

unanswered, as would be the case when management believes that the employee has abused a patient. The answer to such a dilemma is found in placing the employee on suspension pending further investigation. The employee is told that he or she is being taken off the schedule and will be notified as soon as an investigation has been completed. If the employee is called back to work, the employee will get full back pay. Once an investigation has been completed and a decision has been made to terminate the employee a letter notifying the employee of the decision is sent by certified mail. In all disciplinary actions, including termination, the employee should be treated with courtesy.

LABOR RELATIONS AND UNIONIZATION

The National Labor Relations Act (NLRA) of 1935, also known as the Wagner Act, gave workers the right to organize and join unions without fear of retribution from their employers. The law specifically defined certain conduct as unfair labor practices. The NLRA also required employers to bargain in good faith with a union representing the employees. As part of this law the National Labor Relations Board (NLRB) was established as an independent federal agency, which now has 34 regional offices. The NLRB has the authority to conduct union recognition elections and to investigate complaints of unfair labor practices. Since 1974, employees of non-profit health care institutions, who were previously prevented from joining unions, have been extended the same rights as employees in other private businesses.

Election for Collective Representation

Unionization is a collective choice of an organization's employees, who have the collective right to join a union, and they also have the collective right not to join a union. If a union is voted in, however, it then has the exclusive right to represent all the employees in a given **bargaining unit**, which covers categories of employees a union can legitimately represent.

Employees seek union representation mainly because of their ongoing dissatisfaction with employment conditions and their belief that a union would be effective in alleviating at least some of those negative conditions. The main working conditions employees seek to improve include wages, benefits, and perceived unfair treatment from management. In the final analysis, employees who seek to form a union feel powerless to change things that are important to them. They hope to achieve those results

through collective representation. Hence, preventive action through effective leadership and sound human resource practices are the administrator's best defenses against unionization.

Once employees decide to unionize and contact between a small group of employees and union leaders is established, an organizing campaign begins: Union leaders hold employee meetings away from the nursing home premises, and informal leaders among the employees try to persuade their coworkers to sign authorization cards. Signing an authorization card is deemed to indicate the employee's willingness to join the union, although some employees may sign the card just to get a coworker "off their backs." For the NLRB to hold an election, at least 30 percent of the employees in the proposed bargaining unit must sign the authorization cards. As a matter of practice, however, unions seek a much higher number because to win an election the union must get more than 50% of the votes in a subsequent election.

Before an election, the NLRB determines the makeup of the bargaining unit, which is a distinct group of employees who have common employment interests and who may reasonably be grouped together for the purpose of collective bargaining. An election by secret ballot is conducted by NLRB officials in the presence of representatives from the union as well as the employer. All employees who are included in the bargaining unit have the right to vote. If the union wins by a majority vote, the NLRB will certify the union as the legal bargaining representative for the employees. On the other hand, if the union loses the election, it also loses the right to represent the employees.

Unfair Labor Practices

During a unionization campaign, both the employer and the union have the right to present information to employees. Management has the right to inform employees, but all information must be factual. Management representatives may also express their opinions but should not engage in deliberate misrepresentation. The facility's administration, for instance, could make appeals in an effort to convince the employees that joining the union would not be in their best interest. Typical appeals include the following (Bounds and Woods 1998):

- The union can make promises, but it cannot guarantee that it would succeed in delivering on those promises.

- Wages are already good and equal to or better than what the union could negotiate. If the union is voted in, wages and benefits will become negotiable. They may go down, stay the same, or increase.
- Union dues and other costs outweigh the benefits of belonging to a union.
- The union is an outsider, not really attuned to employees' best interests.
- Employees may have to strike even when they do not want to.

In making such appeals, managers must be careful that they do not engage in any **unfair labor practices**, which can be categorized into four areas:

(1) **Promise**. The union can make promises, but management cannot. For example, management cannot promise employees pay increases, better benefits, or other types of rewards in exchange for a 'no' vote. The administrator should, however, continue to follow any preestablished wage increase programs.

(2) **Threaten**. Management cannot make any type of threats. For example, it is illegal to state that the facility will close down if the union is voted in, or that health insurance benefits will have to be curtailed. Intimidating employees with discipline or discharge is also an unfair labor practice. However, supervisors have the right to take any reasonable action to prevent employee solicitation at work stations and during work time. Employees, on the other hand, are free to engage in union solicitation in a break room during break or lunch time.

(3) **Interrogate**. Supervisors cannot ask employees about how they intend to vote, about their past union affiliation, or what may have been discussed at the union meetings. On the other hand, if an employee volunteers information to a supervisor, listening is not illegal. It is only illegal for a supervisor to ask.

(4) **Spy**. It is illegal for management to spy on union meetings or other activities related to the unionization campaign.

Engaging in unfair labor practices during a unionization campaign carries grave risks for management. The union can petition the NLRB to set aside the election and enforce recognition of the union.

Collective Bargaining

Once a union has been certified to represent employees, labor laws mandate that both unions and management negotiate in good faith, a process called **collective bargaining**. This term means that both parties must engage in a genuine process to reach an agreement even though there is no guarantee that an agreement will be reached. Yet when an agreement is reached it must be ratified by a majority vote of the employees in the bargaining unit. The contract specifies the terms and conditions of employment for the workers who are covered under the contract. Some typical areas covered under a union contract include duration of the contract, description of the bargaining unit, wages, benefits, work rules, rights of management, jurisdiction of various jobs, and grievance procedures. Typically, a contract is negotiated for a three-year term. Every contract must be renegotiated at the end of the period it covers.

Contract Administration

Once a union contract has been ratified, the administrator is responsible for ensuring that all supervisors understand its terms. It is important to emphasize the management's rights, which typically include the right to allocate and use resources in a way management sees fit; to give work assignments; to hire, discipline, and terminate employees; and to formulate policies and procedures.

Grievance resolution is an important element of any collective bargaining agreement. "A **grievance** is a formal expression of employee dissatisfaction about some job situation" (Bounds and Woods 1998, p. 413). The union may also protest the way that management has interpreted and enforced certain provisions of the contract. Bringing a complaint to an employee's immediate supervisor is the first step in any grievance procedure. Many grievances can be effectively handled at this level provided that the supervisors are trained in handling grievances.

If the complaint is not resolved, the employee takes the complaint to the union steward. A **union steward** is a unionized employee who works at the facility and who officially represents the union to his or her fellow unionized employees at the workplace. Stewards can employ a lot of discretion in handling grievances and can often be more effective than the employee in getting problems resolved by being more objective. If a grievance is not resolved at this level, a representative from the union office

meets with the administrator in an effort to reach some compromise. If the issue cannot be resolved in this way it is submitted to arbitration, a costly process that both parties try to avoid. **Arbitration** is a process in which a neutral third party—generally, but not necessarily, a retired judge or attorney who may be recognized by a court jurisdiction or be associated with an arbitration service—hears both sides and renders a decision that is binding on both parties (Bounds and Woods 1998).

Strikes and Picketing

Work stoppage as a concerted effort by unionized employees is called a **strike**. The law requires unions to give a ten-day notice to a nursing facility before calling on the employees to go on a strike. The purpose of this requirement is to allow health care facilities to make plans for continuity of patient care. Striking employees often patrol the perimeter of the facility displaying placards that call attention to the labor dispute they have with management. This concerted action is called **picketing**.

An **economic strike** is the most common type of strike. It occurs when the union and management fail to reach an agreement: an **impasse** occurs in the negotiations. Management has the right to hire replacement workers during an economic strike. Striking employees can be replaced either temporarily or permanently. Reinstatement for an employee may occur when a striker makes an offer to return to work with no conditions attached. Reinstatement is not automatic after the strike is over, but preference is given to those who wish to return to work as job vacancies occur.

As a general rule, striking and picketing are not to interfere with the management's right to provide patient care. For instance, picketers may not prevent non-striking workers and supervisors from entering the facility or obstruct delivery trucks delivering essential supplies and food to the facility. Legal remedies are available for dealing with violent strikes and picketing.

EMPLOYMENT LAWS

The purpose of labor laws is to protect the rights of individuals in an employment relationship, which mainly includes hiring, wages, benefits, promotion, and discharge. Hence, many of the legal requirements discussed here are loosely referred to as antidiscrimination laws. These laws

are based on the theory that employment practices should be governed by criteria that are job-related; management's employment decisions should not be based on personal characteristics that have little to do with an individual's ability to do the job. **Employment discrimination** is generally defined as discriminatory action in failing or refusing to hire; in discharging or otherwise discriminating against an individual with respect to terms, conditions, or privileges of employment; or in limiting, segregating, or classifying employees in a way that it deprives an individual of employment opportunity, training, advancement, or status.

Employment-at-Will

Employment laws provide for exceptions to a long-standing legal doctrine called employment-at-will. Historically, the employment-at-will doctrine has asserted that employment is at the will of both the employer and the employee, and that either party may terminate the employment relationship at any time for any reason or for no reason, except when the termination is in violation of a contract. In recent years, however, there has been a growing trend toward a restricted application of this rule (Pozgar 1992). Terminating an employee without cause is also limited by various antidiscrimination laws. Although states vary substantially in applying the at-will rule, additional considerations such as an implied covenant of good faith and fair treatment are increasingly entering into court decisions pertaining to the employment-at-will doctrine (Pozgar 1992).

Equal-Employment Opportunity

Title VII of the Civil Rights Act of 1964 prohibits discrimination on account of race, color, religion, sex, or national origin in any term, condition, or privilege of employment. The Civil Rights Act of 1991 provided for increased financial damages against organizations found guilty of discriminatory practices. The Equal Employment Opportunity Commission (EEOC) has the authority to enforce the various antidiscrimination laws discussed in this section, and to conduct investigations when complaints of discrimination are brought before this agency.

Pregnancy Discrimination

The Pregnancy Discrimination Act of 1978 came about as an amendment to the Title VII of the Civil Rights Act of 1964. The law describes preg-

nancy as a disability, and requires that management consider an employee's pregnancy as any other medical condition would be considered. Accordingly, it makes it illegal to deny sick leave for a pregnancy-related condition. The law also prohibits discrimination against pregnant women in hiring, promotion, or termination, provided that they are able to perform the job.

Age Discrimination

The Age Discrimination in Employment Act was passed in 1967. This act prohibits discrimination in any aspect of employment against individuals between the ages of 40 and 70. The law does not afford protections to people below the age of 40.

Equal Pay

The Equal Pay Act of 1963 addresses the issue of wage disparities based on gender. Simply stated, the law requires that men and women be given equal pay when both perform equal work in the same establishment. Wages between men and women in the same jobs may differ on the basis of factors such as qualifications, seniority, and job performance, but not on the basis of gender alone. Generally, male orderlies and female nurse aides perform similar work and should be paid according to the same wage scale.

Protecting the Disabled

The Americans with Disabilities Act (ADA) of 1990 protects disabled workers against discrimination. The law defines a disabled employee as one who has a physical or mental impairment that substantially limits one or more major life activities, who has a record of such impairment, or who is regarded as having such impairment. A variety of conditions can be classified as disabilities, including hearing loss, emotional illness, heart disease, cancer, and acquired immunodeficiency syndrome (AIDS). The law also protects recovered alcoholics and substance abusers. The ADA requires employers to make "reasonable accommodation" for disabled persons who are otherwise capable of performing the essential functions of a job. **Reasonable accommodation** includes altering facilities and the work environment as well as job restructuring so that the disabled employee is able to perform the essential functions of the job, and it also includes altering or eliminating nonessential aspects of a job.

Family and Medical Leave

The Family and Medical Leave Act (FMLA) of 1993 allows employees twelve weeks of unpaid leave in a twelve-month period for qualified reasons. Qualified reasons include birth of a child, care of a child up to twelve months of age, adoption or foster care for a child, care of a spouse or care of a parent with a serious health condition, or the employee's own serious health condition that prevents the employee from performing the essential functions of the job. To be eligible, the employee must have completed at least one year of employment and worked for the employer for at least 1,250 hours. The law requires that after this unpaid leave the employee be allowed to return to his or her original position or an equivalent position with the same terms of pay, benefits, and working conditions that the employee had before taking FMLA leave.

Harassment

In a general sense, harassment at work occurs in the context of what is termed a "hostile environment" that interferes with an individual's job performance. In principle, unlawful harassment was protected under the Civil Rights Act of 1964, although that law specifically focused on discrimination. The Civil Rights Act of 1991 amended Title VII of the Civil Rights Act of 1964 to specifically include unlawful harassment on the basis of sex, religion, national origin, race, and disability (Sherman et al. 1998). It must be emphasized that even though sexual harassment has received a lot of attention, harassment may also take other forms. In determining harassment, it may sometimes be difficult to decide what may or may not be hostile or offensive. Employee complaints may be one clue to whether something is offensive. Note that harassment may not necessarily come from supervisors. An employee may be harassed by coworkers, visitors, sales people, or clients. Questions that are likely to arise in any litigation over harassment may include whether management knew about the problem or should have known about it, and if anything was done to stop it.

CONCLUSION

Human-resource management is an undertaking that can add substantial value to an organization's services, yet the human asset is often overlooked by

management practices. Many organizational disorders related to human resources can be traced to poor leadership and inflexible policies. Once the underlying dysfunctionality becomes manifest in symptoms such as absenteeism and turnover it takes a lot of time and effort to steer the ship around to the right course. By this time, the dysfunction will have also eroded patient care quality in most instances. Hence, nursing home administrators must receive adequate training in managing human resources. Growing evidence suggests that staff empowerment and self-managed work teams can help overcome some of the problems that beset many nursing homes. For example, nursing home employees are likely to treat residents in the same manner in which the caregivers themselves are treated by management. If caregivers feel nurtured and cared for, they are more likely to be nurturing and caring toward the residents. If caregivers feel valued, they will value the residents (Barba et al. 2002).

DISCUSSION AND APPLICATION QUESTIONS

1. In Exhibit 14-1, what are some alternative ways to create three patient acuity categories using administrative judgment instead of 'squares around the mean' approach?
2. Many experts believe that implementing SMWTs in nursing homes is not easy. What do you think may be some necessary elements for implementing SMWTs? What main problems might a nursing home administrator encounter when implementing SMWTs?

INTERNET RESOURCES FOR FURTHER LEARNING

The Equal Employment Opportunity Commission (EEOC)
   http://www.eeoc.gov/

The National Human Resources Association (NHRA) is a network of local affiliates focused on advancing the development of human resource professionals.
   www.humanresources.org

The National Labor Relations Board (NLRB)
   http://www.nlrb.gov/

REFERENCES

Banaszak-Holl, J., and M.A. Himes. 1996. Factors associated with nursing home staff turnover. *The Gerontologist* 36, no. 4: 512–517.

Barba, B.E., et al. 2002. Promoting thriving in nursing homes: The Eden Alternative. *Journal of Gerontological Nursing* 28, no. 3: 7–13.

Bolton, T. 1997. *Human Resource Management: An Introduction*. Malden, Massachusetts: Blackwell Publishers Inc.

Boone, L.E., and D.L. Kurtz. 1984. *Principles of Management*. 2nd ed. New York: Random House, Inc.

Bounds, G.M., and J.A. Woods. 1998. *Supervision*. Cincinnati, Ohio: South-Western College Publishing.

Brannon, D. et al. 2002. An exploration of job, organizational, and environmental factors associated with high and low nursing assistant turnover. *The Gerontologist* 42 (2): 159–168.

Buddy system can lower turnover, raise morale. 2002. *Staff Leader: Supervision Strategies* 15, no. 9: 1, 11.

Caruth, D.L., and G.D. Handlogten. 1997. *Staffing the Contemporary Organization: A Guide to Planning, Recruiting, and Selecting for Human Resource Professionals*. 2nd ed. Westport, Connecticut: Quorum Books.

Cohen-Mansfield, J., and A.S. Rosenthal. 1989. Absenteeism of nursing staff in a nursing home. *International Journal of Nursing Studies* 26 (2): 187–194.

De Cenzo, D.A., and S.P. Robbins. 1996. *Human Resource Management*. 5th ed. New York: John Wiley & Sons, Inc.

Griffith, J.R. 1995. *The Well-Managed Health Care Organization*. 3rd ed. Ann Arbor, Michigan: AUPHA Press/Health Administration Press.

Hoffman, R. 2001. Lessons learned in creating a successful CAN retention program: One organization's solution to the problem of turnover. *Nursing Homes Long Term Care Management* 50 (4): 26–29.

Institute of Medicine. 2001. *Improving the Quality of Long-Term Care.*, G.S. Wunderlich and P.O. Kohler, Eds. Washington, DC: National Academy Press.

Lescoe-Long, M. 2000. Why they leave. *Nursing Homes Long Term Care Management* 49 (10): 70–74.

Lyncheski, J.E. 2002. Keeping the unions at bay. *Nursing Homes Long Term Care Management* 51 (5): 44–48.

Manard, B. 2002. *Nursing Home Quality Indicators: Their Uses and Limitations*. Washington, DC: Public Policy Institute, AARP.

McCabe, D.M. 1988. *Corporate Nonunion Complaint Procedures and Systems*. New York: Praeger Publishers.

Mondy, R.W., and R.M. Noe. 1993. *Human Resource Management*. 5th ed. Boston: Allyn and Bacon.

Pozgar, G.D. 1992. *Long-Term Care and The Law: A Legal Guide for Health Care Professionals*. Gaithersburg, Maryland: Aspen Publishers, Inc.

Reinhard, S., and R. Stone. 2001. *Promoting Quality in Nursing Homes: The Wellspring Model.* Monograph published by the Commonwealth Fund. www.cmwf.org.

Sherman, A. et al. 1998. *Managing Human Resources.* 11th ed. Cincinnati, Ohio: South-Western College Publishing.

Singh, D.A., and R.C. Schwab. 1998. Retention of administrators in nursing homes: What can management do? *The Gerontologist* 38 (3): 362–369.

Singh, D.A., and R.C. Schwab. 2000. Predicting turnover and retention in nursing home administrators: Management and policy implications. *The Gerontologist* 40 (3): 310–319.

Yeatts, D.E., and C. Hyten. 1998. *High-Performing Self-Managed Work Teams.* Thousand Oaks, CA: Sage Publications, Inc.

Yeatts, D.E., and R.R. Seward. 2000. Reducing turnover and improving health care in nursing homes: The potential effects of self-managed work teams. *The Gerontologist* 40 (3): 358–363.

CHAPTER 15

Effective Marketing and Public Relations

LEARNING MODULES

1. Role of marketing in a changing environment. The basic nature of marketing: What it is and what it is not.
2. Value-based marketing. Perceived value and the role of information. Evolving expectations and value creation.
3. The marketing function viewed as a set of activities and attitudes that permeate the entire organization. The supremacy of customer-orientation over profit-orientation.
4. The goals of marketing, which extend beyond attracting patients to the facility, and include building exchange partnerships.
5. Components of marketing strategy: segmentation, target marketing, positioning, and marketing mix. Purpose and methods of segmentation. Target market selection. Positioning and how to do it. Using the marketing mix as a positioning strategy.
6. Implementing the marketing mix despite challenges that are unique to health care. Tangible and intangible features of the long-term care product. Pricing strategies for certain market

continues

segments. Mitigating the customer's indirect costs. The significance of location and access in marketing. Promotion and its main objectives.

7. Differentiation as a positioning strategy. Is segmentation always necessary? Creating a market niche.

8. Personal selling in preadmission inquiry and in customer relations. Objectives to be achieved during the inquiry process. Facility tour and its purpose. Closing the sale. How to build customer relations.

9. Promotion and public relations and their objectives. Advertising strategies and tools. Obtaining free publicity in the media. Promoting the facility through personal contact, informational materials, and events.

The 1990s and beyond can aptly be labeled as the "age of the customer." Shifts in consumer demand have been the driving force behind changes in the long-term care industry. As pointed out in chapter 6, changing lifestyle expectations of aging Americans are forcing the long-term care industry to rethink some of the traditional concepts of quality of life in nursing homes. Also, during the 1990s, the delivery of long-term care shifted focus from institution-based services to community-based services. Within the institutional continuum itself, settings that are less restrictive than a nursing home, such as assisted living and adult foster care, have enjoyed wide popularity and growth. Patients' individual preferences for receiving services in their own homes have also led to a phenomenal growth of the home-health industry. As the range of long-term care services expands, the continuum of available services from which to choose becomes increasingly more confusing for the consumer. In such an environment marketing becomes a central function, in order to distinctively place a facility's offerings before consumers who are often overwhelmed by the undifferentiated choices.

Marketing is often neglected by nursing home administrators, because many administrators fall victim to what can be called the "word-of-mouth syndrome." Word-of-mouth is actually a powerful communication tool, but without marketing only a small fraction of its full potential is realized. Through marketing administrators can gain clear-cut compet-

itive advantages over those who do not have a marketing function in their organizations.

Marketing is often equated with customer service, advertising, selling, or community relations. These activities are merely some of the action components of marketing, which is much broader in scope. Marketing incorporates a comprehensive strategic conceptualization that calls for developing a plan, carrying out that plan, and taking corrective action as necessary. Because of a fairly widespread misunderstanding of what marketing is, it remains, for many health care facilities, nothing more than a "buzz" word, and some well-intentioned administrators undertake certain haphazard steps and call it marketing. Random "marketing" efforts are frequently undertaken when new competitors enter the market and an existing nursing facility has an increasing number of empty beds that become more and more difficult to fill. In a state of panic, administrators may launch an advertising campaign, start renovating the facility, or plan a facility open house. These efforts may produce temporary results, but often fail to change the long-range outlook.

Marketing must be viewed as an ongoing management strategy, and it must permeate all aspects of a facility's operations. Marketing is not a quick-fix for a major census decline. Marketing involves consistent effort.

MARKETING: ITS PHILOSOPHY AND ESSENCE

The American Marketing Association has furnished one of the most widely accepted definitions of marketing: "Marketing is the process of planning and executing the conception, pricing, promotion, and distribution of ideas, goods, and services to create exchanges that satisfy individual and organizational goals" (American Marketing Association 1995). The marketing process—its planning and execution—is undertaken with the goal of creating exchanges between two or more parties in which each party gives something of value to the other party or parties in the exchange. All parties in the exchange perceive benefits from entering into the exchange. It is not a coincidence that marketing is anchored in the open system philosophy (discussed in Chapter 1).

Although marketing can be applied to any type of exchange, creating an exchange between a business and its customers is often the main focus

of marketing. Peter Drucker (1974), a highly regarded management theo-rist, stated that the purpose of any business is to create customers, and the customers eventually determine what a business is, what it produces, and whether it will prosper. At first thought it may appear as if all customers of nursing home services are looking for the same product, but that is not the case.

Value Perceptions

Successful marketing strategies are anchored in the basic philosophy of delivering value to the customer. The term "value" signifies the worth that is perceived by each party in an exchange. However, value is individual-specific. Each individual tries to determine how his or her needs can be adequately met at the least cost. For example, wide variations exist in how different customers evaluate value when shopping for an automobile. For some consumers, a Mercedes or a Lexus is the best value; for others it may be a Ford Taurus. Some look for value in a brand new vehicle, while others look for the same in a pre-owned car. Similarly, nursing home shoppers determine value by evaluating a number of variables, and not everyone is looking for the same thing. For example, perceived value can vary accord-ing to a facility's size, layout, décor, amenities, location, reputation, owner-ship status (whether the facility is for-profit or non-profit), and price.

Influencing Value Perception

As a first step in marketing, the administrator must understand how value is generally perceived by the community and how the facility and its ser-vices may be packaged to project that value. Drucker (1974) stated that the customer, not the business, determines what value is. However, be-cause the perception of value is not something tangible, it can be shaped by information and education. Customers do not always know how they should evaluate health care services, and many things are not obvious to people when they first visit a facility. Hence, effective marketing should be driven by value-based exchanges (Figure 15-1). For instance, when dis-cussing a potential placement during the inquiry process, understanding the client's needs is essential: Why is the client searching for a nursing home? How soon is a bed needed? How far does the family live? Who will pay? Is cost a barrier? Intake personnel should think about how best the facility can meet the client's needs, and whether the facility can meet those needs in the first place. Intake personnel should provide specific

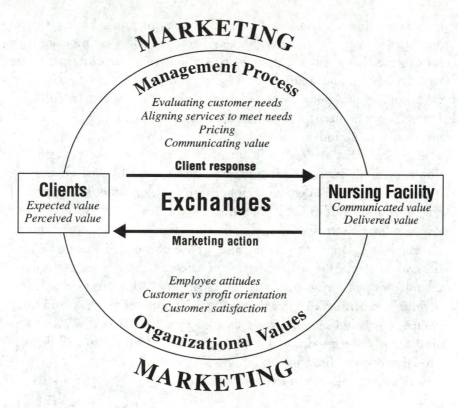

FIGURE 15-1 Marketing Principles Resulting in Value-based Exchanges

information on how the nursing home will address the patient's clinical and social needs, and they should also provide information about the technology the facility has for enhancing care and comfort for patients. Quality-of-life features that emphasize privacy, safety, and comfort must be pointed out by intake personnel to prospective clients. On the other hand, one must be forthright if the facility is not equipped to adequately address what the patient needs. Marketing is, by nature, fundamentally focused on satisfying customer needs and desires. A relentless pursuit to fill vacant beds with little regard for the patient's needs and the facility's ability to serve those needs often turns out to be the wrong approach.

Value Creation

Marketing is not just confined to information and influencing people's perception of value. Marketing has much to do with the creation, promo-

tion, and delivery of value demanded by the customer. Following the open-system concept, effective marketers study changes taking place over time in the characteristics, realities, needs, and values of customers. The term "values" (plural) refers to core beliefs and principles that guide people's thinking and behaviors. Social and cultural change often redefines expectations and needs. Clients' expectations for long-term care are evolving toward more independence, greater control over lifestyle, and living arrangements that are less institutional for the patient. The next generation of well-educated, health-conscious, and financially well-off nursing home consumers will demand emphasis on health promotion, improved amenities and comfort, and on having a voice in the facility's operation. Astute administrators will create value through innovative solutions in nursing-home design, furnishing, and service delivery. Successful administrators of the future will anticipate and respond to change. A facility's complacency in recognizing the forces shaping value creation will risk inviting competitors to enter the market with innovative ideas, and these competitors could snatch away clients. In Drucker's (1974) words, "The aim of marketing is to know and understand the customer so well that the product or service fits him and sells itself" (p. 64). Hence, marketing permeates the very essence of effective management.

THE MARKETING FUNCTION AND ITS GOALS

The concepts just discussed make it clear that marketing is an essential function in long-term care administration. Marketing practices embrace two interrelated principles: (1) Marketing is a function that incorporates a set of marketing activities, and (2) Marketing is an attitude that must permeate the entire organization (Majaro 1993). Figure 15-1 captures these principles.

Functional Activities

As a function, marketing is a continuous management process, which remains dynamic. First and foremost, marketing includes all activities that are necessary for understanding customer requirements and for aligning existing services or creating new services to meet those requirements. Secondly, marketing activities include effective pricing, communication,

and distribution to inform, motivate, and service the markets. Both are "carefully formulated programs, not just random actions" (Kotler and Clarke 1987, pp. 5–6).

Organizational Attitudes and Orientation

Marketing is also an attitude that permeates the entire organization. Although marketing is much more than making a sale, an old business axiom fittingly illustrates the organization-wide attitude that is necessary for marketing, "The sales department isn't the whole company, but the whole company had better be the sales department" (Czinkota et al. 2000). As discussed in previous chapters, positive leadership and human resource practices are essential for building an organizational culture in which all staff members behave according to the values and philosophies desired by the organization's management.

Organizational values provide the underpinnings that define and direct a nursing facility's orientation and thrust. For instance, Majaro (1993) emphasizes "customer orientation" as an organizational value above "profit orientation." Customer orientation requires all personnel to focus their activities and behaviors on satisfying the needs and wants of patients, family members, and visitors. In essence, customer orientation is a proactive style. Customer orientation is primarily centered on a solution-oriented approach that understands problems customers now face, and it also anticipates new issues and concerns that may emerge. Customer orientation presupposes that a primary focus on profits is unwarranted, because by making customer satisfaction its primary mission, a facility can achieve higher profits than by placing its primary focus on profits. The misplaced emphasis on profits helps explain why many nursing facilities are caught in a downward spiral of losing patients, which inevitably translates into lower profitability.

Marketing Goals

According to a well-known marketing theorist, Philip Kotler (1991), "Marketing consists of actions undertaken to elicit desired responses to some object from a target audience" (p. 7). The marketing actions referred to in this definition are associated with the functional aspect mentioned earlier, in which the focus of marketing is on carrying out carefully formulated programs. Kotler's definition also highlights the goal, or "end result," that marketing is designed to achieve.

The desired response from a target audience is the consummation of an exchange based on the value expected and perceived by the target audience (Figure 15-1). An exchange results when the nursing facility is able to communicate value that the client is seeking in a manner that will lead the client to perceive that the expected value will be realized. The exchange continues, however, only when the delivered value equals the value that was communicated to the client.

As pointed out in Chapter 1, effective administrators manage a full cycle of exchanges in four areas:

- obtaining critical resources from the external environment
- attracting clients whose needs would be met by the facility's services
- effective use of resources to adequately meet client needs in terms of quality and satisfaction
- returns to the environment in the form of jobs, taxes (by for-profit entities), competition, and community health

The goal of marketing is to facilitate these exchanges. For example, besides attracting patients, marketing exchanges would also result in successfully recruiting qualified staff members; in obtaining finances at attractive terms for a new construction project; in preserving the facility's licensure, certification, and accreditation status; in attaining higher levels of clinical quality, staff satisfaction, and profits; and in achieving goodwill in the community. Thus, marketing has much broader goals than simply admitting more patients, and marketing includes building the exchange partnerships described in Chapter 2. Most marketing activities are designed to address issues of market competition. Other marketing activities are intended to elicit decisions from family members and other parties to bring patients to a nursing facility. The rest of this chapter will focus on this goal.

MARKETING STRATEGY

Successful marketing requires a core strategy, which is a comprehensive game plan. Simply put, a marketing strategy outlines where and how the nursing facility will compete in the marketplace (Bovée et al. 1995), which requires spotlighting the target customers. How well the nursing facility will compete depends on how well the facility positions itself in

the target market by using an appropriate marketing mix. Figure 15-2 illustrates the steps necessary for developing a marketing strategy.

Segmentation and Target Market

The long-term care market is very diverse, because it includes various community-based services and a continuum of institutional settings. Therefore, identifying and selecting appropriate target markets becomes a nec-

FIGURE 15-2 Steps in Developing a Marketing Strategy

essary strategic step for a facility. To an extent, community-based and institution-based services represent natural segments in the long-term care market, but these broad markets should be further segmented.

Purpose of Segmentation

Value perceptions vary greatly among those who seek nursing home placement. Hence, in nursing home marketing, a large heterogeneous market should be divided into smaller, more homogeneous segments of customers and potential customers. This process of dividing a large market into smaller segments, each with its distinct characteristics, is called **market segmentation**. The purpose of segmentation is to identify distinct market segments of which one or more will constitute the **target market**, which is that part of the overall market from which the nursing facility will create customers. One of the main goals of targeting a small number of market segments is to better understand the needs and desires of customers and to better match the facility's package of services to meet those needs. This goal is easier to accomplish in a client group that is more or less homogeneous than it is to achieve in a diverse group. Once the requirements of the target market are clearly defined, the nursing facility gains the advantage of creating or redesigning services most appropriate for those patients. The more closely a nursing facility can match its services to the value clients are seeking, the more successfully it can market its services and attract patients.

Segmenting by Demographics, Needs, and Preferences

In spite of their degree of functional impairment, most people do not desire to receive care in a nursing home. People go to nursing homes because they need to, not because they choose to do so. Segmentation is achieved by differentiating the needs and preferences of customers. The nursing-home market should be segmented first by demographics, then by clinical needs, and again by client preferences (Exhibit 15-1). For instance, pediatric and geriatric care cannot be mixed unless the facility has distinct areas for such services. Institution-based services have some natural segmentation according to care levels, such as retirement living, assisted living, skilled nursing, and subacute care. Although most nursing homes are confined to delivering skilled nursing care, many nursing homes have captured other segments of the market by adding assisted living, retirement living, or other services along the continuum of care.

EXHIBIT 15–1

Market Segments Based on Demographics, Needs and Preferences

Demographics
Pediatrics
Older adults
Young disabled
Women only
Pay source: personal funds, private insurance, Medicare, Medicaid

Clinical Needs
Short-term rehabilitation
Skilled nursing care
Independent retirement living
Assisted living
Alzheimer's care
Wound care
Head trauma care
Ventilator care
AIDS care
Adult day care

Client Preferences
Facility close to home
Menu selection
High skill mix of staff
High-end private pay
Low-end private pay
Private room
Nonregimented personal routines
Décor and furnishings
Transportation services
Safety
Amenities
Desire for continuing care

Continuing-care retirement communities (CCRCs) cover the entire continuum yet they segment the market on the basis of whether patients have the means to pay an entry fee and whether patients desire to receive continuing care as their health declines. Thus, pay type—whether it is private pay, Medicaid, and Medicare—is another criterion for segmenting the market. Within the private-pay market itself, some subsegments are based on clients' sensitivity to price. Some clients are looking for high-end services and amenities for which they are willing to pay more, whereas other clients are content with more basic services at a cheaper price. The different major types of clients of long-term care discussed in Chapter 2, such as older adults, young disabled adults, and people with AIDS, also constitute market segments. Specialized niches for services such as head trauma care, ventilator care, active rehabilitation, and Alzheimer's care also present an approach to segmenting the market. Clearly, a nursing facility administrator should decide which particular segment(s) of the market the organization can most adequately serve.

Selecting Market Segments

Choice of market segments should not be driven by what the nursing home thinks it would like to have as its target market. Rather, the facility's choice should be based on a careful evaluation of the needs and desires of the target market and on the extent to which the facility possesses the physical structures, equipment, staff competencies, and other resources to address the needs and desires of potential clients. Apart from a facility's strengths and competencies in providing services, market segments can be identified in areas in which unmet needs exist or in areas in which the competitors may be weak. For example, if the target market is large enough for an upscale facility in which clients would receive pampered treatment, such as private rooms, individual telephones and television sets, and restaurant-style table service in a plush dining room, such an operation can fill unmet demand.

To be useful, market segments must be evaluated according to four criteria (Kotler 2000). Each segment must be:

1. **Measurable**. The size and other characteristics of the segments, such as ability to pay and client preferences, must be measurable.
2. **Sizeable**. A segment should be the largest possible homogeneous group worth going after with a tailored marketing program. For

example, in a community with a population of 20,000, segmenting the nursing home market may not make sense.

3. **Accessible**. The facility must be able to effectively reach and serve the market. Because accessibility is governed mainly by the facility's location, the facility should evaluate the needs of its surrounding community. It should also assess how far people may be willing to travel to receive certain services not offered by competitors, and whether clients will travel to the facility's particular location to get those services. For example, people may travel some distance to get specialized services. On the other hand, clients may not want to travel to a facility located in a working-class neighborhood if they are looking for high-end private-pay services.

4. **Differentiable**. The segments should be differentiable according to client needs and preferences. For example, the Green House concept discussed in Chapter 6 is highly differentiated from traditional nursing homes. But differentiation can be achieved in a number of different ways, as discussed later in this chapter.

Market Targeting

Market segmentation does not imply that the facility must target only one segment. How many segments and which particular segments to target will depend on: (1) the segment's overall attractiveness, such as its size, growth potential, and profitability; and (2) the organization's objectives and resources in terms of its mission and competencies (Kotler 2000). In most instances, a nursing facility can pursue three types of targeting strategies:

- Single-offer mass-market coverage
- Single-segment concentration
- Selective specialization

Single-Offer Mass-Market Coverage

Most nursing homes go for a single-offer mass-market coverage, in which market segments are ignored. These facilities offer standard skilled-nursing care, and they try to attract anyone in order to increase the occupancy. As illustrated in Figure 15-3A, one generic product is designed to suit everyone's needs, and little room is given to accommodating client preferences. Such a strategy may work well in communities where the seg-

ments are indistinguishable or the size of different segments is too small to undertake a segmentation approach that would be profitable. In most urban and suburban markets, however, a mass market approach may not produce the results an organization desires.

Single-Segment Concentration

Single-segment concentration (Figure 15-3B) is a targeting strategy in which the facility produces one specialized offering for a single segment. Examples of this strategy include a specialized rehabilitation facility, a facility specializing in head trauma and ventilator care, or a facility catering to high-end private-pay clients. Such a strategy can pose high risks, particularly if a facility launches into specialized offerings based on hunches and assumptions rather than on a thorough study of the market. As an alternative, a facility can produce one specialized offering for different segments. For example, the same level of services is designed to attract private pay, Medicare, and Medicaid clients.

Selective Specialization

Depending on a facility's size, layout, location, and resources, a selective specialization approach may be the most desirable. In this strategy, a facil-

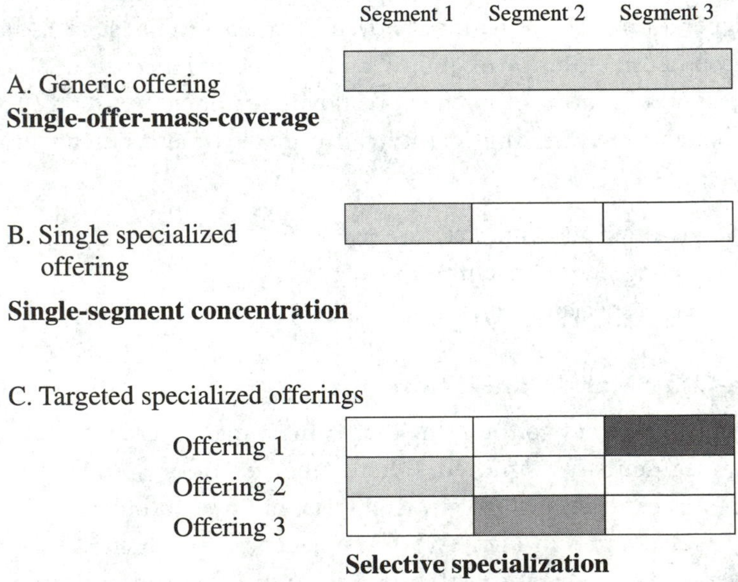

FIGURE 15-3 Market Targeting Patterns

ity produces specialized offerings tailored to the needs and desires of different market segments (Figure 15-3C). As an example, the same nursing facility can offer high-end décor and amenities for wealthy private-pay clients in one section of the facility, short-stay rehabilitation and post-acute services in a separate Medicare section, and Alzheimer's care in a distinct specialized unit.

Positioning

Every facility holds a certain position in the marketplace. Potential customers and key stakeholders form mental images and perceptions of the nursing facilities that they are familiar with, have seen advertised, or have heard about in a media report or from friends and neighbors. People use such perceptions to rank a particular facility and its services in relation to the other facilities in the community. People rank a facility in terms of how favorably they view a given facility.

Positioning refers to staking out a position in the target market (Bovée et al. 1995). Kotler and Andreasen (1996) define positioning as "the act of designing the organization's image and value offer so that the organization's customers understand and appreciate what the organization stands for in relation to its competitors" (p. 191). Positioning starts with a product, such as a nursing home and its services. But positioning is not what is done to the product. Positioning is what a marketer does to the mind of the prospective client. The product is positioned in the mind of the prospective client (Kotler 2000).

An administrator should find out how the facility is positioned, what people think of it and its services, and what type of reputation the facility has in the community. The first step is to determine the extent to which people in the target market are familiar with the facility; the second step is to determine how favorably people feel toward the facility. Obtaining more detailed information about how people may have arrived at forming a particular image of a nursing facility is often necessary. Such detailed information can be collected using techniques such as **semantic differential** (Kotler and Andreasen 1996). In this technique, market researchers select a relatively small set of dimensions that are important to people. The dimensions may include items such as quality of care, reputation, friendliness of the staff, comfort, and décor. Potential clients are asked to rate the facility and its competitors on each of these dimensions. The results show a facility's rank on each of the dimensions in relation to its

competitors. A facility's position is particularly useful within the context of its target market, because this position shows what potential clients think. Management can then decide whether the facility is appropriately positioned. If the facility is not desirably positioned, semantic differential can help management focus its efforts on improving its areas of weakness.

Market repositioning becomes necessary when a change in the existing position is desired. Before a facility can be effectively positioned, the nursing home administrator should put down in writing a "statement of position" and a "positioning statement" (Luther 2001). The **statement of position** specifies how the facility is currently positioned. The **positioning statement** highlights how the facility should be repositioned. The size of the gap between the current and desired positions will dictate the amount of effort and resources necessary for repositioning the facility. Advertising campaigns, news stories in the local media, open houses and facility tours, exchange relationships with the community, and a marketing mix are some of the means that can be used for achieving the desired position.

Marketing Mix

The marketing mix provides the tools necessary for positioning a facility in the target market. The four factors of the marketing mix—product, price, place, and promotion (known as the four P's—Figure 15-4)—are well known, but pose special challenges for implementing them in health care marketing. The next section addresses this issue.

IMPLEMENTING THE MARKETING MIX

In health care marketing, the four P's of the marketing mix do not operate in the same manner as they do for a manufactured product that people can touch, see, try out, and even return if they are not satisfied. The health-care product is for the most part intangible. The primary clients, the people who make the buying decision and evaluate value, are often not the patients themselves, but their surrogates such as family members. Services are produced only when customers are there to receive them, and care delivered to the patients goes mostly unobserved by these primary clients. The product's most desired features, such as quality, are not simple

Product
Differentiation
Tangible characteristics
Intangible factors
Observed and un-
    observed factors
Quality

Price
Direct cost
Ability to pay
Opportunity cost
Psychological costs
Social costs
Third party reimbursement

Target Market
Needs
Preferences

Place
Location
Extramural services
Accessibility
Admission policies
Visiting hours

Promotion
Providing information
Stimulating demand
Advertising
Reassurance
Response to unfavor-
    able news reports
Positive news
    stories

FIGURE 15-4 The Marketing Mix

to objectively define and evaluate. Pricing is often beyond the facility's control, because the facility relies heavily on third-party reimbursement. Place is generally fixed in terms of where the facility is located, its size, and its layout. Promotion presents challenges, because the product is difficult to showcase.

Product

The long-term care product is a package of some tangible but mostly intangible elements. The residential structures, discussed in Chapters 5 and 6, comprise the main tangible component. People can see and feel the living environment. Clients can also taste the food being served, notice the building's cleanliness, smell odors, and to some extent, observe staff

members' attitudes and efficiency. Family members who regularly visit the facility can also observe the patient's personal hygiene and some of the services being provided for the patient. However, a lot more goes unobserved, because clients cannot be in the facility all the time. By extrapolating from what they can observe and sense clients formulate judgments about the care elements that they do not see.

Bovée and colleagues (1995) describe the product component of the marketing mix as a "bundle of value" that meets expectations of customers in the target market. The worth of a product is measured in terms of the benefits it delivers. The benefits to clients can be maximized by effectively managing the structures and processes covered in Part II. Through the administrator's efforts in leading, coaching, training, and coordinating, the various departments of a facility can work together to deliver what customers want in quality, timeliness of service, and responsiveness to their needs. Differentiating the product, which will be discussed later, is another strategy for creating value and positioning the facility in the target market.

Price

Price refers to the cost a consumer bears in exchange for the product or service. Generally, price signifies a direct cost to the customer. In health care, however, third-party financing and reimbursement insulates the customer from the price of services. As pointed out in Chapter 4, the two major payers for nursing home services, Medicaid and Medicare, determine how much they will pay. Therefore, for the most part, the administrator has little control over pricing. Although the consumer bears some out-of-pocket costs to cover deductibles and copayments, these costs are the same regardless of which nursing home the customer chooses. Hence, pricing as a marketing strategy becomes for the most part inconsequential.

There are many reasons why patients are admitted to facilities in which the building and furnishings may not be upscale, even though these patients are covered under third-party reimbursement, which actually entitles them to go to any certified nursing home of their choice. One common reason for admission to facilities that are not upscale is the unavailability of beds at upscale facilities when the patient needs to be admitted. However, customers also assess several types of indirect costs that they weigh against the benefits in determining the value of the prod-

uct they consider purchasing. First, family members face the opportunity cost of time required in traveling to the facility for regular visits. Other indirect costs are psychological costs attributed to feelings of anxiety and guilt family members may have. Clients also incur social costs from the embarrassment of placing a loved one in a facility with a poor reputation. Although travel time is a function of the facility's location in relation to where the family members live, the facility can take steps in helping people overcome their anxiety and guilt through social service counseling, regular communication, and family support groups. The facility should market to the community and to prospective and current clients any such formal programs it may have available. When a facility is spartan in appearance, other features such as friendliness of staff members, security, and other quality of life elements should be emphasized.

Pricing strategies are pertinent in some market segments, such as private-pay, and also in managed care and VA contracting (see Chapter 4). Pricing decisions in these market segments are based on such factors as buyers' willingness and ability to pay, the facility's production costs, and market competition. In the private-pay market, high prices are sometimes used to create a top-of-the-line image, whereas low prices can be used to undercut the competition (Bovée et al. 1995). In contracting with managed care and the VA, pricing can be tricky, because contracts are generally awarded to the lowest bidder in closed-bid contests. A low cost of production relative to its competitors can enable a facility to offer a price that can win a contract. Sometimes, especially in managed-care contracting when open negotiation rather than closed bidding is used, the administrator has more flexibility in pricing.

Place

Place is where services can be purchased, the facility's physical location (Majaro 1993). Choosing the site for building a new facility is a strategic decision, but location also deserves close study when acquiring an existing facility to enter a new market. Another situation in which location is a critical factor is when deciding whether to add more beds to an existing building or to open a new facility at a different location. The cost of capital is often the driving consideration in such decisions, because expanding an existing facility is cheaper than building a new one. But even in growing markets facilities can face low census growth after adding new beds when the critical factor of location has not been adequately studied.

The trend in recent years has been to locate nursing facilities near growing suburban populations.

Although location is the most obvious factor when one thinks of place, in marketing strategy place also refers to the channels of distribution, the mechanisms used for bringing products and customers together to create an exchange. For example, a long-term care facility may offer non-institutional services, such as home health care, hospice services, and meals-on-wheels; these services are taken to wherever the patients reside, regardless of where the facility itself is located.

Place also refers to physical access. For example, easy accessibility and clearly marked signs on adjacent access roads make it easy to find the facility. An adequate number of parking spaces as close as possible to the facility should be reserved for clients. Well-manicured landscaping, well-maintained lawns, flower beds, and adequate lighting draw attention and create a welcoming appeal. Access also refers to the times when a patient can be admitted to the facility. For example, is the facility ready to admit patients in the evenings and on weekends? What does the facility do when a patient needs to be admitted, but no beds are available? The nursing home should develop relationships with hospitals and other long-term care facilities and have policies that facilitate patient admission at all hours. When a facility is full, it can temporarily place the patient in another facility and work out a smooth transfer when appropriate accommodations become available to admit that patient.

In long-term care, place also includes regular contact between the patient and family. Many facilities have unrestricted visiting hours.

Promotion

Majaro (1993) defined promotion as "the communication system that creates awareness of the product, its features and benefits, and its location of purchase, and also reassures the customer after the purchase has taken place" (p. 22). Although this definition is complete in many ways, the objectives of promotion go beyond merely creating an awareness of the nursing facility and its services. Bovée and colleagues (1995) pointed to several objectives to be achieved through promotion:

1. **Providing information**: Information creates awareness, but it also educates and explains how a facility's unique array of services can address problems that potential customers may be facing.

2. **Stimulating demand**: The ultimate goal of all promotion is to influence behavior. Promotion should instill a desire in potential customers to lead them to a purchasing decision when the time comes for placing a patient in a nursing facility.

3. **Differentiating products**: Many nursing homes are alike. A strong promotional program is often what sets these facilities apart. On the other hand, a facility may have differentiated products such as rehabilitation, special dining features, or outdoor events, which can be effectively used for market positioning.

4. **Reminding current customers**: Even existing customers need to be reminded of the facility's benefits in order to prevent those customers from switching to a different facility. Also, once a patient has been admitted to the facility, family members need reinforcement in thinking that they made the right choice.

5. **Countering competitors**: Without engaging in 'name calling' or naming its competitors, a facility can effectively counter promotional campaigns of its competitors.

6. **Responding to negative news**: On occasion even the best nursing homes are likely to become victims of negative publicity focusing on an unforeseen event, or even something that could have been prevented. In such circumstances, not saying anything can be perceived as admission of guilt and create negative public opinion.

7. **Building image**: Positive news stories of events can be powerful elements in building a facility's image.

Promotion should be driven by the three other P's discussed in the previous sections. For example, to emphasize its rehabilitation services a facility may provide factual information on how many days an average patient stays in the facility for active rehabilitation before being discharged home. To emphasize value, a facility may highlight how affordable an attractive and comfortable environment can be. Promotion and advertising must clearly emphasize how to get to the facility, as well as how to contact the facility by telephone and by the Internet. Promotional strategy and tools are discussed later in this chapter.

COMPETITIVE DIFFERENTIATION

Most nursing facilities do not have a sustained marketing program, and those that do often engage in undifferentiated marketing. Also called

"mass marketing," **undifferentiated marketing** purposefully ignores market segmentation and targets the aggregate market using the same marketing mix for the entire market. Mass marketing takes a generic approach by marketing a uniform package of services to the entire market, using the same product to try and appeal to all prospective clients. Because only one product is promoted, without differentiation, marketing costs are minimized. However, this undifferentiated strategy leaves the facility vulnerable to competitors who can differentiate their products. The stereotypical image of nursing homes is pervasive, because most facilities do not differentiate their product offerings from those of their competitors. Marketers refer to this phenomenon as the "me-too" syndrome when nursing facilities operating in the same market provide commonplace services (O'Malley 2001). In a market in which most other nursing homes are "me-too," a facility can gain competitive advantage by distinguishing itself from its competitors. Kotler (1991) asserted that every product and every service, no matter how commonplace, can be differentiated. Innovative architectural designs and methods of service delivery discussed in Chapters 5 and 6 are clear examples of how some nursing homes are differentiating their product offering.

Differentiation Strategy

Differentiation is a competitive strategy in which a facility creates distinctive features that allow customers to distinguish the facility's offer from that of its competitors. Product differentiation can be used effectively for positioning a facility in the target market.

When carefully designed and promoted, distinctive features can create the perception of extra value. For example, two nursing facilities may be similar in their quality of clinical care, but one facility may be able to differentiate itself from the other by offering a choice of menu, a restaurant-style dining experience, or a brunch buffet. Other facilities achieve differentiation by offering an array of support services for family members. In fact, by thinking through their marketing mix, administrators can find numerous opportunities for differentiation; most facilities can be differentiated in one form or another. A facility's affiliation with a hospital or other recognized agency, its layout and atmosphere, its variety of quality-of-life features, its recreation and activity programs, its dietary services, its staff skill-mix, and its staffing levels can all be used for differentiation.

In long-term care marketing, differentiated offerings can be used in three ways, depending on what an organization wants to achieve:

- creating unique value
- segmenting the market
- niche marketing

Creating Unique Value

As already mentioned, distinguishing the facility from other competitors by offering extra value is one use of this strategy, which may be used without segmenting the market. In this case, the facility tries to attract patients by offering extra value that other facilities do not offer. Hence, segmentation is not always necessary, particularly when the market is not large enough for distinctive segments, or when the facility's offerings would appeal to all segments.

Segmenting the Market

Value can also be added by segmenting the market and creating different products and using a different marketing mix for each chosen segment. The main advantage of market segmentation is that it enables facility management to focus on the specific needs of one, two, or more selected market segments. Segmentation, by its very nature, requires differentiation and often provides the logical basis on which to create differentiated offerings.

Niche Marketing

Some long-term care facilities have used the differentiation strategy to concentrate on a single market segment through a high degree of specialization. Examples include Alzheimer's care facilities, rehabilitation facilities, and non-certified upscale facilities that cater to wealthy clients. This type of a concentrated marketing strategy is also called **niche marketing** or niche creation.

PERSONAL SELLING

Marketing activities have both an external and a personal orientation. Activities discussed so far are directed at the outside market, which for the most part is impersonal. Personal selling, called salesmanship in market-

ing literature, requires one-on-one contact with clients. The objective of external marketing is to educate the target audience, build awareness, and position the facility so that when potential customers need its services they will right away think of this facility and will know how to reach it. The buying decision, however, is made only after a personal contact.

The main objective of personal selling is to understand individual needs and offer solutions tailored to meet individual needs. In the process, the facility often learns first-hand how its image is perceived by the clients that it comes in contact with. One of the aims in personal selling is to reinforce a positive image, another aim is to change a negative image with information.

Pre-Admission Inquiry

In almost all instances, the actual buying decision is made only after potential customers have personally visited the facility. Interaction with the facility's staff during this first visit is called the **pre-admission inquiry** process. An overview of this process is included in Chapter 6.

Most customers today have several nursing home choices. It is estimated that a customer visits an average of 3.4 facilities and phones 4.2 facilities before choosing a nursing facility. Also, a growing trend involves not just the adult children but also the spouse of a potential patient in the selection process (Macknick 1998).

Pre-admission inquiry should be a highly professionalized process, a process that requires a sophisticated blend of skills in social services and salesmanship. This process is also highly individualized and should be adapted to the patient's and the family's specific circumstances. Making people feel at ease and taking the time to listen is an art. Only genuine empathy and mutual trust will make people comfortable enough to disclose some very personal information, because nursing home placement is often accompanied by a sense of guilt. Private issues such as the patient's incontinence, dementia, or combativeness are not generally shared with total strangers, nor is information on personal finances. Hence, some "icebreaking" conversation is necessary before discussing sensitive issues.

McKenna (1991) explained that the deluge of claims made by various service providers resulted in confusing people. Customers need reassurance, particularly when they are buying a piece of the future, as they do in purchasing nursing-home services. They are looking for an organization that conveys integrity and has credibility before they will entrust a loved

one to that organization. Therefore, the facility should adequately train all intake workers and back-up personnel.

The facility tour (see Chapter 6) is used primarily to build credibility. This tour should be designed to give a first-hand look into how the facility would meet the multifaceted needs of a patient. With a somewhat informal and personalized approach, the tour should be used to make a connection between the facility and the prospective patient. Key features and services of the facility should be given particular emphasis. For example, a visit to the physical therapy area where other patients are receiving active treatments can be very reassuring. The potential client is often positively impressed when the intake worker introduces the therapist who takes a few minutes to give simple explanations of the therapeutic procedures the prospective patient is likely to receive. Similarly, other key staff members, such as the supervising nurse on the nursing unit, should be introduced to the visitors.

The post-tour concluding interview should highlight the main services that would benefit the patient. Explaining how services are customized for the patient is important, as is explaining how various clinical disciplines interface in a multidisciplinary system. The interview must conclude with what is referred to as "closing the sale." Simply put, closing of a sale is an unobtrusive offer to admit the patient. Macknick (1998) pointed out that an offer to admit the patient is extended in only 2% of the cases when prospects come into the facility for a pre-admission inquiry. Closing the sale is an art and requires confidence. A simple statement, such as "We would be delighted to serve Mrs. Kemple's needs by our excellent staff; when can I call you back?" is all that is required, unless the prospective clients clearly are not interested. The next day, a follow-up telephone call is appropriate.

Customer Relations

Administrators who manage some of the most elegantly furnished and well-decorated facilities sometimes wonder why they lose patients. These facilities often have customer relations problems. On the other hand, some plain-looking nursing facilities are able to maintain full census while their competitors struggle.

Kotler and Clarke (1987) consider the personnel of an organization as the fifth P of marketing (the other four being product, price, place, and promotion, as discussed earlier). Clients often judge quality and their sat-

isfaction with services by how employees interact with them rather than by the technical quality of services, something that clients generally cannot assess. Customers observe the staff's behaviors and attentiveness to tasks; they evaluate the staff's responsiveness to problems; they notice whether the employees are friendly and cheerful; and they rely on the staff for information on their loved one's condition. When they visit the facility, family members also notice how other patients are treated. Family members use such clues to form opinions about the facility's reliability and dependability, because they cannot be at the facility all the time. Negative observations create psychological stress for the potential customers, which dilutes their perception of value.

Following are some suggestions for building better customer relations:

Acknowledgement and helpfulness: Staff members should greet and smile when they pass family members and other visitors. The receptionist should acknowledge with a cheerful greeting anyone who enters the facility and inquire how they can be assisted. Kotler and Clarke (1987) point out that the airlines are known to run all flight attendants, sales agents, and other staff members who have customer contact through "smile school." In the hospitality industry, employees are trained in customer relations and client interactions. Nursing facilities must do the same.

Empathy and compassion: The staff should be trained to understand customer needs and feelings, and how to pay individualized attention to clients. True compassion requires staff members to "be in the customer's shoes" and imagine what the other person must be going through.

Contact and communication: Regular contact and factual updates on the patient's condition build trust. When key family members are informed about how the patient is doing, these family members must also be notified what the staff is doing to address the patient's needs. Timely follow-up by the staff on questions and concerns raised by family members is critical. Professional staff members should not merely inform, they must also educate clients so that expectations are maintained at a reasonable level without making it sound that staff members are giving excuses. This education should include explanations of why certain expectations may be unreasonable. Expectations should be discussed in the context of the facility's operational policies and procedures and quality standards.

PROMOTION AND PUBLIC RELATIONS

The main objective of a promotion (marketing communications) and public relations campaign is to position the nursing facility in the marketplace and to build and maintain a positive image of the facility. **Promotion** is based on effectively communicating a message to present and potential customers. Promotion can be defined as a controlled and integrated program that uses communication methods to effectively present an organization and its services to prospective customers and presents need-satisfying attributes to facilitate sales (Engel et al. 1994). Whereas promotional efforts are targeted at would-be customers, **public relations** or community relations encompass a broader function; they are directed at other key stakeholders and the community at large. Examples of these stakeholders include the facility's staff, community health care agencies, physicians, the local media, legislators and other public officials, and any other agencies the facility considers to be desirable exchange partners. Promotion and public relations work hand-in-hand, and many of the promotional tools can also be used for public relations.

Strategies and Tools

Promotional and public relations goals can be accomplished by using a variety of tools. Developing a uniform strategy, however, is essential in order to communicate the same message through several different channels. The administrator should establish a budget for promotional activities and should also allocate resources for activities such as advertising, printing informational materials, and public relations programs. The administrator should also decide which channels of communication will be the most cost-effective in achieving the promotional goals. An undertaking is **cost-effective** when the benefits achieved are greater than the costs incurred; a facility's cost-effectiveness can be determined by how well the facility does in its efforts to achieve its goals in census development. The facility's budget and resource allocation will also depend on whether the facility considers that the expertise of a professional marketing firm or a public relations firm is necessary.

Advertising

Advertising includes all forms of paid non-face-to-face communication with a target audience. Advertising uses an identified sponsor. Media such

as newspapers, radio, and television are the primary vehicles of advertising, and are considered the most effective vehicles of advertising. But using them is more expensive than using telephone directories, billboards, or the Internet. Advertising incurs investments for which the paybacks are not always known, and advertising's effectiveness can be determined only by how much progress the facility makes toward certain measurable outcomes, such as an increased number of inquiries.

The advertising message needs to be carefully crafted. An ideal message is one that manages to get attention (A), hold interest (I), arouse desire (D), and obtain action (A); this ideal message has what is known as the AIDA framework. The problem, of course, is that ascertaining these attributes is difficult without extensive field testing, which is expensive. However, the administrator can use some innovative approaches, such as testing the message using a focus group consisting of family and staff members. Extensively used in marketing research, a **focus group** consists of about 8 to 12 people who participate in an unstructured session with a skilled moderator to discuss their thoughts and feelings about an issue, an organization, or a service.

The advertising message must include a carefully crafted **selling line** that interprets the facility's positioning statement. The selling line should contain the benefits sought by individuals who make the buying decision (Luther 2001). Yet advertised messages must be free from any misleading statements or claims that may be construed as warranties or promises about clinical outcomes or the quality of care (Becker 2001). Some basic information must be included in all advertisements and printed on all promotional materials. For example, all advertisements and promotional materials must contain the facility's name, logo, street address, location, telephone number, and web address.

Publicity

The term **publicity** refers to free communication of information about the facility and its services, and plays an important role in the facility's promotion and public relations strategy. The fact that the facility does not pay for publicity distinguishes publicity from advertising, and it should therefore be used as a primary channel of promotion. Getting free publicity in the local media is not as difficult as it may sound. Opportunities for publicity can be categorized into three main areas:

- announcements
- human-interest stories
- news events

Announcements

The media play an important public-service informational role, and members of the media are frequently looking for information that would be of interest to the general public. Announcements for programs such as health fairs, health screening, and educational seminars are accepted without charge by many community newspapers and radio stations.

Human-interest Stories

Human-interest stories and follow-up reports on various events are also of interest to the community. Examples include noteworthy events in the lives of certain residents in the nursing home; substantial fund-raising efforts organized by the facility or carried out in collaboration with other local agencies to support foundations such as the American Heart Association, the Alzheimer's Association, or the Arthritis Foundation; celebration of a landmark anniversary of the facility; or a celebrity's visit to the facility. Brennan (1981) reported on examples of numerous human-interest stories published in local newspapers across the country. Some notable stories included residents participating in yoga classes, nursing students training at a local nursing home, a family reunion that included five generations, a resident who served as an altar boy at the local Catholic church, and residents featured in an Easter parade.

News Events

News events featuring the facility, its staff, or residents should be transmitted to the local media. Examples include the facility's outstanding performance on the certification survey, accreditation by the Joint Commission, appointment of a new administrator, ground-breaking for a new facility, or ribbon-cutting for a new service.

Personal Contact

An extremely important part of a facility's promotional strategy is the facility's personal contacts with referral agents. **Referral agents** are professionals in the community who are in a position to influence prospective clients about choosing a facility. Regular personal contact with physicians

and hospital discharge-planners is critical, because these professionals are often consulted by families when they place a loved one in a nursing facility. Personal contact is established when the administrator or other key personnel make presentations before community groups, such as the Rotary Club or a women's auxiliary. Personal contact can be effectively combined with disseminating promotional materials such as business cards, facility brochures, or photo albums.

Promotional Materials

Brochures, business cards, newsletters, photo albums, videos, DVDs, and web sites are commonly used as promotional materials. The quality and content of these materials must be developed with the aim of accomplishing the facility's positioning goals. For instance, positioning high-end services by using an ordinary black-and-white brochure would be counterproductive. On the other hand, a simple facility located in a rural area and known mainly to its local population need not spend money on developing a costly brochure.

In highly competitive markets, different types of promotional materials are necessary, and each one is designed to serve a different purpose. An administrator who meets a physician in the nursing facility's hallway for the first time will give the physician a business card. An administrator will also hand a business card to the receptionist when making a personal call to a physician's office. Brochures are used in a variety of ways: Brochures are included in the packet of information that is handed to prospective clients during pre-admission inquiry; they are kept in the facility's lobby to be picked up by visitors; they are left with hospital discharge planners to be handed out to prospective clients; and they can be distributed to the public during events such as health fairs. The facility's newsletter is a vehicle for regular communication with the staff, current residents and their families, and key stakeholders. Photo albums are left with key referral agents such as physicians and hospital discharge planners to use in promoting the facility's services to prospective clients. Video cassettes or DVDs can be used with likely prospects. Especially when the patient or the spouse cannot personally visit the facility, a video or DVD can be very effective in bringing the facility and its living atmosphere to that potential client. The video or DVD can also be effectively used during speaking engagements to supplement an oral presentation. Use of web sites is now common; web pages can be designed to create a virtual facility tour, using action photographs that include people engaged in various activities. For privacy reasons,

obtain written consent for taking and using photographs of people and avoid identifying individuals in photographs (Miller and Hutton 2000).

Event Promotion

Event promotion is accomplished by organizing programs and special events at the facility, programs and events to which the community is invited. This strategy serves two main purposes: First, it can, depending on the type of event, generate free publicity, often both before and after the event. Second, it creates promotional opportunities by letting key stakeholders and the public see first-hand what the facility is like. Certain events are targeted at specific stakeholder groups, such as a reception for physicians, which may also include social workers and nurses from surrounding hospitals; a special event for nursing students from area colleges; or an event to honor community volunteers. Other events include wider audiences. An open house in conjunction with the dedication of a new facility or a new addition attracts interested audiences. A facility's landmark anniversaries, such as the 5th and the 10th, present excellent opportunities for special celebrations to which the local community should be invited.

CONCLUSION

Marketing can be viewed as the backbone of strategic management, because it bases its value creation on the needs and preferences of customers, who make up one of the strongest forces in the external environment. The value-delivery sequence and all marketing efforts begin with choosing the value desired by a selected target market. The sequence then proceeds with producing that value, promoting that value to the target market, and actually delivering the promised value to clients on a consistent basis. These are critical steps in strategy formulation. The successful facilities of tomorrow will be distinguished by the ones that excel in delivering value in a way that is well-thought-out.

DISCUSSION AND APPLICATION QUESTIONS

1. How does marketing provide a competitive edge to a nursing home?
2. Why do effective marketers study social and cultural change?

3. Discuss some examples of how a nursing facility can deliver better value.
4. Discuss the role of marketing in establishing exchange partnerships with community agencies.
5. How would you develop a marketing strategy at the beginning stages of planning a new facility?
6. How would you formulate a marketing strategy for a facility that is experiencing a loss of market share?
7. Discuss some ways in which a facility may differentiate its offerings by using each element of the marketing mix in both segmented and unsegmented markets.
8. Design a facility tour. How would you emphasize some of the main features of a facility during a tour?
9. How would you improve customer relations with a family member who is "always complaining?"
10. What information will you include in a promotional brochure for a nursing facility? Create an advertising message, and a selling line.

INTERNET RESOURCES FOR FURTHER LEARNING

American Marketing Association
  http://www.marketingpower.com/

American Advertising Federation: Trade association of the advertising industry.
  http://www.aaf.org/

REFERENCES

American Marketing Association. 1995. *Dictionary of Marketing Terms*, 2nd ed., ed. P.D. Bennett. Chicago: American Marketing Association.

Becker, S. 2001. *Health Care Law: A Practical Guide*. 2nd ed. Newark, NJ: Matthew Bender & Company Inc.

Bovée, C.L. et al. 1995. *Marketing*. 2nd ed. New York: McGraw-Hill, Inc.

Brennan, J. 1981. *Public Relations Can Be Fun and Easy Especially for Nursing Home People*. Washington, D.C.: American Health Care Association.

Czinkota, M.R. 2000. *Marketing: Best Practices*. Fort Worth, TX: The Dryden Press.

Drucker, P.F. 1974. *Management: Tasks, Responsibilities, Practices*. New York: Harper & Row, Publishers.

Engel, J.F. et al. 1994. *Promotional Strategy: Managing the Marketing Communications Process.* 8th ed. Chicago: Richard D. Irwin, Inc.

Kotler, P. 1991. *Marketing Management: Analysis, Planning, Implementation, and Control.* 7th ed. Englewood Cliffs, New Jersey: Prentice-Hall, Inc.

Kotler, P. 2000. *Marketing Management: The Millennium Edition.* Upper Saddle River, New Jersey: Prentice-Hall, Inc.

Kotler, P., and A.R. Andreasen. 1996. *Strategic Marketing for Nonprofit Organizations.* 5th ed. Upper Saddle River, New Jersey: Prentice Hall, Inc.

Kotler, P., and R.N. Clarke. 1987. *Marketing for Health Care Organizations.* Englewood Cliffs, New Jersey: Prentice Hall, Inc.

Luther, W.M. 2001. *The Marketing Plan: How to Prepare and Implement It.* 3rd ed. New York: American Management Association.

Macknick, F.J. 1998. Two takes on facility marketing. *Nursing Homes Long Term Care Management* 47 (10): 70–72.

Majaro, S. 1993. *The Essence of Marketing.* New York: Prentice Hall.

McKenna, R. 1991. *Relationship Marketing: Successful Strategies for The Age of The Customer.* Reading, Massachusetts: Addison-Wesley Publishing Company.

Miller, R.D., and R.C. Hutton. 2000. *Problems in Health Care Law.* 8th ed. Gaithersburg, MD: Aspen Publishers, Inc.

O'Malley, J.F. 2001. *Healthcare Marketing, Sales, and Service.* Chicago: Health Administration Press.

CHAPTER 16

Effective Budgeting and Financial Controls

LEARNING MODULES

1. The concept of financial management and financial information systems.
2. Financial accounting: Income statement, balance sheet, and cash-flow statement; what these financial statements are, and what information they contain.
3. Management reports and their use. The technique of variance analysis.
4. Managing revenues based on census and payer-mix.
5. Census range and types of costs. Non-controllable and controllable costs.
6. Controlling labor costs and other expenditures using variance analysis.
7. Inventory management as a tool for controlling costs and maintaining adequate levels of supplies and linens.
8. Managing accounts receivable by minimizing lost reimbursement, write-offs, and the collection cycle.
9. Budgeting revenues, expenses, and operating margin.

Financial management is a critical administrative function that is essential for ensuring a nursing facility's success over the long run. Although financial management is directly associated with the "managing a business" aspect of the administrator's responsibilities (see Chapter 13), financial management also affects the organization's ability to maintain patient-care standards, deliver value, manage the open systems, and carry out other vital functions such as marketing, staff development, and quality-improvement. A nursing facility's vital resources are controlled and conserved through effective financial management.

Financial management encompasses two classical functions of management: planning and control. Financial planning incorporates two types of decisions: (1) What future financial objectives are desirable and achievable? and (2) What resources are needed and how will they be allocated so that the objectives are achieved? Such a process of financial planning is called **budgeting**. Once formulated, the budget becomes a tool for exercising financial control. Managers exercise financial control when they compare the actual operating results against the budget, note unacceptable variances, evaluate reasons for the variances, and take appropriate corrective action. Besides the planning and control functions just described, financial management also includes controlling cash and other assets such as food and supplies inventories.

The planning and control functions associated with budgeting and financial management call for managerial decision-making. Sound decisions require good information. Hence, effective financial management is driven by well-designed systems for analyzing information and reporting on the organization's performance; such systems facilitate budgeting and control processes and help administrators to keep track of cash and inventories. One basic financial information system is the accounting system. Accounting is a professional field in its own right. A nursing home administrator does not need to be an accountant but the administrator must be able to understand the basic accounting statements produced by the accounting system. A well-designed financial information system does more than just simple accounting; this system must also enable the administrator to formulate an annual budget, and to produce various reports to help the administrator understand and manage the financial performance of the facility operations.

ACCOUNTING AND FINANCIAL STATEMENTS

Accounting, more precisely called **financial accounting**, entails recording all financial transactions and preparing standard reports known as financial statements. Each financial transaction is recorded following the well-established double-entry system of debits and credits, and a set of standards called "generally accepted accounting principles" (GAAP). Examples of common financial transactions include revenues derived from providing services; purchases of food, supplies, and other items; expense for salaries and wages; receipt of cash; and payments by cash or check. As explained in chapter 12, most of these routine transactions are recorded by the nursing home's bookkeeping personnel. In addition to the recording of routine transactions, that a bookkeeper can generally handle, an accountant generally makes additional financial entries such as those pertaining to lease or rental arrangements, loans, tax payments, depreciation of assets, and income from investments. Generally, at the end of a specified period, all the financial transactions for that period are summarized in three financial statements: the income statement, the balance sheet, and the cash flow statement. As discussed in subsequent sections, these statements provide concise information on the facility's profitability as well as its economic resources and obligations.

The Income Statement

The **income statement** is also sometimes called "operating statement," "profit and loss statement," or "P&L." Exhibit 16-1 provides an example of an income statement. The income statement furnishes a summary of operations for a given period, such as a month or a year. It has three main sections. In the first section is a listing of the revenue derived from each payer source and the total revenue. The second section lists various expense line-items such as salaries, supplies, raw food, utilities, and advertising. The third section consists of operating income, income taxes, and net income. For non-profit and public facilities that do not pay income taxes, operating income equals net income. In general, net income or net profit equals total revenue minus total expenses (income tax is considered an expense and is added to the total expenses). Thus the income state-

EXHIBIT 16–1

XYZ Nursing Care Facility Income Statement for Year Ended 2003

Net patient revenues:

Private pay	$1,395,540
Private insurance	132,030
Medicaid	1,858,490
Medicare	943,160
Veterans contract	74,600
Total net patient revenue	$4,403,820
Other service revenues	262,120
Rental income	8,040
Income from investments	43,620
Total revenue	$4,717,600

Operating expenses:

Administrative salaries	182,740
Advertising and promotion	14,400
Other administrative	12,240
Nursing salaries	2,294,950
Medical supplies	511,910
Equipment rental	26,400
Dietary salaries	300,370
Raw food	147,020
Dietary supplies	26,400
Dietary chemicals	25,700
Environmental service salaries	274,460
Environmental supplies	38,160
Social services salaries	42,900
Activity salaries	75,220
Activity supplies	5,040
Contracted services	194,290
Fees	46,210
Utilities	53,670
Depreciation	93,650

continues

EXHIBIT 16-1 *continued*

Provision for bad debt	70,230
Other expenses	23,400
Total expenses	4,459,360
Operating income	258,240
Provision for income taxes	77,470
Net income (loss)	$180,770

ment provides valuable information on the profitability of an organization. By identifying revenues by each payer source and by identifying expenses by each type of expense, the income statement provides a summary of how the bottom-line profit was derived. On the other hand, if total expenses exceed total revenue the result is a net loss.

The income statement is of primary importance to most administrators. The balance sheet and the cash flow statement are important to corporate officers and owners.

The Balance Sheet

A **balance sheet** summarizes the financial position of a business organization at a given date, such as the last day of a month or the last day of a year. A balance sheet contains two columns: The left hand column provides a summary of all the **assets** or economic resources of the facility. Total assets constitute the financial value of everything the facility owns. The right hand column has two sections: liabilities and equity. **Liabilities** constitute the facility's economic obligations or debts. Total liabilities constitute the financial value of everything the facility owes to other entities. **Equity**, which is also called owners' equity or stockholders' equity, represents the interests or rights of the owners in a for-profit business corporation. In a non-profit organization, no ownership interest exists. Therefore, **net assets** is the term used by non-profit organizations for the equity portion of the balance sheet. According to the fundamental accounting equation, total assets equal the sum of total liabilities and equity (or net assets). Thus, the two columns of the balance sheet are exactly balanced; the left-hand side equals the right-hand side. See Exhibit 16-2 for an illustration of the balance sheet.

EXHIBIT 16-2 XYZ Nursing Care Facility
Balance Sheet on December 31, 2003

Assets		Liabilities and Equity	
Current Assets:		Current Liabilities:	
Cash	62,350	Accounts payable	44,170
Accounts receivable	981,260	Accrued salaries	32,140
Less allowance for bad debts	70,230	Current maturities of	
Inventories	57,600	long-term debt	41,330
Prepaid expenses	24,400	Long-term debt	13,364,390
		Less current maturities	41,330
Land, buildings, and equipment	23,670,190		
Less accumulated depreciation	8,521,260	Total Liabilities	13,440,700
Other assets	258,990	Equity	3,022,600
Total Assets	$16,463,300	Total Liabilities and Equity	$16,463,300

Cash-Flow Statement

The **cash flow statement** is a summary of actual cash transactions—cash paid and cash received—for a given period, such as a month or a year. The cash flow statement provides information on how much cash was generated and how the cash was used during a given period. This statement identifies the sources of incoming cash and the uses of outgoing cash. Preparing a cash flow statement is necessary because businesses commonly use an accounting method called **accrual-basis accounting**, a method in which revenues and expenses do not match cash inflows and outflows. Revenue is recognized at the time services are rendered although payment for those services is received at a later date. Similarly, expenses are booked as they are incurred even though payments to vendors are generally made at a later date. Certain expenses, such as advertising, may be prepaid for a whole year. In such a case, a cash outflow would occur at the beginning of the year but the expense would be spread out over the entire year.

Note that cash flow is not an indicator of profitability. Cash flow is, however, an important measure of an organization's financial health. A positive cash flow—in which inflows exceed outflows—means that the nursing home has the ability to meet its cash obligations on a timely basis. The facility must have cash to pay the employees on every payday, make payments to vendors according to the terms of credit, make lease payments for building and equipment, and pay loan installments to banks, to name some examples. An organization can face serious financial trouble if it is not able to meet such financial obligations when they are due.

MANAGEMENT REPORTS

The three types of financial statements just discussed do not provide all the information that managers need to control facility operations. The administrator and department managers need detailed reports that can help them monitor the facility's operations and make decisions. **Management accounting** is the term used for the process of preparing reports considered useful for management control and decision-making. Several types of routine management reports may be prepared for a facility's administrator and department managers. Corporate officers also routinely review such reports to evaluate operations. In addition to routine reports, certain non-routine reports may be necessary from time to time.

For example, a *pro forma* report that forecasts anticipated business volume, expected revenues, and anticipated expenses is often necessary before a facility launches a new service. Such a report can help management to decide whether the facility should commit the resources to develop the new service that is being considered.

Financial accounting systems are standardized, and the format of financial statements varies little among different nursing home organizations. Management accounting systems, on the other hand, can have a great deal of variation. The number and types of management reports, as well as their usefulness, depend on the level of sophistication of the financial information systems. Because no standards exist in management accounting, the format of management reports and the level of detail will also vary from one organization to another.

Routine management reports furnish an analysis of operational information. Because the income statement and the balance sheet are summary statements, they lack the details necessary for managing revenues, controlling costs, and monitoring accounts receivable.

Management of revenues and costs is based on a technique called **variance analysis**. A variance is the difference between an actual (realized) numeric value and a budgeted (expected) value. Hence, variance analysis is an examination and interpretation of differences between what has actually happened and what was planned in the budget (Gapenski 2002). The **budget** establishes expectations that become financial objectives that the nursing home administrator is responsible for achieving. Management reports containing variance analyses are valuable tools, because they pinpoint deviations from the budget. These reports enable the administrator to monitor the facility's profitability. Negative variances signify that the actual results are worse than the budget had projected, and such results threaten the expected profitability. Negative variances require follow-up, particularly in areas in which costs are controllable. Such controllable areas are those areas of the operation in which management intervention to reduce costs would not jeopardize quality or violate regulations. For example, labor hours cannot be cut below the minimum staffing levels established by federal and state regulations or cut below the number of staff hours necessary for meeting patients' needs, whichever is higher. Hence, negative variances require careful evaluation and judicious action. Variance analysis and other types of management reports are discussed later in greater detail.

Management of accounts receivable is based on analyzing the receivables by age. Age means the length of time by which an account is past due. Collecting receivables is critical for maintaining adequate cash flows. An **aging report** or aging schedule enables the administrator to monitor past-due accounts that may require follow-up action.

MANAGING REVENUES

Management of revenues is based on two factors:

- **Maintaining expected census levels**: **Census** means the number of patients in a facility on a given day. Each day spent by a patient in the nursing facility is called a **patient day**. Hence patient days over a period represent the cumulative number of days spent by all patients. Patient days amount to a cumulative census over a given period and is also referred to as **days of care**. **Average daily census** is the average number of patients per day over a specific period such as a week, a month, or a year. It is calculated by dividing the total patient days over a period by the number of days in that period (Table 16-1).
- **Achieving the expected payer-mix of patients**: Payer-mix is also called census-mix. This payer-mix is the mix of patients by payer type, such as Medicaid, Medicare, or private pay. Table 16-2 illustrates the payer-mix for a facility, which is also graphically illustrated in Figure 16-1.

Table 16–1 Days of Care and Average Daily Census for a 7-day Period

Day	Daily census
Day 1	121
Day 2	119
Day 3	118
Day 4	117
Day 5	120
Day 6	118
Day 7	120
Patient days	833 (Total census of days 1 through 7)
Average daily census	119 (833 / 7)

Table 16–2 Payer-mix for the Year 2003

Pay type	Patient days	Payer-mix
Private pay	10,998	25.6%
Medicare	5,370	12.5%
Medicaid	25,695	59.9%
Other	861	2.0%
TOTAL	42,924	100.0%
Average daily census	117.6	

The objective of census management is to keep the facility's beds filled. Having more patients in the facility generally translates into more revenue. But simply having more patients is not always enough for achieving revenue targets. A facility may maintain or exceed its expected census levels and yet experience revenue shortfalls because of wide variations in the amount of reimbursement from the various private and public sources of financing discussed in Chapter 4. Medicaid generally maintains the lowest reimbursement rates. Private-pay charges, which are established by the facility, are generally the highest. Exhibit 16-3 illustrates the effect of payer-mix on revenues. Notice that the facility has actually met its bud-

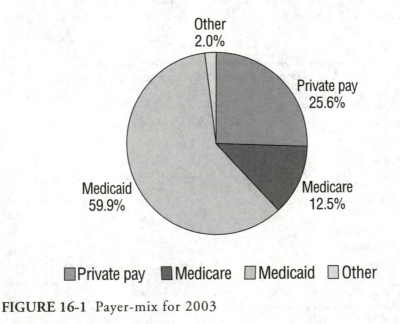

FIGURE 16-1 Payer-mix for 2003

EXHIBIT 16–3

Payer-Mix and Revenue Report
Month of October, 2003

Available beds: 126

	Budget				Actual				Variance		
	Patient days	%	Rates	Revenue	Patient days	%	Rates	Revenue	Patient days	Rates	Revenue
Private pay	903	26.0%	$196.55	$177,430	854	24.6%	$196.55	$167,854	−49	$0.00	−$9,576
Private insurance	104	3.0%	156.00	16,249	73	2.1%	$156.00	11,388	−31	0.00	−4,861
Medicaid	1,805	52.0%	136.00	245,540	1,885	54.3%	$136.00	256,360	80	0.00	10,820
Medicare	521	15.0%	182.00	94,786	526	15.1%	$182.00	95,732	5	0.00	946
Veterans contract	139	4.0%	170.00	23,610	134	3.9%	$170.00	22,780	−5	0.00	−830
TOTALS	3,472	100.0%	$160.60	$557,614	3,472	100.0%	$159.59	$554,114	0	−$1.01	−$3,500
Average daily census	112				112				0		
Occupancy rate	88.9%				88.9%				0.0%		

Note: Occupancy rate = Average daily census / Available beds

geted patient days target of 3,472 and its budgeted 88.9 percent occupancy rate in the month of October. However, shortfalls (indicated by negative variance signs) in achieving targeted private-pay and private-insurance patient days have resulted in a revenue shortfall of $3,500 for the month. Notice that the actual payer-mix produces an average reimbursement rate that is $1.01 lower than the average budgeted rate for each patient day, also a negative variance.

One way to eliminate the revenue shortfall in this case is to increase the overall census by 22 patient days for the month. In this case, 22 patient days times the average reimbursement rate of $159.59 per patient day equals $3,511, which is sufficient to cover the revenue shortfall. Another way to achieve the revenue objective is to realize higher reimbursement rates than the rates projected in the budget. Higher reimbursement rates, however, are often difficult to achieve, because the administrator has little or no control over third-party reimbursement rates. For a substantial number of patients, the rates are established by third parties such as Medicaid and Medicare. Private-pay rates are under management's control, but market factors such as competition from other facilities often limit the administrator's ability to unilaterally raise private-pay rates.

CONTROLLING COSTS

Cost control requires an understanding of three main types of costs: fixed, variable, and semi-fixed (also called step-fixed or step-variable). The three types of costs operate differently within a certain **census range**, which is an anticipated range of patient census. The generic term used in cost accounting for a range of volume or activity such as census is "relevant range." Associating costs with a census range is central to controlling costs without jeopardizing quality of care or demoralizing the staff with staffing shortages. When the concept of census range is employed in planning expenditures, cost expectations are established for an anticipated range of the facility's patient census. A census range should be used, because no one can exactly predict the census for a future time.

Types of Costs

The nature of a particular type of cost can be evaluated on the basis of its relationship to a change in the facility's census. Suppose that costs are

being budgeted for a census range of 108 to 116 patients. Some costs would remain unchanged regardless of whether the facility has 108 or 116 patients. Costs that do not vary with the number of patients within the census range are called **fixed costs**. Fixed costs are non-controllable. For example, regardless of whether the facility has 108 or 116 patients, the facility must still have the same number of RN hours per day (Figure 16-2). Administrative costs, telephone and utilities, rent or lease costs for the building, and maintenance and repairs are other examples of fixed costs.

Variable costs, on the other hand, vary with the change in the number of patients within the census range. For example, if the cost of raw food is $4.00 per patient per day, the food cost would be $432 per day when the facility has 108 patients; it will be $464 per day when the census is 116. Other costs that are considered variable include medical and nursing supplies, dietary supplies, temporary labor, and linens and laundry chemicals. Note that for variable costs, the variable-cost rate (also known as the cost per unit) remains constant. The variable cost rate is expressed as a **per-patient-day cost** (PPD cost), which is a constant amount per patient per day. In the food-cost example, the PPD food cost remains constant at $4.00. To get the total food cost, the PPD cost is multiplied by the number of patients. The total variable costs are controllable. Suppose the facility has been operating with a daily census of 114, and the census drops to 110: The facility must reduce its spending on food from $456 per day to $440 (Figure 16-3), even as the PPD cost remains constant at $4.00. This cost-control technique is not applicable to fixed costs discussed earlier.

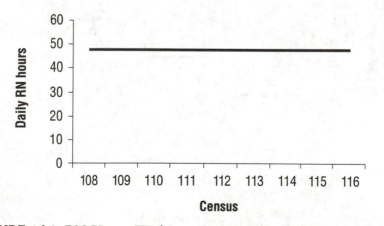

FIGURE 16-2 RN Hours Within a Census Range of 108 and 116.

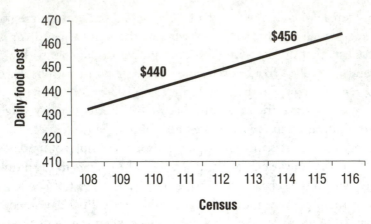

FIGURE 16-3 Food Cost Within a Census Range of 108 and 116.

The third category consists of semi-fixed or step-variable costs. **Semi-fixed costs** remain fixed within parts of the census range; they rise or fall for another part of the census range. Semi-fixed costs are generally encountered in paraprofessional labor hours, such as certified nursing assistant (CNA) hours. The example illustrated in Figure 16-4 assumes that CNAs are scheduled in eight-hour increments. In this example, 360 hours of CNA time is scheduled even though the census may vary between 108 and 110; 368 hours are scheduled when the census increases to 111; an additional eight hours are scheduled only when the census

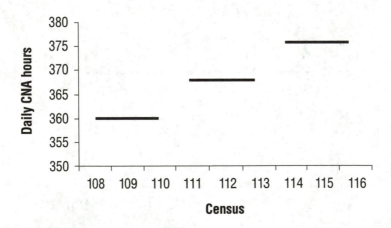

FIGURE 16-4 Nursing Assistant Hours Within a Census Range of 108 and 116.

reaches 114. Like variable costs, semi-fixed costs are also controllable. But unlike variable costs, semi-fixed costs are not controllable for minor fluctuations in census. The example given here assumes that CNAs are assured work for a full shift unless the census drops by three patients, such as from 116 to 113 or from 113 to 110. Depending on management policy, some facilities may treat semi-fixed costs as variable costs. Semi-fixed labor costs can be treated as variable costs, especially when a facility is able to employ adequate part-time staff members who may be called in as needed. Some facilities that do not have this flexibility still treat these costs as variable and a CNA is sent home without completing a full shift if the census drops by as little as one patient. Such a practice can be demoralizing for the staff and contribute to other problems such as absenteeism and turnover.

Controlling Labor Costs

Labor costs have two components: hours of labor and dollars spent on labor. Hours of labor have a direct effect on labor dollars. But the labor-dollar component is also affected by average wages paid to employees. Wages are governed by a facility's wage policies. Competitive pressures may also influence how much a facility may have to pay to hire and retain qualified staff members. Hence, the administrator may have more control over the hours of labor than over total dollars spent on wages and salaries.

Labor costs and other expenditures are controlled using the technique of variance analysis mentioned earlier. Cost control begins with the budgeted figures being adjusted to reflect changes in census. Exhibit 16-4 presents a labor-hour report for a particular nursing unit within a facility. Similar reports would be prepared for other nursing units and departments such as food service, housekeeping, and laundry. A report will also be prepared for the entire facility. A labor-hour report is generally produced every pay period. This report shows budgeted hours, actual hours, adjusted budget hours, and the variance between the adjusted budget and the actual hours. The budgeted hours in this example were based on 532 patient days for the pay period. However, the facility's actual patient days were 504. Therefore, for determining the variances, the budgeted hours must be adjusted for the lower actual census. The actual census is seldom the same as the census that was budgeted. An adjusted budget, which is also called a **flexible budget**, is derived by applying budgeted PPD hours

EXHIBIT 16–4

Labor Hour Report
Pay period: October 11, 2003—October 24, 2003
Department: Nursing (Unit B)

Patient days

Budget	Actual
532	504

	Budget				Actual				Adjusted budget		Variance	
	Regulars Hours	Overtime Hours	Totals Hours	PPD	Regular Hours	Overtime Hours	Total Hours	PPD	Total Hours	PPD	Total	PPD
RN	224	0	224	0.42	224	4	228	0.45	212	0.42	−16	−0.03
LPN	332	4	336	0.63	318	0	318	0.63	318	0.63	0	0.00
CNA	1,762	30	1,792	3.37	1,710	28	1,738	3.45	1,698	3.37	−40	−0.08
Total	2,318	34	2,352	4.42	2,252	32	2,284	4.53	2,228	4.42	−56	−0.11

to the actual patient days. For example, in Exhibit 16-4, the total labor hours under the "adjusted budget" column have been calculated by multiplying the budgeted 4.42 PPD hours by the actual census of 504. A flexible budget extrapolates budgeted variable costs to reflect actual patient days.

Flexible budget = Budgeted PPD hours (or costs) × Actual patient days

Most computer-based accounting and finance programs treat labor hours as variable costs rather than fixed or semi-variable costs. Nevertheless, computer-generated labor hour reports are useful in pointing out the variances. In Exhibit 16-4 the negative variance of 16 hours for RNs indicates overstaffing, but if RN hours are treated as a fixed cost the variance can be ignored. On the other hand, RNs have incurred four hours of overtime that was not budgeted, and this overage calls for follow-up to determine whether this overtime was avoidable. One will also notice that four hours of overtime budgeted for LPNs was not used. One might think that there was a trade-off between LPN and RN overtime, but RN wages are higher than those for LPNs, and this difference would negatively affect the labor dollars, as is apparent from Exhibit 16-5. The budgeted overtime costs for LPNs were $88 for four hours of overtime. For the same four hours of overtime the actual costs for RNs amounted to $106. In such a case the administrator should decide whether circumstances warranted swapping overtime hours.

In Exhibit 16-5, the labor hours shown in Exhibit 16-4 have been converted to dollar costs using the hourly wage rates. For variance analysis, a flexible budget (adjusted budget) is formulated to reflect budgeted dollar costs adjusted for the lower patient day total of 504. Notice in Exhibit 16-5 that even though RN costs are considered fixed, the negative cost variance of $382 is excessive, because the hourly rate has been exceeded by $0.47 per hour. The non-budgeted overtime is partially responsible for the overage. However, the administrator can evaluate the portion of overage attributable to the overtime incurred, and the portion attributable to other causes. The portion attributable to other causes is $0.32 per hour ($17.63 hourly rate under Actual Regular Costs minus $17.31 hourly rate under budgeted Regular Costs). This variance could be the result of market competition that may have become more intense since the budget was finalized. To hire or retain qualified RNs, the facility may have had no choice but to pay higher wages. The remaining $0.15 of the $0.47 variance in hourly rate is attributable to overtime ($17.78 hourly rate under Actual Total Costs minus $17.63 hourly rate under Actual Regular Costs).

EXHIBIT 16-5

Labor Cost Report
Pay period: October 11, 2003–October 24, 2003
Department: Nursing (Unit B)

Patient days	
Budget	Actual
532	504

	Budget						Actual						Flexible Budget		Variance	
	Regular Costs		Overtime Costs		Total Costs		Regular Costs		Overtime Costs		Total Costs		Total Costs		Total Costs	
	Dollars	Hourly rate	Dollars	Hourly rate	Dollars	Hourly rate	Dollars	Hourly rate	Dollars	Hourly rate	Dollars	Hourly rate	Dollars	Hourly rate	Dollars	Hourly rate
RN	$3,877	$17.31	$0	$0.00	$3,877	$17.31	$3,949	$17.63	$106	$26.45	$4,055	$17.78	$3,673	$17.31	−$382	−$0.47
LPN	4,864	14.65	88	21.98	4,952	14.74	4,646	14.61	0	21.92	4,646	14.61	4,692	14.74	46	0.13
CNA	14,184	8.05	362	12.08	14,546	8.12	13,714	8.02	337	12.03	14,051	8.08	13,785	8.12	−266	0.04
Total	$22,925	$9.89	$450	$13.24	$23,375	$9.94	$22,309	$9.91	$443	$13.83	$22,752	$9.96	$22,151	$9.94	−$601	−$0.02

In Exhibit 16-5 the LPN costs are better by $46 than the budgeted costs, a positive cost variance. Even though there is zero variance for LPN hours, cost savings have been realized because of a positive variance of $0.13 in the hourly rate mainly because no overtime was incurred even though it was budgeted. CNA costs appear to be problematic; these costs have a negative variance of $266 even though the variance for hourly rate is positive by $0.04. As shown in Exhibit 16-4, CNA hours have been exceeded by 40, which amounts to an average of 2.9 hours per day during the pay period. The administrator should investigate this variance further; what must be determined is whether managers in the nursing department had the flexibility to schedule part-time staff, or whether the excess staffing was a result of a policy of assuring a full shift to CNAs who are scheduled to work. In spite of the influence of such factors, the fact remains that Nursing Unit B has exceeded its labor budget by $601 during the given pay period. To prevent ongoing budget shortfalls, the facility must build census or reduce costs.

Controlling Non-labor Expenditures

A facility's basic approach to controlling expenses—such as food, supplies, and linens—is also based on variance analysis. However, other types of monitoring and control methods are also used, and these methods are discussed in this section. The technique of variance analysis for expenses is very similar to what has been discussed above. Exhibit 16-6 presents the expense summary for the food-service department. This summary contains variances for the month of October and for the year-to-date totals for 10 months of the year. Although the flexible budget is not shown, the variances are derived from a comparison of the actual expenditures against a flexible budget. As usual, the flexible budget is calculated by multiplying the budgeted PPD costs by the actual patient days. Labor costs for supervisory personnel are considered fixed costs, so a negative variance is produced when the actual patient days are below budget. Similarly, the negative variances for labor cost for operational staff may be ignored if these costs are considered fixed. Details of labor hours and labor costs for the food service department will appear in reports very similar to nursing labor hours and costs shown in Exhibits 16-4 and 16-5. In Exhibit 16-6 the variance for raw food cost is very small, and can be ignored; expenditures for chemicals and small equipment are better than budget; food service supplies, however, require further investigation.

EXHIBIT 16-6

Expense Summary—Food Service Department
Month of October 2003

Patient days

	Month		Year to date	
	Budget	Actual	Budget	Actual
	3,472	3,286	34,564	33,423

	Month				Year to date				Variance	
	Budget	PPD	Actual	PPD	Budget	PPD	Actual	PPD	Month	Year to date
Labor:										
Supervisors	$3,835	$1.10	$3,835	$1.17	$38,350	$1.11	$38,350	$1.15	−$205	−$1,266
Operational staff	13,690	3.94	13,367	4.07	136,900	3.96	134,978	4.04	−410	−2,597
Raw food	13,888	4.00	13,264	4.04	136,873	3.96	132,420	3.96	−120	−65
Chemicals	1,121	0.32	1,012	0.31	11,060	0.32	10,068	0.30	49	627
Food service supplies	1,296	0.37	1,346	0.41	12,789	0.37	13,323	0.40	−119	−956
Small equipment	215	0.06	180	0.05	2,150	0.06	1,956	0.06	23	123
Total cost	$34,045	$9.81	$33,004	$10.04	$338,122	$9.78	$331,095	$9.91	−$783	−$4,135

Expenses should also be monitored by looking at an accounts-payable report. Such a report is generally produced weekly, and it lists all the payables processed by the facility's bookkeeper. The report shows the date when an invoice was processed, the name of the vendor, and the amount paid. Reviewing this report each week may bring to attention anything that may appear out of place.

Inventory Management

Inventory management is an important tool for controlling expenses. Receiving and inventory-control procedures for food items were discussed in Chapter 10. Similar procedures must be adopted for other inventoried items. As an example, a linen inventory control system is presented in Exhibit 16-7. Such a system serves two main purposes: (1) It ensures that the facility always has adequate linens available to serve patients, and (2) It provides a mechanism for linen cost control.

The first of these objectives is achieved by establishing adequate par levels. A **par level** is the number of units of an item the facility should maintain in its inventory, including items in circulation and in storage (the method for establishing linen par levels was discussed in Chapter 11). When the actual count for an item falls below its par level, that item should be replenished.

The second objective of linen cost control is achieved by instituting the two types of inventory control systems discussed in Chapter 10. A **perpetual inventory system** is a continuous record of the available quantity of each linen item. This record maintains a running balance that is updated monthly. The closing inventory at the end of a month equals the beginning inventory (what was on hand at the first of the month, which is the closing inventory from the previous month) plus purchases, minus discards:

$$\textit{closing inventory at the end of a month} = \textit{beginning inventory} + \textit{purchases} - \textit{discards.}$$

The system requires that the person in charge of linens maintain a record of items discarded because of thinning, fading, and tearing. The **physical inventory system** involves actually counting each linen item. Because linens are constantly in circulation, the facility should develop a procedure for counting all linens throughout the facility. A suitable time for taking a physical inventory is when patient care activities have slowed down, generally in late afternoon or during the night. At a given time, the nursing staff should

EXHIBIT 16–7

Linen Inventory on October 31, 2003

	Par levels	On hand October 1	Purchases	Discards	Closing inventory October 31	Physical count October 31	Over/ (short)	To replenish	Replenishment cost Unit cost	Total cost
Bath towels	384	412	0	17	395	406	11		$1.10	
Hand towels	636	507	120	0	627	611	−16	25	$0.58	$14.48
Wash cloths	1,260	966	300	0	1,266	1,009	−257	251	$0.25	$61.70
Bed sheets	504	478	36	14	500	500	0	4	$2.83	$11.32
Pillow cases	252	276	0	6	270	268	−2		$0.91	
Blankets	252	162	0	11	151	154	3	98	$11.95	$1,171.10
Bedspreads	192	178	0	4	174	174	0	18	$13.20	$237.60
Mattress pads	192	230	0	2	228	224	−4		$4.85	
									Total Replenishment Cost	$1,496.20

count all linen items in patient rooms, bathrooms, linen carts, and storage closets on nursing units. At the same time, all soiled linens should be removed to the laundry for washing. These soiled items are counted as they come out of the laundry processing area for folding and storage. Before this count, all items that were processed in the laundry and linens in the main storage room should have been counted. Following this method should produce a fairly accurate count, although there will always be some minor discrepancies. The "over/(short)" column in Exhibit 16-7 shows such discrepancies. For example, the overage of 11 bath towels and shortage of 16 hand towels may be attributed to a miscount, such as counting some hand towels as bath towels. On the other hand, a shortage of washcloths is more significant if the counting was accurate. Such variances in a given month should not cause any alarm, but shortages occurring month after month indicate pilferage or other misuse. The column "to replenish" is the difference between "physical count" and "par levels." This replenish amount shows the number of additional linens the facility must purchase to bring the counts up to par levels. According to Exhibit 16-7, the greatest need is to purchase additional blankets. The administrator should place an order in November to purchase eight dozen blankets. If the budget allows it, the administrator should also purchase eighteen bedspreads in November. The last column in Exhibit 16-7 provides the total cost of bringing current inventory to par levels.

MANAGING RECEIVABLES

Accounts receivable are amounts due from patients and from third-party payers for services that the facility has already provided. Receivables are revenues that have yet to be collected. The income statement, discussed earlier, records all revenues regardless of whether the facility has actually received payment for the services it has performed. A facility that may be profitable on paper may experience serious financial difficulty if the booked revenues remain uncollected. Therefore, managing accounts receivable is one of the critical elements of cash management, which is vitally important for the long-term survival of the facility.

Accounts receivable management has three main objectives (Cleverley and Cameron 2002):

- Minimize lost charges and reimbursement
- Minimize write-offs for uncollectible accounts
- Minimize the accounts-receivable collection cycle

Minimizing Lost Charges and Reimbursement

The term **charge** means a fee that is established by the nursing facility for a particular service or product. The key phrase in this definition is "established by the facility." In contrast, **reimbursement** is the fee established by a third-party payer, such as Medicaid, Medicare, or private insurance. As discussed earlier, the administrator has little or no control over third-party reimbursement rates. The administrator generally has more control over the charges the facility establishes for basic *per diem* (patient day) room-and-board rates and for ancillary services and supplies.

To minimize lost charges and lost reimbursement, the nursing facility must have a census-tallying system to accurately account for all patients in the facility at midnight each day. A **midnight census report** is completed by the nurse in charge on the night shift. This report should be verified by the director of nursing the following morning. The midnight census report is forwarded to the facility's business office, where this report is used for calculating daily revenues for all patients by their respective payer types. Such daily revenue accounting forms the basis for producing monthly bills for each payer. Without adequate controls over daily census accounting, some revenues would be lost.

Charges other than room and board include ancillaries, such as rehabilitation therapies and medical supplies. Most third-party reimbursement rates are now all-inclusive. An **all-inclusive rate** is a bundled fee that establishes a single rate of payment for all services and supplies furnished to a patient. For private-pay patients, however, ancillary items are billed in addition to the basic room-and-board fee. To capture ancillary charges for private-pay patients, the facility must maintain adequate procedures to record all ancillary services and supplies used by each patient.

Minimizing Write-Offs

The accounting term for write-offs is "bad debts." Bad debts represent legitimate revenues, and the facility is entitled to get paid for the services it has already provided. For various reasons, however, the facility is not able to collect all the monies it is owed. After several attempts to collect such outstanding accounts, these accounts are declared uncollectible and are called bad debts. So, a **bad debt** is an amount that is legitimately owed to the facility, but is deemed uncollectible.

Billing errors are the most common reason for which third-party payers reject claims for payment. In other instances, a payer may request evidence for services delivered. In either case, if the facility fails to do adequate and timely follow-up and the dispute over payment remains unresolved, a claim will eventually turn into a bad debt. To minimize such problems, the facility's personnel must thoroughly understand the rules established by each third-party payer. The facility must maintain updated Medicare and Medicaid manuals for reference purposes, and all new personnel must be adequately trained to comply with all rules that pertain to payment. Compliance with rules and regulations and maintenance of appropriate documentation in the medical records are critical to billing and collections.

Although third-party payments constitute the largest component of accounts receivable, the facility must also institute procedures for billing and collecting accounts due from private sources. Deductibles and coinsurance, discussed in Chapter 4, are to be paid privately by the patient. Most nursing home patients have a **responsible party** handling the patient's private financial affairs. Complete information on each patient's designated responsible party, such as a spouse or relative, must be obtained at the time of admission. When the patient is admitted the responsible party is also asked to sign a statement that he or she, as the responsible party, assumes the responsibility to pay all amounts that the patient must pay privately. At the time of admission the facility may also furnish a copy of the facility's credit and collection policy to the responsible party.

Timely billing and follow-up are critical for collecting private monies. The facility must institute collection policy and procedures to be followed by its administrative personnel. The collection policy should outline at what point a collection call should be made, at what point a letter should be sent to demand payment, and at what point an account should be turned over to a collection agency (some of the details were covered in Chapter 12). The policy should also outline at what point and under what circumstances the organization writes off accounts as bad debts (Nowicki 2001). The decision to write off uncollectible amounts is made jointly by the administrator and corporate officers (for facilities affiliated with hospitals or multifacility chains) after evaluating each account that falls within the policy criteria for a bad debt.

EXHIBIT 16-8

Aging Schedule on October 31, 2003

Patient name		0–30 days	31–90 days	91–120 days	over 120 days	Total Outstanding
Adam, B	Private	920	103		1,354	$2,377
	Medicare	3,395	972			$4,367
	Medicaid		2,049		374	$2,423
	Other				127	$127
						$9,294
Blake, C	Private	858	143			$1,001
	Medicare					$0
	Medicaid					$0
	Other	3,579				$3,579
						$4,580
Cooper, D	Private			684		$684
	Medicare					$0
	Medicaid	2,894	320			$3,214
	Other					$0
						$3,898
Total receivables		$708,865	$218,612	$41,125	$112,553	$1,082,237
		65.5%	20.2%	3.8%	10.4%	

Collection period   63.2 days

Minimizing the Collection Cycle

Apart from following procedures to monitor and collect receivables, it is equally important for a facility to establish standards for collection and to determine whether accounts are being collected in a timely manner. An essential tool for monitoring receivables and evaluating performance is called an "aging schedule," also known as an "aging report." An **aging schedule** provides a breakdown of each patient's account by showing the length of time that various amounts within the account have been outstanding. Exhibit 16-8 provides an illustration of an aging schedule. Notice that this exhibit shows the amounts due from each payer type and the age of each amount due. This exhibit also provides totals for the entire facility, and it shows the percentage of the total receivables that have been outstanding in each age category.

The collection cycle for accounts receivable is measured in terms of the **collection period**, which is also called "days revenue outstanding." This measure indicates the number of days worth of revenue that is in accounts receivable, which also indicates the average number of days it takes to collect patient revenues. A collection period evaluates how quickly a facility is able to bill and collect its revenues. This measure should be calculated at the end of each month using year-to-date data. The calculation is as follows:

$$\text{Collection period} = \frac{\text{Total accounts receivable}}{\text{Revenue/Days in period}}$$

Exhibit 16-8 shows that the receivables constitute 63.2 days worth of patient revenues. This result is derived by plugging in the above formula the year-to-date patient revenue of $5,205,696 (not shown) and the 304 days in the period from January through October. The administrator and governing board should decide whether 63.2 days is an acceptable collection period, or whether a shorter period ought to be the standard.

BUDGETING

As stated earlier, the budget ties together operational planning and control functions. Budgeting is the planning phase that involves detailed plans expressed quantitatively in dollar terms; these plans specify how revenues will be generated and what resources will be used during a specified

period (Gapenski 2002). The control phase of the budget is used for the purpose of managing revenues and controlling costs, as discussed earlier. This section focuses on the planning phase of preparing a budget.

The formulation of an operating budget is discussed here; this budget combines forecasts for revenues and expenses and its format is like that of an income statement. The operating budget is generally prepared for an entire fiscal year, and the planning process for this budget often begins three to four months before the current fiscal year ends. The fiscal year is established by the nursing home corporation or its governing body. The fiscal year may or may not coincide with the calendar year, but generally it does.

Budgeting involves making projections for the next fiscal year on the basis of some reasonable assumptions. Throughout the budgeting process one must ask the question, "What can we reasonably expect to achieve?" Answers to this question should incorporate all known variables, such as any foreseeable changes in market competition, trends in the local economy, anticipated Medicare and Medicaid reimbursement rates based on economic and political factors, local labor market conditions for nursing and other personnel, general inflation for consumer products, and results expected from implementing any new strategies, such as a refocused marketing plan or major renovations. Using such assumptions, the administrator must first forecast anticipated census volume by pay type. Projections are also needed for private-pay charges, reimbursement rates from third parties, staffing requirements, wage and benefit costs, and non-labor expenses.

The assumptions just mentioned are applied to some base of reference. A reasonable base to use is what the facility has accomplished in the current fiscal year so far. Current data are often compared to previous year's performance data. Using all this information, managerial judgments are made regarding reasonable projections for the next fiscal year. The budgeting process is greatly facilitated by developing budget worksheets. The worksheets include all major pieces of information on which the budget projections are based.

Budgeting Revenues

The basic equation for a facility's revenue is $R = Q \times P$, where R stands for revenue, Q for quantity (census), and P for price (charge or reimbursement rate). A sample of a worksheet for census forecast is presented in Exhibit 16-9. The first two sections of this exhibit contain historical

EXHIBIT 16–9

Census Projection Worksheet For 2004 budget

	Jan	Feb	Mar	Apr	May	Jun	Jul	Aug	Sep	Oct	Nov	Dec	Year
2002 Average daily census													
Private pay	27.8	28.1	29.1	28.5	27.7	28.0	28.0	27.0	26.6	24.7	23.4	24.0	26.9
Private insurance	2.2	2.2	2.4	2.4	2.5	2.3	2.1	3.0	2.0	3.0	4.0	4.0	2.7
Medicaid	59.6	59.2	59.9	62.9	61.8	63.4	63.9	63.1	64.8	65.2	65.7	63.2	62.7
Medicare	13.4	13.6	15.6	14.9	16.1	16.3	16.6	16.0	16.8	16.2	14.7	13.8	15.3
Veterans contract	4.0	5.0	5.5	5.5	4.5	3.5	3.5	3.0	2.0	2.0	1.0	0.0	3.3
Total	107.0	108.1	112.5	114.2	112.6	113.5	114.1	112.1	112.2	111.1	108.8	105.0	110.9
Occupancy rate	84.9%	85.8%	89.3%	90.6%	89.4%	90.1%	90.6%	89.0%	89.0%	88.2%	86.3%	83.3%	88.0%
2003 Average daily census													
Private pay	22.4	23.1	24.1	23.5	23.7	24.2	26.0	27.0	26.6	27.5			24.8
Private insurance	2.2	2.2	2.4	3.4	4.5	2.3	2.1	3.0	2.0	2.4			2.6
Medicaid	62.6	61.2	59.9	62.9	61.8	65.4	63.9	63.1	64.8	60.8			62.6
Medicare	13.4	13.6	14.6	13.9	16.1	15.2	16.6	16.0	16.8	17.0			15.3
Veterans contract	2.0	2.0	1.0	1.0	0.0	0.0	3.5	3.0	2.0	4.3			1.9
Total	102.6	102.1	102.0	104.7	106.1	107.1	112.1	112.1	112.2	112.0			107.3
Occupancy rate	81.4%	81.0%	81.0%	83.1%	84.2%	85.0%	89.0%	89.0%	89.0%	88.9%			85.2%

continues

EXHIBIT 16–9 *continued*

2004 Average daily census projections

Private pay	26.0	26.0	28.0	29.0	30.0	30.0	31.0	31.0	31.0	31.0	30.0	30.0	29.4
Private insurance	2.6	2.6	2.6	2.6	2.6	2.6	2.6	2.6	2.6	2.6	2.6	2.6	2.6
Medicaid	58.0	58.0	60.0	60.0	62.0	62.0	62.0	62.0	62.0	61.0	59.0	59.0	60.4
Medicare	17.0	18.0	18.0	19.0	19.0	19.0	20.0	20.0	20.0	20.0	20.0	20.0	19.2
Veterans contract	2.0	2.0	0.0	0.0	0.0	0.0	0.0	0.0	0.0	0.0	0.0	0.0	0.3
Total	105.6	106.6	108.6	110.6	113.6	113.6	115.6	115.6	115.6	114.6	111.6	111.6	111.9
Occupancy rate	83.8%	84.6%	86.2%	87.8%	90.2%	90.2%	91.7%	91.7%	91.7%	91.0%	88.6%	88.6%	88.8%

Assumptions:

1. The previous administrator resigned in November 2002. The facility was without a permanent administrator for two months. It is assumed that a temporary drop in census occurred in early 2003 due to this change.
2. A new marketing strategy aimed at private pay clients was implemented in September 2003. It is assumed that private pay census will be slightly higher in 2004.
3. The VA contract will not be renewed once the existing VA patients are discharged.
4. Contract with a new rehab company is expected to increase Medicare census.

and current data for 2002 and 2003. Note that at the time the budget projections for 2004 were made, the census data for 2003 were available only for the period until and including the month of October. The assumptions made for the 2004 projections have been noted on the worksheet. A similar worksheet (not shown) is used for projecting *per diem* rates, and patient revenues are calculated using the revenue formula just presented. Computer-based budget programs calculate the revenues automatically as the census and *per diem* rates are entered into the computer. Finally, estimates for ancillary revenue and other revenues, such as income from investments or rental fees, should be added to the budget to arrive at the total revenue figure.

Budgeting Expenses

Expenses are budgeted for each department separately and then consolidated into a single budget for the entire facility. Separate departmental budgets allow the departmental supervisors to give their inputs into the budgets that they would be responsible for controlling. Projecting labor costs is the most challenging aspect of the expense budget. This task can be simplified if the facility already has pre-established labor-hour standards for different census ranges as illustrated in Figures 16-2 and 16-4. For example, labor hours for maintenance, business office, social services, and activity departments are generally fixed. Housekeeping, laundry, and dietary department hours are usually also fixed, unless census varies substantially. For the nursing department, a method of developing staffing plans based on weighting factors that account for acuity levels of patients was discussed in Chapter 14. To facilitate labor-hour projections, budget worksheets should be developed to record historical data and assumptions used in forecasting.

The administrator and corporate officers should also determine budgetary allowances for overtime, training, and orientation, all of which are legitimate costs incurred in operating a facility. Overtime and orientation costs are partly a function of employee turnover and absenteeism, but these costs may also be incurred for other workload and training needs. Because budgeting is a management planning process, the administrator may consider implementing programs that may effectively reduce turnover and absenteeism. Such programs may require an initial outlay of funds; these funds should be included in the budget in anticipation of

future cost savings. The facility could reasonably achieve these cost savings during the latter part of the next fiscal year. If so, projected labor costs associated with turnover and absenteeism could be reduced in the budget for the latter part of that year.

Once labor hours have been determined, the next step is to project average hourly wages (rates) for each category of employees. The starting point for hourly-rate projections is the actual hourly rates that appear in the current labor-cost reports (See Exhibit 16-5 for an example of these rates). Administrators make projections for the next year based on the facility's wage-increase policies and the labor market conditions in the local area. Once projections for hours and wage rates have been made, labor cost $C = H \times W$, where H stands for hours of labor and W is the average hourly wage rate. As in the case of revenue, computer-based budget programs calculate labor costs automatically as the hours and wage rates are entered.

Finally, all other anticipated expenses should be included in the budget. Fixed costs such as telephone, postage, and insurance would be entered as a constant amount for each month. Costs such as utilities would vary according to hot and cold months, and should be spread out accordingly. Variable expenses are generally projected on the basis of cost per patient day (PPD). For example, if the projected cost for housekeeping chemicals for the 2004 budget is $0.40 PPD, according to the census projected in Exhibit 16-9 the budgeted expense would be $1,309 for January (average daily census of 105.6 × 31 days in the month × .40 PPD expense), and $1,194 for February.

The administrator should also budget for any activities associated with marketing and community-exchange relationships discussed in earlier chapters. In the example presented in Exhibit 16-9, one of the assumptions made for an increased private-pay census is the effect of a new marketing strategy. Any expenses associated with implementing this strategy should be budgeted, the strategy should be carried out, and its results should be evaluated for future planning.

Budgeted Margin

Once all revenues and expenses have been budgeted, the margin (profit or loss) is calculated as

$$Total\ margin = Total\ revenue - Total\ expenses$$

The margin that the administrator is held accountable for achieving is more precisely called an **operating margin**. This operating margin is simply the difference between budgeted revenues and expenses. The operating margin is generally expressed as a percentage:

$$Operating\ margin = \frac{Total\ margin \times 100}{Total\ revenue}$$

Suppose the 2004 budget projected total revenues of $6,658,000 and total expenses of $5,835,000. These projections result in an operating margin of 12.4%. The administrator and the governing body must decide whether this projection is reasonable. Suppose the expectation is 13%. The budget would then require some further tweaking, perhaps both on the revenue and expense sides. In most instances, reasonable modifications are necessary before the budget is finalized and approved by the governing body.

CONCLUSION

Most nursing home organizations consider experience in financial management to be a top qualification when an administrator is recruited, which underscores the importance of financial management in health facility management. The planning phase of formulating a budget is the starting point in financial management. In this phase the administration sets standards against which the actual performance of the operations will be measured. Budget preparation should take into account both internal and external factors and should not be turned into a numbers game. Well-thought-out budgets should provide for adequate resources while also paying attention to the bottom line. However, the top-down process of forecasting census levels, reimbursement, expenditures, and operating margins must be maintained. Well-planned budgets become an important tool for managing revenues and expenditures.

DISCUSSION AND APPLICATION QUESTIONS

1. What is the relationship between (a) accounts receivable and cash flow, and between (b) accounts receivable and income statement?

2. Assume that the private pay charges that were applicable in October 2003 (see Exhibit 16-3) will be increased by 4% on January 1, 2004, and that all third-party reimbursement rates will increase by 3%. Use the census projections in Exhibit 16-9 to calculate the total revenue that will be budgeted for January 2004. Using a spreadsheet calculate the budgeted revenue for each of the 12 months and for the entire year 2004. For each month and for the entire year, show the projected revenue by pay type.

3. Based on revenue projections in (2) above, what should be the total expenses for the year 2004 to earn a net income of 7%? Assume that there are no other revenues.

4. You are given the following information for the year ended December 31, 2004:

	Budget	Actual
Patient days	40955	42456
Total expenses	$6,313,645	$6,675,621

(a) Do a variance analysis after preparing a flexible budget. Assume that all costs are variable.

(b) Now assume that 30% of the costs are fixed and the remaining costs are variable. Do a flexible budget and variance analysis.

(c) Compare the variances in (a) and (b) and explain why the variance in (b) is greater.

REFERENCES

Cleverley, W.O., and A.E. Cameron. 2002. *Essentials of Health Care Finance.* 5th ed. Gaithersburg, MD: Aspen Publishers, Inc.

Gapenski, L.C. 2002. *Healthcare Finance: An Introduction to Accounting and Financial Management.* 2nd ed. Chicago: AUPHA Press and Washington, DC: Health Administration Press.

Nowicki, M. 2001. *The Financial Management of Hospitals and Healthcare Organizations.* 2nd ed. Chicago: AUPHA Press and Washington, DC: Health Administration Press.

CHAPTER 17

Effective Quality and Productivity Management

8. The cycle of data-driven process improvement. All-encompassing, interdisciplinary, and continuous learning aspects of CQI.
9. How to build a quality culture. The Wellspring model as an illustration of quality in action.

Efficiency, productivity, and quality improvement are often regarded as isolated and even contradictory concepts. When the words "efficiency" and "productivity" are mentioned, some people instinctively equate those words with "doing more with fewer resources." Delivery of patient care is particularly **labor intensive**, which means that people have to provide hands-on services that, in most instances, cannot be taken over by technology. Hence, nursing home personnel have a tendency to presume that improved efficiency means working harder, doing more in less time, and constantly rushing to meet patients' needs. Therefore, people commonly assume that quality suffers when greater efficiency is required, and that an organization may achieve higher quality or greater efficiency, but not both. But years of research and experience in various industries have demonstrated that such ideas are flawed.

Through quality management, American medical care delivery has achieved some incredible accomplishments. The average length of stay in hospitals has been drastically reduced and much patient care has shifted from full-service hospitals to less expensive sites such as outpatient surgery centers and rehabilitation hospitals. These changes occurred while some experts were predicting that quality of medical care would suffer. But the dire consequences these experts predicted never materialized.

Modern methods of quality- and productivity-improvement were developed in manufacturing industries. Service organizations, in general, lagged behind the manufacturing sector in implementing these methods. Hospitals, nursing facilities, and other health care organizations were even slower than other service providers in adopting the concepts and methods of quality improvement. Increasingly, however, health care managers have realized that quality of service and productivity can indeed be managed, and that effectively managing these areas can provide a competitive edge to health care delivery organizations.

PRODUCTIVITY AND QUALITY

For all practical purposes, productivity and efficiency are used as synonymous terms. Measuring productivity and efficiency means taking into account the cost of inputs used in the production of certain outputs. Although productivity is often viewed as physical outputs produced in exchange for certain quantified inputs, a sole focus on physical outputs can actually be counterproductive. The notion of outputs must incorporate the quality of the outputs produced, not merely the quantity of outputs.

For simplicity, outputs in a nursing facility are collectively called patient care. However, patient care includes more than medical and nursing care; patient care includes all the other structures and processes covered in Part II. Hence, outputs in a nursing facility encompass the quality of clinical, social, and residential structures, as well as the various patient care delivery processes such as social services; medical care, nursing, and rehabilitation; recreation and activities; dietary services; plant and environmental services; and administrative and information systems. Productivity is enhanced when the most desirable outputs are produced at the least cost for these services.

$$Productivity = \frac{Outputs}{Inputs}$$

$$Productivity\ enhancement = \frac{Desired\ quality}{Minimization\ of\ resource\ inputs} \quad (1)$$

$$or$$

$$\frac{Maximization\ quality}{Unit\ of\ resource\ inputs} \quad (2)$$

Productivity and quality are interrelated. According to current management theory, improved quality can lead to improved efficiency and vice versa. From this perspective, **productivity** is defined as maximization of quality for each unit of resources used in delivering health care. Accordingly, productivity can be expressed as "desired quality at the lowest possible cost" (equation 1 above) or as "highest possible quality for a given cost" (equation 2 above) (Palmer 1991, p. 12). Measuring productivity therefore requires assessing how effectively a nursing facility's resources are used in delivering patient care services. Inefficiency, on the other hand, reduces the opportunity for quality at a given level of resources (Griffith and White 2002).

To borrow language from the manufacturing industry: "It takes just as many resources to make a bad product as it does to make a good one" (Evans and Lindsay 1993, p. 30). In a nursing home, delivering poor patient care would still require the same level of resources as it would to deliver good patient care. In fact, the cost of poor quality can be very high. In the long run, the cost of poor quality may actually far exceed the cost of producing high-quality service. Just think of the many costs associated with low quality. Direct costs can include fines and penalties imposed by regulatory agencies, legal costs incurred in defending against lawsuits, and payment of legal settlements. Indirect costs can have a long-term negative effect on the facility from the erosion of trust in the community, followed by declining reputation, inability to sustain exchange relationships with community partners, and a drop in patient census. Other indirect costs may include increased staff turnover and absenteeism. Costs associated with investigation of complaints are also indirect costs of poor quality.

Finally, productivity requires that quality be managed. Quality improvement is an investment that calls for resources. These resources are wasted if the focus of quality improvement is on the wrong components. On the other hand, appropriately managed quality improvement should enhance the profitability of a nursing facility. Various studies have shown that nursing homes that produce better-quality services are able to lower costs for delivering patient care services because quality improvement often improves processes of care as well as productivity. Even when higher costs are incurred by increasing hours for RNs in relation to other staff, an indirect inverse effect on overall costs is observed through the positive effect of these extra RN hours on outcomes of care (Weech-Maldonado et al. 2003). A higher skill-mix can lead to a reduction in overall costs because of better health outcomes and improved efficiency. For example, through a higher skill-mix care-related problems can be addressed more promptly, better direction can be given to paraprofessionals, and regulatory and legal sanctions can be avoided through improved care.

The Institute of Medicine also concluded that there was little relationship between quality of nursing home care and Medicaid reimbursement policy. Some facilities provided excellent care at the same Medicaid payment rate and with the same payer-mix as other facilities in the same geographic area that provided substandard care. In essence, paying more to

nursing homes will not guarantee higher quality, because many determinants of quality—such as staff attitudes, motivation, efficiency, administrative philosophy, and managerial skills—do not require additional expenditures and are not significantly related to costs (Institute of Medicine 1986; Institute of Medicine 2001).

WHAT IS QUALITY?

Quality in a nursing facility can be defined as the consistent delivery of services that maximize the physical, mental, social, and spiritual well-being of all residents, produce desirable outcomes, and minimize the likelihood of undesirable consequences. Notice that delivery of quality care in the nursing home has four essential components: consistency, total well-being, desirable outcomes, and prevention of undesirable consequences. Quality is compromised when lapses occur in any one of these four areas.

Consistency

The word "consistency" signifies four characteristics that apply to all services described in Part II:

- continuity
- regularity
- uniformity
- reliability

Continuity means that quality must be consistently delivered over time. Variations from one day to another must be kept to a minimum. In practical terms, continuity means that the facility should, among other things, be just as clean on the weekend as it is on a weekday, and that the food served should taste just as good at supper as it does at lunch.

Regularity means timeliness. Regularity emphasizes timely attention to patient needs. Examples of regularity in a facility include regular bed checks for incontinent patients, prompt response to call signals from patients who need staff attention, and timely attention to situations that require the intervention of social services.

Uniformity is sustained delivery of quality not only over time but also across the patient population within the facility. Uniformity means delivering the same caliber of services to all patients regardless of their pay status, race, or any other characteristics.

Reliability is the acid test of consistent quality. Reliability is achieved when quality becomes a part of an organization's culture. Reliability is achieved when a facility's staff can deliver uncompromised quality when no one is watching, because management and family members cannot be in the facility all the time to insure this uncompromised quality. Trust and dependability are built when family members can be free from undue worry about the total well-being of their loved ones.

Total Well-Being

In the nursing home, quality must be based on the holistic concept of health and well-being, described in earlier chapters; this concept emphasizes the well-being of every aspect of what makes a person whole and complete. A holistic approach requires providing services that meet the patient's physical, mental, social, and spiritual needs. Hence, quality includes much more than clinical care; quality must also emphasize all aspects of quality of life. Quality of life has become a vital component of the Requirements of Participation for SNF or NF certification of nursing homes (see Exhibit 3-2). As explained in Chapter 3, periodic inspections have been established for the purpose of monitoring compliance with certification standards and for noting violations of those standards. However, when quality is actively pursued, a facility will take steps to maximize the quality of life for every resident in addition to ensuring the highest levels of medical and nursing care.

Desirable Outcomes

Outcomes are the actual results of a patient's stay in the nursing facility. In health care, outcomes are frequently associated with the results of medical, nursing, and other clinical interventions. An increase in positive outcomes indicates that quality has improved. For example, quality is improved when a greater number of patients than before undergo rehabilitation therapy after orthopedic surgery and return home; there is notable progress with the healing of pressure ulcers that were present when patients were admitted; and patients are weaned off urinary catheters. On the flip side, incidence of pressure ulcers acquired in the facility, prevalence of falls or injuries, frequency of infections, and occurrence of health-threatening weight loss or dehydration are indicators of negative quality outcomes.

Preventing Undesirable Consequences

An important aspect of quality is the system a nursing facility implements to prevent negative outcomes, and how effectively that system is actually used and monitored. Such negative outcomes as accidental deaths and injury from negligence can have catastrophic consequences. Waiting for negative outcomes to occur is obviously not the best approach. Clinical errors, lapses in safety, unsanitary conditions, and untimely maintenance and repairs do not always produce negative consequences, but they often have the potential to cause harm. For example, a patient smokes unsupervised in a smokers' lounge. Even though nothing happens, the situation is really not as innocuous as it may appear. What if the patient was severely burned, or a section of the building had caught fire? The potential devastation is unimaginable.

TECHNICAL AND CONSUMER-DEFINED QUALITY

The above description of quality can be called **technical quality**, which deals essentially with clinical factors. The level of a facility's technical quality depends on its clinical structures, on its processes and practices, and on the technical competence of its health care professionals. The quality of technical performance is evaluated against best practice standards that can be achieved given current scientific knowledge and technology in long-term care delivery (Donabedian 1995). Generally speaking, technical quality is evaluated through expert assessment. However, increasingly, evidence-based practices are being used as a means of reducing inappropriate clinical care and improving patient outcomes (Berlowitz et al. 2001). These best practices are being standardized as **clinical practice guidelines**, which are protocols designed to help practitioners make appropriate health care decisions for specific circumstances (Field and Lohr 1990). The American Geriatric Society and the American Medical Directors Association (AMDA) have developed practice guidelines for the care of the elderly patient. The AMDA has also developed training tools on how to implement the guidelines. The Agency for Healthcare Research and Quality has produced clinical practice guidelines for management of urinary incontinence, prevention of pressure ulcers, treatment of pressure ulcers, post-stroke rehabilitation, and pain management for cancer patients.

The direct consumers of long-term care, i.e., patients and family members, seek technical quality, but they are not equipped to evaluate it, because their observations alone cannot assess the level of clinical quality. Yet consumers do form impressions about a facility's level of quality. Consumers' impressions about quality can be called **consumer-defined quality**. These impressions are based on their personal observations and experiences, what they may hear from other family members, and how the facility's staff interacts and communicates with them. Also, consumers are better able to assess quality-of-life factors than technical quality. Their impressions are also influenced by the aesthetics of the physical premises, cleanliness and comfort, food, activities, staff attitudes, interactions with management, and the facility's accommodation of individual needs and preferences.

It is possible for consumer-defined quality to actually be at odds with a facility's technical level of quality. In general, consumers seek more than technically correct health care. They seek humanistic qualities as well as technical competence (Palmer 1991). Staff interaction with the patient and family, listening for signs of distress, responsiveness, timely exchange of information, respect, empathy, honesty, and sensitivity are key elements of the exchange relationship between the facility and its clients.

Evaluation of total quality must incorporate both the technical side and the consumer side. Client satisfaction has been increasingly recognized as a desirable outcome in various health care delivery settings. Customers' perspective, determined by both residents and family members, is now considered an important element of nursing home quality. This perspective can point to such interpersonal aspects as communications and staff attitudes.

FRAMEWORK OF QUALITY

The management of quality requires an understanding of the framework to guide the improvement of organizational quality. This framework has been credited to the work of Avedis Donabedian (1919–2000). He proposed three domains in which health care quality should be examined: structures, processes, and outcomes. All three domains are equally important in driving quality improvement, and they are closely linked in a hierarchical manner (see Figure 17-1); structures influence processes, and both structures and processes together influence outcomes. Structures and

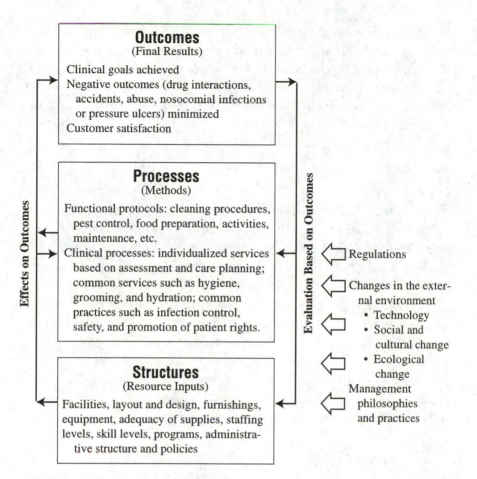

FIGURE 17-1 Framework of Quality

processes in long-term care are shaped by regulations; other changes in the external environment such as new technology, social and cultural change, ecological forces (new infections, antibiotic resistant strains of bacteria, natural events, etc.); and management philosophies and practices.

Structures

Structure provides the necessary foundation without which quality patient care cannot be delivered. In that sense, structure is where quality begins. Structural criteria refer to the availability of resources, such as facilities, equipment, staffing levels, staff qualifications, programs, and the administrative structure (McElroy and Herbelin 1989). Space, build-

ing layout, furnishings, modern equipment, adequate supplies, trained staff, staffing levels and skill-mix, minimum absenteeism and turnover, and facility policies constitute structural elements of quality. The structural elements determine a nursing home's capabilities to deliver an adequate level of care. Inadequate structural quality would negatively affect processes and outcomes.

Processes

Processes are methods used in the production of desired outputs, and how those methods are carried out to produce desired outcomes. Processes entail staff functions, timeliness, accuracy, following established protocols, observation, and taking appropriate action. Each department of the nursing facility must establish functional protocols to aid in the achievement of the process elements of quality. Examples of such protocols include clinical practice guidelines; quality improvement program; room- and hallway-cleaning procedures; pest control; food purchasing, storage, production, and service; building and equipment maintenance procedures; and activities and recreational programming.

The quality of nursing home processes is governed by achieving excellence in the delivery of services that can be classified into three categories: individualized services, common services, and common practices.

Individualized Services

As pointed out in some of the chapters in Part II, patient assessment is the cornerstone on which clinical processes (such as plan of care and the delivery of services) are based to meet individual needs. Individualized care plans establish clinical expectations that guide the delivery of individual care such as administration of medications, nursing treatments, rehabilitation therapies, social interventions, recreational support, special diets, and assistance with designated ADLs. An innovative care planning and care management technique that has been successfully employed in hospitals is clinical pathways; use of this practice is now spreading to other health care settings. A **clinical pathway** is a care-planning tool that outlines important aspects of care necessary for meeting specific outcomes. Pathways are designed for the typical patient from a designated population, such as a patient who has undergone a hip replacement. The pathway is a prewritten document that plots interdisciplinary assess-

ments, interventions, and expected outcomes along a time line (Finch-Guthrie 2000). Clinical pathways promote multidisciplinary teamwork because pathway planning requires input from all disciplines and team interaction is necessary as care delivery progresses along the time line.

Common Services

The second category, common services, consists of routine functional protocols that apply to all patients unless contraindicated in the care plan. Examples include daily hygiene and grooming, scheduled shower or bath, hydration, bedding change, and clean towels. Other types of common services include accurate billing, timely and complete medical records, communication with family about the patient's status, and notification to physicians.

Common Practices

The third category, common practices, include infection control, quality improvement, environmental cleanliness and comfort, safety and security, respect and dignity, privacy, and active promotion of patient rights. Common services and practices are designed to ensure that certain functional protocols are consistently followed to meet the basic needs of all residents and to protect those residents from potential harm or distress.

Outcomes

Outcomes are the final results obtained from using the structure and processes of the facility. Primarily, clinical outcomes are evaluated against individualized care plans to determine whether pre-established treatment and intervention goals have been met. Other outcomes include elements outside the plan of care, and focus mainly on preventing negative incidents such as drug interactions, accidents, alleged abuse, infections, and facility-acquired (nosocomial) pressure ulcers. In almost all cases, outcome issues can be addressed only by a retrospective evaluation of structures and processes and by taking appropriate corrective action.

REGULATORY MINIMUM STANDARDS

Historically, quality in nursing facilities has been defined by standards established for participation in the Medicare and Medicaid programs. Nursing home inspections conducted by the states, known as the survey process, have been used to ascertain compliance with certification stan-

dards (see Chapter 3). Compliance with these standards has been widely used as a proxy for quality.

In 1975, the federal Office of Nursing Home Affairs concluded that certification standards in place at the time had focused mainly on the structural elements of nursing homes, which meant that compliance with existing standards indicated only that the facility had the capacity to provide quality care, but did not necessarily indicate that it delivered quality care. In 1986, the Institute of Medicine produced a landmark study, *Improving the Quality of Care in Nursing Homes*, which concluded that the care provided in the nation's nursing homes was grossly inadequate. This report led to further regulatory changes and the institution of more stringent standards for certification.

Over the years, quality of care in nursing homes has improved, mainly in response to the enforcement of regulatory standards. The survey process, however, has three major limitations: (1) Regulations establish only minimum standards of quality. (2) Nursing facilities cannot be monitored on a continuous basis by regulatory agencies. (3) There are wide variations in survey results, in spite of the government's efforts to standardize the process and train its surveyors. The conclusion here is that quality cannot be improved by regulations alone, even though these regulations have been deemed necessary.

One of the current requirements of participation in the Medicare and Medicaid programs is that the facility establish a quality-assessment and quality-assurance committee. The committee must include the director of nursing, a physician, and at least three other members of the facility's staff. Some major nursing home corporations have based their quality assurance programs on the certification standards, and these corporations internally monitor compliance more frequently than federal regulators do. However, quality improvement should go beyond the federally established minimum standards.

MEASUREMENT AND EVALUATION OF QUALITY

Quality of care remains an unknown entity unless both technical quality and consumer-defined quality are measured. Measurement requires collection of meaningful data, the analysis of that data, and comparison of that data to objective standards of quality. The measurement and evaluation of

quality are geared to pinpoint deficiencies so that corrective actions can be undertaken to improve quality.

Focus on Outcomes

Although structure, process, and outcome data all have a place in measurement of quality, the focus of measurement must be on outcomes. Structural measures only serve to establish a baseline to ensure that staff, facilities, equipment, and organizational features meet at least the minimal necessary conditions for good care (Palmer 1991). Process measures evaluate methods and practices intended to maintain or improve quality. Outcomes, however, define whether quality goals are being met. Once the basic structural and process elements are in place, the focus of measurement must be on outcomes, which can indicate both positive and negative results. When anticipated results are not achieved, administrators must re-examine the structures and processes to determine where the breakdown occurred and what actions should be undertaken to prevent future failures.

Quality measurement can be illustrated by using the example of a meal tray delivered to a patient who requested to have the noon meal in her room. Placing the meal tray before the patient is the main outcome, without which the output would be zero, a total failure of quality, because the patient did not get her meal. But, assuming that a meal tray is delivered, other attributes of this output—such as timeliness of delivery, conformance of the food items placed on the tray with the patient's diet, compliance with the patient's prior indications of likes and dislikes regarding choice of food items, quantity of food served, temperatures of the hot and cold items, the amount of food actually eaten by the patient, and the patient's level of satisfaction with the meal—must be evaluated. Each of these attributes is measurable, so a composite score can be used to quantify the level of quality. The key point is that the notion of quality is meaningless unless outcomes are actually measured.

Measuring Customer Satisfaction

Customer satisfaction is an outcome that characterizes consumer-defined quality. Like technical quality, customer satisfaction can also be measured. Customer satisfaction is best assessed through a satisfaction survey—called a survey instrument—completed by patients and their

surrogates. It is critical, however, that the reliability and validity of the survey instrument be established in order to get meaningful information about customer satisfaction. **Reliability** is the extent to which the same results occur from repeated applications of a measure under identical conditions. Reliability deals with the precision of measurement. Unless a survey instrument delivers reliable results, the results obtained by surveying customers at repeated intervals, such as every year, cannot be compared. For example, if in year one of the survey a facility scored a 7 on a scale of 1 to 10, and in year two the same facility scored a 7.5, improvement in customer satisfaction can be inferred only if the instrument used to assess satisfaction had a high degree of reliability. The **validity** of a survey instrument denotes the extent to which the instrument actually measures what it purports to measure. Reliability in itself does not assure that a measure is valid. An instrument can have very high reliability, but if it has poor validity, the results will be inconsistent with the goals being measured. For example, if a survey instrument measures customers' satisfaction with factors other than those associated with the facility's services, such as satisfaction with location, geographic access, and opinions of friends, such an instrument will be useless in helping the facility improve satisfaction with the facility's services. Appropriate measurement instruments can be designed by health care researchers.

Satisfaction implies subjective quality in the form of judgments by individuals about their experiences with a service. Individually-rated responses from consumer surveys are consolidated to determine an overall score of customer satisfaction. Such aggregated scores derived from all the responses to a survey provide an estimate of the average perceived quality (Lawton 2001). When necessary, survey results can be supplemented with other approaches such as **focus groups**, particularly when further clarification or additional information is needed. Research has demonstrated that there is a high degree of correlation between subjective assessments of satisfaction and key outcomes.

Currently, there are no widely used instruments with proven reliability and validity that measure satisfaction for nursing home residents (Smith 2000). However, some initial efforts in this direction have been made, as illustrated by the Long-Term Care Satisfaction Survey (LTCSS) developed by Norton and colleagues (1996), and the Satisfaction Assessment Questionnaires (SAQs) developed by the American

Health Care Association. Both of these instruments are designed to evaluate the satisfaction of both residents and family members. The LTCSS instrument measures satisfaction in the areas of autonomy, dignity, living area, food, laundry, activities, and overall satisfaction. Patient SAQs have been developed separately for cognitively intact residents, rehabilitation residents, and medically-complex residents (Smith 2000). More recently, family satisfaction surveys have been tested and implemented on statewide basis in Ohio; there are indications that similar efforts may be underway in other states. The instrument recommended for use in Ohio nursing homes consists of a survey with 62 items to evaluate family satisfaction in 13 domains (Ejaz et al. 2003): admission; social services and communication; activities; choice; receptionist and phone; direct care and nurse aides; professional nurses; therapy; administration; meals and dining; laundry; environment; and general areas (overall satisfaction, inclination to recommend facility to others, updates on medical condition, and whether patients or family members were upset by the staff).

Evaluation and Interpretation

Once outcomes have been measured, the results must be interpreted. For instance, a numerical score is meaningless unless its relevance is clearly established. Such interpretation of measurements in this context is called **evaluation**. The goal of evaluation is to transform numerical scores into meaningful information that would be useful for improving quality. Evaluation is always done in relation to some standard. A standard can be anything that management considers acceptable. For example, staff turnover is an inverse and indirect measure of quality; a high score indicates low quality of human resource and leadership practices, and vice versa. Suppose a given nursing home has an annual turnover rate of 30% for licensed nurses. This measure is not very helpful unless it can be interpreted in relation to some standard such as nurse turnover rates in the nursing home industry or within a multifacility corporation or a target established by the administrator and the governing body.

The American Association of Homes and Services for the Aging (AAHSA) has developed a clinical data-analysis program using the Minimum Data Set (MDS). The AAHSA's MDS-Based Quality Improvement System enables individual nursing homes to evaluate their quality based on indicators developed by the Center for Health Systems

Research and Analysis of the University of Wisconsin. This program is available to both members of the Association and non-members. Commercial software programs are also available for assessing quality indicators based on MDS data.

Measuring Quality of Life

For nursing home residents, quality of care and quality of life (QoL) are closely intertwined. Only recently have measures of QoL been developed and tested, mainly through research projects undertaken at the University of Minnesota under the direction of Rosalie Kane. Although QoL is a broad concept and comprehensive measures of all the constructs comprising QoL are not yet available, the work of Kane and colleagues (2001) emphasizes the psychological and social aspects of QoL (wave 2 of this work was still in progress at the time of this writing). These measures are shown in Exhibit 17-1 for illustrative purposes only. The questions are intended to be used for interviews in which nursing-home residents, including those who are cognitively impaired, are asked the actual questions in each of the 11 domains.

QUALITY IMPROVEMENT

The current focus in health care is on **continuous quality improvement** (CQI), which is an ongoing undertaking to improve quality throughout the nursing facility. Also called total quality management (TQM), quality improvement requires total effort involving all employees of the organization. Quality improvement in long-term care embodies six basic principles (adapted from Evans and Lindsay 1993) that form the framework for CQI:

- A facility can be successful only by understanding and fulfilling the needs of customers.
- Leadership in improving quality is the responsibility of the nursing home administrator, with full support from the governing board or corporate officers. Leaders must work toward the aim of establishing a culture of quality.
- Statistical evaluation using factual data is the basis for CQI.
- All functions within the facility must implement CQI.
- Problem solving and process improvement are best performed by interdisciplinary (or multidisciplinary) work teams.

EXHIBIT 17-1

Quality of Life Measures (illustrative only)

Domains, their definitions, and questions for assessing each domain

Note: Depending on the resident's ability to respond, the questions are assessed according to a 4-point scale (often, sometimes, rarely, never) or a dichotomous scale (mostly yes, mostly no), except for the first two questions in the Meaningful Activity scale.

A. Physical comfort. Residents are free from pain, uncomfortable symptoms, and other physical discomforts. They perceive that their pain and discomfort are noticed and addressed by the staff.

1. How often are you too cold here?
2. How often are you so long in the same position that it hurts?
3. How often are you in physical pain?
4. How often are you bothered by noise when you are in your room?
5. How often are you bothered by noise in other parts of the nursing home, for example, in the dining room?
6. Do you get a good night's sleep here?

B. Functional competence. Within the limits of their physical and cognitive abilities, residents are as independent as they wish to be.

1. Is it easy for you to get around in your room by yourself?
2. Can you easily reach the things that you need?
3. If you are anywhere in the nursing home and need a bathroom, can you get to one quickly?
4. Can you easily reach your toilet articles and things that you want to use in your bathroom?
5. Do you do as much to take care of your own things and your room as you can and want?

continues

EXHIBIT 17–1 *continued*

C. Privacy. Residents have bodily privacy, can keep personal information confidential, can be alone as desired, and can be with others in private.

1. Can you find a place to be alone if you wish?
2. Can you make a private phone call?
3. When you have a visitor, can you find a place to visit in private?
4. Can you be together in private with another resident (other than your roommate)?
5. Do the people who work here knock and wait for a reply before entering your room?

D. Dignity. Residents perceive their dignity is intact and respected. They do not feel belittled, devalued, or humiliated.

1. Does the staff here treat you politely?
2. Do you feel that you are treated with respect here?
3. Does the staff here handle you gently while giving you care?
4. Does the staff here respect your modesty?
5. Does the staff take time to listen to you when you have something to say?

E. Meaningful activity. Residents engage in discretionary behavior that results in self-affirming competence or active pleasure in the doing of or watching of an activity.

1. Do you get outdoors: As much as you want? Too much? Too little?
2. About how often do you get outdoors?
3. Do you enjoy the organized activities here at the nursing home?
4. Outside of religious activities, do you have enjoyable things to do at the nursing home during the weekend?
5. Despite your health condition, do you give help to others, such as other residents, your family, people at this nursing home, or the outside community?
6. Do the days here seem too long to you?

F. Relationships. Residents engage in meaningful person-to-person social interchange with other residents, with the staff, or with family and friends who live outside the nursing home.

continues

EXHIBIT 17–1 *continued*

1. Is it easy to make friends at this nursing home?
2. Do you consider that any other resident here is your close friend?
3. In the last month, have people who worked here stopped just to have a friendly conversation with you?
4. Do you consider any staff member to be your friend?
5. Do you think that (name of the facility) tries to make this an easy and pleasant place for families and friends of residents to visit?

G. Autonomy. Residents take initiative and make choices for their lives and care.

1. Can you go to bed at the time you want?
2. Can you get up in the morning at the time you want?
3. Can you decide what clothes to wear?
4. Have you been successful in making changes in things that you do not like?

H. Food enjoyment. Residents enjoy meals and food.

1. Do you like the food at *(name of the facility)*?
2. Do you enjoy mealtimes at *(name of the facility)*?
3. Can you get your favorite foods at *(name of the facility)*?

I. Spiritual well-being. Residents' needs and concerns for religion, prayer, meditation, spirituality, and moral values are met.

1. Do you participate in religious activities here?
2. Do the religious activities here have personal meaning for you?
3. Do you feel your life as a whole has meaning?
4. Do you feel at peace?

J. Security. Residents feel secure and confident about their personal safety, are able to move about freely, believe that their possessions are secure, and believe that the staff has good intentions. They know and understand the rules, expectations, and routines of the facility.

1. Do you feel that your possessions are safe at this nursing home?

continues

EXHIBIT 17–1 *continued*

2. Do your clothes get lost or damaged in the laundry?
3. Do you feel confident that you can get help when you need it?
4. If you do not feel well, can you get a nurse or doctor quickly?
5. Do you ever feel afraid because of the way you or some other resident is treated?

K. Individuality. Residents express their preferences, pursue their past and current interests, maintain a sense of their own identity, and perceive they are known as individuals.

1. Taking all staff together, nurses, aides and others, do staff members know about your interests and what you like?
2. Do staff members know you as a person?
3. Are the people working here interested in your experiences and the things you have done in your life?
4. Does the staff here take your preferences seriously?
5. Do residents here know you as a person?
6. Are your personal wishes and interests respected here?

Source: Quality of life scales for nursing home residents (December 2001). CMS project: Measures, indicators, and improvement of quality of life in nursing homes. Study Director: Rosalie A. Kane; CMS Project Officer: Mary Pratt; CMS Co-project Officer: Karen Schoeneman. Used by courtesy of Rosalie A. Kane, Division of Health Services Research and Policy, School of Public Health, University of Minnesota.

- Continuous learning, training, and education are the responsibility of everyone in the organization, but these activities require support from the top.

Meeting Customer Needs

Quality management is primarily based on understanding who the customers are and then meeting and exceeding those customers' expectations. Here the term "customer" is used in a broad sense; a customer is any entity that receives the product of a transaction. Patients and their families are commonly regarded as customers, and rightly so. But, there are other customers who may not directly receive the products of a transaction, but have a vested interest in the quality of the products. Griffith and White (2002) referred to them as customer partners. They are also

called **external customers**, because they are external to the organization. They include payers (Medicaid, Medicare, managed care organizations, and other insurers); regulatory agencies (state departments of health, agencies on aging, local health and fire departments, and the Joint Commission for Accreditation of Healthcare Organizations); and referral agencies (hospitals, physicians, and others). A nursing facility also has **internal customers**: Internal customers include all personnel who receive information, services, or other professional support from fellow employees. To deliver what external customers expect, these internal customers have to depend on each others' outputs (Bradley and Thompson 2000). Attending physicians, for example, rely on information and support from the facility's nursing staff, and these physicians should be regarded as critical internal customers. The same attending physicians can also be regarded as external customers when they refer patients to the facility. Nursing assistants need the support of professional nurses, and nurses in turn often rely on the nursing assistants to report problems or changes in a patient's condition.

Quality cannot be improved without a strong commitment on the part of all staff to meet the needs and expectations of all customers. Also, the requirements of internal customers should be linked to those of the external customers. If an internal requirement does not in some way help meet external customer requirements, then its value should be questioned (Gaucher and Coffey 1993).

Leadership and Culture

Commitment, leadership, and support from top management play a vital role in establishing the overall tone for CQI. Empirical evidence demonstrates that success in CQI implementation is strongly associated with the commitment and culture of top management. In organizations characterized by top management commitment, turnover at key top-level positions is low, the staff views top management as strong advocates of CQI, leaders are open-minded and communicative, leadership styles are participatory and team-oriented, and top managers demonstrate a clear understanding of CQI principles (Parker et al. 1999).

Executive-level personnel must first understand the concepts of CQI, and then become knowledgeable about the tools, processes, and methods necessary for quality improvement (Baird et al. 1993). Commitment to CQI includes allocation of required resources. Upper management

should then set goals and plans for implementing principles and practices for quality. Upper management must be committed to involving all employees by providing proper training and a reward system for accomplishing quality goals (Evans and Lindsay 1993).

Most experts agree that quality improvement occurs in an organizational culture that values quality. On the other hand, one of the key barriers to change is the conscious or unconscious retention of old beliefs and actions that discourage innovation, creativity, empowerment, or other components of CQI (Gaucher and Coffey 1993). Once a CQI program is underway, both managers and workers should be prepared to accept failures along the way. However, patience and perseverance are necessary. Fear of failure only stifles innovation.

A CQI culture has the following characteristics (Parker et al. 1999):

- CQI is not viewed as a distinct initiative, but as an everyday part of each employee's job.
- Morale is high, and staff turnover is low.
- The staff has a strong sense of pride in the organization.
- Communication is open, and risk taking is rewarded.
- Change is readily accepted.
- Strong team orientation is apparent.

Organizational culture can change only gradually over time. Management must continually emphasize to the staff that quality remains a top priority, otherwise the organization risks losing the commitment of its employees (Evans and Lindsay 1993). Relatively short tenures of nursing home administrators and other key personnel disrupt the cultural continuity that is so essential for CQI. Job-hopping administrators never get to understand the facilities they manage for short durations. Such administrators do a great disservice to the patients and to their profession, because follow-through over time is necessary for building quality and productivity. A culture of quality is built over time with staff stability and consistency. This culture requires empowering leadership that is open to the ideas of others. Managers share organizational power by giving autonomy and discretion over tasks to employees; they build relationships by coaching and mentoring; and they use rewards and recognition to change behaviors that would otherwise stifle quality improvement (Gaucher and Coffey 1993).

Data-driven Process Improvement Cycle

Quality improvement is anchored on a quantitative approach in which data and measurements are used to evaluate the current state of quality, improve processes, and track progress. The Deming cycle, named after W. Edwards Deming (1900–1993), is used to focus on improving processes that would result in improved outputs. It involves four steps: plan, do, study, and act (PDSA). The PDSA cycle is a continuous improvement cycle (Figure 17-2) that can be applied to any process, using data to identify key process problems.

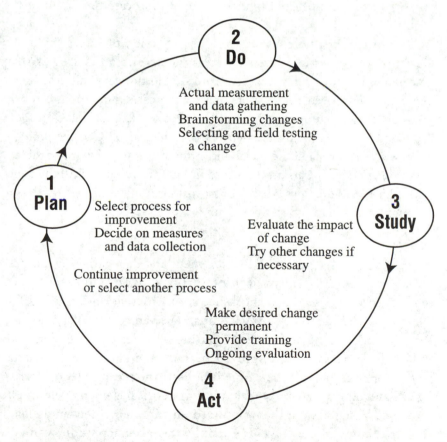

FIGURE 17-2 The PDSA Cycle

Plan

The "plan stage" consists of studying the current situation, gathering appropriate data, and planning for improvement. The plan stage focuses on uncovering quality problems and selecting a specific area for improvement. Initially, it may be best to address small-scale problems that would facilitate learning the PDSA process and build the confidence of employees in applying this process. If benchmarks or standards are available, variations are measured to determine how much current outcomes deviate from the standards. Decisions are made about what type of ongoing measurements or data collection are needed. For example, nursing assistants who serve meals to residents may report frequent meal-tray errors, but only data collection can provide quantitative information on the number and types of errors to indicate the extent of the problem.

Once the PDSA system is learned, the selection of topics should be driven by priorities in addressing areas where outcomes are less than acceptable. Improvement in patient care should outweigh all other goals of a quality-improvement program. Answering certain questions can help focus on the most important topics (Vitale and Vengroski 1993): Does the problem interfere with the delivery of quality care? Can the problem be solved with available financial and human resources? Is the problem common enough to warrant the effort and cost to solve it? Will the benefit of improved outcomes outweigh the cost of monitoring and correcting the problem? Is it a high-risk concern?

Do

The "do stage" involves actual measurement and data gathering. Sources of data may be the facility's own internal records and information systems, special surveys, logs, checksheets, or observational studies. The data can be charted using flow diagrams, cause-and-effect diagrams, and various types of statistical charts. Charting provides a clear understanding of the process to be improved because the charts help visualize trends and the magnitude of deviations from acceptable standards. Charts and diagrams can also help pinpoint critical elements that can be improved. Changes are then discussed and implemented on a small-scale trial basis. In the previous example, tray accuracy studies can be a useful diagnostic tool for evaluating the quantity and seriousness of diet

errors, both from the standpoint of quality of care and quality of life (Dowling and Cotner 1988). Such studies may also point to where in the process the breakdowns occur. In the "do stage" of the PDSA cycle, a critical step in the process where the breakdown occurs is chosen for testing an intervention that could alleviate the breakdown. For example, in the meal delivery system a checker may be assigned at the end of the tray line to check all items on the meal trays against diet cards for individual patients.

Study

The "study stage" requires an evaluation of the changes that have been made in a selected process and the effect of those changes on quality improvement. This stage requires ongoing data collection to determine the effectiveness of implemented changes, and the extent of improvement. If the changes do not produce at least some improvement, other changes should be discussed, tried, and tested. In the meal tray example, ongoing data collection will tell whether the change results in reducing diet errors and whether the change should be made permanent.

Act

The "act stage" deals with implementing a change after the value of that change has been confirmed. New practices are institutionalized by training all staff members who are affected by the changes and by communicating, updating policies and procedures, and monitoring to ensure that the improved methods become routine.

The PDSA process is repeated to further improve the same process, if outcomes show the need for additional improvement, or to address a different area of concern. Ongoing use of the PDSA cycle produces continuous improvement in quality.

Encompass All Functions

CQI must focus on all departmental functions in the facility. Because the major functions covered in Part II are interdependent, total quality can only be achieved by applying CQI to every function. CQI requires scrutiny of interdepartmental communications, process interlinkages, and horizontal coordination between the various organizational units, all in the context of meeting the expectations of internal and external customers.

Interdisciplinary Work Teams

The interdependency of functions in a facility underscores the need for an interdisciplinary approach to quality improvement. A team approach to quality improvement is likely to make the process unbiased, systematic, and thorough. The team approach can be accomplished by formulating a quality-improvement committee comprised of individuals representing every discipline. Under the leadership of the administrator or a consultant, the composition of the committee should change as new quality issues are addressed. As different staff members get the opportunity to be on the team, the team becomes a mechanism for building a culture of quality in the organization, in training staff, and in building a sense of ownership in quality improvement. Once the CQI is well established, more than one team can work on different quality-improvement projects.

Hiring a consultant may be necessary for CQI, especially when a facility initiates a CQI program. The consultant can evaluate the cultural aspects of the organization that could pose barriers to the success of a CQI program. When substantial barriers are foreseen, the administrator is in a better position to develop a strategy for gradual change. The consultant can also be instrumental in training the staff at all levels, including senior management. Such organization-wide training is how CQI programs are almost always formally begun. Training is necessary to reach a common understanding about CQI, clarify goals, and establish reasonable expectations.

Continuous Learning

A well-developed CQI program involves the participation of all staff members at all levels of the organization. Continuous learning then becomes institutionalized alongside continuous improvement of quality as employees discover improved methods and play a role in implementing them. The results of PDSA cycles should be shared with all affected staff. In an interdisciplinary environment, employees get to better understand how their actions affect the work of others, and how their actions in turn affect the expectations and satisfaction of external customers.

QUALITY CULTURE

The end result of CQI is the emergence of an organization-wide culture of excellence. When quality is institutionalized, it produces an organiza-

tional culture that retains and attracts like-minded staff members who are dedicated to delivering excellence. In such an environment, all employees receive social and psychological gratification by knowing that others are better off because they, the employees, have chosen to put excellence first and foremost. Management recognizes the contribution of these employees by expressing appreciation in various forms, including financial rewards. The reward system is designed so that it promotes cooperation and team effort, not envy and competitiveness. As such, the reward system does not exclude any member of the organization. Finally, such a nursing facility gains a community-wide reputation for excellence that is recognized by all external exchange partners. But, even at this stage, facility management continues to seek ways to improve structures, processes, and outcomes. Management ensures the satisfaction of customers through a firm commitment to never-ending improvement in quality.

In studying the ongoing pursuit of quality, some thoughts from Deming are noteworthy. Deming is counted among the greatest pioneers of the quality-improvement movement. Many books on CQI have reproduced, in one form or another, his fourteen principles of quality improvement. These principles are directed at management attitudes and actions, because Deming believed that quality breakdowns were attributable to management, not workers. Much of the earlier discussion in this chapter incorporates these principles. The following thoughts summarize the remaining pertinent requirements that are also necessary for building a culture of quality in nursing facilities:

- **Create constancy of purpose toward improvement of product and service, with the aim to become competitive in the market**. A facility must create value to remain ahead of the competition. Because $Value = \dfrac{Quality}{Cost}$, cost reduction efforts that reduce quality are likely to decrease value. On the other hand, improving quality may increase cost somewhat, but value is enhanced when quality is improved to a greater extent than costs are increased (Lighter and Fair 2000). Hence, CQI efforts should aim to increase both quality and productivity.
- **Cease dependence on inspections to improve quality**. Eliminate the need for inspections on a mass basis by building quality into the

product (service) in the first place. Inspection should be used as an information-gathering tool for improvement, not as the principal tool for quality control (Evans and Lindsay 1993).

- **Drive out fear, so that everyone may work effectively for the organization**. Fear may promote short-term gains, but longer-term accomplishments are less likely, because workers spend more time inventing ways of avoiding difficult situations than in finding methods of increasing output. Empowerment rather than threats should be used to motivate employees (Lighter and Fair 2000). CQI should be used to find process problems, not to assign blame to workers; otherwise they would spend their time covering up problems for fear of being blamed for problems.

- **Break down barriers between departments**. Internal competition for raises, performance ratings, and recognition can be counterproductive. Incentives associated with CQI should promote cooperation and teamwork, not competition.

- **Eliminate slogans and exhortations**. Posters and slogans assume that all quality problems are attributable to people. They overlook the fact that most quality problems are systemic and cannot be improved through posters, slogans, or the wearing of happy-face buttons. Attacking problems rather than workers, understanding the causes of problems, and using statistical thinking and training to improve processes are necessary for achieving higher quality.

- **Eliminate quotas.** Standards and quotas that workers are often held up to are generally used punitively. These standards and quotas are born out of short-term perspectives, and create fear. A quota, such as requiring each nursing assistant to take sole responsibility for a predefined number of patients, promotes short-cuts in quality in order to reach a numerical goal. Once numerical standards are achieved, there is no incentive to continue production or to improve quality. When these standards are not achieved workers become frustrated and resentful (Evans and Lindsay 1993).

- **Remove barriers to pride in workmanship**. Hourly workers such as nursing assistants, housekeepers, dishwashers, and laundry workers are often treated by management as commodities. Pride in workmanship can be achieved through teamwork and continuous improvement strategies when workers are treated as valuable resources, not as commodities. According to Deming, there are three

categories of employees: most work within the system, some are outside the system on the superior side, and others are outside the system on the inferior side. While superior performers should receive special compensation, inferior performers need extra training or they should be replaced (Evans and Lindsay 1993).

WELLSPRING: QUALITY IN ACTION

The Wellspring program was introduced in chapters 6 and 14 as an example of a model that incorporates the concepts of enriched living environments and empowered work teams. The Wellspring program also provides an example of how the principles of CQI can be applied to achieve higher quality by integrating top management commitment, organization-wide participation, organization of the staff into self-managed work teams, and data-driven methods for quality improvement. The project has successfully demonstrated that quality can be improved without increasing costs of input, thus dispelling the notion that quality can only be produced at higher cost. By forming a consortium, participating facilities realize cost savings through collaboration, resource sharing, and common learning. Quality indicators are employed to quantify quality of care, with the goal of continually raising results. The Wellspring program has developed specific training modules for physical assessment, incontinence care, fall prevention, skin care, pressure-ulcer prevention, nutrition, restorative care, and behavior management. The proven strategies of this program have also been made available to other facilities under licensing agreements with Wellspring Innovative Solutions, Inc. (Manard 2002).

CONCLUSION

The Minimum Data Set has been instrumental in bringing data-based clinical quality measurement to skilled nursing facilities. The next step, beyond MDS-based quality assurance, is the institution of standardized care-planning and evidence-based processes of care delivery that have been in use in other health care settings. The underlying premise of evidence-based protocols is that standardizing work processes decreases care variability and improves outcomes (Finch-Guthrie 2000). As discussed earlier in this chapter, clinical practice guidelines are a means of reducing inappropriate med-

ical care and improving patient outcomes, and the value of these guidelines is being increasingly recognized by the medical community. However, implementation of standardized guidelines is particularly challenging in nursing homes, because care delivery in nursing homes requires interdisciplinary decision making, and as much as 70% of the care is provided by paraprofessionals who have little formal training. Interdisciplinary decision-making can be facilitated by using clinical pathways. Although the use of clinical pathways in long-term care is not well established, their use can improve care delivery especially in subacute care settings (Riley 1994).

From a public policy perspective, nursing homes continue to receive criticism on account of lapses in quality of care. At least according to one recent analysis, the historical reliance on government regulation has not ensured nursing home quality. One major weakness of regulation-driven quality improvement in nursing homes has been the lack of standardization of the survey and enforcement processes (Winzelberg 2003). There are no easy answers, but the historical emphasis on increased regulations and inspections alone is unlikely to produce the results that both policymakers and the public hope for. The long-range answer to improved quality lies in a clear understanding of what quality is, and the adoption of well-recognized principles and methods of quality improvement. These initiatives must come from nursing home leaders. Public policy, on the other hand, must support outcomes research to help develop and use evidence-based guidelines for patient care delivery.

DISCUSSION AND APPLICATION QUESTIONS

1. Introducing a CQI initiative into a nursing facility is often associated with start-up costs, which in some instances may be quite substantial. For example, adopting the Wellspring program may cost $50,000 or more. What other direct or indirect costs may be associated with the adoption of CQI?

2. How would you evaluate whether spending a substantial amount of money on CQI is worth it?

3. Design a short questionnaire that could be given to family members to assess consumer-defined quality.

4. As the administrator of a skilled nursing facility, how would you determine whether the facility is ready for CQI adoption?

INTERNET RESOURCES
FOR FURTHER LEARNING

American Medical Directors Association
  http://www.amda.com/info/

MDS-Based Quality Improvement System (American Association of Homes
  and Services for the Aging)
  http://www.aahsa.org/public/4pgflyer.htm

The Wellspring Program (Wellspring Innovative Solutions, Inc.)
  http://www.wellspringis.org/

REFERENCES

Baird, R., et al. 1993. The implementation of total quality. In *The Textbook of Total Quality in Healthcare,* eds. A.F. Al-Assaf and J.A. Schmele. Delray Beach, FL: St. Lucie Press: 91–101.

Berlowitz, D.R., et al. 2001. Clinical practice guidelines in the nursing home. *American Journal of Medical Quality* 16, no. 6: 189–195.

Bradley, M.G., and N.R. Thompson. 2000. *Quality Management Integration in Long-Term Care.* Baltimore: Health Professions Press, Inc.

Donabedian, A. 1995. The quality of care: How can it be assessed? In *Quality in Health Care: Theory, Application, and Evolution,* ed. N.O. Graham. Gaithersburg, MD: Aspen Publishers, Inc.: 32–46.

Dowling, R., and C. Cotner. 1988. Monitor of tray error rates for quality control. *Journal of the American Dietetic Association* 88: 450–453.

Ejaz, F.K., et al. 2003. Developing a satisfaction survey for families of Ohio's nursing home residents. *The Gerontologist* 43, no. 4: 447–458.

Evans, J.R., and W.M. Lindsay. 1993. *The Management and Control of Quality.* St. Paul, MN: West Publishing Company.

Field, M.J., and K.N. Lohr. 1990. *Clinical Practice Guidelines: Directions for a New Agency.* Washington, DC: National Academy Press.

Finch-Guthrie, P. 2000. Care planning for older adults in health care settings. In *Assessing Older Persons: Measures, Meaning, and Practical Applications,* eds. R.L. Kane and R.A. Kane, 406–437. New York: Oxford University Press, Inc.

Gaucher, E.J., and R.J. Coffey. 1993. *Total Quality in Health Care: From Theory to Practice.* San Francisco: Jossey-Bass Publishers.

Griffith, J.R., and K.R. White. 2002. *The Well-Managed Health Care Organization.* 5th ed. Chicago: Health Administration Press and Washington, D.C.: Association of University Programs in Health Administration.

Institute of Medicine. 1986. *Improving the Quality of Care in Nursing Homes.* Washington, DC: National Academy Press.

Institute of Medicine. 2001. *Improving the Quality of Long-Term Care.* Eds. G.S. Wunderlich and P.O. Kohler. Washington, DC: National Academy Press.

Kane, R.A., et al. 2001. *Quality of Life Scales for Nursing Home Residents.* CMS project: Measures, indicators, and improvement of quality of life in nursing homes. Unpublished manuscript.

Lighter, D.E., and D.C. Fair. 2000. *Principles and Methods of Quality Management in Health Care.* Gaithersburg, MD: Aspen Publishers, Inc.

Lawton, M.P. 2001. Quality of care and quality of life in dementia care units. In *Linking Quality of Long Term Care and Quality of Life,* eds. L. Noelker and Z. Harel, 136–161. New York: Springer.

Manard, B. 2002. *Nursing Home Quality Indicators: Their Uses and Limitations.* Washington, DC: Public Policy Institute, AARP.

McElroy, D., and K. Herbelin. 1989. Assuring quality of care in long-term care facilities. *Journal of Gerontological Nursing* 15, no. 7: 8–10.

Norton, P.G., et al. 1996. Satisfaction of residents and families in long-term care: I. Construction and application of an instrument. *Quality Management in Health Care* 4, no. 3: 38–46.

Palmer, R.H. 1991. Considerations in defining quality of health care. In *Striving for Quality in Health Care: An Inquiry into Policy and Practice,* eds. R.H. Palmer, A. Donabedian, and G.L. Povar, 3–58. Ann Arbor, MI: Health Administration Press.

Parker, V.A., et al. 1999. Implementing quality improvement in hospitals: The role of leadership and culture. *American Journal of Medical Quality* 14, no. 1: 64–69.

Riley, S.A. 1994. Clinical pathways: A basic tool for subacute care. *Nursing Homes Long Term Care Management* 43, no. 6: 35–36.

Smith, M.A. 2000. Satisfaction. In *Assessing Older Persons: Measures, Meaning, and Practical Applications,* eds. R.L. Kane and R.A. Kane, 261–299. New York: Oxford University Press, Inc.

Vitale, B.A., and S.M. Vengroski. 1993. *Quality Assessment and Improvement in Long-Term Care: A Continuous Process.* Philadelphia: F.A. Davis Company.

Weech-Maldonado, R., et al. 2003. Does quality of care lead to better financial performance?: The case of the nursing home industry. *Health Care Management Review* 28, no. 3: 201–216.

Winzelberg, G.S. 2003. The quest for nursing home quality: learning history's lessons. *Archives of Internal Medicine* 163, no. 21: 2552–2556.

GLOSSARY

Abuse: (1) Willful infliction of injury, unreasonable confinement, intimidation or punishment with resulting physical harm, pain, or mental anguish to a patient. (2) Fraud committed against a public program such as Medicare or Medicaid.

Accounts payable: Money owed to vendors from whom goods, supplies, and services have been purchased on credit.

Accounts receivable: Amounts that remain to be collected by the facility for services rendered.

Accreditation: Based on voluntary compliance with standards, accreditation of a nursing facility by the Joint Commission on Accreditation of Healthcare Organizations (JCAHO).

Accrual-basis accounting: The commonly used method of accounting in which revenues and expenses do not match cash inflows and outflows. Revenue is recognized at the time services are rendered although payment for such services is received at a later date. Similarly, expenses are recorded as they are incurred even though payments to vendors may be made at a later date.

Acquired Immune Deficiency Syndrome (AIDS): AIDS develops when a person infected with the human immunodeficiency virus (HIV) undergoes a breakdown of the immune system and becomes susceptible to serious illness and death from other viruses, parasites, fungi, and bacteria.

Activities of daily living (ADL): The most commonly used measure of disability. ADLs determine whether an individual needs assistance in performing six basic activities: eating, bathing, dressing, using the toilet, maintaining continence, and getting into or out of a bed or chair (transferring). Grooming and walking a distance of eight feet are sometimes added to evaluate self care and mobility.

Activity: Active or passive involvement of patients in any activities, outside the activities of daily living, that provide meaning and personal enrichment.

Acuity: The level of severity of a patient's condition. For example, patients who require intensive services are referred to as those having a higher level of acuity in relation to those who require less care.

Acute care: Short-term, intense medical care for an episode of illness or injury often requiring hospitalization.

Acute conditions: Episodic conditions that require short-term but intensive medical interventions.

ADA: The American Dietetic Association. It registers dieticians and approves associate degree programs for dietetic technicians.

ADLs: See **activities of daily living**.

Administrative law: Rules and regulations formulated by the departments or agencies of the executive branch of government to carry out the intent of **statutory law**.

Administrator-in-training (AIT): An internship with a certified **preceptor** required for an **NHA** license in some states.

Adult day care: A daytime program of nursing care, rehabilitation therapies, supervision, and socialization that enables elderly people to remain in the community and live with family. Services are generally provided on weekdays between 7 a.m. and 6 p.m. to individuals who return home in the evening.

Adult foster care: Small, family-run homes licensed to provide room, board, supervision, and personal care to non-related adults who are unable to live independently. These neighborhood homes are also called "group homes."

Advance directive: A written statement prepared by a **competent** individual indicating his or her desires for medical treatment in case the patient loses the capacity to make decisions.

Ageism: Prejudicial treatment of the elderly based on stereotypes and misconceptions.

Agent: Someone authorized to act on behalf of another (a **principal**); for example, a corporation generally authorizes the **NHA** to represent it or to act on its behalf.

Aging in place: For patients whose functional status has declined, continuing to provide for their long-term care needs in their existing setting, without transferring them to a facility that provides higher level of services.

Aging report (aging schedule): A report that includes a breakdown of each uncollected patient account (see **accounts receivable**) by showing the length of time that various amounts have been outstanding.

Agitation: A disruptive behavior such as yelling or meaningless motion that creates disruptions.

AIDS: See **Acquired Immune Deficiency Syndrome**.

AIT: See **administrator-in-training**.

All-inclusive rate: A bundled fee which includes in a single rate all services and supplies furnished to a patient. See **bundled rate.**

Almshouse: See **poorhouse**.

Alzheimer's disease: An irreversible degenerative **dementia**.

Ambulation: Moving about.

Ambulatory: Being able to move about.

Ambulatory care (ambulatory services): Services that require the patients to come and receive needed services at a community-based location. In a broader context, ambulatory care can be any outpatient service such as a visit to the physician's office or clinic or outpatient surgery.

Ancillaries: Services and products, such as rehabilitation therapies, pharmaceuticals, catheters, dressings, incontinence pads, oxygen, etc. which can be billed separately to **private-pay patients** in addition to the basic room-and-board rate.

Antisepsis: Removing or destroying **microorganisms**.

Aphasia: Inability to speak.

Arbitration: A process in which a neutral third party hears both sides in a dispute and renders a decision that is binding on both parties.

Area Agency on Aging: Agencies established in local communities under the 1973 amendments to the Federal Older Americans Act of 1965 to address the needs of Americans aged 60 and over. Among other services, these agencies assess clients' needs and determine eligibility for services best suited to meet their needs.

Asepsis: Absence of harmful microorganisms called **pathogens**. It refers to the practice of clean procedures, such as handwashing.

Assault: A threatening act in which physical contact need not occur, but the assaulted individual reasonably believes that the aggressor is capable of an imminent physical act. See **battery**.

Assessment: The process by which health care professionals attempt to reliably characterize the patient's physical health, functional abilities, cognitive functioning, psychological state, social well-being, and past and current use of formal services.

Assets: The financial value of everything a business owns, as shown on the **balance sheet**.

Assisted living: A residential setting that provides personal care services, 24-hour supervision, scheduled and unscheduled assistance, social activities, and some nursing care services.

Audiologist: A health care professional who is specially trained and licensed to provide direct clinical services to individuals with hearing or balance disorders.

Autism: A complex developmental disability that typically appears during the first three years of life, and is the result of a brain disorder. It affects the person's social interaction and communication.

Average daily census: The average number of inpatients per day over a period of time such as a week, a month, or a year.

Baby boomers: People born between 1946 and 1964. This age group constitutes approximately 70 million Americans who will start retiring around 2010. By 2030, when all the baby boomers will have retired, experts predict that they will severely strain the nation's health care system.

Bad debt: An amount that is legitimately owed to the facility, but is deemed uncollectible.

Balance sheet: A financial statement that summarizes the financial position (**assets**, **liabilities**, and **equity**) of a business organization at a given date, such as the last day of a month or the last day of a year.

Bargaining unit: Employee categories that a union can legitimately represent.

Battery: An action in which intentional touching occurs without consent from the other individual. See **assault**.

Bed-hold: When a patient is temporarily out of the facility (at a hospital or with family), but the bed is being held and must be paid for.

Benefit period: Under Part A of Medicare, it refers to a period of time which begins when a patient is hospitalized for a particular spell of illness, and ends when the patient has not been an inpatient in a hospital or has received skilled nursing care in a **SNF** for 60 consecutive days for that particular spell of illness.

Biophilia: The human tendency to pay attention to, affiliate with, and respond positively to nature.

Bioterrorism: The use of chemical, biological, or nuclear agents to inflict harm on relatively large civilian populations by rogue individuals or groups.

Board-and-care homes: Very basic long-term care homes that provide physically-supportive dwelling units, monitoring, or assistance with medications, supervision, and light care with **ADLs**, but do not provide nursing care. These facilities are also called **domiciliary care facilities** or **shelter care facilities**.

Board of directors (board of trustees): See **governing body**.

Breach of contract: A civil wrong involving the violation of a specific agreement between two parties.

Budget: A tool for exercising financial control. It sets expectations which become financial objectives that the nursing home administrator is responsible for achieving.

Budgeting: The process of financial planning.

Bundled rate: A price that includes all services a patient may require.

Capitation: Payment of a predetermined rate per person to include all covered services.

Cardiologist: A physician who specializes in the treatment of heart diseases.

Care plan: See **plan of care**.

Case management: A centralized coordinating function in which the special needs of older adults are identified and a trained professional determines which services would be most appropriate, determines eligibility for those services, makes referrals, arranges for financing, and coordinates and monitors delivery of care to ensure that clients are receiving the prescribed services. Case management helps link, manage, and coordinate services to meet the varied and changing health care needs of elderly clients.

Case-mix: Mix of patients with different acuity levels. Patients who are more seriously ill require more intensive use of resources and incur greater cost to the facility.

Cash flow statement: A summary of actual cash transactions—cash paid and cash received—for a month or a year.

Census: Number of patients in a facility on a given day.

Census-mix: See **payer-mix**.

Cerebral palsy: A **developmental disability** caused by brain damage occurring before or during childbirth.

Certificate of need (CON): Determination by a state planning agency whether additional beds are needed or not. Based on this determination, new construction is approved or disapproved.

Certification: (1) Federal authorization required for a facility to admit Medicare and Medicaid patients. **SNF** certification is for Medicare, **NF** for Medicaid, and dual certification is for both. (2) A process by which a non-governmental agency or association recognizes the competence of individuals who have met certain qualifications as determined by the agency or association.

Chemotherapy: The use of anti-cancer (cytotoxic) drugs to destroy cancer cells. Chemotherapy drugs may be given on their own, but often several drugs may be combined.

Charge: A fee which is established by the nursing facility for a particular services or product.

Chiropractor: A licensed practitioner who holds a Doctor of Chiropractic (DC) degree. Chiropractors treat patients through chiropractic manipulation which includes manipulation of the spine, physiotherapy, and dietary counseling.

Chronic condition: A medical condition that persists over time, is generally irreversible, and can result in complications if left untreated.

Civil law: Body of laws governing private legal affairs, such as private rights and duties, contracts, and commercial relations.

Claim: A bill submitted to the fiscal intermediary claiming payment for services provided.

Clinical pathway: A care planning tool that outlines in a time sequence important aspects of care necessary for meeting specific outcomes.

Clinical practice guidelines: Evidence-based standardized protocols indicated for the treatment of specific health conditions.

Clinical structure: Structures and processes designed to address the medical needs of patients.

Closed system: An orientation that emphasizes only internal organizational relationships while ignoring the interaction with the external environment. Closed system management is essentially focused on organizational set up, productivity, efficiency, cost control, profitability, and quality.

CMS (Centers for Medicare and Medicaid Services): An agency of the federal Department of Health and Human Services.

Collective bargaining: Good faith negotiation between a union and management.

Common law: Body of legal principles and precedents that have been handed down in the form of court decisions.

Community advisory board: Composed of key community leaders, the community advisory board functions as the "eyes and ears" for the facility. Through their influence, the advisory board members can also assist the administrator form meaningful partnerships with community agencies.

Comorbidity: The simultaneous presence of two or more health problems.

Competent: Legal qualification necessary for entering into a contract and for giving informed consent. Legal incompetence would include being a minor or having mental incapacity due to mental illness, mental retardation, dementia, or substance abuse.

Complementary services: Services that are not directly rendered by the facility in which the patient resides, but are necessary to address the total health care needs of a patient. Complementary services are necessary for delivering **total care.**

Consideration: Something of value promised to another in exchange for something else of value.

Continuing care retirement community (CCRC): An organization offering various elder-care living options on one campus. Living and care arrangements can range from independent living in separated cottages to skilled nursing care in an adjoining facility.

Continuous quality improvement (CQI): An ongoing undertaking to improve quality throughout the nursing facility. It is also called total quality management (TQM).

Continuum of long-term care: The full range of long-term care services that increases in the level of acuity and complexity from one end to the other—from informal and community-based services at one end of the continuum to the institutional system at the other end.

Contract: A legally binding agreement between two or more parties to carry out a legal purpose.

Control: A management function which involves monitoring progress, evaluating results against the objective, assessing deviations, and taking corrective action.

Controlled substances: Narcotics, stimulants, depressants, hallucinogens, anabolic steroids, and chemicals that are governed by the Controlled Substances Act (CSA), Title II of the Comprehensive Drug Abuse Prevention and Control Act of 1970. Except as provided under the law, their possession and use are illegal.

Copayment: An amount an insured must pay **out of pocket** each time a health care service is used.

Corporate law: Statutes defining the rights and responsibilities of corporations.

Corporation: A legal entity that is regarded as separate from its owners.

Cost-effectiveness (cost-efficiency): An undertaking is cost-effective when the benefits achieved are greater than the costs incurred.

Crime: An offense committed against the general public regardless of whether only one or more individuals have been wronged. Examples include theft, murder, disorderly conduct, and sexual abuse. Medicaid and Medicare fraud are also criminal offenses.

Criminal law: A branch of law that defines crimes and provides for their punishment.

Cross-contamination: Transfer of disease-causing organisms through contact with a dirty surface, unwashed hands, or insects.

Custodial care: Basic care that includes routine assistance with ADLs but does not include active medical or rehabilitative treatments. Such care is provided when a patient's health or function is not likely to improve.

Days of care: Cumulative **census** over a given period of time. Also called **patient days**.

Deductible: An amount the patient must first pay each year (or at the beginning of a **benefit period** for Medicare) before any amount of benefits would be payable by insurance.

Defendant: A party against whom a lawsuit is brought, or a party accused of committing a crime.

Deficiency: A nursing facility's failure to meet any of the federal standards associated with the Requirements for Participation. Deficiencies are also evaluated in terms of their severity and scope. Severity is evaluated in the context of actual or potential harm and negative health outcomes. Scope refers to how widespread a problem is in the facility.

Delirium: A state of mental confusion which often manifests itself in the form of disorientation, incoherent speech, and physical agitation.

Dementia: A generic term that describes chronic or progressive mental dysfunction that results in complex cognitive decline. These cognitive changes are commonly accompanied by disturbances of mood, behavior, and personality.

Dermatologist: A specialist physician who treats infections, growths, injuries, and other disorders related to the skin.

Developmental disability: Physical incapacity that generally accompanies mental retardation and often arises at birth or in early childhood.

Differentiation: A competitive strategy in which a facility creates distinctive features that allow customers to distinguish the facility's offer from that of its competitors.

Directed plan of correction: Measures imposed by the state regulators to bring a facility into compliance with federal **certification** standards, particularly when a **plan of correction** developed by the facility is considered inadequate.

Disability: (1) See **handicap**. (2) A person's inability to perform one of more **activities of daily living**.

Discharge planner: A social worker employed in a hospital's discharge planning department to facilitate a smooth transfer of patients to an appropriate setting after discharge from the hospital.

Distinct part: A section of a nursing home that is distinctly certified from the rest of the facility. For instance, a distinct part may have **SNF** certification whereas the rest of the facility may be non-certified.

Docket: An annotated meeting agenda that lists the items to be discussed and also provides some pertinent details and explanations for each item.

Do-not-resuscitate (DNR) order: An **advance directive** in which a person specifies that he or she does not wish to have heartbeat or breathing restored in the event of a cardiac or respiratory arrest.

Domains of practice. Broad areas of a nursing home administrator's responsibilities as established by the National Association of Boards of Nursing Home Administrators (NAB) for the purpose of developing the national licensure exam. The five domains are resident care management, personnel management, financial management, environmental management, and governance and organizational management.

Domiciliary care facilities: See **board-and-care homes**.

Dual certification: Federal **certification** that authorizes a facility to admit both Medicare and Medicaid patients.

Durable power of attorney: A written document that provides a legal means for a patient to delegate authority to someone else to act on the patient's behalf even after the patient has been incapacitated.

Dysarthria: Slurred or unintelligible speech due to muscle weakness or other problem.

Dysphagia: Difficulty in swallowing due to a dysfunction in any phase of the swallowing process.

Economic strike: A common type of strike by union workers that occurs when the union and management fail to reach an agreement.

Edenizing: Changing a nursing home's environment by implementing the principles developed by the **Eden Alternative**.

Eden Alternative: A cultural change that advocates converting nursing home interior surroundings into habitats based on the lessons of nature to create vibrant and vigorous settings. It is based on the belief that the companionship of pet animals, the opportunity to give meaningful care to other living creatures, and the spontaneity that marks an enlivened environment have therapeutic values.

Effectiveness: Success in achieving certain output goals.

Efficiency: A measure of outputs in relation to the resources used in producing the outputs.

Emphysema: A chronic condition characterized by damaged air sacs in the lungs. The resulting reduction of surface area available for gas exchange makes breathing difficult and makes the heart work harder to circulate blood through the lungs. All these changes make less oxygen available to the body.

Employment discrimination: Failing or refusing to hire; discharging or otherwise discriminating against an individual with respect to terms, conditions, or privileges of employment; or limiting, segregating, or classifying employees in a way that it deprives an individual of employment opportunity, training, advancement, or status when such actions are in violation of a law.

End-of-life care: Hospice services for the terminally ill.

Enteral nutrition: Delivery of liquid food through a tube directly into the stomach.

Entrée: The main dish on a menu.

Environmental assessment: The formal process of analyzing and evaluating the potential impact of external trends on the organization.

Environmental scanning: Using various formal and informal processes to identify, on an ongoing basis, significant trends and events in the **external environment**.

Epidemic: Excessive prevalence of a negative health condition.

Epilepsy: A brain disorder in which signals sent by nerve cells become disturbed, causing strange sensations, emotions, convulsions, muscle spasms, or loss of consciousness.

Equity: Also called owners' equity or stockholders' equity, it represents the interests or rights of the owners in a for-profit business corporation.

Esophagostomy tube: A small tube that enters a surgical incision on the side of the neck and is generally removed after each feeding. The tube allows food to enter the esophagus and then flow down into the stomach.

Ethics committee: A **multidisciplinary** forum that may include the administrator, a nursing representative, a physician, social worker, activity director, clergy, an ethicist, a legal representative, and others if necessary. The committee's purpose is to discuss situations and resolve issues in view of what is best for the patient.

Evacuation: Removal of patients and vital equipment from an unsafe area to a safe area during a fire or other emergency situation.

Exempt employees: Salaried workers who are exempt from overtime provisions of the Fair Labor Standards Act.

Extended care unit (ECU): See **transitional care unit**.

External environment: Social, political, economic, technological, informational, and ecological forces that are external to the organization.

False imprisonment: Unlawful restriction of freedom.

Felony: Crime of a serious nature that is subject to a jail term of more than one year.

Financial accounting: The recording of all financial transactions and the preparation of financial statements.

Financing: Means by which patients receiving services in nursing facilities pay for those services.

Fiscal intermediary: Private insurance companies contracted by Medicare to process **claims** from providers.

Fixed cost: A cost that does not vary with the number of patients. These costs are non-controllable.

Flexible budget: An adjusted budget which is based on the budgeted census, but budgeted costs are transformed to reflect the actual census.

Focus group: A group of about eight to twelve people who participate in an unstructured session with a skilled moderator to discuss their thoughts and feelings about an issue, an organization, or a service.

Fraud: Harm or loss caused by willful misrepresentation.

Gastrostomy tube (G-tube): A mechanism for delivering nutrition through a tube that passes through a surgical opening in the abdomen and into the stomach.

General partnership: There is no limit on the potential liability of the partners.

Geriatrics: A branch of medicine that deals with the problems and diseases that accompany aging.

Gerontology: An area of knowledge that deals with the understanding of the aging process, the changes accompanying aging, and the special problems associated with aging.

Governing body: Also called 'board of directors' or 'board of trustees,' it has the ultimate legal responsibility for a facility's operations.

Green House: A small freestanding facility designed to house six to ten residents who live together in a homelike setting. Generally, a number of Green Houses are arranged around a central skilled nursing facility which provides support services.

Grievance: A formal expression of employee dissatisfaction about some job situation.

Group homes: See **adult foster care**.

Guardian: Someone who is legally empowered and charged with the responsibility to make decisions in the patient's best interest, when the patient is not legally **competent** to act for himself or herself.

Handicap: According to law, a physical or mental impairment which substantially limits one or more of a person's major life activities.

Health screening: Early detection of health problems through regular exams and tests so that early treatment can be provided to prevent complications and ensuing disability.

Health policy: Government decisions pertaining to the financing of health care, distribution of resources, and the delivery of services.

Hemiplegia: Total paralysis of one half of the body: the arm, leg, and trunk on the same side.

Hemodialysis: A routine treatment necessary for patients whose kidney function has failed. During dialysis, the patient's blood is allowed to flow through a machine with a special filter that removes waste.

HIV: See **Human Immunodeficiency Virus**.

Holistic model: A philosophy of health care that emphasizes the well-being of every aspect of what makes a person whole and complete. It proposes that clinical and other services should not focus merely on a person's physical and mental needs, but should go beyond in meeting the needs of the whole person. It considers the social and spiritual aspects of an individual's life to be just as important as the physical and mental aspects.

Home health care: Services such as nursing, therapy, and health-related homemaker or social services brought to patients in their own homes because such patients do not need to be in an institution, and are generally unable to leave their homes safely to get the care they need.

Hospice: A cluster of special service for the dying. It blends medical, spiritual, legal, financial, and family-support services.

Hotel services: Generally meals, housekeeping, laundry, and maintenance services provided to patients in hospitals and long-term care facilities.

Human Immunodeficiency Virus (HIV): A virus that gradually destroys the body's natural immune system designed to fight infections and disease.

Hydration: Adequate fluid intake to prevent dehydration.

Hypertension: High blood pressure.

IADL: See **instrumental activities of daily living**.

Iatrogenic: Caused by the process of medical care.

ICP: See **infection control practitioner**.

Impasse: A situation describing a failure to reach an agreement by union and management representatives.

Imprest amount: A fixed amount, such as $400 or $500, to meet a facility's petty cash needs. Funds used are replenished periodically. Cash and vouchers always total the imprest amount.

Incident: Any unexpected negative occurrence involving a patient, staff, or visitor.

Income statement: Also called 'operating statement' or 'profit and loss statement' (P&L), it furnishes a summary of revenues, expenses, and profitability for a given period of time.

Incontinence: Inability to control bowel and/or bladder function.

Incorporation: Formation of a **corporation**, which requires filing of articles of incorporation (called a charter or certificate of incorporation in some states) with the proper state authority.

Infantilization: Treating older adults as children.

Infection control: A comprehensive program to prevent the transmission of infections protecting the residents, the staff, and visitors from contracting infections while in the facility.

Infection control practitioner: Generally a **registered nurse** who is responsible for overseeing the facility's **infection control** program.

Infectious waste: A general term for waste that can pose a hazard to human health. It includes pathological waste and sharps.

Informal care: Unpaid services provided by family and others.

Informed consent: (1) The right of a patient to understand the diagnosis, planned course of treatment, optional treatments and their benefits and

risks, and to make an informed choice about medical care including the right to refuse treatment. (2) Consent by a patient to authorize release of information from his or her medical record based on the patient's understanding of what information will be released and what use will be made of the information.

Injury: Physical, financial, or emotional harm.

Inpatient services: Health care services provided on the basis of an overnight stay in a facility.

In-service: An educational session.

Instrumental activities of daily living (IADL): Activities considered necessary for independent living. Among the IADLs are doing housework, cooking, doing laundry, grocery shopping, taking medication, using the telephone, managing money, and moving around outside the home.

Integrated health system: A local or regional health services conglomerate, usually built around a major hospital that offers a range of health care services by linking hospitals, clinics, and managed care organizations.

Intentional tort: A willful act that violates the rights or interests of others.

Interdependence: A state of living together (symbiosis) in a mutually beneficial relationship.

Interdisciplinary: See **multidisciplinary**.

Interpretive guidelines: Federal interpretation of the **Requirements of Participation** contained in the current edition of the State Operations Manual produced by the Centers for Medicare and Medicaid Services.

Intimacy: (1) A person's privacy during visits with family, friends, or counselors. (2) Sexual intimacy. (3) Closeness or proximity of the caregiver to the dependent elder which goes beyond mere familiarity.

Jejunostomy tube (J-tube): A surgically placed tube that enters the small intestine for the delivery of specialized nutritional formulas.

Joint venture: A separate organization formed jointly by two or more existing entities for pursuing a common purpose.

Leadership: Inducing people to act for certain goals that represent the values and motivations—wants, needs, aspirations, and expectations—of both leaders and followers.

Learned helplessness: A psychological state in which patients believe that they can no longer do anything for themselves and must depend on others.

Liabilities: The financial value of everything a business owes in debts and obligations, as shown on the **balance sheet**.

Liability: Potential damages ensuing from legal action.

Libel: A written false report intended to defame another person. See **slander**.

Licensed practical (or vocational) nurse: An LPN or LVN is a professional nurse who has completed a state-approved program in practical nursing, which is generally one or two years in duration, and has passed a national written examination.

Licensure: Licensing of a health care facility or a health care professional in accordance with state laws which require that certain conditions be met for the granting of a license.

Life Safety Code: Rules and standards developed by the National Fire Protection Association to specify numerous fire safety and other elements of building construction, fixtures, and furnishings that nursing facilities must comply with.

Limited partnership: Limits the individual liability of partners.

Living will: An **advance directive** specifying a person's wishes regarding medical treatment in the event this person becomes incompetent.

Long-term care: Long-term care includes a variety of services that are specifically tailored for meeting the needs of individuals who have disabilities that prevent them from functioning independently.

Long-term care facility: A facility, commonly referred to as a nursing home, that is duly licensed to provide long-term care services.

Managed care: A system of health care delivery which aims to make health services more cost-effective by managing utilization of services and payment to providers.

Management accounting: Preparation of routine and special reports considered useful for management control and decision-making.

Management by objectives (MBO): A system of management which is based on a joint agreement between supervisors and employees on what specific and measurable objectives would be accomplished over a given period of time, at the end of which the supervisors evaluate individual employees based on the accomplishment of these objectives.

Margin: Total profit (or loss) as a percent of total **revenue**.

Market segmentation: See **segmentation**.

Marketing: Actions undertaken to elicit desired responses to some object from a target audience.

Marketing mix: The four factors—product, price, place, and promotion (known as the four P's)—which are operationalized to position a facility in the target market.

Mastectomy: Surgical removal of a breast.

MBO: See **management by objectives**.

MDS: See minimum data set.

Meals-on-wheels: A program funded through the Older Americans Act to deliver one hot noontime meal five days a week to Americans aged 60 and older (and their spouses) who are unable to prepare a nutritionally balanced meal for themselves.

Medicaid: A jointly-funded federal-state health insurance program for the indigent.

Medical model: Delivery of health care that places its primary emphasis on the treatment of disease, relief of symptoms, and intensive use of medical technology, with little emphasis on the promotion of optimum health in a holistic context.

Medicare: A federal program of health insurance for the elderly and some disabled persons.

Mental retardation: Subaverage intellectual functioning that is long term and incurable.

Menu cycle: A specified period of time, generally three to four weeks, during which the main items on the menus are not repeated. At the end of this period, the same daily menus are repeated in the same order.

Metropolitan Statistical Area (MSA): The U.S. Bureau of Census has defined an MSA as a geographic area that includes one of the following: (1) one city with a population of 50,000 or more, or (2) an urbanized area of at least 50,000 inhabitants and a total MSA population of at least 100,000 (75,000 in the New England Census Region).

Microorganism: A living organism that cannot be seen with the naked eye.

Mid-level providers: Also called non-physician practitioners (NPPs), these are clinical professionals who practice in many areas similar to those in which **primary care physicians** practice but who are not trained as physicians. Examples include **nurse practitioners**, physician assistants, and certified nurse midwives.

Midnight census report: A census tallying mechanism in which the nurse-in-charge on the night shift counts all patients in the facility at midnight.

Minimum data set (MDS): A set of standardized screening elements that must be assessed for each patient admitted to a **skilled nursing facility**.

Misappropriation of resident property: Deliberate misplacement, exploitation, or wrongful, temporary, or permanent use of a resident's belongings or money without the resident's consent.

Misdemeanor: Crime of a less serious nature than a **felony**. It is punishable by a jail term of less than one year.

Mission: Closely connected to its **vision**, an organization's mission emphasizes the key benefits that would accrue to patients and their families, employees, and the community as the organization strives to achieve its strategic objectives.

MR/DD: See **mental retardation** and **developmental disability.**

MS: See **multiple sclerosis**.

Multidisciplinary (or interdisciplinary): A team approach to problem solving or delivery of care in which all key disciplines, such as nursing, food service, therapy, social work, and activities, participate and make joint decisions.

Multisensory stimulation: See **Snoezelen**.

Multiple sclerosis (MS): A disorder of the central nervous system (brain and spinal cord) involving decreased nerve function. It involves repeated episodes of inflammation of nervous tissue in certain areas. The inflammation destroys the covering of the nerve cells in that area. The disorder most commonly begins between 20 to 40 years old, and is one of the major causes of disability in adults under age 65.

Nasoduodenal tube: A mechanism for delivering nutrition through a tube that passes through the patient's nose and goes down into the duodenum, the first part of the small intestine.

Nasogastric tube (NG-tube): A method of delivering nutrition through a tube that passes through the nasal openings, down to the esophagus, and into the stomach.

Neglect: Failure to provide to a patient goods and services necessary to avoid physical harm, mental anguish, or mental illness.

Negligence: Failure to exercise the degree of care that a reasonable person would have exercised in similar circumstances.

Nephrologist: A physician who specializes in kidney diseases, kidney transplantation, and dialysis therapy. Nephrology is classified as an internal medicine subspecialty.

Net assets: For a non-profit organization, net assets = total assets − total liabilities.

Neurological: Associated with the nervous system.

NF (nursing facility): Federal certification which authorizes a facility to admit **Medicaid** patients.

NHA: See **nursing home administrator**.

Niche marketing: Concentrating on just one market segment by specializing in a particular service.

Noncertified: A facility that is not certified to admit Medicare and/or Medicaid patients.

Nonexempt employees: Workers who are paid an hourly rate, which must at least equal the minimum wage established under law. Nonexempt employees are also entitled to overtime pay.

Non-profit: A form of ownership in which the entity must serve a charitable purpose in exchange for tax-exempt status. Non-profit organizations are prohibited by law from distributing profits to any individuals.

Nosocomial: A negative health condition that can be attributed to the process of health care delivery.

Nurse practitioner (NP): An individual who has completed an advanced program of study leading to nursing competence in an expanded role, which includes taking patients' comprehensive health histories, assessing health status, performing physical examinations, and formulating and managing a care regimen for acute and chronically ill patients. Some NPs specialize in **geriatrics**.

Nursing home administrator (NHA): As an agent of the **governing body**, a full-time NHA is responsible for the day-to-day management of a nursing facility.

Nutritional screening: Identifying patients who may be at risk for nutritional problems. Such patients may include those who sustain weight loss, the ones on therapeutic diets, and those having difficulty eating.

Occupancy rate: Percent of total beds occupied.

Occupational therapy: Therapies designed to help temporarily or permanently disabled individuals improve their ability to perform tasks in their daily living and working environments. Occupational therapists not only help clients improve basic motor functions and reasoning abilities, but also compensate for permanent loss of function by assisting patients in performing activities of all types, ranging from using a computer, to caring for daily needs such as dressing, cooking, and eating. Physical exercises may be used to increase strength and dexterity, while paper and pencil exercises may be chosen to improve visual acuity and the ability to discern patterns. A client with short-term memory loss, for instance, might be encouraged to make lists to aid recall. A person with coordination problems might be assigned exercises to improve hand-eye coordination. For those with permanent functional disabilities, such as spinal cord injuries, cerebral palsy, or muscular dystrophy, therapists instruct in the use of adaptive equipment such as wheelchairs, splints, and aids for eating and dressing. They also design or make special equipment needed at home or at work.

Ombudsman: A trained professional who works independently with area nursing home residents and their families in resolving concerns they may have about their lives in a facility. Under the Federal Older Americans Act, every state is required to have an ombudsman program to address complaints and to act as advocates for residents in long-term care facilities.

Oncology: A medical specialty dealing with cancers and tumors.

Open system: A management orientation that recognizes the effects of external environmental factors and views internal operations in relation to changes in the **external environment**.

Operating margin: See **margin**.

Ophthalmologist: A physician who specializes in the treatment of diseases and injuries of the eye.

Opportunity cost: Foregone value of time that could have been used for something more productive.

Optician: An optical technician who generally holds an associate's degree in opticianry. An optician dispenses and fits eyeglasses.

Optometrist: A licensed professional who holds a Doctor of Optometry (OD) degree and is trained to diagnose and treat vision problems and

other eye disorders. They most commonly prescribe eyeglasses and contact lenses.

Orthopedist: A physician who specializes in correcting deformities of the skeletal system, and may surgically repair bones and joints.

Out of pocket: Costs to be paid by the recipient of health care services. Main examples are **deductibles** and **copayments**.

Outcome: An actual result obtained from medical, nursing, and other clinical interventions.

Outpatient services: Any health care services that do not require an overnight stay in a facility.

Package price: See **bundled rate**.

Palliative care: Medical care focused on relieving pain and discomfort.

Par level: The number of units of an item the facility should maintain in the inventory, including items in circulation and storage.

Paraprofessional: A caregiver who generally does not require a license or professional certification to practice, and works under the supervision of a professional. Examples include certified nursing assistants and therapy assistants.

Parenteral nutrition: Delivering a special liquid nutritional formulation directly into the blood stream, when the gastrointestinal tract is not functioning properly.

Parkinson's disease: A progressive disorder of the central nervous system affecting over 1 million people in the United States. Clinically, the disease is characterized by a decrease in spontaneous movements, gait difficulty, postural instability, rigidity, and tremor. Parkinson's disease is caused by the degeneration of certain neurons in the brain.

Partnership: An association of two or more individuals or organizations for the purpose of carrying out a business for profit. The partners share profits as well as the expenses and liabilities of the partnership.

Pathogen: Disease-causing organism.

Pathological waste: Human waste that may contain human tissue or body fluids.

Patient's bill of rights: A printed handout listing the rights of patients as residents of a nursing facility. The Patient Self-Determination Act of 1990 requires that patients be informed of their rights.

Patient days: Number of patients each day in the facility cumulated over a specified period of time. Also called **days of care**.

Payables: See **accounts payable**.

Payer-mix: Also called **census-mix**, it refers to the mix of patients by payer type, such as Medicaid, Medicare, private pay, etc.

Per diem: Per day, such as a *per diem* rate of **reimbursement**.

Per patient day: A revenue or cost amount for each patient day.

Person-centered care: A philosophy of care delivery in which caregivers empower the patients to assert their rights and preferences.

Personal care: Basic assistance with light **ADLs** and services such as meals and recreation.

Physical therapy: Evaluation and treatment modalities designed to increase, restore or maintain range of motion, physical strength, flexibility, coordination, balance, and endurance. Physical therapists also teach positioning, transfers, and walking skills to promote maximum function and independence within an individual's capability.

Picketing: A concerted action by striking union employees in which they patrol the perimeter of a facility displaying placards calling attention to a labor dispute.

Pilferage: Small-scale theft of relatively inexpensive items.

Pioneer Network: A national organization which began as a grassroots movement of caregivers, consumer advocates, and others who were concerned about the quality of life in nursing homes. The organization advocates cultural change in nursing facilities through educating, sharing of ideas, and forming coalitions with stakeholders such as regulators, **ombudsmen**, consumers, and care professionals.

Plan of care (care plan): A written plan developed through team participation of various professional disciplines to clearly outline how each identified need of a given patient will be addressed and what specific goals will be accomplished.

Plan of correction (POC): The facility's written response to each **deficiency** cited during a **survey**, outlining exactly how the facility will correct the deficiency.

Plaintiff: Party who brings a lawsuit before a court to seek damages or other legal remedies.

Podiatrist: A physician who treats patients with diseases or deformities of the feet.

Policy agenda: In the public domain, a set of priorities on which political action is based.

Poorhouse: County-run institutions during colonial times where the destitute of society, including the elderly, the homeless, the orphan, the ill, and the disabled, were given food and shelter, and conditions were often squalid.

Portion control: Accuracy in serving food according to pre-established quantities.

Positioning: Staking out a position in the **target market**.

Position statement: In developing a marketing strategy, it describes how the facility should be positioned in the market.

PPD: See **per patient day**.

Pre-admission inquiry: Interaction with the facility's staff during the first visit a potential client makes to get information about the facility.

Preceptor: A nursing home administrator who meets prescribed qualifications and has been certified to mentor **AIT** interns.

Pressure ulcer: Also referred to as a pressure sore or decubitus ulcer, it is a localized area of soft-tissue injury resulting from compression between a bony prominence and an external surface.

Prevalence: The number of cases of a negative health condition or disease in a given population that are present at a certain point in time.

Principal: An entity that appoints an **agent**.

Primary care: Basic, routine, continuous, and coordinated medical care rendered by a primary care physician or a mid-level provider such as a physician's assistant or nurse practitioner.

Primary care physician: A physician in general practice, such as family practice, general internal medicine, general pediatrics, and obstetrics and gynecology.

Private-pay patients: Patients in a nursing home who have a personal or private source of funding to pay for the services. These patients do not qualify for public funding such as Medicare or Medicaid.

Productivity: Maximization of quality for each unit of resources used in delivering health care.

Programming: Structured methods of delivering needed services.

Promotion: A controlled and integrated program using communication methods that would effectively present an organization and its services to prospective customers, and would present need-satisfying attributes to facilitate sales.

Prospective payment system: A method of **reimbursement** based on **case-mix** so that facilities incurring a more intensive use of resources for treating more complex conditions are paid more.

Protected healthcare information: Under the provisions of the Health Insurance Portability and Accountability Act of 1996, it is defined as individually identifiable health information that relates to the past, present, or future physical or mental health of, or the provision of healthcare to, a patient.

Provider: Any individual or organization that provides services generally covered under health insurance (including Medicaid and Medicare), e.g., physicians, hospitals, skilled nursing facilities, dentists, laboratories, pharmacies, and providers of durable medical equipment.

Public facility: A facility owned by the government.

Public relations: Also called community relations, public relations is a formal program of communication with external **stakeholders** and the community at large.

Publicity: Non-paid communication of information about the facility and its services.

Punitive damages: Damages awarded in excess of the actual losses suffered by a **plaintiff**.

Quadriplegia: Paralysis of all four extremities and usually the trunk.

Quality: Consistent delivery of services that maximize the physical, mental, social, and spiritual well-being of all patients, produce desirable outcomes, and minimize the likelihood of undesirable consequences.

Quality of life: The total living experience which results in overall satisfaction with one's life. The integration of social, environmental, and personal factors—including safety, comfort, personal preferences, dignity, interpersonal relations, and pain management—into the delivery of care. These factors are considered just as important and desirable as better health.

***Qui tam*:** A provision in the False Claims Act which allows any person (called a *qui tam* relator) who has knowledge that a person or an entity is

submitting false claims can bring a lawsuit on behalf of the government, and share in the damages recovered as a result of the lawsuit.

RAI: Resident Assessment Instrument.

RAP: See resident assessment protocol.

Reality orientation: A form of therapy for confused or disoriented individuals which consists of reiteration of the person's identity, orientation to time and place, and reinforcement of consistency in daily routine. Repeated attempts are made to draw the person into conversation, using simple questions, pictures, or whatever may spark their interest.

Reasonable accommodation: Actions such as alteration of facilities and the work environment as well as job restructuring to focus on the essential functions, and altering or eliminating nonessential aspects of a job in order to accommodate a disabled employee.

Receivables: See **accounts receivable**.

Referral agents: Professionals in the community who are in a position to influence prospective clients about choosing a facility.

Registered nurse (RN): A professional nurse who has completed an associate's degree, a diploma, a bachelor's degree, or a master's degree in nursing, and has been licensed as a registered nurse.

Regulations: Administrative interpretations of statutes, containing details on carrying out the statutes. Regulations carry the force of law.

Rehabilitation: Provision of therapies to either restore lost functioning or maintain existing levels of functioning and prevent further deterioration.

Reimbursement: (1) Fee established by a third party. (2) Payment to a provider for services rendered.

Reliability: Reliability of a measurement system reflects the extent to which the same results occur from repeated applications of a measure.

Reminiscence: Remembering, and in some way reliving past experiences is considered important for emotional well-being. Photo albums, memorabilia, and old news clips can be used as aids.

Requirements of Participation: Federal standards which a facility must comply with in order to be certified to admit Medicare and/or Medicaid patients.

Resident assessment protocol (RAP): According to the **MDS** process, each **trigger** requires the use of the RAP to carry out further assessment.

Resident council: An independent, semi-formal body made up of all residents who are able to participate. The purpose of this forum is to empower the residents so they can have a say in the operations of the facility.

Residential structure: It emphasizes making the living environment homelike.

Resource utilization groups (RUGs): A classification system designed to differentiate **SNF** patients by their levels of resource use. Medicare uses the RUG categories to determine the *per diem* **reimbursement** rate.

Respiratory therapy: Evaluation and treatment of patients with breathing disorders. It includes providing temporary relief to patients with chronic asthma or **emphysema**, as well as emergency care to patients who are victims of a heart attack, **stroke**, drowning, or shock. To treat patients, respiratory therapists use oxygen or oxygen mixtures, chest physiotherapy, and aerosol medications. To increase a patient's concentration of oxygen, therapists place an oxygen mask or nasal cannula on a patient and set the oxygen flow at the level prescribed by a physician. Therapists also connect patients who cannot breathe on their own to **ventilators** that deliver pressurized oxygen into the lungs. They insert a tube into a patient's windpipe; connect the tube to the ventilator; and set the rate, volume, and oxygen concentration of the oxygen mixture entering the patient's lungs.

Respite care: Any temporary long-term care service (adult day care, home health, or temporary institutionalization) that focuses on giving family caregivers time off while the patient's care is taken over by the respite care provider.

Respondeat superior: Also called "vicarious liability," it is a legal doctrine which holds a corporation liable for the tortious acts of its employees.

Responsible party: A person, such as a spouse or relative, who handles a patient's private financial affairs.

Restorative care: A combination of physical activity and recreational programming to help long-term care patients maximize their existing abilities. Restorative programs help promote the highest level of functioning through individualized programs that include assisted mobility, feeding/eating programs, functional activities, optimal communication, and social interaction.

Restraint: A safety device used to restrict a person's freedom of movement.

Revenue: Amounts earned by a nursing facility from the delivery of services. Revenue is recognized at the time services are rendered even though the actual payment for such services is received at a later date.

Reverse mortgage: A type of loan against the equity in the home. It is available to people 62 and older who own their home, and have few or no mortgage payments left.

Risk adjustment: It accounts for the expected consumption of health care resources in accordance with the patients' health status.

Risk factor: Any attribute that is known to increase the probability of a negative outcome in the future. Examples of negative outcomes include developing a disease, acquiring a negative health condition (such as being injured in a fall), and institutionalization.

Risk management: The identification, analysis, and reduction or prevention of risks.

Safety zone: An area beyond the fire door away from the point of origin of the fire.

Sanitizing: Killing harmful organisms by exposure to high temperatures or chemicals. For example, utensils can be sanitized by immersing in hot water at 170° F or by using chlorine or iodine at recommended strengths. Other approved chemicals are used for sanitizing floors and equipment.

Secondary disability: Functional loss of capabilities that were previously unaffected.

Segmentation: The process of dividing a large market into smaller segments in order to identify the **target market**.

Selective menu: A menu generally offering two choices for **entrée**.

Self-managed work team (SMWT): A group of employees who are together responsible for performing a range of tasks, including scheduling, planning of tasks, and monitoring the team's performance.

Self-perpetuating board: A **governing body** that itself selects new members to succeed the ones who would no longer serve.

Selling line: A carefully-crafted brief message used in advertising to interpret the facility's **positioning statement**.

Semantic differential: A technique used by market researchers in which people are asked to rate a facility and its competitors on dimensions such as quality, reputation, friendliness of staff, comfort, décor, etc.

Senior center: A local community center for older adults where seniors can congregate and socialize. Many centers offer a daily meal. Others sponsor wellness programs, health education, counseling services, information and referral, and some limited health care services.

Sensory stimulation: Therapy to stimulate the senses in patients with dementia, or those in comatose or vegetative states. It may involve use of stuffed animals for tactile stimulation, sounds, taste and smell, or visual stimulation.

Septicemia: Also called blood poisoning, septicemia is a rapidly progressing and life-threatening infection due to the presence of bacteria in the blood.

Sharps: Disposed objects that can cut or puncture, such as needles, blades, broken glass, and nails.

Shelter care facilities: See **board-and-care homes**.

Sick-role model: Proposed by Talcott Parsons, in the sick role the patient is expected to relinquish control to medical personnel, and comply with their directions.

Skill-mix: The ratio of a particular skill type to the total staff. For example, the ratio of registered nurses, licensed practical nurses, and nursing assistants to total nursing staff.

Skilled nursing care: Medically oriented care provided by a licensed nurse. It includes monitoring of subacute and unstable **chronic conditions**, evaluation of the patient's care needs, and nursing and therapy treatments.

Skilled nursing facility: A long-term care facility that is equipped to provide skilled nursing care.

Slander: An oral false report intended to defame another person. See **libel**.

SNF (skilled nursing facility): A long-term care facility certified to admit Medicare patients.

Snoezelen: A Dutch term for multisensory stimulation through soft music, aroma therapy, textured objects, colors, and food.

Social structure: In long-term care, it refers to the facility's responsibility to enable its patients to maintain their individuality within a stable communal environment and find meaningful social relationships within that environment.

Social support: A variety of assistive and counseling services to help people cope with situations that may cause stress, conflict, grief, or other emotional imbalances. The goal is to help people make adjustments and learn to deal with changed circumstances in their lives.

Social work designee: A person who does not possess a bachelor's of social work (BSW) degree but has a related academic degree. In some states, such a person may be employed as a social worker with adequate consultation from a qualified social worker.

Sole proprietorship: Single owner who has not incorporated the business.

Speech-language pathology (Speech therapy): Therapy focusing on individuals with communication problems, including disorders of speech, language, feeding, and swallowing.

Spend down: To qualify for **Medicaid**, individuals who may have too much income or assets may incur medical and/or remedial care expenses to become "medically needy."

Spina bifida: A disabling birth defect in which the spine fails to close properly.

Standard precautions: General infection control precautions to be used when delivering hands-on care to any patient, or when handling soiled articles of linen and clothing. It requires the use of gloves, gowns, and masks as necessary to avoid contact with body fluids.

Stakeholder: Any constituent group that has an interest in what a nursing facility stands for and what outcomes it produces.

Statement of position: In developing a marketing strategy, it describes the existing market position of a facility.

Statute of limitations: A deadline prescribed by law to file a lawsuit.

Statutory law: Statutes passed by various legislative bodies, such as the U.S. Congress, state legislatures, or legislative bodies of local governments.

Stoma: An artificially created opening in the body.

Strategy: A decision that defines an organization's future direction in response to changes in the **external environment**.

Strike: Work stoppage as a concerted effort by unionized employees.

Stroke: A sudden interruption in the blood supply of the brain. Most strokes are caused by an abrupt blockage of arteries leading to the brain

(ischemic stroke). Other strokes are caused by bleeding into brain tissue when a blood vessel bursts (hemorrhagic stroke).

Subacute care: Various medical-surgical, oncological, rehabilitation, and other specialty services for patients who no longer need **acute care** but require more nursing intervention than traditionally included in **skilled nursing care**.

Substantial compliance: A level of compliance with the **Requirements of Participation** such that any identified **deficiencies** would pose a risk of only minimal harm to patient health and safety.

Substitute services: Other long-term care options that clients may choose from, such as home health care instead of a skilled nursing facility.

Survey: An inspection by the state's department of health to verify compliance with state and federal standards.

Swing bed: A hospital bed that can be used for **acute care** or **skilled nursing care** depending on fluctuations in demand.

Target market: Sector of the market that is composed of target customers.

Third party: A payer other than the patients and their families. Examples of third-party payers are insurance companies, managed care, Medicare, Medicaid, and VA.

Thriving: Living life to the full.

Tort: A civil wrong other than a breach of contract.

Total care: Recognizing any health care need that may arise and ensuring that the need is evaluated and addressed by appropriate clinical professionals. When evaluation and treatment are beyond the nursing home's scope of services, referral must be made to an external provider.

Transfer: (1) Movement of a patient from one surface to another, such as from bed to chair, or from wheelchair to car seat. (2) Movement of a patient from one facility to another.

Transitional care unit (TCU): A hospital-based subacute care unit.

Transmission-based precautions: Infection control precautions to follow when caring for patients who have a communicable disease. These precautions are used in addition to **standard precautions**.

Trigger: An actual problem or risk factor for potential functional problems discovered during the **assessment** process using the **MDS**. Such a 'red flag' requires additional review and assessment.

Undifferentiated marketing: It is also called 'mass marketing' because it ignores market **segmentation**, and targets the aggregate market using the same **marketing mix**.

Unfair labor practice: An action declared as illegal under the National Labor Relations Act.

Union steward: A unionized employee working at the facility who officially represents the union on issues involving the labor contract.

Upcoding: Billing for services that procure a higher reimbursement than the services actually provided, and which should have been billed at a lower rate of reimbursement. It is a **felony** under the fraud and abuse law.

Validation therapy: Many old people, especially before death, want to return to the past to wrap up loose ends. Demented patients often "live in the past." The theory behind this therapeutic approach is that validation or acceptance of the values and beliefs of a person, even if they have no basis in reality, helps the individual come to grips with the past. The therapy involves listening with empathy. In the absence of such therapy, the person is likely to withdraw. So, if a 70 year old man says that he is a senior in high school, and has to go to school so he can run the 100 yard dash —a validation therapist accepts it as real.

Validity: Denotes the extent to which a measurement system actually measures what it purports to measure.

Value (singular): The value or worth that is perceived by each party in an exchange. Value is created when the facility produces benefits that exceed, or at least equal, the inputs brought by outsiders into the exchange.

Value network: A total pattern of values received, generated, and distributed through an organization's ongoing relationships with its clients and stakeholders.

Values (generally plural): Core beliefs and principles that guide people's thinking and behaviors.

Variable cost: A cost that varies with the change in the number of patients.

Variance analysis: A financial management technique which uses the difference between an actual (realized) value and budgeted value to examine variances between what has actually happened and what was planned in the budget.

Ventilator: A mechanical device for artificial breathing. The device forces air into the lungs.

Vicarious liability: See *respondeat superior*.

Vision: A compelling picture of how an organization will look and function when its main objectives are achieved.

Vital signs: Generally, body temperature, pulse rate, blood pressure, and respiratory rate are referred to as vital signs. Any abnormalities in these measures triggers further clinical evaluation.

Wage garnishment: Any legal or equitable procedure through which some portion of a person's earnings is required to be withheld by an employer for the payment of a debt.

Walk-in clinic: A freestanding **outpatient** clinic where patients are seen on a first-come-first-served basis without prior appointments.

Wayfinding: Incorporation of features that can help people find their way with relative ease within a large institution.

Zoonosis: Transmittal of infections from vertebrate animals to humans.

INDEX

Page numbers followed by t denote tables

DATE DUE